T0305299

The Capital Markets

The Capital Markets

Evolution of the Financial Ecosystem

GARY STRUMEYER

WITH
EXECUTIVE EDITOR,
SARAH SWAMMY, Ph.D.

WILEY

Published by John Wiley & Sons, Inc., Hoboken, New Jersey.

Published simultaneously in Canada.

Library of Congress Cataloging-in-Publication Data is available:

ISBN 978-1-119-22054-1 (Hardcover)
ISBN 978-1-119-22057-2 (ePDF)
ISBN 978-1-119-22056-5 (ePub)

Cover Design: Wiley
Cover Image: © bluebay/Shutterstock

Printed in the United States of America.

10 9 8 7 6 5 4 3 2 1

*All royalties from this book will be donated
to the Robin Hood Foundation.*

Contents

Preface   xi

Acknowledgments   xiii

About the Author & Executive Editor   xv

About the Contributors   xvii

PART ONE

Introduction and Tools

CHAPTER 1
The Early 21st-Century Evolution of Global Capital Markets   3

Jack Malvey

CHAPTER 2
The Role of Global Capital Markets   20

Christian A. Edelmann and Shasheen Jayaweera

CHAPTER 3
How the Global Financial Crisis Transformed the Industry   52

Christian A. Edelmann and Pete Clarke

CHAPTER 4
Cash Bonds and Futures   64

Amir Sadr

CHAPTER 5
Risk in Capital Markets   89

Peter Reynolds and Mike Hepinstall

CHAPTER 6
Enablers for Robust Risk Management in Capital Markets   **110**

Swati Sawjiany

CHAPTER 7
Making Markets Work   **120**

Eric Czervionke

PART TWO

Capital Markets Products

CHAPTER 8
Money Markets   **157**

Randy Harrison and Paul Mandel

CHAPTER 9
Repurchase Agreements   **184**

Karl Schultz and Jeffrey Bockian

CHAPTER 10
U.S. Treasury and Government Agency Securities   **205**

Lee Griffin and David Isaac

CHAPTER 11
Government-Sponsored Enterprises and Federal Agencies   **210**

David Isaac and Francis C. Reed, Jr.

CHAPTER 12
Inflation-Linked Bonds   **232**

Henry Willmore

CHAPTER 13
Mortgage-Backed Securities   **239**

Patrick Byrne

CHAPTER 14
Corporate Bonds   **254**

Marvin Loh

CHAPTER 15
Preferred Stock 286
Sarah Swammy

CHAPTER 16
Distressed Debt Securities 296
Michael McMaster

CHAPTER 17
Securitization 304
Daniel I. Castro, Jr.

CHAPTER 18
Asset-Backed Securities 312
Daniel I. Castro, Jr.

CHAPTER 19
Non-Agency Residential Mortgage-Backed Securities (RMBSs) 329
Daniel I. Castro, Jr.

CHAPTER 20
Commercial Mortgage-Backed Securities (CMBSs) 348
Daniel I. Castro, Jr.

CHAPTER 21
Collateralized Debt Obligations (CDOs) 361
Daniel I. Castro, Jr.

CHAPTER 22
Structured Investment Vehicles (SIVs) 381
Daniel I. Castro, Jr.

CHAPTER 23
Collateralized Loan Obligations (CLOs) 389
Mendel Starkman

CHAPTER 24
Municipal Bonds 419
Fred Yosca

CHAPTER 25
Equities 435

David Weisberger

CHAPTER 26
Cash Equities in the Secondary Market 458

Eric Blackman and Robert Grohskopf

CHAPTER 27
Exchange-Traded Funds (ETFs) 469

Reginald M. Browne

CHAPTER 28
Equity Capital Markets 481

Daniel C. de Menocal, Jr.

CHAPTER 29
Interest Rate Swaps 503

Amir Sadr

CHAPTER 30
Interest Rate Options 523

Amir Sadr

CHAPTER 31
Commodities 548

Bob Swarup

CHAPTER 32
Currency 571

Simon Derrick

CHAPTER 33
Conclusion 578

Gary Strumeyer and Christian Edelmann

Index 591

Preface

Throughout my career in financial services as an author, educator, and sales executive, and president of a broker dealer, I continue to be amazed by the lack of understanding that the average person has about the evolution of our global capital markets ecosystem. This condition, if left unchecked, can easily become untenable and dangerous in our highly regulated, hyperconnected, tech-saturated world. This book—the first of its kind post–Financial Crisis—will serve as an antidote to this condition. I have assembled the right team—practitioners, academics, and economists—to present clearly in these pages the fundamentals necessary for both professionals and nonprofessionals to learn about what makes up our capital markets ecosystem.

Gary Strumeyer

NOTE: Supplementary materials are available on www.wiley.com/go/strumeyer under "Downloads".

Acknowledgments

First and foremost I wish to single out the driving force behind our literary adventure by expressing my deepest appreciation and unqualified gratitude to our consummate editor in chief, Dr. Sarah Swammy. Through her ability to find, recruit, and sign the best, most qualified authors, combined with her benevolent taskmaster persona and her laser-like focus on submitting the final drafts well in advance of the original deadlines, she brought to life the vision of this book and ensured the high quality of its contents. She shares with me my belief in the power of thought leadership and motivated the host of talented writers and thinkers to bring this project home with efficiency, speed, and grace. Thank you, Sarah, for your many contributions to this work—chief among them keeping me ahead of schedule.

Specials thanks are due to Alberto Baptiste and Peter Borish. Al got the ball rolling by providing us with key resources early in our progress. He was integral in kicking off this endeavor, enabling us to attract industry leaders as contributors. I am also grateful to Peter for his guidance, insight, and connecting us with the Robin Hood Foundation.

I would also like to express my gratitude to all of my friends and colleagues who shared their experience, market insight, time, and contacts to make this book comprehensive and successful: Joe Gaziano, Larry Harris, Ron Hooey, Joe Keenan, Dena Mandara, Lenny Scotto, and Sam Schwartzman.

Thanks, again, to all of the contributors not only for their brilliant submissions but for helping us to identify the trends and subject matter relevant to the evolving financial ecosystem.

Gary Strumeyer

About the Author & Executive Editor

GARY STRUMEYER

Gary M. Strumeyer is the former president of BNY Mellon Capital Markets, LLC, a registered broker-dealer subsidiary of The Bank of New York Mellon Corporation ("BNY Mellon").

Gary spent over 30 years with BNY Mellon. He began his career in municipal bond sales before becoming sales manager of the newly formed Capital Markets subsidiary in 1996. In 2008, Gary was appointed president of BNY Mellon Capital Markets, LLC. Under his leadership, Capital Markets has evolved into a full-service, multifaceted, institutional broker-dealer.

Gary served on BNY Mellon Operating Committee and Executive Steering Committee of BNY Mellon's Women's Initiative Network where he was a mentor and sponsor. Formerly, Gary served on the board of directors of the Cambodian Children's Fund and was a member of the National Association of Securities Dealers (NASD) Corporate Debt Market Panel.

He is a former adjunct professor of economics and finance at New York University's School of Professional Studies, and author of *Keys to Investing in Municipal Bonds*, and *Investing in Fixed Income Securities: Understanding the Bond Market*.

Mr. Strumeyer holds a BS in Management and Economics, and an MBA in Finance from New York University.

SARAH SWAMMY

Sarah Swammy is a managing director, business manager, and head of supervision for BNY Mellon Capital Markets, LLC, a registered broker-dealer subsidiary of The Bank of New York Mellon Corporation ("BNY Mellon"). Sarah's prior roles include CAO of Global Markets and principal overseeing the sales and trading businesses of BNY Mellon Capital Markets, LLC. Sarah joined Capital Markets from Deutsche Bank Securities, Inc., where she was an advisory compliance officer. She has also held compliance positions at both CSFB and Barclays Capital, Inc.

Sarah is a member of BNY Mellon Capital Markets Board of Managers, and serves as a member of New York Institute of Technology School of Management's Executive Council. She is a former member of the Touro College of Education's Graduate Advisory Board and a former member of the Executive Steering Committee for BNY Mellon's Women's Initiative Network.

Sarah holds a BS in Business Administration and an MS in Human Resources Management and Labor Relations from New York Institute of Technology, an MA in Business Education from New York University, and a Ph.D. in Information Studies from C.W. Post. She is also an adjunct instructor teaching C-Suite Leadership in the Integrated Marketing Graduate program at New York University School of Professional Services.

About the Contributors

Eric Blackman
Partner, Gartland and Mellina Group, Regulatory & Compliance Practice
20 years of financial services experience in management consulting, corporate strategy, equity trading, regulatory compliance, risk management and control, cost take outs, acquisition due diligence, business process re-engineering, program and project management and enterprise data management.

Prior to Gartland and Mellina, Eric spent eight years as an internal consultant for BYN Mellon, Bear Stearns Asset Management and Morgan Stanley driving strategic efforts which were intended to grow revenues, increase efficiencies and reduce costs. Prior to Morgan Stanley, Eric spent three years at KPMG Consulting focused on advisory and implementation services for front and back office projects. Prior to KPMG, Eric worked for three years as an equity trader and advisor to the specialists and market makers on the Pacific Stock Exchange floors. Eric began his career at Donaldson, Lufkin and Jenrette in their retail brokerage division.

Eric is a graduate of Muhlenberg College with a B.A. in Political Science. He has previously held the Series 7, 63 & 55 licenses and is a member of the Association for Strategic Planning (ASP), Association of Internal Management Consultants (AIMC), Financial Services Business Transformation Roundtable (FSBT) and The Data Management Association of NY (DAMA-NY). Eric is a frequent speaker at Capital Markets conferences and Dodd Frank/Regulatory impact forums.

Jeffrey Bockian
Managing Director, BNY Mellon
Jeffrey Bockian is managing director of BNY Mellon Corporate Treasury's Funding and Short-Term Investments Group. As part of his responsibilities, he oversees liquidity and collateral management activities, including trading of repurchase agreements. From 2012 to 2016, Bockian was global head of Securities Finance Portfolio Management at BNY Mellon. Prior to that, he was executive vice president and head of Finance Trading in the Capital Markets Division of Countrywide Financial Corporation, which he joined in 1998. Before joining Countrywide, Bockian was a vice president in the fixed-income division at Morgan Stanley, New York, where he traded mortgage-backed securities options and derivatives and other OTC and listed rates products. For the three years prior to joining the Trading Department,

Bockian managed the Mortgage-Backed Securities, Commodities, and Futures Operations Departments. He is a graduate of New York University.

Reginald M. Browne
Senior Managing Director, Cantor Fitzgerald
Reginald M. Browne is a senior managing director overseeing the exchange-traded funds business at Cantor Fitzgerald, which facilitates about one trillion dollars in trades annually. Mr. Browne has been featured in major business publications and regularly speaks at industry conferences. He is widely known as "The Godfather of ETFs" because of his influence helping bring to market nearly 25 percent of the ETFs listed in the United States. Mr. Browne has more than three decades of Wall Street experience. Prior to joining Cantor Fitzgerald, Mr. Browne was managing director, co-global head of the ETF group at Knight Capital Group and a senior vice president and co-head of the ETF group at Newedge USA, a division of Société Générale and Crédit Agricole CIB. He also worked at Susquehanna International and O'Connor and Associates. Mr. Browne earned his bachelor's in business administration from La Salle University, where he currently serves as a trustee. In January 2015, Mr. Browne was appointed to the Equity Market Structure Advisory Committee.

Patrick Byrne
Managing Director and Senior Portfolio Manager, BNY Mellon
Patrick Byrne is a managing director and senior portfolio manager in the BNY Mellon Investment Portfolio Management Group. Prior to his current role Mr. Byrne was the Head of Institutional Fixed-Income Asset Management and a chief investment officer (CIO) at BNY Asset Management. Mr. Byrne set strategy and oversaw all fixed-income products. He was a member of the BNY Asset Management's Investment Policy Committee as well as the Fixed-Income Strategy Committee. He began his career at Salomon Brothers working on the mortgage-backed securities trading desk. Mr. Byrne also held mortgage trading positions at Chase Securities and Mabon Securities. He graduated with a BS in finance/economics from Fordham University, and obtained an MBA from the University of Notre Dame.

Daniel I. Castro, Jr.
President and Founder, Robust Advisors, Inc.
Daniel I. Castro, Jr. is the founder of Robust Advisors, Inc., an independent consulting company focusing on structured finance markets. Robust Advisors provides due diligence, valuation, expert witness, litigation support, and general consulting services to banks, broker-dealers, hedge funds, insurance companies, issuers, originators, and trustees. Mr. Castro has been involved in the fixed-income and structured finance markets for over 30 years. Mr. Castro has been on both the sell-side and buy-side of the market, and has a thorough understanding of both the big picture and

the nuances. From 1991 to 2004, he ran Merrill Lynch's Structured Finance Research Group (1991–2004). He was the top-ranked analyst for ABS strategy in the industry multiple times according to the *Institutional Investor* industry poll. Prior to founding Robust Advisors, Mr. Castro led structured finance teams at BTIG LLC, a FINRA registered broker-dealer; GSC Group, an investment management firm that also served as a CDO fund manager; and Huxley Capital Management. He also served on the board of directors of the American Securitization Forum. Mr. Castro earned an MBA in finance from Washington University, preceded by a BA in government from the University of Notre Dame.

Daniel C. de Menocal, Jr.
Former Managing Director Equity Capital Markets, BNY Mellon Capital Markets, LLC (Retired)
Daniel C. de Menocal, Jr., is a former managing director, who headed the equity capital markets business of BNY Mellon Capital Markets, LLC, a broker-dealer subsidiary of The Bank of New York Mellon Corporation. His principal business included managing primary and secondary market equity offerings for public corporations. Beginning in 2005, he was instrumental in developing the market for at-the-market equity offerings for the electric utility and REIT industries. Mr. de Menocal has had over 40 years' experience in banking, fixed-income sales, public finance, and investment banking. He began his career at Irving Trust Company in 1975.

Eric M. Czervionke
Partner, Corporate and Institutional Banking, Finance & Risk, Oliver Wyman
Eric M. Czervionke is a Partner in Oliver Wyman's New York Office. As a member of the firm's Corporate and Institutional Banking and Finance & Risk practices, he advises global banks, broker-dealers, custodians, and financial market infrastructure providers on strategy, mergers & acquisitions, product design, operations, regulatory change, and risk management.

Prior to joining Oliver Wyman, Eric held positions at the Bombay Stock Exchange, where he led the exchange's Corporate Strategy function and Information Products business, and at Merrill Lynch, where he was a member of the firm's Corporate Strategy and Business Development group. While at Merrill Lynch, Eric supported a number of strategic acquisitions, divestitures, and integrations, including the post-merger integration efforts following Merrill Lynch's acquisition by Bank of America.

Eric holds a B.S.E. in Operations Research & Financial Engineering, magna cum laude, with certificates in Finance, Engineering Management Systems, and Applied Mathematics from Princeton University.

Simon Derrick
Managing Director and Head of Global Markets Strategy, BNY Mellon
Simon Derrick is a managing director of The Bank of New York Mellon and is head of the bank's Global Markets Strategy team. Mr. Derrick established the team 17 years ago and has been responsible for its development into one of the pre-eminent voices in the FX markets. His views on "currency wars" and on developments within the Euro-zone are frequently quoted in the financial media. Prior to heading up BNYM's currency strategy team, Simon ran The Bank of New York's European FX sales team for four years. Previously, he worked in sales and proprietary trading roles at Midland Bank (now part of HSBC), Banque Indosuez (now part of Crédit Agricole Corporate and Investment Bank), and Citibank. He is an honors graduate in geography from University College London.

Christian A. Edelmann
Partner, Global Head of Corporate & Institutional Banking, and Global Head Wealth & Asset Management, Oliver Wyman
Christian A. Edelmann is a partner based in the London office and the head of Oliver Wyman's Corporate & Institutional Banking (CIB) and Wealth & Asset Management (WAM) practices. Prior to his current role, Mr. Edelmann was based out of Hong Kong, running Oliver Wyman's business in Asia-Pacific. He has worked in depth with major financial institutions in North America, Europe, Asia, and the Middle East, covering a broad range of sell- and buy-side institutions as well as market infrastructure players. Among other projects, he has advised a broad set of clients on strategy and business model optimization. Mr. Edelmann is the author of various recent Oliver Wyman landmark publications, including the 2015 and 2016 editions of the annual publication with Morgan Stanley on Wholesale Banking & Asset Management as well as a joint report with the Fung Global Institute on Asia Finance 2020. He regularly acts as a speaker at leading industry events and is a recurrent commentator on CNBC and Bloomberg TV. Mr. Edelmann holds a master's degree in law (summa cum laude) and a master's degree in business and economics (insigni cum laude) from the University of Basel in Switzerland. He has also earned the CFA (Chartered Financial Analyst) and the FRM (Financial Risk Manager) designations.

Pete Clarke
Partner, Corporate & Institutional Banking, New York
Pete Clarke is a Partner in the Corporate & Institutional Banking practice in Oliver Wyman's New York office. Pete has over 10 years of experience in capital markets and consulting to leading financial institutions in the US and Europe, focusing on capital markets and investment banking. He has broad expertise in strategic reviews, responses to new regulation spanning risk capital, leverage, liquidity and funding, balance sheet efficiency and commercial due diligence for private equity and

alternative investment firms, concentrating on capital markets and wholesale banking targets. Pete has also contributed to published articles and reports, co-writing the annual joint Oliver Wyman-Morgan Stanley outlook research report in 2012 and Financial Resource Management Point of View report in 2014. Pete holds a first class honours degree in Economics from the University of Warwick and a Licence in Economics (Erasmus Programme) from the Université Paris I Panthéon-Sorbonne. Pete joined Oliver Wyman in 2010. He previously worked for Deutsche Bank in the Financial Institutions Group.

Lee Griffin
Senior Treasury Trader, BNY Mellon
Lee Griffin is a senior treasury trader at BNY Mellon Capital Markets LLC. Mr. Griffin has been Trading treasuries for five years. He was a senior rates trader for BNY Mellon Markets in Tokyo, and has previously traded USD denominated covered bonds and Supra Sovereign Agencies, as well investment grade corporates. Mr. Griffin currently focus on longer end of the rates curve. He provides market color, and analysis in addition to his role managing BNY Mellon Capital market's treasury market making strategy and rates hedging strategies. Mr Griffin attended New York University where he majored in Economics. He holds FINRA series 7 & 63 licenses.

Randy Harrison
Managing Director, BNY Mellon
Randy Harrison is managing director responsible for short-term debt origination at BNY Mellon, where he started in November 2015. Before joining BNY Mellon, Mr. Harrison was a founding partner of Acacia Asset Management. From 2001 to 2014, Mr. Harrison was managing director, global head of Short-Term Credit at Citigroup, where he led the U.S. commercial paper, euro commercial paper, and brokered CDs businesses for seven years. Prior to Citigroup, he was a vice president at Goldman Sachs in New York from 1987 until 2001, where initially, he was a financial institutions credit analyst in risk management and then lead asset backed commercial paper origination in the firm's fixed-income division. He served as an executive-in-residence at the University of Richmond from 2014 to 2016. Mr. Harrison earned a BA in English Literature from the University of Virginia and an MBA from the University of Virginia's Darden School.

Mike Hepinstall
Partner, Oliver Wyman
Mike Hepinstall is a Partner in Oliver Wyman's Finance & Risk practice in New York. He works with leading US and global financial institutions to help them advance their risk analytics capabilities, and embed better risk information into decisions. His projects run from high-level framework design or review/redesign, to sophisticated technical model development, including the management of large

programs. He has led a variety of teams through the development of frameworks and models for credit, market and operational risk measurement, capital stress testing, balance sheet optimization for trading, marketing spend optimization for retail banking, and a variety of other applications. He earned dual bachelor's degrees from the University of Pennsylvania, where he studied International Studies and German Studies, and from the Wharton School, where he studied Finance and Public Policy.

David Isaac

David Isaac is the Head Government Agency Trader at BNY Mellon Capital Markets LLC. Mr. Isaac has been trading Government Agency and Supra Sovereign debt for 15 years. Prior to joining BNY Mellon, David worked at UBS Investment Bank and BNP Paribas. He received his BS in Business Administration from SUNY Maritime Colleges and his MBA from the École Nationale des Ponts et Chaussées in Paris, France. He holds FINRA series 7, 24 & 63 licenses.

Robert Grohskopf

Mr. Grohskopf has 25+ years of Financial Services experience in equity sales and trading and hedge fund management. Bob has held numerous senior executive positions, including Executive Member of the Global Equity Management Committee, Global Head of Cash Equities Trading and Sales Trading, and Hedge Fund Managing Member. He has a proven track record of managing complex and fragmented businesses in transition, recognizing operating inefficiencies, integrating acquired businesses, and developing and implementing strategies to maximize profitability. During his extensive front-office career, Bob has developed in-depth market function expertise. Bob holds a B.S. in Forest Management from Rutgers University and an M.B.A. from Virginia Tech. He previously held the Series 24, 7 and 63 licenses.

Shasheen Jayaweera
Principal, Corporate & Institutional Banking, Oliver Wyman
Shasheen Jayaweera is a principal in the financial services practice in Oliver Wyman's New York Office. Mr. Jayaweera has more than seven years of experience in consulting, primarily to leading financial institutions across the United States, Asia, and Australia, focusing on corporate and institutional banking, and specializing in capital markets infrastructure. Mr. Jayaweera's experiences and expertise range across capital markets infrastructure strategy and post-trade processes, corporate banking strategy, transaction banking strategy, corporate front-office organization, and regulation. Shasheen holds a first-class honors degree in economics and a bachelor's degree in commerce (finance and accounting) from the University of New South Wales in Australia and has completed executive education at Wharton and INSEAD.

Marvin Loh
Managing Director and Senior Global Market Strategist, BNY Mellon
Marvin Loh is a managing director at BNY Mellon Markets Group, where he is the firm's senior market strategist. Mr. Loh monitors market, industry, and credit developments, and formulates their impact on a wide range of asset classes. Prior to joining BNY Mellon, he was the director of research at W.R. Hambrecht, a boutique investment bank that pioneered the auction IPO process. Mr. Loh assembled an *Institutional Investor*-ranked research team that focused on identifying disruptive business models that could provide above-average, long-term investment returns. Mr. Loh has held senior analyst roles at Oppenheimer and Company, Decision Economics, Fidelity Investments, Financial Guaranty Insurance Company, and the Federal Reserve Bank of New York. His credit and equity coverage has included analysis of the finance, specialty finance, healthcare, technology, energy, and utility sectors. Mr. Loh graduated from New York University, where he obtained his MBA in finance and a BS in finance and economics.

Jack Malvey, CFA
Former Chief Global Markets Strategist, BNY Mellon
Jack Malvey is the former chief global markets strategist and director of the BNY Mellon Center for Global Investment and Market Intelligence for BNY Mellon Investment Management, two positions that were created when he joined BNY Mellon in March 2011. Mr. Malvey led a team responsible for capturing and researching investment trends, market activity, and economics. He focused on developing a global investment and market knowledge platform that helped capture and communicate investment opinions and analysis. In addition to holding the Chartered Financial Analyst designation, Jack belongs to the Financial Management Association, the New York Society of Security Analysts, the Fixed Income Analysts Society, Inc., and the Society of Quantitative Analysts. Jack is a former president of the Fixed Income Analysts Society and was inducted into the Fixed Income Analysts Society's Hall of Fame in November 2003. Jack received an AB in economics from Georgetown University and did graduate work in economics at the New School for Social Research in New York.

Paul Mandel
Paul Mandel spent his entire 33-year career at J.P. Morgan Securities LLC, predominantly in the Short Term Fixed Income division. He ended his career as an Executive Director and Business Manager after serving as short term salesperson; national sales manager; short term loan trading manager; North America Fixed Income Business Manager; and Business Manager/Manager of eCommerce activities for Short Term Fixed Income. As Short Term Fixed Income Business Manager, Paul was responsible for developing eCommerce/eTrading strategies and systems and overseeing matters relating to P&L, compliance, legal/regulatory, new product development and audit.

In addition, he was part of the team that led JPMS's response to the Global Financial Crisis of 2008. Paul received his BA from New York University, MA and Master of Philosophy from Columbia University and MBA from Columbia University Business School. Paul is now retired but engaged in part-time eCommerce consulting work.

Michael McMaster
Managing Director and Chief Compliance Officer, BNY Mellon
Michael McMaster is a Managing Director and Chief Compliance Officer for BNY Mellon Capital Markets, LLC, a broker-dealer affiliate of BNY Mellon, Chief Compliance Officer for BNY Mellon's Broker Dealer Services Division and is also the Head of BNY Mellon's Shared Services Compliance Group which services its broker-dealer affiliates and swap dealer. Prior to joining BNY Mellon in 2010, Mr. McMaster was Counsel for Rabobank (a Dutch banking organization) handling securities regulatory matters and Rabobank's U.S. Medium-Term Note Issuance Programs as well as Chief Compliance Officer for Rabo Securities USA, Inc., the U.S. broker-dealer affiliate of Rabobank. From 1998 to 2002, Mr. McMaster worked for BNY Capital Markets, Inc.—a predecessor entity to BNY Mellon Capital Markets, LLC—and held the position of Chief Compliance Officer. Mr. McMaster also held positions as Counsel and Chief Compliance Officer for Libra Securities LLC and was an Assistant District Attorney in the King's County (Brooklyn, NY) District Attorney's Office. Prior to moving into legal and compliance positions, Mr. McMaster was a Collateralized Mortgage Obligation trader for Tucker Anthony. He graduated with an undergraduate degree in Finance from Manhattan College and received his J.D. from New York Law School. Mr. McMaster is an adjunct professor at New York Law School and is Chairman of the Compliance Committee for the New York City Bar Association.

Francis C. Reed, Jr.
Global Regulatory Strategist, FactSet Research Systems
Francis C. Reed, Jr., is an experienced capital markets professional with extensive fixed-income trading, structuring, and sales expertise at top-tier investment banks like Morgan Stanley, UBS, Lehman Brothers, and Barclays Capital. Presently, Mr. Reed is a global regulatory strategist at FactSet Research Systems. He is an industry author and speaker on topics including debt capital markets, financial regulatory reform, housing reform, and public policy matters. Mr. Reed has managed institutional trading and sales teams for large complex investors like U.S. government-sponsored enterprises (GSEs), European Supranationals/Sovereigns/Agencies (SSAs), central banks, commercial banks, hedge funds, insurance companies, and asset managers. Mr. Reed holds an MBA in finance from Fordham University and a BS in marketing from Fairfield University. He is a founding board member of The Children's Fund for GSD Research, a 501c3 non-profit charitable organization committed to finding a cure for GSD, a rare genetic condition afflicting his daughter: www.CureGSD.org.

Peter Reynolds
Partner, Financial Services Finance & Risk, Oliver Wyman
Peter Reynolds is a partner in the finance and risk practice based in Oliver Wyman's Hong Kong office. Mr. Reynolds has worked in depth with major financial institutions across Asia, the United States, Europe, and the Middle East, leading large engagements across the full spectrum of risk and finance topics for leading banks and insurers. He joined Oliver Wyman in February 2004 from a generalist strategy consulting firm. Peter holds a bachelor's degree from Oxford University in history and economics, and an MBA with distinction from INSEAD.

Karl Schultz
Vice President, BNY Mellon
Karl Schultz is a vice president on the funding and short-term investments desk in the Corporate Treasury at BNY Mellon, where he trades repurchase agreements and other secured financing transactions. Prior to his current role, he spent close to eight years trading repo for MBS-related products at Countrywide Securities Corporation and three years trading corporate investment grade bonds at Morgan Stanley Asset Management. Mr. Schultz holds an MBA from the Stern School of Business at New York University and is a CFA Charterholder.

Amir Sadr
Chief Operating Officer, Yield Curve Trading, LLC
Amir Sadr received his Ph.D. in 1990 from Cornell University with thesis work on the foundations of probability theory. After working at AT&T Bell Laboratories until 1993, he started his Wall Street career at Morgan Stanley, initially as a vice president in quantitative modeling and development of exotic interest rate models, and later on as an exotics trader in Derivative Product Group. He founded Panalytix, Inc., in 1997 to develop financial software for pricing and risk management of interest rate derivatives. He has worked at Greenwich Capital, HSBC, and Brevan Howard US Asset Management in Connecticut. Since 2009, he has been the COO of Yield Curve Trading, LLC, a boutique proprietary trading firm. Dr. Sadr is the author of *Interest Rate Swaps and Their Derivatives: A Practitioner's Guide* (Wiley, 2009), and has been an adjunct professor at NYU School of Professional Studies, where he taught courses on swaps and derivatives.

Swati Sawjiany
Partner, Oliver Wyman
Swati Sawjiany is a partner in Oliver Wyman's financial services practice, based out of their New York office. Ms. Sawjiany has worked on client engagements in North America, Europe, and Asia, primarily across corporate and institutional banking, market infrastructure, and retail banking with a focus on finance and risk technology and operations. Ms. Sawjiany has an MBA from INSEAD, a master's in information systems management from Carnegie Mellon University, and a bachelor's in engineering from Mumbai University.

Mendel Starkman
Managing Director, BNY Mellon

Mendel Starkman, CFA, is a managing director at BNY Mellon Corporate Treasury, where he co-manages the bank's investments in collateralized loan obligations (CLOs) and supports investment activities in other U.S. and European structured credit products. In addition, Mr. Starkman works on the integration of various regulatory requirements that pertain to Corporate Treasury's investment activities. Prior to joining BNY Mellon, Mr. Starkman was a senior structured credit analyst at Dynamic Credit Partners, LLC (DCP), where he analyzed and invested in subordinate tranches of CLOs and in complex or distressed structured credit products, and participated in the origination and management of eight structured credit vehicles. During the financial crisis, Mr. Starkman helped manage DCP's consulting business and continued in that role when the business was acquired by Duff and Phelps. Prior to joining DCP, Mendel worked at at Corinthian Partners, LLC, and E. Magnus Oppenheim and Company, Inc. Mendel holds an MBA in finance and investments from Baruch College of the City University of New York, and has earned the right to use the Chartered Financial Analyst designation.

Bob Swarup
Principal, Camdor Global

Bob Swarup is a respected international expert on financial markets, investment strategy, alternatives, asset-liability management, and regulation. He is the founder of Camdor Global, an advisory firm that works with institutions and investors around the world on strategic investment, risk management, ALM, and business issues. Dr. Swarup was formerly a partner at Pension Corporation, and chief risk officer at Thought Leadership. Dr. Swarup holds a Ph.D. in cosmology from Imperial College London and an MA (Hons) from the University of Cambridge. He has written extensively on diverse topics, and edited *Asset-Liability Management for Financial Institutions: Balancing Financial Stability with Strategic Objectives*. His latest book is the internationally acclaimed bestseller *Money Mania*, which covers two millennia of financial crises and the lessons to learn (Bloomsbury, 2014).

David Weisberger
Managing Director, IHS Markit

David Weisberger is a managing director at IHS Markit with responsibility for the firm's trading analytic products. These include transaction cost analysis, venue analytics, and best execution measurement products as well as the firm's research signals business, which utilizes a combination of fundamental, econometric, and proprietary datasets to rank equities across several hundred factors globally. Prior to this, Mr. Weisberger had over 29 years of direct experience in electronic equity trading including, most recently, as the executive principal for Two Sigma Securities (TSS). TSS is a registered market maker in over 7000 NMS securities, and Mr. Weisberger was instrumental in building Two Sigma Securities' various trading businesses. He started his career in technology as an architect of portfolio trading systems and progressed to direct responsibility for building Salomon Brothers international portfolio trading business. In 2000, he became the global architect of the market making system for Salomon Smith Barney, ran the Best Execution Committee for the firm, and later ran both the statistical arbitrage group and then Citi's Lava trading subsidiary, which was one of the first Smart Order Routers developed in the U.S. equity market.

Henry Willmore
Inflationist LLC

Henry Willmore founded Inflationist LLC in 2005 in order to provide high-frequency analysis of inflation for participants in the U.S. inflation-linked bond market. He has been producing research on this market since its inception in 1997. Before starting Inflationist LLC, he was the Chief U.S. Economist at Barclays Capital. Prior to that, he was a senior economist at The Chase Manhattan Bank. He holds a Ph.D. from MIT and an undergraduate degree from Oberlin College.

Fred Yosca
Head, Municipal Trading, BNY Mellon

Mr. Yosca has been with BNY Mellon Capital Markets and its predecessor firms for 43 years. During the course of his career he has had supervisory responsibility for fixed-income trading, municipal bond underwriting, and market risk monitoring. As head trader he managed the day-to-day activities of traders in all of the firm's fixed-income asset classes. Mr. Yosca has extensive experience trading the bonds issued by the State of New York, its agencies, authorities, and political subdivisions as well as overseeing the firm's competitive underwriting for issuers within the State. Mr. Yosca earned a bachelor of science degree from Cornell University and a master's of business administration from St. John's University. He is a former president of The Municipal Bond Club of New York and had run the club's Bond School for two years.

The Capital Markets

CHAPTER 1

The Early 21st-Century Evolution of Global Capital Markets

The Great Transition Era

Jack Malvey

INTRODUCTION

The pace of economic evolution varies and is told in real time by fluctuating global capital markets. New technologies arrive, displacing old ways. Political frameworks oscillate between centralized and decentralized approaches to economic affairs. Regulators shift between more or less economic and market oversight. Economic policies alternate between stimulus and restraint. Corporate finance trends swing between high and low financial leverage. Healthier, longer-living people migrate in search of better opportunities. Economies rise and fall. Industries soar and skid. Firms come and go. Institutional and individual investment philosophies adapt to new products like ETFs and revisions in expected return and risk tolerance assumptions. Currencies and commodities climb and descend based on general economic prospects and idiosyncratic market conditions like demand and supply. Changes in market psychology favor some economic and industry groupings over others.

The signs of economic evolution are all around us and often can be seen more clearly through a long-term lens. Each one of us has a unique, personal, observational journey. Although oblivious at the time, I grew up in a kind of U.S. economics laboratory. At the peak of the Baby Boom years, in the early 1960s, the intersection of three major highways in sprawling suburban Northern New Jersey persuaded developers to launch three full-sized malls. A fourth mall was added in the early 1970s. Routes 17 and 4, which ran north–south, also were flanked by a nearly continuous strip of car dealerships, diners, camping stores, bathroom fixture and tile sellers, furniture stores, and even a bowling alley and a roller-skating rink. Paramus, New Jersey, where Routes 17 and 4 met the Garden State Parkway, quickly transformed from a truck-farm center selling produce like corn and tomatoes, which it had been until the late 1950s, into a post–World War II American shoppers' paradise.

Particularly during the holiday season, the density of the highway traffic and the scarcity of mall parking spaces provided a real-time indicator of general economic conditions. The famous circular flow diagram from Economics 101 was fully enacted. People worked and earned so that they could shop. Even in the tender years of our adolescence, my childhood friends and I questioned the adult population's apparent dedication to the "shop-until-you-drop model" in often heavily congested malls.

Somehow, this retail business model regularly failed over the years. Despite their alluring decorative displays in this hubbub of prodigious economic activity, most of the retailers of my youth have long vanished. Gimbels, Bamberger's, Korvettes, Ohrbach's, Sterns, Alexander's, Herman's Sporting Goods are all gone, killed by a combination of excessive debt; overexpansion into too many malls; business-cycle downturns; the arrival of less expensive competitors; and, for the fortunate few, acquisition by nimbler firms.

This life-cycle pattern of industries and firms is hardly confined to retailers. Over the past half century, industry sectors like airlines, auto manufacturers, communications, conglomerates, financial institutions, mining, media, oil and gas producers, railroads, real estate, and technology providers have all experienced bouts of intoxicating prosperity, periods of abject gloom, and mass extinction events. Popular industry stalwarts like Pan Am, TWA, McDonnell Douglas, American Motors, Circuit City, Chemical Bank, Texaco, Penn Central, GTE, Dalton's, and Digital Equipment have disappeared.

Similar transformative structural and cyclical tides have rippled through regional economies, sovereign nations, and non-U.S. firms. Designated as China's first Special Economic Zone, Shenzhen, China, sprouted from a town of 330,000 in 1980 to a metropolitan area of 18 million by 2016. While among the most spectacular growth stories of the past four decades, Shenzhen does not stand alone. The skylines of Seoul, Tokyo, Bangkok, Singapore, London, New York, and many other urban centers have been re-sculpted by the erection of new structures that look like the cover of a science fiction novel set in the 23rd century.

Like the forensic criminologists on the popular *C.S.I.* TV programs, the task of the capital markets profession (economists, corporate financial managements, portfolio managers, security analysts, and strategists) is to search for explanatory clues to government, industry, and issuer success and failure across the vast global financial system of at least $405 trillion on May 31, 2016, on the way to $4.0 quadrillion by 2050, as shown in Figure 1.1.

FIGURE 1.1 Capital markets: Growth industry; global financial asset choice set: May 31, 2016, and projected to 2050*
*Projected cagr as shown above based on our historically derived assumptions. 1) Barclays fixed income indices data as of May 31, 2016, except U.S. commercial and industrial loans (May 25, 2016), non-agency U.S. MBS (December 31, 2015), and cash and cash-like (see below); 2) Global equity market capitalization per Bloomberg; 3) Data as of June 30, 2015, per Preqin; 4) U.S. data as of December 31, 2015, and non-U.S. real estate estimated from U.S. share of global GDP; 5) Notional amounts outstanding and gross market value data per BIS as of December 31, 2015, and may not add up exactly to total due to rounding; 6) Cash and Cash-Like: Sum of M2 money supply for Brazil, Canada, China, Eurozone, Hong Kong, India, Japan, Russia, Singapore, U.K., and U.S. and converted to U.S.$ using most recent data and exchange rates as of May 31, 2016; dates of most recently published data do not exactly match. Global Financial Asset Choice Set intended to be a representation of various market values as defined by the footnotes above and should not be construed as a complete representation of all assets or markets. Sum of asset class components and all asset classes may not add up exactly to total due to rounding.
Source: BNY Mellon using data from FactSet, Bloomberg, Barclays Live, IMF, BIS, Preqin, Raconteur.net, and Reserve Bank of India

Global Cash Financial Market Value Size (U.S.$ Billion)			
	5/31/2016	CAGR (%)	12/31/2050
Total Debt[1]	**128,509**		**1,202,155**
Multiverse Index	48,989		696,111
U.S. Aggregate Index	18,940	6%	142,084
Pan-European Aggregate	14,659	8%	209,903
Asian-Pacific Aggregate	9,689	10%	261,680
Global High Yield	2,317	10%	62,584
Canadians	1,157	3%	3,216
Euro Yen	13	3%	35
Other	2,214	6%	16,609
Global Inflation-Linked Securities Index	2,518	5%	13,609
Global Capital Securities	725	2%	1,438
U.S. Municipal Bond Index	1,429	5%	7,721
Global FRNs	841	1%	1,186
Russia, India, and China Aggregate Indices	3,518	10%	95,002
Short-Term Indices	4,865	6%	36,497
Non-Agency U.S. MBS, U.S. Hybrid ARMs	641	4%	2,487
U.S. Commercial & Industrial Loans	2,060	4%	7,996
Cash and Cash-Like[6]	62,924	5%	340,107
Total Equity	**67,275**		**698,305**
Global Common Equity[2]	63,110	7%	655,073
Private Equity Funds[3]	4,165	7%	43,232
Total Debt and Equity	**195,785**		**1,900,460**

Global Real Estate Asset Value Size (U.S.$ Billion)			
	5/31/2016	CAGR (%)	12/31/2050
Real Estate/Land[4]			
Non-U.S. Real Estate	146,107	7%	1,516,558
United States	48,912	5%	264,369
Total	**195,019**		**1,780,927**

Global Derivatives[5]	Size (U.S.$ Billion)			
	Notional	Market Value	CAGR (%)	
Commodities	**1,320**	**297**		**1,605**
Gold	286	75	5%	405
Other commodities	1,034	222	5%	1,200
Currencies	**70,446**	**2,579**		**30,472**
Forwards and forex swaps	36,331	947	6%	7,104
Currency swaps	22,750	1,345	8%	19,259
Options	11,365	287	8%	4,109
Credit Default Swaps	**12,294**	**421**	**10%**	**11,370**
Interest Rate Contracts	**384,025**	**10,148**		**274,107**
Forward rate agreements	58,326	114	10%	3,079
Swaps	288,634	8,993	10%	242,886
Options	37,065	1,042	10%	28,143
Equity Derivatives	**7,141**	**495**		**13,369**
Forwards and swaps	3,321	147	10%	3,970
Options	3,820	348	10%	9,399
Other	**17,685**	**558**	**10%**	**15,071**
Total	**492,911**	**14,499**		**345,995**

Grand Total	**405,302**		**4,027,382**

Long-term predictive success hinges on a command of politics, demographics, history, economics, finance, quantitative methods, technological knowhow, and psychology.

The pursuit of capital market diagnostic excellence can be daunting. A weekday never passes for financial markets without fresh releases providing economic, industry, issuer, rating agency, central bank, and regulatory information. This data torrent can sometimes obscure the more important determinants of capital market valuations and induce random-walk noise trading.

For example, the interpretations of local central bank governors' speeches may be quickly canceled out by the remarks 24 hours later by another governor from the same central bank. An inordinate emphasis can be placed on highly volatile and often subsequently revised economic statistics like the U.S. monthly employment report.

CAPITAL MARKET MISSION AND KEY CAPITAL MARKET QUESTIONS

It's generally accepted that all categories of investors seek to optimize their risk-adjusted returns, income, or capital preservation in accordance with their chosen time horizon, risk tolerance, and bespoke portfolio constraints (e.g., environmental, social and governance (ESG) standards). Concurrently, all types of financial security issuers seek to limit their cost of capital. The myriad competing investor and issuer quests is sorted out in the capital markets.

The main function of global capital markets is to match capital savers with capital needers. In most societies, there are some governments, individuals, and enterprises that do not spend their entire income. These delayers of consumption thereby save. In contrast, there are governments, individuals, and firms that spend more than their income. If such spending is partially dedicated to the funding of existing enterprise expansion and the formation of new businesses, then such excess spending is deemed to be investing.

Through this around-the-clock market process, the value of every stock, bond, currency, commodity, real estate unit, and collectible is established. Most of these determinations are made via some form of electronic exchange. But many also are formed through various types of auctions.

As usual, the textbook condensation of complex activities does not fully illuminate the activities, excitement, and consequences of the capital markets mission. The study of capital markets can help shed light on some of society's important questions like:

- Why are construction cranes working almost continuously in certain cities, while nearly invisible in other urban centers?
- Why do retail clothing stores and restaurants come and go at such a high turnover rate?
- Why do some businesses last for decades?
- Where does the capital come from to sponsor the creation of new firms and technologies that improve the quality of life for billions of people?
- What explains the vast difference in borrowing rates among nations?
- What is the proper balance between fiscal and monetary policy?

- Should nations strive for a strong or weak currency?
- Should a firm finance its expansion through common stock, preferred stock, senior debt, junior debt, or convertible debt?
- Why do certain works of art sell at more than $100 million? How are prices determined for rare coins, stamps, antiques, and sports memorabilia?
- Where does the money come from that pours into institutions like mutual funds, hedge funds, endowments, insurance companies, and pension funds? And what are these institutions really trying to accomplish with their money?
- Will ZIRP (zero-interest rate policies) and NIRP (negative-interest rate policies) by central banks really prove effective in stimulating advanced economy growth?
- Will global banks be able to smoothly "normalize" their policies in the late Teens/early Twenties without inflicting an economic growth pause and chilling, perhaps only briefly, capital market risk-taking?
- Will virtual currencies and block chain methods become more prevalent?
- Does inadequate liquidity, especially for credit instruments, pose a systemic risk for markets?
- Are global trade flows helped or hurt under various types of trade agreements?
- What are the principal causes of slow productivity growth despite a near-unanimous sense of accelerated technological change so far in the 21st century?
- What are the best future career fields? Will the arrival of more robots significantly displace huge portions of the workforce?
- How should portfolios be diversified, and how often should asset class allocations be adjusted?
- Who will pay and how much to curb climate change?
- Will long-living retirees have sufficient financial resources to fund their post-working lives?

POST–GREAT RECESSION, GLOBAL CAPITAL MARKETS CHART A MORE CONSERVATIVE COURSE

Approaching a decade after its onset in 2007 and more than seven years after its supposed conclusion in 2009, the Great Recession and its aftershocks continue to reverberate through the global financial system. In various forms, social unrest ferments from Iraq to Syria to Turkey to Greece to Belgium to France to England and to the United States. This lurking social unrest spills over into unexpected plebiscite outcomes, like the United Kingdom's decision in June 2016 to leave the European Union.

In many parts of the world, good jobs and real wage advances remain scarce. Advanced economy growth dawdles below historic post-recession norms (3.0% or greater GDP growth for at least two-to-four consecutive quarters). Despite ebullient "techno-optimistic" celebrations of coming mammoth industry disruptions authored by big data, 3D printing, nanotechnology, biotechnology, social media, smart communications, fintech, driverless vehicles, robotics, artificial intelligence, virtual currencies like bitcoins, and drones, productivity gains dwindle in a slow-moving economic current characterized as secular stagnation. The skewed distribution of wealth draws rebuke from political populists and the Vatican. Vast new immigration flows perturb long-term residents of some nations. Equities and risky credit asset values ride a bumpy roller-coaster. Precious metals sky, retreat, and then bounce. Energy prices descend to multi-decade lows in 2016 courtesy of fracking, while interest rates tumble to multi-century troughs as shown in Figure 1.2 and even fall into unprecedented negative territory for Japan and large parts of Europe. The U.S. dollar, yen, and the euro engage in seesaw contests to ascertain the least favorite major currency of all, while China aspires to global reserve currency status.

Chronic wariness rules the capital market mindset in the Teens. And little wonder. "Manipulated" market valuations (especially suppressed bond yields) rest on pillars of unprecedented economic stimulus largesse, especially from central banks. Policymakers are assailed for doing too little or too much. In many investment arenas, the search for portfolio alpha generation has morphed into sideline-standing, index-hugging capital preservation. Returns from alternative investment strategies, particularly by macro hedge funds, have proven less bountiful and consistent.

The strategic-outlook haze seldom has been thicker. Inspired by ideological and theological divisions, geopolitical uncertainties abound in this new "multipolar world" of the early 21st century. The menu of proposed political and economic remedies to exit this "high state of uncertainty" grows ever longer.

Deep structural forces shift the tectonics of the global financial system. A multiple-generation escalation of financial leverage in all forms has crested and begun to recede,

FIGURE 1.2   Record low G4 10-year interest rates (%): 1871 to June 27, 2016*
*Germany, Japan, U.K., and U.S.; closest substitute available used when 10-year government bond yield data unavailable.
Source: BNY Mellon using data from Global Financial Data and Bloomberg

albeit at a glacial pace. While undeniably an overall benefit, globalization comes with a price in the form of displaced industries and workers. EM economies converge to advanced economy status through their ascent of the production value chain. Systemic uncertainties, especially in financial services, have bred a well-intentioned quest by regulators to suppress potential instability through additional oversight. Stoking echoes of the 19th century and the 1930s, the efficacy of capitalism has even been called into question.

The progression to the mid-21st century likely will follow a hybrid of three main scenarios: first, an unlikely return to the Goldilocks milieu of bounding risky asset valuations during the mid-1980s and mid-1990s; second, a perpetuation of chronic malaise for advanced economies spanning all of the Teens and consuming much of the Twenties (see Japan's experience since 1989); third, and closely related to the second scenario, a muddle-through, risk on/risk off, range-mired global financial system mainly waiting for the passage of time to eventually rekindle dormant animal spirits.

This "Great Transition" of the global financial system poses vast implications for financial industry business models. The ill-prepared, rooted mainly in the traditions of the past, will be "reengineered" into "adaption capitulation" or obsolescence. "Fast-mover adaptation assimilants" will seize their fields.

ACCURATE FINANCIAL ERA DEFINITION HELPS CHART BUSINESS AND PORTFOLIO STRATEGY

Most intellectual disciplines assign a broad label to each major phase of their historical evolution. While unable to match the taxonomic diversity of geology and biology, physics and economics can be divided roughly into classical, modern (neoclassical), and postmodern periods. This practice of "era categorization" extends to financial markets, where the capricious ebb and flow of business and valuation cycles gives rise to an abundance of defining labels.

For any field, especially financial markets, no single universal label completely fits an era. Nonconforming theoretical and information outliers often coexist with mainstream perspectives. Despite centuries of convergence, the fortunes of local economies frequently deviate from the global norm. And secular global financial market labels usually fail to encompass the prospects of technological advances, productivity enhancements, and history-altering geopolitical events like the rise of the "Arab Street" in 2011 and ISIS/ISIL in 2014. Instead, many professionals, who know they cannot reliably predict the price of a 10-year Treasury a week in advance, place too much faith in multi-decade forecasts of economic parameters like growth, deficits, interest rates, savings, and investments generated by linear data extrapolations via spreadsheet analytics. History convincingly shows the fallacy of overreliance on secular forecasts of financial market metrics to characterize an era. For example, the U.S. government falsely was thought as recently as 2000 to be running budget surpluses for as far as the eye can see.

The sources and appropriate remedies for the profound and repeated systemic financial malfunctions from the onset of the Asian Financial Crisis in 1997 through the dot-com bubble in the late 1990s and its collapse in 2000, the U.S. corporate governance deficiencies in 2001–2002, the real-estate bubble detonating, financial-deleveraging Great Recession of 2007–2009, and its damaging offspring, the Sovereign Credit Crisis of 2010–2012, have been thoroughly parsed. Like the multidiscipline excavations of the root causes of the Great Depression of the 1930s, the search for deeper interpretations equipped with historical forensics, especially the persistence of "anticipation failure" by the policymaker and investor consensus, will occupy scholars for decades. Triggered by the difficult experiences of 1997–2011, especially 2007 through early 2009, and reinforced by a multitude of lingering uncertainties, a neither first, nor last, "New Conservative Financial Consensus" has dawned in this "Great Transition Era" that will long endure in our opinion.

For policymakers and strategic investors, the formation of expectations about the future format of the global financial system should rank higher than the mental exhaustion incurred from absorbing the ever-changing, herd-dominated tactical prophecies of capital market values. The contemplation and ultimate selection of a strategic template to define a financial era can enhance the forecasting prowess and ensuing organizational success of capital market institutions. Multiple candidates like "Capitalism 4.0," "The Rise of EM," "The Grand Convergence, "The Great Deleveraging," "The Consumer Bust," "The Clash of Generations," "The Age of Financial Reform," "The Post–Great Recession," and "The Second Great Contraction" vie for the best title to encapsulate this 2007–2030 era. Each holds a valid yet partial claim on characterizing this unfolding period in capital market history. Paralleling recent political reorientations in the United States and parts of Europe, "The Great Transition Era" serves as the most comprehensive portrayal of the present and medium-term financial milieu in our view.

Under the aegis of this Great Transition Era, economic policymaker, regulatory, legislative, credit rating agency, and even judicial overseers have switched from a minimalist, do-not-tamper-with-legal-market-activities approach to a cautious, interventionist, prophylactic philosophy focused on sound banking rules, higher capital requirements, liquidity fortification, and discovery of willing or unintended malfeasance. "Expected risk" now takes precedence over "expected gain." The first question has become "what can go wrong?" rather than "what's the upside?" The maintenance of liquidity and minimization of valuation volatility have climbed the "micro" financial decision-making checklist. Ironically on a macro basis, the application of the "New Conservative Financial Consensus" has entailed the pursuit of prosperity through fiscal austerity consistent with a political repudiation of Keynesian economics.

Economic, market, industry, and issuer forecasts are justifiably viewed as malleable projections of the future, dependent upon model mechanics and the regular recalibration of assumption inputs. The daily din of instantaneous, conjectural reactions to new financial system data has been properly classified as occasionally useful "background noise," to be methodologically overridden by rigorous analyses. The heady pace of financial innovation from the mid-1970s through the mid-Oughts, which featured the introduction of Treasury futures and options, ABS, CMOs, swaps, modern high-yield and emerging-debt markets, and CDS has stalled in the Teens. The global financial system has installed new antiviral software, expelled toxic components like certain structured credit products such as CDOs, and has rebooted with higher defensive firewalls.

By definition, a *consensus* does not imply unanimity. Indeed, anti-consensus, contrarian investment strategies frequently reap generous rewards. Accordingly, all aspects of the "Next-Generation Financial System" will not be found in harmony during "The Great Transition Age." Risk-taking has not been entirely vanquished. The pursuit of absolute and relative returns, an increasingly more arduous chore in the late Ought-Teens regime of low interest rates, demands the assumption of some portfolio risks. And as evidenced by the gradual globalization and asset class range extensions of the portfolio management choice set for plan sponsors, sovereign wealth funds, and endowments, the steady march out of the "nominal risk curve" has not and will not be curtailed by the "New Conservative Financial Consensus." But this seeming contradiction can be quickly resolved by switching to a "risk-adjusted framework." Anachronistic portfolio constraints, from local market-only anchors to credit-quality restrictions and asset-class eliminations, probably impinge risk-adjusted alpha over the long run more than active management errors.

THE GREAT TRANSITION AGE UNFOLDS

In the aftermath of all major financial calamities, pledges to more cautious, systemic–stress mitigating, safety-first methods are widely promulgated and willingly embraced by policymakers and survivors. The longevity of such "professions of prudence" is usually proportional to the magnitude of the dislocation. Given the colossal damage inflicted by the Great Depression of the 1930s, many capital market institutions in the 1970s still could be found navigating in accordance with four-decade-old, conservative financial philosophies. As a result, restrained government and corporate financial leverage, tepid consumer borrowings, and plan sponsor preference for higher bond than equity allocation generally prevailed until the early 1980s. The global financial system of 1945–1972 still regularly succumbed to local recessions and negative reappraisals of key capital market values. But the periodicity of shocks and amplitude of valuation responses paled in comparison to the successor era of 1973–2016, inaptly once thought to be emblematic of a "Great Moderation" macroeconomic triumph.

As with its more severe predecessor in the 1930s, the painful Great Recession of 2007–2009 and malingering uncertainties like the growing probability of European and U.S. recession recidivism in the late Teens/early Twenties, augmented by the United Kingdom's departure from the European Union, have inspired a well-warranted embrace of government, policymaker, corporate, consumer, investor, and institutional financial conservatism. An outbreak of fiscal rectitude has descended upon European and U.S. governments. Corporate capital cushions and liquidity provisions have been fortified. Consumer spending growth has waned in advanced economies, while savings have blossomed. To the benefit of the global financial system, the recent "lessons learned" and re-learned (see Figure 1.3) will inform mainstream economic, issuer, portfolio, legislative, and regulatory policies throughout the Teens and beyond.

In some ways, little learning progress has been made over the past century. In Bruner & Carr's *The Panic of 1907: Lessons Learned,* the following catalysts for

- Inadequate big-picture thinking about economic/capital market evolution and risk.
- Like industries and individual firms, global economic and global financial systems periodically require tweaking and even major overhaul.
- Ignorance/ignoring of rich capital market history of past two centuries can be highly hazardous to portfolios.
- Global trade and capital flow imbalances are not sustainable infinitely.
- Residential and commercial real estate valuations do not continuously escalate and are highly correlated.
- Reoccurring systemic and idiosyncratic credit misdiagnoses continue to plague world financial system.
- Government, financial institution, and consumer financial leverage have risk limits and need to be recalibrated lower.
- Excessive reliance on short-term financing.
- Complete consideration of high fluctuations in liquidity.
- Regular fallibility of institutions (certain financials, rating agencies, regulators), financial risk models, risk surveillance.
- Antiquated regulatory and government oversight methodologies need overhaul, with enhanced global coordination and additional scrutiny of rating agencies and certain types of alternative managers.
- Rate of financial innovation exceeded "comprehension speed limit."
- Inter-asset-class correlations can be disturbingly high.
- Hazards of yield maximization and understaffed asset management firms.

FIGURE 1.3 Lessons Re-learned from Great Recession (2007–2009)

the Panic were cited: complexity of system architecture; buoyant growth for a while; inadequate safety buffers; adverse leadership; real economic shock; excess fear and greed and strange behaviors; and failure of collective action.[1] Hopefully, variations of the same lessons are not reintroduced in yet-to-be-written histories of future severe panics, manias, and crashes. But such optimism may be misguided. As John Kenneth Galbraith wrote in *A Short History of Financial Euphoria* in 1993, "Recurrent speculative insanity and the associated financial deprivation and larger devastation are, I am persuaded, inherent in the system. Perhaps it is better that this be recognized and accepted."[2]

Guided by the Grand Convergence of political, economic, finance, and portfolio management methods, the world economy ironically has become more asymmetric since the mid-1990s. Advanced economies did not miss a beat during the Asian Financial Crisis of

---

[1] Robert F. Bruner and Sean D. Carr, *The Panic of 1907: Lessons Learned from the Market's Perfect Storm* (Hoboken, NJ: John Wiley & Sons, 2007).
[2] John Kenneth Galbraith, *A Short History of Financial Euphoria* (New York: Penguin, 1994).

1997–1998. And the Great Recession largely spared emerging nations thanks to a commodity price bloom until 2015. EM economic ascendance likely will persist well into the 2020s. But having bottomed in 2009, advanced economies are envisioned to deliver below full potential growth of 1.5%–2.0% out to 2025.

In the Q2 2009 through Q2 2015 recognition of this AE economic rebound, unfolding conservative financial era, and gusher of restorative liquidity injected by monetary policymakers, risky financial asset valuations recorded extraordinary gains as shown in Figures 1.4 and 1.5 (global financial asset returns by decade). Volatility for most financial asset classes tumbled. Emerging market valuations boomed. Adjusting for record European, Japanese, and U.S. corporate cash holdings, effective corporate financial leverage dipped. Money markets normalized. The lowest interest rates since the 1950s inspired a massive surge in debt refundings and trimmed borrowers' cost of debt capital. Steep yield curves abetted financial institution recovery. Corporate mergers and acquisitions rose. Rating downgrades and defaults plummeted.

NO TRANSITIONS ARE FRICTIONLESS

While vastly improved from early 2009, global financial conditions in the late Teens are hardly idyllic. Structural aftermath questions linger. Bonds arguably entered bubble territory in 2010 and remain partially disconnected from fundamentals thanks to the policy ministrations of central banks. Greece tottered on the brink of de facto default in 2015 and could still instigate a systemic "European Contagion" across its periphery sufficiently potent to trip up a few key major banks and to derail the euro. The United States barely sidestepped a perilous excursion into unprecedented default territory on August 2, 2011, earning an S&P AAA to AA+ rating rebuke along the way, as Washington struggled to overcome a vast ideological divide to raise the U.S. government debt ceiling. Great Britain voted to leave the European Union on June 23, 2016. The Brexit process may be emulated in France, Holland, Italy, and TBD. Scotland may conduct another referendum to leave the United Kingdom, and Northern Ireland may opt to merge into the Republic of Ireland. Several additional European sovereigns and portions of the U.S. public finance sector like Puerto Rico require fiscal remediation. Real estate has recovered slowly in parts of the world and may already be cyclically peaking in some areas. Structural unemployment resists easy resolution in the United States and Europe.

The frayed Washington Consensus has inspired new flavors of capitalism and mildly reinvigorated a long-settled debate about the merits of globalization. A global legion of experts and official overseers has introduced a lengthy and sometimes contradictory prescription list of regulatory cures, often without confirming benefit-cost analyses. Acute political partisanship, though genuine, is side-by-side with and often obscures intense battles among income levels and commercial interests protecting and expanding their benefits and privileges. In several Western democracies, a contentious, intransigent political process thwarts the crafting of compromise and application of intelligent solutions, like using the tax code to incent production and restrain consumption, to complex political-economic problems.

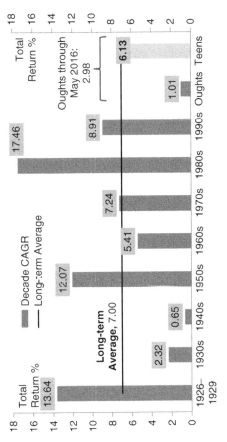

Periodic Compound Average Annual Growth Rates (%)

	1926–1999	1946–1999	1970–1999	1980s	1990s	Oughts	2010–May 31, 2016	Oughts through May 31, 2016	2016
Global Equity	9.34	11.19	12.11	20.77	9.09	-2.60	6.90	1.01	-0.27
Global Bond	4.79	5.48	9.07	12.03	8.08	5.84	4.48	5.30	4.07
Global Financial Asset	7.91	9.07	11.12	17.46	8.91	1.01	6.13	2.98	1.53

	1926–May 31, 2016	1980–May 31, 2016
Global Equity	7.76	8.35
Global Bond	4.88	7.88
Global Financial Asset	7.00	8.42

FIGURE 1.4 Nominal global financial asset returns by decade*: 1926 to May 31, 2016

*Global Financial Asset: 60% weighted return of Global Equity and 40% weighted return of Global Bond. Global Financial Asset portfolio is rebalanced monthly. Global Equity: from 1926 to 1987, Global Financial Data World Total Return Index (U.S.-dollar) is used; MSCI-Hedged World U.S.-dollar Index from 1988 to current. Global Bond: from 1926 to 1986, Global Financial Data Global Total Return Government Bond Index; from 1987 to 1989, Barclays Global Treasury Index; from 1990 to 1998, Barclays Global Aggregate Index; from 1999 to 2016, Barclays Multiverse Index is used. Global Bond U.S.-dollar hedged after 1986 and Global Equity U.S.-dollar hedged after 1987. Financial asset total return series begins in 1926; Global Equity total return except from 1988 to current.

Source: BNY Mellon using data from Global Financial Data, FactSet, Barclays Live, and Bloomberg

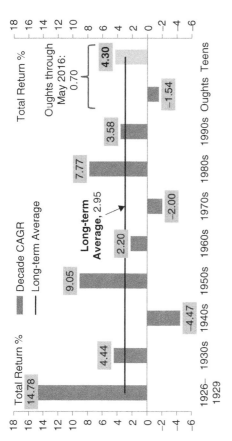

Periodic Compound Average Annual Growth Rates (%)									
	1926–1999	1946–1999	1970–1999	1970s	1980s	1990s	Oughts	2010–May 31, 2016	Oughts through May 31, 2016	2016
Global Equity	5.11	4.97	3.96	–2.26	10.80	3.75	–5.06	5.06	–1.22	–1.16
Global Bond	0.46	–0.41	1.14	–2.07	2.78	2.79	3.16	2.68	2.97	3.15
Global Financial Asset	3.45	2.97	3.04	–2.00	7.77	3.58	–1.54	4.30	0.70	0.63

	1926–May 31, 2016	1980–May 31, 2016
Global Equity	3.93	3.33
Global Bond	0.91	2.87
Global Financial Asset	2.95	3.39

FIGURE 1.5 Real global financial asset returns by decade*: 1926 to May 31, 2016

*Global Financial Asset: 60% weighted return of Global Equity and 40% weighted return of Global Bond. Global Financial Asset portfolio is rebalanced monthly. Global Equity: from 1926 to 1987, Global Financial Data World Total Return Index (U.S.-dollar) is used; MSCI-Hedged World U.S.-dollar Index from 1988 to current. Global Bond: from 1926 to 1986, Global Financial Data Global Total Return Government Bond Index; from 1987 to 1989, Barclays Global Treasury Index; from 1990 to 1998, Barclays Global Aggregate Index; from 1999 to 2016, Barclays Multiverse Index is used. Global Bond U.S.-dollar hedged after 1986 and Global Equity U.S.-dollar hedged after 1987. Financial asset total return series begins in 1926; Global Equity total return except from 1988 to current. *Source:* BNY Mellon using data from Global Financial Data, FactSet, Barclays Live, and Bloomberg

15

Secular outlook confidence gained and then waned since the chaos of early 2009. In turn, tactical market sentiment has oscillated in a bipolar pendulum between recovery euphoria and reoccurring bouts of doubt sufficient to entertain economic contraction conjectures. Corporate and consumer animal spirits remain subdued in the late Teens. All layers of the global financial system continue to deleverage, a most welcome trend for both debtors and creditors. But this "debt-downsizing adjustment" will require years to complete and leave scars as evidenced by peripheral Europe and all layers of U.S. governments. As manifest in the proliferation of long-term forecasts, outlook horizons have never been longer and risk-mitigation culture seldom has been more worshiped. Abetted by technology, macro and micro risk vigilance has been generationally and possibly permanently enhanced. The ever-stronger interdependence of the global financial system has been widely acknowledged and has induced an erosion of regional and asset-class siloization. In turn, this has bred a desire for greater global policymaking and regulatory harmonization.

The blueprint for the Next-Generation Global Financial System has been cast; the detailed construction and adoption phases have begun. Business models will require major recalibration, both in anticipation and after detailing of new regulatory rules. To the possible detriment of arresting structural unemployment in the United States and Europe, the ability of accommodative monetary policy to offset fiscal conservatism remains unknown. The forecast divide between possible deflation now/inflation later for advanced economies has not been resolved.

Guided by a desire to invest in rapid economic growth and a quest for yield maximization, global trade and capital flow imbalances persist in favor of emerging-market nations and may worsen with potential deployment of currency and trade protectionist policies. The endurance of export-driven Modern Mercantilism and low-saving Western Consumerism cannot be predicted. A grand rebalancing ultimately must be implemented; the economic mechanisms and especially political willingness to achieve sustainable global capital flow equilibrium are unclear. As displayed by soaring values for precious metals and bitcoins again in 2016, confidence in the ability of certain major currencies, like the U.S. dollar, to serve as a permanent store-of-value rather than a depreciating asset has diminished. While highly unlikely to lose its role in the foreseeable future, the status of the U.S. dollar as the world's reserve currency will continue to be questioned as an inevitable transition to a multipolar world economic regime unfolds. And until full resolution of several European sovereign credit concerns, the destiny of the European currency union and the euro will entice conjecture about the modern meaning of "risk-free government securities."

A potential strategic upward reset by the early Twenties of medium- and long-term interest rates on possible inflation reignition in advanced economies, a broad asset allocation shift from bonds to equities, and further economic normalization have inspired apprehension of higher debt capital costs and refunding roadblocks for some debt asset classes like lower-quality credits. The fates of the mortgage-finance agencies, Fannie Mae and Freddie Mac, are obscured by political considerations. Bond market perturbations likely will emanate from the Fed's slow march to higher short-term interest rates over the late Teens and eventual paring of its quantitative-easing balance sheet horde of U.S.

debt securities. The capability of emerging-markets to sustain their enviable surge over the past decade and to withstand embryonic inflation and a possible retreat of hot capital flows has been called into question.

The exponential rise of algorithmic trading has not peaked. In the spirit of efficiency maximization, heeding the siren's call of allegedly superior quantitative methods, and ironically sometimes at the expense of rigorous fundamental differentiation, high-speed trading has shrunk investment horizons at many institutions. Except for ETFs, next-generation contingent bank capital structures like CoCos, and Islamic Finance, new financial product innovation largely has stalled since 2007. Securitization and derivitization have regressed into the plain-vanilla methods of the 1990s. And as demonstrated in 2001, a terrorist shock and sudden escalation of geopolitical risk could dim expectations at any time. The specter of systemic cyber-disruption has become more real.

THE NEW CONSERVATIVE FINANCIAL CONSENSUS SPEEDS THE TRANSITION TO THE NEXT-GENERATION GLOBAL FINANCIAL SYSTEM

Over the coming decade of the Twenties, the increasingly complex and inseparably interwoven global economy and global financial system face a gauntlet of deep adjustments. The accelerating geographic rearrangement of manufacturing, resource, technology, services, health care, and education introduces profound questions about the structural destiny of the global and, even more so, many local economies. In advanced economies, the combination of escalating entitlement obligations emanating from aging populations and a concurrent desire to rein in government deficits can only be rectified through some politically challenging combination of benefit reductions and tax increases. The construction of new measures of international and national economic vitality would aid in smoothing the path to a 21st-century fiscal rectitude that eschews pork-barrel spending, targets benefits only to those truly in need rather than the politically potent, and funds projects after rigorous cost-benefit analyses. And as demographics and fiscal constraints stretch social safety nets in advanced economies, many emerging economies will grapple with their initial fabrication.

Globally, long-run savings may not match burgeoning infrastructure investment demand from a rising middle-class in emerging nations. The possible scarcity of investment capital may escalate capital costs and crowd out some traditional borrowers from financial markets. The global flow of human capital in pursuit of superior economic opportunity accelerates with each passing generation and engenders difficult-to-forecast economic and social knock-on effects. Attempts to arrest global climate change will shape government, industry, issuer, and investor decision-making in a yet-to-be determined manner. For instance, the rate of acceptance of electric cars and alternative energy sources like solar and wind will help determine the longevity of high dependence on fossil fuels. And the anticipated opening of the Arctic Passage will charge lower-cost trade between Europe and Asia. Meanwhile, geopolitical risks in the Middle East loom as a constant presence.

Akin to the discovery quest for dark matter, the search for and retention of asset management excellence (risk-adjusted absolute returns and relative-value alpha) will become more difficult. Many traditional informational advantages have been dissipated by technology, new analytics, the substitution of expert independent research providers for generic sell-side research, enhanced macro-market expertise by supranational organizations (e.g., BIS, IMF, World Bank, Asian Development Bank), local central banks, and a prodigious expansion of a more proficient 24/7 financial media. And absolute returns have been compressed in a sea of surfeit liquidity, sponsored by stimulative-minded central banks.

This ongoing upgrade of the global financial system under the auspices of a conservative mantle will extend beyond the Teens. This lengthy transition will not be without cost. While espousing the virtues of free markets, nation-state participation in economic affairs will advance. As firms compete in brand power, product quality, and costs, nations will vie to attract business via modest corporate tax rates, low real wages, and high-quality human capital. Central bank oversight likely will be increased, leading to the possible politicization of monetary policy. The regenerative bypass of traditional-banking endeavors, under the well-intentioned guidance of Basel III, to raise capital and liquidity, to the less-regulated, shadow banking system will reintroduce systemic vulnerabilities. European and U.S. economic performance may remain subdued for a long period as institutional and retail balance sheets embrace deficit and debt diets. The social consequences of extended austerity ultimately will become conspicuous as evidenced by the late 2011 flurry of disjointed protests and the 2016 presidential campaign of Bernie Sanders directed against Wall Street and big banks. To the detriment of the restraining prudence of moral hazard, a handful of key systemically important financial institutions effectively will stay too big to fail. At the potential expense of liquidity and allowing for some resurrection of the shadow banking, the world financial system has become lumpier with rising aggregations of investment capital in sovereign wealth funds and very large asset management firms. And periods of pronounced secular adjustment always re-sort economic, industry, and issuer leaders and trailers, often in unpredictable ways.

STURDIER GLOBAL FINANCIAL SYSTEM PROMOTES WORLD ECONOMIC GROWTH

Conservatism alone does not immunize the global financial system from setbacks. Structural adjustment frictions will not dissipate. Business cycles will persist and possibly feature shorter-duration amplitudes accompanied by waves of high volatility. Complete global financial, environmental, and tax regulatory harmonization remains a distant goal. The eventual abatement of massive monetary and fiscal stimulus in the late Teens/early Twenties may spur a minor, temporary growth retreat and diminution of systemic liquidity. Some risk complacency will cyclically reoccur when markets enjoy a long spell of relative calm, new enlistees join the capital market profession, and partial amnesia of 2007–2009 sets in at some institutions. Individual economies and asset classes occasionally will stampede upward at rapid velocities prior to bubble bursts. Periodic and sometimes negative short-term fluctuations of capital market parameters are an inevitable feature of capitalism.

Financial systems are always partially beholden to the governments that set up the laws and rules that guide their operations. Just as professional athletic contests require referees, financial system regulation is an unavoidable accomplice to sound, fair, unbiased, and competitive free markets. Optimal financial markets should promote the general welfare of society through efficient capital allocation to its most productive applications and not facilitate capital detours into schemes like international tax arbitrage. Successful financial systems hinge on a balanced approach by governments. Insufficient oversight can encourage fraud, waste, capital destruction, and less-than-optimal economic growth. Conversely, excessive and capricious government oversight can chill innovation and willingness to take risk by businesses, entrepreneurs, and investors.

Nonetheless as a consequence of the Great Recession, this unfolding conservative re-sculpting of the global financial system into a sturdier edifice will reduce the chances of systemically perilous mishaps, especially along the instigating vectors of the late Oughts. Future economic historians may well cite the evolutionary-stimulative consequences of the Great Recession under the aegis of a New Conservative Financial Consensus as a more important legacy than the containment of its numerous catalysts. A robust, generally stable, efficient global financial system underpins world economic progress. This will reinvigorate strategic confidence, augment capital raising, sharpen capital allocation, spur innovation, unleash new asset management methods, and help speed global economic growth. Eight decades elapsed between the Great Depression and the Great Recession. Hopefully as a result of this Great Transition Age, the distance to the next global financial system spasm of similar magnitude will measure at least eight decades. The global financial system of the late Teens has not attained perfection, but it's far sounder than its predecessors. And its successor iterations over the next two decades will be even sturdier.

Introduction and Tools

The Role of Global Capital Markets

Christian Edelmann and Shasheen Jayaweera

INTRODUCTION

This chapter provides an introduction to the participants, products, and functioning of global capital markets (Figure 2.1). We also discuss the important role capital markets play in supporting economic growth and development. We start with a detailed discussion of key participants and how capital markets support their economic activities. We then introduce the main product groups offered, describing their key features and uses. Next, the various types of markets are explained, covering how they facilitate the funding and investing needs of participants. Finally, we conclude with a discussion of why capital markets are critical for economic development.

THE BASIC PRODUCTS OFFERED IN CAPITAL MARKETS

In a narrow definition, capital markets offer two types of funding products to issuers, equities and debt (also called fixed income) through both primary (initial issuance of securities) and secondary (ongoing trading of securities) markets. In a broader definition, capital markets include the trading of physical assets (e.g., commodities) in addition to currencies and derivatives.

Equities

Equities, commonly known as *shares* and *stocks*, represent an ownership interest in a corporation, hence the term *share* as each security is a share of ownership. Shares have the same limited liability rights of the corporations they represent, which means that the liability of share owners is limited to their investment amount. Shares are initially created when a corporation is formed, whereby the owners can choose the number of shares appropriate for the corporation's plans and valuation. At this point the corporation is known as a private corporation as all the shares are held by a close group of investors.

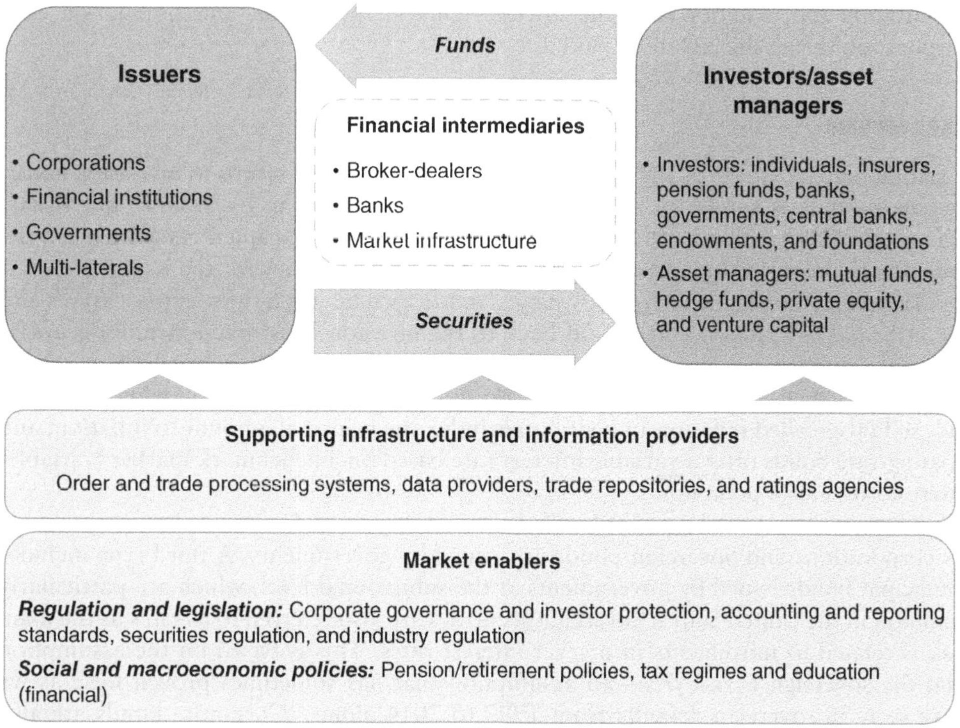

FIGURE 2.1 Capital markets environment
Source: Oliver Wyman

As corporations grow, some may choose to become a *public* corporation, or one that is *listed* on a public stock exchange, where members of the public can openly buy or sell shares. This process is known as *listing*, where existing or additional shares may be created and offered to the public through an *initial public offering* (IPO).

Shares entitle their holders to a share of the dividends declared by the board of directors to be distributed from the corporation's profits. Likewise they also generally entitle owners to a vote on critical decisions at annual general meetings. Shares can be created in different *classes* with differing rights. There are two broad classes of shares, *common* and *preferred*. Preferred shares typically have a higher claim on dividends and on the assets of a firm in the event of liquidation, but typically have no voting rights and have a fixed dividend that will not rise with earnings.

Following an IPO, shares are traded on stock exchanges and their valuation is subject to supply and demand, which in turn is influenced by the underlying fundamentals of the business, macroeconomic factors such as interest rates, and market sentiment.

The return to shareholders is a function of both the dividends paid to them from the corporation's profits, and of any movements in the share price (capital growth).

Importantly too, equities have the lowest rights in the default and liquidation of a corporation, being the last to be paid out.

Fixed Income

Fixed-income securities, as the name suggests, promise a *fixed* return to investors. Fixed-income funding is similar in nature to the provision of a loan by a bank, but issuers manage to attract a broader investor base through tapping into capital markets, generally lowering the required interest rate or improving non-price terms for the issuer.

Fixed-income securities typically have a *maturity* date when the security expires and the *principal* or loan amount is paid back to the investor. Most fixed-income securities also offer interest rate payments (known as *coupons*) at regular intervals. Some types of securities such as zero-coupon bonds do not pay out any coupons, while inflation-indexed (also called inflation-linked) bonds index the principal amount to inflation, and floating-rate bonds offer a variable interest rate based on a benchmark market (variable) interest rate plus a premium.

There are two broad types of bonds based on the issuer: Corporate bonds are issued by corporations and Sovereign bonds are issued by governments. A third type includes municipal bonds issued by governments at the subnational level, which are particularly common in the United States. Sovereign securities are also referred to as *rates* as the main risk is related to movements in market interest rates. This is based on the assumption that the sovereign is *risk free*—an assumption that has sometimes proven false as we have seen 30 sovereign defaults from 1997 to 2014 alone.[1] Corporate bonds are also known as credit securities as they also entail credit risk in the underlying issuer.

Fixed-income securities are also tradable in the market and are thus subject to market price movements. Given that the interest rate payments are largely fixed, any decline in market interest rates raises the effective yield of the security (coupon payment as a percentage of value of the security). As a result, there would be increased demand for the security, driving its price higher and reducing its yield. Thus, the prices of fixed-income securities typically move inversely to movements in market interest rates. Furthermore, a change in sentiment about the credit quality of an issuer can result in a decline in the value of those securities.

Foreign Exchange and Commodities

Foreign Exchange (FX) relates to the trading of currencies in exchange for other currencies. The most basic form of FX transaction is a *spot* trade where two currencies are agreed to be exchanged immediately at an agreed rate (although the settlement may take further time based on settlement standards). However, the bulk of FX-related transactions happen in the form of derivatives contracts and these will be discussed in the next section.

---

[1]Moody's "Sovereign Default and Recovery Rates, 1983–2013," April 11, 2014.

FX is frequently broken down into G10 (comprising the 10 largest developed countries) and EM (currencies of all other countries). Trading volumes and market activity tend to be concentrated in the former.

Commodities represent basic goods, typically used in production and commerce. There are many types of commodities traded, with each commodity represented for contract purposes using a variety of sizes and qualities based on historical conventions. When commodities are traded on an exchange, they must conform to strict quality criteria to ensure standardization of each unit. The key groups of commodities include (with common examples):

- Agricultural (e.g., corn and soybeans)
- Animal products (e.g., cattle and hogs)
- Energy (e.g., crude oil and natural gas)
- Precious metals (e.g., gold and silver)
- Base metals (e.g., iron and copper)

Commodities are also largely traded in the form of derivatives contracts.

Derivatives

Securities can be classed also as *cash* and *derivatives*. Cash securities represent direct ownership or claims on assets such as part of a corporation or a financial obligation from an issuer. Derivatives, as the name suggests, are securities that derive their value from an underlying asset such as other securities, indices, commodities, or currencies (FX).

Derivatives typically represent future claims on assets, for example, if a commodity is bought forward via a forward contract. Hence they are heavily used for hedging purposes by a wide variety of market participants. Hedging involves offsetting some form of risk, such as potential future changes in interest rates or the potential change in the price of a commodity. When used as a hedging tool, derivatives effectively transfer the risk in the underlying asset to a different party. As such, derivatives can also be thought of as providing a form of insurance. Derivatives are also used as a form of (leveraged) investments.

The most common types of derivatives are briefly outlined below:

- *Forwards:* Forwards represent binding contracts for the sale or purchase of a fixed quantity of an asset at a fixed point of time in the future. Forwards are most commonly used in the FX and commodities markets. Once the initial contract has been agreed, it can then also be traded, with its value changing relative to the movements in the underlying asset. As an example, airlines often enter into forward contracts to minimize fuel price risks as fuel represents one of their largest costs. Forwards are traded in over-the-counter (OTC) markets.
- *Futures:* Futures are similar to forwards except that their contract terms are standardized and they are traded on exchanges. Futures are also available on many index products including stock indices.

- *Options:* Options, as the name suggests, provide the right (but not obligation) for the contract holder to either buy (known as a *call* option) or sell (*put* option) a certain fixed quantity of an asset either before or at a fixed expiry date at a fixed price. Options can help provide a *floor* price for certain assets (i.e., through owning a put option which guarantees a certain sale price) or a ceiling price (i.e., through a call option which guarantees a maximum purchase price) for certain assets thus minimizing risks faced by the option holder.
- *Swaps:* Swaps are contracts by which two parties agree on the swapping or exchange of two assets or commitments at some point in time. The most common form of swaps are interest rate swaps (IRSs). These contracts swap the interest rate payment commitments between two counterparties. The two main types of IRSs include *float for fixed* where a floating interest rate commitment is swapped for a fixed interest rate commitment and *float for float* involving the swapping of a floating rate based on one benchmark rate with another. Both involve fixed notional or principal amounts upon which the rates are calculated. Other frequently used swap contracts include FX swaps or cross-currency interest rate swaps.

CAPITAL MARKETS AS A SUBSTITUTE FOR BANK LENDING

We described the narrow definition of capital markets as the provision of funding to issuers. In that sense, capital markets serve similar functions to traditional banking. Banks facilitate the provision of funds to customers to support their economic activities. Banks traditionally raise their own funding through customer deposits, and thus match investors supplying funds with issuers requiring funds. They also help transform the maturity or term profile required by each of these parties, with investors typically seeking to part with their funds mostly for short periods and issuers looking for longer-term funds.

Banks traditionally relied on their deposits for a significant proportion of their lending; thus deposits were the primary limit on lending. However, now, under most modern fractional reserve banking systems (which we will not detail here), banks have the unique ability to also create money. To highly simplify the process, when a bank creates a loan (an asset on its balance sheet), it simultaneously also creates a deposit in the loan customer's account (a liability on its balance sheet). The deposit is effectively new money, created by the bank, which the customer can then utilize. This is known as the *money creation effect*. Banks could theoretically offer unlimited lending and create unlimited new money; however, they face several regulatory restrictions on their activities. These regulations result in banks having to optimize between several constraints to their lending and deposit-taking activities based on the quality and quantity of loans, deposits, other funding and capital (can largely be thought of as shareholders' equity and reserves). In effect the deposit base and capital position of a bank serve as key restrictions on overall lending growth. The main regulations have converged globally around the Basel accords and local requirements. These regulations will be discussed further in Chapter 3 but are briefly discussed here:

- *Leverage ratio:* Constrains the ability of a bank to leverage its balance sheet, thus representing a constraint on lending in relation to capital. The leverage ratio is defined as a bank's highest quality capital (Tier 1 capital) divided by its exposures (on–balance sheet exposures, derivatives exposures, securities financing exposures, and off–balance sheet exposures). Basel III sets the leverage ratio at 3%.
- *Liquidity coverage ratio:* Requires banks to hold an amount of highly liquid assets (e.g., cash and government bonds) generally equal to 30 days of net cash-flow. This requirement helps ensure that banks can meet any immediate cash shortages through the sale of their liquid assets. Liquid assets generally do not include lending, and so this requirement also restricts lendable assets.
- *Capital adequacy ratio:* Sets a minimum capital requirement based on a bank's risk-weighted assets. Riskier lending and assets generate higher capital requirements. This requirement also further constrains the amount of lending banks can engage in based on their capital.
- *Loan-to-deposit ratio:* In many emerging markets, lending is also directly constrained by the size of deposits based on the loan-to-deposit ratio. An example is Indonesia, where Bank Indonesia, the central bank, enforces a maximum loan-to-funding ratio of 94% at the time of writing. Here, funding includes demand deposits, time deposits, medium-term notes, floating rate notes, and bonds that are issued by banks.

Given the constraints faced by banks, capital markets offer an important alternative source of funding for issuers and alternative investment options for investors. From an issuer perspective, fixed income securities allow a broader range of funding options compared to bank loans. They are highly customizable and allow for a broader issuer base enabling issuers to raise funds which banks may not be willing to provide in the form of a loan given constraints discussed above. Of course, capital markets also offer the option of raising equity funding, which is not available generally from banks. From an investor perspective, both fixed-income securities and deposits can offer a *fixed* return. However, fixed-income securities allow investors to also take corporate credit risk, create a more diversified portfolio, and access different points on the risk/return profile, whereas deposits, which tend to be at least partially insured, typically offer the lowest return for investors.

The mix of bank lending and other forms of capital markets financing differ significantly between countries as demonstrated in Figure 2.2. Countries with more advanced and *deeper* capital markets such as the United States and the UK see larger shares of capital markets financing when compared to countries like India, China, and South Africa. Countries like Egypt and Nigeria almost completely rely on bank lending with relatively limited capital markets. In some emerging markets such as those in South and Central America, bank lending is extremely difficult to obtain for many businesses, resulting

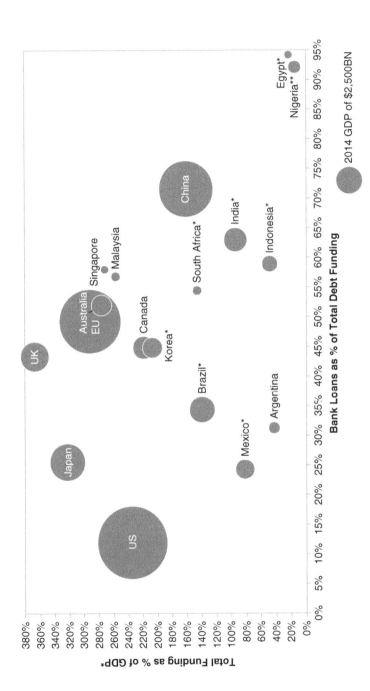

Total funding is the total sum of equity funding, corporate and sovereign bonds. and bank loans
*Total funding calculated from international debt securities and domestic debt securities
**Domestic debt securities data is not available

FIGURE 2.2 Funding structure in selected economies (2014, total funding as a % of GDP, bubble size 2014 GDP)
Sources: IMF, BIS, EIU, World Bank, Oliver Wyman analysis

in total funding markets being skewed toward larger firms that utilize capital markets. Capital markets utilization can also vary significantly within countries. Japan's overall funding, for example, is overall largely biased toward capital markets. However, for corporate funding, Japan relies largely on bank loans. This is, however, masked as Japan's financial institutions and government are large users of capital markets.

KEY PARTICIPANTS IN CAPITAL MARKETS

Capital markets consist of five basic stakeholders:

The Key Stakeholders in Capital Markets

1. Issuers (principally corporations, financial institutions, government and multilateral organizations) that seek funding for business activities
2. Investors who seek a financial return on their investment, and/or seek liquidity
3. Financial intermediaries that ensure an efficient flow of money from investors to issuers
4. Supporting infrastructure and information providers that sustain capital markets by providing critical information to market participants
5. Regulators and governments that provide the required legal framework and rules enabling the activities of all other participants

Issuers

Issuers represent the demand for funding in capital markets and seek to obtain funding for a variety of reasons, differing based on the type of issuer. In general, issuers seek funds to develop or maintain economic projects which generate cash-flow. The cash-flow from these projects is partly used to pay for the cost of funding obtained. There are four main categories of issuers: financial corporations, non-financial corporations, sovereigns/governments, and quasi-sovereigns or international multilateral organizations.

Overall, corporations are by far the largest issuers of capital markets and we differentiate here between financial and non-financial corporations as their needs and use of funds, along with the type of funds used, can differ considerably. Each of these issuers will be discussed in more detail now while the types of capital markets products they use will be covered in the next section.

Corporations (Non-Financial Institutions)

Non-financial corporations include both listed (public) and unlisted (private) firms. These firms require funds for carrying out their various economic activities with funding requirements typically differentiated between the term required:

1. *Long-term capital:* Longer-term investments include the construction of factories, purchasing or developing equipment, acquiring other firms, and funding research and

development—typically investments which generate cash-flows which span beyond one-year. Specific funding products can include term loans (from banks) and/or a combination of equity funding and fixed-income bonds. The specific choice and mix of funding chosen will depend on the rates and terms available and their suitability to the issuer.

2. *Short-term capital:* Typically classed as *working capital* and used for purchasing of items and inputs to production which are expected to be sold within one year. Working capital is typically largely funded either through short-term working capital loans, overdraft facilities, and credit cards (for smaller firms) provided by banks and other financial institutions or through short-term capital markets products such as commercial paper.

Participation in debt capital markets generally requires a credit rating, which is typically only available to larger firms with sufficient historic financial information. On the other hand, a range of companies access equity funding, with some exchanges even catering exclusively to smaller companies.

Financial Corporations

From an issuer perspective, financial corporations include banks, thrifts (also known as *savings and loans* in the United States), building societies, and credit unions, but also to a lesser extent, investment managers such as fund-managers. Financial corporations are also significant users of capital markets and are highly involved as intermediaries, too. While many of them have investment needs as corporates (e.g., for branches or IT systems), we highlight two distinct funding purposes:

1. *Asset-liability management (ALM):* ALM is the process of managing structural mismatches between assets and liabilities on the balance sheet. In a bank, these include the balancing of lending and/or investments (assets) and deposits and other non-equity funding (liabilities). ALM is also a vital function of financial institutions such as insurers and asset managers which have significant maturity transformation roles or frequently changing assets and liabilities. Mismatches arise and change on an intraday basis due to the changing profile of assets and liabilities (e.g., short-term deposits vs. longer-term loans) and market movements (e.g., changing interest rate curve and FX movements). Capital markets are actively utilized to manage and balance these mismatches as they occur (e.g., an increase in longer-term loans may be balanced with longer-term funding). In recent years, significant equity raisings have also been conducted by banks to strengthen their balance sheets.

2. *Investment leverage:* Some investment managers such as hedge funds will utilize capital markets for generating leverage on their investments—essentially raising funding from capital markets in the form of debt, enabling them to invest more than the sum of their investors' funds with the aim to generate higher *leveraged* returns. Using derivatives can be an alternative form of *synthetic* leverage.

Sovereigns/Governments

Sovereigns and *governments* (used interchangeably) are also significant users of capital markets in most economies globally although smaller in aggregate than corporates. In larger economies such as the United States, governments at all levels including the federal/national, state/province, and local/municipal level are active users of capital markets while in smaller economies, typically only the national and state governments are in a position to seek funding through capital markets. In some smaller economies and in emerging or developing markets, governments typically are the largest issuers in capital markets. Governments typically require funding from capital markets for two broad uses:

1. *Non-capital expenditure (government final consumption expenditure):* In many cases, government expenditure on consumption items which directly provide goods and services to their population (including on health care, education, defense, and social security) exceeds general government income (including personal and business taxation, duties, fees, and asset sales). In this situation, the government's budget is said to be in deficit. Governments typically need to borrow funds from capital markets to fund this gap and ensure essential public services can be provided.
2. *Capital and infrastructure project development (government gross capital formation):* Governments are also primarily responsible for providing infrastructure such as highways, airports, hospitals, and schools. These, too, may require borrowing funds from capital markets if funds cannot be provided from general government income. Some of these projects may generate ongoing revenue streams in the future, which will assist in covering their borrowing costs.

A third but related point is that during times of economic stress (such as recessions), governments often use fiscal measures such as increasing public spending (both consumption and capital), aiming to create extra demand and stimulate economic growth to lift their economies out of recession.

While we have classified governments under issuers, governments can also be investors. In certain countries, where governments accumulate surplus budget funds or foreign exchange surpluses, these are also invested through capital and other markets, typically through central banks or sovereign wealth funds (SWFs), which we will cover under investors.

Government securities are typically issued by their Treasury departments. However, certain sizable government entities which engage in significant financial activities may also seek funding on their own. These include, for example, the Federal National Mortgage Association (FNMA) or "Fannie Mae" in the United States, a publicly traded corporation, which is a *government-sponsored entity* (GSE) and supports the national mortgage market.

Quasi-Sovereigns/International Multilateral Organizations (MLOs) Quasi-sovereigns or international multilateral organizations (MLOs) are typically owned and managed by multiple governments with activities focused on projects in multiple nations with significance to more than a single government. Examples include the World Bank Group, the European Bank for Reconstruction and Development (EBRD), the International Monetary Fund (IMF), and regional development banks such as the African Development Bank (AfDB) and the new Asia Infrastructure Investment Bank (AIIB). These institutions largely provide funding to governments in developing and emerging markets to foster economic development, largely for infrastructure or trade and related projects. Some MLOs also provide funding directly to corporates and financial institutions under special programs related to their wider national development agendas. They borrow funds from international capital markets at lower costs than what individual loan recipient countries can typically borrow at.

Furthermore, issuers also use capital markets when they want to sell assets. For example, a corporation may want to divest or de-merge part of its business and seek new owners for the business. A government may want to privatize a national asset and raise funds for other purposes, thus using capital markets to facilitate the sale and receive funds from investors.

Investors and Asset Owners

Investors or asset owners represent the supply of funding in capital markets and seek to obtain a return for supplying funds to issuers. Figure 2.3 compares a selection of countries from around the world and their investors' assets expressed as a share of GDP. Investor assets vary widely, with advanced economies having significant investment funds and emerging and developing economies much smaller pools of funds. Some countries like the UK and Singapore are hubs for investment management due to financial infrastructure, legal environments, and tax reasons and have higher-than-average investment funds available. Others such as Australia have strong mandatory pension savings regimes and countries such as Japan have strong savings cultures boosting funds.

Investors can be any individual or institution which is in possession of funds and seeks to generate a return from those funds. We see seven types of investors. Individual investors (category 1 below) represent persons (also referred to as retail investors). Institutional investors, on the other hand, invest on behalf of pools of underlying clients, or represent large institutions such as governments. Institutional investors (categories 2–7 below) can typically be very powerful forces in capital markets given the size of funds they represent and their trading activity can influence the activities of issuers (i.e., the strategy and behavior and politics of the underlying issuer firms, and even governments). Institutional investors are thus seen as exceptionally important and issuers from firms to governments dedicate significant time and effort to ensure their confidence and understanding of the issuer's strategies and activities. The key categories of investors are outlined in the following sections.

1. Individuals Individuals have a variety of options for generating returns from their savings. In most countries, the largest investments made by individuals are typically their homes. Individuals may choose to keep any extra savings funds in bank accounts, although these typically yield lower than other options on average. As a result, individuals

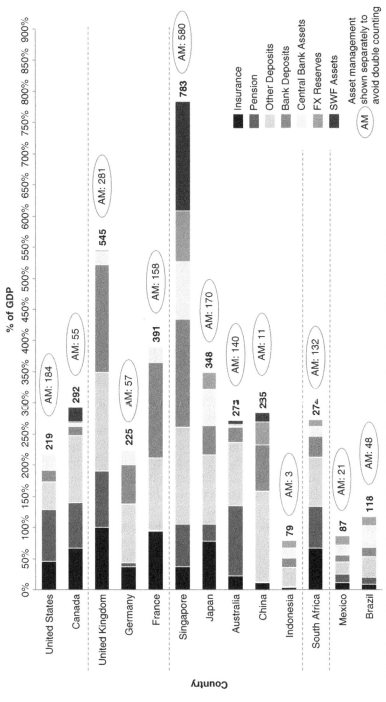

FIGURE 2.3 World investment structure (2014, % of GDP)

Source: Oxford Economics, World Bank, IFIC, Lipper Data, EFAMA, APRA, Nomura Research Institute, Indonesian Financial Services Authority, Alexander Forbes, Towers Watson, Reuters, Funds Society, OECD, EIU, Axco, ECB, IRS, and Oliver Wyman analysis

Note: Latest available data used with most data based on 2014, although some inputs leverage 2012, 2013, and 2015

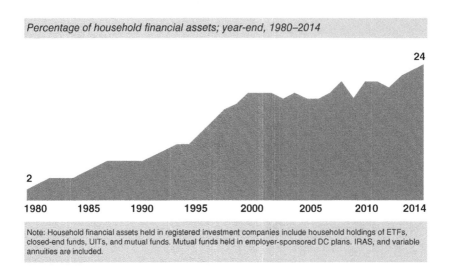

FIGURE 2.4   Share of household financial assets held in investment companies
Source: Investment Company Institute and Federal Reserve Board

increasingly participate in capital markets, either directly, such as the purchase of equities or bonds through a broker, or indirectly, through placing their funds with an asset manager. Figure 2.4 demonstrates that individuals in the United States are increasing investing their savings through investment management companies, a trend which is also observed in many other countries.

     With the prevalence of online brokers, and the diversification of their offerings, retail investors can now directly participate in many capital markets products. Retail capital markets activity is largely concentrated in equities given their ease of access, low fees, and typically less complex products. Retail investors can easily trade ETFs and basic derivatives such as stock options and contracts for difference (CFD) while in some markets fixed-income securities are also easily accessible through brokers.

2. Insurers   Insurers collect premiums from their policyholders and use these proceeds to invest in assets which will eventually support the payment of claims according to insured events such as life events (death, terminal or critical injury, etc.), property and casualty (fire, injury, etc.) and health events (hospitalization, medical care, etc.) by their claim-holders.

3. Pension Funds   Pension funds aggregate the retirement savings of individuals. For pensions which are managed and provided directly by employers, the pension fund represents the employer's contributions to meet their future pension obligations to their employees. Individuals and/or their employers make regular contributions to these funds, usually as a proportion of monthly pay, and this is invested to grow over their working life. Given their size in some countries, pensions represent a powerful class of investors. Upon retirement, individuals either withdraw their pension for usage, or convert their pension fund into an annuity which pays regular cash-flows. In an increasing number of nations, contributions to pensions are mandated, including Australia (Superannuation), USA (401K), UK (Workplace Pensions), and Singapore (Central Provident Fund) to mention a few. Governments have realized that as the share of the working-age population declines and as people live longer, the government is less able to fund extensive social security programs and that individuals will need to be responsible. As such, pensions represent a sizable share of available funds and are very important given the millions of individuals who rely on them for retirement income and for saving governments from extensive social security payments. Pensions originally were largely structured as *defined benefit* where investors were guaranteed a fixed benefit or payment based on their incomes or regular contribution amount. Given fluctuations in asset prices and difficulty in forecasting, together with the fact that life expectancy has increased significantly in the past 50 years, pensions are increasingly adopting a *defined contribution* structure, where the benefit is dependent on both contributions and the investment performance of the pension.

4. Banks Banks invest in capital markets products as part of their asset-liability management (ALM) process (see "Financial Corporations" for an overview). However, banks need to be prepared for any short-term shortages in liquidity and thus are required to hold a significant amount of highly liquid assets (set to be at least 100% of net stressed cash-flows over a 30-day period under the Basel Liquidity Coverage Ratio rules). This should ensure that in the event of a liquidity crisis, banks can convert these assets into cash in capital markets relatively quickly to cover cash shortfalls.

5. Governments Governments can generate surplus funds, either through budget surpluses, through asset sales (national firms, or commodities, etc.), or through foreign exchange surpluses. Many governments have created state funds tasked with investing these funds, known as *sovereign wealth funds* (SWFs). The investment of these funds is extremely important given that their income supports national budgets and national investment in infrastructure and facilities such as schools and hospitals. Given the size of these funds, they must tap capital markets to source appropriately sized investments.

6. Central Banks Following the financial crisis of 2008, central banks have become significant investors in capital markets through the use of *quantitative easing* (QE). QE involves the purchase of securities (largely government securities) from banks to reduce yields and enable banks to increase lending activity with the additional funds in order to stimulate economic growth. The United States (Federal Reserve), Europe (European Central Bank), and Japan (Bank of Japan) have all extensively used QE over the past decade to stimulate economic activity.

Some central banks also have significant funds which are used to manage their exchange rates, of which the Chinese State Administration of Foreign Exchange (SAFE) and the Hong Kong Monetary Authority (HKMA) are two key examples. These funds are utilized to buy and sell securities (largely high-grade government debt, but also increasingly some equities) globally and locally both to effect local exchange rates and to invest their funds and generate a return. SAFE is estimated to manage over US$3 trillion in assets at the time of writing, much of it accumulated through China's large trade surpluses over the past decade.

Central banks also participate widely in capital markets as part of their role to implement monetary policy and in some cases as part of their role in managing exchange rates. In many countries, central banks manage the key overnight reference interest rates through trading activity in overnight repo markets, effectively setting the rates banks lend to each other overnight. Repos, short for *repurchase agreements,* are short-term collateralized loans made between two parties where one party borrows money in return for securities (the collateral) and agrees to buy back the securities at a fixed time. Repos are vital instruments for short-term financing in many capital markets. Through repo and reverse-repo (the opposite transaction flows to a repo) trading activity, central banks can manage the demand and supply for money and thus the cost of money or the interest rates. Central banks also can influence interest rates through the interest they pay on funds deposited by banks in special accounts at the central bank, known as reserve accounts, for settling payments.

7. Endowments and Private Foundations   Endowments are trusts made up of funds, usually donated, and dedicated to provide ongoing support for the activities of certain (typically nonprofit) institutions. The most well-known endowments include those established to support universities or charitable not-for-profit organizations. Endowments invest their funds through capital markets and supply a portion of the investment returns to support their beneficiary institution, occasionally also utilizing some of the funds when investment incomes may be low.

Investors/asset owners may directly manage their capital markets investment decisions (using brokers or trading platforms to execute these decisions), or place their funds with asset managers who make investment decisions for asset owners based on various investment strategies. Asset managers either offer segregated and bespoke mandates to institutional investors or aggregate investible funds from numerous investors into funds, each with clearly defined investment policies and principles.

There are four types of basic fund structures:

1. *Mutual funds:* Mutual funds typically issue units, each representing a proportion of the total fund, allowing investors to purchase an investment in the fund based on their desired size. Mutual funds can be structured as closed-ended or open-ended. Closed-ended funds issue a fixed number of units when a fund is launched. They are normally listed on a stock exchange and investors are only able to enter and exit by buying and selling existing units in the fund, with units priced by the market. Closed-ended funds commonly utilize leverage in their investments. Open-ended funds do not have a fixed number of units and thus can accept new investments (through the creation of new units) or redemptions (through reducing the number of units) based on demand for investing in the fund. Under the 40 Act in the United States and UCITS regulation in Europe, these funds offer daily liquidity for investors. A more recent phenomenon includes exchange-traded funds

(ETFs). Units of the fund are listed and can be bought and sold by investors like any other security. Most of these ETFs are *passive* funds tracking an index and in return come with lower fees than *actively* managed mutual funds. ETFs are typically managed to trade within a close spread to their net-asset value, unlike closed-ended funds where market sentiment can cause values to diverge significantly from the value of their assets. Open-ended funds also trade based on their net-asset value.

2. *Hedge funds:* Hedge funds seek to generate a positive return in all market conditions. As a result, hedge funds will often have complex investment strategies, utilizing a broad variety of investment products spanning many asset classes, including significant usage of derivatives. In contrast to mutual funds they face fewer investment restrictions. Therefore, in most countries they are not accessible to all (retail) investors.

3. *Private equity funds:* Private equity (PE) funds make medium- to long-term equity investments in both listed and unlisted corporations. Typically, the PE fund's aim is to take an active role in managing the firm and to fix issues and improve the firm's profitability. Typically PE firms will aim to achieve a controlling stake in an investment where they seek to significantly influence management. Once performance is improved, PE funds aim to offload their investments, either through a sale to another firm, or through an IPO at a higher valuation, generating superior returns. A subclass of PE firms includes *buyout firms*, which aim to purchase companies outright.

4. *Venture capital funds:* Venture capital (VC) funds also largely make equity investments. While similar to PE investments in many ways, venture capital is provided at a much earlier stage than typical private equity investments, usually to promising startup businesses with little or no revenues. As such, there is a high degree of risk associated with venture investing. VC funds typically offer a range of support services to assist in building their businesses, ranging from management training to marketing and partnership support. The investment styles of VC funds can differ considerably, with some taking highly active roles in management while others are more passive at least initially. Both venture and PE funds typically are open to only wealthy investors given the risks involved and the longer-term nature of investments.

Financial Intermediaries

Financial intermediaries enable capital markets to operate across the full breadth of products facilitating the matching of the specific needs of investors and issuers. There are five main categories of intermediaries in capital markets: banks (investment banks), broker-dealers, exchanges and clearing organizations, custodians, and central securities depositories. Apart from banks and broker-dealers, these intermediaries are also known as *market infrastructure*.

Banks (Investment Banks) In the section "Key Participants in Capital Markets," we discussed the function of banks as investors and issuers. Banks also play two further significant functions in capital markets. These include the investment banking function (discussed in this section), and the broker-dealer function (discussed in the next section).

The investment banking function supports firms to raise funding from capital markets and to also broker mergers and acquisitions deals between firms. There are three subfunctions within investment banking broadly:

1. *Equity capital markets (ECM):* The ECM division of an investment bank is responsible for supporting issuers to raise funds through the issue of equities to the public. ECM teams are usually specialized by industry to enable them to effectively determine the value of the issuing firm and its securities. ECM divisions also maintain large networks of potential investors to support distribution of the securities. ECM teams also support firms in issuing ongoing equity capital raisings, through rights issues, for example. As part of the ECM function, investment banks often *underwrite* the securities, or agree to buy a pre-agreed level of the securities if they fail to attract sufficient interest from investors. There are many types of underwriting commitments, with the most broad, a *firm commitment* committing the underwriter to purchase all securities not issued. Other forms of underwriting insulate the underwriter from various risks associated with underwriting, including minimum levels of investor demand.

2. *Debt capital markets (DCM):* The DCM division supports issuers to raise debt financing for corporate and government issuers. Similar to ECM teams, they are often specialized to ensure they can accurately determine the right structure and pricing for debt issuances based on the unique characteristics of the issuer and the prevailing market conditions. In certain markets, some of the largest dealers are also denoted, typically by the Department of Treasury as *primary dealers*. These dealers represent the only dealers which may directly transact with the Treasury department or national central bank in government securities. Typically only the largest and most well-managed dealers are allowed this privilege.

3. *Mergers and acquisitions (M&A):* M&A teams support clients in merging with or acquiring other firms, and also divesting parts of their business. While not directly a capital markets activity, M&A transactions often require significant financing and often collaborate with ECM and DCM teams.

Broker-Dealers Broking (brokering) and dealing are two separate functions although they are often discussed together given that their core functions are complementary and often offered in an integrated manner. Broking essentially involves the execution of capital market transactions without taking on any risk. It is also called *acting on an agency basis* when dealing in equities and *riskless principal* when dealing in the fixed-income markets. In essence, brokers connect two parties to a transaction, either through a trading medium such as an exchange, or directly as in over-the-counter transactions. For this service they charge a commission.

Dealers in contrast act on a *principal* basis, willing to use their own balance sheet to make a market for clients (known as market-making). Dealers quote a *spread* for each security they are willing to trade in. The spread refers to the difference in the price they would be willing to buy or sell a security at. Dealers thus may have to sometimes serve as the counterparty to a trade until a further counterparty is found. Banks can now largely only undertake such *principal* transactions for their clients under the "Volcker Rule" in the United States and its equivalents elsewhere. These rules prevent banks from putting their own capital at risk in high-risk short-term trading transactions which are not directly related to benefiting their clients (known as *proprietary trading*) to increase profits.

A subset of brokers are inter-dealer brokers who only look to serve broker-dealers themselves as their clients.

Broker-dealers also provide advice to their clients on which investments to make, often supported by teams of research analysts. The research reports of broker-dealers are highly important in supporting investor participation through the dissemination of trade ideas while also keeping a close check on the performance of issuers. Research has generally been bundled into brokers' trading commissions and thus not charged for separately, although recent reforms under Europe's MiFID II could see research unbundled and charged for separately to minimize potential conflicts of interest and increase transparency for end investors.

Exchanges, Clearinghouses, and Central Counterparties (CCPs) Exchanges are venues where buyers and sellers of securities meet to transact/trade in those securities. Today, most exchanges, particularly for equities, are almost completely virtual; however, some still maintain *trading floors* where traders representing the brokers of buyers and sellers physically meet and agree to trades. Historically exchanges were typically specialized in certain asset classes, the most well-known of which are stock exchanges where equities are traded. Other key exchanges include commodities-focused exchanges such as the Chicago Mercantile Exchange (CME). Increasingly, exchanges have been diversifying over the past decade, with credit fixed-income products, *exchange-traded* funds, and a host of derivatives offered on exchanges. Several exchange groups such as the London Stock Exchange (LSE) and Intercontinental Exchange (ICE) have formed exchange groups with multiple asset classes.

Following the execution of a trade, there are two key post-trade processes conducted: clearing and settlement. The Bank of International Settlements (BIS) defines clearing as "the process of transmitting, reconciling and, in some cases, confirming payment orders or security transfer instructions prior to settlement, possibly including the netting of instructions and the establishment of final positions for settlement." In essence, clearing is the process of preparing to complete or settle a trade and involves confirming several administrative and legal details between the counterparties and their brokers. The BIS defines settlement as "the completion of a transaction, wherein the seller transfers… securities or financial instruments to the buyer and the buyer transfers money to the seller." In essence, settlement involves the completion of the trade, thus recording the changes in ownership of the security and undertaking of relevant payments.

Clearinghouses are defined by the BIS as "a central location or central processing mechanism through which financial institutions agree to exchange payment instructions or other financial obligations. The institutions settle for items exchanged at a designated time based on the rules and procedures of the clearing house." In essence, clearinghouses carry out the clearing stage of a trade preparing for settlement. In the United States, all equities are cleared through the Depository Trust and Clearing Corporation (DTCC) group centrally while multiple clearinghouses exist for other securities, including CME Clearing and ICE Clear. Europe and Asia are more fragmented with multiple clearinghouses, including for equities. Equities clearinghouses are mostly owned by exchanges.

Clearing houses can assume an additional role of acting as *central counterparties* (CCPs) serving as a direct counterparty to all trades for each side or "an entity that is the buyer to every seller and seller to every buyer of a specified set of contracts" as defined by the BIS. Both the buyer and seller's contracts are novated, in essence, their contract is replaced with two contracts between them and the CCP, and thus are not exposed to risk of either counterparty defaulting. The CCP, serving both sides of numerous trades is able to undertake considerable netting between transactions to minimize exposure, and accepts collateral from each party of the trade to ensure deliveries are met. Netting refers to the process of consolidating multiple positions into a single position, resulting in each party only having to make a single transaction based on the net value of multiple transactions. The benefits from netting alone can be very large, substantially affecting the economics of a trade.

Figure 2.5 depicts the basic trade flow with and without a CCP.

Central Securities Depositories Central securities depositories (CSDs) are registrars responsible for maintaining the original ownership records for securities and facilitating the settlement and transfer of securities between owners. Traditionally, securities were issued on paper with the owners' names registered and stored in large safes by the owners. Trading was complex with certificates having to be physically delivered. As trading volumes increased, storage of the certificates was first centralized and then digitized and today almost all securities globally are stored in electronic databases maintained by CSDs. Transfers of securities are now done through electronic book-entry, that is, changing the ownership of securities electronically without moving physical documents.

An international central securities depository (ICSD) is a central securities depository that facilitates cross-border settlement of securities from various domestic markets. ICSDs were originally set up to manage clearing and settlement of the Eurobond business for which there was no supporting market infrastructure. Since their creation over 30 years ago, the business of ICSDs has expanded to cover most domestic and internationally traded instruments, including investment funds. ICSDs usually operate through direct or indirect (via local agents) links to local CSDs. Clearstream Banking in Luxembourg, Euroclear Bank, and SIX SIS in Switzerland are considered ICSDs. Clearstream and Euroclear together dominate the European ICSD/CSD market.

Custodians Custodians are banks that are responsible for holding assets such as capital markets securities on behalf of investors. In their *safe-keeping* or *custody* role, custodians ensure that the assets of clients managed by large investment firms are held safely and accurately in their names. In their *asset-servicing* role, custodians also support the clearing process, corporate actions processing (such as dividends and stock splits), tax advice, and also assist with transaction accounting and reporting. Typically, investment fund assets and collateral for trades are safeguarded by a third-party so that they are separated from the assets of the investment manager protecting the underlying investors, and to ensure

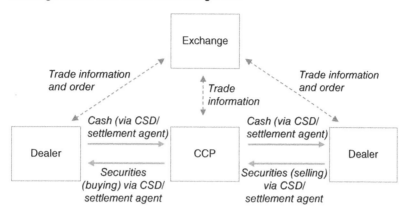

Exchange-traded inter-dealer trade using a CCP

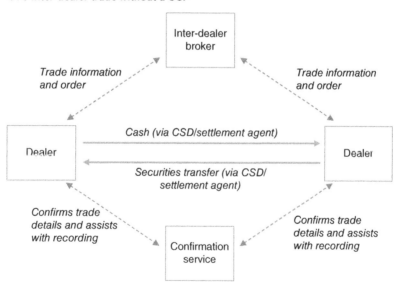

OTC inter-dealer trade without a CCP

FIGURE 2.5   Basic trade flow example with and without a CCP

that they are transacted within the bounds of their various investment mandates. A few large global banks such as BNY Mellon and JP Morgan dominate the custodian industry. There are two types of custodians:

- *Global custodians* safeguard assets for their clients in multiple jurisdictions around the world and are generally the first level through which institutional investors and broker-dealers engage in the clearing and settlement process. Global custodians maintain accounts at multiple local CSDs and/or sub-custodians covering most geographical markets or link to local sub-custodians. Global custodians also offer several value-added services, including the optimization of client collateral, collateral processing, and reporting.

■ *Sub-custodians* offer similar services to global custodians except that they are typically limited to one or a few local markets. They thus can facilitate access to local markets to clients using global custodians which have limited local presence. Market participants could connect to sub-custodians either directly or through global custodians with their role being protected by local regulations. Sub-custodians also provide more customized local services, including the handling of localized withholding taxes.

Figure 2.6 depicts how each of these intermediaries support the processing of an exchange-based trade.

Supporting Infrastructure and Information Providers

Several other important institutions also exist that support the smooth operation of global capital markets and their broader ecosystem of participants. We have provided a brief overview on some of these institutions here:

■ *Order and trade processing system providers:* These systems support market participants in making and then managing trade orders. They also support the processing of the trade order, including matching orders between the buy- and sell-side, completing order information, and confirming settlement details to settle and complete the trade. Given the complexity and volumes of trades, particularly in OTC markets where trading is highly customized, these systems are essential. A host of firms offer varying solutions, with most solutions offering highly specialized services catering to one part of the trade value chain for certain participants and for a subset of securities. There has been a trend for broadening of solutions across the value chain in recent years and hence some consolidation as participants seek to minimize complexity.

■ *Data providers:* Significant volumes of data are required for markets to operate efficiently and effectively. Numerous data providers exist and support data requirements across the full value chain of capital markets from client onboarding and due-diligence, to economic and market research, to trade price discovery and portfolio management. Several providers exist, often specializing based on the types of markets and securities covered. Some of the most well-known names include Bloomberg, Standard & Poor's Capital IQ, and Thomson Reuters.

■ *Trade repositories:* OTC markets have traditionally been highly opaque given the lack of a central exchange. Given that trades can also take days to settle, and the frequency of trading, tracing the true final owners of securities can be complex as securities change hands. An example was during the financial crisis of 2008 when large defaults such as that of Lehman Brothers highlighted that often the total outstanding values of OTC positions were difficult to estimate and that all counterparties were also difficult to immediately identify. Trade repositories were introduced to centralize the

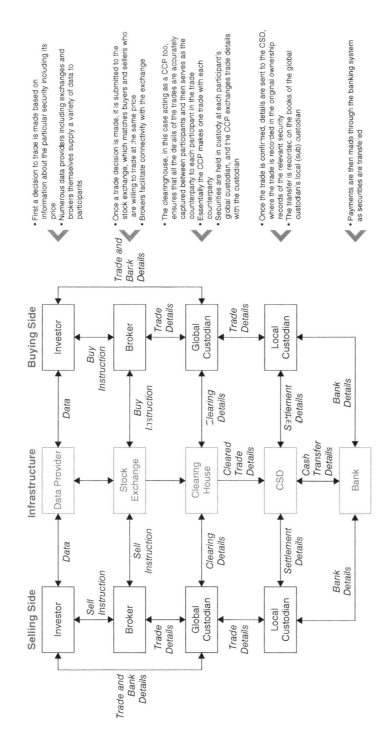

FIGURE 2.6 Simplified example of exchange-based trade and the role of key intermediaries
Source: Oliver Wyman

- First a decision to trade is made based on information about the particular security including its price
- Numerous data providers including exchanges and brokers themselves supply a variety of data to participants

- Once a trade decision is made, it is submitted to the stock exchange, which matches buyers and sellers who are willing to trade at the same price
- Brokers facilitate connectivity with the exchange

- The clearinghouse, in this case acting as a CCP too, ensures that all the details of the trades are accurately captured between participants and then serves as the counterparty to each participant in the trade
- Essentially the CCP makes one trade with each counterparty
- Securities are held in custody at each participant's global custodian, and the CCP exchanges trade details with the custodian

- Once the trade is confirmed, details are sent to the CSD, where the trade is recorded in the original ownership records of the relevant security
- The transfer is recorded on the books of the global custodian's local (sub) custodian

- Payments are then made through the banking system as securities are transferred

collection and reporting of trade data. Trade repositories store information on all outstanding OTC trades with reporting increasingly mandated globally, allowing regulators and counterparties to have clear, verified, and comprehensive information. In many cases trade repositories are owned and/or operated by clearinghouses or stock exchanges.

- *Ratings agencies:* Ratings agencies assess the credit risk (risk of a default on borrowings) of borrowers. These agencies play a vital role in capital markets assisting investors with guidance on the risk that an issuer may default. Ratings are primarily expressed as a grade based on the probability of default, and while primarily applied to debt markets, are also very helpful for equity markets. Ratings are applied both at the issuer level (corporations, multilaterals, and sovereigns) and can also be generated for individual debt securities based on the structure and terms and class of the security. Issuers pay close attention to their credit rating as the costs of borrowing are closely related to their rating, and also as some investors may only be permitted to invest in rated and more favorably rated securities (e.g., investment grade).

TYPES OF MARKETS

Primary and Secondary Markets

Primary markets refer to the initial issuance of equity and debt securities, where the securities are newly created (or *originated*) and then *issued* to the market for subscription. The processes for issuance of equities, credit, and government securities was discussed earlier.

Following the initial creation of the securities, subscriptions, and their listing, the ongoing trading of securities on exchanges is referred to as the *secondary market*. The primary and secondary markets can be seen as substitutes in some ways, as investors can choose to invest in newly created securities or buy existing traded securities, as shown in Figure 2.7. However, each security type can differ considerably.

Secondary market volumes drastically exceed primary markets as they represent the ongoing trading of securities over time for equities. This also holds for many classes of bonds although many bonds are lightly or rarely traded (held to maturity). Both primary and secondary market volumes can fluctuate significantly. Primary market issuance in equities, for example, is highest when economic conditions are best and when issuing companies can demand a higher price. Primary equity markets can sometimes virtually shut down when economic times are challenging. Secondary market volumes, both for equities and fixed income, can also change drastically during periods of economic uncertainty when market participants are changing their expectations and making significant shifts to their portfolios.

Figures 2.8 and 2.9 depict primary and secondary market activity levels in the United States. Primary issuance can be very volatile as market sentiment changes. For example, following the financial crisis of 2008, appetite for investing in new equity issuances almost disappeared, dropping by over 80% from 2007. Issuance volumes have risen since as

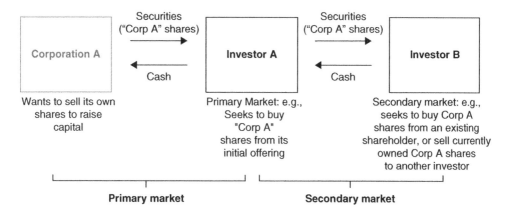

FIGURE 2.7 Example of primary and secondary markets
Source: Oliver Wyman

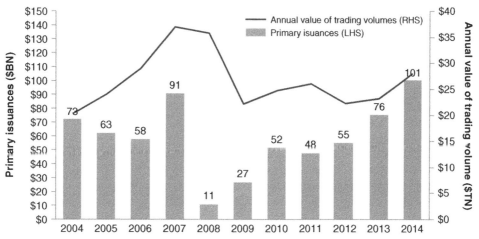

Note: Trading volume value represent daily average volumes multiplied by 252 trading days per year for the NYSE and Nasdaq exchanges only. Primary issuances represent all exchanges reporting within SIFMA

FIGURE 2.8 U.S. equities trading and issuance volumes
Source: SIFMA

economic growth and the outlook improved. Trading volumes followed a similar path. Fixed-income issuance increased significantly following the crisis as the U.S. government had to borrow heavily to fund its budget deficit.

Exchange and Over-the-Counter (OTC) Markets

Exchange markets are those where securities are traded over an exchange serving as an intermediary to match buyers and sellers of securities. These include stock, futures,

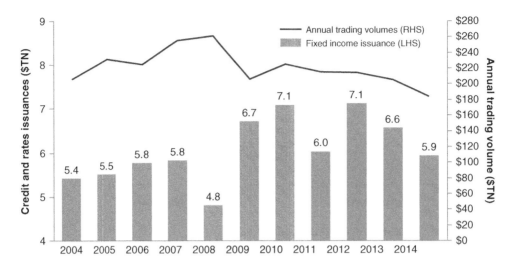

FIGURE 2.9 U.S. fixed-income trading and issuance volumes
Source: SIFMA; trading volumes represent daily average volumes multiplied by 252 trading days per year

commodities, and other products. Exchanges provide real-time data on the demand and supply for each listed security in their *order books,* which display the volume of each security type available for sale/purchase and the corresponding prices asked/offered. Trades are made when there are matching prices from buyers and sellers. Note that the order book, however, does not reveal who the buyers and sellers are. Securities listed on exchanges are standardized in that there are generally only a few (typically between one and three) classes of securities for each issuer. Furthermore, the size of each security unit is typically small, allowing relatively small amounts to be traded at a time. Given the level of standardization, securities transactions are typically settled electronically (mostly within three days of the trade), with buyers and sellers typically having no knowledge of each other. Furthermore, given securities are more standardized and bid and offer prices are visible and published, there is a high degree of price transparency.

OTC markets refer to the trading of contracts through a dealer network as opposed to on a centralized exchange. OTC contracts are typically highly customized (non-standardized) and there is a broad array of securities available within each asset class. Furthermore, each security is typically larger in value and they are thus typically only traded by wholesale investors. There are two main types of OTC traded securities: fixed-income securities and OTC derivatives.

A single listed corporation, for example, may have hundreds (or even thousands for the largest corporations) of fixed-income instruments issued, each issued at a different time, for a differing term, with a differing face value and coupon payment. As a result liquidity is more dispersed and less suitable to a central order book approach.

The vast majority of derivatives also trade on OTC markets, with only equity derivatives having a significant presence on exchange markets. Given the high degree of customization, varied liquidity, and large trade sizes in OTC markets, pricing can be an art and rely on complex formulas together with significant judgment. Banks and brokers employ numerous Sales and Trading staff who specialize in certain asset classes, and often certain geographies for certain asset classes to serve the trading needs of clients.

Given the high degrees of customization and involvement of significant manual effort for OTC transactions, trades can typically take longer to settle. Significant amounts of manual verification work are required for trades to be processed, including for the details of counterparties to be exchanged, for trade contract details to be verified, for payments to be processed, and for the trade to be recorded. One factor which exacerbated the effects of the 2008 financial crisis was that, facing default, several banks and other market participants struggled to trace the final counterparties to many of their OTC derivatives transactions and struggled to completely settle outstanding trades. This led to the virtual freezing of market trading activity, increasing risk to all participants. A key pillar of reform efforts since the crisis has focused on increasing automation of trade processing, mandatory clearing (through a central counterparty), improved (and increasingly mandated) trade reporting, and the centralization of trade, counterparty, and settlement details. As an example, the bulk of interest rates and credit default swaps are now centrally cleared with regulations introducing penalties for uncleared swaps in the form of increased and/or mandatory exchange of margin.

While exchange trading is virtually electronic at this time, OTC trading is becoming increasingly electronic to reduce risks and to increase speed and accuracy. Major dealers offer proprietary platforms for their clients known as dealer-client platforms, allowing their clients to quickly access their pricing information and to process trades. Alternative types of exchanges have also been emerging rapidly. One such type is a *swap execution facility* (SEF) in the United States (in Europe, SEFs are comparable to *multilateral trading facilities* or MTFs). SEFs are non-exchange venues facilitating the trading of swaps between many member participants. SEFs allow greater price and trading transparency by allowing participants to see other participants' bids and offers and the movement in prices and volumes.

Figure 2.10 shows how trading venues vary by asset class and the variety of trading options available. Trading is increasingly facilitated through electronic means such as exchanges and trading platforms versus manual means such as voice brokers, although the most complex assets still require more manual processing.

Dark pools are a further category of markets. Dark pools are a type of *alternative trading system* (ATS) in U.S. regulation, and fall under *multilateral trading facilities* (MTFs) in Europe. Dark pools are a type of exchange where traders can buy and sell securities privately without revealing their identities and without revealing transactions to the public.[2] Dark pool trading has increased significantly in recent years, rising to over

---

[2]Aubrey Gallo, "Development Article, Dark Pool Liquidity," *Review of Banking and Financial Law*, 29, (2009), 88.

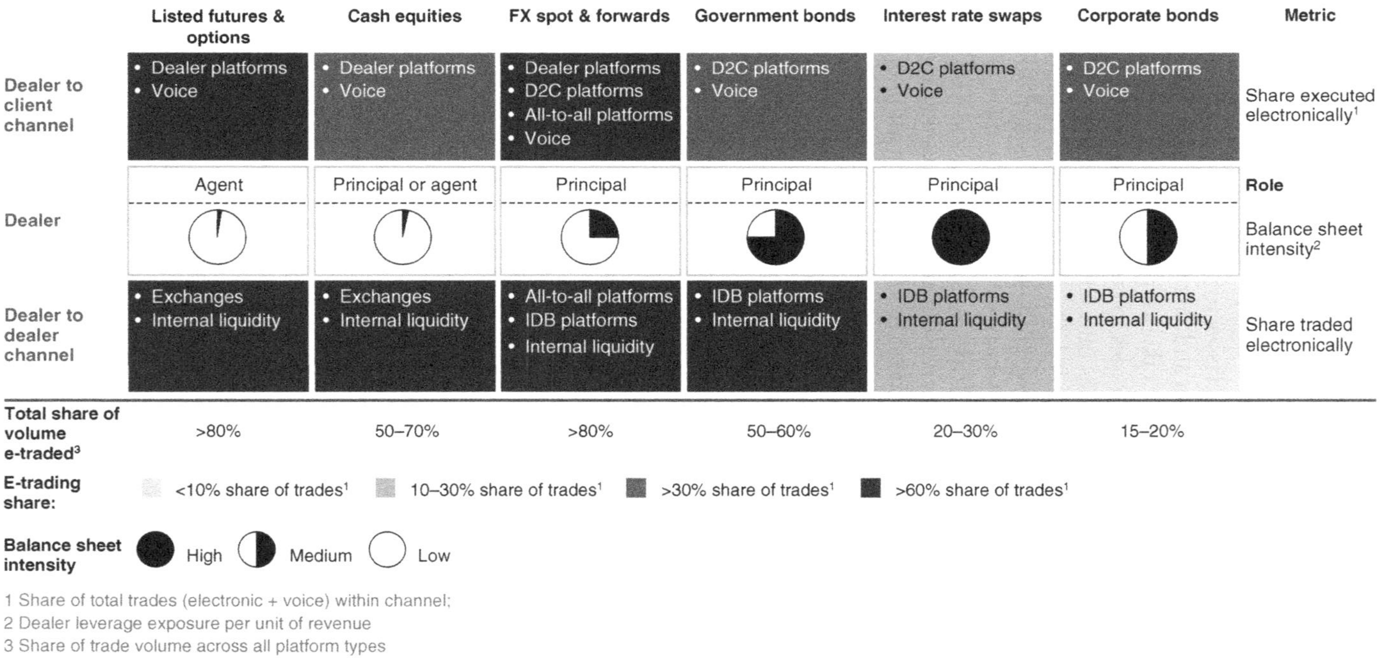

	Listed futures & options	Cash equities	FX spot & forwards	Government bonds	Interest rate swaps	Corporate bonds	Metric
Dealer to client channel	• Dealer platforms • Voice	• Dealer platforms • Voice	• Dealer platforms • D2C platforms • All-to-all platforms • Voice	• D2C platforms • Voice	• D2C platforms • Voice	• D2C platforms • Voice	Share executed electronically[1]
							Role
Dealer	Agent	Principal or agent	Principal	Principal	Principal	Principal	Balance sheet intensity[2]
Dealer to dealer channel	• Exchanges • Internal liquidity	• Exchanges • Internal liquidity	• All-to-all platforms • IDB platforms • Internal liquidity	• IDB platforms • Internal liquidity	• IDB platforms • Internal liquidity	• IDB platforms • Internal liquidity	Share traded electronically
Total share of volume e-traded[3]	>80%	50–70%	>80%	50–60%	20–30%	15–20%	

E-trading share:
- <10% share of trades[1]
- 10–30% share of trades[1]
- >30% share of trades[1]
- >60% share of trades[1]

Balance sheet intensity: High · Medium · Low

1 Share of total trades (electronic + voice) within channel;
2 Dealer leverage exposure per unit of revenue
3 Share of trade volume across all platform types

FIGURE 2.10 Penetration of election trading by asset class (relevance of different trading models by asset class)

Sources: Oliver Wyman, proprietary data and analysis; Euromoney, BIS, Celent

30% of trading by some estimates in the United States,[3] and 10% in Europe.[4] Proponents of dark pools argue that they allow for larger trades without disrupting regular markets, and improve liquidity, particularly for larger orders. However, opponents of dark pools argue that they reduce transparency, reduce liquidity, and can lead to pricing impairments.

CAPITAL MARKETS DEVELOPMENT

As discussed throughout this chapter, capital markets provide an important source of funding for several types of issuers thus supporting their economic activities and growth. In essence, capital markets channel capital to productive investments. The larger the capital market, the more investment that can be supported, and the more investment supported, the more capital and infrastructure in the economy, which results in increased economic output. As such, building and maintaining robust capital markets is often a key priority to support economic growth.

Capital markets offer a diverse range of investment opportunities, helping investors achieve increased portfolio diversification. This helps to support a better matching of the needs of investors with those of issuers. Furthermore, capital markets can help support more longer-term investment opportunities. The diversification of investment opportunities and increased investment expertise required can stimulate the development of the local asset management industry. With fund managers, pension funds, and insurers growing, economies can benefit tremendously from increased access to new financial products provided by these firms. Furthermore, these firms offer additional options for transforming maturity (more longer-term investment appetite to fund longer-term funding needs) and for matching investors and issuers, contributing to more effective markets. In the longer run, the provision of this range of asset management services, combined with more individual ability to directly invest, can decrease dependence on social welfare.

The diversification of investment opportunities also diversifies the sources of credit and associated risks. Rather than being concentrated in firms that banks choose to lend to, credit risk is spread across a range of issuers and projects. Furthermore, with a broader base of investors, credit risk is also diversified across the issuer base, placing less stress on the banking system. This can improve stability during difficult economic conditions.

---

[3] Jacob Bunge, "Market's Dark Side Expands to More Than 3-Year High in July," *Wall Street Journal Blog* (July 31, 2013, 6:04 PM), http://blogs.wsj.com/moneybeat/2013/07/31/stock-markets-dark-side-expands-to-more-than-3-year-high-in-july/?KEYWORDS=dark+pools.

[4] Anish Puaar, "Financial News: Dark Pool Trading at Record Levels in Europe," *Wall Street Journal* (Aug. 12, 2013, 3:33 AM), http://online.wsj.com/article/BT-CO-20130812-701291.html.

Even countries that boast large capital markets are on a constant path of reform to continue to drive improvements, as demonstrated through recent reform efforts across major advanced economies. This section provides a brief overview of the drivers of capital markets development. We draw heavily on recent work completed by Oliver Wyman and the World Economic Forum on capital markets development in this section.[5]

In essence, capital markets development rests on three pillars:

1. *The breadth and depth of investment opportunities available (issuer side):* The level of participation in capital markets by issuers and the extent to which they utilize capital markets vs. other forms of funding (e.g., bank loans, private funding and retained earnings). The broader the issuer base (across types of issuers, types of projects, variety of industries, levels of maturity), the broader the range of investment opportunities in the market. Advanced markets like the United States provide a wide range of such opportunities. Individual investors, for example, can choose to invest in almost any sector through the stock market and in firms with varying levels of maturity. They can also invest in a variety of government debt (largely through fund managers), and also in infrastructure projects through a variety of methods.

2. *The breadth and depth of the investor base:* The range of investors available to provide funds to issuers through capital markets and the size of investible assets. As discussed earlier, investors have a broad range of preferences across risk, return, term, cashflow, etc. The broader the investor base, and the larger the availability of funds to invest, the larger the range of investment opportunities that can be supported.

3. *The strength of supporting market infrastructure, regulations, and supervision:* Effective capital markets require a strong regulatory and legal framework given the complexity of products and their economic significance. These frameworks guide standards around disclosure, issuance criteria, and investment manager duties, for example. They are vital for building trust across the numerous participants and standards to understand the products available with consistency. Furthermore, they facilitate the development of strong, reliable market infrastructure including stock exchanges and other trading venues, ratings agencies, and data sharing. These will be discussed further in the next section of this chapter, and then in detail in a subsequent chapter.

A range of options are available to improve each of these three pillars and we'll next briefly discuss these options. However, none of these options can be truly successful

---

[5]World Economic Forum and Oliver Wyman, "Accelerating Emerging Capital Markets Development: Corporate Bond Markets" (April 2015). Also consulted: Oliver Wyman research and analysis to support roundtables and industry discussions jointly held by Oliver Wyman and World Economic Forum capital markets.

on their own. For example, several initiatives can be undertaken to increase issuer participation, but unless investor participation is also improved, issuers will not be able to successfully raise the funds they seek. Capital markets are an ecosystem, and a combination of policies and actions across each of the key pillars is required to drive development.

Increasing Issuer Participation

Equity Markets First, initiatives targeted at streamlining the listing process can help to facilitate increased issuer participation. However, these initiatives should also ensure that adequate disclosure standards are maintained. The listing process involves registration, prospectus preparation, and approvals, all of which can be costly and take significant time. Furthermore, for smaller firms seeking to list, these processes can be even more costly, deterring use of equity markets. Second, the privatization of *state-owned enterprises* through public offerings can dramatically increase equity participation particularly when equity market depth is limited. As further larger firms are listed, the depth of investment options rises, drawing more investors and thus encouraging more firms to list. Singapore and Malaysia both followed this route. Third, even in the most advanced economies, *small-to-medium enterprises* may struggle to source capital, finding the listing process too expensive and onerous. Furthermore, they may struggle to draw attention in the midst of bigger names. Many countries have seen separate exchange markets develop to cater to smaller firms while some exchanges have created specific segments to bring more attention to smaller firms, including Korea, Thailand, China, Malaysia, South Africa, and Singapore. Finally, a further policy commonly undertaken includes facilitating broader types of listed investments, from infrastructure funds to other exchange-traded funds (ETFs).

Fixed Income Many of the policy initiatives discussed above for equity markets also apply to fixed-income markets. However, given the closer substitutability to bank loans, investor participation is much more a function of relative cost. Approval and security issuance processes are all extremely important, too.

Increasing Investor Participation

Improving investor participation likewise is complex; investors require a broad range of capital markets products (see discussion on increasing issuer participation). Furthermore, there also needs to be sufficient wealth in an economy for investment. An early method of stimulating investor participation includes opening up markets to more foreign capital. This requires FX and capital account liberalization and so must also be coordinated closely with macroeconomic policy. Singapore and Korea both were strong proponents of this approach. However, foreign capital can also be volatile, being drawn away during uncertain economic times, and should be carefully balanced with growing domestic investor participation, too. Initiatives to boost savings also vastly support investor participation. Countries which have mandatory pension savings programs have amassed significant savings, also further boosting the asset management industry. Likewise, initiatives to boost the wider adoption of insurance further support increased participation. Finally, investor education initiatives can also support broader awareness of savings and investment, increasing particularly retail use of asset management, and also direct capital markets participation. Countries such as the United States, UK, Australia, and New Zealand have wide-ranging investor education programs boosting participation.

Strengthening Supporting Infrastructure and Regulatory Framework

Needless to say, a strong regulatory and supervisory framework with clear, fair, and prudent standards for governing capital markets is fundamental. As discussed earlier, capital markets involve a multitude of supporting infrastructure, from exchanges to ratings agencies, from data providers to custodians. Trust is a fundamental characteristic and ensuring the stability and robustness of each of these institutions, together with ensuring the highest standards of their work, is fundamental for strong capital markets. As mentioned earlier, even the most advanced economies are still continuing to refine their capital markets frameworks. This process is unlikely to pause as markets, their products, and their participants evolve. The details of regulation and market infrastructure will be covered in subsequent chapters.

Capital markets also facilitate improved market discipline and transparency. Public fundraising involves high disclosure and transparency standards together with improved corporate governance. Issuers are subject to market sentiment with the price of their securities directly affected by their performance, hence keeping them focused on effectively managing their organizations. In effect, capital markets can also serve as a barometer of economic risks based on how investments are being priced. Increasing credit spreads can be a result of increasing credit risks, as are declining equity prices, suggesting the outlook for firms may be declining.

While vital to economic development, capital markets also are subject to market forces and have proven to be extremely volatile. During the Financial Crisis of 2008, global credit markets shut down temporarily or came close to shutting down. Equity markets can also fluctuate vastly as market sentiment shifts, significantly affecting the value of investments of pensions and other investments while also impacting consumer confidence and the ability for firms to source new equity funding. Thus, while capital markets support economic activity and growth, they can also harm it, and as a result, effective regulation of capital markets is vital. In the years since 2008, there has been a renewed (and more coordinated) focus on stringent regulation globally. A more detailed discussion on relevant global regulations will be covered in a subsequent chapter.

Figure 2.11 depicts the growth of capital markets globally since 1990. Even in this relatively recent timeframe, the growth of capital markets is evident across all participants despite significant fluctuations along this journey.

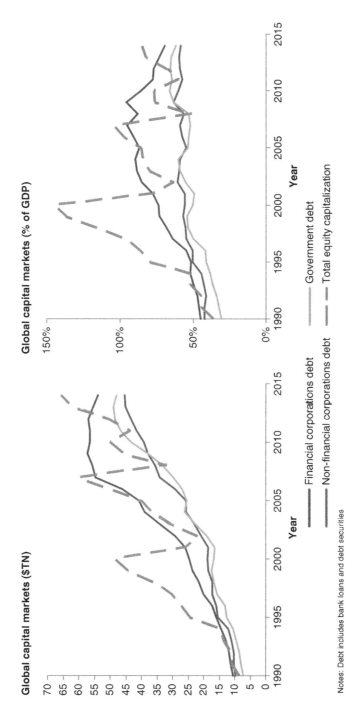

FIGURE 2.11 Global capital markets size, 1990–2014
Sources: EIU, WFE, BIS, IMF, Oliver Wyman analysis

CHAPTER 3

How the Global Financial Crisis Transformed the Industry

Christian Edelmann and Pete Clarke

Capital markets have changed fundamentally following the global financial crisis. In this chapter we discuss the transition from the pre-crisis period, when investment banks enjoyed record profit levels, to the world we observe today. We discuss in detail the main measures that the regulators introduced following the crisis and their impact on investment banking business models. We conclude with a discussion on the effects of these changes on the functioning of capital markets.

THE SITUATION PRIOR TO THE GLOBAL FINANCIAL CRISIS

Sales and trading in fixed income and equity instruments and primary market investment banking activities enjoyed a period of tremendous growth from 2000 to 2007. Industry revenues almost doubled to $300bn over this period. This compares to global GDP, which rose 60% in nominal terms over the same period. Investment banks posted record profits and advertised high targets for shareholder returns on equity.

This strong industry growth had several drivers. Benign economic conditions and strong economic growth in most regions globally accelerated asset accumulation and drove up investor appetite for risk assets. Liberalization of banking structures and of national financial systems meant that banks could benefit from a wider array of funding sources and compete in a wider range of markets, leading many to acquire smaller rivals along the way. Financial innovations, such as the invention and adoption of new kinds of derivatives and structured products, and the increased use of leverage when running capital markets operations, enhanced the financial toolkit that banks could deploy to generate revenues.

Banks also managed financial resources in a simpler way than today. Most banks primarily focused on generating revenues and converting leverage into profit. Banks generally manage to "economic capital" as the firm's scarce resource, measuring capital needed using internal statistical models that captured various drivers of risk and resource consumption. Minimum capital requirements imposed by regulators were rarely binding (for example, the expectations of banks' investors as to what tier-1 capital ratio to maintain were often more stringent than the regulatory minimum ratios), and liquidity was readily accessible in the markets. The usage of capital, leverage, liquidity, or funding was sometimes allocated internally for the purposes of performance measurement and resource prioritization, but the respective trading desks had to cope with relatively few constraints.

And more broadly regulatory constraints were not as stringent as today. For example, there was little in the way of monitoring or capitalization of derivative positions, or meaningful restraints on the amount of total leverage that wholesale banks could deploy. Because of this, banks allocated financial and operational resources to those businesses earning the highest return on economic capital—as a result, growth in structured derivatives, securitization, prime brokerage, and structured credit all accelerated. Equally, a looser standard of governance existed in the back office, with derivatives collateralization often less than complete and over-the-counter derivatives had significant settlement backlogs.

In this way, the wholesale banking industry's growth in revenues and profits was driven as much by the relatively permissive regulatory environment and looser financial resource management as by the macroeconomic and market conditions.

OVERVIEW OF REGULATION INTRODUCED 2008–2015

The global financial crisis had many causes and expressed the weaknesses of the financial system in many different ways. Both standalone broker models and global universal banks sustained heavy losses and either went bankrupt, sold themselves to competitors, or in many cases needed public bailouts. However, it was largely the standalone investment bank models that ceased operations altogether as the universal bank models benefited from diversification—although these banks, too, sustained very heavy losses in a few cases. Example weaknesses within the wholesale banks that were identified by regulators included:

- Hidden leverage in the system built up through the use of derivatives, which were largely treated as off–balance sheet exposures and were often not fully capitalized
- Insufficiently sensitive and often underestimated market risk capital charges for traded capital markets products
- A lack of accounting for counterparty credit risk in derivative exposures, which were often less than fully collateralized and without sufficient capital
- A lack of robust liquidity and funding risk frameworks at banks, with an overreliance on short-term funding backing up often less-liquid assets
- While still small in absolute terms, a growing reliance on proprietary trading and/or principal risk-taking to boost profit generation within the context of banking structures often funded partially through retail deposits
- Insufficient compliance and controls frameworks, leading to several large scandals, including the Libor interest rate rigging affair

To tackle these weaknesses, global and national financial regulators introduced a raft of regulatory reforms, the bulk of which were accounted for at the global level by Basel 2.5 and Basel 3, in the United States by the Dodd-Frank Act, and in Europe by regulatory reforms such as EMIR or MiFID as well as various country-led initiatives such as the Vickers reform in the UK. While the cumulative weight of regulatory reforms runs to several thousand pages, the principal ambitions from the regulators can be summarized as:

- Increasing the amount and quality of capital that banks (especially banks deemed systemically important) use to back their assets
- Restricting leverage in banks' balance sheets, that is, the ratio of debt to equity
- Improving the liquidity positions of banks
- Ensuring more stable funding (i.e., promoting a longer-term funding structure with less reliance on short-term wholesale funding)
- Limiting risk-taking, in particular preventing banks with retail deposits from taking proprietary trading risks
- Upgrading governance standards, enabling a fundamental change in bank governance and the way boards interact with both management and regulators

These ambitions were expressed in various new post-crisis rules and approaches. Some prominent examples include:

- Higher standards of capitalization ratios, expressed by core equity and tier-1 ratios, that is, the amount of capital a bank needs to hold for a given amount of risk-weighted assets. Basel 3, one of the cornerstones of post-crisis global financial regulation, forced up minimum ratios to an 8% minimum total capital ratio, plus a 2.5% capital conservation buffer. For many global banks this was a significant hike in the amount and capital—but also in the quality of capital, as previously there had been a large amount of hybrid capital and other capital types allowed to count towards banks' capital, versus the newer approach of a much tighter definition of *core* capital, that is, primarily tangible common equity.
- Introduction of additional capital buffers for the most complex banks. As part of the authorities' stated desire to tackle the issue of "too big to fail" in the wake of the crisis, after rescues of financial institutions and failures of complex organizations, new rules also forced the most complex financial institutions to hold additional capital buffers of up to 2.5% of RWA (on top of the capital conservation buffer).
- As well as needing to hold more capital for a given level of RWA, risk weightings for assets also increased. The set of regulations known as Basel 2.5 increased market-risk-weighted assets. Within Basel 3, new charges for counterparty credit risk were introduced. More recently, newer rules such as the Fundamental Review of the Trading Book and the move to a *standardized approach* for risk-weighted assets caused further increases in the amount of capital which banks must use.
- As a complementary measure to the risk capital ratios, Basel 3 introduced the leverage ratio, which was intended to be a measure of total exposures regardless of risk profile. The Basel 3 leverage calculations brought much of previously off–balance sheet

activity into the capitalized perimeter. Although many market participants expected the leverage ratio to be intended to be a backstop to the risk capital requirements, the introduction of the leverage ratio has turned out to be a major focus for banks with large capital markets operations, in many cases necessitating widescale optimization programs and putting pressures on balance sheet and inventory.

■ Because several of the large stress events of the financial crisis were liquidity related, regulators introduced the *liquidity coverage ratio* (LCR). It requires banks to hold an amount of highly liquid assets (e.g., cash and government bonds) generally equal to 30 days of net cash outflow. This requirement is supposed to ensure that banks can meet any immediate cash shortages through the sale of liquid assets. Liquid assets generally do not include lending, and so this requirement also restricts lendable assets. In the current interest rate environment this has led to a situation where the cost of funding can be higher than the yield on these liquid assets.

■ The *net stable funding ratio* (NSFR) was designed to strengthen banks' funding positioning by forcing a terming out of the funding profile of banks. The NSFR is yet to be fully phased in and is again expected to increase banks' overall cost of funding capital markets positions.

■ The Volcker Rule in the United States stamped out much previous proprietary trading activity and oriented the industry toward a more client activity–focused revenue-generation model.

■ In derivatives, the whole infrastructure of trading was overhauled. Dodd-Frank in the United States and MiFID in the EU mandated much of the market for simpler derivatives to be executed electronically on exchanges or so-called swap execution facilities (SEFs), which includes centralized clearing.

■ Regulators combined many of the new measures above into consolidated stress-tests which require banks to hold adequate levels of capital and liquidity to survive simulated periods of severe market volatility. The Fed's Comprehensive Capital Analysis and Review (CCAR) program in the United States has become a major focus point for all large financial institutions.

Many of these regulations were intended to be implemented globally with consistent standards. While a certain amount of initial harmonization was achieved, along several dimensions regional fragmentation of rule application started to appear, for instance, in the timelines for pushing derivatives to be cleared, with the United States leading the way and Europe initially lagging behind. Many regulators have also deployed tougher standards on their home country banks, the "Swiss finish" by FINMA, the Swiss capital markets regulator, being the most prominent example. In summary, the regulatory landscape has become more patchwork and hence increased the complexity of operating international investment banks. It also led to the occasional accusations of an uneven playing field between banks of different jurisdictions.

IMPACTS ON BUSINESS MODELS

The regulatory reform landscape, in combination with stagnant GDP in many markets, particularly in Europe, has started to significantly impact business models. It has affected the industry's revenue-earning capacity, it has led to a significant increase in costs of operations, and we are starting to see an impact on competition and concentration levels in the industry. We explore these three trends in this section:

1. Reduced revenue-earning capacity
2. Increased cost of operations
3. Changing competitive landscape

Reduced Revenue-Earning Capacity

The year 2009 marks a high point in industry revenue generation from a historical viewpoint. In this year, massive rebounds in asset positions from the previous nadirs of the years before were coupled with a partial return of positive investor sentiment following authorities' interventions, supercharging market flows. Many banks had hoped for a fast and sustained recovery and had started to set hiring targets on growth mode again. Total wholesale banking revenues exceeded $315bn in 2009, yet by 2015 industry revenues had fallen away 30% to $220bn. Over the same period, global GDP grew in nominal terms by 30%.

Accounting precisely for the fall in revenue generation is challenging, but the decline is driven at least in part by four factors: more stringent regulation pushing the sell-side (investment banks) to reduce their presence, a particular set of macroeconomic conditions discouraging institutional and corporate clients from risk taking or hedging, a general downward pressure on margins in dealing in sales and trading products, and a fall in risk appetite by the management of investment banks. Things have been aggravated by a so-far-unmaterialized hope for a last-man-standing advantage, resulting in banks retaining business with subpar economics for too long.

For example, the introduction of the leverage ratio has lessened returns in balance sheet–intensive businesses such as repo (repo and reverse-repo financing outstanding by U.S. government securities primary dealers has fallen from $6.5tn to $4.0tn over 2008–15). Higher counterparty risk charges have dented returns in structured derivatives where several banks have downsized or ceased operating.

However, the decline in industry revenues is by far not only driven by the change in the regulatory environment; it has also had macroeconomic drivers. For instance, the post-crisis period was characterized by central banks injecting liquidity into the financial markets on an unprecedented scale, which collapsed interest rates and dampened volatility in asset prices for several years. A prolonged period of ultra-low interest rates has been supportive for economic growth and for certain wholesale business lines such as DCM. However, for most other business lines the low-volatility, low-spread environment has dented wholesale banking returns by limiting institutional clients' interest in participating in the markets. For instance, the relatively flat shape of yield curves has dampened demand for hedging products while the decrease in credit spreads over the same period has lessened the incentive for investors to take on relative value trades.

More, margins that the investment banks have been able to generate in making markets in equity and fixed-income and investment banking products have declined in many products. One reason for this is transparency. The move to push standardized derivatives onto swap execution facilities shifted derivatives from historically being bilaterally negotiated between dealers and clients toward looking more like exchange-traded instruments, and clients were able to achieve tighter pricing as a result in many instances. Another reason is electronification. Improvements in trading technology have encouraged a higher percentage of assets to be traded electronically, although at different rates of growth for different asset classes, and this has also aided new types of non-bank competitors to break into the market-making business, pressuring the average margin per trade that banks could hope to extract. This has been particularly pronounced in FX, where so-called multi-dealer platforms now hold more than 35% of the market.

Understandably, the period 2009–15 has also been marked by a noticeable increase in bank shareholder risk aversion. Banks have themselves acted to enhance risk management standards, to strengthen the capital base through both equity and hybrid capital, to more tightly limit trading desks' use of capital, funding, and liquidity, and to more tightly monitor and limit value-at-risk for trading activities. While this risk-aversion aims to make the banking group safer, tighter risk limits also constrain the ability of trading desks to benefit from arbitrage or risk-taking opportunities.

Increased Cost of Operations

As a result of the regulatory reform agenda, banks now need to manage their business against a varied set of financial constraints as shown in the following (Figure 3.1).

In a world of multiple binding constraints, pursuing activity in one area consumes capacity to pursue activities in others—that is the essence of the optimization challenge. However, it is extremely unlikely that any institution will find itself up against all binding constraints at once. This creates a comparative advantage that can be used to pursue new opportunities. For example, an investment banking business with an outsized repo financing book may be up against the leverage-based capital constraint, but consumes relatively low levels of RWA (risk-based capital) or liquidity and funding. This will generate capacity to pursue more RWA-consumptive business (e.g., structured) or more liquidity- and funding-consumptive business (e.g., mortgages) with a relative pricing advantage over risk-based capital or liquidity and funding constrained competitors, all else equal. Moreover, risk–return comparisons are extremely sensitive to changes in interest rates, which make it even more difficult to draw strategic conclusions.

Against this backdrop, investment banks' strategy setting is increasingly encompassing both franchise- and resource-driven decisions. Franchise-driven decision making has always been a feature of strategic planning—identifying and prioritizing the "crown jewels" of the franchise where the business enjoys genuine competitive advantages, be they client types, product groups/structures, or geographies. Multidimensional resource-driven decision-making is the new frontier, requiring a deeper understanding of how the pursuit of crown jewels creates advantages or disadvantages in the pursuit of other opportunities (and ultimately drives economics).

Banks are responding to this challenge in different ways. Almost all have been upgrading their internal information environment, so that calculations on how much

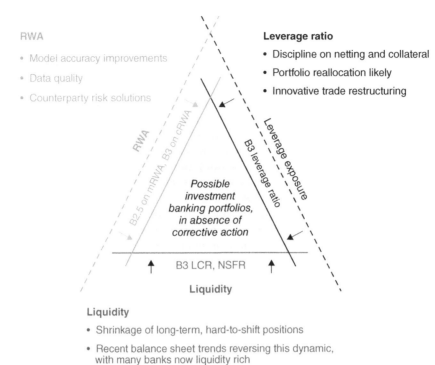

RWA

• Model accuracy improvements

• Data quality

• Counterparty risk solutions

Leverage ratio

• Discipline on netting and collateral

• Portfolio reallocation likely

• Innovative trade restructuring

Possible investment banking portfolios, in absence of corrective action

B3 LCR, NSFR

Liquidity

Liquidity

• Shrinkage of long-term, hard-to-shift positions

• Recent balance sheet trends reversing this dynamic, with many banks now liquidity rich

FIGURE 3.1 Possible investment banking portfolios, in absence of corrective action

different clients and products are consuming across risk capital, liquidity, and balance sheet can be produced quicker, more accurately, and at a more granular level. Most banks have re-educated their front office, such that salespeople, traders, and originators are now cognizant of the financial resource implications of positions they are about to create. And a significant subset have started to pass these financial resource costs down to the position level, such that the economics of positions are fully loaded in terms of financial resource costs.

As a result of this, we have seen the cost of operating these businesses going up. Banks have significantly invested in their risk management and compliance capabilities. Running the regulatory reform agenda such as CCAR, the stress-test operated by the Fed in the United States, can cost tens of millions of dollars. This is happening at a time when banks need to invest in new (digital) capabilities and to "keep the lights on" for—in many cases—hundreds of legacy systems, which can date back to the 1980s. With the future regulatory landscape now clearer, but with new regulations such as the Fundamental Review of the Trading Book set to make the way risk and finance interact with infrastructure even more important, many banks are looking to rationalize their technology estates—again with post-crisis regulation the driving force.

More, as local regulators step up their efforts to protect home market interests such as depositors, costs of operating in any additional country have gone up tremendously. This is triggered by local capital, liquidity, and funding requirements. In various countries, there are also local language reporting requirements or needs to store data locally which can lead to duplications or inefficiencies when aiming to run a global business.

Changing Competitive Landscape

The shape of investment banks' participation in the markets is evolving in two ways: The banks are becoming more selective in their product and client portfolios, and non-banks are picking up some of the value chain.

Because of the new regulatory and market pressures, banks have taken a harder look at their own areas of excellence and areas where they lag peers in service provision and this is increasing the dispersion in competitive models. Whereas in the pre-crisis period, many banks had similar business models leveraging similar strengths, this is no longer true. Looking at the top 20 financial institutions active in sales and trading and investment banking, many different models are observable. Some are corporate-focused models, typically leveraging strong fixed-income capabilities such as Rates and FX, looking into adjacencies in transaction banking (e.g., payments cash management, trade finance) to provide a more comprehensive offering to their CFO and corporate treasurer clients. Some are focused on serving institutional investors, primarily with equities capabilities, whereas others are more wealth-focused, catering to the needs of (ultra)-high-net-worth clients in combination with asset and wealth management arms. Others again are specialists in emerging markets assets and service models with depth in certain geographies and emerging markets products.

All of this has led to a large amount of competitive flux which continues to shake up the competitive structure. As shown in Figure 3.2, the market could see as much as 5% of market share open up in the latest round of strategic restructuring exercises, less than half of which is currently in flight. To put this in context, the market share released in the wave of restructurings and exits from fixed-income businesses over 2010–14 was equivalent to 4–5% of industry revenues.

Historically, wholesale banks often dominated the entire value chain of securities market-making (e.g., client coverage, content and advisory, connectivity, execution, post-trade, clearing and settlement, collateral management). The larger market share competitors generally still do, but several smaller institutions are taking a far more selective approach to the value chain and are dropping out of some activities altogether while non-bank financial institutions have been picking up market share.

A proliferation in non-bank market makers has arisen, partially caused by the pressure on bank returns causing retrenchment, and partially caused by improved efficiency in vended solutions enabling more agile trading systems infrastructure in a quasi-startup environment. Non-bank proprietary trading firms, electronic market makers, and alternative trading venues now play an important role in securities trading. For instance, Citadel, a hedge fund, was the third biggest market maker by number of trades in U.S. interest rate swaps in Q1 2015. And in May 2016 it was announced that

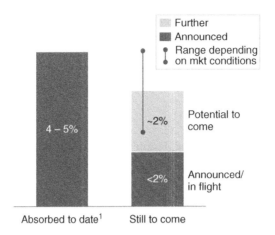

FIGURE 3.2   Market share sacrifice is linked to strategic repositioning (2010–14 and going forward, %)

XTX Markets, a computerized trading firm, had risen to fourth in the Euromoney FX rankings. This represents a powerful new source of competition for wholesale banks and one that threatens to disintermediate traditional business models; on the other hand, it also represents an opportunity for a potentially more collaborative relationship between wholesale banks and non-bank operators.

In most individual business lines within investment banking, concentration has increased. In specific product categories such as Credit and Securitized products, concentration levels have shot up materially (Securitized product sales and trading revenues top-5 concentration has increased 10 percentage points over this period). As more banks are likely to exit entire business lines, we may end up with rather oligopolistic markets. This may at one point shift the regulatory agenda more toward sustaining a minimum level of competition and avoiding further fallouts—a big task in a business that comes with significant economies of scale.

HOW IT IMPACTS THE FUNCTIONING OF CAPITAL MARKETS

The forces of change imposed on investment banks have also had a broader impact in the securities industry as a whole. There has been a clear shift in value capture. Since 2006 sell-side revenues have fallen by 20%, whereas buy-side revenues have risen 45% and market infrastructure has stayed flat. Banks cutting capacity and de-risking is an important factor. But the macroeconomic climate has also supported this shift as quantitative easing has translated into strong asset growth benefiting asset managers. Low volatility and weak economic recovery continue to depress sell-side revenues. Revenue capture by market infrastructure providers—including custodians, execution venues, clearinghouses, and data providers—is broadly flat, albeit with significant shifts within this group, mainly toward the tech and data providers.

But risks have also been shifting. The sell-side is continuing to de-risk across the board, while risks in the market infrastructure (MI) layer have grown with the introduction of central clearing and initial margins.

The biggest shift has been toward the asset owners. While liquidity provision by banks is falling, AuM in daily redeemable funds has grown rapidly, up 76% since 2008, with >45% of all globally managed assets now sitting in daily redeemable funds, up by 3 percentage points since 2008, with increased investment in less liquid asset classes (e.g., high-yield credit). With the continued growth of defined contribution (DC) an even larger share of total industry assets sit in retail-related funds, although DC structures such as 401(k) plans in the United States are stickier since investors can only switch funds rather than redeem outright.

Yet in this new environment, execution conditions have also changed, particularly in cash bond markets. Here, the principal focus lies with liquidity, that is, the ease with which clients can buy and sell securities with limited market impact within a given time period.

Credit trading is a key focus point today, with the prospect of rising U.S. rates adding an additional amount of urgency to the debate. A confluence of a significant surge in primary issuance since the crisis, a strong growth in mutual fund holdings with daily liquidity, and markedly lower dealer inventory levels combines to prompt many market participants to fear a liquidity-related market dislocation in credit. Debt issuance has grown at a 10% CAGR globally since 2005; primary issuance in 2014 was 2.4 times 2005 levels. Mutual funds offering daily liquidity have more than doubled their holdings of U.S. credit since 2005 and now hold 21% of outstanding securities, compared to 11% in 2005. And dealer balance sheet in corporate credit is down 30% globally since 2010 and we expect another 5–15% to come out.

The ultra-low interest rate environment pushed investors toward higher-yielding assets, creating strong demand for corporate credit, while issuers have looked to take advantage of attractive financing terms and to move away from pressured bank lending. Some of the strongest growth has been in HY markets. While there is evidence to suggest little degradation in liquidity in terms of standard measures (for instance, bid–ask spreads or total volumes traded), there is equally much anecdotal evidence that a lack of risk appetite and capacity means that it is harder to execute large ("block") trades that would traditionally require a dealer to take principal risk and hold a position over a period of time.

The pressures come from a number of sources:

- Most directly, capital and funding costs on dealer inventories have increased 4 to 5 times.
- Many dealers also cite the massive contraction in activity in the single-name CDS market as a key factor making it harder to hedge and manage risk in corporate bonds

(single-name CDS volumes have dropped ~70% in response to specific regulatory pressures).

■ Many also cite concerns around proprietary trading limits (e.g., Volcker) and earnings volatility as another constraint on risk appetite.

■ Many market participants feel that increased requirements on transparency (such as TRACE in the United States) have made providing liquidity through market making more challenging (for example, by recycling risk back into the market in the given "transparency window" once a position has been taken).

■ Some also feel that increased buy-side concentration in credit and the growth of passive strategies (e.g., trackers, ETFs) have contributed to an environment of more correlated flows.

The concern is that while holdings of corporate bonds have materially shifted toward mutual fund structures that offer daily liquidity to their investors, the liquidity of the underlying assets has significantly reduced—although there is actually considerable debate about whether market liquidity has actually reduced so far or whether the impact would only be materially felt in a period of market stress. Dealer inventory is now down to less than 1% of outstanding credit securities globally, or circa 1.5% of mutual fund AuM. In 2005 these statistics were ~2.5% and ~19%. Put differently, a recent IMF study suggested it could take 50–60 days for full liquidation of a U.S. high-yield fund, compared to the 7-day limit for redemption payments on U.S. funds.

On one hand, improvements in financial technology have enabled the proliferation of electronic sales, which has enabled faster and easier trading for clients at a lower cost than the older voice models. Electronic trading platforms have also introduced new trading protocols, which have benefited market liquidity by increasing the pool of potential participants. On the other hand, the regulatory reforms have driven banks to decrease the total size of trading inventory in products such as investment-grade and high-yield bonds, where banks were the traditional matchers of buyers and sellers of bonds. Because of this smaller presence of wholesale banks in the market, there is much anecdotal evidence that institutional investors are finding buying and selling bonds in large size more challenging than 10 years ago; and many investors who are not finding challenges in buying and selling bonds today are concerned that in a market volatility or crisis situation, liquidity conditions would dry up completely as the market-clearing infrastructure that previously existed could cease to function in any meaningful way.

Moreover, electronic trading and new marketplaces will grow—but will not entirely solve the fundamental concerns. There are a host of initiatives underway to increase electronic trading, establish new data networks, launch new agency execution models, and create new marketplaces. However there are limitations to how far electronification will go in fixed-income markets in the next few years given instrument heterogeneity. For example 15% of volume in credit is electronically traded today, and even aggressive estimates see it as unlikely to grow to more than 25%. More importantly, electronification doesn't improve liquidity in tail events, per se; this would require more fundamental changes to increase standardization, which in turn would bring trade-offs for issuance flexibility and investment portfolio construction.

As with much in finance, there are not many easy solutions to the liquidity conundrum as policymakers face an unresolved conflict among regulators' desires to reduce the riskiness and interconnectedness between banks, to ensure that asset managers have sufficient liquidity to deliver on promises to their investors, and to preserve companies' flexibility to issue in a wide range of markets and tenors. Yet resolution of this conundrum is critical to ensure capital markets remain effective channels of funding to support the global recovery.

CHAPTER 4

Cash Bonds and Futures

Amir Sadr

In order to price and manage the risk of any fixed-income product including bonds, swaps, and interest rate derivatives, one requires a basic knowledge of discounting, interest rates, and sensitivity measures such as duration.

TOOLS OF THE TRADE

Consider a 1-year loan of $100 at an interest rate $r = 4\%$. In 1 year's time, the lender will receive the original amount lent, $100, and the interest of $4 = \$100 \times 4\%$, for a total of $104. The interest payment is in compensation for use of the money, i.e., the lender could have used the $100 for other purposes, maybe a lucrative investment, and hence needs to get compensated for this opportunity cost.

Now, consider a 2-year loan at the same annual interest rate of $r = 4\%$. The 1-year future value of it is $104, and the 2-year future value is $104 \times (1 + 4\%) = \$108.16$. The $8 is the interest for 2 years, $4 per annum, and the extra $0.16 is due to *compounding* effect: receiving *interest on interest*.

One can enter into loans with a stated annual interest rate, but with the interest paid and compounded multiple times per year. In general, the Future Value, FV, on a horizon date of a loan A at an annual interest rate of r, *compounded m times a year*, for N whole compounding periods is

$$FV = A \times (1 + r/m)^N.$$

For example, if $m = 1$, we have annual compounding, $FV = A \times (1 + r)^N$, and N is the number of years until the future horizon date. If $m = 2$, we have semi-annual compounding (standard for U.S. Treasury securities), $FV = A \times (1 + r/2)^N$, and $N = 2 \times T$ is the number of whole semi-annual periods until the horizon date (T years from now).

The above formula can be generalized to incorporate horizon dates that are not a whole number of compounding periods away. We compute T as the number of years between the investment date and the horizon date, according to some day count basis, and come up with:

$$FV = A \times (1 + r/m)^{m \times T}$$

As we compound more and more often, in the limit we reach *continuous* compounding:

$$FV = \lim_{m \to \infty} A \times (1 + r/m)^{m \times T} = A \times e^{rT}$$

An alternative to using compounded interest rates is to use *simple* interest rates:

$$FV = A \times (1 + r \times T),$$

where T is the number of years (can be fractional) to the horizon date. Simple interest rates are usually used for *Money Market* instruments, that is, fixed income instruments with maturity less than or equal to 1 year.

The above formula is for *add on* simple interest rates. US Treasury Bills use the *discount* simple interest rate:

$$A = FV \times (1 - r \times T),$$

where T denotes the fraction of time from settlement date to maturity date, quoted Actual/360.

Consider a transaction where we today pay PV and receive FV at some future date T. We can compute the *Internal Rate of Return (IRR)* of this transaction via the following:

$$PV = \frac{FV}{(1 + r/m)^{m \times T}}.$$

In the above transaction, r is implied *Yield to Maturity (YTM)* or IRR of this transaction, *quoted* with m compoundings per year. By using a consistent quote convention for *YTM*, one can compare the attractiveness of different loans—investments from the lender's point of view.

If $FV = 1$, the PV is simply the *Present Value* of unit payment at T. Note that Present Value (PV) and Future Value (FV) are simply inverses of each other:

$$PV = 1/FV, FV = 1/PV.$$

DISCOUNT FACTORS

Consider a security that pays $100 in 1 year with no other interim cash-flows. This is an example of a zero-coupon bond, the most basic instrument in fixed income. The market price of this bond equates the 1-year Discount Factor.

In general, denoting the zero coupon bond price maturing T years from today by $ZC(T)$, we can express its implied YTM for T, $y(T)$, and the discount factor, $D(T)$, as follows:

$$D(T) = ZC(T) = \frac{1}{(1 + y(T)/m)^{m \times T}}$$

where $y(T)$ is the zero coupon rate quoted with m compoundings per year.

Note that while interest rates and implied YTM's can be quoted using different frequency and day count conventions, the actual investment (PV dollars in, FV dollars out) and any interim cash-flows remain the same. In order to *compare* different investments (loans), one would need to compare them using the same metric, that is, YTM's with same quote convention. However, in order to *price* future cash-flows, all we need are Discount Factors.

PRICE-YIELD FORMULA

Discount Factors are the fundamental building blocks for valuing fixed-income securities. Given a series of known cash-flows $(C_1, \ldots, C_N)$ to be received at various times $(T_1, \ldots, T_N)$ in the future, if we know the discount factor $D(T_i)$ for each payment date T_i, then today's value of this package is:

$$PV(\text{Portfolio of Cash-flows}) = \sum_{i=1}^{N} C_i D(T_i)$$

For example, today's price P of a T-year bond paying an annualized coupon rate C, m times a year (so $N = T \times m$ payments left) is

$$P = \sum_{i=1}^{N} \frac{C}{m} D(T_i) + D(T_N).$$

The standard bond pricing formula is based on *Flat Yield* assumption: it assumes that there is a *single* zero coupon rate, y, applicable to all cash-flows of the bond, regardless of how far the payment date is, and that all interim cash-flows can be reinvested at this rate. With this assumption, $D(T_i) = 1/(1 + y/m)^i$, and we get the classical bond pricing formula:

$$P(C, y, N, m) = P = \sum_{i=1}^{N} \frac{C/m}{(1 + y/m)^i} + \frac{1}{(1 + y/m)^N}$$

$$= \frac{C}{y}\left(1 - \frac{1}{(1 + y/m)^N}\right) + \frac{1}{(1 + y/m)^N}.$$

The above formula is for when there are $N = T \times m$ *whole* future coupon periods left. For a bond in the middle of a coupon period, the discount factors get modified as $D(T_i) = 1/(1 + y/m)^{i-w}$ where w measures the *accrued* fraction (measured using some day-count convention: Act/Act, Act/365, ...) of the current coupon period:

$$P = \sum_{i=1}^{N} \frac{C/m}{(1 + y/m)^{i-w}} + \frac{1}{(1 + y/m)^{N-w}}$$

$$= (1 + y/m)^{w} \left[\frac{C}{y} \left(1 - \frac{1}{(1 + y/m)^{N}} \right) + \frac{1}{(1 + y/m)^{N}} \right].$$

The above formula is the *Dirty (Invoice/Gross/Full) Price* of a bond, that is, how much cash is needed in order to purchase this bond. The Dirty price of a bond is the discounted value of its remaining cash-flows. The standard Price/Yield formulae simply express this by assuming a flat yield and expressing all discount factors as a function of this hypothetical yield y.

Figure 4.1 shows the graph of Price as a function of YTM. As can be seen, when YTM equals the coupon rate, the price of the bond is *Par* (100%). Also, note that as

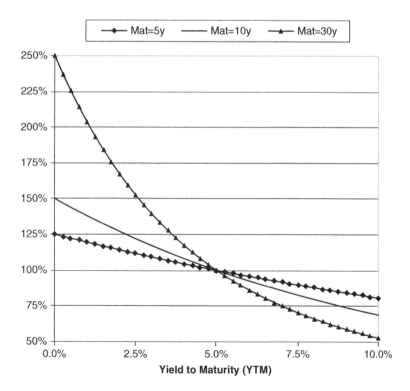

FIGURE 4.1 Price-yield graph for a 5% semi-annual coupon bond for different maturities

yields approach zero, then the price of a bond simply becomes the sum of the remaining cash-flows with no discounting.

The graph of a Dirty Price of a bond versus time to maturity T is discontinuous, with drops equal to paid coupon on coupon payment dates. This makes sense, since the present value of *remaining* cash-flows should drop when there is one less coupon. For bond traders focused on the quoted *price* of a bond, this drop in price—while real in terms of PV of *remaining* cash-flows—is artificial in terms of worthiness/value of a bond, and they prefer a smoother measure. By subtracting the *accrued interest*, wC/m, from the dirty price, one arrives at the *Clean/Quoted Price*:

$$P_{Clean} = P_{Dirty} - w\frac{C}{m}$$

$$= (1 + y/m)^w \left[\frac{C}{y} \left(1 - \frac{1}{(1 + y/m)^N}\right) + \frac{1}{(1 + y/m)^N} \right] - w\frac{C}{m}.$$

Figure 4.2 shows the evolution of the Clean and Dirty prices for a 2y 5% semi-annual coupon bond as we get closer to maturity while holding yields constant for 3-yield scenarios: $y = 7.5\%$ leading to a *Discount Bond* $(C < y)$, $y = 2.5\%$ leading to a *Premium Bond* $(C > y)$, and $y = 5\%$ leading to a *Par* $(C = y)$ bond. Notice the *Pull-to-Par Effect* for the bond regardless of the assumed yield scenario: A Discount bond gets pulled *up* to par, while a Premium bond gets pulled *down* to par.

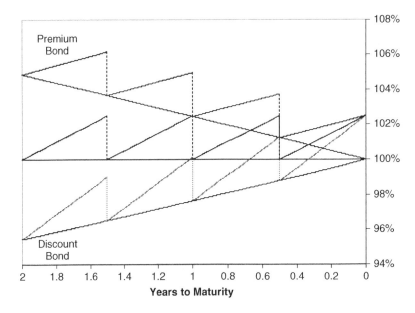

FIGURE 4.2 Clean/Dirty price evolution for a 2y 5% semi-annual coupon bond in unchanging yield scenarios

U.S. TREASURY DEBT OBLIGATIONS

The U.S. Treasury regularly auctions 1-month, 3-month, 6-month Bills; 2-year, 3-year, 5-year, 7-year, 10-year Notes; and 30-year Bonds. The new issue and existing U.S. Treasury debt obligation comprise the largest, safest, and most liquid bond market in the world. Table 4.1 shows the characteristics of the *current* treasuries on trade date 8-Oct-2015.

Let us consider the life cycle of a typical 2-year U.S. Treasury note. Two-year notes are auctioned monthly with last day of month as their coupon and principal dates. If any of the payment dates falls on a weekend, then the payment is paid on the next good business day. The other salient dates are the Announcement Date, Auction Date, and Issue (first Settlement) Date. From its Announcement date until Auction date, a 2-year note will be considered *When-Issued (WI)* and trade based on yield since the coupon rate is only known at auction time. After the auction, it starts trading based on price, and becomes the *Current* or *Active* or *On-the-run* 2y note, replacing the old 2y note. From auction date until the Issue Date, it will have a forward settlement date, and thereafter it will have a $T + 1$ settlement date. It remains the current/active 2y until the next 2y auction towards the end of next month, when it will be replaced by a new 2y issue, and will then become the *off-the-run* old 2y.

Example 4.1 On Thu, 8-Oct-2015, the current 2y U.S. Treasury (CT2 from now on) has a coupon of 0.625% with maturity date 30-Sep-2017. It is trading at clean price of 99-31+ for (T+1) settlement date of Fri 9-Oct-2015:

$$P_{Clean} = (99 + 31.5/32)/100 = 99.984375\%.$$

The bond's Issue Date is Wed, 30-Sep-2015, and hence has 9 days of accrued interest on settlement date. U.S. Treasury securities use the "Actual/Actual" convention for fractional first periods and accrued interest:

$$w = \frac{\text{Actual number of days from LastCpn/IssueDate to Settlement Date}}{\text{Actual number of days in current coupon period}}$$

$$= \frac{9\text{-Oct-}2015\text{–}30\text{-Sep-}2015}{31\text{-Mar-}2016\text{–}30\text{-Sep-}2015} = \frac{9}{183},$$

TABLE 4.1 U.S. Treasury *Currents* on 8-Oct-2015 Trade Date

U.S. Treasury	Mat. Date	Cpn Rate	Clean Price	Yield	PV01 (cents)	Mod. Dur (yrs)	Conv.
CT2	30-Sep-2017	0.625%	99-31+	0.63296%	1.960	1.96	4.83
CT3	15-Oct-2018	0.875%	99-262	0.93554%	2.964	2.96	10.34
CT5	30-Sep-2020	1.375%	99-286	1.39618%	4.788	4.79	25.77
CT7	30-Sep-2022	1.75%	99-257	1.77927%	6.526	6.54	47.44
CT10	15-Aug-2025	2%	99-02	2.10576%	8.808	8.86	87.41
CT30	15-Aug-2045	2.875%	98-20	2.94444%	19.594	19.78	504.51

Its accrued interest is then $(0.625\%/2) \times (9/183)$ and the dirty price is:

$$P_{Dirty} = P_{Clean} + w \times C/2$$
$$= 99.984375\% + (9/183) \times (0.625\%/2)$$
$$= 99.999744\%.$$

Its semi-annual yield (0.63296%) is computed by backing out (trial and error, or a root-search method such as Newton-Raphson) the y that solves:

$$99.999744\% = \frac{0.625\%/2}{(1+y/2)^{1-w}} + \frac{0.625\%/2}{(1+y/2)^{2-w}} + \frac{0.625\%/2}{(1+y/2)^{3-w}} + \frac{0.625\%/2}{(1+y/2)^{4-w}}$$
$$+ \frac{1}{(1+y/2)^{4-w}}$$
$$= (1+y/2)^{\frac{9}{183}} \left[\frac{0.625\%}{y} \left(1 - \frac{1}{(1+y/2)^4} \right) + \frac{1}{(1+y/2)^4} \right].$$

If you bought $100 million face/principal of this treasury on 8-Oct-2015, then you need to pay $99,999,743.85 to seller on 9-Oct-2015 by 3pm (before the Fed-Wire closes). This amount includes accrued interest of $15,368.85.

PV01, PVBP

Bond prices fluctuate in response to market conditions. When market yields rise, the bond's fixed coupon rate becomes less attractive relative to new market rates, and the bond value drops accordingly. Alternatively, when market yields drop, then a fixed rate bond's coupon becomes more attractive and the bond value increases. The sensitivity of a bond price to changes in interest rates, known as the market risk, is the primary source of risk to a bond holder. Other risks include credit risk, liquidity risk, inflation risk, and re-investment risk.

The change in price is usually expressed in *cents*, that is, units of 1/10,000, or for a principal of $100 = 10,000 cents. For example, when holding a $1,000,000 face of a bond, and the price increases by *5 cents*, one has made $1,000,000 \times 5 \times 0.0001 = 500. For U.S. Treasuries, units of 1/32nd of 1% (1/3200) (also called Treasury Ticks, or ticks for short) are usually used. In this case, when holding a $1,000,000 face of a bond, and the price moves by 1 tick, one has made $1,000,000 \times 1 \times (1/3200) = $312.50 = 3.125$ cents. Therefore, each U.S. Treasury tick equals 3.125 cents.

It is the standard to consider price changes due to 1 basis-point (bp, $0.0001 = 1\%$ of 1%) move in yields/rates, giving rise to *PV01*: the change in Present Value of the bond due to 1 basis-point change in implied yields, sometimes called *Risk*, or DV01 for Dollar-centric folks:

$$PV01 = \frac{dP}{dy} \times 0.0001,$$

where dP/dy is the first derivative of the bond price formula with respect to yield.

In Bond-land, PV01 is defined as the negative of the above, so that a positive PV01 signifies a long position in the bond.

A little bit of algebra gets us

$$\frac{dP}{dy} = (1 + y/m)^w \left[\frac{C}{y^2} \left(\frac{1}{(1+y/m)^N} - 1 \right) + \frac{N}{m}(\frac{C}{y} - 1)\frac{1}{(1+y/m)^{N+1}} \right]$$
$$+ \frac{w}{m+y} P_{Dirty}(y)$$

Modified Duration is defined as the *percentage* change in price, that is,

$$\text{Modified Duration} = -\frac{1}{P_{Dirty}} \frac{dP}{dy},$$

and has unit of years. While it makes sense for bonds, since swaps can have zero PV, it does not extend to swaps and interest rate derivatives, and we will stay with PV01.

A concept similar to PV01, but not identical to it is *PVBP*: Present Value of 1 bp. This is the change in price due to changing the coupon rate by 1 bp:

$$PVBP = 0.0001 \times \frac{dP_{Dirty}}{dC}.$$

PVBP is equivalent to PV'ing a 1 bp per annum annuity, paid m times a year, and can be expressed via the *Annuity Formula*:

$$PVBP = 0.0001 \times \frac{(1 + y/m)^w}{y} \left(1 - \frac{1}{(1+y/m)^N} \right).$$

For par bonds $(C = y)$, receiving 1 bp extra in coupon is almost equivalent to yields dropping by 1 bp, and that's why PV01 and PVBP are sometimes used interchangeably in practice. For non-par bonds, however, the difference can become significant, see Figure 4.3, and the appropriate formula should be used depending on the application.

CONVEXITY

Looking at price-yield graph of a bond, we observe that PV01 at a given yield is the slope of the curve at that point. We also observe that the graph is not linear and

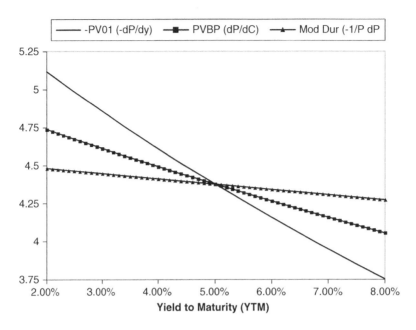

FIGURE 4.3 PV01, PVBP, Modified duration for a 5y 5% semi-annual coupon bond

has positive curvature, and as bond yields move, so does the slope or the PV01. The *Convexity* of a bond is a measure of the curvature of the price-yield graph, and is defined as the second derivative of price with respect to yield, that is, how PV01 changes as yields move.

$$\text{Convexity} = \frac{d^2 P}{dy^2} = \frac{-w}{(m+y)^2} P_{Dirty} + \frac{w}{m+y} \frac{dP}{dy}$$

$$+ \frac{N(N+1-w)}{m^2} \frac{1 - C/y}{(1+y/m)^{N+2-w}} - \frac{2CN/(my^2)}{(1+y/m)^{N+1-w}}$$

$$+ C \frac{(1+y/m)^w}{y^3} \left(1 - \frac{1}{(1+y/m)^N} \right) \left(2 - \frac{wy}{m+y} \right).$$

PV01 and Convexity can be used to estimate the price change due to a small change (Δy) in yields. Let Δy be the number of bp's change in yields. We have

$$\text{Price Change} \approx \text{PV01} \times \Delta y + 1/2 \times \text{Convexity} \times \left(\frac{\Delta y}{10,000} \right)^2.$$

In practice, however, one is primarily interested in the PV01, ignoring the convexity effect in the above equation except for long maturity bonds, or for large yield movements.

Using the above first order approximation, one can relate the changes in yields to P&L: *Each 1 bp change in yields translates to approximately PV01 cents change in value.*

Example 4.2   Continuing with Example 1, let us compute the above sensitivity measures for U.S. CT2 trading at 99-31+ ($y = 0.63296\%$) for settlement on 9-Oct-2015 with Dirty Price of 99.999744%. Using the above formulae ($N = 4$, $m = 2$, $w = 9/183$, $C = 0.625\%$), we get:

$$\frac{dP}{dy} = -1.9598749,$$

$$\text{PV01} = -0.019598749\% = -1.9598749 \text{ cents},$$

$$\text{Modified Duration} = \frac{-\text{PV01}}{P_{Dirty}} = 1.95988 \text{ years},$$

$$\text{PVBP} = 0.0001 \times \frac{dP}{dC} = 1.98458 \text{ cents},$$

$$\text{Convexity} = \frac{d^2P}{dy^2} = 4.8287.$$

We can estimate the price change due to a small, say 10bp, change in yields:

$$P(y - 10bp) - P(y) \approx \text{PV01} \times (-10) + 1/2 \times \text{Convexity} \times \left(\frac{-10}{10,000}\right)^2$$

$$= 0.019598749\% \times 10 + (1/2)(4.8287)(-0.0010)^2$$

$$= 0.19598749\% + 0.000241\% = 0.196229\%,$$

leading to an estimate of $P(y - 10bp) = 100.18060393\%$. Compared to actual $P(0.53296\%) = 100.18060417\%$, we see that the difference is quite small (0.00076% of 1/32nd, or $0.24 for $100 million face). Note that since the PV01 of this bond is 1.96 cents, we would have expected the price change to be $= 19.6 = 10 \times 1.96$ cents, in line with the above results.

YIELD CURVE

The collection of on-the-run (actives) and off-the-run U.S. Treasuries spans a collection of about 250 outstanding bonds, each with its own maturity, coupon, price, and issue size. The interrelationship between these bonds and their relative prices and yields provide a rich universe for trading, hedging, and speculating on interest rates. Figure 4.4 shows a sample snapshot of the U.S. Treasury yield curve.

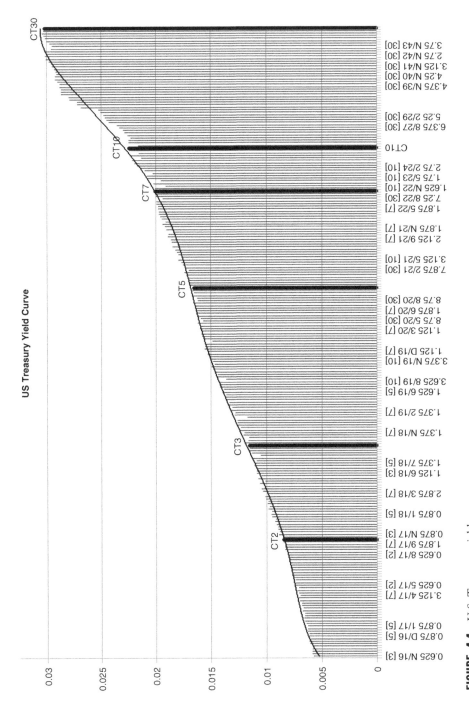

FIGURE 4.4 U.S. Treasury yield curve

Since all UST bonds are issued by the same entity and have the same credit, one would expect that the UST yield curve should be perfectly smooth. However, in practice, each bond has its own supply and demand dynamics, with the actives being the most liquid and in demand, especially in times of crisis and flight to quality, with diminishing liquidity as they become an off-the-run issue. This can cause two bonds with close maturity and coupon characteristics, say 5y vs. the old-5y, to trade at too wide a yield differential.

There are other factors for a specific bond's yield to differ from similar adjacent bonds: It might be the candidate for delivery for a U.S. Treasury futures contract, *Cheapest-to-deliver*; a bond fund might be liquidating a portfolio in response to redemption requests, resulting in cheapening of a whole sector; the issue might be in high demand due to borrowing needs of a large number of short sellers; its coupon might be much higher than similar maturity bonds, resulting in its flat YTM being lower (coupon effect).

A bond's richness or cheapness usually does not last long: There are always investors such as bond funds who are impervious to specific issues and just want to buy highest yielding or cheapest bonds in a sector. They will eventually step into the market and help normalize the yield differential between similar bonds. Also, speculators and relative value traders will buy cheap bonds and sell rich ones against them, waiting for the yields to converge to a smooth shape.

The above situations lead to three dominant category of trades: *out-right trades*, *curve trades*, and *curvature/butterfly* trades. An outright trade is based on taking a position or hedging market risk relative to the overall level of yields, for example buying 100 million 10y bond. A curve trade is taking position on the slope of the yield curve, while a butterfly trade is taking position on the relationship of a bond's yield relative to yields of a shorter and a longer maturity bond. Curve trades can be within a sector, for example, an old-2y vs. triple-old 2y, or between different sectors, say, 2y vs. 5y. Similarly, butterfly trades can be within a sector or span sectors.

SAMPLE TRADES

Example 4.3   Yield Curve Trade   Using prices in Table 4.1, we observe that the 2's-10's curve is trading at 147.28 bp (= 2.10576% − 0.63296%), which a trader might feel is too steep compared to their historical relationship, and with a view that the imminent fed tightening will cause the 2y yields to rise by more than the increase in 10y yields, i.e., the 2y will *lead in a selloff*. The trader can express this *bear-flattening* view by selling CT2 and buying CT10 in PV01-equal amounts, that is 4.49413 (=8.808/1.960) units of CT2 for each unit of CT10:

$$N_{2y} \times PV01(2y) = N_{10y} \times PV01(10y).$$

For example, if one sells $449.13 million CT2 versus buying $100 million of CT10, one is long a spread-PV01 risk of $88,080 (=$100,000,000 × 8.808 × 0.0001) or 8.81 cents per each 1 bp steepening of 2's-10's Treasury yield curve. Note that this trade is impervious to the overall level of rates: there is little PL (some convexity PL) if the whole yield curve moves up or down by the same amount, *parallel shift*, so there is no *outright* risk.

Another common trade is a *Butterfly* trade, which is a way of expressing a view on the difference between slopes of the yield curve at different points, that is on the *Curvature* of the yield curve. For example, looking at Figure 4.4, a trader might feel that 2's/5's is too flat compared to 5's/10's, that is, 5y is trading too rich relative to 2y and 10y. In this case, one can enter into a 2-5-10 butterfly by buying CT2, selling the (rich) CT5, and buying CT10 so that each spread leg (CT2-CT5, CT5-CT10) is PV01-equivalent.

Example 4.4 Butterfly Trade Using prices in Table 4.1, the 2-5-10 butterfly is trading at

$$5.4bp = (1.39618\% - 0.63296\%) - (2.10576\% - 1.39618\%)$$

$$= 2 \times 1.39618\% - 0.63296\% - 2.10576\%$$

which a trader might think is too low compared to history, see Figure 4.5. A simple trade would be to sell the (rich) *belly*, CT5, and buying the *wings*, CT2 and CT10. This is equivalent to buying the 2's-5's curve and selling 5's-10's curve in equal Spread-PV01 amounts: buying N_1 CT2 versus selling N_2 CT5 (buying 2's-5's curve), while simultaneously selling an additional N_2 CT5 versus buying N_3 CT10 (selling 5's-10's curve), so that

$$N_1 \times PV01(2y) = N_2 \times PV01(5y) = N_3 \times PV01(10y),$$

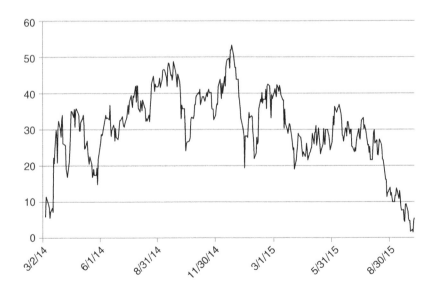

FIGURE 4.5 2y-5y-10y butterfly (bp)

The principals then become N_1 2y, $-2N_2$ 5y, and N_3 10y, sometimes referred to as equal weight or *2 in the middle* butterfly. For example, for a $100 million sale of CT5, one has to buy $122.1 million CT2 and $27.18 million CT10 for an equal-weight butterfly trade.

A more common curvature trade is to regression-weight each curve leg. For example, if a regression analysis shows that for each 1 bp movement in 2's-5's, there is typically a 0.8 bp movement in 5's-10's, then one would weight the butterfly so that

$$PV01(2's - 5's\ Curve) = 0.8 \times PV01(5's - 10's\ Curve),$$

that is, one has to underweight the 2's-5's leg due to its higher volatility, resulting in purchase of $108.57 million CT2 and $30.2 million CT10 for a sale of $100 million CT5. Notice that compared to the equal weight butterfly, we are buying less CT2's and more CT10's for the same amount of CT5's in the belly.

In general, a *Regression-Weighted Butterfly* between 3 points of yield curve is expressed as

$$\frac{m}{1+m} \times (y_2 - y_1) - \frac{1}{1+m} \times (y_3 - y_2)$$

where m is the regression slope of $y_3 - y_2$ versus $y_2 - y_1$:

$$(y_3 - y_2) = m(y_2 - y_1) + b + Error,$$

with the principals satisfying:

$$N_1 = \frac{PV01_2}{PV01_1} \times \frac{m}{1+m} N_2$$

$$N_3 = \frac{PV01_2}{PV01_3} \times \frac{1}{1+m} N_2.$$

FORWARD PRICES: CASH AND CARRY

At a given time t, the value of an asset A for *spot* (cash) delivery is obviously $A(t)$. However, if we need the asset only at some future time $T > t$, then we can enter into a *forward* contract. Such a forward contract for some specified delivery price, K, has a value today. From a buyer's point of view, if K is too large, then the forward contract is an agreement to buy an asset in the future at an inflated price, and hence has negative value. Similarly, if K is too small, then one is buying an asset in the future on the cheap, and the value of the forward contract is positive. The delivery price K which would make the contract have zero value today is called the *Forward Price* of the asset, and is denoted by $F_A(t, T), T \geq t$.

Notice that there are two dates here: trading date t, and forward delivery date $T > t$. On any given trading date t, we can graph $F_A(t, \cdot)$ as a function of forward dates T, and come up with *Forward Curve* of the asset at t. Obviously, if $T = t$, then we have the spot/cash price of the asset: $F_A(t, t) = A(t)$. We can think of the Forward Curve as the *indifference* curve of the asset: Given all the information today, we are indifferent between paying $A(t)$ for the asset today, or agreeing to pay $F_A(t, T)$ at some future delivery date T.

For a fixed forward delivery date T, the Forward Price at any trading day $t \leq T$ will fluctuate depending on market conditions. At the delivery date, of course, the forward price will coincide with the spot price: $A(T) = F_A(T, T)$. Since the forward price fluctuates on any trading day, the value of a given (seasoned) forward contract with a fixed delivery price K will also fluctuate. For example, assume it is January 1, and an asset is trading at 100, and its forward value for delivery on March 31 is 101. We might enter into this contract at 101 with no exchange of money (just a handshake). For the next three months, the value of this contract will fluctuate, depending on each day's market perception of the March-31 (forward) delivery price of the asset. At the maturity of the contract, if the spot price of the asset is higher than 101, then the contract has positive value, since it enables a long to gain the asset for lower than its market value. Similarly, if the spot price is lower than 101, then the contract has negative value, since it obligates the long to buy an asset for higher than its market value. Depending on the contract, one can either cash-settle, or take/make physical delivery of the asset at the *agreed* rather than the actual spot price.

One might think that determining the T-forward value would involve forecasting of the T-realized price of the asset. However, a simple *cash-and-carry* argument shows that we can determine the forward value of an asset without resorting to forecasting: At the inception of the contract, t, as far as the seller is concerned, he has to deliver the asset at time T in exchange for the (to be determined) forward value $K = F_A(t, T)$. He can conceptually buy that asset today t at $A(t)$ by taking a loan—potentially collateralized by the asset—with maturity T and hold on to the asset till maturity. At maturity, he will deliver the asset, receive the amount K agreed upon at time t and fixed thereafter, and repay the $A(t)$ loan plus the interest. As long as K equals the loan and interest, he will have no risk. So the forward price, K, must equal the loan amount plus its interest.

In general, the cash-and-carry argument shows that the forward value of an asset is the spot value *plus* the cost of carrying the asset *minus* any income that accrues to the holder of the asset, properly future valued to the forward date:

$$F_A(t, T) = A(t) \times (1 + r \times (T - t)) + FV(\text{Interim CF's})$$

where r is the simple funding rate for asset A at t for T. If the asset can only be carried via an un-collateralized risk-free loan, then the forward prices can be related to risk-free interest rates, or equivalently their implied discount factors:

$$F_A(t, T) = A(t)/D(t, T).$$

FORWARD RATES

A forward rate-lock agreement is an agreement for a loan starting in the future, but with the interest rate of the loan agreed upon today. If both counterparties to the loan agree on some rate, and shake hands on the loan with *no exchange* of money today, that rate is called the breakeven or *Forward Rate*. One might think that in order to come up with it, we ought to have a good idea as to what the future interest rates would be. After all, if we agreed to some rate today and in future the prevailing interest rates were very different, one side would be very happy, while the other side would feel foolish, and unemployed.

Before losing all hope, though, we can appeal to a simple replication argument to compute forward rates. Specifically, assume that the underlying future loan is for the period $[T_1, T_2]$ in the future, and the interest is computed on a simple basis. Starting with \$1 today, it will be worth $FV(T_1) = 1/D(T_1)$ at T_1, which can then be reinvested at the locked rate $f([T_1, T_2])$ until T_2, so the terminal value of \$1 investment is

$$1/D(T_1) \times (1 + f([T_1, T_2]) \times \Delta T)$$

at T_2, where ΔT is the duration of the loan period in years according to the rate's day-count. Alternatively, a \$1 investment can be guaranteed to be worth $FV(T_2) = 1/D(T_2)$ at T_2. Lack of arbitrage requires that these should be worth the same amount in the future:

$$\frac{1}{D(T_1)} \times (1 + f([T_1, T_2]) \times \Delta T) = \frac{1}{D(T_2)},$$

or equivalently,

$$D(T_2) = D(T_1) \times \frac{1}{1 + f([T_1, T_2]) \times \Delta T},$$

leading to the following formula for simple forward rates:

$$f([T_1, T_2]) = \frac{D(T_1)/D(T_2) - 1}{\Delta T}.$$

Example 4.5 Let the 3-month and 6-month deposit rates be quoted at 1% and 1.5% respectively. Ignoring day counts, we can calculate the "3-month rate, 3-months forward," $f([3m, 6m])$, as follows:

$$(1 + r_{6m}/2) = (1 + r_{3m}/4) \times (1 + f([3m, 6m])/4)$$

$$(1 + 1.5\%/2) = (1 + 1\%/4) \times (1 + f([3m, 6m])/4)$$

$$f([3m, 6m]) = 4 \times \left(\frac{(1 + 1.5\%/2)}{(1 + 1\%/4)} - 1 \right) = 1.99501\%$$

which is reasonable: If we think of interest rates as growth rates of money, then if \$1 grows at rate of 1% for the first 3 months, and simultaneously grows at rate 1.5% for the first 6 months, then our first estimate for its growth rate between 3 and 6 months would be 2%, and the above result bears that intuition.

For a given tenor/term, ΔT, say 3-months, a graph of $f([T, T + \Delta T])$ versus T, is called the *Forward-ΔT Rate Curve*. If there is no uncertainty about future interest rates, say if God came and told us what the 3-month financing rates would be in 3 months and every 3 months thereafter, then the forward-3m rates have to equal these God-given known rates. If not, for any quarterly period, one would borrow at the lower rate (whichever one: locked rate or God-given rate), and lend at the other (higher) rate, creating a sure profit. *The forward rate curve then is the implied path of short-term rates if interest rates are deterministic.*

In the presence of uncertainty, the realized future interest rates can differ from the previously locked forward rates. For realistic (random) interest rates, the forward rate curve can still be interpreted as the *expected* future interest rates, however, this interpretation is only a first-order understanding of them, and further qualifications need to be made.

Forward Rates and Discount Factors

We saw that knowledge of the Discount Factor Curve determines all forward rates. Conversely, given a sequence of forward rates spanning a series of dates $0 = T_0 < T_1 < T_2 < \ldots$, one can iteratively use the above relationship to compute discount factors: $D(T_0) = D(0) = 1$,

$$
D(T_{n+1}) = 1 \times \frac{1}{1 + f([T_0, T_1])\Delta T_0} \times \cdots \times \frac{1}{1 + f([T_n, T_{n+1}])\Delta T_n}
$$

$$
= \prod_{i=0}^{n} \frac{1}{1 + f([T_i, T_{i+1}])\Delta T_i}, \qquad \Delta T_i = T_{i+1} - T_i,
$$

using simple rates. Therefore, the Forward Rate curve and the Discount Factor curve are interchangeable, and knowledge of one completely determines the other.

EXTRACTING THE DISCOUNT FACTOR CURVE

The yield-to-maturity is based on the assumption that all cash-flows of a bond can be discounted back to today using the same flat YTM. In reality, yields of zero coupon bonds, *Zero or Spot Rates*, show a usually upward sloping term structure. It is often desirable to extract a single discount factor curve and price all cash-flows of a bond appropriately according to each cash flow's discount factor and zero rate. When priced off of this single curve, we can then measure the relative rich/cheapness of existing bonds, or calculate hypothetical price and yield of non-existent—say constant maturity treasuries—or back out implied forward rates such as 5y, 5y nominal and breakeven rates.

Bootstrap Method

A standard method of constructing the discount factor curve is to *Bootstrap:* Arrange the benchmark (usually the actively traded and liquid) instruments into increasing maturity, and starting with the shortest maturity, derive the discount factors for its cash-flow dates up to its maturity, and move on to the next instrument. Since the next instrument may have cash flows that precede prior instruments' maturities, we will use the already-constructed discount factors for these—if there are no existing discount factors for a particular date, we will use an interpolation method to get its discount factor—and estimate the remaining discount factors. An example will be helpful:

Example 4.6 Assume we are quoted the market rates appearing in Table 4.2.

Starting with $D(0) = 1$, we can extract the 6m discount factor as follows (we are ignoring all calendar and date details):

$$D(6m) = 1/(1 + 0.30\%/2) = 0.998502.$$

The 1y SA YTM is 0.55%, meaning a 1y bond with SA coupon of 0.55% should price par:

$$100\% = (0.55\%/2)[D(6m) + D(1y)] + (100\%)D(1y).$$

Since we have already obtained $D(6m) = 0.998502$, the above equation has only 1 unknown, and we solve for $D(1y) = 0.994519$.

The 2y SA YTM is 0.625%, hence,

$$100\% = (0.625\%/2)[D(6m) + D(1y) + D(1.5y) + D(2y)] + (100\%)D(2y).$$

In solving the above, we already have $D(6m)$, $D(1y)$, but we need to solve for 2 unknowns: $D(1.5y)$ *and* $D(2y)$. It might seem that we are stumped, since there is one equation and 2 unknowns. This is where interpolation comes into play: We can assume that the discount factor curve is a piece-wise linear function, and hence

$$D(1.5y) = (1/2)D(1y) + (1/2)D(2y).$$

With this interpolation method, we just need to solve for the single unknown $D(2y)$, which after a bit of algebra, we get as $D(2y) = 0.987589$, and we then calculate $D(1.5y) = 0.991054$. Continuing along in this fashion, we get the following set of discount factors and forward-6m rates shown in Table 4.3.

TABLE 4.2 Inputs for Bootstrap Method

6m Simple Rate	0.30%
1y SA YTM	0.55%
2y SA YTM	0.625%
3y SA YTM	0.90%
5y SA YTM	1.40%

TABLE 4.3 Bootstrapped Discount Factor Curve

T	DF(T)	SA YTM	f([T,T+6m]
0y	1.0		0.300%
6m	0.998502	**0.300%**	0.801%
1y	0.994519	**0.550%**	0.699%
1.5y	0.991054	0.600%	0.702%
2y	0.987589	**0.625%**	1.454%
2.5y	0.980462	0.789%	1.464%
3y	0.973335	**0.900%**	2.147%
3.5y	0.963	1.074%	2.170%
4y	0.952664	1.207%	2.194%
4.5y	0.942328	1.313%	2.218%
5y	0.931992	**1.400%**	0.000%

Armed with a discount factor curve, we can calculate the fair value of a high-coupon, say 5%, 5y bond:

$$(5\%/2)[D(6m) + D(1y) + \cdots + D(4.5y) + D(2y)] + (100\%)D(5y) = 117.488\%$$

which implied YTM of 1.369%. Note that this high-coupon bond's YTM is 3.1bp lower than 5y par yield (1.40%), which is called the *High-Coupon Effect:* In an upward sloping yield curve, for 2 identical maturity bonds, the one with the higher coupon has a lower yield if priced off of the same discount curve.

CARRY, ROLL-DOWN

The Price-Yield formulae were based on *Spot* ($T + 1$ for US) transactions. If instead one wants to agree on a *Forward Price* today, but take ownership of a bond at a later (forward) date, one is entering into a *forward* transaction. Since the Forward Price has to be set today, one resorts to a cash-and-carry argument to arrive at the fair forward price.

The forward seller can conceptually buy the bond today, finance it to the forward delivery date, and deliver the bond to buyer, receive the previously agreed-upon forward price, settle the financing cost, and be free. Also, if there are any coupon payments before the forward date, then a (fair) seller needs to future-value these coupon payments to the forward date. Hence the fair Forward Price, *FP*, of a bond is:

$$FP_{Dirty} = P_{Dirty} + \text{Financing cost} - FV(\text{Coupon Income}).$$

As bonds are usually financed via repo markets, the Future Value of any coupon income is calculated using the repo rate, r. Hence, for UST bonds, we have:

$$FP_{Dirty}(T_{Fwd}) = P_{Dirty} \times \left(1 + r\frac{T_{Fwd} - T_s}{360}\right) - \sum_{i=1}^{M} \frac{C}{2}\left(1 + r\frac{T_{Fwd} - T_i}{360}\right),$$

where $T_1, \ldots, T_M$ are the payment dates of the intermediate coupons (if any) from the settlement date T_s to the forward date T_{Fwd}.

The *Forward Yield* is the implied YTM of the forward price using the forward settlement date. The *Price Carry* (sometimes called Dollar-Carry, or just Carry), is the difference between the current (spot) clean price and the forward clean price:

$$\text{Price Carry} = P_{Clean} - FP_{Clean}(T_{Fwd}),$$

while the *Yield Carry* (again sometimes just called Carry), is the difference between the forward and spot yields:

$$\text{Yield Carry} = \text{Forward Yield--Spot Yield}.$$

If there are no intermediate coupon payments between spot and forward settlement dates, we can simplify the general Forward Price Formula as:

$$FP_{Clean}(T_{Fwd}) = P_{Clean} + P_{Dirty}(T_s) \times r \times \frac{T_{Fwd} - T_s}{360} - \frac{C}{2} \frac{T_{Fwd} - T_s}{D},$$

where D is the Actual number of days in the current coupon period.

If the yield carry is positive, then one can buy the bond spot, finance it in repo to the forward date, and as long as its actual yield on the forward date is lower than the forward yield, one can close out the position by selling the bond for a net profit. Hence, the yield carry is a measure of the cushion in yield movements (from spot) for a long position in this bond to be profitable. A high positive carry is a signal that yields have to move by a lot from their spot (today's) values before a long position in a bond loses money.

In general, for a positively sloped yield curve where spot yields are higher than repo rates (after adjusting for the difference in their quote convention, Act/Act vs Act/360), purchasing a bond and earning the higher yield while financing it via the lower repo rate leads to *Positive Carry*. This investment strategy is sometimes called "Riding the Yield Curve," which in essence is equivalent to betting against the forward yields: the ride is profitable if future yields turn out to be lower than what was implied by the forwards.

Yield carry is sometimes called the amount of unfavorable *Parallel Shift* in the yield curve before one loses money. This is not exactly correct, since it ignores the *Roll-Down Effect*, that is, it ignores the fact that the bond on the forward date has a shorter maturity than when bought today. Therefore one is comparing the spot yield of a longer bond to the forward yield of a shorter bond. To compare apples to apples, one then computes the *Yield Roll-Down* (sometimes just called roll-down) as the difference between spot yield of the bond, to the spot yield of another bond whose maturity is shorter by the length of the investment horizon (Forward Date-Spot Date):

$$\text{"n"-Month Roll-Down} = y(T) - y(T - \text{"n"-Months}),$$

where T is the maturity of the bond under consideration, and $y(T)$ its YTM. The amount of parallel shift protection is the sum of yield carry and yield roll-down.

Example 4.7 Continuing with U.S. Treasury CT2 with clean price quoted at $P = 100\text{-}31+$, $y = 0.63296\%$ on trade date 8-Oct-2015, and settlement date 9-Oct-2015, let us compute its forward price/yield 3 months forward, for forward settlement date of Monday 11-Jan-2016, using a term financing rate of 0.25%. Since there is no intermediate coupon between settlement date and forward date, we can compute the forward clean price as

$$FP_{Clean}(11\text{-}Jan\text{-}2016) = P_{Clean} + P_{Dirty} \times 0.25\% \times \frac{N}{360} - \frac{0.625\%}{2}\frac{N}{D},$$

where $N = 94$ is the actual number of holding days (9-Oct-2015 to 11-Jan-2016), and $D = 183$ is the number of days in the current coupon period (30-Sep-2015 to 31-Mar-2016):

$$FP_{Clean}(11\text{-}Jan\text{-}2016) = 99.984375\% + 99.999744\% \times 0.25\% \times \frac{94}{360} - \frac{0.625\%}{2}\frac{94}{183}$$
$$= 99.889133\% = 99 - 28+,$$

leading to a forward yield of 0.68993%. The yield carry is 5.7 bp's.

If there was a bond today with maturity 30-Jun-2017, with a yield of 0.60296% (3bp's lower), then the 3m-roll-down would be computed as 3bp, for a total of 8.7 bp parallel shift (carry + roll-down) protection.

U.S. TREASURY FUTURES

U.S. Treasury futures are standardized exchange-traded contracts based on the forward prices of a *basket* of deliverable bonds. For example, the 5y treasury future contract with Dec 2015 delivery can be physically settled by delivery of any of the bonds in Table 4.4.

TABLE 4.4 5y Delivery Basket; Trade Date: 8-Oct-2015, Fut Price: 120-106; Last Del. Date: 6-Jan-2016; Repo Rate: 0.25%

Cpn Rate	Mat. Date	Clean Price	Conv. Factor	Gross Basis (/32nds)	Prc Carry (/32nds)	Net Basis (/32nds)	IRR
1.375%	02/29/20	100-121	0.8317	9.5	8.8	0.7	0.164%
1.375%	03/31/20	100-07	0.8287	15.9	8.7	7.2	−0.654%
1.375%	04/30/20	100-05+	0.8258	25.6	8.7	16.8	−1.869%
1.5%	05/31/20	100-251	0.8276	38.2	9.7	28.6	−3.325%
1.625%	06/30/20	101-055	0.8297	42.7	10.6	32.1	−3.743%
1.625%	07/31/20	101-042	0.8269	52.1	10.6	41.5	−4.921%
1.375%	08/31/20	100-005	0.8141	65.7	8.8	57.0	−6.937%
1.375%	09/30/20	99-286	0.8113	72.6	8.7	63.9	−7.834%

The short counterparty has many choices for delivery, the main ones being which bond and when to deliver: At any time during the delivery month (plus 3 business days after the delivery month for the 2y and 5y contracts), so from 1-Dec-2015 to 6-Jan-2016, the short can deliver any of the bonds in the basket. In positively sloped yield curves, it is typically advantageous to deliver on the last possible day, 6-Jan-2016, so the timing option is of small value. However, the option of selecting any of the bonds in the basket, known as *quality option* makes this contract a nuanced one.

On any delivery date, if the short decides to deliver, she will certainly deliver that day's *cheapest to deliver*. Without any adjustments, this bond will typically be the one in the basket with the lowest coupon and shortest maturity, and would usually not change during the 3-month active life of the contract. However, the treasury futures contract is designed to give each bond in the basket a chance to be deliverable. This is achieved by assigning a conversion factor to each bond to adjust for coupon and maturity differentials. This conversion factor is set to make all bonds have the same price—and hence equally deliverable—if their yields were the same (currently set at 6%). The clean *Invoice Price* charged by the short for delivering a specific bond is then the *adjusted* futures price: $P_{Fut} \times CF$, where CF is the conversion factor of the delivered bond.

On any given date t prior to delivery, the Invoice Price, $P_{Fut}(t) \times CF$, for any deliverable bond cannot be higher than its forward price FP(Del. Date), or there would be an arbitrage opportunity: A speculator could sell the futures contract at t for $P_{Fut}(t)$, and buy that bond forward at the forward price FP(Del. Date). On delivery date, she would collect the higher invoice price, $P_{Fut}(t) \times CF$ plus accrued interest, pay the lower forward price agreed before at t, FP(Del. Date), plus the same accrued interest, and transfer the bond from the forward seller to the futures buyer for a risk-less profit of

$$P_{Fut}(t) \times CF - FP(\text{Del Date}) > 0.$$

Therefore $P_{Fut}(t) \leq FP(\text{Del Date})/CF$ for any bond in the delivery basket. This leads to the following upper bond:

$$P_{Fut}(t) \leq \min\left(\frac{FP_1(\text{Del Date})}{CF_1}, \frac{FP_2(\text{Del Date})}{CF_2}, \ldots, \frac{FP_N(\text{Del Date})}{CF_N}\right),$$

when there are N bonds in the delivery basket.

The *Futures basis* of a bond is its current price versus its Invoice Price. This is slightly different than the typical definition of *Basis*—spot price less the forward price, which is just the cost of carrying the bond. Since the short in the contract owns the timing and quality options, and no option is given away for free, the futures price is somewhat lower than the minimum of the converted prices, with the difference being the market price of these options. Note that as one approaches the last delivery date, the value of these options decreases to zero, and on the last delivery date, the futures price equals the lowest converted price. However, prior to final delivery, as yield levels change, so does the market's estimate of the likely CTD, and its potential to change (switch option).

For each bond in the basket, the *Gross Basis*, is defined as

$$GB = P_{Clean} - P_{Fut} \times CF$$

while the basis net of carry, *Net Basis*, is defined as

$$NB = GB - Price\ Carry$$
$$= P_{Clean} - Price\ Carry - P_{Fut} \times CF$$
$$= FP - P_{Fut} \times CF$$

Net basis of a bond is the cost to the short for selling the future and hedging the sale by buying the bond spot and financing it in a term repo to delivery date. Since the short can select any of the bonds in the basket to hedge, she would select the bond that has the lowest cost. Therefore, market practitioners designate the bond with the lowest net basis as the most likely one to be delivered, i.e., the CTD bond.

Another way of searching for the CTD is to calculate the *Implied Repo Rate (IRR)*, i.e., the hypothetical return on a spot bond purchase, sale of the futures contract, and delivery of the bond for $P_{Fut} \times CF$. Assuming no intermediate coupon payments between now and the delivery date, the cash flows are $P_{Clean} + AI_1$ for the purchase price (investment), and $P_{Fut} \times CF + AI_2$ for the redemption amount, where AI_1, AI_2 are the settlement date's and delivery date's accrued interest respectively. Solving for the simple implied interest rate, we have the IRR:

$$IRR = \left(\frac{P_{Fut} \times CF + AI_2}{P_{Clean} + AI_1} - 1 \right) \Big/ (N/360),$$

where N is number of days between settle date and delivery date. Since the short can pick any of deliverable bonds in the above transaction, she would select the one with the highest IRR, and that bond becomes the market's estimate of the CTD bond.

Example 4.8 Looking at Table 4.4, let us compute the GB, NB, and IRR of the first bond, which has the lowest NB and highest IRR, and hence is the current CTD.

$$GB = (100 + 12.125/32)\% - 0.8317 \times (120 + 10.75/32)\% = 0.2955\%$$
$$= 9.5\ ticks\ (/32nd's)$$
$$P_{Dirty} = (100 + 12.125/32)\% + 1.375\%/2 \times 39/182 = 100.526228\%$$
$$N = N_1 = 6\text{-Jan-}2016 - 9\text{-Oct-}2015 = 89$$
$$D_1 = 29\text{-Feb-}2016 - 31\text{-Aug-}2015 = 182$$
$$Price\ Carry = (1.375\%/2) \times (89/182) - 100.526228\%(0.25\%)(89/360) = 0.27223\%$$
$$= 8.8\ ticks(/32nd's)$$

$$NB = 9.5 - 8.8 = 0.7\,ticks(/32nd's)$$

$$N_2 = 6\text{-Jan-}2016 - 31\text{-Aug-}2015 = 128$$

$$AI_2 = 1.375\%/2 \times (128/182) = 0.48352\%$$

$$IRR = \left(\frac{(120 + 10.75/32)\% \times 0.8317 + 0.48352\%}{100.526228\%} - 1 \right) \Big/ (89/360) = 0.1637\%$$

A basis trade consists of simultaneous buying/selling of a bond and taking the opposite position in the futures contract. For example, buying/selling the 5y basis of a bond means buying/selling $A principal of the bond and selling/buying $A/100,0000 \times CF$ number of futures contracts (each contract has a notional of $100,000). Note that this is just the gross basis of the bond which includes the optionality premia. The basis of a bond is only known with certainty on the last delivery date when there is no more optionality and equals its price versus the converted price of the CTD—the basis of CTD is obviously zero at expiry. Prior to expiry, the basis includes the carry and the premia for all the options (delivery, quality,...) that have been conferred to the short.

Figure 4.6 shows the basis of CTD and two other bonds in the December 5y basket (Table 4.4) at the last delivery date versus the potential parallel yield curve movements between trade date and expiry date. For example, on trade date 8-Oct-2015, the UST 1.375% Feb/20 is the CTD. It remains the CTD at expiration even with 275 bp parallel

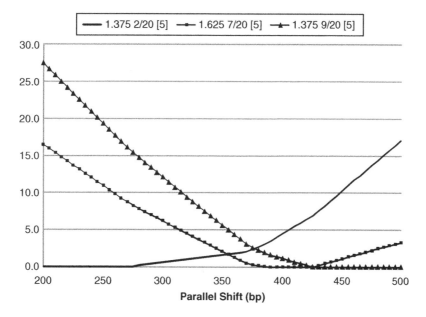

FIGURE 4.6 Basis (/32nd's) of three sample bonds at last delivery date vs. parallel shift

move up in yields, where at that point another issue becomes the CTD, and UST 1.375% Feb/20's basis is no longer zero.

The basis of CTD at expiration looks like a hockey stick with multiple breaks. This is typical when yields are below the assumed contract yield of 6%, and it is why a short basis position (long futures) is usually hedged by buying a single or a series of put options on the futures contracts at various strikes (275 bp out-of-the-money, 375 bp's out-of-the-money, ...). On the other hand, if one sells the basis and not hedge it, then one is selling options and betting that the CTD will not change (no switch).

Example 4.9   Assume that on 8-Oct-2015, a trader sells $100 million basis of the then CTD, UST 1.375% Feb/20 for 9.5 ticks: Sell $100 million of the bond for 100-121, and buy 832 ($\approx 0.8317 \times 100{,}000{,}000/100{,}000$) 5y Dec contracts for 120-106, and repo the bond to delivery date 6-Jan-2016 at term repo rate of 0.25%. Looking at Figure 4.6, he decides that it is unlikely that rates will back up by 275 bp from trade date to 6-Jan-2016, and decides not to hedge it.

On 6-Jan-2015, assume that his view is borne out and the UST 1.375% Feb/20 is still the CTD. Then he gets delivered the bonds, buys back his short, and his profit in the trade is the net basis at trade date: $100{,}000{,}000 \times 0.7/3200 = \$21{,}875$.

In actual practice, the 5y contract stops trading on 31-Dec-2015 and its price gets frozen and no longer tracks the CTD. Also the short needs to just deliver the notional amount of the contract on any deliverable bond: $83.2 million. That's why as soon as the contract stops trading, a basis seller buys back the *tail*: $16.8 million ($100–$83.2 million) of the bond one is short to cover the *tail risk*.

CHAPTER 5

Risk in Capital Markets

Peter Reynolds and Mike Hepinstall

INTRODUCTION

The capital markets provide an invaluable mechanism within the economy to enable private- and public-sector investment and growth by facilitating the allocation of resources and sharing of risk. Such activities by their very nature require careful and appropriate risk management. The level of complexity and speed inherent within modern capital markets firms make sound risk management extremely important, as problems can emerge and escalate quickly. Particularly, following the financial crisis, there has also been an elevated regulatory focus on risk management practices, risk measures, and capital requirements.

This chapter provides a comprehensive overview of the risk management and measurement approaches used within capital markets firms. Where regulatory concepts are introduced, the focus is primarily on regulations that apply to banks active in the capital markets; however, the underlying risk management principles apply to non-bank capital markets firms as well. This chapter will outline a common taxonomy used to parse risks into digestible types, review the major metrics used to measure and monitor risk, provide a brief overview of the regulatory environment, and discuss the intersection of risk and strategy.

The risk metrics section includes more detailed reviews of market and counterparty risk measures that are uniquely important to the capital markets, and provides an introduction to other relevant risk types such as operational risk and liquidity risk.

Even the in-depth sections of this chapter only skim the surface of the thinking, practice, and approaches used to measure, monitor, and react to risks. Thousands of books, academic papers, regulatory rules, and other thought-pieces have been written about risk management, and the approaches continue to evolve. This chapter provides an introduction to key concepts of that world. Finally, it closes with some thoughts on the future of risk management.

OVERVIEW OF RISK MANAGEMENT IN CAPITAL MARKETS

Defining Risk

Given its importance, there is surprisingly little consensus on the definition of *risk*. Early debates center on the distinction between "risk" and "uncertainty," with a view that risk needs to be inherently quantifiable.[1] This thinking has evolved notably with Holton (2004),[2] who proposes that risk exists when there is uncertainty about potential outcomes and those outcomes have an impact on utility.

For the purposes of this chapter, we define risk as uncertainty around future expectations of earnings. We should highlight that risk is in the *deviation* from expectations. Within a distribution of potential outcomes, the expected value may be negative (for example, a bank may anticipate that there will be expected losses on a loan portfolio). But this is not in itself risk, as the expected value is known and it can be priced into the transaction at inception. Risk is an unexpected value: the volatility around that expectation.

A Taxonomy of Risks

In their paper from 2007,[3] Schuermann and Kuritzkes define a mutually exclusive, collectively exhaustive taxonomy of risk (Figure 5.1). They use this to determine the proportion of earnings volatility attributable to each risk-type. This serves as a good starting point for parsing risk into digestible types that can be measured and monitored.

- **Market risk** is the earnings impact of a change in the market value of a position held by an institution. This risk-type is most clearly seen in activities that involve principal investment (e.g., hedge funds and private equity firms). The failure of Long

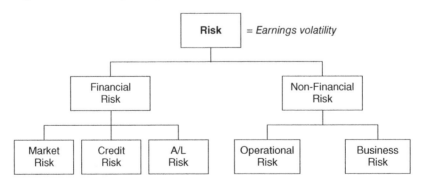

FIGURE 5.1   Taxonomy of Risks
Source: Oliver Wyman

[1]See, e.g., F. H. Knight, *Risk, Uncertainty and Profit* (New York: Hart, Schaffner & Marx, 1921).
[2]Glyn A. Holton, "Defining Risk," *Financial Analysis Journal*, 60(6), (2004), 19–25.
[3]http://fic.wharton.upenn.edu/fic/papers/06/0605.pdf.

Term Capital Management in 1998, documented by Roger Lowenstein,[4] serves as a quintessential case study on losses resulting from market risk.

▪ **Credit risk** is the set of risks resulting from the default of other parties to whom you have exposure. In commercial and retail banking, this risk mainly arises from defaults of those to whom a bank has lent money. Within the capital markets, credit risk largely stems from defaults by trading counterparties resulting in nonperformance on their contractual obligations, such as those arising from derivative contracts. This is known more specifically as *counterparty* credit risk. For example, firm A may hedge an equity market risk exposure by purchasing put options from firm B, where the put references the same equity security. Yet even if the option is in the money, firm A may lose the value of that option in the event that firm B defaults and does not fulfill its obligation under the contract.

As a high-profile example, much of the fallout from the collapse of Lehman Brothers in 2008 stemmed from concern that losses arising from one counterparty default could be large enough to destabilize other counterparties, leading to a chain of further defaults.

▪ **Asset–liability risk**, also known as liquidity risk, stems from a potential mismatch between a firm's asset and liability profile. Such a mismatch may lead to a firm being unable to meet short-term financial demands. This risk may arise when a firm has a material portion of short-term funding (e.g., overnight repo) supporting long-term assets (e.g., multi-month derivative contracts). If such an institution undergoes a crisis of confidence and short-term funding becomes unavailable, long-term assets may not be able to be liquidated in time, at a sufficient price to meet obligations. The failure of Bear Stearns is a good example of this risk.

▪ **Operational risk**, as defined by the Bank of International Settlements, is "the risk of loss resulting from inadequate or failed internal processes, people, and systems, or from external events."[5] Such losses are referred to as non-financial, as they are not driven by market prices, although they can be significantly influenced by market movements. For example, Société Générale lost EUR 4.9BN in 2008 due to rogue trading by Jerome Kerviel and a lack of adequate internal processes and controls. Other examples of operational risk include systems breakdowns, data hacking, and business practice lawsuits.

More recently two subsets of operational risk have been the subject of close scrutiny: *conduct risk* and *model risk*. Conduct risk is the risk that losses may occur due to misconduct of employees of a bank, for example, the selling of inappropriate products to consumers. Model risk is the risk that errors in models or in their use lead to losses (e.g., by incorrectly pricing trades or drawing other faulty business decisions from model output).

▪ **Business risk** is the risk caused by uncertainty in profits due to changes in the competitive, economic, or sociopolitical environment. Examples include increased costs

---

[4]Roger Lowenstein, *When Genius Failed* (New York: Random House, 2001).
[5]BCBS 2005, §644.

and/or decreased revenue opportunities arising from regulatory changes, margin erosion or market share loss from increased competition, or the ramifications of a prolonged low interest rate environment.

Since the financial crisis, the approach to measuring and managing risk has materially evolved.

First, there has been an increased focus on the connections among various risk types, including more stringent approaches to handling correlation across risks. This has included greater regulatory emphasis on broad-based stress tests—exemplified by the U.S. Federal Reserve's CCAR process, which considers major macroeconomic shocks that could influence multiple categories of risk.

Second, the prior focus on capitalization, which is the buffer held to mitigate all risk-types covered above, has been expanded. Many new measures are much more blunt, and purposefully do not seek to risk-weight assets (e.g., the leverage ratio), reflecting the view that models of risk are inherently limited. In addition, the regulatory focus has extended beyond capital to also include buffers for liquidity and funding risks ("asset–liability risk" in the framework above). This reflects the reality that many of the major firms that failed during the financial crisis did so primarily due to liquidity and funding issues, rather than pure insolvency.

Risk management as a discipline, and regulators in particular, have also taken a broader look at the overall interconnectivity of the whole financial system. This includes the designation of a number of non-banks as systemically important financial institutions (SIFIs) covered by banking regulation, as well as reviews of the "shadow" banking sector (e.g., repo markets, non-bank financial intermediaries). Furthermore, the overall functioning of the markets—including depth of liquidity—has been under close review to ensure that the financial system is sound.

Organizational Structures in Place to Manage Risks

The organization of controls and structures within capital markets firms has evolved materially over the past 20 years. The core principle used is that of "three lines of defense":

1. The first line responsible for risk management is the business itself—in capital markets firms, that is the front office. Much work has been done to ensure that appropriate controls are in place to govern the day-to-day activities of traders and bankers. Furthermore, incentives and compensation plans were altered to align the remuneration of traders and bankers with the risk goals of the firm (i.e., compensation claw-back provisions). Often, this first line is heavily supported by the middle office and product control functions.

2. The second line is responsible for ensuring that policies, procedures, and controls are firmly in place to measure and monitor risks. This includes establishing the firm's risk appetite, developing risk measurement models, monitoring risk measures, and liaising with regulators. Segregation of the lines of defense is critical. In most major

capital markets firms, the second line reports to a chief risk officer (CRO), who has a direct line to both the CEO and board of directors.

3. The third line of defense is Internal Audit, which provides independent testing and evaluation of the effectiveness of risk management, control, and governance processes, and independent advice to management and the board of directors on improving such effectiveness. Internal audit provides an independent evaluation of both the first and the second line of defense.

Capital markets firms often maintain a matrix risk reporting structure for the second line, the first dimension of this matrix being the primary lines of business—with a *risk officer* dedicated to ensuring that each business unit is appropriately managed, and acting as the primary point-of-contact for the business line management team. The second dimension in the matrix is based on risk type, with a risk officer charged with ensuring that the aggregate risk profile of the business is appropriate for each risk type incurred. Recently, a third dimension has grown in importance, as national regulators increasingly require global firms to "ring fence" their businesses in each geography, and hence regional risk officers are of growing importance.

In order for the risk organization to be effective, a clearly established set of policies and procedures needs to be put in place. Policies and procedures must be supported by a clear risk appetite statement, limit framework, robust risk measures, and systematic reporting of the risks and associated actions taken to mitigate these risks. Key risk measures, limits, and risk mitigation actions are reported through to a clearly defined committee structure, leading up to the board of directors, who often have a standalone risk committee.

METRICS USED TO MEASURE AND MONITOR RISK

At the core of risk management is a set of metrics comparing the ratio of risk to the buffer held by an institution against that risk. Quantification of these metrics requires two sets of calculations: (1) determining what qualifies as a buffer for the risk in question; and (2) quantifying the potential risk itself, and comparing this to the buffer to ensure adequate protection.

Key Buffers Against Risk in Capital Markets Firms

In order to mitigate risks, banks hold two distinct but related forms of cushion: capital and liquidity.

Through time, banks have failed or have required government assistance because they had shortfalls in capital, lack of liquidity, or a combination of the two. In addition, liquidity and capital shortfalls can blend together in times of stress, with perceptions of inadequate capital leading to liquidity shortfalls, and liquidity shortfalls leading to inadequate capital. All key stakeholders in capital markets firms, including regulators and investors, maintain a keen focus on ensuring adequate capital and liquidity levels.

Capital   In its simplest form, capital is the equity in a bank's balance sheet: the difference between assets and liabilities. If assets decline in value, capital is the cushion that banks hold against these losses.

Bank balance sheets are complex. A bank's total capital is made up of various types of capital, including:

- Tier 1 capital, which is seen as a core measure of financial strength, composed of:
  - Core equity capital (common stock)
  - Disclosed reserves/retained earnings
  - Certain forms of nonredeemable, noncumulative preferred stock
- Tier 2 capital is supplementary capital that either (a) is already set aside for known losses (rather than being a cushion for unexpected losses); or (b) shares characteristics with debt rather than equity. It is composed of:
  - Evaluation reserves
  - General loan-loss reserves
  - Other undisclosed reserves
  - Hybrid capital instruments and subordinated term debt

Recently, banks have issued a number of contingent convertible capital instruments (CoCos). These are hybrid securities that convert from debt-like instruments to equity-like capital on specific trigger events designed to capture stressful environments. Depending on the precise nature of these contractual triggers, these instruments can be classed as either additional Tier 1 or Tier 2 capital.

Most jurisdictions set a regulatory minimum for each type of capital defined previously. In general, these minimum levels are presented as a percentage of risk-weighted assets (RWA). Risk-weighted assets are defined in a later section. Banks seek to be as efficient as possible in terms of required capital, as the cost of equity is generally higher than the cost of debt.

Liquidity   Following the recent financial crisis, the focus of regulators and risk management practitioners turned to capital adequacy measurement and management. Shortly thereafter, liquidity and funding management became the focus through many regulatory initiatives.

Capital and liquidity are distinct but related. While capital is fundamentally a measure of the solvency of a bank (the difference between assets and liabilities), liquidity reflects the ability a bank has to find the liquid resources (usually cash) to meet demands. A bank can be solvent from an accounting perspective, maintaining adequate capital, but still face a material crisis due to lack of liquidity. Indeed, most recent cases of bank failure have manifested themselves through liquidity, rather than capital, shortfalls.

Measures of asset liquidity for banks essentially have two dimensions:

1. Measures of assets held in cash (in currency or on deposit with central banks) or securities that are readily convertible to cash, such as U.S. government discount notes or U.S. Treasury bills.

2. Measures of the maturity profile of less liquid assets. While liquidity crises can be sudden, they are rarely instant. As a result, a number of less liquid assets are likely to mature in the window under consideration, generating additional funds for the bank.

As with capital, liquidity is costly, as expected returns on short-term highly liquid positions, such as cash, are low relative to the alternatives.

Since liquidity risk arises from mismatches of assets and liabilities, the measurement of funding stability is also critical to liquidity risk management. Both asset-side and funding measures of liquidity are further detailed later in this chapter.

BRIEF OVERVIEW OF REGULATORY LANDSCAPE

The financial system plays a critical role in the functioning of the modern economy. When healthy, it provides businesses and consumers access to the capital markets to fund their growth opportunities—be it a new factory, a new home or car, and so on. When the financial system is unhealthy, such growth opportunities may be systematically forgone, resulting in slower growth, recession, or even depression.

As a result, banks have unique access to government support, including access to central bank funding such as the funding window at the U.S. Federal Reserve. Given this, and the importance of their role to the economy as a whole, banks are subject to comprehensive regulation by multiple bodies.

At a global level, regulation is developed by the Basel Committee on Banking Supervision, a sister organization of the Bank for International Settlements (BIS), which was established in 1930 and is headquartered in Basel, Switzerland. The Basel Committee has played a central role in development of new capital and liquidity standards for financial services firms. These capital accords are referred to in shorthand as "Basel accords," and have evolved through time:

- Basel 1,[6] established in 1988, was primarily focused on ensuring that banks had adequate capital to withstand credit risk events. The simple framework proposed five categories of assets, each with different risk weights ranging from 0% to 100%. Banks were required to hold capital above 8% of their risk-weighted assets.
- A Market Risk Amendment[7] was added to Basel 1 in 1997, to include market risks within the regulatory capital landscape. The amendment established a standardized measurement method, covering all major capital markets exposures (rates, equities, foreign-exchange, commodities, and options). In addition, for the first time, the amendment also proposed allowing firms to develop internal models to measure market risk.

---

[6]http://www.bis.org/publ/bcbsc111.pdf.
[7]http://www.bis.org/publ/bcbs24.pdf.

- Basel 2,[8] finalized in 2004, completely revised the proposed capital framework. The capital adequacy framework was updated to include three separate pillars: minimum requirements, supervisory review, and market discipline. The minimum capital requirements were materially adjusted in the following aspects:
  - Granular standardized approaches to credit risk capital
  - The option to develop internal ratings-based approaches to capital
  - A framework for capitalization of securitizations
  - Addition of operational risk capital
  - Major updates to trading book capital
- "Basel 2.5" is shorthand used to refer to the 2009 revisions to the market risk framework.[9] Again, a number of risk-weights in the standardized measures were adjusted. In addition, a set of approaches for internal models to quantify "specific risk" were added.
- Basel 3[10] was established in 2010–11 following the crisis, and again refreshed certain capital requirements. Most significantly, however, the framework was revised beyond capital to add a liquidity coverage ratio and net stable funding ratio, aiming to address liquidity risk in regulated entities.

The global regulatory landscape continues to evolve markedly. The BIS has conducted a fundamental review of the trading book (FRTB),[11] which resulted in proposals to remove a number of the more complex modeling approaches for market risk, establish capital floors, and move management of market risk to the desk-level. Further capital proposals are also under development for both the standardized approach to credit risk[12] as well as specific approaches to counterparty credit risk.[13] These recent regulatory proposals present a clear trend toward limiting the use of internal models to determine regulatory capital.

While the global regulatory framework is the product of negotiation and agreement across major central banks, the implementation of the rules falls to national regulators. The precise national interpretation of rules may differ by geography. In the United States, a web of regulatory bodies exists. Within the capital markets space, these bodies include:

1. Securities and Exchange Commission (SEC)
2. Financial Industry Regulatory Authority (FINRA)
3. Federal Reserve System (Fed)
4. Office of the Comptroller of the Currency (OCC)

---

[8] http://www.bis.org/publ/bcbs107.htm.
[9] http://www.bis.org/publ/bcbs158.pdf.
[10] http://www.bis.org/bcbs/basel3.htm.
[11] http://www.bis.org/publ/bcbs265.pdf.
[12] http://www.bis.org/bcbs/publ/d347.pdf.
[13] http://www.bis.org/publ/bcbs279.pdf.

5. Federal Deposit Insurance Corporation (FDIC)—for those institutions that are deposit-taking (e.g., Bank of America, JP Morgan, Citi)
6. Commodities Futures Trading Commission (CFTC)

Each of these bodies, as part of their supervisory mandate, is able to develop and enforce regulation. In some cases this is done by implementing global regulations—for example, the FDIC, Federal Reserve Board, and the OCC have jointly implemented the Basel requirements in the United States.

In a number of cases regulation is local rather than global. For example, the Volcker Rule[14] prohibiting capital markets firms from engaging in proprietary trading was part of the Dodd-Frank Act, and hence only applies to firms with a U.S. presence. Furthermore, the supervisory process itself may be materially different based on geography. In the United States, for example, Dodd-Frank mandated stress-testing as the primary tool used by regulators to ensure appropriate capital adequacy and robustness in risk management processes. This manifests itself through the annual Comprehensive Capital Analysis and Review (CCAR). CCAR requires major bank holding companies (BHCs) and intermediate holding companies (IHCs) of large foreign-owned banks to estimate the impact on income statements and balance sheets of a severely adverse economic scenario, and demonstrate adequacy of capital though this stressed forecast.

Outside of the United States, multiple regulatory agencies have evolved post-crisis. They have a keen focus on real-world stress testing of banks. Similar to CCAR, these stress tests act as a tool for determining adequate capital. Examples include the European Union–wide stress tests run by the European Banking Authority (EBA) and the Bank of England stress testing of UK banks, run by the Prudential Regulation Authority (PRA). Furthermore, additional regulations have required international firms to ring-fence and manage risk for their local legal entities on a standalone basis, reducing the fungibility of moving capital across regions.

METRICS FOR MAJOR RISK TYPES

A number of analytical techniques are used to determine the riskiness of a bank's positions. In many cases, these are directly used to determine a risk-weighted assets (RWA) estimate, which can then be compared to capital.

Market Risk Metrics

Risk Factors as Building Blocks of Market Risk Changes in the market value of traded instruments are typically explained by the use of pricing models, which relate a position's market value to a set of individual market-derived inputs known as *risk factors*. For example, using the classic Black-Scholes model for a call option, the risk factors would

---

[14] § 619[1] (12 U.S.C. § 1851) of the Dodd–Frank Wall Street Reform and Consumer Protection Act.

include the stock price, discount curve, expected dividends, and implied volatility (the strike price and maturity would also be key static inputs, but not risk factors).

The use of risk factors is instrumental to the aggregation of market risk measurements across a portfolio of various instruments. Extending the above example, the translation of the option position into a set of risk factor sensitivities allows a risk manager to understand how its sensitivity to an equity price shock combines with other direct long and short positions to form overall portfolio sensitivities and conduct portfolio-level scenario analysis. Such sensitivities may be linear or nonlinear.

Value at Risk (VaR)   Value-at-Risk (VaR) is a measure of the risk of loss on a specific portfolio of liquid assets in a trading book, for a given portfolio, probability, and holding period. VaR is defined as the threshold of a one-sided confidence interval, such that the probability of a mark-to-market loss exceeding this threshold is equal to a specified probability threshold (Figure 5.2). For example, if a given portfolio has a 1-day holding period and has a 99% confidence level VaR of $1 MM, this means that on average, a daily loss exceeding $1 MM should happen in only 1 out of 100 trading days.

Typically, VaR is computed assuming a static portfolio, that is, assuming no new positions or hedges are taken on and no existing positions or hedges are exited during the horizon.

Framework Variations in Modeling VaR   There are multiple methods for creating the distribution of portfolio gains and losses needed to calculate VaR. We review several of the alternatives. Models generally follow one of three broad frameworks:

1. A "delta-normal" parametric framework, in which all position sensitivities to risk factors are approximated as linear, all risk factor distributions are approximated as normal, and all dependence structures between risk factors are approximated as fixed correlations. The advantage of this framework is simplicity: If all those assumptions

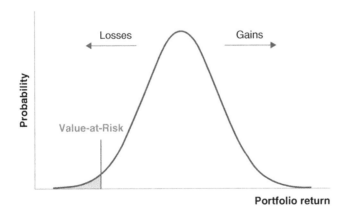

FIGURE 5.2   Illustrative Calculation of VaR
Source: Oliver Wyman

hold, VaR can be expressed by an analytic formula and calculated quickly without simulation. But these assumptions rarely hold completely, and the inaccuracy of these assumptions weighs heavily against the use of such a framework for sophisticated trading books.

2. A Monte Carlo simulation framework, in which risk factor distributions are estimated from historical data (and may take a variety of non-normal distributions) and then combined via simulation in which correlated random draws are taken for each risk factor. After the portfolio value is computed for each of a large number of simulations, a percentile can be computed from the simulation results. This form of aggregation is in principle very flexible for complex distributions and nonlinear sensitivities, but the tradeoff is that it can be highly computationally demanding—to the point that if valuation calculations are individually time-consuming, repeating them across tens or hundreds of thousands of simulation paths can be prohibitive.

3. A historical simulation framework, in which the joint distribution of risk factor changes is approximated by simply drawing from the past 1–3 years of returns over a particular holding period (e.g., 1-day or 10-day). In the example of 1-day holding period returns, if there are 250 trading days in a year (rounded for simplicity), a 2-year historical VaR would be calculated by drawing from the last 500 daily returns. Each of those 500 historical days can be viewed as a separate scenario that could apply to today's portfolio, in the sense that the movements observed in each risk factor from that day can be mapped into potential movements today. This can be done without explicitly estimating the shape of the distribution assumptions or the correlation between risk factors—instead, both are empirically matched to a specific historical window. By utilizing fewer scenarios, this approach is also less computationally challenging than the Monte Carlo simulation.

Selection of Holding Period Another core building block of any VaR model is the selection of the appropriate holding period to use for analysis. Given that the VaR framework measures potential changes to the portfolio assuming no rebalancing, the selection of a longer holding period will generally lead to a higher VaR-based risk measure. However, since trading books turn over quickly and tend to be managed closely, this fundamental modeling assumption becomes less representative of reality when it is applied to longer horizons.

While classical VaR models generally do not relax the assumption of a static portfolio, the rapid turnover of positions is one reason why VaR model time horizons are generally short. Historically, many trading businesses internally used a 1-day VaR metric for internal management reporting, alongside a 10-day VaR metric for regulatory capital and the associated reporting. Some other businesses use intermediate values (e.g., 2- or 3-day VaR).

However, each of these is a fairly one-size-fits-all metric, where highly liquid assets that could be managed down or hedged within hours are commingled with less liquid positions that would take significantly longer.

Percentile Threshold versus Expected Shortfall In its classic definition as noted above, VaR refers to threshold value, that is, the size of loss beyond which there is only an $x\%$ chance of exceeding that loss within a certain period of time.

Another measure that has emerged over time is Expected Shortfall (ES), which measures the expected value (i.e., probability-weighted average) of all the potential losses that are *beyond* a certain percentile of the distribution. Since VaR measures the threshold value while ES measures the values beyond it, for any given value of x, ES will give a larger dollar-loss figure than VaR. ES has certain benefits for risk management purposes; in particular it always considers the most extreme potential losses, whereas VaR is mostly insensitive to differences in risk that are beyond the threshold value.

For instance, say that one trading desk (A) has entered a trade that pays off $5 MM in 99.9% of cases, but loses $1 BN in 0.1% of cases, while another (B) has a position that pays off $5 MM in 99% of cases, but loses $100 MM in the other 1%. Using a 99% VaR, the risk in position B would be captured well but A could slip under the radar as its risk only arises further out in the tail than was considered. ES would capture them both, weighing the larger loss potential of A against the higher likelihood of loss in B.

Limitations of VaR While VaR models are commonly used in risk management, they also have significant limitations, including:

- As noted above, the threshold definition of VaR is fairly insensitive to risks that are beyond the specified percentile.
- Inferences of risk factor distributions are generally drawn from past market movements, which are not necessarily indicative of the future. In particular, key market variables like equity index prices, credit spreads, and FX rates have all exhibited periods of low volatility followed by periods of high volatility, so recent calm does not necessarily signal future calm in the market. Similarly, certain market risk factors have also shown high correlation during some years and low correlation during others. As a result, VaR may significantly understate or overstate risk depending on the time period used.
- For credit-sensitive trading exposures, VaR models may not adequately capture certain price risks associated with credit events (e.g., default), which may be meaningful risks even if they have not occurred to a given issuer in the historical window.
- The choice of a single time horizon (e.g., 10 days) for a VaR model is generally a simplification rather than a reflection of instrument-specific risks that may unfold over different horizons.

Regulatory Measures Aimed at Addressing Shortcomings of VaR In response to the financial crisis, global regulators have taken additional measures—first through Basel 2.5, and subsequently through the proposals arising from the Fundamental Review of the Trading Book—to address its limitations. Comparing the post-FRTB capital proposals against Basel 2, key enhancements include:

- Regulatory capital models will be adjusted to use an Expected Shortfall (ES) metric instead of threshold VaR.
- Using a stressed calibration of the return distributions for Expected Shortfall, that is, a period of significant financial stress rather than simply the most recent year or two.

- For credit-sensitive trading exposures, adding a separate default risk charge (DRC) to address the default risks not captured in VaR. Banks may use separate internal models to compute this charge based on the 99.9% threshold value from the probability distribution of default-related credit losses. To capture the shape of this distribution, such models must take into account not only the individual probabilities of default of different issuers, but also the correlations between the creditworthiness of different issuers, which may be higher if issuers are in the same industry or region. Where banks do not receive approval to use internal DRC models, prescriptive standardized add-ons will be applied.
- ES-based regulatory capital models will be adjusted to differentiate the holding periods used for assessing the market risk associated with different factors, depending on assessments of the liquidity and depth of markets in those risk factors.

In addition to modeling of general and specific risks covered previously, capital markets firms are also required to identify risks not in VaR/ES (RNIVs) and to ensure that they are appropriately capitalized.

Market Risk Stress Testing In addition to VaR or ES, risk managers also use other complementary measures for market risk. Several of these are variants of stress testing, including scenario analysis. Generally, in stress tests, instead of attempting to define an entire probability distribution for possible losses, the focus is on defining specific hypothetical situations and then using valuation models and other analytic tools to determine the impact the scenario would have on the portfolio. By considering hypothetical scenarios, stress tests can help risk managers to assess risks that have not occurred but may materialize in the future. On the other hand, stress tests are limited to whatever scenarios have been considered (not completely exhaustive). Nonetheless, to develop a robust stress-testing framework, risk managers often consider three categories of scenarios:

1. Single-factor scenarios, such as simple parallel shifts up or down in a yield or spread curve, or shocks to equity index values, which are useful for identifying/confirming major sensitivities and concentrations.
2. Targeted multifactor scenarios (e.g., equity price and equity volatility shocked at once to capture cross-risks, i.e., the situation where a change in one risk factor leads to increased or decreased sensitivity to another risk factor). Alternatively, different yields or spreads may be shocked to different degrees in a way that exposes a basis risk (i.e., where opposite exposures to two related risk factors fail to offset as expected).
3. Complete market environment scenarios, which, given the large number of risk factors to stress simultaneously, are often selected from historical events that caused major market disruptions. Custom scenarios may also be designed to explore a hypothesized vulnerability.

Another common risk measure used to evaluate credit risk concentrations in a trading portfolio (equivalent to a form of stress testing) is to simply identify and monitor the top 10, 20, or 50 counterparty exposures, ranked by the total loss incurred if each counterparty were to immediately jump to default. One or more alternative Loss Given Default (LGD) assumptions are used when utilizing this approach (e.g., JTD_100, JTD_50, JTD_0, JTD_worst).

Counterparty Credit Risk Metrics

Counterparty risk can be defined as the risk of a financial loss due to the potential default of a trading counterparty. It arises mainly from two types of activity:

1. Derivatives trading (e.g., swaps, options)
2. Securities financing (e.g., repo/reverse repo, margin lending against client portfolios)

Compared with the credit risk that arises from lending, counterparty risk presents an additional measurement challenge as the value of exposures fluctuates through time and is dependent on market movements. It can be helpful to think of counterparty risk as a mixture of market risk and credit risk—indeed, the tools used to measure and manage counterparty risk incorporate some elements from each, as well as some unique concepts.

For instance, concentration of exposure to any one entity or group of related entities is a major consideration across credit risk types whether arising from lending or counterparty activity. For credit risk management purposes, many organizations define total exposure limits and reporting to combine lending and counterparty activities.

On the other hand, like market risk, the potential variability in exposure to a given counterparty can be expressed in a VaR-like measure. Such measures are commonly used in internal risk reporting, and in some cases also embedded in contractual margin requirements (discussed further in the following).

Exposure Definitions and Measurement   Given that exposure can vary over time, the management and capitalization of counterparty risk typically considers both *current exposure* and *future exposure*.

In the case of an uncollateralized derivative, current exposure can be measured simply as:

$$Current\ Exposure = \max (0,\ Market\ Value)$$

where the derivative's market value could be either positive or negative, but only positive market values create exposure to the counterparty.

Future exposure is a somewhat more nebulous concept since the future is uncertain and there are typically multiple time horizons of interest between the present and the maturity of a position (or portfolio of positions under one netting agreement). We use this term broadly to encompass a family of distinct metrics, some key members of which are defined more precisely in Table 5.1.

As shown, potential future exposure (PFE) is strongly analogous to VaR, except that it refers to the upper tail of potential market values at a particular future date, rather than the lower tail of potential changes in value over a particular horizon from today.

TABLE 5.1 Metrics and Their Corresponding Equations

Metric	Equation
Expected exposure (EE)	$EE_t = E[\max(0,\ MV_t)]$
Effective expected exposure	$EEE = \max\limits_{t\in[0,maturity]} (EE_t)$
Potential future exposure (PFE)	$PFE_t(\alpha) = x$ *such that* $P(MV_t < x) = \alpha$ where α is a confidence level such as 95% or 99%
Maximum PFE/Peak PFE	$Peak\ PFE = \max\limits_{t\in[0,maturity]} (PFE_t)$

When setting risk management limits on individual counterparties, it is common to utilize PFE-related measures as they provide advance visibility into the more extreme possible exposure concentrations that could result from unexpected market movements.

Credit Valuation Adjustment (CVA) Measurements of counterparty exposure are also intrinsically related to a second key counterparty risk concept, the Credit Valuation Adjustment (CVA). CVA measures the difference between the market value of a particular derivative contract and the market value the same contract would have had if the counterparty (or both the counterparty and the firm)[15] had zero probability of default.

A simplified example will illustrate:

A derivative contract is structured such that there are two potential outcomes: In 50% of cases, the counterparty will owe the firm $15 MM, and in the other 50% of cases, the firm will owe the counterparty $10 MM. Assuming no credit risk on either party and a short enough horizon that discounting is immaterial, the NPV of the contract is $2.5 MM. Yet if the counterparty has a 10% chance of defaulting (with no recoveries), this decreases the positive contribution to NPV by 10%*50%*$15 MM or $750 K. If the firm itself has a 1% chance of defaulting (with no recoveries), this decreases the negative contribution to NPV by 1%*50%*$10 MM or $50 K. Netting these two effects, the bilateral CVA would be –$700 K and the final derivative value would be $1.8 MM.

In general mathematical form, unilateral CVA can be expressed as:

$$CVA = \iint\limits_{scenarios,\,time} Max(0, MV_t)\, PD_t LGD_t$$

If the scenarios of MV, PD, and LGD are completely independent of each other (which may not necessarily hold in all cases), then this can be simplified to the more tractable expression below:

$$CVA = \int\limits_{time} EE(t)\, PD_t LGD_t$$

---

[15]Unilateral CVA refers to the effect on value from the counterparty's credit risk alone. Bilateral CVA refers to the effect of adjusting for the credit risk of your own firm as well as that of the counterparty.

Prior to the global financial crisis, measuring CVA had already become a common accounting practice, used to create a reserve for expected credit losses on derivatives, which could be viewed as analogous to loan loss reserves. However, the approach to estimating the counterparty's PD and LGD could either be a historical/actuarial approach or a market-driven approach derived from spreads, such as from traded CDS contracts. In recent years, the market-driven approach has come to dominate, at least where the counterparty's spreads are observable or can be inferred from comparable companies and indices.

While CVA considers the possibility of default, it does so from an expected value point of view, so considering our definition of risk as "deviations from expected," CVA is not in that sense a risk measure but simply a pricing or valuation measure. However, *changes* in CVA do present a second form of risk, since such changes affect the fair value of the firm's positions and ultimately flow through to earnings. In an environment where the counterparty PD is derived from the counterparty's market-observed spreads, counterparty spread volatility can be a major driver of variations in CVA, and hence another source of risk to earnings.

Many firms have also expanded a similar approach to adjust derivatives valuations for other effects beyond CVA, such as the risk of their own default (debt valuation adjustment, or DVA), and the cost of funding the positions (funding valuation adjustment, or FVA). Further valuation adjustments for cost of capital (KVA) and margin (MVA) have even been considered. The term *XVA* is used as a catchall for the set of all valuation adjustments on derivatives.

Managing Counterparty Risk   There are a number of contractual mechanisms by which counterparty risk can be mitigated, if not entirely eliminated:

- Right of offset and netting provisions—where the firm and counterparty owe each other certain gross amounts, these allow the firm not to make gross payments that would be owed back by the counterparty, reducing exposure from a gross to net basis.
- Guarantees, especially from central counterparties (clearinghouses).
- Collateral held as margin, under agreements such as a Credit Support Annex (CSA).
- Haircuts applied to collateral posted.
- Rating-based triggers that may require greater overcollateralization if the counterparty is downgraded, or allow the firm to terminate the contract at that point.

Collateral posted and held as margin is an important element in both cleared and bilateral derivative trading. For instance, a clearinghouse will generally require each of its counterparties to post two forms of margin:

1. *Initial margin* covers potential future exposure and hence is more driven by estimates of volatility in the risk factors.
2. *Variation margin* is the additional collateral posted directly to cover price movements that change the current exposure.

Wrong-Way Risk   Wrong-way risk refers to the situation where a counterparty's exposure is strongly correlated, or even causally linked, to its Probability of Default (PD) and/or Loss Given Default (LGD). When this is the case, multiplying independent estimates of exposure, PD, and LGD together does not give a sufficient measure of expected loss, because under the scenarios that generate the most exposure, PD or LGD is also higher.

For illustration, consider a simple example where there are two equally probable scenarios: one in which exposure = $100, PD = 20%, LGD = 100% and another in which exposure = $10, PD = 0% and LGD = 0%. The first scenario leads to loss of $20 and the second $0, for an average of $10. Whereas if exposure, PD, and LGD were each averaged and then multiplied as though independent, the expected loss computed as $60*10\%*50\% = \$3$ would be understated.

The most severe examples of wrong-way risk are when the counterparty is directly affiliated with an issuer whose securities are referenced on a derivative or used as collateral. This is referred to as "specific wrong-way risk," and is generally addressed through controls to restrict such transactions, or provide no credit for such collateral, rather than advanced measurements.

However, broader forms of general wrong-way risk can lurk where there are underlying economic drivers that affect, but do not fully determine, both the counterparty's creditworthiness and the exposure. Examples include:

- Counterparty is in the same sector as underlying (e.g., oil & gas).
- FX trades where the counterparty and the exposure are both more sensitive to a particular foreign economy.

In the presence of general wrong-way risk, firms may make further adjustments to their exposure or LGD estimates to be more consistent with values conditional on default, or adjustments to their PD or LGD estimates to be more consistent with values conditional on a scenario that would drive high exposure.

The opposite of wrong-way risk is sometimes referred to as "right-way risk" (i.e., when a key factor that could lead to an increase in exposure would also lead to an improvement in counterparty creditworthiness). This can sometimes be seen in commodity hedging with certain corporate clients (e.g., where the client's profits are correlated to a commodity price, and the derivatives used for hedging involve paying the client a fixed price for a certain volume of that commodity). In principle, right-way risk may reduce CVA or other measures of counterparty risk.

Liquidity Risk Metrics

Basel 3 introduced two distinct metrics to measure and manage liquidity risk, the Liquidity Coverage Ratio (LCR) and the Net Stable Funding Ratio (NSFR).

1. The LCR is designed to ensure that banks would have necessary liquid resources to survive a 30-day market crisis. It is calculated as the ratio of high-quality liquid assets to projected cash claims. Assumptions are made as to the quality of assets,

with differentiated haircuts applied to values of certain assets, as well as rollover rates on assets scheduled to mature in the 30-day window. Further, liabilities such as retail deposits are categorized into levels of "stickiness" (i.e., the amount that are expected to persist through a financial crisis to support the asset base). The minimum LCR is specified at 100% by Basel, although national regulators have discretion over thresholds. In practice, banks will generally choose to ensure they have a buffer above the required minimum.

2. The NSFR is designed to ensure banks have appropriately stable sources of funding. It is calculated as the ratio of stable sources of funds (Tier 1 and 2 capital, other preferred shares, liabilities with maturities >1 year, and portions of certain other liabilities such as deposits) to assets, adjusted to reflect their ability to be liquidated. As with the LCR, the requirement is for banks to have an NSFR above 100%. Again, banks are likely to target additional buffers.

In addition to the metrics above, firms are also expected to conduct periodic stress testing of their liquidity profile. As an example, in the United States, the Federal Reserve Board conducts a comprehensive liquidity analysis and review (CLAR) process to evaluate the liquidity position and liquidity risk management practices at the largest firms.[16]

Operational Risk Metrics

Since the financial crisis, the banking sector has seen a number of significant operational risk losses. The most noteworthy high-profile cases included rogue trader Jérôme Kerviel at Société Générale, unauthorized or unknown risk positions put on by the "London Whale" at JP Morgan Chase, and legal fines levied on firms related to the mis-selling of financial assets.

The Basel 2 accords outline seven categories of operational risk events:

1. Internal Fraud—misappropriation of assets, tax evasion, intentional mismarking of positions, bribery
2. External Fraud—theft of information, hacking, third-party theft, forgery
3. Employment Practices and Workplace Safety—discrimination, workers compensation, employee health and safety
4. Clients, Products, and Business Practice—market manipulation, antitrust, improper trade, product defects, fiduciary breaches, account churning
5. Damage to Physical Assets—natural disasters, terrorism, vandalism
6. Business Disruption and Systems Failures—utility disruptions, software failures, hardware failures
7. Execution, Delivery, and Process Management—data entry errors, accounting errors, failed mandatory reporting, negligent loss of client assets

---

[16]http://www.federalreserve.gov/bankinforeg/srletters/sr1507.htm.

Basel 2 also outlines two key approaches to quantification of operational risks:

1. The advanced measurement approach (AMA) allows a firm to develop internal modeling of operational risks.
2. The standardized approach, which defines "beta factors" for specific banking business lines. These can be simply used to estimate the capital required, based on the aggregate level of gross income.

In addition to the regulatory metrics, recent focus has once again been on stress testing and scenario analysis to test the vulnerability of firms to operational risk losses.

Internal Metrics

Beyond regulatory requirements, capital markets firms have developed their own in-house approaches used to measure, monitor, and manage risks. These range from simple exposure levels, which are easily understood, to more complex internal "economic capital" measures that attempt to combine multiple risk types in a common metric. In addition, real-world scenario analysis is often used. For example, a firm may analyze the impact of a default by two of its largest counterparties or customers.

THE INTERSECTION BETWEEN RISK AND STRATEGY

Risk Appetite

Capital markets firms use a "risk appetite" statement to express the firm's risk tolerance in the context of their overall risk framework. This is a communication tool used with both internal and external stakeholders—including regulators and the board of directors. A firm's risk appetite statement is a starting point for business units to assess the products and services offered to clients, and to analyze the trade-offs of risk versus return on a day-to-day basis.

Limit Frameworks

A limit framework is often set up to translate a firm's risk appetite to an operational level. For example, specific limits are assigned at the desk and trader levels. The limit framework is continuously monitored by Risk to ensure that each trader is in compliance with the limit structure. Risk also maintains a formal process for the management of breaches.

Linking Management of Limited Resources to Strategy

Given the limited nature of, and costs associated with, financial resources (liquidity, funding, capital), Risk, Treasury, Finance, and the Front Office need to work hand in hand to optimize these scarce resources and maximize shareholder returns. This is often done by multiple mechanisms—one more top-down and another bottom-up.

A top-down approach involves measuring returns on one or more of these financial resources for each line of business, and using the comparison of relative returns to inform strategic plans to grow certain businesses more quickly, challenge underperforming units to make do with fewer financial resources, or exit businesses that are expected to continue to underperform.

A bottom-up approach involves creating internal mechanisms to charge businesses for the financial resources they use, at costs that may be higher for the scarcest financial resources. When these costs are pushed down, essentially every business is challenged to find and root out the constituent activities that drive a greater share of their resource usage than their share of profits and expand those that yield greater share of profits. Those activities may be distinguished at a much more granular level (e.g., offering of specific product subtypes, or even covering specific clients).

Risk-Adjusted Returns Metrics

Given the relationship between risk and returns, banks look to be appropriately compensated for the risk they take, using a measure of *risk-adjusted returns* for optimizing business decisions as well as for management reporting. Since there is no single industry-standard approach, firms often tailor their choice of metric to fit their business models.

FUTURE OUTLOOK

Effective risk management is, and will remain, critical to the success of capital markets businesses. If anything, the importance will continue to increase as firms become increasingly interconnected. This trend is driven by the velocity of trading in an electronic age, as well as post-crisis consolidation of the larger capital markets firms. Ongoing product development will only add further complexity to the product-set, and hence risk management will need to continue to evolve to provide effective control and balance.

Metrics and regulatory requirements will continue to evolve through time; thus in highly competitive markets, risk management functions will need to be:

- *Agile and creative:* Given the continued evolution in products, and ever-changing macro- and microeconomic environments, managing risks effectively requires agility to reflect changing product characteristics, and imagination to test what might go wrong. In some cases, this will require a broadening of the current capabilities of risk teams.
- *Connected to strategy:* Risk needs to be not only a control and compliance function, but also an advisor and enabler for the business to grow and succeed. Especially in an era of tightened margins and constrained financial resources, the risk function needs

to partner with the first line in identifying and considering risk-return tradeoffs. This requires risk to be embedded, ex-ante, in the development of the strategic direction of the firm.

- *Pragmatic enablers of decision making:* Risk management in capital markets requires careful balancing of complexity with real-world management of risk. The advent of stress testing, for example, represents a much more digestible output than many of the complex economic capital models that had come before. Risk functions need to continue to develop metrics and reports that enable senior management to understand the risk–return trade-offs embedded in their business, and take action.

CHAPTER 6

Enablers for Robust Risk Management in Capital Markets

Process, Technology, and Data

Swati Sawjiany

INTRODUCTION

As discussed in earlier chapters, capital markets activities by their very nature require careful and appropriate risk management. The global financial crisis exposed the need for improved and more stringent risk management practices at financial services firms; firms have responded by investing in upgrades to their risk management processes, technology, and data environments.

The pace of regulations and complexity remains daunting. As a result, the cost of compliance is higher than at any point in recent history, operational and technology risks are plentiful, and the need for more timely and accurate analytics is pervasive.

With this backdrop, risk processes, technology, and data are playing and will continue to play a critical role in the stability and efficiency of capital markets business models. This chapter provides an overview of the risk management and measurement processes, technology, and data capabilities required at capital markets firms. Following this introductory section are the following topics:

- The typical *capital markets risk processes* executed at large financial institutions
- The technology capabilities and systems architecture required to support capital markets risk activities
- Key data sets used for capital markets risk management and core principles associated with effective management of risk data

OVERVIEW OF CAPITAL MARKETS RISK MANAGEMENT PROCESSES

To execute on demands placed on capital markets risk management teams, firms must institute appropriate risk policies and governance that are implemented in the

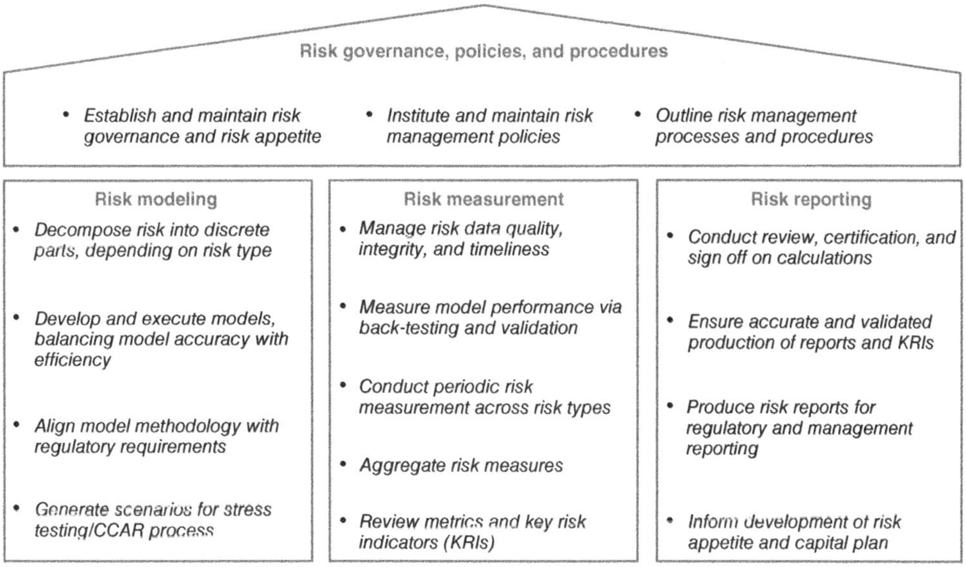

Risk governance, policies, and procedures

- Establish and maintain risk governance and risk appetite
- Institute and maintain risk management policies
- Outline risk management processes and procedures

Risk modeling	Risk measurement	Risk reporting
• Decompose risk into discrete parts, depending on risk type	• Manage risk data quality, integrity, and timeliness	• Conduct review, certification, and sign off on calculations
• Develop and execute models, balancing model accuracy with efficiency	• Measure model performance via back-testing and validation	• Ensure accurate and validated production of reports and KRIs
• Align model methodology with regulatory requirements	• Conduct periodic risk measurement across risk types	• Produce risk reports for regulatory and management reporting
• Generate scenarios for stress testing/CCAR process	• Aggregate risk measures	• Inform development of risk appetite and capital plan
	• Review metrics and key risk indicators (KRIs)	

FIGURE 6.1   Illustrative process architecture for large capital markets risk management function
Source: Oliver Wyman

organization day-to-day via procedures and processes. Figure 6.1 depicts a typical process architecture for a large capital markets risk management function.

Risk Governance, Policies, and Procedures

Risk governance refers to the mechanisms that a firm uses to assess and implement decisions related to market, credit, liquidity, and operational risks inherent in capital markets business. The risk governance framework at a bank typically involves various stakeholders at different levels of the firm, including the board of directors and senior executives across various business, risk, and corporate functions, such as finance and audit.

Capital markets firms, encouraged by regulators globally, organize and govern their risk management practices using a *three-lines-of-defense* model. The three lines of defense typically include risk-taking, risk-oversight, and risk-assurance activities. Broadly, the first line is made up of the risk takers—business line heads who must own and track the risks they generate. The second line is an independent body, typically the capital markets risk function that sets risk-taking limits and ensures that all risks are being appropriately managed across the organization. The third line, usually internal audit, verifies the efforts of the other two functions to ensure that nothing falls through the cracks so that policies, processes, and other controls are being adhered to.

The effectiveness of the three-lines-of-defense model depends upon: (1) clarity of roles and responsibilities/accountabilities across all stakeholders; (2) segregation of duties to promote independence in risk management; and (3) appropriate review and challenge that is built into the governance framework at all levels of the organization.

The capital markets risk function needs to outline its approach and strategy to risk management on a periodic basis (at a minimum annually, given the rapidly evolving capital markets business and regulatory landscape). In other words, the risk function needs to quantify and articulate how much risk the firm is willing to take across all risk types, and outline specific actions that management should undertake when the firm approaches or exceeds agreed-upon risk thresholds. The activity of identifying and quantifying risks manifests in a *risk appetite statement* with permissible risk levels for each risk type. Furthermore, *risk policies*, which are guiding principles used to set the direction of the risk management function across all risk types, are developed and maintained to remain in sync with the business's strategy and the firm's risk appetite statement.

Capital markets risk management procedures and processes translate policies into specific and tangible steps, according to which day-to-day activities can be performed. Procedures also need to ensure that the firm has in place an effective system of controls, reasonably designed to identify and mitigate risks.

Risk Modeling, Measurement, and Reporting

A firm's ability to effectively monitor risk across risk types (i.e., credit, market, liquidity, and operational risk) requires key capabilities, namely: sound risk model methodology, model development, model validation, and the ability to respond to specific business and regulatory analyses. Although modeling methodologies vary by risk type, there are foundational elements that need to be considered:

- *Decomposing risk into discrete parts:* Dividing the analytical problem into manageable subparts (e.g., for market risk methodology, segmenting models by asset class; for credit risk methodology, segmenting models by market segment/obligor).
- *Balancing model effectiveness and efficiency:* Evaluating the complexity of the model methodology, number of models required, and the accuracy/predictive power of the model, taking account of constraints such as the availability and quality of modeling data, number of resources available, and the timeliness of model development.
- *Aligning methodology with regulatory requirements and firm's accounting practices:* As risk management models are developed and then validated, it is essential that they achieve the desired performance requirements of the risk function and are consistent with the firm's accounting practices while also adhering to guidelines and expectations set by the regulators.

Example: A robust market risk function would typically entail execution of the following processes:

- Development of a model methodology for calculation of Value-at-Risk (VaR) and Stressed Value-at-Risk (SVaR)
- Development of pricing models and sensitivities for the asset classes in the bank's portfolio and within the capital markets risk function's purview

- Development of stress testing and scenario generation calculations
- Model calibration and measurement of model performance (e.g., via backtesting)
- Execution of applicable ad-hoc risk analyses
- Periodic validation of market risk models in line with the firm's model validation policies

Risk IT teams collaborate with risk modelers to implement models and methodology into robust technology platforms and systems. This enables risk managers to:

- Effectively manage and oversee market data (e.g., security price, bond price), position data (e.g., number of shares), and reference data (e.g., CUSIP, ISIN), which feed into risk systems
- Execute risk measurement processes on a periodic basis—real-time/daily for market risk, upon specific events/triggers (e.g., changes in corporate structure) for credit risk.
- Perform backtest runs to ensure models are performing and responding as expected/designed.
- Review risk metrics and key risk indicators (KRIs) that are calculated, to ensure conformance with risk limits.

The aggregation of risk metrics into insightful risk reports and KRIs is vital to senior management's ability to effectively monitor and consequently mitigate risk across all material risk types. Senior management usually sets the frequency of risk management report production and distribution. The frequency of risk management reports reflects the needs of the recipients, the nature of the risk reported, and the speed at which the risk can change. In summary it depends on the importance of reports in contributing to sound risk management and effective and efficient decision making across the bank.

Risk reporting is a key capability that comprises the following processes:

- Certifying and signing off on results (e.g., daily VaR and SVaR calculations) to maintain risk measurement accuracy and confirm that risk managers believe the results are appropriate for reporting and disclosure purposes.
- Producing risk reports that accurately and precisely convey aggregated risk data; reports need to be reconciled and validated prior to senior management review. Ideally, reports should include an appropriate balance between risk data, analysis and interpretation, and qualitative explanations.
- Producing risk reports for regulatory reporting; this particular process entails multiple checks and validations by risk managers and senior management to ensure completeness and accuracy of results.

In addition to the above, the risk function needs to ensure it is closely managing and responding to more targeted regulatory requests as well as broader regulatory mandates.

As discussed in earlier chapters, regulators in the United States and in Europe view stress testing as the primary tool to ensure appropriate capital adequacy and robustness in risk management processes. *Note:* In the United States this manifests itself through the annual Comprehensive Capital Analysis and Review (CCAR).

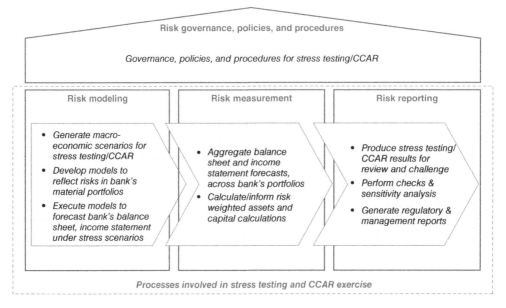

FIGURE 6.2 Illustrative processes for stress testing and CCAR exercise
Source: Oliver Wyman

Key processes performed as part of the stress testing and CCAR exercise align with the process architecture outlined previously, comprising the following categories: *risk governance, policies, and procedures,* as well as *risk modeling, measurement,* and *reporting.*

Figure 6.2 details the specific processes performed for stress testing and CCAR within each of these process categories. The key differentiation here is that as part of the stress testing and CCAR exercise, risk is modeled, measured, and reported in order to estimate the impact on the bank's income statements and balance sheets under stress scenarios and demonstrate adequacy of capital under stressed scenarios.

TECHNOLOGY CAPABILITIES AND IT ARCHITECTURE TO SUPPORT CAPITAL MARKETS RISK

Running capital market risk management processes requires a substantial technological investment as it necessitates putting in place a robust set of systems and applications for risk analytics and risk data management. Given the complexity of calculations and degree of data processing performed on a daily basis, key risk systems and applications take several months and often years to develop and test before releasing to users for day-to-day use. Banks may choose to develop these systems in-house (i.e., "build"), leveraging their internal IT teams, or may choose to implement an IT solution that is provided and implemented by a risk technology vendor (i.e., "buy"). *Build-versus-buy* decisions are typically made by risk and IT senior management in advance of any systems implementation, and each approach has its own pros and cons.

Capital markets risk functions that depend on internally developed systems may face challenges with ongoing maintenance (i.e., keep the lights on or KTLO enhancements), especially when it comes to legacy systems that were developed in archaic software development languages for which developers are scarce, and on inflexible infrastructures. The benefits of developing risk systems internally are that a bank may be able to incorporate custom business requirements and ensure that the system is compatible with its technology landscape.

As new financial technology vendors emerge, banks are increasingly leveraging opportunities to implement IT solutions developed by risk technology vendors (i.e., commercial off-the-shelf technology). This provides the risk function with access to innovative, flexible, and modular technology solutions, often incorporating market best practices and evolving regulatory requirements with future releases and upgrades.

Capital markets IT architecture can be viewed through several lenses, namely: *contextual view, conceptual view, logical view,* and *technical view*. Each of these IT architecture views is described ahead:

- *Contextual view:* Focuses on establishing core IT design principles to serve as guardrails for the other architectural views; all risk systems should be modular and should be able to seamlessly interface/interact with each other.
- *Conceptual view:* Outlines key functional and nonfunctional requirements/features requested by users, independent of systems, products, geographies, and technologies.
- *Logical view:* Outlines the systems and applications that house the functional and nonfunctional requirements. This view also typically entails a representation of information and data flows between systems and applications.
- *Technical view:* Translates the above systems and application architecture in the logical view to infrastructure and implementation requirements (i.e., hardware needs).

The logical view is the most commonly used lens to represent capital markets risk technology architecture. Within the logical view, the capital markets risk-IT landscape comprises the following layers:

- *Data sourcing and storage layer:* Entails sourcing of end-of-day, intraday, and historical market and trade/position data as well as product and client reference data. This layer stores and archives input data as well as output data in the form of results and risk metrics, at the most granular level. Systems in this layer will need to meet data management guidelines set by regulators.
- *Preprocessing layer:* This layer is responsible for validating the completeness and accuracy of market data and trade/position data prior to running any risk system. For market and trade/position data that is incomplete the system may apply an interpolation or proxy approach to create a complete data set/data time series.

- *Calculation layer:* This layer is the most computationally intensive and receives input data from the data sourcing and preprocessing layers for calculation and analytics purposes. The output from this layer, in the form of risk metrics, is relayed to the data storage layer. From a calculation perspective, example components can include product/asset pricing calculations (e.g., interest rate curve construction), scenario generation for various use-cases (e.g., historical scenarios for VaR, CCAR, stress testing), simulation of VaR results, analytics for sensitivities, and backtesting analyses.

- *Risk aggregation layer:* This layer performs the essential task of aggregating risk calculations and outputs produced in the calculation layer. Examples include calculation of capital and risk-weighted assets for Basel 2.5, Volcker, and other regulatory requirements. Aggregation of risk metrics to determine limit breaches also takes place in this layer.

- *Reporting and presentation layer:* Making decisions based on risk metrics requires a distinct reporting and presentation layer, which can provide report generation and analytics data visualization capabilities for both regulatory and management reporting purposes. The majority of capital markets risk strategy and decisions will be conducted as a result of the organization's interaction with this particular layer.

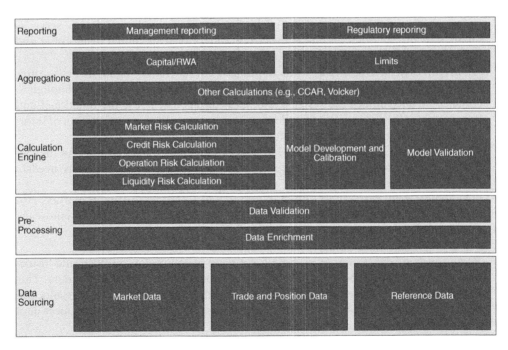

FIGURE 6.3 Risk IT architecture
Source: Oliver Wyman

DATA CAPABILITIES TO SUPPORT CAPITAL MARKETS RISK

Data is a critical but often underappreciated component of capital markets risk management—it is what fuels risk management engines. Typically, most risk management calculations require 7–10 years of historical data for robust model development and validation activities. Furthermore, the quality of the risk measurement/output is only as good at the input data sets; in other words, inaccurate input data typically results in inaccurate risk metrics. Thus the availability of historical data across most risk types and the quality control of large-scale data sets present major data management challenges for capital markets institutions.

Capital markets institutions expend substantial human and financial resources to access, source, consolidate, format, and validate risk data. More recently, most capital markets institutions have developed data management strategies to adequately address the abovementioned data challenges. A data strategy comprises the following:

- Principles used to govern the sources and uses of data
- Capabilities required to govern and manage data in an effective and efficient manner
- Technology to enable data management capabilities

Data Governance Principles

One of the key lessons learned from the global financial crisis was that banks' data architectures were inadequate to support the broad management of financial risks. Many banks lacked the ability to aggregate risk exposures and identify concentrations quickly and accurately at the bank group level, across business lines, and between legal entities. In response, the Basel Committee issued regulation "BCBS 239" for effective risk data aggregation and risk reporting.

Many in the industry recognize the benefits of improving a bank's risk data aggregation and reporting capabilities, as a result strengthening its ability to support better informed decisions. The associated benefits include gains in efficiency, reduced probability of losses, enhanced strategic decision-making, and, ultimately, increased profitability.

The key principles for achieving effective risk data management are focused on establishing:

- A robust data governance that enables comprehensive, accurate, complete, and timely risk reporting.
- A data architecture and IT infrastructure that fully supports the firm's risk data aggregation capabilities and risk reporting practices not only in normal times but also during times of stress or crisis.
- Capabilities to generate accurate and reliable risk data to meet normal and stress/crisis reporting accuracy requirements. Data should be aggregated on a largely automated basis so as to minimize the probability of errors. Ideally, the firm should be able to capture and aggregate all material risk data across the group.

- Data that is available by business line, legal entity, asset type, industry, region, and other groupings that permit identification and reporting of risk exposures, concentrations, and emerging risks.
- Capabilities to generate aggregate risk data that meets a broad range of on-demand, ad-hoc risk management reporting requests, including requests during crisis situations, requests due to changing internal needs, and requests to meet supervisory queries.

Data Management Capabilities

In order to achieve and implement the principles described above, firms design, build, and maintain fundamental risk data management capabilities that span the lifecycle of risk data. Typical capabilities in this space include:

- Data strategy and governance outlines the risk function's data mandate/requirements, oversight committees, resources, and organization structure. Additionally the governance structure details the roles and responsibilities of the risk data group as well as business owners of the data (i.e., data stewards).
- Data operations delineate the various data lifecycle management processes, encompassing risk data sourcing of inputs from various internal and external sources/ systems, data staging and transformation into desired formats, data validation for accuracy, integrity, and completeness, data loading and provisioning to models/ analytics systems, data aggregation of results, reconciliation of results, and storage and archiving of inputs and results.
- Overlaying the above data operations are processes to measure, monitor, and escalate data quality and performance to the risk function's stated data requirements.
- The appropriate data architecture and IT systems need to be implemented to support data management activities. Each component of the data lifecycle may be executed on multiple systems and platforms, increasing the complexity associated with risk data quality and management.

Technology to Enable Data Management Capabilities   Most large capital markets firms have embarked on the important journey of bolstering their data management capabilities and streamlining their data and IT architectures. Firms have implemented or are investing in new tools and technologies to enable more seamless management, aggregation, and visualization of large volumes of risk data. Depending on the stage of the data lifecycle, the types of systems and tools may vary:

- Risk data warehouses, operational data stores, and data lakes are types of repositories used for risk data storage and staging.
- Various tools for data profiling, ETL (extract, transform, load), and validation are available.
- Data processing technologies such as Hadoop for distributed processing of large data sets, as well as enhancements in hardware platforms enable faster analytics.

■ Business intelligence tools enable slicing and dicing of risk metrics, allowing senior executives to drill down to more granular levels of risk reporting when needed.

The velocity (speed of data delivery), volume (amount of data processed), and variety (the range of data sets leveraged) of data in capital markets is increasing at a relentless pace. Banks are beginning to explore opportunities and evaluate use cases/applications for big data in capital markets. *Big data* is defined as a strategy and/or technology deployment that addresses data problems that are too large or complex for traditional database technologies. Capital markets tend to largely deal with structured data sets from a multitude of defined sources—clients, counterparties, market data vendors, and market infrastructure players. However, recently, the use of unstructured data is becoming increasingly popular—for example, for risk analytics, client analyses, sentiment analyses, and market surveillance (e.g., asset price, volatility, liquidity trends).

LOOKING FORWARD

Emerging technology enablers such as high-frequency trading (HFT)[1] platforms and blockchain[2] are putting increasing pressure on capital markets risk functions to proactively identify, monitor, and mitigate risks in a timely manner, and within accelerated timeframes—previously from days/hours to now minutes/seconds. For capital markets risk, this has major implications on the frequency (e.g., intraday, real-time) and complexity of risk analytics, as well as the sophistication of underlying data and technology, in order to remain current and effectively monitor risks in the market.

Thus the next generation of risk management will involve the automated intraday and near-real-time calculation, aggregation, and reporting of risk exposures and KRIs across the entire capital markets institution for various risk types—market, counterparty, liquidity, and so on, by product, geography, client, and business unit. Capital markets risk will need to have the ability to perform more frequent what-if analysis, stress-testing, and liquidity studies to test a broad set of risk assumptions and macroeconomic scenarios. Finally, in order for risk managers to be effective they will require sophisticated tools that synthesize and articulate complex, interrelated portfolio, counterparty, market, and liquidity events into insightful and timely alerts and reports.

---

[1]High frequency trading (HFT): A type of algorithmic trading characterized by high speeds, high turnover rates, and high order-to-trade ratios that leverages high-frequency financial data and electronic trading tools.
[2]Blockchain: A data structure that makes it possible to create a digital ledger of transactions, that is shared among a distributed network of computers.

CHAPTER 7

Making Markets Work

The Critical Role of Market Infrastructure

Eric Czervionke

INTRODUCTION

Every day trillions of financial transactions between counterparties are made smoothly and seamlessly. We have come to expect smoothly functioning markets and often give little thought to the many operational steps that take place after a trade is made. In fact, most people are blissfully unaware that there is a vast technological infrastructure underpinning our financial system, operated by hundreds of financial market infrastructure institutions that span jurisdictions and markets. These critical institutions literally make our markets work.

This chapter focuses on the post-trade activities that take place after securities and derivatives trades are made and will highlight the market infrastructure providers involved in these activities along the activity chain. There are complex regulatory and market structure nuances that exist across jurisdictions and even markets within jurisdictions. These subtleties make market infrastructure an interesting topic to explore, but also mean that we are forced to describe the key activities at a relatively high level in order to focus on those elements that are common.

We will focus primarily on infrastructure in two areas: securities market infrastructure and derivatives markets. While we will attempt to highlight differences across jurisdictions where possible, to keep this discussion manageable we will take a largely U.S. and European perspective.

Regulation has long been a driver of change in the market's underlying infrastructure. This was the case during the 1970s "paperwork crisis", when U.S. regulators encouraged the move from paper to electronic book-entry recordkeeping, in the early 2000s when regulators encouraged the proliferation of competition among regulated exchanges, many of which had been virtual monopolies for decades, and now in the 2010s when post-crisis regulatory reforms have had a very significant impact, particularly on derivatives market infrastructure. While all of these changes have by and large been beneficial for the market, they have created a very complex web of actors and processes.

This post-trade ecosystem works extremely well but, its current structure, created through decades of incremental evolution, is constantly evolving and highly complex.

Innovative developments, such as the blockchain, purport to be able to address this complexity by vastly simplifying portions of this infrastructure, potentially disrupting many of the key actors in the post-trade value chain along the way. Regardless of the outcome, the next decade will be an interesting one as the infrastructure continues to evolve in response to regulatory and market forces.

SECURITIES MARKET INFRASTRUCTURE

We will start our exploration of the post-trade market infrastructure landscape with securities markets. Securities comprise cash-traded financial instruments that are issued by entities such as corporations and governments for the purpose of raising capital. Instruments may be equity, debt such as bonds, shorter term money market securities, or more exotic instruments. The type of security most familiar to the average retail investor is common stock, issued by a corporation and listed at a regulated national stock exchange.

In most jurisdictions, active markets exist for the secondary trading of securities, and we will explore in this section the execution venues and supporting post-trade market infrastructure that facilitates the actual legal transfer of these securities after a trade is made.

Exchange and OTC Markets

Depending on the type of security, secondary market trading of securities will take place either on a nationally recognized exchange or on an off-exchange trading venue. Off-exchange venues are referred to colloquially in the industry as OTC (i.e., over-the-counter) markets.

In nearly all jurisdictions, equity securities must be formally listed on a nationally registered and regulated stock exchange. Historically, secondary trading of equity securities would only take place at the stock exchange where the equity security was listed. In most markets now, however, equity securities will trade at multiple stock exchanges (including those that did not list the security) as well as at OTC marketplaces. This has greatly increased competition among execution venues and ultimately resulted in lower execution costs for market participants.

Debt and money market securities also trade on exchanges, although in many jurisdictions OTC marketplaces are more common than exchanges for the secondary market trading of these instruments.

Key Actors Along the Securities Trade Lifecycle

There are many market infrastructure providers along the post-trade activity chain that ultimately make securities trading possible, as highlighted in Figure 7.1. These providers include:

- *Securities trade execution venues:* Marketplaces that match the orders of buyers with those of sellers, ultimately resulting in a legally binding, executed trade. We will focus on three types: exchanges, alternative trading venues, and inter-dealer brokers.

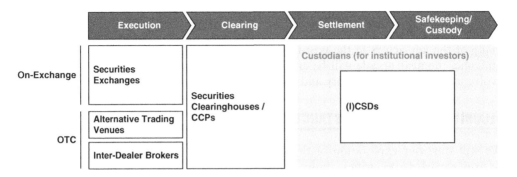

FIGURE 7.1   Overview of major securities market infrastructure providers by activity
Source: Oliver Wymann

- *Securities clearinghouses:* Institutions that compare trade details, net trading positions, and often step in as a central counterparty (CCP) for trades. We will highlight the differences between clearinghouses and CCPs.
- *Securities settlement systems, central securities depositories (CSDs), and custodians:* Institutions that manage the electronic records of security ownership and ultimately record the transfer of ownership from one entity to another. We will focus on CSDs, international CSDs (ICSDs), and custodians, noting that these are the primary institutions managing both recordkeeping and securities settlement.

As an illustration of the typical securities post-trade process, Figure 7.2 provides an overview of the main steps involved in a typical U.S. cash equity broker-to-broker trade.

The key steps in this process are largely common across markets and jurisdictions, and include:

- *Trade execution:* Execution of a securities trade will take place either at a regulated securities exchange or off-exchange at any number of possible OTC execution venues. Common OTC execution venues include various types of alternative trading venues and IDBs.
- *Securities clearing:* In many markets, particularly for corporate and equity securities, after trade execution, trades are typically cleared at a securities clearinghouse. The clearinghouse will confirm and match trade details, net positions across market participants, and often act as a central counterparty (CCP) to all trades.
- *Securities settlement:* Settlement for most securities is ultimately effected at a central securities depository (CSD) or, in the case of institutional investors, at a custodian bank. Securities settlement will take place typically as a delivery-versus-payment (DVP) transaction in either central bank or commercial bank money.
- *Money Settlement:* For those securities settlement systems that do not operate on a real-time gross settlement (RTGS) basis in central bank money, net settlement in central bank money may take place later in the settlement day, typically through intermediary *settlement banks* that may or may not be affiliated with the broker-dealer counterparty to the trade.

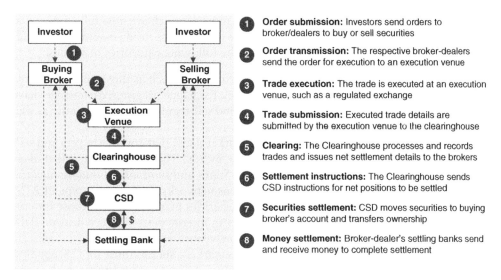

1 **Order submission:** Investors send orders to broker/dealers to buy or sell securities

2 **Order transmission:** The respective broker-dealers send the order for execution to an execution venue

3 **Trade execution:** The trade is executed at an execution venue, such as a regulated exchange

4 **Trade submission:** Executed trade details are submitted by the execution venue to the clearinghouse

5 **Clearing:** The Clearinghouse processes and records trades and issues net settlement details to the brokers

6 **Settlement instructions:** The Clearinghouse sends CSD instructions for net positions to be settled

7 **Securities settlement:** CSD moves securities to buying broker's account and transfers ownership

8 **Money settlement:** Broker-dealer's settling banks send and receive money to complete settlement

FIGURE 7.2 Illustrative securities post-trade process
Source: Oliver Wyman (*Note:* Illustration is modeled after a typical U.S. equity broker-to-broker trade.)

It is important to note that the process for settling security trades for institutional investor counterparties in many jurisdictions, including the United States, is more complex than the broker-to-broker process outlined in Figure 7.2. More intermediaries are involved in the process, including investment managers and custodians, necessitating additional post-trade infrastructure to facilitate the trade confirmation and affirmation/matching process.

For the remainder of this section, we will review the main market infrastructure actors along the securities post-trade lifecycle at length in the subsequent subsections, focusing on:

- Securities trade execution
- Securities clearing
- Securities settlement and safekeeping

Securities Trade Execution

Trade execution refers to the act of matching a buyer with a seller to consummate a trade. For centuries, securities trade execution has taken place predominantly at organized exchanges where buyers and sellers would meet at a physical location to trade. For a long time, the role of the exchange has been to list securities, create rules around their trading, and act as a central location for trade. Historically, these physical venues were open only to members, who were often brokers and dealers in securities.

This conception of the brokers club where traders would shout orders at one another is now long antiquated. Advances in technology and changes in market structure have introduced new types of trade execution venues, most of which are now fully automated and electronic. While there are differences across jurisdictions, trade execution for securities now takes place predominantly in one of the following categories of venues:

- *Securities exchanges:* Nationally registered exchanges, such as those operated by the New York Stock Exchange[1] and London Stock Exchange. Registered exchanges have the unique power to list corporate securities and self-regulate the issuing entity as well as exchange members.
- *Alternative trading venues:* Off-exchange marketplaces that connect buyers and sellers of securities directly, often via electronic means. These venues are called *alternative trading systems* (ATSs) in the United States and *multilateral trading facilities* (MTFs) in Europe. Electronic communications networks (ECNs) are a type of ATS.
- *Inter-dealer brokers (IDBs):* In some OTC securities markets, such as those for corporate bonds, IDBs play an important role as an intermediary between dealers. IDBs now operate both voice and electronic trading venues.
- *Broker-dealer internalizers:* In some securities markets, such as those for U.S. equities, a substantial amount of client trade flow is internalized within broker-dealers and never reaches an organized securities exchange or alternative trading venue. Since this activity takes place within a broker-dealer itself, we do not categorize this as market infrastructure and will not discuss this activity in detail within this chapter.

Given subtle and often confusing differences in both the terminology and underlying nuances of the market structure across jurisdictions and products, it can be challenging to navigate the different types of trading venues. As an example, Figure 7.3 provides an overview of the key types of trading venues for U.S. equity securities.

The lines between securities exchanges and ATSs, and in particular ECNs, have been blurred in recent years as many of the legacy stock exchanges such as the New York Stock Exchange (NYSE) and NASDAQ have acquired ECNs. Moreover, other legacy ECNs, such as DirectEdge (i.e., EDGX, EDGA), have applied for and received registered exchange status. It is worth to note that *dark pools* are regulated as ATSs within the United States and that a significant amount of trading volume never reaches an organized exchange or ATS, as it is internalized first at the executing broker-dealer.

While today's trading venue infrastructure is complex and varies across jurisdictional and product boundaries, there have been a number of common themes in recent years:

- *Automated trading:* Venues have become increasingly electronic and automated. In major markets, particularly for equities, virtually all trading volume is now executed over automated electronic platforms.
- *High-frequency trading:* In recent years, there has been a proliferation of high-frequency trading (HFT) driven by advances in technology (e.g., faster telecommunication networks, greater computing power, increased availability of market data)

---

[1]The New York Stock Exchange was acquired by Intercontinental Exchange (ICE), an Atlanta-based exchange conglomerate with its origins as a futures exchange. The deal closed in 2013.

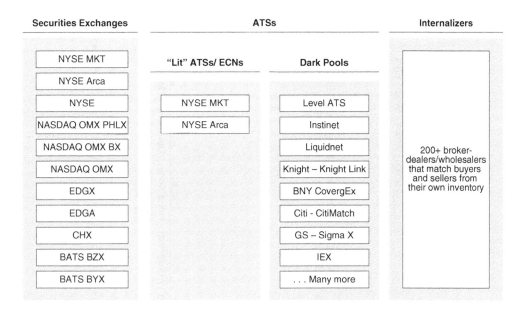

FIGURE 7.3 Case study: U.S. equity execution venues by type (as of August 2014)
Sources: Oliver Wymann, SEC

as well as changes in trading venue practices (e.g., maker-taker pricing, colocation). Market liquidity has generally improved, although there have been some relatively high-profile cases of market abuse from this activity.

- *Trading venue consolidation:* Trading venues have gradually been consolidating across products and geographies. There are now a few large conglomerates such as NYSE-ICE, NASDAQ, and Deutsche Boerse that each now operate in many national markets and offer multiple types of trading venues to their customers.

Securities Exchanges Securities exchanges are organized markets where broker-dealers meet to trade securities among themselves. They are organized in the sense that there are specific sets of rules and regulations that all trading members must follow. They are also closely controlled and regulated by the local financial authorities, for example, by the Securities and Exchange Commission (SEC) in the United States in order to guarantee fair and equal treatment of all market participants.

Some of the more historically well-known exchanges include the New York Stock Exchange (NYSE), NASDAQ, London Stock Exchange (LSE), and Deutsche Boerse. In recent years, exchanges in Asia, most particularly in China, have grown rapidly relative to their developed market peers and now rival the largest American and European stock exchanges in terms of the number and value of shares traded. Figure 7.4 highlights the ten largest stock exchanges that report to the World Federation of Exchanges (WFE) by value

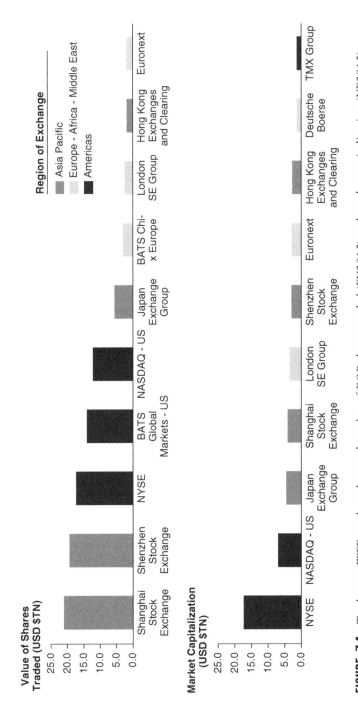

FIGURE 7.4 Ten largest WFE stock exchanges by value of EOB shares traded (FY2015) and market capitalization (YE2015)

Sources: Oliver Wyman, World Federation of Exchanges (WFE); Electronic Order Book (EOB) trades only (*Note:* Excludes exchanges such as Deutsche Bourse that do not report to the WFE.)

of electronic order book (EOB) shares traded and by market capitalization, a measure of the total market value of all shares listed on the exchange.

Exchanges have stringent admission criteria. These criteria apply to both trading members and companies whose shares are listed on the exchange. Before a security can be traded on an exchange, it must be admitted for trading via the exchange's formal listing process. To have its shares listed, a company must be large enough for there to be a market in its shares and it must agree to abide by the listing rules of the particular exchange. Listing rules typically include disclosure requirements, such as those aimed at keeping the market informed of its activities and the public reporting of profits and other financial information periodically. Additionally, securities traded on exchange need to have a minimum level of standardization and acceptable liquidity, which is typically measured by the amount of trading conducted in a particular issue over a fixed period of time.

Those securities not admitted for trading on exchanges are instead traded in OTC markets. In general, by historic precedent, most equity securities (e.g., stocks) are typically traded on exchange, and most debt securities (e.g., bonds) are traded in OTC markets. There are of course many exceptions to the rule. For example, stocks that are not liquid enough to be traded on-exchange are also traded OTC, and bonds that are very liquid, such as government bonds, may be traded on-exchange. The recent trend, however, has been for more and more securities to be traded on-exchange, regardless of their liquidity.

Revenue Model In general, a securities exchange generates revenue from different activities revolving around the trading of securities listed on its exchange. The three most traditional sources of revenue for securities exchanges are the following:

- *Trading fees:* Fees charged on trades that are generally either fixed fee or dependent on the size of the trade, defined by value traded or number of shares traded. In both cases, exchanges will generate more revenue when trading activity is higher and therefore more trades are processed. Some exchanges employ a *maker-taker* fee model in which the exchange pays its members a rebate to provide (i.e., "make") liquidity and charges a fee to remove (i.e., "take") liquidity.
- *Issuer and member fees:* Fees collected from companies issuing securities and trading members at the exchange. The more issues listed on the exchange and the more trading members, the higher these fees are at an exchange. An additional second-order revenue effect from increasing listings is the incremental trading fee revenue earned on new listings.
- *Market data and analytics:* Fees charged to access the raw trading data that is generated from trading activities. Exchanges capture data on traded prices (i.e., Level 1 data) and on the depth of the exchange's order book (i.e., Level 2 data), which is sold directly to market participants and to market data vendors for distribution.

Trading volumes and therefore revenues typically are more correlated with market volatility than market values. For example, trading activity can be relatively high, even as market values are declining. Exchanges recently have been trying to diversify their revenue to other sources that are not so strongly linked to general market conditions and therefore provide greater revenue stability.

Exchange Competition In several developed markets, most notably the United States, Canada, and Europe, the traditional securities exchange model has been under attack by non–exchange trading venues, referred to as *alternative trading venues*. These venues, often electronic, offer very similar trade execution capabilities often with additional benefits for institutional traders.

In the United States in particular, the proliferation of non–exchange trading venues has led to increased competition and has led to an increasingly fragmented trade execution landscape. In some cases, some of these new entrants, such as BATS and DirectEdge, have since become registered exchanges and now are full competitors to the traditional exchanges. Figure 7.5 highlights the dramatic shift in trading volumes from 1998 to 2013. During this period, NYSE and NASDAQ, the two dominant securities exchanges, lost considerable market share to a combination of new exchange entrants and alternative trading systems (ATSs). While not necessarily harmful to the market, these trends have created competitive pressure on the traditional exchange model and created a more fragmented market structure in the United States.

Alternative Trading Venues Alternative trading venues are non–exchange trading venues that compete with the traditional stock exchange model. Competition with the traditional exchange model used to be quite difficult when physical proximity to other traders was required to create an organized marketplace. However, with the advent of computing and telecommunications technologies that now allow trading to occur electronically outside the confines of a physical exchange, there has been a significant proliferation in non–exchange trading venues.

Regulators have been attempting to keep pace with this change and have repeatedly overhauled regulations to better account for the evolution of the market structure. Two of the most notable developments were the formal designation of alternative trading systems (ATSs) in the United States and multilateral trading facilities (MTFs) in Europe.

Alternative trading venues can either be "lit," in which trading interest is publicly displayed, or "dark," in which trading interest is either non-public or non-displayed. The industry refers to alternative trading venues that offer dark liquidity as *dark pools*. Dark pools can be broadly classified as exchange sponsored, broker-dealer sponsored, or independent.

Alternative Trading Systems (ATSs) in the United States An ATS is a U.S. regulatory term for a non–exchange trading venue and is broadly equivalent to a multilateral trading facility (MTF) in Europe, with some notable differences. For example, ATSs do not perform self-regulation, do not necessarily provide public pre-trade transparency, and do not necessarily set rules governing the conduct of ATS subscribers, in contrast to MTFs.

ATSs in the United States are regulated as broker-dealers and are not subject to the same regulatory regime as traditional national registered stock exchanges. ATSs

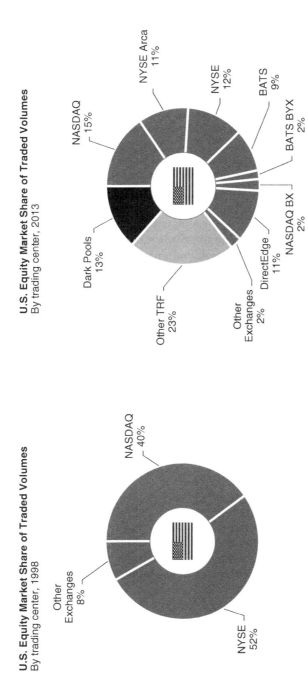

U.S. Equity Market Share of Traded Volumes
By trading center, 2013

NYSE Arca
11%

NYSE
12%

BATS
9%

BATS BYX
2%

NASDAQ BX
2%

DirectEdge
11%

Other
Exchanges
2%

Other TRF
23%

Dark Pools
13%

NASDAQ
15%

U.S. Equity Market Share of Traded Volumes
By trading center, 1998

NASDAQ
40%

Other
Exchanges
8%

NYSE
52%

FIGURE 7.5 U.S. equity market share of traded volumes by trading center (1998 vs. 2013)
Source: Oliver Wyman (*Note:* "Other TRF" includes broker capital commitments and internalizations.)

are generally electronic but do not necessarily have to be according to the regulation. ATSs broadly fall into the following two categories:

1. *ECNs:* Electronic communications networks (ECNs) are a type of ATS that trades listed stocks and other exchange-traded products. Unlike dark pools, ECNs display orders in the consolidated quote stream. As ATSs, ECNs are required to register with the Securities and Exchange Commission (SEC) as broker-dealers and are also members of the Financial Industry Regulatory Authority (FINRA), an industry self-regulatory organization. To place orders directly with an ECN, one must be an ECN subscriber. Typically, only broker-dealers and certain institutional traders are permitted to become ECN subscribers. Individual investors must have an account with a broker-dealer subscriber to place an order on an ECN. An execution occurs when the price of a buy order and the price of a sell order intersect on the ECN.[2]
2. *Dark pools:* Dark pools are ATSs that, in contrast to ECNs, do not provide their best priced orders for inclusion in the consolidated quotation data. In general, dark pools offer trading services to institutional investors and others that seek to execute large trading interest in a manner that will minimize the movement of prices against the trading interest and thereby reduce trading costs. Dark pools can vary quite widely in the services they offer their customers. For example, some dark pools, such as block-crossing networks, offer specialized size discovery mechanisms that attempt to bring large buyers and sellers in the same NMS stock together anonymously and to facilitate a trade between them. Most dark pools, though they may handle large orders, primarily execute trades with small sizes that are more comparable to the average size of trades in the public markets.[3]

Multilateral Trading Facilities (MTFs) in Europe Introduced in 2007 by the Markets in Financial Instruments Directive (MiFID), multilateral trading facilities (MTFs) are a specific type of European alternative trading venue. MTFs are multilateral systems, operated by an investment firm or a market operator, that bring together multiple third-party buying and selling interests.

The origin of the MTF regulation in Europe, as with comparable regulation in the United States, was driven heavily by a regulatory objective of diminishing the monopoly power of the single national stock exchanges in Europe and providing more easily accessible, pan-European trading platforms.

MTFs have fewer restrictions surrounding the admittance of financial instruments for trading relative to regulated markets, allowing participants to exchange more exotic products. They do not have a listing process and cannot change the regulatory status of a security. In comparison with other trading venues, MTFs are noted for high trading speeds and relatively low execution costs. Most of the MTFs are jointly owned and built

---

[2]SEC website.
[3]SEC Concept Release on Equity Market Structure (January 21, 2010).

by one or more of the large investment banks. These banks often trade on the MTFs on their own account or promote them with their institutional clients. Chi-X, BATS, Turquoise, and Alternext are all examples of MTFs.

Inter-Dealer Brokers (IDBs) Inter-dealer brokers (IDBs) act as brokers for brokers and facilitate transactions in cash security instruments such as bonds and stocks, as well as currencies and derivatives. With respect to securities, their role is typically to help match buyers and sellers of large blocks of securities that are generally unable to be traded on exchange.

In general, IDBs play an important role in the markets they operate, which are often less transparent than on-exchange markets. A primary role of the IDB is to provide anonymity for the participating dealers. IDBs also facilitate the trading of highly illiquid and complex products.

There are few large IDBs in the market, the leading ones being ICAP, TullettPrebon, BGC, and Tradition. The fact that there are not many players in the IDB space helps make the process more efficient by concentrating liquidity: By contacting only one IDB a broker-dealer automatically gets good exposure to all other broker-dealers in the market.

With respect to cash securities, IDBs play a large role in the secondary trading of bonds. As illustrated in Figure 7.6, historically the role of the IDB was to facilitate anonymous trading between dealers in the inter-dealer market, typically through voice communication channels. This market structure has evolved considerably with IDBs now offering voice and electronic channels as well as access to other trading participants beyond dealers, including hedge funds, market makers, and other non-dealer liquidity providers.

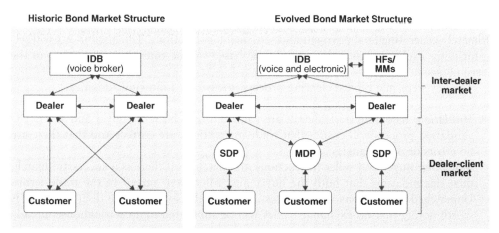

Note: SDP = Single-Dealer Platform, MDP = Multi-Dealer Platform, HFs = Hedge Funds, MMs = Market Makers

FIGURE 7.6 Historic and current role of the IDB in the bond markets
Source: Oliver Wyman; graphic adapted from the paper "BIS: Electronic Trading in Fixed Income Markets (January 2016)"

Figure 7.6 also highlights another trend, which is the proliferation of single-dealer platforms (SDPs) and multi-dealer platforms (MDPs). In markets such as those for bonds, where the historic client channel was voice, SDPs and MDPs act as electronic trading platforms where clients can access quotes from one or multiple dealers, respectively. SDPs are typically owned by the broker-dealer and provided to their clients. MDPs may be owned independently or by a consortium of broker-dealers.

Securities Clearing

After a securities trade is executed, the next step in the trade lifecycle is clearing. Before settlement, that is, the exchange of securities against payment, there are a number of operational steps that must first be performed. Clearing is formally defined as the process by which payment orders or security transfer instructions are transmitted, reconciled, and in some cases, confirmed prior to settlement. Importantly, clearing also typically involves the netting of individual trade instructions and calculation of net obligations to be settled. It is important to note that clearing is a distinct function from settlement, although *clearing* and *settlement* are often imprecisely used interchangeably.

Securities clearing activities can be conducted bilaterally or centrally via systems known as clearinghouses or CCPs. In most mature markets there is a central clearinghouse or CCP that facilitates the central clearing process for the market. Clearinghouses may be independently owned and operated or directly affiliated with an exchange. They may clear one or more products and some may clear both securities and derivatives.

Examples of major securities clearinghouses/CCPs include NSCC and FICC in the United States, and LCH.Clearnet and Eurex Clearing in Europe.

Clearinghouses   Clearinghouses capture and process trade details from counterparties, ultimately generating final payment and settlement instructions. The institutions will settle for items exchanged at a designated time based on the rules and procedures of the clearinghouse.

The key steps in a typical clearing process involve the following activities:

- *Validation:* Incoming trade details are validated with both the buyer and seller. The validation process will ensure that trade instructions are correct and that there are no errors or discrepancies.
- *Matching:* Buyer and seller instructions are matched. If there is a successful match, then this indicates that both the buyer and seller have agreed to the trade terms. Unmatched transactions will be investigated for the source of the discrepancy. It is worth noting that on-exchange trades will be submitted to a clearinghouse already matched.
- *Pre-settlement risk management:* In many cases, where the clearinghouse assumes risk management functions, the buyer's cash availability and seller's asset availability will be assessed to determine whether settlement can take place.
- *Calculation of net obligations:* The clearinghouse in most cases will calculate net security settlement and money payment amounts, aggregating individual transactions in a given security as well as payments into one net obligation per counterparty.

- *Transmission of settlement instructions:* On the settlement date, the clearinghouse will pass settlement instructions to the settlement system where settlement actually takes place. This will typically be at a central securities depository (CSD).

In the above model, it is worth noting that the clearinghouse does not take on any counterparty risk, which remains between the buyer and seller. In this model, the clearinghouse merely acts as a facilitator in creating matched and validated settlement instructions, in many cases netting obligations down to a net value.

CCPs Central counterparties (CCPs) are a special type of clearinghouse where the clearinghouse acts as the buyer to every seller and the seller to every buyer. The legal process by which the CCP steps in between each transaction between buyer and seller is called *novation*. Once novation occurs, the CCP acts as a central counterparty between every buyer, and after this process is complete all buyers and sellers have counterparty risk only with the CCP, not with each other. Having a single counterparty has numerous advantages, including netting benefits, simplification of credit monitoring, and the reduction of systemic risk in the event of a single counterparty failure. However, this comes at the expense of having a single point of failure making robust risk management at these institutions particularly important.

The CCP takes on significant counterparty risk in this model. Theoretically, all obligations are equal and opposite, and the CCP's net exposure is zero. However, in practice, the CCP is subject to market and liquidity risks that must be carefully managed to avoid insolvency in a member default scenario.

CCPs manage their risk through a number of activities, which include:

- *Initial and variation margin:* Collecting margin, that is, securities or cash collateral, at the onset of the trade or periodically (i.e., typically daily) between trade date and settlement date to reflect changes in market value of the exposure
- *Default fund:* Collecting default fund resources that are sufficient to withstand a default scenario comprising the failure of one or more of the CCP's largest counterparties
- *Client porting:* Having pre-established client porting provisions and mechanisms that facilitate the seamless transfer of customer positions from one clearing member to another in the event of a member default
- *Collateral haircuts:* Applying haircuts on collateral received for margin and default fund resources to cover market risks associated with any change in the underlying market value of the collateral

Beyond concentrating counterparty credit risk and reducing capital charges to its members, a CCP has the additional benefit of facilitating multilateral netting, as highlighted in Figure 7.7.

In the classic gross settlement model, all trades are settled individually and directly between market participants. This is both operationally inefficient as well as inefficient from a liquidity management perspective, as liquidity needs can swing wildly throughout the day as payments go in and out due to gross settlement. Importantly, CCPs enable multilateral netting, further reducing the number of payment obligations down to one per day, dramatically simplifying both settlement operations and liquidity management.

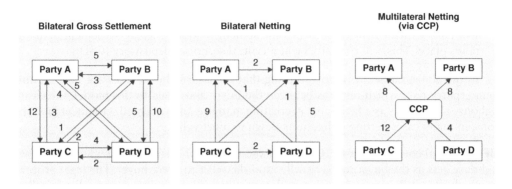

FIGURE 7.7   Illustration of impact of multilateral netting on settlement
Source: Oliver Wyman (*Note:* Each arrow represents a payment flow and assumes that the corresponding value of security is simultaneously transferred.)

As with a clearinghouse, once net settlement obligations have been computed for a given counterparty, instructions will be submitted to the settlement system, again, typically a CSD for settlement. The next section discusses the securities settlement process in detail.

Securities Settlement and Safekeeping

In order to complete a trade, ownership of the security must ultimately be transferred from the seller to the buyer. The process by which the seller transfers a security against payment received from the buyer is known as settlement. Most investors and institutions do not hold securities in physical possession, but rather rely on an agent bank or securities depository to hold securities on their behalf for safekeeping. While there was a time when securities were held in physical form, nearly all securities are now held electronically in book entry form.

Settlement Models and Conventions   In practice, securities settlement now occurs as electronic book entry transfers and generally takes two forms depending on whether settlement occurs on a transaction-by-transaction basis or on an aggregate basis:

1. *Gross settlement* involves settlement of securities on a transaction-by-transaction basis. Gross settlement can take place either on a real-time basis (referred to as *real-time gross settlement*, or RTGS) in which case securities settle continuously throughout the day, or alternatively on a batch basis at a designated time. Batch settlement involves the deferral of set of transactions to a designated time during the day. As multi-batch settlement slices become more frequent this second settlement approach begins to resemble RTGS.

2. *Net settlement* involves accumulating all buying and selling transactions into one net buy or sell transaction. At the end of the settlement day, in a net settlement system, each institution receives either one credit or one debit per security account reflecting the net of all buy and sell transactions executed during the day. Net settlement involves a delay until the end of the day, but this approach generates both operational and liquidity efficiencies for market participants.

As we have already described, securities settlement[4] involves the simultaneous, final, and irrevocable receipt of securities against a corresponding delivery of payment. This concept, called *delivery versus payment* (DVP), is an important industry concept and its implementation in modern settlement systems results in significantly reduced settlement risk. Settlement risk arises when one counterparty delivers securities or value as per the trade agreement, but the other counterparty does not, potentially resulting in losses for the counterparty that has not received value or securities as expected.

Three broad types of DVP models exist as defined by the Bank of International Settlements (BIS),[5] namely:

1. *DVP Model 1 (gross simultaneous settlement):* Systems that settle transfer instructions for both securities and funds on a trade-by-trade (i.e., gross) basis, with final (i.e., unconditional) transfer of securities from the seller to the buyer (i.e., delivery) occurring at the same time as final transfer of funds from the buyer to the seller (i.e., payment). Example systems using this model include Euroclear in Belgium and Clearstream in Germany.
2. *DVP Model 2 (gross settlement of securities, net funds transfer):* Systems that settle securities transfer instructions on a gross basis, with final transfer of securities from the seller to the buyer (i.e., delivery) occurring throughout the processing cycle, but that settle funds transfer instructions on a net basis, with final transfer of funds from the buyer to the seller (i.e., payment) occurring at the end of the processing cycle. Example systems using this model include DTC in the United States and CDS in Canada.
3. *DVP Model 3 (net simultaneous settlement):* Systems that settle transfer instructions for both securities and funds on a net basis, with final transfers of both securities and funds occurring at the end of the processing cycle. Example systems using this model include CETIP in Brazil and CDSL and NSDL in India.

Depending on the market, securities may settle on the same day that the transaction is made (called *trade date plus zero*, or T+0, in industry terms) or may settle on a

---

[4]There are a few exceptions when free of payment (FOP) delivery is acceptable. For example, when a customer transfers securities from one custodian to another, no exchange of value is required as no securities have been bought or sold.

[5]"A Glossary of Terms Used in Payment and Settlement Systems" (BIS, 2013).

fixed number of days after the trade date, such as T+3. Settlement conventions vary considerably by jurisdiction and even within jurisdictions. For example, in Europe, equity securities settle T+2 and government securities settle T+1.

Securities Safekeeping Intermediaries Figure 7.8 highlights the different types of relationships that customers (i.e., buy-side institutions, broker-dealers, etc.) can have with the key intermediaries in the securities safekeeping layer, which include CSDs, ICSDs, and global/local custodians.

The important points to note are that:

- Securities are ultimately held in book-entry form at national Central Securities Depositories (CSDs). CSDs in many (but not all cases) limit the types of institutions that can be members of the depository and hence most institutions and individuals must obtain the services of an intermediary to perform securities safekeeping services on their behalf.
- Typically, only local legal entities are allowed access to a country's CSD (the main exception being links with other (I)CSDs). As a result, international customers wishing to hold securities and settle securities transactions will need to do so through a local custodian or through a global custodian or ICSD that has sub-custody relationships with a local custodian or direct links to the national CSD.
- For large, global institutional asset managers, there is a clear efficiency gain to hold securities with a *global custodian*, who can provide custody and settlement services to a wide variety of markets through a network of direct and sub-custody relationships.
- Importantly, the ultimate location of settlement (i.e., where book-entry transfer actually takes place) is often a function of where the counterparty to the trade has its

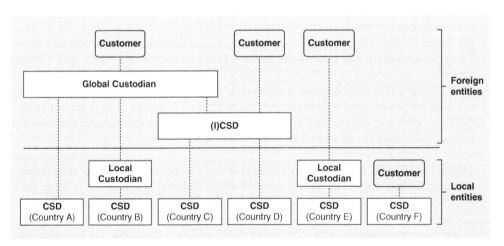

FIGURE 7.8 Representative securities safekeeping chains that can exist for local and cross-border settlement
Source: Oliver Wyman, BIS

account. For example, if the buyer and seller of a security both have an account at the same global custodian, no settlement will take place at a CSD. The transaction will merely be settled internally at the global custodian.

Many good books have been written on the topics of global custody and safekeeping, so we will focus the rest of this section on providing a brief overview of the key market infrastructure institutions providing securities safekeeping and settlement services, namely:

- Central securities depositories (CSDs)
- International central securities depositories (ICSDs)
- Custodians (covering both local and global custodians)

CSDs A *central securities depository* (CSD) is an organization holding securities in the lowest level in the securities safekeeping chain. CSDs maintain source records about which securities exist and who owns them. Today these records are in electronic form in order to enable their book-entry transfer, that is, changing of the ownership of securities electronically without the movement of physical documents. CSDs generally also provide other services around settlement and custody. In most jurisdictions, CSDs are still largely national monopolies and as a general rule every country has one dominant institution CSD. However, exceptions to this rule do exist, as is the case in India, where there are two national CSDs, each affiliated with one of the two national securities exchanges.

CSDs provide several core services to their clients, including:

- *Safekeeping:* The primary function of a CSD is the safekeeping or custody of securities. A CSD may include safekeeping for one type of security (e.g., equities) or multiple types (e.g., equities and corporate bonds).
- *Settlement:* The transfer of ownership between participants in the CSD will take place in book entry form at the CSD through its *securities settlement system.*
- *Income collection:* The CSD will collect dividend and interest payments from a security issuer's paying agent and ensure that these payments are credited to participants holding the respective security.
- *Corporate actions:* The CSD is responsible for processing any corporate actions, such as stock splits and dividend payments, working with issuing and paying agents to do so.

ICSDs An *international central securities depository* (ICSD) is a special type of central securities depository that was originally set up to settle Eurobond trades but has since evolved to facilitate the settlement of international and various domestic securities. Clearstream Banking in Luxembourg, Euroclear Bank in Germany, and SIX SIS in Switzerland are considered ICSDs.

Since their creation over 40 years ago, the business of ICSDs has expanded to also cover most European domestic and internationally traded instruments, including investment funds. They usually operate through direct or indirect (via local agents) links to local CSDs. Clearstream and Euroclear together dominate the European ICSD market.

ICSDs are similar conceptually to CSDs, in that they facilitate the safekeeping and settlement of securities. However, one major difference between these entities is that the ICSDs are structured as banks whereas CSDs as not. As a result, ICSDs are able to provide credit to its participants as well as provide other banking services related to securities settlement that many CSDs are not able to provide.

The ICSDs provide a variety of services, many of which are highly overlapping with that of CSDs:

- *Notary/issuer services:* Initial bookkeeping to enable book-entry transfer, assistance in setting up a new security, and shareholder identification
- *Settlement:* Domestic and cross-border settlement in bonds, equities, and funds, both on-exchange and OTC
- *Custody:* Safekeeping of physical and electronic securities, administration, asset servicing and corporate actions (dividend, coupon, proxy voting, etc.), and tax advice
- *Deposit and withdrawal:* Services involving a relationship between the transfer agent, issuers, and the CSD; also covers the CSD's role in the underwriting process
- *Collateral management and lending:* Services such as securities lending and borrowing (as agent and principal), collateral management, tri-party repo, repo margin management, and derivatives margin management
- *Banking services:* Specialized foreign exchange services, cash management, securities financing, and account services (subject to banking license requirements)
- *Other services:* Reporting, accounting connectivity, fund management, and information services

Custodians Custodians are banks that provide access to clearinghouses and CSDs for their investor clients. They act and hold accounts on behalf of their clients and keep their clients' assets under custody, which essentially means safekeeping and servicing them. Custodians are referred to as *global custodians* if they also provide asset safekeeping services for their clients across multiple jurisdictions. This is done via accounts at multiple local CSDs covering most geographical markets or by using local sub-custodians. The largest global custodians include BNY Mellon, State Street, JP Morgan, Citi, and BNP Paribas.

Local custodians, also called *regional custodians*, are banks that provide sub-custody services to global custodians or custody services directly to local and foreign investors. Regional custodians are typically present in only their local market and do not have access to a range of CSDs. Moreover, they typically provide a more basic service offering than global custodians.

DERIVATIVES MARKET INFRASTRUCTURE

While post-crisis regulatory reforms have made derivatives market infrastructure more closely resemble that of the securities markets, there are still several fundamental differences. These differences are driven in part by post-trade processing requirements that are unique to derivative instruments as well as differences in the evolution of the underlying market structure.

On a superficial level, derivatives trading, clearing, and settlement appears at first to be similar to that of securities. Like securities, derivatives may be traded on or off of regulated exchanges. Moreover, clearinghouses and CCPs exist to perform clearing and central counterparty functions for portions of the market. Settlements do take place that involve the exchange of cash and in some cases securities or physical assets.

While several of the concepts for derivatives trading, clearing, and settlement are similar to those for securities, there are a number of notable conceptual differences.

- Derivatives are not issued and traded like securities; rather, they are created either by a derivatives exchange or by market participants through bilateral contracts; accordingly, there is no such concept as a derivatives depository.
- Derivative contracts are not "sold"; rather, a counterparty will typically enter into an equal and offsetting transaction that either extinguishes the obligation or offsets the associated risk exposure.
- Derivative contracts do not settle in full shortly after trade execution; rather, the contracts remain open and must be risk managed until termination or exercise, requiring periodic exchanges of margin or collateral.
- In most cases, derivatives do not involve physical delivery of an underlying asset, as most contracts are settled for cash value; a CSD or ICSD is only involved when securities are posted as margin or collateral to a derivatives CCP or counterparty.
- Historically, the OTCD market has been largely opaque, although that is changing with the regulatory mandate to introduce trade repositories.

Regulatory Developments

Leading up to and during the 2007/2008 financial crisis, global regulators became increasingly concerned by the large volumes of OTC derivatives between counterparties and the systemic risk these interdependent exposures created between financial institutions. The crisis in particular exposed a number of risks created by the OTC derivatives market, most notably:

- Insufficient market transparency
- Inadequate and nonstandard collateralization practices
- Relatively cumbersome operational processes
- Uncoordinated default management

In an effort to address these concerns, the G20, a forum consisting of central bank governors from 20 major economies, agreed to reform the OTC derivatives markets in 2009 with the Financial Stability Board (FSB) assuming responsibility for global oversight of this effort, which ultimately requires regulatory implementation at the local level of the member countries. There are five key elements of the reform agenda for OTC derivatives:[6]

1. Trade reporting for all OTC derivatives
2. CCP clearing of all standardized OTC derivatives

---

[6] Financial Stability Board (FSB), "OTC Derivatives Market Reforms: Tenth Progress Report on Implementation" (November 4, 2015).

3. Exchange or electronic platform trading of all standardized OTC derivatives
4. More stringent and standardized margin requirements for uncleared OTC derivatives
5. Higher capital requirements for OTC derivatives that are not centrally cleared

The first three of these reforms has led to new market infrastructure being created to fulfil these newly required market functions, which include, respectively, trade repositories, OTC derivatives CCPs, and electronic trading platforms for OTC derivatives.[7] Each of these new pieces of infrastructure will be discussed in this section in greater detail.

The net effect of these reforms is that the OTC derivatives market structure now more closely resembles that of the exchange-traded and cleared-securities and derivatives markets. Ultimately, this will result in greater market transparency as well as regulatory oversight.

Overview of Derivatives Market Infrastructure

The market infrastructure for derivatives is organized differently for the exchange-traded derivatives (ETD) and OTC derivatives (OTCD) markets, as highlighted in Figure 7.9. However, the key activities performed are similar across both markets.

Exchange-Traded Derivatives (ETD) The market infrastructure for ETD is relatively consistent across jurisdictions. Trade execution for ETD occurs exclusively at derivatives exchanges, where contracts are standardized and where trades are typically executed via an electronic trading platform operated by the exchange. Trading parties typically remain anonymous. Since derivatives are created by the exchange, executed trades will either add new open contracts (i.e., new open interest) or offset existing open contracts.

Once trades are executed, a derivatives clearinghouse, which may or may not be owned and operated by the derivatives exchange, will manage the clearing process and

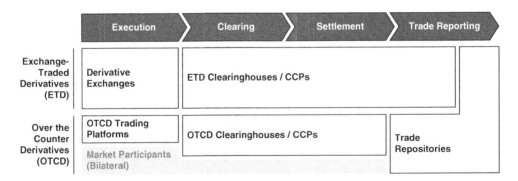

FIGURE 7.9 Overview of major derivatives market infrastructure providers by activity

[7]For example, SEFs in the United States and OTFs in Europe.

typically also step in as a central counterparty (CCP). The CCP manages risk at a participant level, collecting margin as required for open positions and generating settlement instructions for any required payments or deliveries.

In most countries, including the United States, the trade reporting function is performed by the derivatives exchange and/or CCP, although in Europe reporting to an ESMA-registered trade repository is mandatory for both ETD and OTCD trades.

OTC Derivatives (OTCD) The OTC derivative (OTCD) market infrastructure differs from that of ETD, although in recent years it has come to more closely resemble that of the exchange-traded market. Instead of being created by an exchange, OTC derivative contracts are created through standard legal documentation, most commonly via one of several *master agreements* published by the International Swaps and Derivatives Association (ISDA). OTC derivative contracts can be either standard (i.e., having a common set of standard terms) or nonstandard (i.e., more bespoke contracts with less standardized and typically more complex terms).

OTC derivative contracts are privately negotiated between market participants on a bilateral basis and historically did not rely on centralized electronic trading venues for execution. Many OTC derivative contracts are still executed bilaterally, particularly those that are nonstandard with more bespoke terms. However, as jurisdictions implement the G20 reforms, a larger percentage of OTC derivative contracts are traded on new electronic trading platforms, most notably swap execution facilities (SEFs) in the United States and organized trading facilities (OTFs) in Europe. These electronic trading platforms allow market participants to quote prices competitively and provide more transparency around price formation.

Historically, OTC derivative transactions were processed bilaterally with clearing, associated risk management functions, and settlement being performed between trading counterparties. Today, however, at the behest of regulators, a growing percentage of OTCD contracts are centrally cleared, particularly those that are standardized in nature.

As nations implement the G20 reforms, a growing number of trade repositories have emerged for the reporting of OTC derivative transactions. These trade repositories are mandated at the national level and are in existence in a large number of jurisdictions already. It is expected that all OTC derivatives will eventually be reported to a national trade repository.

Central bank payment systems and agent/custodian banks play a role in the settlement of money payments, either from market participants to derivative clearinghouses/CCPs or between market participants for bilateral uncleared OTC derivatives. ICSDs and CSDs have less of a role to play than they do for securities settlement, although occasionally securities are required to be transferred either as collateral, or less frequently for delivery.

The remainder of this section explores the key market infrastructure providers across the derivatives activity chain, focusing on derivatives trade execution, clearing and settlement, and trade reporting.

Derivatives Trade Execution

The way in which derivatives trades are executed varies based on whether the derivative is exchange traded or traded over-the-counter (OTC). Exchange-traded derivatives are standardized contracts and must be executed on the issuing derivatives exchange. OTC derivative contracts have historically been traded bilaterally between counterparties through voice and proprietary electronic channels as well as inter-dealer brokers. More recently, however, as regulators have introduced central clearing and trade execution mandates for standardized derivatives, there is an emerging class of new exchange-like trading platforms for the execution of OTC derivatives.

There are two primary types of market infrastructure institutions involved with the execution of derivatives, namely:

1. Derivatives exchanges
2. Trading platforms for OTC derivatives (e.g., SEFs, OTFs, and ETPs)

Derivatives Exchanges   Trading and execution of exchange-traded derivatives occurs on derivatives exchanges. Exchange-traded derivative products consist predominantly of futures and options contracts on a wide range of underlying reference assets, which include: equity securities and ETFs,[8] commodities, currencies, and interest rates.

Derivatives exchanges historically focused on a limited subset of underlying asset classes, although acquisition activity over the past two decades has led to significant industry consolidation. The largest global derivatives exchanges are now part of exchange conglomerates, which may include multiple derivative and security exchanges. For example, the Intercontinental Exchange (ICE), after its acquisition of the New York Stock Exchange, now owns and operates several commodity futures exchanges as well as several security and equity derivatives exchanges. Similarly, the Chicago Mercantile Exchange owns and operates four derivatives exchanges whose contracts cover futures and options spanning currencies, rates, commodities, and stock indices. Figure 7.10 provides an overview of some of the major derivatives exchanges by number of futures and options contracts traded in 2015.

Contract Standardization   Derivatives exchanges create standardized contracts for trading on their respective exchanges. In contrast to the OTC derivatives market, market participants have no ability to alter the terms of the exchange-traded derivative contracts. Derivatives exchanges also typically attempt to minimize the number of contracts related to a specific underlying and risk exposure type. The standardization of contracts, as well as a finite number of contracts on a given underlying, helps to boost liquidity in any given contract, since market participants seeking to buy or sell that particular exposure must trade in one of a few specific contracts (Table 7.1).

---

[8]For our purposes, we define *equities* as including futures and options on single stocks, equity indices, and ETFs.

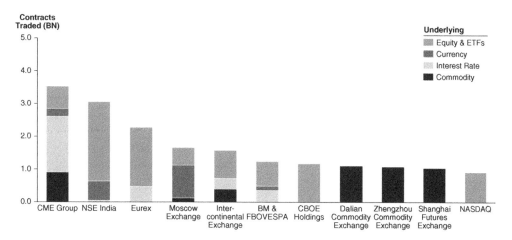

FIGURE 7.10 Major derivatives exchanges by number of contracts traded (2015)
Source: World Federation of Exchanges, Oliver Wyman

TABLE 7.1 Example Contract Terms for a Soybean Futures Contract

Contract Term	Description	Example: CME Soybean Futures
Contract Unit	Size of each contract	5,000 bushels
Price Quotation	Price quotation convention	Cents per bushel
Trading Hours	Hours during which contract trading takes place	Sun–Fri, 7pm–7:45am CT Mon–Fri, 8:30am–1:20pm CT
Minimum Price Fluctuation	Minimum amount that a contract price can move	¼ of once cent per bushel ($12.50 per contract)
Listed Contracts	Listed contract months available for trading	January (F), March (H), May (K), July (N), August (Q), September (U), and November (X)
Settlement Method	Method of settlement—typically cash or physical delivery	Deliverable
Termination of Trading	Day when trading halts on a particular contract	Business day prior to the 15th calendar day of the contract month
Last Delivery Date	Last calendar date on which delivery is accepted	Second business day following the last trading day of the delivery month
Grade and Quality	Details on how quality of physical asset delivered relates to price	#2 Yellow at contract price, #1 Yellow at a 6-cent/bushel premium, #3 Yellow at a 6-cent/bushel discount

Source: Chicago Mercantile Exchange. Available at: http://www.cmegroup.com/trading/agricultural/grain-and-oilseed/soybean_contract_specifications.html [Accessed February 20, 2016]

Exchange-traded contracts may be settled either by physical delivery of the underlying or by cash settlement. However, most market participants will exit a deliverable contract for cash prior to the contract termination date so as to avoid the need to receive or deliver the physical underlying.

The most actively traded exchange-traded derivative contracts tend to be futures contracts. With some notable exceptions (e.g., U.S.-listed stock, and ETF options), liquidity for a particular contract type tends to concentrate in one derivatives exchange. Table 7.2 highlights the five most actively traded contracts by underlying type. While the number of contracts traded is a good overall proxy of the relative demand for a particular product, differences in contract size can make these statistics misleading across

TABLE 7.2 Five Most Actively Traded ETD Contracts by Underlying

Underlying		Contract	Exchange	Domicile	Contracts Traded (2014, in millions)
Equity Index	1	CNX Nifty Options	NSE India	India	972.7
	2	SPDR S&P 500 ETF Options	*Multiple*	US	609.1
	3	Kospi 200 Options	KRX	Korea	462.0
	4	S&P Sensex Options	BSE	India	439.1
	5	E-mini S&P 500 Futures	CME	US	425.0
Commodity	1	Steel Rebar Futures	SHFE	China	408.1
	2	Rapeseed Meal Futures	ZCE	China	303.5
	3	Soy Meal futures	DCE	China	205.0
	4	Silver Futures	SHFE	China	193.5
	5	Brent Crude Futures	ICE (Europe)	UK	160.4
Currency	1	USD/RUB Futures	MOEX	Russia	656.5
	2	USD/INR Futures	NSE India	India	294.0
	3	USD/INR Futures	BSE	India	171.6
	4	USD/INR Futures	MCX-SX	India	112.5
	5	USD/INR Options	NSE India	India	98.8
Interest Rate	1	Eurodollar Futures	CME (CME)	US	664.4
	2	10 YR Treasury Note Futures	CME (CBOT)	US	340.5
	3	One Day Inter-Bank Deposit Futures	BM&FBovespa	Brazil	286.1
	4	5 YR Treasury Note Futures	CME (CBOT)	US	196.4
	5	Euro-Bund Futures	Eurex	Germany	179.1

Source: Futures Industry Association (FIA). Available at: https://fimag.fia.org/sites/default/files/content_attachments/2014%20FIA%20Annual%20Volume%20Survey%20%E2%80%93%20Charts%20and%20Tables.pdf [Accessed February 20, 2016]

exchanges and in particular across regional markets. For example, the average contract size of USD/INR futures across the three Indian derivatives exchange is $1,000 USD compared to €125,000 for EUR/JPY futures traded on CME.

Open Interest Exchange-traded derivative transactions are not trades involving the exchange of a physical asset in the classical sense, as is the case with securities transactions. Rather, an exchange-traded derivative transaction either creates a new exposure or offsets (i.e., cancels) an existing one. Hence, when a market participant buys or sells a derivative contract there is only one of three possible outcomes:

1. A long exposure is created (when buying)
2. A short exposure is created (when selling)
3. A long or short exposure is reduced (by selling or buying, respectively)

Accordingly, derivative contracts are created by the exchange as needed when a market participant buys a contract creating a new exposure and destroyed as a market participant sells a contract that offsets an existing exposure. *Open interest* is the total amount of long exposure across all participants in the derivatives exchange and can be thought of as the number of contracts created by the exchange net of any contracts that have been closed out or that have been delivered. This concept is best illustrated through a simplified example.

As can be seen in the simplified example in Table 7.3, the volume of contracts traded on a derivatives exchange by construction must be greater than or equal to the contract's open interest. Typically, open interest in a particular contract is many orders of magnitude less than the total number of contracts traded, as market participants continually increase and reduce their exposures through trading.

This exposure reduction is an attractive feature of the exchange-traded derivatives market and is also in stark contrast to OTC derivatives markets, where exposures are offset by new derivative transactions without cancellation of any existing contracts (unless trade-compression services are utilized). Moreover, this concept makes it difficult to directly compare the size of the ETD and OTCD markets, as OTC derivatives are typically held until expiration (which can be many years) even when offset economically by other transactions. Some estimate that reported OTC derivatives notional

TABLE 7.3 Open Interest and Traded Volume Calculation

Trade	Trade Details	Open Interest	Volume
1	Participant A buys 3 contracts from Participant B who sells	+3	+3
2	Participant C buys 2 contracts from Participant D who sells	+2	+2
3	Participant E buys 2 contracts from Participant A who sells	0	+2
4	Participant D buys 1 contract from Participant A who sells	−1	+1
5	Participant B buys 2 contracts from Participant F who sells	0	+2
	Total:	4	10

outstanding may be reduced by 75–95%[9] if one were to take into account offsetting economic exposures, although this number has been declining recently with increased usage of OTCD CCPs and trade-compression services.

Central Clearing of Exchange-Traded Derivatives   Exchange-traded derivatives are almost universally centrally cleared, most frequently through a CCP. In most cases, the clearinghouse or CCP is directly owned by the same conglomerate that owns the derivatives exchange. Prominent examples include CME Clearing (which clears for each of CME Group's four derivatives exchanges), and ICE Clear US, which clears for ICE's U.S. futures markets. There are some notable exceptions to this vertically integrated exchange/clearinghouse model. For example, U.S.-listed equity options trade at multiple derivatives exchanges, but all utilize a common, participant-owned utility CCP, the Options Clearing Corporation (OCC). In general, industry clearing costs are less expensive when performed by a centralized utility than when directly compared to costs at a vertically integrated clearinghouse or CCP.

Trading Platforms for OTC Derivatives   OTC derivative contracts were historically exempt from regulation and traded *over the counter* on a bilateral basis between counterparties, rather than on regulated exchanges. Derivative dealers would create derivative contracts on behalf of their end-user clients as well as create contracts with other dealers to hedge residual risk or to take on a risk position. Contract terms could be negotiated and customized based on the needs of the end-user client or risk being hedged. Much of this business was conducted by voice over telecommunications networks with limited transparency into the market, in stark contrast to markets traded on regulated exchanges.

This lack of transparency was identified by regulators as a major contributor to the global financial crisis, as regulators and market participants did not have adequate information to identify and assess market exposures and counterparty relationships. Accordingly, the leaders of the G20 nations made a commitment to migrate all standardized derivative contract trading to electronic trading platforms. An increasing percentage of OTC derivative contracts that are more suitable to standardized terms are now being traded on electronic platforms. More exotic, bespoke OTC derivatives are still traded bilaterally, given the need to tailor terms to the specific needs of the counterparties involved.

Implementation of the G20 commitment to migrate most standardized OTC derivative contract trading to organized trading venues is underway, although progress is uneven across jurisdictions.[10] As of early 2016, the United States, European Union, and Japan were the furthest along in implementation.

United States: Swap Execution Facilities (SEFs)

- In the United States, the Dodd Frank Act introduced the legal requirement that standardized OTC derivatives eligible for clearing also be traded on electronic facilities. These facilities, called swap execution facilities (SEFs), are multilateral trading venues

---

[9]Chicago Mercantile Exchange, "Derivatives Market Landscape: Spring 2014."
[10] "OTC Derivatives Market Reforms: Tenth Progress Report on Implementation" (FSB, Nov. 2015).

that feature multi-dealer request for quote (RFQ) functionality as well as operate an open limit order book (LOB).

- Development of the regulatory framework to implement the SEF requirement was left to the CFTC and SEC, with the CFTC covering non-security-based swaps and the SEC covering security-based swaps, respectively. To make matters somewhat more complicated than they ought to be, each regulatory body has taken their own approach to implementing these rules, with the:
  - CFTC finalizing its rules on SEFs in June 2013 and implementing in February 2014 a mandatory trade execution rule for certain interest rate and credit default swaps subject to the CFTC's clearing requirement.
  - SEC proposing rules on the registration and regulation of security-based SEFs in February 2011, but with no final rule yet released as of the beginning of 2016
- SEFs have already begun changing the market structure of the OTC derivatives market in the United States. Most notably, SEFs have:
  - Increased pre-trade price transparency and competition by allowing market participants to compare prices from multiple dealers on one platform
  - Changed the relationship between dealers and end-users by permitting end-users to compete directly with dealers in the provision of liquidity

Data exists on the transaction volumes at U.S. SEFs since the 2014 trade execution mandate. As highlighted in Figure 7.11, notional value traded on SEFs has remained relatively constant across the three major swap categories.

In theory, the new SEF rules were designed in part to create new opportunities for other market entrants to compete within the execution segment for OTC derivatives. However, in practice, the majority of the new SEF entrants are in fact incumbent electronic inter-dealer brokerage platforms that have been repurposed to adhere to the SEF rules, as highlighted in Figure 7.12.

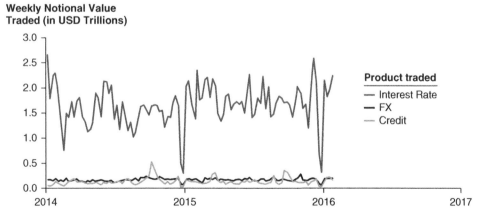

FIGURE 7.11 Notional value traded at U.S. SEFs by product type
Source: FIA SEF Tracker (Issue #22, as of January 26, 2016), Oliver Wyman analysis

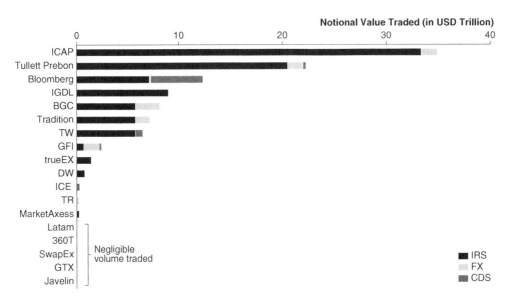

FIGURE 7.12 SEFs by notional value traded in 2015
Source: FIA SEF Tracker (Issue #22, as of January 26, 2016), Oliver Wyman analysis

European Union: Organized Trading Facilities (OTFs) The European equivalent of a swap execution facility (SEF) is called an organized trading facility (OTF), which is a new type of permitted trading system introduced under MiFID II, in addition to multilateral trading facilities (MTFs) and regulated markets. There is still work to be done to harmonize the EU and U.S. regimes for OTC derivatives trade execution, as these two competing regimes do not perfectly overlap conceptually. Some notable differences include the fact that OTFs can be designed to trade products other than swaps, including equities, commodities, and non-swap derivatives, among other differences.

Japan: Electronic Trading Platforms (ETPs) In Japan, the equivalent term for an SEF/OTF is *electronic trading platform* (ETP). Mandatory trading on ETPs was slated to begin in September 2015 for JPY vanilla interest rate swaps. ETPs are conceptually similar to SEFs/OTFs, again with some subtle but specific differences. ETPs must have an *order book* or RFQ functionality with no fewer than three counterparties. Voice is still an acceptable protocol, despite the fact that these are being dubbed "electronic" platforms.

Clearing and Settlement of Derivatives

As with the securities trade lifecycle, the next steps in the trade lifecycle for derivatives involves clearing and then settlement of the contract. While the concept of clearing is similar for derivatives (i.e., trade details must be matched and validated), the concept for settlement is not. With a securities transaction, settlement involves the delivery of cash in exchange for the receipt of a security. For derivatives there is no such analogous concept.

Derivative contracts are "created" (either by an exchange or through bilateral agreement) and must be risk managed through their life until they mature. Counterparty risk between buyers and sellers of derivatives therefore remains open throughout the life of the derivatives contract. The primary way risk is managed is through the upfront transfer of cash/collateral, which in ETD markets is called *initial margin* and in OTC markets called the *independent amount*, and through periodic margin payments, called *variation margin*, which are typically made in cash. Some select products, such as options, may involve the upfront payment of cash from the buyer to the seller. Collectively, these cash and collateral transfers throughout the life of the derivative contract can be thought of as the settlement process.

This settlement process must be managed by the back offices of the counterparties involved, as is the case with bilateral OTC derivatives, or by central counterparties (CCPs) that are either part of the derivatives exchange or a separate CCP for the clearing of OTC derivatives. Since bilateral clearing does not involve separate market infrastructure, the rest of this section focuses on the two major types of market infrastructure institutions that support the clearing and settlement of derivatives, namely:

- ETD clearinghouses
- OTCD clearinghouses

ETD Clearinghouses   Exchange-traded derivatives such as futures and options are almost universally centrally cleared by a clearinghouse, and in many cases that clearinghouse will also act as a CCP. The clearinghouse may be part of the same organization as the exchange, as is the case at CME and ICE, or may be a separate independent organization, as is the case with U.S. equity options that trade on multiple U.S. exchanges but are cleared at the Options Clearing Corporation, an industry-owned utility.

Members of the derivatives exchange may or may not also be members of the associated derivatives CCP. In the case where an institution is a member of the derivatives exchange but not of the ETD clearinghouse, the institution must access the clearinghouse through an intermediary, called a *general clearing member*. A General clearing member is a financial intermediary that provides clearing services both for its own account and for clients, as opposed to a *clearing member*, which may only provide these services on its own account.

In some cases a client may have an *execution broker* that is different from the general clearing member that is acting on their behalf to clear trades at the clearinghouse. Responsibilities of the general clearing member in relation to its client differ by jurisdiction. In general, in Europe there is more of a principal model where the general clearing members act as principals on behalf of brokers. In the United States, there is a pure agency relationship between the general clearing member and its client, with a broker's margins being channeled through the general clearing member on a gross basis.

There are several key functions that a derivatives CCP must perform with the most crucial ones being:

- *Registration and novation of the transaction:* Once a derivatives trade is submitted to the derivatives clearinghouse, if it is acting as a CCP, the clearinghouse will insert itself between the buyer and seller through a process known as novation.
- *Collection of initial margin:* At the onset of the trade, the CCP will ask for a deposit on open positions, called initial margin (IM), which can be in the form of CCP-eligible securities or cash.
- *Periodic collection of variation margin:* Over the life of the contract, the CCP will collect periodic variation margin (VM) payments based on the profit or loss on open positions. VM is typically calculated at least daily and is usually settled in cash.

It is important to note that ETD clearinghouses usually calculate margin payments on a portfolio basis rather than on an individual contract level. In this way they are able to take into account relationships between positions that result in netting benefits.

OTCD Clearinghouses OTC derivatives clearinghouses have been around for some time. For example, LCH.Clearnet has been clearing OTC interest rate swaps since 1999. However, OTC derivatives clearing has gained significant momentum in recent years given the G20 policy objective around the clearing of OTC derivatives.

OTCD clearinghouses function in the same manner as ETD clearinghouses, with respect to the core clearing and settlement functions. The main difference is that OTC derivatives by definition do not trade on-exchange and hence must be submitted to the OTCD clearinghouse. In several cases market participants have several OTCD clearinghouses to choose from.

As Table 7.4 highlights, there are a large number of OTCD clearinghouses that will clear the five core OTC derivative products. The majority of these OTCD clearinghouses are existing ETD clearinghouses that are now offering services to clear OTC derivatives. Pooling ETD and OTCD positions at one clearinghouse may in some cases come with margin efficiencies where there are offsetting risk exposures.

While OTCD clearing has gained momentum recently, there is still a significant way to go before there is widespread market adoption. As we have discussed previously only a few jurisdictions have put in place trading and clearing mandates for OTCD. Accordingly, this segment of the market infrastructure is likely to continue to evolve as regulations are finalized and market participants settle on an acceptable market structure.

Trade Repositories for Derivatives

Regulators and supervisory authorities require accurate and up-to-date information to gain a clear picture of the markets they oversee. Traditionally, regulators have had a clear view into the exchange-traded derivative markets, as data on every transaction is stored and available at the derivatives exchanges and CCPs where these transactions are centrally traded and cleared, respectively.

TABLE 7.4 Major OTCD CCPs by Jurisdiction and OTCD Product Cleared

Jurisdiction	OTC Derivative CCP	CO	CR	EQ	FX	IR
United States	CME Group	•	•			•
	ICE Clear Credit LLC		•			
	LCH Clearnet LLC					•
	OCC			•		
Eurozone	CME Clearing Europe	•				•
	ICE Clear Europe Ltd.		•		•	
	LCH.Clearnet Ltd.	•		•	•	•
	LCH SA		•			
	LME Clear Ltd.	•				
Brazil	BM&F Bovespa	•	•	•	•	•
Russia	CJSC JSCB National Clearing Centre	•	•	•	•	•
India	CCIL				•	•
China	Shanghai Clearing House	•			•	•

Source: "OTC Derivatives Market Reforms: Tenth Progress Report on Implementation" (FSB, 2015). CO = Commodity, CR = Credit, EQ = Equity, FX = Foreign Exchange, IR = Interest Rate.

In contrast, the OTC derivatives markets were historically opaque, as trading took place bilaterally between counterparties (often over the phone) with no mechanism in place to consolidate data across market participants for reporting to regulators. As the 2007–08 financial crisis unfolded, regulators did not have access to trade-level position data across the OTC derivatives markets and were therefore in a very poor position to assess the systemic risks inherent in these markets, both in aggregate and at the market participant level.

The G20 OTC derivatives reforms addressed these concerns directly by establishing a commitment among G20 nations to create the regulatory framework and associated infrastructure for the trade reporting of all OTC derivatives. The G20 nations are now in the process of implementing these regulatory requirements, with progress varying by jurisdiction.

Trade Repositories Trade repositories capture and retain key trade-level information related to open OTC derivative contracts. Depending on the jurisdiction, trade repositories may also collect data on exchange-traded derivative transactions, as is the case in the European Union, giving regulators a complete picture across both the ETD and OTCD markets without the need to aggregate data from multiple sources. Trade repositories provide services to both market participants and regulators, which include:

- Acceptance and confirmation of data, which may come from multiple sources, including derivative exchanges, derivative clearinghouses/CCPs, SEFs/OTFs, or directly from market participants.

- Recordkeeping and storage of the underlying transaction-level data.
- Public and proprietary reporting on the underlying data collected; in some jurisdictions, such as the United States, this includes near real-time dissemination of data.
- Maintenance of data privacy and integrity; and provision of access to regulators for reporting, monitoring, and analysis purposes.

As Table 7.5 highlights, many of the larger trade repositories are subsidiaries of existing market infrastructure providers, including derivatives exchanges, (I)CSDs, and SEF operators. As OTC derivatives trade reporting regulations were first implemented in the United States, market infrastructure providers headquartered in the United States have had a head start in developing the requisite infrastructure and accordingly have a broader presence across jurisdictions as they were able to largely leverage the infrastructure built

TABLE 7.5 Major OTC Derivatives Trade Repositories by Parent Company

Parent Company	Parent Domicile	Trade Repository Legal Name	Markets Served*						
			AU	CA	EU	HK	JP	SG	US
Bloomberg	US	BSDR LLC							•
Chicago Mercantile Exchange (CME)	US	Chicago Mercantile Exchange (US) Inc.	•	•					•
		CME Trade Repository (UK) Ltd.			•				
Depository Trust Clearing Corporation (DTCC)	US	DTCC Data Repository (US) LLC				•			•
		DTCC Derivatives Repository (UK) Ltd.			•	•			
		DTCC Data Repository (Japan) KK					•		
		DTCC Data Repository (Singapore) PTE Ltd.	•					•	
Intercontinental Exchange (ICE)	US	ICE Trade Vault (US) LLC				•			•
		ICE Trade Vault Europe (UK) Ltd.			•				
Clearstream/ Iberclear[11]	Luxem.	REGIS-TR (Luxembourg) S.A.			•				
London Stock Exchange (LSE)	UK	UnaVista (UK) Ltd.			•				
CSD of Poland (KDPW)	Poland	Krajowy Depozyt Papierów Wartosciowych S.A. (KDPW)			•				

*Country abbreviations: AU = Australia, CA = Canada, EU = European Union, HK = Hong Kong, JP = Japan, SG = Singapore, and US = United States.
Source: "OTC Derivatives Market Reforms: Tenth Progress Report on Implementation" (FSB, 2015).

[11]Regis is a joint venture between Iberclear, the Spanish central securities depository (CSD), and Clearstream, the international central securities depository (ICSD) based in Luxembourg.

for U.S. swap data reporting purposes. DTCC in particular has built a global network of regulator approved OTC derivative trade repositories and now operates across seven jurisdictions.

Differences between U.S. and European Implementation   In the United States, trade repositories are known as *swap data repositories* (SDRs), as defined in the Dodd-Frank Act. SDRs must be registered by either the CFTC or the SEC, depending on the type of swap. Only OTC derivatives are required to be submitted to SDRs, as regulators have access to exchange-traded derivatives data directly from the derivatives exchanges. While there are two parties to each swap transaction U.S. regulators require submission from only one to satisfy the trade reporting requirement. This simplifies submission, particularly for swap end-users that are not financial institutions.

Within the EU, ESMA has direct responsibility for the registration, supervision, and recognition of trade repositories. In contrast to the United States, the trade reporting requirement extends beyond OTC derivatives to exchange-traded derivatives, and submission requirements extend to all market participants, including both financial and nonfinancial participants. Both parties to a given derivative transaction must report their trade, creating duplicate submissions.

European trade repositories are obligated to report aggregate position and notional statistics publicly. Figure 7.13 provides an overview of the relative size of the six currently registered trade repositories operating in the EU based on the number of open OTC derivatives positions currently reported. DTCC's global trade repository is currently the largest by position count and captures a significant portion of dealer-reported OTC derivatives trades, particularly those that are not currently cleared. Univista, CME, and Regis all complete largely through capturing captive trade reports through their relationships with existing OTCD clearinghouses.

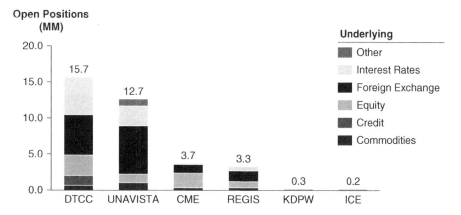

FIGURE 7.13   European trade repository open OTC derivative positions by underlying
Source: Public EMIR reporting data from each repository, Oliver Wyman analysis; as of date 2/12/2016 for all trade repositories except Univista; Univista as of date 2/9/2016

The Road Ahead for Trade Repositories   While a large percentage of jurisdictions now have a regulatory framework in place for the reporting of OTC derivatives trades, global regulators still have much work to do to harmonize reporting across the various jurisdictions so that an accurate global view of the OTC derivatives market can be constructed. In many cases, the competition among trade repository providers that regulators enthusiastically promoted has created operational challenges, particularly around the aggregation of data. Some of the key challenges that regulators are still working through include:[12]

- Problems with data quality and the absence of critical fields such as *unique transaction identifiers* (UTIs) and *unique product identifiers* (UPIs) required to match transactions
- Challenges in aggregating data cross-trade repositories (domestically and cross-border)
- Legal restrictions on the ability for foreign authorities to access domestically held data

CONCLUDING REMARKS

The post-trade landscape is constantly changing and the great changes that have occurred over the past 20 to 30 years are not likely to slow down any time soon. Even more change is on the horizon, fueled by both regulatory objectives and market forces, but also more interestingly by a growing realization, driven largely by new financial technology providers, that much of the post-trade infrastructure could be rationalized and re-architected. As these developments begin to materialize, market infrastructure will continue to be an exciting space to watch for some time to come.

---

[12] "OTC Derivatives Market Reforms: Ninth Progress Report on Implementation" (FSB, 2014).

Capital Markets Products

CHAPTER 8

Money Markets

Randy Harrison and Paul Mandel

Much of the U.S. economy relies on the scale and efficiency of the money markets. This is one of the most important financial markets that keeps our U.S. government, our local governments, and agencies, corporations, banks, other financial institutions, and broker-dealers functioning smoothly for the benefit of its stakeholders and clients. The U.S. money markets include capital markets debt instruments with maturities of one year and less. Enormous cash flows are transacted daily in money market products that are readily accepted by investors due to the money market's liquidity, short duration, and strong credit quality. The Federal Reserve Bank is a significant strategic participant in the U.S. money markets and through its actions implements interest rate policies that impact the broader capital markets, including the bond and stock markets as well as the foreign exchange market. The principal purpose of the money markets from an issuer's perspective is to enable the federal government and domestic corporations to fund their short-term cash needs, principally working capital. Investors who seek short-term investment securities known for high credit quality that typically can be quickly converted to cash look to the money markets. This chapter will focus on the most significant instruments that comprise the U.S. money markets: fed funds, repurchase agreements, Treasury bills, agency securities, commercial paper, certificates of deposit, Eurodollar deposits, short-dated municipal notes, and variable-rate demand notes.

The end of this chapter will examine the impact of money market products during the Global Financial Crisis of 2007 and 2008. This financial crisis permanently altered the money markets in many ways. In the wake of the crisis, sweeping changes were made to regulations governing money market funds as well as to rules dictating how banks fund themselves. Prior to the financial crisis, there were several products, such as *structured investment vehicles* and *auction rate securities*, that ceased to be viable after stresses in the financial system caused investors to desert these money market instruments, resulting in the virtual evaporation of market liquidity. The financial crisis also significantly altered how money market participants, both issuers and investors, view the overall liquidity of money market instruments.

The U.S. money markets create the market for the efficient transfer of capital from lenders to borrowers for short durations. Money market securities are debt instruments with short-term maturities typically ranging from overnight to one year. Massive sums of capital can be transferred rapidly and easily from investors, or lenders, to borrowers for relatively short periods of time. Institutions (such as corporations, banks, and municipalities) with short-term borrowing needs can meet these needs by maintaining access to the money markets and raising funds when required. Similarly, investors with excess cash (such as high-net-worth individuals, money market funds, banks, corporations, and municipalities) can maximize their returns yet maintain liquidity by investing in money market securities. Most money market securities are very liquid and have a high credit quality and low interest rate risk. As a largely institutional market, money market trading activity is often comprised of very large amounts, with trades in the tens or even hundreds of millions of dollars being common. Active secondary markets allow most money market securities to be traded prior to maturity if an investor has a more immediate need for cash. The interest rates of these instruments are largely influenced by Federal Reserve policy more than any other sector of the fixed-income market. Because of their high credit quality, money market securities allow investors to enhance returns on cash while also maintaining liquidity and preserving capital. While investors managing large cash balances often invest directly in money market instruments, investors who lack the scale or expertise will invest in money market funds that in turn investing on behalf of a pool of investors are active participants in the money markets. In particular, retail investors do not typically invest directly in all money market instruments but instead invest through money funds (although retail investors will often purchase commercial paper, T-bills, and CDs).

FEDERAL FUNDS MARKETS

The federal funds (or *fed funds*) market is used by banks for borrowing and lending of bank reserves. The fed funds market is central to the overnight market for credit for banks in the United States. The Federal Reserve seeks to influence its target fed funds rate through its execution of monetary policy to achieve its statutory objectives for monetary policy—maximum employment, stable prices, and moderate long-term interest rates—as defined in the Federal Reserve Act. The current and expected interest rates on fed funds have significant influence on the levels of all other money market rates. Even long-term fixed-income market rates are influenced by this benchmark short-term rate.

Most of the reserves held by banks consist of deposits with the Federal Reserve System. The market exists due to the fact that on many occasions certain banks will have more deposits than they need to meet the Fed's reserve requirements. Alternatively, some banks find themselves in need of cash and use the fed funds market to manage those reserves. The interest rate payable to the lending bank is termed the federal funds rate or fed funds rate. Banks negotiate the rates depending on the supply and demand of cash availability for that day. This rate may be higher, lower, or the same as the fed funds target, depending on market conditions. Working on instructions from banks, the Fed transfers funds from one bank's account to another.

The key characteristics of fed funds are as follows:

- Fed funds are short-term borrowings, typically overnight.
- Fed funds are settled between depository institutions within a single business day.
- Only the depository institutions that are required to hold reserves with Federal Reserve banks (member banks) can borrow or lend fed funds. So, for instance, a non-bank corporation cannot participate in the fed funds market. Institutions that are permitted to transact fed funds include commercial banks, savings and loan associations, credit unions, U.S. branches of foreign banks, and U.S. government agencies.
- When a bank or other financial institution borrows fed funds, that borrowing is exempt from both reserve requirements and interest rate ceilings.
- Fed fund loans are uncollateralized obligations and are not guaranteed by the U.S. government but obligations of the borrowing bank.

On any given day, the fed funds market rate reflects the point where the aggregate demand for reserves is in equilibrium with the aggregate supply of reserves. The Federal Reserve Bank publishes the "Fed Effective" rate for the previous business day each morning on its public website.[1] This Fed Effective rate represents the weighted average of all fed funds transactions for that day. Aggregate demand for bank reserves is determined by the public's demand for demand deposits against which banks hold reserves. One of the factors affecting this demand is the overall level of money market rates. The aggregate quantity of reserves by the public falls as money market interest rates rise, since the opportunity cost of holding idle, non-interest-bearing assets will increase. On the supply side of bank reserves, the Federal Reserve is the key force. Through open market operations (sales and purchases of Treasury securities) the Fed injects or extracts reserves from the system. Through its open markets operations, the Federal Reserve is able to influence the federal funds rate.

The fed funds target rate is the base rate to which other money market rates are anchored. Consequently, an increasing fed funds rate will tend to lead all other money market rates higher.

REPURCHASE AGREEMENTS

A repurchase agreement transaction (repo) is the sale of securities to a repo investor with an agreement by the seller to repurchase the securities on an established future date at a fixed price that includes accrued interest to that date. A repo transaction is essentially a secured loan of cash collateralized by securities acceptable to the cash lender for a term and rate mutually agreeable by the counterparties, the lender and the borrower. Repo

[1]https://www.federalreserve.gov/releases/h15/20160524/.

transactions are documented under the terms of a *master repurchase agreement*, which governs the rights and responsibilities of each counterparty in the sale and repurchase of the securities. Under the master repurchase agreement, the seller of the securities does not lose title to the securities collateralizing the repo and continues to receive any principal and interest payments due on the securities. The seller of the securities (the party borrowing the cash) is considered to be engaging in a repo. The purchaser of the securities (the party lending/investing cash) is described as entering into a reverse repurchase agreement (*reverse repo*). In other words, the same transaction is either a reverse repo or repo, depending on whether the party is the lender or borrower of securities.

A transaction in the repo market is a secured loan where the seller of the securities is borrowing funds from the buyer and pledging the securities as collateral. Repo transactions combine the concept of outright sales and purchases with that of secured loans. The repo rate then is commonly quoted as an interest rate (on a yield basis).

Repo transactions typically have maturities from overnight to 90 days. While the vast majority of repo transactions are traditionally overnight transactions, as the result of recent regulations, broker-dealers and banks are now seeking to structure repos with longer maturities (greater than 90 days). Sometimes repo counterparties can trade on an "open" maturity under which repo agreement continues to roll for an unspecified term until closed out by either counterparty.

The negotiated interest rate depends largely on the creditworthiness of the counterparty borrowing against the securities and the quality of the underlying securities. Interest rates on repo transactions are also influenced by the overall money market, including the fed funds rate, availability of securities (collateral), and cash available to be invested. Like all interest rates, repo rates are set by this supply/demand tug-of-war.

Since repurchase agreements are close substitutes for federal funds borrowings, rates on repos and fed funds often move in tandem. These fluctuations between rates on repos and fed funds reflect many variables, including Federal Reserve policy, availability of collateral, economic conditions, and the perceived health of the broker-dealer community.

Transactions are generally conducted between financial and nonfinancial institutions. Most repo transactions are executed in sizes well into the millions of dollars. Repo transactions in excess of several hundred million dollars are not uncommon. Securities broker-dealers are the largest borrowers of cash in the repo market, often using the repo market to finance their Treasury, government agency, corporate bond, mortgage, and money market securities positions. Rather than borrowing on an unsecured basis, broker-dealers and banks instead pledge their trading securities as collateral. Investor counterparties on these transactions are primarily institutions with excess cash that they need to invest. These investors include money market funds, banks and thrifts, pension funds, municipalities, and corporations. High-net-worth individuals with significant liquidity may also invest in repos. A common theme among all these investors is a desire for a high credit quality, collateralized investment. Most securities lent in the repo market are deemed to be *general collateral* because they are not in special demand in the market and are readily available. Some repo counterparties may have a short-term need for a particular security (called a *special*) to settle a trade or to borrow to engage in a short sale. Interest rates paid on these special security repos is lower for the securities lender than on general collateral repos (in other words, the borrower of the cash/lender of the security will pay a lower rate to borrow money since the security being lent is more valuable or harder to find).

Most repos today are transacted as *tri-party repos*. In tri-party repo, the securities lender (cash borrower) delivers their collateral to the securities borrower (cash lender) at an account of a third-party custodian bank. The custodian collects and holds the securities, calculates that there is sufficient collateral to cover the cash lending according to the formulas detailed in the repo agreement, and sends the cash to the securities lender. When the repo matures, the custodian transfers the collateral back to the securities lender and repays the securities borrower their cash plus interest. Tri-party repo was structured to reduce repo settlement risk and standardize transaction processing. Tri-party repo allows broker-dealers and banks to lend as much of their available collateral as necessary and securities borrowers no longer need to check collateral lists and prices as the custodians now do this on their behalf in an automated fashion. Before tri-party repo came into being, collateral had to be delivered to each securities borrower's custodial account and typically both parties to the repo would prefer larger blocks of securities (as opposed to large lists of small pieces).

U.S. TREASURY BILLS (T-BILLS)

U.S. Treasury bills (T-bills) are short-term securities issued by the U.S. Treasury that mature in one year or less from their issue date. T-bills and other longer-term debt are issued to fund our federal government, or to refinance older debt as it matures. T-bills are backed by the full faith and credit of the U.S. government and possess virtually no default risk. Because of the low credit risk, T-bills yields are lower than other money market instruments. The spread between T-bills and non-U.S. government money market instruments, such as commercial paper or certificates of deposit, will increase and decrease with varying economic conditions. For example, a weaker economy could tend to raise the difference, or spread, between the rates on T-bills and commercial paper of a comparable maturity as investors will prefer to have to T-bills, the safest money market instrument. Under such conditions the price of T-bills would be bid up, causing the yield to drop.

T-bills are non-callable and due to the sheer size of the market are considered to be the most liquid money market security. The liquidity of the T-bill is demonstrated by the fact that the spread between the bid and offer is extremely small: often a fraction of a basis point (a basis point being 1/100 of 1 percent). The ability of investors to easily buy and sell this security is an attractive feature of investing in T-bills, allowing investors an opportunity to liquidate their T-bills prior to maturity at little or no cost.

Unlike many other money market instruments, interest generated by U.S. T-bills is exempt from state and local income taxes for a U.S.-based investor. Investors purchase T-bills for a price less than their par (face) value, or at a discount.[2] When T-bills mature

---

[2]Note that in the near-zero rate environment that has existed since the Global Financial Crisis of 2007–08, T-bills (and discount notes) sometimes actually traded at negative interest rates. As a result, the investor would have had to pay more than par value and would have only received back the face value.

they are redeemed at par value. The interest is the difference between the purchase price of the security and what is paid at maturity. For example, if an investor bought a $100,000 26-week Treasury bill for $97,500 and held it until maturity, the investor would receive $100,000 back. The interest earned would thus be $2,500.

Treasury bills can be purchased at the weekly auctions conducted by the U.S. Treasury, or in the secondary (after-sale) securities market. About one week before each auction, the Treasury issues a press release announcing the security to be auctioned, the amount of the issue, the auction date, and other relevant information. Typically, weekly offerings of three- and six-month T-bills are announced on a Tuesday, with the actual auction conducted on the following Monday. Delivery and payment (settlement) normally take place Thursday of the same week.

Investors can submit a bid for T-bills either noncompetitively or competitively, with a minimum purchase amount of $10,000. The vast majority of individual, nonprofessional investors enter noncompetitive bids.

All T-bills are issued in book-entry form (an entry in an electronic ledger) and settle on the *government wire*. You can hold your Treasury securities either at a bank custodial account or directly with the Treasury Department through Treasury Direct.

GOVERNMENT-SPONSORED ENTERPRISES/FEDERAL AGENCY SECURITIES

Government-sponsored enterprises (GSEs), more commonly known as federal agencies, are financing entities set up by Congress to make loans to specific groups such as farmers or homeowners. The debt issued by these entities is normally sponsored by, but not guaranteed by, the U.S. government. These securities are instruments of those particular GSEs and are not a direct obligation of the U.S. government. Nevertheless, the debt of these GSEs is viewed as strong credits, based on limited lines of credit from and a perceived tie to the U.S. government. It is important to note that there are GSEs, such as the Government National Mortgage Association (Ginnie Mae), which are an actual division of the U.S. government. As such, Ginnie Mae securities come with a full-faith-and-credit U.S. government guarantee.

Although GSEs issue debt across the entire yield curve, their short-term issuance is a significant sector of the money markets. While the debt comes in a variety of forms, the most popular issues are known as discount notes (also known as *discos*). Discos are short-term obligations issued at a discount from face value with maturities ranging from overnight to one year. Similar to T-bills, discos have no periodic interest payments or a coupon, which means that the investor buys these securities at less than par and at maturity receives the note's face value at maturity.

The agencies offer billions in new issue securities each morning, through their *window* programs and auctions. Window postings are a listing of specific agency issuance needs for that day (amounts, maturities, and rates). An agency dealer can see those new issue offerings on the agency's screen and then fill investor orders by purchasing the new issue discos from the issuers. Discos are also issued in book-entry form and settle via the government wire. These notes are the primary short-term funding tools of GSEs. Federal agencies that issue discos include: Federal Home Loan Bank (FHLB), Federal National Mortgage Association or Fannie Mae (FNMA), Federal Farm Credit Bank (FFCB), Federal Agricultural Mortgage Corporation or Farmer Mac (FAMC), Federal Home Loan Mortgage Corporation or Freddie Mac (FHLMC), and Tennessee Valley Authority (TVA). These institutions issue discos to raise short-term funds to lend out for their various missions.

The disco market is another large and liquid market. On a daily basis, the U.S. disco dealers bid and offer billions of these short-term securities. Enormous quantities of notes are regularly traded under very competitive conditions and sold with razor-thin margins. Government agency discount notes are widely purchased by large institutions, including money market funds, municipalities, and corporations. High-net-worth individuals can also invest in discount notes as a slightly higher-yielding alternative to T-bills.

GSEs can also issue callable notes with maturities of 13 months or less, giving the agencies the ability to call the notes prior to maturity. The investor is normally rewarded with a higher yield for providing the agency with this call option.

COMMERCIAL PAPER

Commercial paper (CP) is a short-term, unsecured promissory note issued primarily by three issuer types: (1) corporations, (2) financial institutions (including banks), and (3) special-purpose vehicles funding high-quality assets (also known as *asset-backed commercial paper*, or ABCP). The CP market is an attractive source of funds for issuers since it provides a lower-cost funding alternative to bank loans. According to data gathered by the Federal Reserve Bank, the size of the U.S. CP market has consistently been over $1 trillion in recent years (http://www.federalreserve.gov/releases/cp/outstanding.htm). Before the Global Financial Crisis unfolded in 2007, the CP market had exceeded $2 trillion. The events of 2007 and 2008 had a significant impact on size of CP market, the regulatory framework of the market's largest class of investors, money market funds, and banks' need for short-dated (under 90 days) funding.

CP maturities typically range from overnight up to 270 days, averaging around 30 days. Many issuers continuously roll over their CP to fund working capital needs while other issuers use their CP program more episodically for special purposes (such as to finance a merger, interim financing for a development project, or the purchase of assets). CP investors, like other short-term investors, are typically more concerned about protecting the return of their principal investment rather than maximizing their return. As a result, only those CP issuers with investment-grade ratings are able to easily access the investor market. Instead of using long-term debt ratings, CP market participants use short-term ratings from Moody's (P1, P2, or P3), S&P (A1+, A1, A2, or A3), and Fitch (F1+, F1, F2, or F3) as a framework for rating the credit strength of issuers (for a fuller description of the ratings' evaluation, see ahead).

Issuers that are highly rated can raise billions of dollars quickly and efficiently without incurring Securities and Exchange Commission (SEC) registration fees and avoid the extensive disclosure requirements, including the creation of detailed offering memoranda that are required for longer-dated debt and equity securities. It is important to note that when CP was initially introduced and became popular as an investment alternative, CP maturities were limited to a maximum of 270 days in order to avoid the registration requirements of the Securities Act of 1933. By issuing a security with a maturity of 270 days or less, the issuer could take advantage of the exemption the act provided for short-term securities to come to market more rapidly. CP issued in this manner was exempt from registration under the Securities Act of 1933, pursuant to Section 3(a)(3). Section 3(a)(3) CP may be issued for normal working capital purposes, has a minimum denomination of $100,000, and may be sold to any investor (including individuals). Short "offering memoranda" would be made available to investors and these offering memos would be generic to the CP program, rather than to each note or issuance.

In order to allow issuers to use CP for non-working-capital purposes, CP programs were created that were also exempt from registration but were deemed to be *private placements* under rule 4(2) of the Securities Act of 1934. Paired with the resale safe harbor called 144a, CP has mostly shifted to a regulatory type known as 4(2)/144a or more recently called 4(a)(2). These types of CP programs are issued using a "private placement memorandum," can be issued with maturities of up to 397 days, may only be sold to *qualified institutional buyers* (QIBs, mostly large institutions with investment assets exceeding $100 MM), and have a minimum denomination of $250,000.

CP can be sold directly by issuers or through the broker-dealer community. Investors consist of a large and diverse group of institutional buyers, including money market funds, corporations, municipalities, and even some high-net-worth investors. These investors earn competitive rates that normally exceed those of T-bills, discos, and money market funds. Investors in the CP market are almost entirely institutions. Thus, while minimum denominations are normally $100,000 or $250,000 (depending on the regulatory type), typical transactions are in the tens or hundreds of millions of dollars.

Similar to T-bills and the discos, CP is normally issued on a discount basis rather than on an interest-bearing basis. On a discount basis, CP is purchased at a discount to par and then receives face value at maturity. The difference between the price paid and face value is the imputed interest earned by the investor. Thus, CP interest rates are quoted on a discount basis. However, the true yield of discounted CP, or the money market equivalent yield, is actually higher than the discount rate. Through a mathematical adjustment the discount rate is calculated to generate a money market equivalent yield to allow an investor to compare different types of securities (i.e., discounted vs. interest-bearing) using an equivalent rate basis. While CP can be issued as interest-bearing, this is not typically the case. However, issuers have recently become interested in creating longer-dated structured CP that may include floating rate and callable or puttable features that improve the capital and regulatory treatment for the liabilities for some issuers while providing investors with enhanced yields. When CP is issued as an interest-bearing note, the investor pays the face value and at maturity receives the face value plus accrued interest, which may be paid at maturity or periodically.

CP is usually issued with a specific maturity date. If an investor needs their funds prior to the maturity date, it is possible to sell the CP back to a dealer for that issuer's program. The dealer can then identify another investor who may purchase the note for its remaining maturity at a current market price, which may be less than or more than the original purchase price (adjusted for accretion as may be the case). Most issuers use CP dealers to distribute their paper. However, some issuers choose to sell their paper directly to investors without using a dealer. According to market data maintained by the Federal Reserve, approximately 10% to 15% CP is sold by an issuer directly to an investor. These issuers are referred to as direct issuers.

As noted above, there are three issuer types: (1) corporations, which in 2016 account for approximately 25% of the total CP market, (2) financial institutions (including banks), accounting for approximately 50% of the market, and (3) asset-backed CP (ABCP), which accounts for approximately 25% of the market. Trends in CP outstandings can be viewed on the Federal Reserve's website.[3] The issuer category types are as follows:

- *Financial institutions* include banks, insurance companies, securities firms, and finance companies. Banks are the most active of all in the financial institutions category. European banks are the most active financial issuers in the U.S. CP market, followed by Asian banks who all use the CP market to fund their banking activities. Insurance companies utilize the CP market to finance premium receivables and short-term expenses. Securities firms use CP as a low-cost funding mechanism and alternative to repos and money market loans. Finally, finance companies use CP to fund the loans that they make to businesses and consumers.

- *Corporations* include any nonfinancial firm such as industrial, technology, public utility, or service companies. These corporations use CP as short-term financing for current assets such as accounts receivable and inventory. CP can also be used to fill longer-dated financing needs such as funding for capital projects or acquiring another company. Often CP is used to fund longer-dated assets before term financing is arranged in the bond market. Because CP allows highly rated issuers to quickly raise large amounts, in some cases billions of dollars, the product allows an issuer flexibility to access the bond market at the most opportune time rather than being forced to access the debt or equity market at the time of the cash need, which may be less optimal.

- *Asset-backed commercial paper* (ABCP), in contrast to conventional CP issued by corporations or financials, is backed by defined pools of assets. The creditworthiness of ABCP is dependent upon the quality of the underlying assets as well as the structure of the asset-backed program (e.g., credit enhancement, such as liquidity facilities provided by a bank, which may be necessary to achieving program ratings of A-1/P-1). When they are structured, almost all high-grade ABCP programs are rated with a "1" (A-1+ or A1/P-1/F1) by at least two rating agencies. Lesser-rated programs will generally find a shallower market with their higher perceived risk profile.

---

[3] http://www.federalreserve.gov/releases/cp/outstanding.htm.

The first ABCP programs were established in the mid-to-late 1980s. By August 2007 the ABCP market had grown to $1.2 trillion, accounting for 55% of the CP market outstanding at that time. In 2007 there were many ABCP programs that funded mortgage-backed assets. There were also ABCP structures that did not have bank liquidity facilities to fully cover that program's CP outstanding. When investors lost confidence in an ABCP program's assets or its structure as the financial markets began to seize up, these programs were no longer able to sell CP to investors and had to liquidate their assets. Many of these less-than-full-liquidity programs were not able to successfully liquidate their assets to repay all of their debt, which caused a loss of confidence in ABCP structures as a whole. As the markets recovered, beginning in 2010, the ABCP slowly recuperated. Currently, the ABCP market is much smaller than in the early 2000s, accounting for $220 billion or approximately 25% of the CP market (Figure 8.1). Those structures that had funding difficulties in 2007 and 2008 were eventually terminated. Currently, the typical ABCP program is sponsored by a commercial bank rated at least A-1/P-1/F1 and has a liquidity facility, usually from the sponsoring institution, that is equal to 100% of the CP outstanding. The structures that characterize the market today are similar to the program structures that were seen in the markets in the 1980s. The ABCP structures in the market today successfully withstood the financial crisis without any credit issues and are still viewed favorably by many money market investors.

ABCP programs are created as special-purpose corporations (SPCs). An ABCP structure using an SPC usually has a *de minimus* amount of capital backing it. Instead, the CP note holder is relying on the quality of the underlying assets and the credit enhancement or liquidity facilities that back the structure. The credit enhancement is either in the form of a bank credit facility that covers a portion of defaulted assets or in the form of overcollateralization, which means that the amount of assets that are collateralizing the SPC exceed the outstanding paper. Virtually all ABCP programs have liquidity backup

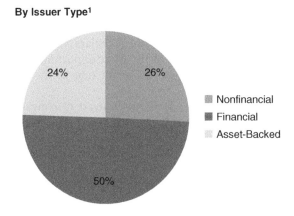

FIGURE 8.1 ABCP volume
[1]As of March 9, 2016. Board Of Governors of the Federal Reserve System website statistics

facilities equal to the face amount of CP outstanding. The facility is normally provided by the bank administrating the ABCP program. Most ABCP programs can be characterized as multi-seller programs. Although typically there is one sponsoring bank that administers the program, there are numerous clients of that bank who will sell their assets into the ABCP program to be funded by the ABCP. Through the issuance of ABCP, the administering banks' corporate customers receive funding from the CP market and pledge their accounts receivable, for example, to the ABCP program. These programs are used to finance trade receivables, consumer loans such as credit cards or auto loans, warehousing of commercial assets, and many other types of high-quality assets. ABCP programs provide their investors with monthly "investor reports" or "pool reports" that detail the ongoing performance and quality of the assets owned by the SPC.

All CP programs are often rated by an independent rating agency or agencies for creditworthiness. Rating agencies, including Moody's Investors Service and Standard & Poor's and Fitch Rating Services, have short-term ratings protocols, similar to the ratings on longer-dated corporate and municipal bonds and other long-term debt. The highest quality CP has the ratings: A-1/P-1/F1 or A-1+/P-1/F1+. A-1+ A-1 and F1+ are the highest short-term ratings given to CP by Standard & Poor's, Moody's, and Fitch respectively, while P-1 refers to the highest rating given by Moody's Investors Service. These short-term debt ratings are opinions of the rating agencies as to the ability of issuers to repay their short-term obligations in a timely manner, since even a delay of several days is considered a technical default.

A Moody's issuer rating of P-1 (Prime-1) indicates that Moody's believes that the issuer has a superior ability to repay its senior short-term debt obligations. According to Moody's, P-1 repayment ability will often be evidenced by such qualities as "leading market positions in well-established industries, high rates of return on funds employed, conservative capitalization structure with moderate reliance on debt and ample asset protection, broad margins in earnings coverage of fixed financial charges and high internal cash generation, and well established access to a range of financial markets and assured sources of alternate liquidity."[4] Issuers rated P-2 (Prime-2) have a strong (but not superior) ability for repayment of senior short-term debt obligations. This will normally be evidenced by many, but not all, of the characteristics cited with Prime-1. According to Moody's, "Earnings trends and coverage ratios, while sound, may be more subject to variation. Capitalization characteristics, while still appropriate, may be more affected by external conditions. Ample alternate liquidity is maintained."[5] The lowest short-term rating, which still correlates with long-term investment-grade ratings, is P-3 (Prime-3), where the issuer's ability to repay is deemed "acceptable" even though "variability in earnings and profitability may result, however, in changes in the level of debt protection measures."

Standard & Poor's maintains a similar short-term rating system to Moody's, with A-1 designating that the "degree of safety regarding timely repayment is strong." Those

---

[4] moodys.com.
[5] moodys.com.

issuers with even stronger safety characteristics are denoted with a "+" sign for a rating of A-1+. (Moody's has no such "+" designation.) Issues rated A-2 indicate that capacity for timely payment is satisfactory, although the relative degree of safety is not as high as for issues designated A-1. Issues carrying the A-3 designation have adequate capacity for timely repayment. However, A-3 issues are more vulnerable to the adverse effects of changes in circumstances than obligations carrying the A-2 and A-1 designations. Issues rated below A-3/P-3 are deemed more speculative and are not frequently issued in the market.

These rating agencies are designated by the SEC as *nationally recognized statistical rating organizations* (NRSROs), which rate fixed-income instruments, including CP programs.

Almost all CP programs are backed by bank liquidity facilities. As a condition to providing a rating to a CP issuer, the rating agencies require that an issuer have access to bank liquidity lines that will allow the issuer to repay the CP in the event that investors suddenly stop purchasing that program. These liquidity facilities will not lend in the event of a bankruptcy of an issuer. The liquidity is meant to only cover liquidity risk (the risk that investors are not willing to buy the paper due to market conditions) rather than credit risk (the risk that an issuer defaults on its obligations).

Because credit quality is a paramount concern to short-term investors, especially to money market mutual funds, many of those investors limit their purchases of CP to only the top-quality programs. Those programs are denoted as "Tier 1," which means that the CP programs have a "1" or "1+" rating by at least two NRSROs. Thus, programs that have ratings of A-1 (or A-1+) by Standard & Poor's, P-1 by Moody's, or F1 (or F1+) by Fitch (or any combination of the above) are Tier 1 CP Programs. Tier 1 CP, according to the Federal Reserve, constitutes approximately 90% of all CP outstanding today. Most of the remaining 10% of the CP market is Tier 2 (any combination of two of the following: A-2, P-2, or F2). While there are a few programs with ratings of A-3, P-3, or F3 that are able to fund in the CP market, there is limited demand for this end of the credit spectrum, being a speculative sector of the CP market. An issuer rated non-investment grade, or with short-term ratings below A-3/P-3/F3 and long-term ratings below Baa3/BBB–/BBB– or not rated at all, is rarely able to find buyers in CP market. Given that a primary motivation for CP investors is preservation of their investment principal, the market is primarily accessible to issuers with higher ratings (Figure 8.2).

Given the size and the importance of the CP market to the broader economy, the Federal Reserve Board compiles weekly data on the market, including issuance volume by different categories. The Federal Reserve Board also tracks rates and publishes several different CP indices in the CP section of its website, www.federalreserve.gov. These rate composites include, for example, average issuance costs for AA-rated corporate names, financial issuers, and A-2/P-2-rated issuers.

Figure 8.3 graphs data compiled by the Federal Reserve, illustrating the CP yield curve, discount rate spread, discount rate history, as well as CP outstanding.

Figure 8.4 represents a snapshot of the CP yield curve. This curve shows how much added return the investor receives by buying longer-maturity paper. The yield curve is steeper for the lower-rated Tier 2 names than it is for Tier 1 rated issuers. The steeper

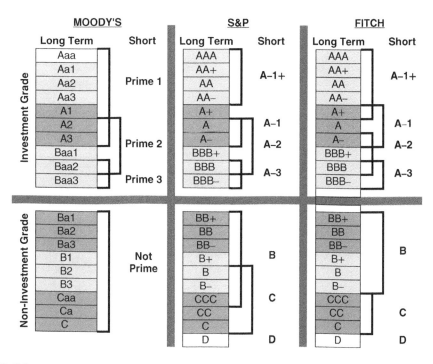

FIGURE 8.2   Market breakdown by ratings

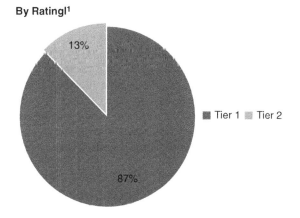

FIGURE 8.3   Fed data of rates
[1] As of March 9, 2016. Board of Governors of the
Federal Reserve System website statistics

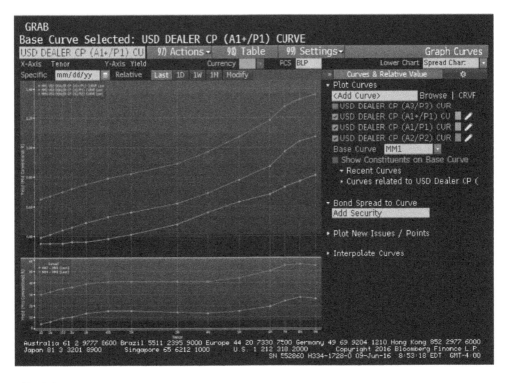

FIGURE 8.4   Yield curve from Fed website

curve for lower-rated CP indicates that investors require higher compensation when extending their maturity exposure to credits they perceive as higher credit risk.

Figure 8.5 quantifies the quality spread, or additional yield paid by lower-rated Tier 2 issuers. We see that at certain points in time the spread increased dramatically (mid-2001) as many investors avoided lower-rated CP and shifted funds to borrowers that were perceived as more creditworthy. When credit quality concerns emerge (for instance, due to a bankruptcy or widespread credit downgrades within an industry), some Tier 2 investors reduce their holdings of this paper while others stop buying certain credits all together.

Declining demand for Tier 2 paper would cause the price of this paper to drop and the issuer's interest rate to rise. Supply and demand will ultimately cause investors to find equilibrium, the rate at which investors feel they are being adequately compensated for the additional risk. Some buyers may require a higher rate to account for the higher perceived risk while other investors purchasing the CP may choose to remove it from their holdings.

Based on Figure 8.6 we see that U.S. corporate CP outstanding has continued to increase as a percentage of the total CP market since the Global Financial Crisis in 2007 and 2008.

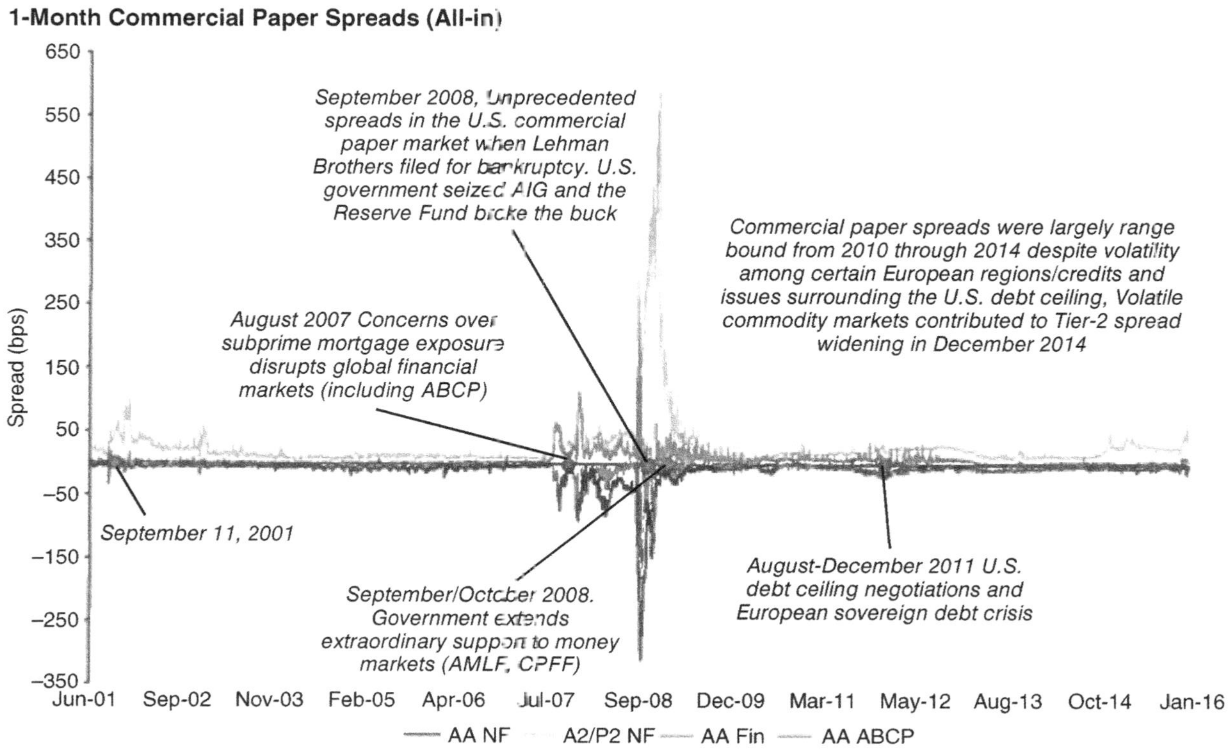
1-Month Commercial Paper Spreads (All-in)
Spread (bps)
650
550
450
350
250
150
50
−50
−150
−250
−350
September 2008, Unprecedented spreads in the U.S. commercial paper market when Lehman Brothers filed for bankruptcy. U.S. government seized AIG and the Reserve Fund broke the buck
Commercial paper spreads were largely range bound from 2010 through 2014 despite volatility among certain European regions/credits and issues surrounding the U.S. debt ceiling, Volatile commodity markets contributed to Tier-2 spread widening in December 2014
August 2007 Concerns over subprime mortgage exposure disrupts global financial markets (including ABCP)
September 11, 2001
September/October 2008. Government extends extraordinary support to money markets (AMLF, CPFF)
August-December 2011 U.S. debt ceiling negotiations and European sovereign debt crisis
Jun-01
Sep-02
Nov-03
Feb-05
Apr-06
Jul-07
Sep-08
Dec-09
Mar-11
May-12
Aug-13
Oct-14
Jan-16
AA NF
A2/P2 NF
AA Fin
AA ABCP

FIGURE 8.5 Historical rate spread
Source: Federal Reserve as of 1/4/16.

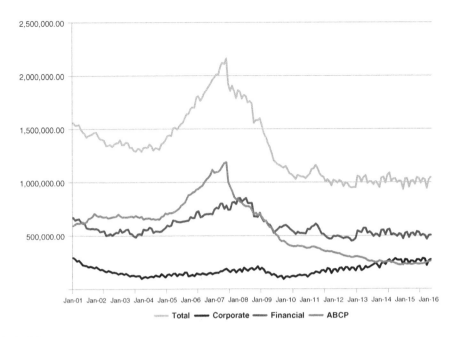

FIGURE 8.6   Outstanding commercial paper by issuer type

CERTIFICATES OF DEPOSIT

A certificate of deposit (CD) is a bank obligation payable on a specific maturity date. Funds are deposited with a bank by investors for a specified period of time during which the funds will earn interest at a specified interest rate. Interest earned can be paid either periodically or at maturity along with the return of principal. Unlike the CP or repo markets, which are largely institutional, CDs can be sold to either institutional investors or retail investors.

Retail CDs

Retail CDs are considered low-risk investments, since the Federal Deposit Insurance Corporation (FDIC) guarantees up to $250,000 per depositor per insured bank for each account ownership category (account party). This puts the risk of these obligations on par with other obligations of the U.S. government. If an individual has more than $250,000 at a specific bank, the excess amount is not FDIC-insured and repayment is dependent solely on the creditworthiness of the deposit bank. Because FDIC rules limit deposit insurance to $250,000 per depositor per institution, an individual wanting to maintain FDIC insurance on deposits can open CD accounts with multiple banks.

The FDIC was formed as a response to the massive bank failures in the Great Depression of the early 1930s. Since its inception, no depositor has lost a single cent of funds that were insured as a result of bank failure (only investors who held CDs in excess of the insured amount over $250,000 have ever lost funds as a result of a bank failure). FDIC-insured CDs are considered to be virtually risk free.[6] As of June 2016, the FDIC held insurance funds totaling $75 billion and insured $6.7 trillion of deposits in U.S. banks and thrift deposits.

The FDIC only insures CDs and other bank deposits. It does not insure mutual funds, securities, or other types of investments that banks may offer.

A retail investor may also consider using a network of banks to invest FDIC-insured CDs in excess of $250,000. Promontory Interfinancial Network, for example, administers a network of member banks nationwide that offer the Certificate of Deposit Account Registry Service (CDARS). Through a proprietary computer system operated by the Promontory network, member banks match customer CDs in amounts under $250,000 to obtain FDIC coverage for their customers. With CDARS, banks can offer a customer up to $10 million in FDIC coverage and customers can enjoy the convenience of managing all of their CDs in a single account.

CDs can be purchased directly from a financial institution or through broker-dealers and CD brokers, either on the phone or through the Internet.

Brokered CDs

An individual investor can also purchase a CD from a broker-dealer, referred to as a brokered CD. Although purchased from a different source other than a bank, a brokered CD is the same instrument as one that is purchased directly from the issuing bank, but purchased through a broker-dealer. Brokered CDs are eligible for the same $250,000 deposit insurance as a CD purchased directly from a bank. These CDs are often held in a broker-dealer custody account with an individual investor's other securities.

Institutional CDs

For institutions and high-net-worth individuals who invest in CDs in excess of the FDIC insurance limit, the investor must analyze the creditworthiness of the bank.

Moody's, Standard & Poor's, and Fitch all analyze the creditworthiness of individual banks and publish ratings for investors. However, these ratings may be interpreted in a different manner from traditional analysis of corporate and municipal bonds. Moody's Investors Service, for example, publishes *Bank Financial Strength Ratings,* giving their opinion of banks' soundness and overall safety. Unlike conventional short-term analysis, Moody's does not address the probability of timely repayment, but includes "bank-specific elements such as financial fundamentals, franchise value, and business and asset diversification." Moody's does not take into account the probability that the bank will receive external government support. Moody's publishes a gradation scale from "A" (exceptional financial strength) to "E" (very weak financial condition).

---

[6]FDIC.gov.

Fitch has developed a unique procedure to assess the individual financial strength of the institution, as well as the likelihood and source of external support should the institution experience financial difficulties. Balance sheet integrity, profitability, and risk management are some of the variables that are reviewed.

There are other rating services that rate banks as well. These firms often use formulas based on a variation of *CAMEL* analysis (capital, assets, management, earnings, and liquidity), assigning a letter grade or numerical ranking that indicates the relative safety of each institution. Usually these types of ratings will only use quantitative metrics and exclude subjective factors.

Floating-rate CDs, in contrast to conventional fixed-rate CDs, offer investors interest rates that change periodically throughout the CD's term. The rates typically float with a common benchmark (such as the London Inter-Bank Offer Rate (LIBOR), 3-month T-bill rates, or prime rate) and are designed to allow the investor to take advantage of rising interest rates or to match floating-rate liabilities with floating-rate assets.

Callable CDs possess a call feature, which means that the bank that issues the CD can choose to repay, or call, the CD after a specified amount of time prior to maturity. Remember, only the issuing bank, not the investor, can call a CD prior to maturity. So giving the issuing bank a call option benefits the bank at the expense of the investor. The bank will tend to call the CD during a period of lower interest rates, returning the investor's money, which will have to be reinvested at lower rates. Therefore, when purchasing a callable CD, the investor should expect additional yield to compensate for selling a call option.

CDs are issued by a variety of different types of banks:

- Domestic CDs are issued by U.S-based domestic banks.
- Yankee CDs are issued by U.S. branches of foreign banks or agencies. For instance, a CD issued by the New York branch of a French bank is a Yankee CD. Yankee CDs are not FDIC insured.
- Euro CDs are any U.S.-dollar CD issued outside of the United States. For instance, a CD issued branch by the London branch of a Japanese bank is a euro CD. All euro CDs, even for U.S. banks, are not FDIC insured.

EURODOLLAR DEPOSITS

Eurodollars are dollar-denominated bank deposit liabilities not subject to U.S. banking regulations or under the jurisdiction of the Federal Reserve. Eurodollar deposits are offered by depository institutions not located in the United States (i.e., foreign banks as well as foreign branches of U.S. banks). Eurodollar deposits are illiquid in that they cannot be sold to another investor or dealer and can only be redeemed early with a significant penalty. As a result, the vast majority of Eurodollar deposits are very short-term, almost exclusively overnight. Current regulations on U.S. banks penalize liabilities that are shorter than 90 days and so U.S. banks have mostly exited the Eurodollar market. The remaining issuers of Eurodollar deposits are mainly European, Canadian, and Asian banks. The entities that invest in these deposits are large corporations (domestic, foreign, and multinational), money market funds, some high-net-worth individuals, and central banks of national governments.

The term *Eurodollar deposits* reflects the fact that at one time these deposits were held entirely in Europe. However, the term is no longer region-specific. Eurodollar deposits now refers to any dollar-denominated deposit held anywhere outside of the United States. While the majority of Eurodollar deposits are still held in Europe, they can also be held at other offshore locations such as the Cayman Islands, the Bahamas, Bahrain, Canada, Hong Kong, Japan, the Netherlands Antilles, Panama, and Singapore. Regardless of where they are held, these deposits are referred to as Eurodollars. Eurodollar deposit rates are often tied to the LIBOR. Rates are usually quoted as a spread to LIBOR. While Eurodollar deposit rates are sometimes fixed, it is more common that they pay interest on a floating-rate basis, corresponding to a LIBOR benchmark, such as three- or six-months LIBOR. As the benchmark LIBOR rate increases or decreases, so does the Eurodollar deposit rate.

MUNICIPAL NOTES

Municipal notes are short-term obligations issued by municipalities to meet cash flow borrowing needs. Municipal notes normally mature in a year or less and pay interest at maturity. In analyzing the creditworthiness of a municipality, great emphasis is placed on cash flow since it is the primary source to repay the note. An investor must assess whether there will be enough cash on hand when the notes come due or whether the notes can be successfully rolled over. The most common types of municipal notes are tax anticipation notes (TANs), revenue anticipation notes (RANs), tax and revenue anticipation notes (TRANs), and bond anticipation notes (BANs).

- Tax anticipation notes (TANs) are issued in anticipation of future tax collections.
- Revenue anticipation notes (RANs) are issued in anticipation of some form of revenue other than taxes, such as state aid. For example, school districts are major issuers of RANs, because in many instances a significant portion of their budget consists of state aid.
- Tax and revenue anticipation notes (TRANs) are issued in anticipation of a combination of both taxes and other sources of revenue, such as state aid.
- Bond anticipation notes (BANs) are issued in anticipation of a future longer-term bond issuance. BANs may very often be rolled over, or refinanced, before the issuer ultimately floats a bond issue. Therefore, issuer access to the bond market is the primary source of repayment.

All things being equal, TANs, RANs, and TRANs are considered more creditworthy than BANs, since the payment of the former three types of notes is not contingent upon access to financial markets and the revenues used to repay the notes is assessable. Even if the municipality has access to the market, rolling over an issue during a period of high short-term interest rates may very well prove to be a financial strain for the issuer. Nonetheless, BANs, like the other three short-term obligations, are still backed by the full faith and credit of the municipality.

TANs, RANs, and TRANs are considered cash flow notes or seasonal borrowing notes. These instruments allow municipalities to meet various liquidity needs throughout the fiscal year. For example, a school district needing to purchase materials or make payroll or capital improvements prior to the beginning of the school year in advance of tax inflows would issue a TAN to bridge the expense-revenue timing mismatch.

When analyzing municipal note issuers, both Moody's and Standard & Poor's often designate special short-term ratings, taking into account questions such as the projected cash flow for the upcoming period and the sources, quality, and probability of the of repayment. The rating agencies will also review a municipality's tax collection history to see if the municipality is collecting sufficient taxes in a timely manner. They will also consider whether a municipality is relying on a disproportionate amount of revenue coming from one source, such as state aid or a major industrial taxpayer. The rating agencies will also assess whether the municipality is relying too heavily on short-term debt.

These ratings, MIG1 and SP1+, for example, may also be assigned in addition to the municipality's underlying long-term rating. Occasionally, it is possible for an issuer with an average or below-average underlying rating to receive the top short-term rating. For example, a municipality with a long-term investment grade rating of A2 nonetheless receives an MIG1 short-term rating on its note issues. What Moody's is saying in effect is that while certain challenges may persist that could threaten the municipality's long-term creditworthiness, the sources of repayment for the notes are adequate.

VARIABLE RATE DEMAND NOTES

A variable rate demand note (VRDN) is a long-term tax-exempt municipal bond (maturities can be as long as 30 years) that is structured like a short-term security in that it has a long-term maturity, a floating interest rate, and the note has a purchase demand feature enabling the investor to "put" the note back to the issuer on demand. These bonds are often issued to fund industrial development and pollution-control projects, as well as education, housing, health care, and transportation needs using a quasi-governmental agency such as a development authority as an issuing authority (although the debt obligation is owned by the ultimate user of the funds). Such agencies typically promote industrial development in a particular area by allowing a corporate or nonprofit entity to borrow money at favorable tax-exempt interest rates as an incentive to develop industry in the authority's district. In virtually all cases, highly rated bank guarantees are structured into the note, assuring timely repayment of interest and principal of the VRDN.

VRDNs are distributed by a remarketing agent, whose principal responsibility is to find a buyer for the notes, known as remarketing the notes, when the current holder wishes to liquidate (put) them. The remarketing agent maintains the ability at various intervals—daily or weekly—to adjust the coupon rate on the bonds to ensure that the bonds are able to be sold to an investor at par. Hence, the rates on VRDNs track short-term tax-exempt rate trends very closely. Since the investor has the unconditional ability to put the notes at various intervals (such as daily, weekly, or quarterly), these long-term notes are treated as short-term instruments due to the put feature.

The following example helps to illustrate and clarify how a VRDN works:

XYZ Widget Company wishes to build a factory in New York City. It applies to the New York City Industrial Development Agency (NYC IDA) for the authorization to issue bonds through the agency at the advantaged tax-exempt interest rates. Meeting the criteria for issuance—the factory will create jobs in New York City—the NYC IDA issues the bonds on behalf of XYZ Widget Company. Because the creditworthiness of XYZ is not widely known by the investing public, a highly rated bank is engaged to provide credit support to the bonds through a direct-pay *letter of credit*. Then a broker-dealer is appointed to sell and remarket the notes to investors. During the term of the note, investors who wish to put their notes must notify the broker-dealer in advance and, if the remarketing agent is unable to resell the notes, the letter of credit will be drawn upon to repay the investor. The letter of credit also guarantees the investor against default of principal and interest.

- *The note:* New York City Industrial Development Agency (for XYZ Widget Company), maturing July 1, 2030
- *Backing of the note:* Letter of credit—AAA bank, as well as the credit of XYZ Widget Company (not the NYC IDA)
- *Interest rate:* Variable rate, adjusting weekly (every Wednesday)
- *Remarketing agent:* ABC broker-dealer
- *Notification period:* Five business days prior to the tender date

Although the actual maturity of the note in this example is 2030, the investor in effect is purchasing a weekly investment. While the stated issuer is the NYC IDA, the real backing on the bonds is the direct-pay letter-of-credit bank. The letter-of-credit bank expects to be repaid by XYZ Widget Company.

Primarily purchased by money market funds, corporations, and high-net-worth individuals, VRDNs are viewed as an alternative to tax-exempt money market funds and other short-term tax-exempt instruments due to their liquidity and credit characteristics.

MONEY MARKET FUNDS

Money market funds are the largest single category of money market investors. These funds are also known as 2a-7 funds because they are governed by the Rule 2a-7 of the Investment Company Act of 1940. Rule 2a-7 seeks to protect investors by lowering money market fund risks. To accomplish this, Rule 2a-7 requires money market funds to own:

- Only the highest credit quality debt instruments (i.e., Tier 1)
- Instruments that mature in 397 days or less

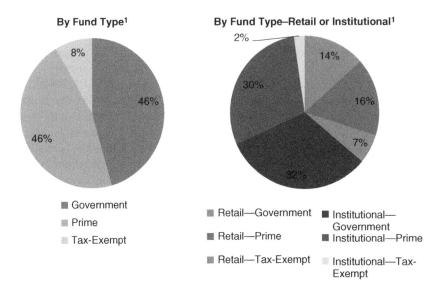

FIGURE 8.7 Two pie charts of breakdown of money market funds: three pies and six pies
[1]As of March 9, 2016. Investment Company Institute website statistics
Source: Investment Company Institute website

- A portfolio with a maximum average duration of 60 days
- No more than 5% of its total portfolio invested in any one issue (except for government securities, GSEs, and repo)

As of May 2016, money market funds held approximately $2.7 trillion of assets, comprised of $1.4 trillion of government-backed funds (primarily funds invested in U.S. government and agency securities), $1.1 trillion of prime funds (largely high-quality corporate credits as well as U.S. government and agency securities), and $200 billion of tax-exempt funds (primarily municipal credits). Whether government, prime, or tax-exempt, money market funds can be further categorized as either retail or institutional (Figure 8.7). Retail funds are sold to individuals while institutional funds are sold to institutional investors.

While government money market funds must be almost entirely invested in U.S. government securities or repurchase agreements that are fully collateralized by U.S. government securities, municipal funds are primarily invested in debt securities of state and local agencies and municipalities. Although focused on high-quality securities, prime funds invest in a broad range of products and are active participants in each of the products discussed in this chapter (Figure 8.8).

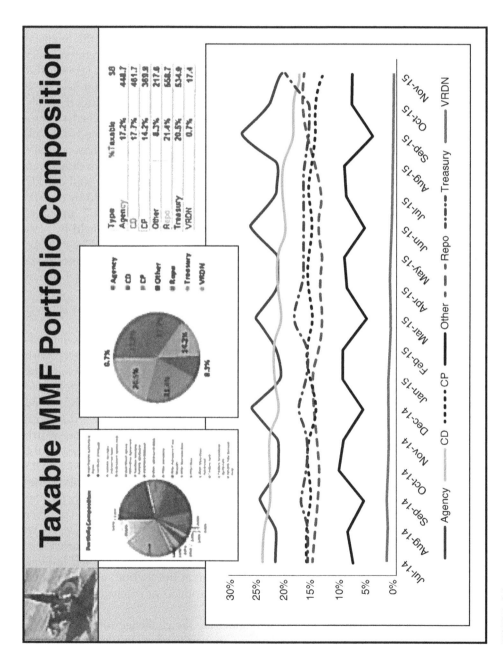

FIGURE 8.8 Pie chart of products
Source: Peter Crane presentation, p. 4

HOW THE FINANCIAL CRISIS OF 2007 AND 2008 CHANGED THE MONEY MARKETS

The Global Financial Crisis of 2007 and 2008 had a significant impact on the regulation and the subsequent market practices in the money markets. While difficulties in the non-agency mortgage-backed securities market was a primary casualty of the financial crisis, evidence of the financial crisis began to unfold in the money markets in the summer of 2007. Due to concerns about the increasing presence of impaired mortgages in ABCP programs, investors began to reduce their purchases of the ABCP vehicles that held these securities. At that time, many of these ABCP vehicles had bank liquidity facilities that only backed a small portion of their issuance. These partial-liquidity, asset-backed vehicles were referred to as structured investment vehicles (SIVs). Money market funds (as well as other domestic and foreign institutional investors) were the primary purchasers of SIV paper. Because the SIVs held highly rated securities at that time, which were thought to be highly liquid, market participants expected that these securities could be sold quickly for a price close to par. Unfortunately, the assumption that the securities held by the SIV would maintain their value and liquidity was falsely placed. In August 2007, investors increasingly concerned about the non-agency mortgage-backed securities held by SIVs stopped investing in SIVs, closing off the expected liquidity in that market. The investor pullback from SIVs in August 2007 was one of the first visible cracks in the financial system that ultimately led to failure of several financial institutions, most notably Lehman Brothers on September 15, 2008.

In some cases, governments, including the Federal Reserve, stepped in to support individual financial institutions and markets such as the repo and CP markets.

Auction rate securities (ARSs) were another product that ended up not having sufficient market liquidity. ARSs were long-term financial instruments like VRDNs (with final maturities up to 30 years) that were structured like short-term securities through the utilization of a Dutch auction process to provide the tender option for the ARS holder. Investor holding periods were typically intervals of 7, 28, 35, and 120 days. ARSs could be either auction rate preferred or straight auction rate debt. They were issued as both tax-exempt and taxable instruments. Investors such as corporations and high-net-worth individuals, seeking a higher-yielding alternative to conventional short-term investments, were the primary investors in ARS. In most cases, the assets that were funded in ARS were of good quality, for example, student loans or long-term municipal bonds. However, when investors feared that the ARS Dutch auction process would potentially fail and not provide them with an opportunity to turn their investment into cash, given the other constrictions of the markets at the onset of the financial crisis, the ARS product ceased to be a viable market and that market seized up much in the way that the SIV market did. As a result, almost all of the institutional investors in these securities were left holding ARSs (as there were no other purchasers to take them out at the auction) until they were either refinanced by their issuers using other financing products or reached maturity and paid off.

The importance of liquidity was also highlighted by the challenges of several large commercial and investment banks and one large money market mutual fund in late

2008. It was the practice at the time for the largest commercial and investment banks to raise a significant portion of their funding in the institutional money markets. These large commercial and investment banks used very short-dated instruments such as repo, institutional CDs, and commercial paper to fund a significant portion of their balance sheets. These financial institutions were largely funded by large institutional investors, including money market funds and other financial institutions. When investors became increasing concerned about the credit quality of the large commercial and investment banks, they began to shorten maturities and reduce their exposures to these financial instruments. This lack of confidence became self-fulfilling. On September 15, 2008, the large investment bank, Lehman Brothers, could not meet its maturing debt obligations and, as a result of its lenders refusing to roll over Lehman's obligations, filed for bankruptcy. Similar to the investors in SIVs and ARS, the investors in Lehman had lost confidence that Lehman would be able to continue to fund itself due to concerns about its asset quality. When investors stopped investing in Lehman's debt, Lehman was not able to convert its assets into cash quickly enough to pay off its obligations, leading to its demise.

The failure of Lehman had a domino effect on the markets and other financial institutions. Short-term investors had lost confidence in the markets and wanted to make sure that they were not exposed to another potential failure so they converted much of their portfolio holdings to cash and government securities. One large money fund with $65 billion of assets, the Reserve Primary Fund, was caught holding $785 million of Lehman Brothers CP, thereby causing the value of the fund's assets to fall below par and creating a crisis of confidence for the Reserve's investors. All money market funds are regulated under the Securities and Exchange Commission's Rule 2-a7, which was designed to ensure that a money fund's portfolio be managed to maintain a *constant net asset value* of 100 cents on the dollar, or par. If a fund's assets became worth less than par, its assets would no longer be sufficient to return all of the money to investors at par.

When a money market mutual fund finds itself in the position that a drop in its asset value prevents it from repaying its investors at par, it is referred to as breaking the buck. The term *breaking the buck*, comes from the idea that money market fund investors expect to receive a dollar (plus a dividend) back for each dollar they invest. When a fund realizes that it does not have enough in net asset value to repay investors at par, it must place a moratorium on investor withdrawals to allow for an orderly liquidation of the fund. In September 2008, the Reserve Primary Fund had to halt investor withdrawals when it realized that its assets were insufficient to allow the funds to be returned at par, largely due to the Lehman failure. While no other money market fund broke the buck at the time, investors in other funds became concerned that their funds could also be holding assets that were not worth par. And as investors withdrew their money from other money market funds, each of those funds had to sell assets in order to meet investors' liquidity demands, which had a cascading effect on market liquidity.

The widespread rush of investors, particularly institutional money fund investors, to liquidate their holdings and withdraw funds out of money market funds created a related issue. Investor withdrawals caused money market funds to have to rush to liquidate their assets at the same time. With the largest class of money market investors all selling assets at the same time, and therefore an insufficient number of large investors willing to buy, values of the assets being liquidated deteriorated rapidly across all asset classes. Deteriorating asset values, which were in part caused by mass money market fund liquidations, increased the risk that other funds would break the buck. As more investors began to pull their investments, the U.S. Treasury acted quickly to provide market liquidity and also provided a temporary guarantee of all eligible 2a-7. In order to participate in the program, eligible funds had to apply and pay a fee. This action slowly turned the tide and restored investor confidence in money funds. With a U.S. government guarantee, investors became comfortable that they would be able to get their money back and investors no longer felt the need to liquidate their money funds and a more serious run on money funds was averted.

The U.S. Treasury's guarantee of money market funds was temporary. But the potential for an all-out run on the money market funds caused the U.S. Treasury and SEC to conclude that the 2a-7 rules that govern money market funds needed to be stricter in order to make money funds more stable during future periods of market stress. In 2010, the SEC implemented extensive rules that required money market funds to maintain a higher percentage of their assets in more liquid securities and hold a smaller percentage of Tier 2, or lower-rated, securities.

Rule 2a-7 was further amended (effective in October 2016) to require institutional prime and municipal money market funds to be deemed as *variable or floating net asset value* instead of guaranteeing a *constant (par) net asset value*. The SEC believed that if investors were accustomed to seeing the net asset value of their fund float with market value changes in the fund's assets, albeit with potentially limited variability in price, those investors would be less susceptible to withdrawing money out of money market funds in times of market stress. Because the SEC determined that retail prime or municipal money market funds were less prone to mass investor withdrawals than institutional prime or municipal money funds, the amendments would allow retail funds to continue to offer a constant net asset value. Other important provisions of the SEC's Money Market Fund Reform now require that institutional prime money funds have the ability to charge investors a fee for withdrawing money from a fund in a time of market disruption. The rules also provide for "gates," which allow a fund to hold back all or a portion of investors' funds during a time of a market crisis.

As we have seen, the Global Financial Crisis of 2007 and 2008 had a significant impact on how banks and other financial institutions managed their short-term funding and investing. Banks were overly reliant on short-term funding in their use of short-dated CDs, CP, and the repo market. In September 2008, when short-term investors began to reduce their exposure to financial institutions, there were many large institutions that became concerned about their ability to continue to fund themselves. Like the investors in money market funds, investors in bank instruments also became concerned that their investments were at risk and began to limit their exposures. The U.S. Treasury, the Federal Reserve, and other federal governmental entities quickly established numerous programs designed to give investors confidence that banks would be able to repay their short-term obligations. While these temporary emergency measures successfully prevented other major bank failures after Lehman Brothers, global banking regulators began to revise the entire bank regulatory framework to reduce the risk of bank failures in the future. While many of the new regulations, such as the Dodd-Frank Act, increased the amount of capital that banks were required to hold, other regulations limit the maximum percentage of short-term borrowings a bank could have as well as other liquidity management practices for banks.

CONCLUSION

The Global Financial Crisis of 2007 and 2008 profoundly changed much of how the money markets function. In its aftermath, several money market products disappeared and regulations governing money market products became more stringent. The reforms also served to shrink the scope of the money markets by penalizing the leveraging of assets and consolidating the number of money market funds. However, these changes in the market and its practices have ultimately made the money markets more resilient and presumably better positioned to withstand future market stresses. The U.S. money markets are still central in providing corporations, financial institutions, and governmental entities with a needed source of short-term funding while also providing investors with a liquid and relatively safe place to invest their cash with a fair market rate of return. As such, short-term money market products and the money markets as a whole are critical cornerstones to the smooth functioning of the U.S capital markets and the entire global economy. The money markets are the oil in the gears of our economic engine.

CHAPTER 9

Repurchase Agreements

Karl Schultz and Jeffrey Bockian

INTRODUCTION

A *repurchase agreement* is a financing transaction executed when a holder of securities sells them to an investor and simultaneously agrees to repurchase them at the same dollar price on a specified future date. The difference between the sale price and the subsequent repurchase price represents interest over the period. In effect the seller of the securities is borrowing funds from the buyer and repaying the loan when the securities are repurchased. The term *repo* is used to describe the transaction from the perspective of the borrower or seller of the securities. The lender of the funds or purchaser of the securities initially is engaging in a reverse repurchase agreement (reverse repo). Repo transactions can alternatively be viewed as the economic equivalent of secured loans, where the seller of the securities is in effect borrowing funds from the buyer and pledging the securities as collateral. However, despite some economic similarities, repurchase agreements differ from secured loans as repos feature title transfer of collateral from the seller to the buyer. In contrast, a secured loan typically operates under a pledge structure in which the borrower retains ownership of the securities upon which the lender retains a lien. Another key difference between repos and secured loans is that repos are generally exempt from stay under the bankruptcy code. That means in an event of default, such as the failure of the seller to repurchase the collateral on the repurchase date, the buyer may endeavor to sell the collateral to recoup the monies owed without having to wait for permission of the bankruptcy court.

The rights and other obligations of buyers and sellers are usually detailed in a governing legal document called a *master repurchase agreement* (MRA).[1] A single properly

---

[1] In the United States, the standard agreement used is the Securities Industry and Financial Markets Association's (SIFMA) Master Repurchase Agreement, which is based on New York law. Global counterparties often use SIFMA's Global Master Repurchase Agreement (GMRA), which is based on English law. See SIFMA for more details on documentation: Securities Industry and Financial Markets Association, Master Repurchase Agreement, http://www.sifma.org/services/standard-forms-and-documentation/mra,-gmra,-msla-and-msftas/.

executed MRA may be used to govern any number of transactions between a buyer and a seller and allows bespoke terms and conditions, including the security descriptions, purchase and repurchase prices, and transaction dates, all of which are required to be evidenced in written confirmations between the parties. Together, the MRA and confirmations constitute conclusive evidence of the agreed terms between the buyer and seller unless specific objection is communicated promptly after receipt of the confirmation.

In a repo agreement the two participants engaging in the transaction are known as *counterparties*. The securities and other assets underlying the transaction are called the *collateral*. On the *settlement date*, the selling counterparty will deliver securities to the buying counterparty, who in turn will deliver cash proceeds to the seller. The cash proceeds delivered at settlement are called the *repo principal*. The *repo rate* is the interest rate charged and used to determine the cash proceeds due back to the buyer on the *repurchase date*, also known as the *maturity date*. On this date, an unwind process occurs in which the seller returns the cash proceeds with accrued interest and the buyer returns the collateral.

Repo trade tenors represent the length of time between the start and maturity of repo transactions and tend to be short term, but the bespoke nature of repo transactions allows deals to be structured for almost any tenor. Trades structured to mature in one business day are referred to as *overnight repos*. Trades structured with fixed tenors of more than one day are known as *term repos*. Term trades of one week to one year are the most common, but longer terms are quite possible. Alternatively, counterparties might not establish a predetermined maturity date for a repo transaction. This type of transaction is terminable *on demand*, and is often referred to as being placed *on open*. When a trade is on open, on a daily basis the counterparties may agree to extend the maturity an additional day or allow the trade to mature. Trades placed on open allow counterparties to transact in a series of overnight repos without incurring the costs and risks associated with delivering securities back and forth.

An additional nuance with term repo trades involves the periodic income distributions on the underlying collateral, including coupon payments, bond amortization payments, and dividends. Typically the MRA dictates that these payments will be remitted to the seller as though the repo transaction had not occurred. These payments normally decrease the value of a security, as in the case of amortizing bonds, and will require additional collateral be posted to maintain the loan-to-collateral value ratio.

MECHANICS OF A REPO TRADE

To illustrate the mechanics of a repo transaction, suppose a hedge fund owns $10 million par of U.S. Treasury securities (T)2.50 2/15/2046, and would like to use this security as collateral to obtain repo financing from March 10 to March 29. A repo dealer quotes a repo rate of 53 basis points, which the hedge fund accepts.

On the settlement date of March 10, the two counterparties will agree on the current market price of the bond and use it to calculate the repo's principal value. Assume on

March 10, the security has a price without accrued interest of 95.625. To calculate the purchase price or repo principal,

Purchase Price or Repo Principal = [Notional Amount or Par Value] × Market Price

or

$$\$9,562,500 = \$10,000,000 \times 0.95625$$

As the seller, the hedge fund will deliver $10 million par value of T 2.50 2/15/2046 to the repo dealer, who, as buyer, will deliver cash proceeds of $9,562,500 to the hedge fund.

On the maturity date of March 29, the trade will unwind. The repo dealer will return the collateral and the hedge fund will deliver the original proceeds plus accrued interest to the dealer. To calculate the repo interest, or price differential:

Price Differential = Repo Principal or Purchase Price × Repo Rate × (# days/360)

or

$$\$2,674.84 = \$9,562,500 \times .0053 \times 19/360$$

The repurchase price the hedge fund owes to the dealer is therefore

$$\$9,565,174.84 = \$9,562,500 + \$2,674.84$$

An important aspect of calculating interest is the day-count convention. U.S. dollar–denominated repo transactions, like other dollar-denominated money market instruments, follow an actual number of days/360 day-count convention rather than a 30/360 day count. Day-count calculations normally follow the standards and practices based on the currency underlying the transaction. For example, while USD repos follow an actual/360 approach, British pound sterling and Canadian dollar transactions use an actual/365 convention.

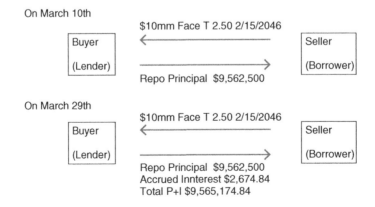

FIGURE 9.1 REPO Trade Example

MARGINING TRADES

A key risk to the buyer in a repo trade is the potential for the value of the collateral to decline substantially in a short period of time. For example, a buyer could make a $100 million loan collateralized by $100 million worth of bonds. If the value of the bonds decreased by 10% before the maturity of the trade and the seller defaulted, the buyer would not be able to sell the collateral in the market at a price high enough to recover the purchase price.

To protect themselves, buyers often require repo transactions to be margined. *Margin*, commonly known as the *haircut*, involves the seller providing collateral valued greater than the cash proceeds. Collateral underlying a trade is marked to market on a daily basis. Shortfalls can result in a margin call, which are met with the delivery of cash or additional collateral. This helps ensure that in the event of a seller default, the buyer holds ample collateral that can be sold at prevailing market prices to recoup the original repo principal.

Margin is typically quoted as a percentage applied to the collateral. The margin percentage is set based on several factors: credit quality, volatility, and liquidity of the underlying collateral. Lower-quality, highly volatile, illiquid securities will be subject to the largest haircuts while haircuts on high-quality, less volatile, highly liquid securities will be far less. For example, agency pass-through mortgage-backed securities, such as Fannie Mae or Freddie Mac issues, might require a 5% haircut while riskier mortgages such as private-label whole loan collateralized mortgage obligations (CMOs) might require more than a 10% haircut. Trade tenor can also factor into the margin rate, with longer maturities requiring higher haircuts. Additionally, the credit rating of the selling counterparty might affect margin rates. All things being equal, a buyer might require more margin from a highly leveraged hedge fund than from a highly rated, well-capitalized bank.

Calculating Repo Principal with Margin

As previously mentioned, required margin on a trade is quoted as a percentage that is applied to the collateral. Margin therefore adds a new dimension to calculating repo principal. Two approaches can be used in practice. The *additive* approach adds the margin percentage to collateral required against repo principal. The *subtractive* approach subtracts the margin percentage from the collateral value to obtain repo principal.

Additive Approach

The additive approach is the industry convention and preferred method among repo market practitioners. This approach adds the quoted margin percentage to a 100% value of the collateral to determine the total market value of securities required for given repo principal. For example, if a buyer requires a 5% haircut on a trade, a seller will need to provide collateral worth 105% of the repo principal. Alternatively, a buyer who demands a 7% haircut would need the seller to deliver securities worth 107% of the value of the repo principal.

$$\text{Market Value of Required Collateral} = \text{Repo Principal} \times (1 + \text{Margin Rate})$$

where

$$\text{Market Value} = \text{Par} \times \text{Market Price}$$

or for mortgages,

$$\text{Market Value} = \text{Original Face} \times \text{Mortgage Factor} \times \text{Market Price}$$

When a trade does not require margin (i.e., has a margin rate of 0%, the repo), principal is equal to 100% of the market value of the collateral.

To demonstrate, suppose an investor wanted to obtain $50 million of financing using the agency debenture FNMA 1.125 10/29/18 with a market price of 99 ½ as collateral. The buyer requires a 2% haircut. Using equation (1) to determine how much of this bond is needed yields:

$$\text{Par} \times .9950 = \$50,000,000 \times (1 + .02)$$

$$\text{Par} \times .9950 = \$50,000,000 \times 1.02$$

$$\text{Par} \times .9950 = \$51,000,000$$

$$\text{Par} = \$51,000,000/.9950$$

$$= \$51,256,281.41 \text{ or } \$51,257,000 \text{ rounded to the nearest } 1,000$$

To generate repo principal of $50 million against this issue, a buyer would require the seller to deliver $51,257,000 par to properly collateralize the repo transaction.

The previous example showed how much of a given security would need to be delivered to meet a specific repo principal. Now suppose an investor owns a bond and would like to know how much repo principal would be generated by financing the entire position. This equation can be rearranged algebraically to determine the repo principal using a given amount of a security as collateral by

$$\text{Repo Principal} = \frac{\text{Par} \times \text{Market Price}}{(1 + \text{Margin Rate})}$$

For example, suppose the investor owned $25 million par of the FNMA 1.125 10/29/18 from the previous example, again with a market price of 99 ½. The buyer now requires a 5% haircut. Using this equation the investor can determine the repo principal attainable using this agency debenture as collateral. Specifically,

$$\text{Repo Principal} = \frac{\$25,000,000 \times 99.50}{(1 + .05)}$$

$$\text{Repo Principal} = \$24,875,000/1.05$$

$$= \$23,690,476 \text{ or } \$23,690,000 \text{ rounded to the nearest } 1,000$$

Subtractive Approach

Occasionally, market participants subtract the margin percentage from the collateral value to obtain the repo principal. For example, if the haircut is 5%, the loan will be for 95% of the collateral's market value.

$$\text{Repo Principal} = \text{Market Value} \times (1 - \text{Margin Rate})$$

where

$$\text{Market Value} = \text{Par} \times \text{Market Price}$$

or for mortgages,

$$\text{Market Value} = \text{Original Face} \times \text{Mortgage Factor} \times \text{Market Price}$$

For example, if an investor wanted to use $50 million face of a bond priced at 100, and the haircut was 2%, these bonds would support a repo principal of

$$\text{Repo Principal} = \$50,000,000 \times 1.00 \times (1 - .02) = \$49,000,000$$

The appeal of this method is its simplicity. However, as stated earlier the market convention is to use the additive approach. An additional consideration is that each approach results in a different repo principal. All things being equal, sellers will get greater leverage using the additive approach. Using the previous collateral example of the FNMA 1.125 10/29/18 with a market price of 99½, we saw that the repo principal of $50 million required $51,257,000 in par with a 2% margin rate. If the subtractive approach is applied, the same par amount of securities would yield repo principal of $49,980,700:

$$\text{Repo Principal} = \$51,257,000 \times .995 \times (1 - .02) = \$49,980,700$$

This is almost $20,000 less than the result obtained from the previous method. In fact, to obtain repo principal of $50 million desired in the first example would require $51,277,000 in par. Table 9.1 displays the different outcomes of the two approaches using a 5% margin rate and bond prices at premiums, par, and discounts. In each case the repo principal is greater using the additive approach.

MARKET PARTICIPANTS

While repo market participants may have unique needs, they can generally be grouped into several categories: natural buyers (cash providers), natural sellers (cash users), those who both buy and sell, those focusing on specials trading (providing and sourcing specific securities), and finally, the Federal Reserve, which will be discussed in a later section.

TABLE 9.1 Different Outcomes of the Subtractive and Additive Approaches

Subtractive Approach			
Par	100,000,000	100,000,000	100,000,000
Price	99.00	100.00	101.00
5% Margin	0.95	0.95	0.95
Loan	94,050,000	95,000,000	95,950,000
Additive Approach			
Par	100,000,000	100,000,000	100,000,000
Price	99.00	100.00	101.00
5% Margin	1.05	1.05	1.05
Loan	94,285,714.29	95,238,095.24	96,190,476.19
Difference	**235,714.29**	**238,095.24**	**240,476.19**

Natural buyers include a wide range of cash-rich investors with short-term investment horizons and low risk tolerances. Such investors are willing to accept relatively low yields compared to other money market instruments to obtain the additional safety provided by repo collateral. Natural buyers include money market funds, asset managers, pension funds, insurance companies, government-sponsored entities (GSEs), corporations, and municipalities. For example, the maximum weighted average portfolio life for a money market fund is currently 60 days.[2] Short-term instruments such as repos are often a natural fit.

While natural buyers use repos as a safe place to invest cash on a short-term basis, natural sellers use repos to achieve low-cost funding. By providing collateral and executing repos with short tenors, sellers often achieve favorable financing costs compared to longer-term and unsecured financing alternatives. Natural sellers include hedge funds, asset managers, and real estate investment trusts (REITs). Such investors often employ financial leverage to increase portfolio returns and repo markets often provide such leverage. Conversely, natural buyers such as money market mutual funds and corporate treasurers utilize the repo market to maximize their return on short-term cash.

Financial intermediaries, particularly securities broker-dealers, often engage as both sellers and buyers in the repo markets. For example, a broker-dealer may use repos to obtain low-cost financing for its securities inventory and to fund its operations. At the same time, broker-dealers may perform reverse repos as a way of providing clients

---

[2]See Securities and Exchange Commission Money Market Fund Reform, Final Rule 2010 and Final Rule 2014, for more details related to limitations placed on money market funds. See Securities and Exchange Commission Money Market Fund Reform, Final Rule 2010 (https://www.sec.gov/rules/final/2010/ic-29132.pdf) and Securities and Exchange Commission Money Market Fund Reform, Final Rule 2014 (https://www.sec.gov/rules/final/2014/33-9616.pdf).

financing for securities purchases. To obtain the financing needed to make these loans, the broker-dealer will simultaneously use the collateral obtained in reverse repo transaction as collateral on a new repo trade. This is known as running a matched book. Similar to broker-dealers, large banks will engage in both lending and borrowing in the repo markets (and often through the banks' own securities dealer). Eager for revenues, a bank will provide financing as a client service. At the same time, that bank may be borrowing in the repo markets as a tool to manage its own internal liquidity.

While it is intuitive to understand the borrowing and lending of securities to manage cash requirements, market participants also access the repo markets to borrow securities to meet specific needs. The most basic of these needs is borrowing specific securities to cover shorts. Traders often sell securities they do not own for a multitude of reasons. For example a trader may expect the price of a bond to go down and therefore sells it with the intention of buying it back when the price decrease materializes. A market maker may be short because of customer orders. A corporate bond trader may short a benchmark Treasury to hedge the interest rate risk associated with a long corporate bond position. Similarly, a swap dealer may short a Treasury bond to hedge a swap position. Regardless of the reason for the short, the ultimate purchaser on the other side of the trade expects delivery. The repo market provides a deep, highly liquid venue for traders to cover short positions. A detailed discussion follows in a later section, "General Collateral and Specials."

RISKS ASSOCIATED WITH REPO TRANSACTIONS

There is a common misperception that because repo transactions are collateralized, they are considered risk free. Although collateral provided by the seller mitigates risk to the buyer, it does not entirely eliminate it. A broad understanding of risks inherent in repo trades as well as tools available to reduce the risks is therefore essential.

Counterparty Risk

In repo transactions, both participants are exposed to one another's counterparty risk.[3] For instance, suppose that between the inception of a transaction and its maturity the seller experiences financial difficulties and is unable to repay the repurchase price. To be made whole, that buyer could sell the collateral in the open market. However, what if the value of the collateral declined beyond the margin level of the trade? The proceeds of the sale of the collateral would be less than the principal amount and the buyer would be exposed to a loss. From a seller's perspective, suppose the buyer defaults. While the seller has received the defaulting counterparty's cash, a loss exposure exists if the market value of the collateral, including the margin securities, is greater than the trade's principal. Several market conventions exist to mitigate such credit risk exposures.

---

[3]Counterparty risk is also referred to as credit risk.

As discussed earlier, the most common protection demanded by cash providers is that collateral underlying a trade be worth more than the principal amount. As discussed earlier, the additional collateral is known as *margin* and is based on a *haircut percentage,* or simply haircut on a trade. The amount of margin required can range from less than 1% to higher than 50% depending on the quality of the collateral, the tenor of the transaction, the creditworthiness of the borrower, and general economic conditions.

A second protection against counterparty risk used with term trades is margin maintenance activities, which typically feature daily mark-to-market (MTM) of the underlying securities. As valuations decline, a purchaser can require the seller to deliver additional collateral. As valuations increase, sellers may request return of excess collateral to ensure trades are not over-collateralized. The daily margin maintenance process protects both counterparties and ensures the proper balance between the collateral required and the principal balance.

Finally, initial and ongoing counterparty due diligence and credit analysis and the establishment of credit exposure limits are essential in mitigating counterparty risks. Many large participants in repo markets, such as broker-dealers and asset managers, will have a dedicated department responsible for conducting these analyses. In-depth reviews of financial statements, current leverage usage, and portfolio construction among other factors will lead to decisions about counterparty exposure limits. Overall, limits on total financial exposure, acceptable collateral, maximum tenors, and margin requirements can be set to mitigate credit exposure.

Liquidity Risk

A key risk in repo markets, one terribly underestimated by market participants leading into the financial crisis of 2008, is liquidity risk. Essentially, this is the risk that existing short-term financings will not be renewed by lenders and replacement sources of financing will become unavailable. This may occur during periods when short-term funding is critically needed, resulting in a period of increased stress for the borrower. Liquidity risk arises from financing long-term assets using short-term liquidity, where repos need to be rolled into a new transaction. The inherent risk is that the seller may not be able to find a counterparty willing to execute a new repo transaction. For example, an investor owns a bond that is rated BBB and engages in an overnight repo transaction with a large commercial bank. The bond is downgraded to BB and the commercial bank does not want to provide financing (roll over the repo) for this now non-investment-grade bond. The investor would now have to find a new counterparty to provide financing for the downgraded bond. If one does not materialize, the investor may be forced to sell that asset in a stressed market at a fire-sale price.[4] Now consider if multiple creditors feared that a particular borrower's liquidity was disappearing. Collectively they may begin to refuse to renew repo trades, further exacerbating the stress.

---

[4]A fire sale refers to a sale of assets at low prices.

The speed at which short-term liquidity can disappear became very apparent during the financial crisis; thus new regulations from Dodd-Frank to Basel III have impacted both the buyers and sellers of repo securities.[5] These regulations sought to address this risk through channels such as increased capital requirements intended to limit banks' overall leverage to sellers of these securities. Additionally, a pillar of the Basel III initiatives is the *net stable funding ratio* (NSFR), the intention of which is to reduce banks' reliance on short-term funding, notably repo, in favor of longer term debt.[6] While these affect sellers, money fund reforms mandated by the Securities and Exchange Commission target the buyers by requiring shorter maturities and limiting exposure to lower rated credit.[7] These reforms cumulatively reduce leverage in the system, thereby lowering the risk of contagion in periods of shrinking liquidity.

Interest Rate Risk

Inherent in all fixed-income trading, including repo transactions, is the risk stemming from movements in interest rates. This is called interest rate risk, and impacts the repo markets from several angles. When the markets are in a rising rate environment, those who borrow cash are exposed to higher borrowing costs each time a financing trade matures and is rolled into a new financing trade. If the longer-term asset used as collateral in a repo transaction earns a fixed rate, these successive increases in finance costs quickly reduce the carry earned on the asset. If the short-term interest rates rise above the yield earned on the long-term asset, that investor is exposed to negative carry on the position. From the perspective of the buyer who enters a term reverse repo, if market interest rates rise faster than the buyer anticipated, the buyer risks holding a portfolio of reverse repo transactions yielding less than prevailing market rates. This represents missed opportunities.

A declining interest rate environment also affects participants. Buyers are exposed to decreasing margins. As short-term repo transactions mature, these buyers can only replace them by entering new repo trades at the new lower yields. For sellers who use term repos, if interest rates decline faster than expected, the sellers may find themselves committed to paying higher yields than the prevailing market rates.

Interest rates also have a significant impact on values of the underlying collateral. For example, if a portfolio of bonds collateralizes a repo trade and interest rates were to suddenly rise, those bonds can be expected to decline in price. Depending on the

---

[5]Basel Committee on Banking Supervision, "Basel III: A Global Regulatory Framework for More Resilient Banks and Banking Systems," December 2010 (http://www.bis.org/publ/bcbs189.pdf); "The Liquidity Coverage Ratio and Liquidity Risk Monitoring Tools," January 2013 (http://www.bis.org/publ/bcbs238.pdf); and "The Net Stable Funding Ratio," October 2014 (http://www.bis.org/bcbs/publ/d295.pdf).

[6]For a detailed discussion of the net stable funding ratio, please refer to the Basel Committee on Banking Supervision's "Basel III: The Net Stable Funding Ratio."

[7]For a detailed discussion on money market reform, please refer to the Securities and Exchange Commission's Money Market Fund Reform Final Rule 2010 and Final Rule 2014.

duration of those bonds, the price decline could trigger margin calls and require additional collateral to be posted. This reduces the amount of potential collateral available for further leveraging.

Market participants have several tools to mitigate these risks. A highly liquid and customizable option is overnight indexed swaps (OIS). These swaps, with the floating leg tied to an overnight index, such as effective fed funds rates, allow users to convert short-term transactions to either a fixed or floating rate. Other options include fed funds and Eurodollar futures contracts, options on these contracts, and forward rate agreements (FRAs).

DELIVERY CONVENTIONS

An additional facet of a repo transaction involves the delivery method of the cash and collateral. The distinction between delivery methods divides the repo market into two broad segments: the bilateral repo market and the tri-party repo market.

Bilateral Repo

In a *bilateral repo*, typically referred to as *delivery versus payment* (DVP), the counterparty selling the collateral will deliver the physical securities to the buyer's account in exchange for the buyer wiring the cash proceeds to the seller's account. A key reason for collateral buyers to transact bilaterally is gaining control of the collateral. Intuitively, access to the collateral is a powerful protection in the event of default. However, a more common motivation is the buyer's ability to use the collateral. Rights granted to the buyer in the master repurchase agreement typically include the ability to sell, transfer, and rehypothecate securities. The right to reuse or pledge collateral to a third party, known as *rehypothecation*, is an important aspect of bilateral repo. An obligation still exists to return the securities at the maturity of the repurchase agreement, but prior to maturity those securities may be used for a range of purposes. For example, a security bought in repo may be used to cover a short sale. Alternatively, the buyer of a security could in turn sell that security to another counterparty in a second repo transaction to raise new liquidity. In fact, dealers running matched books often buy collateral in a reverse repo from a client and then use that same collateral in a repo to finance the loan to the client, earning a spread between where it buys and sells.

There are implications of bilateral transactions, however, notably transaction costs, operational considerations, and operational risk. Since collateral is delivered back and forth between buyers and sellers, often daily, participants must pay transactional costs associated with making these deliveries.

Operational considerations also exist. For example, both counterparties need the ability to properly price collateral to ensure the collateral value accurately reflects the repo principal. For term repos, both counterparties need to be able to conduct a daily mark to market and issue margin calls. Bilateral repos are operationally intensive and most often done with a *cash settlement*,[8] meaning repo principal and collateral deliveries occur on the same day as the transaction date. This imposes extremely tight timeframes to complete all necessary operational steps, such as pricing collateral and calculating repo principal.

Furthermore, operational risk exists. If for any reason a delivery in either direction is not made, it is known as a *fail*. If the seller of the collateral fails to deliver the securities to the buyer, the buyer will not deliver the repo principal. Although the seller did not receive the repo principal, the seller is still committed to paying the price differential. Economically, this may be viewed as paying interest on a loan without receiving the loan proceeds. If the repo matures, but the buyer fails to return the collateral to the seller, the seller will not return the repo principal and price differential. Those proceeds will be available for overnight investment by the seller, and the buyer will lose the opportunity to invest that cash for a day.

Tri-Party Repo

A second segment of the repo market, and one used heavily by the broker-dealer community to finance inventories, is tri-party repo. As its name suggests, three parties are involved (Figure 9.2). The first two are the buying and selling counterparties, while the

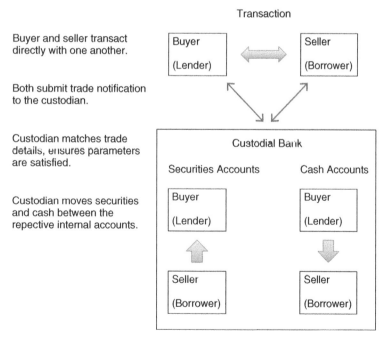

FIGURE 9.2 Tri-party flows

---

[8]Cash settlement is also called *same-day settlement*.

third party, which is typically a large clearing bank,[9] acts as a custodian on their behalf. In a bilateral repo, actual delivery of cash and securities is made between the buyer and seller. In a tri-party trade, the counterparties maintain custodial cash and securities accounts at the clearing bank. Rather than make the physical delivery of cash and securities to each other, the cash and securities remain under the custody of the clearing bank, which upon matching instructions from the buyer and seller makes internal transfers between the respective accounts of the two counterparties.

Tri-party repo offers several advantages to participants. To begin, the custodian offers a layer of protection to both counterparties while providing a range of services. Clearing banks involved as custodians typically have the infrastructure in place to gain operational efficiencies. Services provided include collateral pricing, calculating daily markings to market, margining trades, and ensuring collateral posted meets the guidelines stated the master repurchase agreement's collateral schedule.[10] A key advantage stemming from the clearing bank's infrastructure is the ability for sellers to use smaller denominations as collateral on a trade. For example, if a dealer held $100 million in bonds, but in issue sizes of $1 million, bilateral repo would be operationally challenging, especially for overnight repos. Each bond would need to be priced to calculate repo principal before 100 individual bonds could be delivered. But using a tri-party trade, this issue is trivial since the clearing bank is able to quickly price the securities, calculate principal, and allocate collateral within the trade parameters. Another advantage of tri-party repo is that instead of actual delivery, an internal journal entry on the books of the clearing bank is made. Since physical deliveries of securities are not made in a tri-party trade, transactions costs are lower than in a bilateral repo. Furthermore, the risk of failing to deliver is eliminated since collateral remains with the custodian.

In addition to standard tri-party, a second tri-party product is available to participants in the inter-dealer broker market called *general collateral finance* (GCF) repo. The GCF service is operated by the Fixed Income Clearing Corporation (FICC),[11] which guarantees settlement of trades upon notification. Unlike a standard tri-party where the buyer and seller are known to one another, GCF trades anonymously, or blind. Further, collateral types are restricted to securities that settle on the Fedwire Securities Service,

---

[9]Almost all domestic tri-party activity is done using BNY Mellon or JP Morgan Chase. For more see Adam Copeland, Darrell Duffie, Antoine Martin, and Susan McLaughlin, "Key Mechanics of the U.S. Tri-Party Repo Market," FRBNY Economic Policy review, https://www.newyorkfed .org/medialibrary/media/research/epr/2012/1210cope.pdf; see also Kenneth D. Garbade, Frank M. Keane, Lorie Logan, Amanda Stokes, and Jennifer Wolgemuth, "The Introduction of the TMPG Fails Charge for U.S. Treasury Securities," FRBNY Economic Policy Review, October 2010, https:// www.newyorkfed.org/medialibrary/media/research/epr/10v16n2/1010garb.pdf.

[10]Embedded in the master repurchase agreement and tri-party agreement is a document called the *collateral schedule*. The collateral schedule details the parameters for acceptable collateral as well as margin requirements for each collateral asset type.

[11]FICC is a subsidiary of DTCC that provides trade-matching clearing, risk management, and netting for a range of government and government agency securities, including repurchase agreements. For more information visit the FICC page at http://www.dtcc.com.

and each asset class trades using a unique CUSIP. A key advantage of GCF is the ability to net trades. For example, a dealer could sell $1 billion in Treasury GCF in the morning and repurchase $750 million Treasury GCF in the afternoon. The positions would net, leaving the dealer with an exposure of $250 million in Treasury GCF. This allows dealers flexibility in managing their positions.

GENERAL COLLATERAL AND SPECIALS

The repo markets play a unique and crucial role in the U.S. Treasury market, providing not only a way to finance positions, but a way for investors and traders to obtain specific Treasury issues. Often, counterparties engage in a transaction to be collateralized by Treasuries where both the buyer and seller are more interested in the asset class as opposed to specific issues. In this case, the counterparties are said to be trading *general collateral* (GC). Market participants frequently use the term *GC rate* when referring to financing rate for Treasury securities. GC refers to any Treasury bond, note, or bill, but excludes TIPS and STRIPS. Further, participants can deal in "under-ten" GC, meaning any Treasury with a maturity of less than ten years remaining.[12] The reason for the distinction is that bilateral trades are done in par values as opposed to market values. Since long-term bonds can trade at large premiums, it is possible for a seller to deliver a bond worth well beyond what the buyer was expecting. Imagine a trade for $1 billion and the seller delivers a bond with a price of 145-00. The loan would be for $1.45 billion when the expectation was for $1 billion in loan proceeds. Additionally, some tri-party schedules place higher margin rates on longer-duration bonds. Buying a bond to put in a tri-party could require the buyer to post more collateral than received in the bilateral trade if there is a margin mismatch.

An active market also exists for the borrowing and lending of specific Treasury issues. Traders will often sell bonds they do not own, which is known as shorting a bond. Delivery of the bond to the end buyer is still expected, and the U.S. Treasury imposes a steep penalty fee on sellers who fail to deliver bonds to buyers as a way of ensuring a sound and functioning Treasury market.[13] Traders that need a specific issue are often willing to lend cash at below-market rates in order to obtain the desired bond. That bond develops a scarcity value. When this happens, the bond is said to *trade special*, called *on special* or simply *special*. Rates in the specials market are highly dependent on the supply-and-demand dynamics for a particular issue, and can range from a couple of basis points below the GC rate to several percentage points below the GC rate. Demand for a particular bond might cause that bond to trade at negative rates in the specials market, meaning buyers will pay the seller simply to obtain that specific issue. It is important to understand that the more special a bond, the lower the repo rate for that bond since

---

[12] Market participants can also trade in under five year, under one year, and Treasury bill collateral, although the market preference is for under ten year.

[13] See Garbade et al. for a greater discussion of the U.S. Treasury's TMPG fail charge.

from an economic viewpoint the buying counterparty is willing to provide financing at lower rates to obtain the special bond.

The most heavily traded issues in the specials market tend to be the current on-the-run benchmarks and the most recent off-the-run issues.[14] Traders and investors often prefer these benchmarks for their liquidity and duration characteristics. These issues are shorted for a number of reasons. For example, a corporate bond trader might short benchmark Treasuries to hedge interest rate risk of the trading book. A corporate Treasury might short a bond ahead of a debt issuance to lock in a rate. An asset manager might short a particular benchmark Treasury to change the duration of a fixed-income portfolio. In each of these cases, the short position will need to be borrowed.

The supply and demand of a special will affect the rate. Benchmark issues often follow the Treasuries auction cycle, with specialness increasing over time. This is because with the passage of time, the benchmark issues slowly become part of longer-term portfolios that may not necessarily be willing to lend the bond. This decreases the supply and increases the specialness. Alternatively, current market sentiment expecting interest rates to rise and bond prices to fall might result in larger short positions. This will increase the demand to borrow those shorted bonds, increasing the specialness of a bond.

DETERMINANTS OF REPO RATES

Several dynamics affect repo rates. Some are systemic, affected by the overall rate environment, and others are specific to an individual transaction. It is imperative that market participants understand the drivers of repo rates.

Market Factors

Repo rates are shaped by the same macroeconomic conditions that influence the short end of the yield curve. For example, expectations regarding potential fed funds target rate cuts or rate hikes are quickly translated into repo rates, particularly term repos. However, some market forces are particularly relevant to repo rates.

Money Supply and Demand

An important factor influencing the repo rate is the supply-and-demand function for short-term money. The repo rate tends to rise in situations where the supply of money available decreases or the demand for money increases. In these cases, sellers in need of

---

[14]The most recently issued Treasury is known as the current or on-the-run issue. The U.S. Treasury currently issues 2-year, 3-year, 5-year, 7-year, 10-year, and 30-year bonds. The newest 2-year therefore is the "on-the-run two." As time passes and the Treasury issues a new 2-year, the previous on-the-run becomes an off-the-run issue. The most recent off-the-run is usually referred to as old, for example, the "old 2-year," and the issue before that as the double-old.

liquidity are forced to compete for fewer available dollars, which is done by paying higher rates to buyers. The supply of money can decrease for a number of reasons. For example, the Federal Reserve through its open-market operations may drain reserves. The U.S. Treasury might increase the size of its bill, bond, or note auctions, in which case money that was available to invest in repo markets is reallocated to purchase the new Treasury securities. Another reason may be optimistic market sentiments result in outflows from money market funds into longer-term assets. Demand may increase for many reasons as well. If, for instance, broker-dealer inventories increased, demand for financing might increase in tandem.

In situations where the supply of money increases or the demand for money decreases, the repo rate tends to decrease. In these instances, the increase in money available to be lent or a decrease in borrowing demand means lenders will need to compete for borrowers, usually by offering lower financing costs. Increased supply may be the result of many things. Suppose overall market sentiment turned sour, and fearful investors shift investments into money market funds. These money market fund inflows represent an increase in supply as these funds would need to find short-term investments for the new money. Demand might decrease for several reasons as well. For instance, a large deleveraging by banks or broker-dealers could lead to significantly lower demand for borrowed funds.

AVAILABILITY OF COLLATERAL

Collateral plays an essential role in the repo markets. Often, counterparties favor, or are possibly required to have, certain types of collateral. For example, a municipality with idle cash in its operating account may only be able to accept Treasuries as collateral versus a loan, or a bank may prefer to hold Treasuries on its balance sheet to meet regulatory requirements such as HQLA minimums. Because of these preferences, repo rates can be impacted by supply-and-demand functions of the underlying collateral. Decreases in the supply of collateral and increases in demand for collateral tend to decrease the repo rate on that collateral asset class. This is because investors buying collateral are in effect lending money. To meet specific collateral needs, these participants are willing to lend money at lower rates in exchange for the desired collateral, driving down the rate in the process. An example of this dynamic is Treasuries that trade special because of a large number of short positions. Sometimes a large volume of Treasury GC is traded in tri-party transactions. Since collateral in a tri-party trade is not rehypothecated as it is in bilateral trades, this removes GC supply and occasionally creates shortages. When the repo rate drops sharply due to a shortage of available collateral, repo market participants call this a *collateral squeeze*.

Balance Sheet Constraints

The regulatory response to the financial crisis of 2008 included many reforms aimed at increasing capital requirements, reducing reliance on short-term financing, and reducing overall leverage in the banking system. Under the Basel III framework, securities financing transactions, including repo, are now included in a bank's exposure measure.[15] As such, banks are required to hold additional costly equity capital to support the repo businesses. Banks and their affiliated broker-dealers therefore must assess the costs of any transaction that will grow their balance sheet. As balance sheets shrink, a reduction in the capacity to execute marginal trades can potentially increase the repo rate.

Because banks and dealers often dramatically reduce the size of their balance sheets on dates used for reporting financial results, the balance sheet effect is most visible at quarter-ends. Additionally, on these reporting dates, banks and dealers prefer to reserve their balance sheet capacity for higher quality collateral, such as U.S. Treasuries. As a result, transactions extending over these dates, especially for collateral deemed undesirable, will see these preferences reflected in the repo rate.

Transaction-Specific Factors

Several aspects of an individual transaction will affect the quoted repo rate. The underlying collateral will have by far the largest impact on the rate. Safer, higher quality collateral warrants lower rates than riskier collateral. When assessing collateral quality, buyers may look at many dimensions of that collateral, including risk of the asset class, price volatility, secondary market liquidity and trading volumes, default risk, and credit rating. These factors are built into the repo rate quoted by buyers.

A term premium is typically built into the repo rate. The amount of this premium will depend on several factors. In general, longer tenors require higher rates to reflect the uncertainty associated with longer-time horizons. The additional spread is dependent to a large degree on the steepness of the yield curve at the time of trade execution. Additionally, calendar events that occur during a trade's tenor may be incorporated into the rate (i.e., Federal Reserve Interest Rate Policy Meeting, Treasury Refunding).

THE FEDERAL RESERVE AND REPO

The Federal Reserve often implements monetary policy by conducting open-market operations utilizing repo and reverse repo facilities. Its purpose is to influence the level of reserves, or liquidity in the financial system, consistent with the targeted fed funds rate mandated by the Federal Open Markets Committee (FOMC). As discussed previously, higher levels of money supply lead to lower interest rates while lower levels lead to higher interest rates. To achieve the FOMC fed funds target, the Open Markets Trading Desk at the Federal Reserve Bank of New York will execute repos or reverse repos to increase or decrease liquidity to the banking system. The Federal Reserve adds money to the system using its repo facility, and removes money using the reverse repo facility.

---

[15]Please see the Basel Committee on Banking Supervision piece, "Basel III: A Global Regulatory Framework for More Resilient Banks and Banking Systems," for a more detailed discussion of capital and leverage initiatives.

Some clarity needs to be given to the language chosen by the Federal Reserve. For example, when the Fed announces that it will conduct a repo operation, it is actually the Fed's counterparty that is doing the repo. Thus in a Fed repo, the Fed buys collateral and sells cash. In the same way, when the Fed announces a reverse repo, the counterparty is actually buying (reversing in) securities sold by the Fed. This use of terminology can be confusing, and market participants must understand what action is actually being done by the Federal Reserve.

Repo

When the Fed conducts a repo operation, it is typically done on an overnight basis. While term repos can be employed with a tenor not exceeding 65 days, most term repos have a tenor of less than two weeks. In conducting its operations, the Fed will accept competitive bids for three different collateral types: Treasury general collateral (GC), agency debentures, or agency MBS collateral. All winning bids will receive the stop-out rate. The transactions will then settle in the tri-party markets.

Federal Reserve repos decrease the overnight rate in two ways. First, since the Fed is providing cash by buying collateral, it increases the cash position at the counterparty. This increases the money supply, resulting in decreased overnight rates. Second, since the trades settle tri-party, the operation effectively removes collateral from the banking system, decreasing the supply of collateral. All things being equal, declines in collateral availability will cause repo rates to decline.

Reverse Repo

Utilizing its overnight reverse repurchase agreement facility (ON RRP), the Fed engages in bilateral transactions where bonds from its System Open Market Account (SOMA) portfolio are sold to counterparties, thereby removing money from the system and replacing it with securities. By reducing money supply, overnight interest rates should rise.

The RRP program has become an important tool for the FOMC. The Federal Reserve responded to the financial crisis of 2008 by implementing three rounds of quantitative easing, which increased the size of the Fed's balance sheet to $4.5 trillion, and a zero interest rate policy. The RRP addresses the challenge of changing gears and raising rates with unprecedented liquidity in the system. The rate on the program, set by the committee, acts as a floor to interest rates. Since the Fed is viewed as a risk-free counterparty, and the collateral received is U.S. Treasuries (gilt-edged), a risk-averse investor will not lend to a riskier counterparty at a lower rate. Thus the RRP allows the Fed to increase interest rates while retaining a massive balance sheet.

REPO AND BOND CARRY

The interest rate carry, which is the difference between the accrued coupon and the financing expense, is an important factor in determining the price of a bond. The daily carry can be expressed as

Daily Carry = Daily Accrued Coupon Interest − Daily Financing Interest Expense where

$$\text{Daily Accrued Coupon Interest}$$
$$= \text{Original Face} \times (\text{Annual Coupon}/2) \times (1 \text{ day}/\text{Days in Period})$$

and

$$\text{Daily Financing Interest Expense} = \text{Loan Proceeds} \times \text{Repo Rate} \times (1 \text{ day}/360)$$

For the trader, the profit or loss on a particular trade will be the difference between the purchase price and the sale price, plus the total carry earned over the holding period.

In an upward-sloping yield curve environment, the coupon on the bond is typically higher than the overnight repo rate used to finance the bond. This leads to positive carry. If the financing cost is higher than the accrued coupon, it is referred to as negative carry. Negative carry can also occur when a trader takes a short position by selling a bond he or she does not own. In this case, during the period when the trader is short the bond accrues daily coupon interest that will need to be paid when the short is covered. This cost is offset since the trader will be able to take the proceeds and lend them at the overnight repo rate.

To demonstrate, suppose on January 13, 2016, a U.S. Treasury trader buys $100 million face of the T 2.25 11/15/2025 for a dollar price of 101-12.[16] The purchase is financed by selling the collateral in the repo market at an overnight repo rate of 35 basis points. The following day, the trader sells the bonds outright at a price of 101-13. Given these details,[17] the profit can be calculated and attributed to price change and carry on the trade. First, since the bond is held and financed overnight, the daily carry can be calculated as

$$\text{Daily Accrued Coupon Interest} = \$100,000,000 \times (.0225/2) \times (1/182)$$
$$= \$6,181.32$$
$$\text{Daily Financing Interest Expense} = \$101,745,879.12 \times .0035 \times (1/360)$$
$$= \$989.20$$

so that daily carry equals

$$\text{Daily Carry} = \$6,181.32 - \$989.20 = \$5,192.12$$

---

[16]Treasury prices are quoted in percentage of par and 32nd of a percentage point. A price of 101-12 equates to a price of 101.375%.

[17]For the T 2.25 11/15/2015, there are 182 days between the coupon dates of November 15, 2015, and May 15, 2015. Additionally, bonds purchased on January 13 will settle on the next business day, in this case January 14. Therefore, there are 60 days of interest accrued since November 15, which equates to $370,879.12 ($100 million × (.0225/2) × (60/182)). This is added to principal of $101,375,000 (or $100 million * 101.375%) to give net proceeds of $101,745,879.12 that will be due to the seller and be the required amount to be financed.

Adding the daily carry to the profit from selling the bond for a 1/32 of a point increase in price gives a total profit on the trade of

$$\text{Total Profit} = \$100,000,000 \times [(1/32)/100] + \$5,192.12$$
$$= \$31,250.00 + \$5,192.12 = \$36,442.12$$

As can be seen, carry comprises almost 15% of the total P/L on the trade.

Now suppose a trader takes a short position and sells a bond not held in inventory. If the trader fails to deliver the bond to the buyer, the trader is exposed to a penalty fee.[18] To avoid this, borrowing the bond using a reverse repo covers the short position. Assume on January 15, 2016, a trading desk sells short $100 million original face of the T 1.125 1/15/2019 at a price of 100-04. The bond trades special and can be borrowed at a repo rate of 15 basis points. The next business day, January 19, 2016,[19] the desk covers the short outright by purchasing the bonds at a price of 100-02.

On the settlement date, the purchaser will pay for the bonds and the desk will receive proceeds of

$$\text{Total Proceeds} = \text{Principal} + \text{Accrued Coupon Interest}$$
$$\text{Principal} = \$100,000,000 \times 1.00125 = \$100,125,000.00$$
$$\text{Accrued Coupon Interest} = \$100,000,000 \times (.01125/2) \times (4/182) = \$12,362.64$$
$$\text{Total Proceeds} = \$100,137,362.64$$

Simultaneously, the desk will borrow the bond using a reverse repo and loaning the cash proceeds at an overnight rate of 15 basis points. The following day, the purchase to cover the short settles. Simultaneously, the reverse repo will unwind and the desk will receive the loan proceeds plus accrued interest. These proceeds will be used to pay for the bond purchased outright, which in turn will be delivered to the counterparty that lent the bond. The flows can be seen as follows.

For the interest earned on the reverse repo,

$$\text{Reverse Repo Interest Earned} = \$100,137,362.64 \times .0015 \times (1/360) = \$417.24$$

---

[18]Prior to the financial crisis, short sellers were able to sell Treasury securities and fail to deliver the securities to the buyer at the settlement date without any explicit penalty. A "dynamic fails charge" implemented by the Treasury Market Practice Group in May 2009 intended to curb this practice. Dealers who fail to deliver bonds sold short face a daily charge, currently 3.00%. Short sellers are more inclined to pay specials rates, even at negative levels, to ensure short positions are covered. For more, see Garbade, Keane, Logan, Stokes, and Wolgemuth.

[19]In this example, the trade dates occur on the Friday before and the Tuesday following the Martin Luther King Day holiday. With T+1 settlement, the trades settle on January 19 and 20 respectively.

For the purchase of the bond, principal and accrued interest equal

$$\text{Principal} = \$100,000,000 \times 100.0625\% = \$100,062,500.00$$

$$\text{Accrued Coupon Interest} = \$100,0000,000 \times (.00125/2) \times (5/182) = \$15,453.30$$

$$\text{Total Proceeds} = \$100,077,953.30$$

Note that the accrued coupon interest on the sale is lower than the accrued coupon interest on the purchase by $3,090.66. In the first example when the trader was long the bond for one day, the trader earned the coupon interest. However, in the case of the short sale, the buyer on the other side of the short sale earns the coupon interest, which effectively is paid by the short seller. The short does benefit somewhat. Instead of paying interest to finance a bond, the short is able to use the proceeds to lend and earn interest. But since the yield curve is upward sloping, and the bond shorted traded special, the interest income from the reverse repo was less than the accruing coupon interest, resulting in negative carry of

$$\text{Carry} = \$3,090.66 + \$417.24 = \$(2,673.42)$$

The negative carry, added to profit from the change in price, gives the short sale a final profit of

$$\text{Total P/L} = \$62,500 - \$2,673.42 = \$59,826.58$$

CONCLUSION

Repurchase agreements are an effective tool for participants in the short-term markets. Counterparties in need of financing are able to source liquidity by selling assets in the repo markets to cash-rich investors in need of short-term investments. Additionally, those in need of specific securities to deliver against short positions are often able to borrow those issues in the repo specials markets. Furthermore, the Federal Reserve often implements monetary policy by conducting open-market operations utilizing repo and reverse repo facilities.

The future of repo markets will be closely tied to changes in the regulatory environment following the financial crisis of 2008. Rules such as the net stable funding requirement will require many participants to shift their financing from short-term instruments such as repo into longer-term debt. Regulations designed to shrink bank balance sheets such as the supplemental leverage ratio could result in less appetite to allocate balance sheet to low-yielding short-term assets. While these changes may reduce the size of the repo markets, repurchase agreements will still play an important role in finance.

For more, see Securities Industry and Financial Markets Association, Master Repurchase Agreement, http://www.sifma.org/services/standard-forms-and-documentation/mra,-gmra,-msla-and-msftas/.

CHAPTER 10

U.S. Treasury and Government Agency Securities

Lee Griffin and David Isaac

FEATURES OF U.S. TREASURY SECURITIES

U.S. Treasury securities are direct obligations of the U.S. government, backed by its full faith and credit. Proceeds from the sale of these securities are used to finance the activities of the federal government and to refund its outstanding debt. Since Treasuries are generally considered to be free of credit risk, they serve as a "safe haven" credit during times of economic or geopolitical tumult and are widely held by investors around the world. Given the perception of Treasuries' lack of credit risk and their ubiquity they serve as the benchmark security for the global fixed-income markets.

In addition to credit quality, the most important feature Treasuries offer is liquidity. Liquidity is measured by the ease with which a financial asset can be converted to cash without a substantial change in its price. There is a large and active secondary market for U.S. Treasuries, supported by primary dealers and institutional investors around the world. (A primary dealer is a large bank or securities dealer recognized by the Federal Reserve Bank as a market maker in U.S. Treasuries. Primary dealers are required to bid for a portion of every Treasury auction.) Unlike many fixed-income products, it is possible to obtain bid and offered quotes at any time on virtually any U.S. Treasury security.

For U.S. taxpayers, one last selling point is that interest on U.S. Treasuries is exempt from state and local income taxes (but are subject to federal tax).

In summary, investors in Treasuries have taken credit risk and geopolitical or event risk off the table. The sole remaining risk category to contend with is interest rate risk. Implicit in our understanding of the yield curve is the concept that time equals risk; that is, the greater the tenor of a bond, the greater its sensitivity to changes in interest rates. Therefore the interest rate risk of the 30-year U.S. Treasury bond is far greater than that of the 10-year note, which in turn is more risky than the 5-year note, and so on. Taken to its logical conclusion, then, the safest vehicle in the world of fixed income is a one-week U.S. Treasury bill.

TYPES OF TREASURY SECURITIES

Treasury Bills (T-bills)

Treasury bills (T-bills) are the shortest term debt obligations of the U.S. Treasury with maturities of one year or less. One-month, three-month, six-month, and one-year T-bills are sold directly to the public by the Treasury. Treasury bills are sold at a discount from face value. At maturity, the investor redeems the bill for full face value. The difference between the purchase price and the amount that is paid at maturity represents the investor's interest. For example, if you buy a $100,000 (face or par value) 26-week T-bill for $99,250, at maturity you will receive $100,000. The difference of $750 represents your interest. Interest on T-bills accrues based on the actual number of days between purchase and maturity and each year is assumed to contain 360 days.

Treasury Notes and Bonds

Notes mature in more than a year, but not more than 10 years from their issue date. The Treasury offers three kinds of notes: fixed rate, floating rate, and inflation linked. (For discussion of floating-rate bonds, see the FRN section to follow. For discussion of inflation-linked bonds see the TIPS section.) Fixed-rate Treasury notes are currently issued in terms of 2, 3, 5, 7, and 10 years. Interest is paid semiannually with no call option prior to maturity. T-notes are normally traded in multiples of $1,000 but can be traded in denominations as small as $100. The term *Treasury bond* refers generically to debt issued with a 30-year maturity. Other than its tenor, the long bond has the same characteristics as Treasury notes.

TIPS

In January 1997, the Department of the Treasury introduced Treasury Inflation Indexed Securities, often referred to as Treasury Inflation Protected Securities (TIPS), a new form of notes and bonds whose principal is tied to the rate of inflation.

Simply stated, TIPS adjust the principal paid to the investor to keep pace with the rate of inflation. While these securities pay a fixed rate of interest, the principal amount of the bond is adjusted for inflation. In exchange for this inflation protection feature, the investor accepts an interest rate on the bond lower than traditional Treasuries of similar maturity. Over the life of the bond, semiannual interest payments are based on the new inflation-adjusted principal, not the original face value. If consumer prices rise, the inflation-adjusted principal will increase, as will the interest payments received. Conversely, if consumer prices fall, the inflation-adjusted principal will decrease. In this instance, investors will receive smaller interest payments than they would have if the rate of inflation had increased or stayed the same. In the event that consumer prices actually decline (deflation), the Treasury offers a safeguard: Upon maturity, the bondholder will be paid the greater of either the inflation-adjusted principal or the original face value, guaranteeing a return to the investor of at least the original principal amount invested.

The inflation rate used to adjust the principal is the Consumer Price Index (CPI), the Bureau of Labor Statistics' nonseasonally adjusted monthly measure of price changes in a basket of goods and services.

TIPS are currently issued with maturities of 5, 10, and 30 years and can be purchased in the new issue market by placing a competitive or noncompetitive bid through the standard Treasury auction process (see discussion of the auction process that follows). Secondary markets of previously issued TIPS exist but they are not traded as frequently as traditional on-the-run Treasuries.

Like all Treasury notes and bonds, TIPS are exempt from state and local income taxes. At the federal level, investors will be taxed both on the coupon payments and on any inflation increase to the principal value in the year that it occurs. Because of this tax treatment, investors should consider purchasing TIPS for their tax-deferred accounts. It should be noted that if deflation causes a reduction in the principal amount, the IRS allows the investor to reduce his or her taxable interest income expense by the amount of the principal reduction. If the reduction exceeds the amount of semiannual interest payments for that year, the investor can carry forward the deduction to subsequent years until it is used up.

Investors considering an investment in TIPS generally begin their analysis by comparing the yield differential between TIPS and a comparable maturity fixed-rate Treasury bond. That difference is sometimes called a breakeven inflation rate. If a traditional 10-year Treasury yields 2.5 percent and a new 10-year TIPS bond yields 2 percent, then the difference of 0.5 percent is the breakeven inflation rate. If the average annual inflation rate over the 10-year life of the bond exceeds 0.5 percent, the TIPS bond should outperform the traditional 10-year Treasury. So, the larger the breakeven inflation rate, the more expensive the TIPS bond.

Treasury STRIPS

Treasury STRIPS are the most common type of zero-coupon bond derived from U.S. Treasury securities. Zero-coupon bonds are issued at a discount to face value and pay no interest during the life of the bond. Instead, the interest payments are realized as incremental increases in the principal value of the bond and are payable at maturity. STRIPS are not issued by the U.S. Treasury; rather they are created by the Treasury by stripping the semiannual interest payments of existing coupon-bearing bonds and repackaging them as new securities. Since the security of the new bond is derived from the full faith and credit pledge of the U.S. government to pay the interest on its debt, STRIPS are considered to be Treasury debt. STRIPS maturities range from one month to as long as 30 years.

FRNs

In January 2014 the Treasury began to issue floating-rate notes (FRNs) in response to regulatory changes that encouraged money managers to allocate a greater portion of their assets to government securities, and the Treasury Department's desire to lower their borrowing cost. FRNs are a borrowing structure commonly used by corporations and GSEs, as well as some foreign governments, but the U.S. government had never utilized the structure before. Treasury FRNs are currently issued quarterly with a two-year maturity and quarterly interest payments. Like other structures they are issued and mature at par and trade in minimum quantities of $100. Where FRNs differ from other Treasury bonds is in the way the quarterly interest payments vary each period depending on changes in the reference rate.

When the Treasury Borrowing Advisory Committee (TBAC) was originally discussing the idea of issuing FRNs there was considerable debate about what reference rate to use.[1] In corporate bonds the London Interbank Offered Rate (LIBOR) is the most commonly used reference rate, but as LIBOR is a credit based rate it would not be appropriate for Treasury debt. The TBAC considered using either the average price of *general collateral* (GC) repurchase trades or the stop level of the monthly three-month T-bill auction. In the end, it was decided to use the stop level of the monthly three-month bill given its more extensive historical data, an expectation of lower rates, and the fact that GC is sometimes pushed higher by credit-related problems. The auction process for FRNs is similar to the process for standard fixed-coupon notes, with the major difference being that the bid is quoted as the premium over the reference rate that the bidder requires to lend to the Treasury. This spread over the benchmark rate is referred to as the discount margin (DM). As in every other auction, the Treasury seeks to minimize its borrowing cost and will award bonds to those bidders who submit the lowest DM.

The use of FRNs diversifies the structure of Treasury's borrowing, reduces its borrowing costs, and provides more stable funding. FRNs offer benefits to lenders as well. Chief among them is the measure of inflation protection that FRNs provide. If inflation rises, one would expect the rates on the three-month T-bill to rise as well, pushing up interest payments on all outstanding FRNs and easing the drag of higher inflation.

TREASURY AUCTIONS

The U.S. Treasury accesses the primary market through regularly scheduled auctions throughout the calendar year. Auction dates are announced by the Treasury about one week before each auction. Information on upcoming auctions is available through the financial press, broker/dealers, and the Bureau of Public Debt website.

The Treasury department uses a Dutch auction (aka single-price auction) process to sell its debt to the public. This process also sets the initial interest rate for the newly issued securities. The Treasury conducted over 270 auctions, issuing over $7.0 trillion in securities in 2015. Under the Dutch auction process, each successful bidder is awarded securities at the same price, which is equal to the highest accepted rate or yield. In other words, the

---

[1]Ezechiel Copic, Luis Gonzalez, Caitlin Gorback, Blake Gwinn, and Ernst Schaumburg, *Liberty Street Economics*, Federal Reserve Bank of New York, April 21, 2014. http://libertystreeteconomics .newyorkfed.org/2014/04/introduction-to-the-floating-rate-note-treasury-security.html# .V6iQzVcXqQp.

final price of the security being auctioned is the lowest price (or highest yield) necessary to sell the entire offering. When investors participate in an auction for a Treasury security, they must decide whether they will submit a competitive or a noncompetitive bid. In a competitive bid the bidder states what amount of securities he or she will purchase and the minimum yield level he or she will accept. Depending on the range of bids received, the Treasury may reject a competitive bid, fill it in part, or award the bidder with the full amount bid for.

The terms of bidding in a Treasury auction are as follows: The minimum denomination for all bidders is $1,000 with increments in multiples of $1,000. The maximum amount that may be bid by a noncompetitive bidder is $1 million for T-bills and $5 million for Treasury notes, bonds, and TIPS. There are no quantity restrictions for competitive bidders with one exception: No bidder may purchase more than 35% of the offering.

Once the auction is closed, all noncompetitive bids that comply with the auction rules are immediately accepted. The competitive bids are then sorted from lowest to highest yield and accepted in that order until the entire allotment of securities being offered has been reached. All bidders, competitive and noncompetitive alike, then purchase the securities at the same rate, the highest accepted yield.

Participants in Treasury auctions can bid using two different methods. Individual investors can submit noncompetitive bids directly with the government through a program called TreasuryDirect (www.treasurydirect.gov). An investor using this method buys Treasuries directly from the government, bypassing the broker/dealer community in the process. Alternatively, individuals may place orders in an auction through their financial institutions as well. Institutional investors and dealers participate in auctions using the Treasury Automated Auction Processing System (TAAPS) to place bids for customers and for their own accounts.

CONCLUSION

The rates at which the U.S. Treasury borrows money, whether in bills, notes, or TIPS, are the basis for the rates that every other U.S. dollar borrower pays and form the backbone of the global financial system. On the short end of the maturity curve, bills are a widely used reference rate, and on the long end, Treasury bonds are among the safest long-term investments available. Following the global turmoil of the 2008 financial crisis Treasuries have been in high demand from global investors seeking the safety of U.S. government debt and as a result yields across the curve have steadily declined. As of this writing, yields have fallen to their lowest levels ever. However, with many of the alternatives such as high-quality government bonds in Europe and Asia trading at negative yields, it is not unreasonable to believe that the U.S. government's borrowing costs will continue to remain below the long-term average in the near future. U.S. Treasuries will continue to represent a risk-free rate of return and be among the most important benchmarks in the global financial system.

CHAPTER 11

Government-Sponsored Enterprises and Federal Agencies

David Isaac and Francis C. Reed, Jr.

INTRODUCTION

Government-sponsored enterprises (GSEs) are chartered by Congress, and in some cases given lines of credit from the Department of Treasury to provide a continuous, low-cost source of capital to specific types of borrowers, most notably, homeowners, farmers, and students. Some GSEs are publicly owned and traded in the equity market while others are corporations wholly owned by the U.S. government. GSEs are a uniquely American concept—a symbol of American idealism, resourcefulness, and optimism combined with free-market capitalism. Commonly referred to as *U.S. agencies*, the debt securities issued by the GSEs are publicly traded across the globe. The security for agency debt falls into two general categories: (1) explicitly guaranteed by the full faith and credit of the U.S. government, and (2) supported by, but not guaranteed by, the U.S. government. (See Table 11.1.) Two of these agencies, the Federal National Mortgage Association (FNMA or Fannie Mae) and the Federal Home Loan Mortgage Corp. (FHLMC or Freddie Mac), were instrumental in the creation of one of the largest and most liquid markets in the world, the mortgage-backed securities or MBS market. Collectively, the success of the GSEs has contributed greatly to the unprecedented expansion of the U.S. debt market as the dominant force in global fixed income.

AGENCY BONDS

As mentioned earlier, GSE bonds and Federal Agency debt issuance are commonly lumped together and referred to as *agency bonds*. They are regarded as secure investments due to their special status as institutions chartered by Congress and/or their particular government guarantee mechanism.

The Federal Agencies listed in Table 11.1 are *explicitly* guaranteed, backed by the full faith and credit of the U.S. government. Explicit issuer guarantee is essentially a

TABLE 11.1 Government-Sponsored Enterprises and Federal Agencies

Issuer	Ratings	Ownership	Guarantee Status	Role	Debt Tax-Exempt Status
Fannie Mae	Aaa/AAA	Government-Sponsored Enterprise (GSE), under conservatorship of FHFA	None	Provides liquidity to primary mortgage market	None
Freddie Mac	Aaa/AAA	Government-Sponsored Enterprise (GSE), under conservatorship of FHFA	None	Provides liquidity to primary mortgage market	None
FFCB	Aaa/AAA	Government-Sponsored Enterprise, borrower owned	None	Provides American agriculture with sound and dependable credit	State & Local
FHLB	Aaa/AAA	Government-Sponsored Enterprise, owned by member banks	None	Supports residential mortgage lending and related community investment through its member institutions	State & Local
Farmer Mac	Aaa/AAA	Government-Sponsored Enterprise, Stockholder-owned company,	None	Provides capital and lender competition to American agriculture and rural communities	None
TVA	Aaa/AAA	Government-Sponsored Enterprise, a corporate agency of the U.S. Government	None	Provides wholesale power to municipal and cooperative institutions, industries. and governments	State & Local
Ginnie Mae	Aaa/AAA	Federal agency	U.S. Treasury	Provides liquidity to the U.S. mortgage market	None
HUD	Aaa/AAA	Federal agency	U.S. Treasury	Provides capital and lending to urban communities	None
FICO	Aaa/AAA	Federal agency	U.S. Treasury	Savings & Loans Bailout of the 1980s	State & Local
RefCo	Aaa/AAA	Federal agency	U.S. Treasury	Savings & Loans Bailout of the 1980s	State & Local
PEFCO	Aaa/AAA	Federal agency	U.S. Treasury	Supports the exports off U.S. goods and services	None
OPIC	Aaa/AAA	Federal agency	U.S. Treasury	Provides financing for projects in developing countries	None
IBRD	Aaa/AAA	Supra-National (member countries)	None (Multilateral Development Bank)	Provides medium- and long-term financing to governments and other entities	None

"maintenance guarantee," meaning the guarantor is economically responsible for the guaranteed entity and its activities. That the guarantee exists suggests that the entity has sufficient financial cover to meet its debt obligations in a timely manner. The GSEs listed in Table 11.1 are assumed to be *implicitly* guaranteed by the tax authority of the U.S. federal government. Agency bonds are debentures, unsecured debt instruments not collateralized by specific assets such as a pool of mortgages as is the case with MBS.

Despite their high level of credit quality, agency bonds do not have the same level of market efficiency as U.S. Treasury securities. Explicit-guarantee agency bonds trade at a small yield premium above comparable U.S. Treasury bonds because they lack the same degree of liquidity. Implicit guaranteed agency bonds trade with a larger yield premium for the same reason as well as the fact that investors are assuming additional credit risk. Additionally, factors such as the size and structure of a particular agency issue may reduce the number of participants involved in the marketplace with a commensurate drop in liquidity.

Thanks to their conservative underwriting standards and solid credit-monitoring policies, issuers of agency bonds share the same credit rating as the U.S. government: Aaa by Moody's, AAA by Fitch, and AA+ by Standard & Poor's. Short-term debt is rated P-1 by Moody's, A-1+ by Standard & Poor's, and F1+ by Fitch. Farmer Mac continues to be unrated, as it is the only GSE that has never requested an official rating from an outside rating agency.[1]

OVERVIEW OF GOVERNMENT-SPONSORED ENTERPRISES; HOUSING GSEs

The primary regulator of the Housing GSEs—Fannie Mae, Freddie Mac, and the Federal Home Loan Bank system—is the Federal Housing Finance Agency (FHFA). The FHFA was created by the Housing and Economic Recovery Act of 2008. The role of the FHFA was previously handled by the Office of Federal Housing Enterprise Oversight (OFHEO) and the Federal Housing Board (FHB). There was additional regulatory oversight from the Department of U.S. Housing and Urban Development (HUD), a federal agency.

The FHFA was established to strengthen and better coordinate the oversight of the activities of the Housing GSEs during the mortgage crisis of 2008. One of the FHFA's most important powers was the ability to place the aforementioned GSEs in conservatorship or receivership, if necessary.[2] That is exactly what happened to Fannie Mae and Freddie Mac in September 2008. The losses sustained in their mortgage portfolios had left Freddie Mac and Fannie Mae unable to fulfill their missions without government assistance. Both entities remain in conservatorship to this day.

---

[1] Farmer Mac, www.farmermac.com.
[2] Federal Housing Finance Agency, "History of Fannie Mae & Freddie Mac Conservatorships," http://www.fhfa.gov/Conservatorship/pages/history-of-fannie-mae--freddie-conservatorships .aspx.

Federal National Mortgage Association (FNMA or Fannie Mae)

Fannie Mae is a shareholder-owned company chartered by Congress on February 10, 1938. Fannie Mae became a private shareholder company in 1968 and since September 2008 has been under the conservatorship of the U.S. government and regulated by the Federal Housing Finance Agency (FHFA).

Fannie Mae's mandate is to support the liquidity and stability of the secondary mortgage market. Fannie Mae carries out this public policy mission not through directly lending money to home buyers, but by securitizing mortgage loans underwritten by mortgage lenders.[3] To qualify, individual mortgage loans must conform to Fannie Mae's underwriting standards. These loans are then pooled into mortgage-backed securities for sale to investors. Fannie Mae also maintains a retained portfolio of mortgage investments, which include both mortgage-related securities and whole-loan mortgages. Prior to being placed into conservatorship, Fannie Mae (and Freddie Mac) carried out an essential role in refinancing and modifying underwater loans, in order to support the affordable housing mission. Fannie Mae funds its mortgage portfolio through the issuance of debt securities in the international capital markets; these debt securities vary in term, size, and structure.

Federal National Mortgage Corporation (FHLMC or Freddie Mac)

Freddie Mac was chartered in 1970 to stabilize the U.S. residential mortgage markets and promote homeownership and affordable rentals. Its statutory mission is to provide liquidity, stability, and affordability to the U.S. housing market.[4] Freddie Mac does not make loans directly to homebuyers, but instead buys mortgage loans from approved lenders and either securitizes the loans (into Freddie Mac MBS) or holds them for its retained portfolio.

Freddie Mac continues to aid the housing market and the broader economy by making liquid mortgage markets for lenders and trying to mitigate foreclosures. It was placed into conservatorship simultaneously with Fannie Mae in September 2008. Both entities are regulated by the Federal Housing Finance Agency (FHFA), whose goal is to bring both GSEs back to solvency and mitigate systemic risk. Freddie Mac continues to issue debt on a regularly scheduled basis in order to fund investments for its mortgage portfolio and, ultimately, work toward its public mission. Similar to Fannie Mae, Freddie Mac relies heavily on callable debt issuance to fund and hedge its portfolio mortgage holdings and new purchases.

HISTORY OF FANNIE MAE AND FREDDIE MAC

The Federal National Mortgage Association (FNMA), known as Fannie Mae, was established in the aftermath of the Great Depression to provide regional banks with federal

---

[3]Fannie Mae, www.fanniemae.com.
[4]Freddie Mac, http://www.freddiemac.com/corporate/company_profile/.

money to finance home mortgages in an attempt to raise levels of homeownership. By making Federal Housing Administration (FHA) insured mortgages available to banks and other loan originators, Fannie Mae created an active and viable secondary mortgage market.

Fannie Mae was immensely successful in increasing homeownership, raising home prices and helping to lift people out of poverty. This allowed it to hold a monopoly over the secondary mortgage market for decades.[5]

Over time, the structure and ownership of Fannie Mae changed in response to continuing controversy over the concept of federal subsidies encouraging private homeownership.[6] In 1954, the Federal National Mortgage Association Charter Act made Fannie Mae into a "mixed-ownership" corporation. The federal government now held the preferred stock while private investors held the common stock.

Due to a combination of economic and political factors, Fannie Mae was converted to a privately held corporation in 1968.[7] The economically destructive combination of rising U.S. unemployment and dramatically increasing U.S. national debt to fund the Vietnam War became the drivers of this change to remove Fannie Mae's activity and debt from the federal budget.[8] The 1968 change also created the Government National Mortgage Association (GNMA or Ginnie Mae).

Ginnie Mae, which remains a government organization, supports FHA-insured mortgages as well as Veterans Administration (VA) and Farmers Home Administration (FHA) insured mortgages. Ginnie Mae is the only home-loan agency explicitly backed by the full faith and credit of the U.S. government.

In 1970, the federal government authorized Fannie Mae to purchase conventional mortgages, the same year it went public on the New York and Pacific Exchanges. The year 1970 also saw the creation of the Federal Home Loan Mortgage Corporation (FHLMC or Freddie Mac), to compete with Fannie Mae and thus facilitate a more robust and efficient secondary mortgage market.[9]

FEDERAL HOME LOAN BANKS (FHLB)

Another New Deal program, the Federal Home Loan Banks (FHLBs), was established by the Federal Home Loan Bank Board, pursuant to the Federal Home Loan Bank Act of 1932. FHLBs were established in order to provide funds and liquidity to many different types of financial institutions. The institutions needed to purchase stock from their member FHLB in order to be a member.[10]

---

[5]Fannie Mae, www.fanniemae.com.
[6]*Financial Times*. "A History of Freddie Mac and Fannie Mae," September 8, 2008, www.ft.com/cms/s/0/e3e1d654-5288-11dd-9ba7-000077b07658.htm.
[7]Fannie Mae, www.fanniemae.com.
[8]Federal Housing Finance Agency, "History of the Government Sponsored Enterprises," Office of Inspector General, http://fhfaoig.gov/LearnMore/History.
[9]Ibid.
[10]Ibid.

The Federal Home Loan Banking system is a national network of 11 regional Federal Home Loan Bank offices:

1. Atlanta
2. Boston
3. Chicago
4. Cincinnati
5. Dallas
6. Des Moines (absorbed the Seattle FHLB in June 2015)
7. Indianapolis
8. New York
9. Pittsburgh
10. San Francisco
11. Topeka

See Figure 11.1.

The 11 FHLBs are each cooperatively owned and governed by their member financial institutions, numbering some 7,300 regulated financial institutions located in all 50 states as well as the U.S. possessions and territories. The membership includes small community banks, regional banks, savings and loan associations, commercial banks, credit unions, and insurance companies.

The FHL banks raise money to fund member lending through the daily sale of debt securities in the global capital markets. The Office of Finance located in Reston, Virginia, acts as the central debt issuance facility, conduit, and servicer for the regional FHLBs. The debt is sold through an international network of underwriters, or as direct placements. Interest from FHLB bonds are exempt from state and local taxes for U.S. investors.

FHLB debt securities are known as consolidated obligations that are "joint and severally" owned by all of the banks. In other words, if any individual bank was not able to meet its obligations, the other banks would be required to cover that debt.

Proceeds from debt sales enable member financial institutions to extend mortgage credit to U.S. homebuyers and fund economic development projects at the local level. Purchasers of FHLB debt securities include commercial banks, central banks, mutual funds, corporations, pension funds, government agencies, and individual investors.

The Federal Housing Finance Agency (FHFA) regulates the FHLB system and the Office of Finance. The FHFA is responsible for monitoring the ability of the FHLB system to sustain its core business within prudent risk limitations while fulfilling its public policy mission.

OVERVIEW OF GOVERNMENT-SPONSORED ENTERPRISES; NON-HOUSING GSEs

While the Housing GSE may be more well known by the general public, there are numerous other entities that have been created by Congress to reduce the cost of capital for certain sectors of the economy.

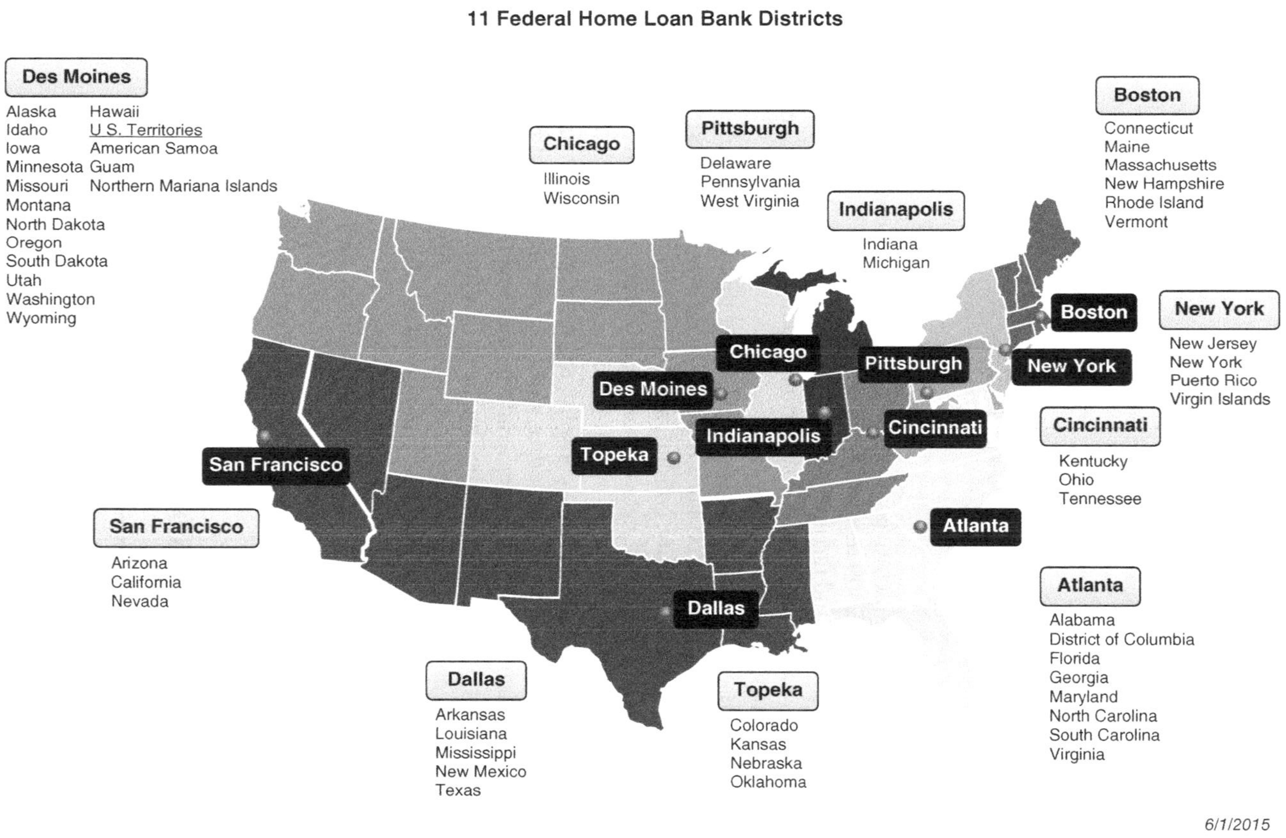

11 Federal Home Loan Bank Districts

Des Moines

Alaska   Hawaii
Idaho   U.S. Territories
Iowa   American Samoa
Minnesota   Guam
Missouri   Northern Mariana Islands
Montana
North Dakota
Oregon
South Dakota
Utah
Washington
Wyoming

San Francisco

Arizona
California
Nevada

Chicago

Illinois
Wisconsin

Pittsburgh

Delaware
Pennsylvania
West Virginia

Indianapolis

Indiana
Michigan

Boston

Connecticut
Maine
Massachusetts
New Hampshire
Rhode Island
Vermont

New York

New Jersey
New York
Puerto Rico
Virgin Islands

Cincinnati

Kentucky
Ohio
Tennessee

Atlanta

Alabama
District of Columbia
Florida
Georgia
Maryland
North Carolina
South Carolina
Virginia

Topeka

Colorado
Kansas
Nebraska
Oklahoma

Dallas

Arkansas
Louisiana
Mississippi
New Mexico
Texas

6/1/2015

FIGURE 11.1 Map of Federal Home Loan Banks districts
Source: Federal Housing Finance Agency (www.fhfa.gov)

Federal Farm Credit Banks (FFCBs)

Now over 100 years old and considered the first GSE chartered in the United States, the Farm Credit System was established by Congress in 1916 to provide a reliable source of credit for the nation's farmers and ranchers. Today, the Farm Credit System provides more than one-third of the credit needed by those who live and work in rural America.[11]

The Federal Farm Credit banks are a unique cooperative structure of member-owners with three branches:

1. System banks
2. System associations (members/borrowers)
3. Funding corporation

The System banks consist of four banks that operate jointly to handle asset, liability, and risk management of the system:

1. AgFirst
2. AgriBank
3. FCB of Texas
4. CoBank

Unlike commercial banks, Farm Credit banks above do not take deposits. Funds for loans are instead raised by issuing debt securities, the proceeds of which are used to help satisfy the financing needs of the 78 member banks and associations.[12] Currently the four System banks issue debt on a joint and several basis (similar to FHLB).[13] Interest on these bonds is generally tax exempt at the local level for domestic investors.

The Federal Farm Credit Banks Funding Corporation plays the role of the fiscal agent for the System banks. It is responsible for issuing, marketing, and handling Farm Credit Debt Securities on behalf of the System banks. Specifically, the Funding Corporation is in charge of determining amounts, maturities, interest rates, terms, and conditions for the securities. These securities are then distributed by the funding groups. The Funding Corporation can be thought of as the financial spokesperson for the System and is responsible for accounting and reporting service, as well as financial disclosure and the release of certain financial information. Again, this is similar to the role that the Office of Finance plays for the Federal Home Loan banks.

Headquartered in Jersey City, NJ, the Federal Farm Credit Banks Funding Corporation issues a variety of Federal Farm Credit Banks Consolidated System-wide Debt Securities (Farm Credit Debt Securities) on behalf of the Farm Credit System Banks. Maturities

---

[11]Federal Farm Credit Banks Funding Corporation, "About Us: Overview," www.farmcredit funding.com/ffcb_live/overview.html.
[12]Farm Credit Administration, "Number of FCS Banks and Associations by Type and District as of July 1, 2016," www.fca.gov/info/number_of_fcs_institutions.html.
[13]Federal Farm Credit Banks Funding Corporation, "About Us: Overview," www.farmcredit funding.com/ffcb_live/overview.html.

range from overnight to 30 years and structures include discount notes, floating-rate notes, bullets, and callable/putable notes.

Farm Credit System institutions are federally chartered under the Farm Credit Act and are regulated by the Farm Credit Administration (FCA), an independent agency of the U.S. government Executive branch. The borrowers, as a cooperative network, own the System. The Farm Credit System Associations offer loans, leases, and financial services to qualified borrowers and the Farm Credit System banks provide capital to those retail associations. For example, CoBank, one of the FFCB System banks, provides direct financing to large agribusinesses, cooperatives, and rural utilities.[14]

The debt securities are not direct obligations of the U.S. government; rather they are "joint and several obligations" of the four banks that comprise the overall Farm Credit System.

The debt is insured by the Farm Credit System Insurance Corporation. During the Farm Crisis of the 1980s, defaults of loans made to farmers increased as a result of high interest rates and low crop prices. To allay concerns about the solvency of the Farm Credit banks, the Farm Credit Act was amended in 1988 to establish the corporation to insure the timely payment of principal and interest on the system-wide debt.[15]

Federal Agricultural Mortgage Corporation (Farmer Mac)

Created by the Agricultural Credit Act of 1987, the Federal Agricultural Mortgage Corporation, commonly known as Famer Mac, is a federally chartered, private corporation (NYSE: AGM) responsible for guaranteeing the timely repayment of principal and interest to investors in the agricultural secondary market. This secondary market allows a lending institution to sell a qualified farm real estate loan to an agricultural mortgage marketing facility, or pooler, which packages these loans, and sells to investors securities that are backed by, or represent interests in, the pooled loans.

Farmer Mac is regulated by the Farm Credit Administration, which also regulates the Federal Farm Credit banks. Farmer Mac is distinct from Farm Credit and has its own charter, balance sheet, and management. Farmer Mac is a private corporation as opposed to a nationwide cooperative network of borrower-owned lending institutions. Another key difference between the two organizations is that most Farm Credit System institutions are primary lenders to borrowers in rural America, whereas Farmer Mac serves as a secondary market for lenders that extend credit in rural America.

Farmer Mac debt issues are not state and local tax exempt as is the case with Federal Farm Credit Bank and Federal Home Loan Bank debt issuance. Ultimately, Farmer Mac is not liable for any Federal Farm Credit System debt obligation or security. Likewise, no Farm Credit System institution is liable for any debt obligation of Farmer Mac. As mentioned previously, Farmer Mac debt is not rated.

---

[14] Ibid.

[15] Farm Credit Administration, "History of FCA and FCS," https://www.fca.gov/about/history/historyFCA_FCS.html.

Tennessee Valley Authority (TVA)

TVA was established by Congress in 1933 to develop the Tennessee Valley region. It was designed by President Roosevelt as part of a greater effort to lift the nation out of the depths of the Great Depression. TVA has dealt with a number of vital issues in the Tennessee Valley over the years, including power production, navigation, flood control, malaria prevention, reforestation, erosion control, and energy conservation.[16]

TVA has not received any appropriations from Congress since 1959 due to political pressures. It finances all of its programs through power sales and the occasional sale of bonds in the capital markets. TVA's debt is currently subject to a statutory limit of $30 billion outstanding.[17] Interest from TVA securities is exempt from state on local taxes.

Student Loan Marketing Association (Sallie Mae)

Sallie Mae was fully privatized into the SLM Corporation in 2004 (NASDAQ: SLM); it presently provides consumer banking services. Originally, designed to support the guaranteed student loan program created by the Higher Education Act of 1965, the Student Loan Marketing Association, commonly known as Sallie Mae, was chartered by Congress in 1972 as a government-sponsored enterprise. Sallie Mae previously originated federally guaranteed student loans originated under the Federal Family Education Loan Program and worked as a servicer and collector of federal student loans on behalf of the Department of Education.[18]

In 2014, Sallie Mae split into two publicly traded entities; its loan-servicing operation and most of its loan portfolio were split off into a separate, publicly traded entity called Navient Corporation (NASDAQ: NAVI).

OVERVIEW OF FEDERAL AGENCIES

Government National Mortgage Association (Ginnie Mae)

Despite carrying the "Mae" in its name, Ginnie Mae is not a GSE but a government-owned corporation that is part of the Department of Housing and Urban Development (HUD—see ahead). The Government National Mortgage Association was created in 1968 when Fannie Mae was split into two different entities. Ginnie Mae was tasked with guaranteeing the mortgage-backed securities (MBS) issued by other government

---

[16]Tennessee Valley Authority, "About TVA: Our History," www.tva.com/About-TVA/Our-History.
[17]*State of North Carolina v. Tennessee Valley Authority*, "Expert Report of Susan F. Tierney, PhD: The Financial Feasibility and Reasonableness of Reducing NOx and SO2 Emissions from TVA's Coal-Fired Power Plants," October 26, 2006, http://www.ncdoj.gov/getdoc/f275bf3e-b5bf-4b34-ab5f-b8fc37f61a1c/Tierney-Expert-Report.aspx.
[18]Sallie Mae, "About: Who We Are," www.salliemae.com/about/who-we-are/history/.

agencies, mostly the Federal Housing Association (FHA) and the Veterans administration (VA). Fannie Mae (and later, Freddie Mac) was responsible for guaranteeing conventional mortgages not guaranteed or insured by government agencies.[19]

MBSs insured by Ginnie Mae have always had the explicit backing of the U.S. government. Ginnie Mae does not need to issue debt securities in the financial markets due to its direct government link. Moreover, Ginnie Mae has never needed a government bailout. An understanding of the credit and ownership differences between Ginnie Mae and its GSE colleagues, Fannie Mae and Freddie Mac, is crucial to understanding the collapse of the housing market in 2008. This topic is addressed in detail later in this chapter.

Department of Housing and Urban Development (HUD)

The United States Department of Housing and Urban Development (HUD) is a Cabinet-level department of the U.S. federal government. HUD was established by the Urban Development Act in 1965 as part of the Great Society program. Its core mission is to promote homeownership, support community development, and increase access to affordable housing.[20]

HUD debt is backed by the full faith and credit of the U.S. government but is infrequently issued. At the beginning of 2016 it had approximately $6.2 billion in outstanding debt.[21]

Financing Corporation (FICO)

The Financing Corporation (FICO) was created by Congress in response to the U.S. Savings and Loan (S&L) crisis during the 1980s in an attempt to recapitalize the insolvent Federal Savings and Loan Insurance Corporation (FSLIC).[22] FICO assumed all of the assets and liabilities of the FSLIC Resolution Fund after it was abolished by the Financial Institutions Reform, Recovery, and Enforcement Act of 1989 (FIRREA). The Resolution Trust Corporation Refinancing, Restructuring, and Improvement Act of 1991 terminated FICO's borrowing authority.

Resolution Funding Corporation (REFCO)

The Resolution Funding Corporation (REFCO) is a government-sponsored enterprise that provides funds to the Resolution Trust Corporation (RTC). RTC was established by Congress as part of the Financial Institutions Reform, Recovery, and Enforcement Act of

---

[19]Ginnie Mae, "About Us: Who We Are," www.ginniemae.gov/about_us/who_we_are/Pages/our_history.aspx.
[20]U.S. Department of Housing and Urban Development, "HUD History," http://portal.hud.gov/hudportal/HUD?src=/about/hud_history.
[21]Bloomberg.com.
[22]Ibid.

1989 (FIRREA) to finance the bailout of the savings and loan industry. REFCO ceased issuing bonds in 1991 with approximately $30 billion outstanding of long-term debt.[23]

Private Export Funding Corporation (PEFCO)

The Private Export Funding Corporation was created in 1970 with the support of the U.S. Department of Treasury, and the Export-Import Bank of the United States (Eximbank). PEFCO's shareowners include most of the major commercial banks involved in financing U.S. exports, industrial companies involved in exporting U.S. products and services, and financial services companies. PEFCO's goal is to increase the funding available for financing the export of U.S. goods and services by making dollar-denominated loans to foreign importers.[24]

PEFCO has approximately $6.5 billion in debt outstanding to support this mission. Interest payments are directly guaranteed by Eximbank, which is an Executive Branch agency of the U.S. government.[25]

PEFCO long-term debt is rated AAA by Moody's and Fitch consistent with their U.S. sovereign rating. Standard & Poor's downgraded its rating on PEFCO's Secured Notes to A+ in light of increased risk to PEFCO's business model as a result of the ongoing debate in the U.S. Congress over Eximbank's charter.[26]

Overseas Private Investment Corporation (OPIC)

The Overseas Private Investment Corporation (OPIC) was established in 1971 as an agency of the U.S. government and is organized with a corporate structure. OPIC's funding is appropriated and reauthorized on a regular basis by Congress. OPIC is able to finance itself through its operations. It has operated on a self-sustaining basis at no net cost to American taxpayers since its inception.

OPIC serves the role of providing development financing, operating in over 150 countries around the world. OPIC provides medium- to long-term financing through direct loans and loan guaranties to eligible investment projects in developing and emerging countries where conventional institutions are reluctant or unable to lend. In addition, OPIC offers political risk insurance and support for private equity investment funds.

OPIC is another infrequent issuer with approximately $6.5 billion in debt outstanding as of 2015. The debt consists largely of 5- to 15-year floating-rate notes that carry sinking funds and/or put options. Its authority to guarantee and insure U.S. investments abroad is backed by the full faith and credit of the U.S. government.[27]

---

[23]Ibid.

[24]Private Export Funding Corporation, "About: Overview," http://pefco.com/about/overview.html.

[25]Ibid.

[26]Bloomberg.com

[27]OPIC, "Who We Are," www.opic.gov/who-we-are/overview.

International Bank for Reconstruction and Development (IBRD)

The International Bank for Reconstruction and Development (IBRD) is an arm of the World Bank, founded in 1944 to aid Europe's recovery from World War II. As such, it is more properly classified as a *supra-sovereign* agency. The IBRD provides loans to developing countries for capital programs and to promote sustainable, equitable, and job-creating growth to reduce poverty on a global basis.[28]

To fund these development projects in member countries, World Bank bonds are issued through the IBRD in a variety of currencies and structures. The World Bank's borrowing requirements are primarily determined by its lending activities for development projects.[29]

IBRD debt is not covered by an explicit guarantee of the U.S. government, but does carry the same ratings as U.S. GSEs and agencies. Structured like a cooperative, the IBRD currently has 186 member countries and is headquartered in Washington D.C. The five largest shareholders are the United States (17% of total voting power), Japan (8%), Germany (5%), France (4.5%), and the United Kingdom (4.3%).[30]

IBRD debt along with other supra debt like the International Finance Corporation (another arm of the World Bank) and the Inter-American Development Bank are becoming more popular among investors as issuance from the U.S. housing GSEs continues to shrink in the wake of the 2008 subprime mortgage crisis.

TYPES OF AGENCY DEBT

GSE issuers over the years have utilized different methods to issue debt, including Dutch auctions as well as a robust negotiated underwriting process. The type of issuance is largely determined by the size, scale, maturity, and structure of the bond being issued.

The basic debt types found in the agency market include:

- Discount notes
- Bullets
- Agency benchmark programs
- Floating-rate notes
- Callables
- Medium-term notes

Figure 11.2 is an example of the debt profile one of the larger issuers, FFCB.

---

[28]World Bank, "About: What We Do," http://www.worldbank.org/en/about/what-we-do/brief/ibrd.

[29]Ibid.

[30]World Bank, "World Bank Group Finances," https://finances.worldbank.org/Shareholder-Equity/IBRD-Voting-Shares-Column-Chart/wf2k-zkn9.

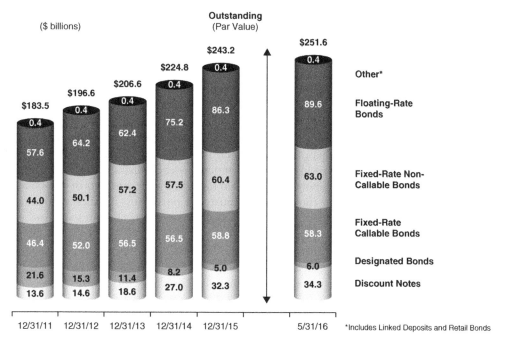

($ billions)

Outstanding
(Par Value)

FIGURE 11.2 Federal Farm Credit Debt Security issuance snapshot
Source: Federal Farm Credit Funding Investor Presentation 5/2016

Discount Notes

Agency discount notes (DNs) range in maturity from overnight to 360 days. Issued at a discount to their face value (similar to Treasury bills), discount notes do not pay coupon interest. At maturity the notes are redeemed at par or 100% of face value. The difference between the issue price and face value constitutes the interest paid to the bondholder. Discount notes are only issued by the GSEs. The "Big 3" issuers, Fannie, Freddie, and Home Loan, issue discount notes weekly to a selling group of banks and brokerage firms through a competitive bidding process. The Big 3 issuers and the Farming GSE's (Farm Credit and Famer Mac) also post discount note offerings with a wide variety of maturity and settlement dates on an electronic offering page known as the Window on a daily basis.

Bullets

Bullets are a common type of agency bond with a stated maturity, a fixed-rate coupon, and payment schedule and no call options. Bullet maturities generally range from 1 to 30 years and pay interest semiannually. However, there are rare exceptions where the coupon convention is on a monthly, quarterly, or annual basis.

Agency Benchmark Programs

Agency benchmark programs are large syndicated bullet debt issues sold by the GSEs. In the late 1990s, amid declining U.S. Treasury issuance, Fannie Mae and Freddie Mac saw the opportunity for growth. Overall, the 1990s was a decade of declining federal deficits and a commensurate reduction in Treasury debt issuance as well as increased domestic and global demand for U.S. Treasury paper. Fannie Mae was the first to seize the opportunity to exploit this supply/demand imbalance by trying to become the U.S. dollar–denominated debt issuance global benchmark. Freddie Mac quickly followed suit.

During this period there was rapid growth in the U.S. housing market, which was a boon to Fannie Mae's and Freddie Mac's fortunes. To capitalize on the increases in demand for mortgage financing, both GSEs needed to source large amounts of capital for mortgage pool creation and for their retained mortgage portfolios. To succeed, Fannie Mae knew they needed to change the funding model to incorporate features such as:

- Commitment to a curve term structure
- Consistent size—large and global debt issuance across the curve
- A published issuance calendar—transparency and predictability of supply across global markets
- Non–U.S. dollar issuance to address global investors
- Development of a futures market to promote liquidity
- Development of a funding or repo market

The majority of GSE debt is issued by Fannie Mae, Freddie Mac, Home Loan, and Farm Credit. Fannie and Freddie are unique in that they serve a similar single purpose and have a centralized process and operation. FHLB and FFCB are more regional in mission and decentralized in structure. The member cooperative structure of FFCBs and the FHLBs presented unique challenges in the form of less issuance scale and less commitment to issuance maturity and type. Following is a brief summary of each of the four major GSEs global note programs.

Fannie Mae Benchmark Note and Freddie Mac Reference Note Programs   Benchmark notes and reference notes are issued or auctioned according to a predetermined calendar on a monthly basis in maturities ranging from 3 months to 30 years. A core dealer group is responsible for issuing or bidding on the following structures.

- Benchmark/reference bills—short-term discount notes
- Benchmark/reference bullets—intermediate and long-term bullets
- Callable benchmark notes—intermediate and long-term callable notes (no longer issued)

FHLB Global Notes and TAPS Programs
- Global notes are issued on a monthly basis according to a predetermined calendar across a 2- to 10-year curve in minimum size of at least $1 billion.

- TAP notes are issued on a quarterly basis across a 1- to 10-year curve. Individual issues are often reopened to aggregate the most common maturities.

FFCB-Designated Bonds Program   Designated bonds are issued on a periodic basis across a 2- to 10-year curve and distributed through a core group of dealers.

Floating-Rate Notes   Floating-rate notes (FRNs or *floaters*) are another commonly issued structure. Floaters are tied to an index and pay interest on a quarterly basis, consistent with a reference rate or index. They are generally issued in maturities ranging from three months to three years.

Some of the most common types of GSE FRN reference rates include:

- 1-, 3-, 6-, and 12-month London Inter-Bank Overnight Rate (LIBOR)
- The BLS consumer price index (CPI) inflation gauge
- Prime bank lending rate
- Federal funds rate

Callable Notes

Callable note issuance has been very popular with the GSEs since the early 1990s and was spurred by the dramatic growth in the mortgage securitization market during that time. Callable notes were the perfect vehicle to feed the growth of the U.S. mortgage market because they replicate the characteristics of the retained mortgages held in the investment portfolios of the issuing GSEs. From an investor's perspective, callable bonds offered a higher yield spread relative to bullets.

To fulfill their mission of facilitating affordable residential housing in the United States, Fannie Mae and Freddie Mac guarantee and purchase residential mortgage loans. Typical mortgages have stated final maturities of 15 and 30 years, but expected durations are considerably shorter, given the mobility of today's homebuyers and borrowers' ability to pre-pay or refinance. For example, the data compiled by the GSEs reveal that a current market 30-year mortgage has an expected duration of just 7 years.[31] This mismatch between stated mortgage maturity and expected duration, known as a *duration gap*, can create asset–liability funding problems for mortgage lenders.

For the GSEs this occurs when the net duration of the retained mortgage portfolio (asset) differs from the net duration of the funding portfolio (liability). Large duration gaps can lead to excess cash reserves not being deployed efficiently or, conversely, delays and possible defaults on principal and interest payments. To prevent this from occurring, the GSEs have come to rely on increased callable note issuance.[32]

As stated earlier, callable debt offers an investor a yield premium over a similar bullet maturity. This pickup in yield or spread is achieved without sacrificing credit quality.

---

[31]Freddie Mac, "Product Overview: Callable Debt," http://www.freddiemac.com/debt/pdf/callable-debt_brochure.pdf.
[32]Ibid.

A characteristic of callable notes is negative convexity, which limits price appreciation potential, but also acts as a price cushion during times of rising rates. However, for buy-and-hold investors with flexibility on duration targets, callable notes can be a very attractive alternative to similar GSE bullet bonds.

Medium-Term Notes   Another major category of fixed-rate bonds issued by the GSEs is medium-term notes (MTNs). The main feature of these bonds is their flexibility. These securities can be either fixed, step, or floating rate and come in a wide range of maturities and structures. Issues are usually created based upon investor inquiry and dealer interest based upon historical demand for particular structures. Medium-term notes are continuously available for underwriting for the three major GSEs. The opportunity to underwrite MTNs for the other GSEs and agencies occurs selectively or not at all.

The term *medium-term note* can be misleading, as they are not limited to midrange maturities. MTNs are issued with final maturities of 6 months to 30 years. Deals are usually negotiated underwritings with one or more broker-dealers involved. Due to their smaller deal sizes and vast variety of structures, MTNs may offer less liquidity than larger global issues.

COST-BENEFIT ANALYSIS OF CALLABLE NOTES

Callable note structures give the issuer of a bond the right, but not the obligation, to redeem the security beginning on a predetermined date or schedule of dates (known as call dates) prior to the final maturity. The buyer of the callable bond has in effect purchased a bullet bond and simultaneously sold a "synthetic" call option to the issuer. This call option is referred to as synthetic because it is embedded in the security and doesn't exist otherwise. The value of the call option is driven by the market volatility and is priced as a swap on an option, known as a swaption. Also affecting the value of this option are factors such as the style of call option (American, Bermudan, or European), the length of the call protection period, and the spread between the bond's coupon rate and the current market rate of securities with similar structures. The aggregated influence of these factors determines whether the option is in-the-money, at-the-money, or out-of-the-money. The option's value is paid to the investor in the form of additional yield above that of a noncallable bond with similar maturity. In other words, the buyer of a callable bond may be viewed as betting that yields will remain relatively stable or perhaps even rise slightly. If correct, the issuer's call option will be out-of-the-money, enabling the investor to capture the yield spread over noncallable bonds until maturity.

Callable bonds can be problematic to professional investors for a variety of reasons related to the duration uncertainty and convexity issues including:

■ Reinvestment risk
■ Extension risk
■ Negative convexity and par compression risk

Reinvestment Risk

Duration uncertainty is the primary concern facing the callable bond investor. Having sold the call option, an investor does not know if the bond will be redeemed prior to maturity. Referred to as call risk or reinvestment risk, this occurs when interest rates fall and issuers exercise their in-the-money call options. Having been called out of their investment before maturity, the investor is then faced with the prospect of reinvesting at a lower rate of return.

Extension Risk

The risk that the life of a callable bond extends beyond initial expectations is referred to as extension risk. Rising interest rates imply a longer duration for callable bonds. Portfolio managers with duration targets seek to maximize returns without exceeding duration thresholds. Purchasing callable notes priced to the expected duration is an effective way to employ this strategy. The risk of extension beyond the duration and out to the final maturity date will generally occur in periods of rising rates, denying the investment manager the opportunity to reinvest at higher rates.

Negative Convexity and Par Compression

Callable notes have a unique "pull-to-par" dynamic that can work both for and against the investor. The embedded call option acts as a cap on upside price potential by shortening the duration as rates decline. This phenomenon where a bond's price rises less for a downward move in yield than its price declines for a commensurate upward move in yield is known as negative convexity. Alternatively, the embedded call option acts as a downside price cushion to the callable bond. Embedded call options have both intrinsic and time value, so even as the intrinsic option value declines in a rising rate environment, the time value remaining in the option helps limit the downside price action relative to comparable bullet bonds. Therefore, par compression works to effectively limit both the upside and downside price action of callable bonds. Although not necessarily a desired or even planned-for outcome, par compression can benefit an investor by limiting some of the downside risk during extreme market moves.

Partial Call Bonds

While the vast majority of callable notes are callable "in whole," meaning the entire bond is redeemed if called by the issuer, some notes are callable only "in part." As part of an issue is called, a value is assigned to reflect the percentage of the original principal amount that is still outstanding. This value is referred to as a *factor*. Despite offering a slightly higher rate of return relative to wholly callable notes, factor bonds are a minor presence in the markets and trade infrequently. Difficulty experienced by many accounting systems in accurately tracking and reporting factor values are a further impediment to the trading of partial call bonds.

THE 2008 FINANCIAL CRISIS

The 2008 financial crisis has its origins in the real estate market, specifically the subprime mortgage market. Irresponsible and predatory lending practices by banks and mortgage originators, encouraged by government policies dating back to the 1980s that sought to expand homeownership to more of the population, created an unsustainable housing bubble. By the 1990s, a decade of declining federal debt and relaxed federal banking legislation and regulatory oversight, excessive real estate risk-taking had become the order of the day. The rigorous mortgage lending standards of the past were cast aside by bankers, who rushed to increase mortgage creation by extending credit to less-than-prime borrowers, often with little or no documentation.[33]

In early 2000, all manner of high-risk exotic mortgages became available. These loans were marketed to high-risk buyers who never would have been able to buy a home in the past. Lenders then sold these mortgages to investment banks to be repackaged into pools for securitization. These new collateralized bonds were sold in turn to numerous types of investors around the world.

Despite the dubious nature of the collateral, most of these bonds were given AAA ratings. Most investors would not have bought these mortgage securities or collateralized debt obligations (CDOs) without a AAA rating from one of the three major ratings agencies. Of course, fees to rate the bonds were paid to the ratings agencies by the very same investment banks that created the products in the first place.[34]

With a seemingly insatiable homebuyer demand for credit and investor appetite for these mortgage products, the mortgage lenders and investment banks fueled the flames of the housing bubble. Everything was fine as long as house prices kept going up.

As the mortgage market changed, so did Fannie Mae and Freddie Mac. They were mandated by the federal government to further increase homeownership by guaranteeing and purchasing subprime mortgages into their ballooning retained portfolio.

In 2006–2007 interest rates began to rise, and home prices soon peaked and began a downward spiral. As is the fate of all market bubbles, this one burst. As prices collapsed, defaults and foreclosures increased dramatically. In many parts of the United States, prices fell more than even the most aggressive models ever forecasted. A relatively small portion of the loans contributed to a disproportionate part of the losses.

The two giant GSEs, Fannie Mae and Freddie Mac, were at the heart of all of this. At the time they owned or guaranteed approximately 40% of the $12+ trillion mortgage market.[35] Efforts had been made in the U.S. Congress going back to the late 1990s to

---

[33]Robin Blackburn, "The Subprime Crisis," *New Left Review*, 50 (March–April 2008), https://faculty.washington.edu/sparke/blackburn.pdf.

[34]Council on Foreign Relations, "The Credit Rating Controversy," February 19, 2015, http://www.cfr.org/financial-crises/credit-rating-controversy/p22328.

[35]Congressional Budget Office, "Fannie Mae, Freddie Mac, and the Federal Role in the Secondary Mortgage Market," December 22, 2010, www.cbo.gov/publication/21992.

curtail or eliminate Fannie and Freddie's activities or, potentially, to privatize or even eliminate them. This effort failed thanks to extensive lobbying of Congress by the GSE's consultants and political action committees. Along with the other players in the mortgage industry, they continued to assume more risk with little fear of the consequences thanks to their implied federal backing.[36]

Conservatorship of Fannie Mae and Freddie Mac

As mentioned earlier, the FHFA placed Fannie Mae and Freddie Mac into conservatorship in September 2008 when they were on the verge of insolvency. Conservatorship is the "legal process in which a person or entity is appointed to establish control and oversight of a company in an effort to restore it to solvency."[37] The FHFA would strive to carry on Fannie and Freddie's business as well as preserve and conserve the assets and property of both companies.

No time frame has been given as to when this conservatorship may end. The issue remains a point of contention with many in Congress and the financial community.

Several actions have been taken by the conservator to nurse the companies back to health:

Cash Injection: On Sept. 8, 2008, the U.S. Treasury pledged up to $200 billion in cash to help the companies cope with mortgage default losses.

Senior Preferred Stock Purchase Agreement: The FHFA prompted Fannie Mae and Freddie Mac to the issue to the Treasury new senior preferred stock and common stock warrants amounting to 79.9% for each institution at $0.00001 per share.[38] Needless to say, this greatly reduced the current shareholder stock value.

The Treasury agreed to purchase additional preferred stock in Fannie Mae on a quarterly basis when required to address any negative net equity as per the Senior Preferred Stock Purchase Agreement (SPSPA) between Fannie Mae, Treasury, and FHFA. In return, Fannie Mae and Freddie Mac pay a dividend to the Treasury. This agreement helps to ensure that Fannie Mae and Freddie Mac remain adequately funded and can continue to pay their direct obligations as scheduled.

Obligations: The Company's obligations will be paid in the normal course of business during the Conservatorship. The Treasury Department, through the secured lending credit facility and the SPSPA, has significantly enhanced the ability of

---

[36]Ibid.

[37]Federal Finance Housing Agency, "FAQs: Questions and Answers on Conservatorship," www
.fhfa.gov/Media/PublicAffairs/Pages/Fact-Sheet-Questions-and-Answers-on-Conservatorship
.aspx.

[38]Federal Finance Housing Agency, "Senior Preferred Stock Purchase Agreements," http://www
.fhfa.gov/conservatorship/pages/senior-preferred-stock-purchase-agreements.aspx.

the Company to meet its obligations. "The Conservator does not anticipate that there will be any disruption in the Company's pattern of payments or ongoing business operations."[39]

Company Stockholders: "During the conservatorship, the Company's stock will continue to trade. However, the powers of the stockholders are suspended until the conservatorship is terminated. Stockholders will continue to retain all rights in the stock's financial worth as determined by the market."[40]

De-Listing: The FHFA, in June 2010, directed Fannie and Freddie to delist their outstanding shares from the NYSE. Both companies' shares had hovered just above the $1/share minimum for some time. Since then the stocks have continued to trade on the Over-the-Counter Bulletin Board.

Dividend: Fannie Mae and Freddie Mac have continued to pay dividends to the U.S. Treasury over and above each of the bailout amounts lent through the crisis. As of this writing, Fannie Mae and Freddie Mac's combined dividend payments to the U.S. Treasury totaled $236.4 billion versus the $187.4 billion total combined bailout cost. Fannie Mae, as of March 2016, has paid a total of $148.5 billion in payments to the Treasury, well above its $116.1 billion bailout.[41] Freddie Mac has paid a total of $98.2 billion, also well above its $71.3 billion bailout.[42]

Reduction of Fannie Mae and Freddie Mac's Retained Mortgage Investment Portfolio By 2008 Fannie Mae and Freddie Mac had become two of the largest debt issuers in the world. The combined $1.5 trillion+ combined portfolios presented too much of a systemic risk to the nation. Under FHFA regulation and the Purchase Agreement with the Treasury, as amended on August 17, 2012, both Fannie Mae and Freddie Mac's mortgage-related investments portfolio were subject to a cap beginning in 2013 that decreases by 15% each year until the cap reaches $250 billion. Prior to the August 2012 amendment, the portfolio was subject to a cap that decreased by 10% each year.[43] As a result, the debt issuance of these two large GSE's has mirrored the reduction in their retained portfolios.

CONCLUSION

The story doesn't end here. Conservatorship was never meant to be a long-term solution. U.S. housing policy remains controversial among policymakers, academics, and

---

[39]Federal Finance Housing Agency, "FAQs: Questions and Answers on Conservatorship," www .fhfa.gov/Media/PublicAffairs/Pages/Fact-Sheet-Questions-and-Answers-on-Conservatorship .aspx.

[40]Ibid.

[41]Fannie Mae, "Progress Q1 2016," May 5, 2016, http://www.fanniemae.com/resources/file/ aboutus/pdf/q12016_progressreport.pdf.

[42]Freddie Mac, "Multifamily Securitization," March 31, 2016, http://www.freddiemac.com/ multifamily/pdf/mf_securitization_investor-presentation.pdf.

[43]Freddie Mac, Investor Presentation, May 2016.

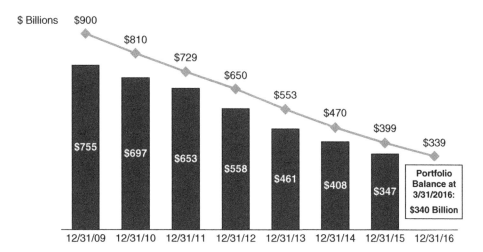

FIGURE 11.3   Fannie & Freddie's shrinking retained portfolio
Source: Freddie Mac Investor Presentation, May 2016

regulators in Washington, DC, and throughout the country. There are very real ideo-logical divides on the issue. Democrats generally support social mechanisms to promote broad U.S. homeownership, acknowledging it as an integral component of the American Dream. Republicans consider such social engineering contrary to the free-market capi-talism upon which our country was established. At the time of this writing, the political divide shows no sign of narrowing and represents the largest hurdle in the long-running housing policy debate.

To date, there have not been any structural changes to the GSEs or to the future of Fannie Mae and Freddie Mac, nor have any serious legislative proposals been enacted. The Administration and Congress have discussed reforming the housing agencies, but no action has been taken. The nature of housing GSE reform is highly uncertain, in that there is no agreed-upon plan, either for what should be changed or for how it should be changed. That is, should the new model be more public in nature, more private, or just regulated in a better way? This uncertainty represents a real political or headline risk on top of the already complex and inherent financial-related risks.

CHAPTER 12

Inflation-Linked Bonds

Henry Willmore

nflation-linked bonds were first issued by the United States Treasury Department in 1997. They are designed to provide investors with an asset that compensates them for inflation. The principal of those bonds is indexed to the consumer price index (CPI). Interest payments are also effectively indexed through the application of a fixed interest rate to the indexed or adjusted principal. Inflation-linked bonds appeal to a variety of investors, including pension funds, many of which have to make payments tied to the rate of inflation. In addition, inflation-linked bonds provide diversification for investors who hold other assets such as equities and conventional bonds.

Inflation-linked bonds are popularly known as TIPS (Treasury inflation-protected securities) in the United States. As of the end of 2015, public holdings of TIPS totaled $1.168 trillion. Gross issuance was $155 billion in 2015.[1] In recent years, the Treasury Department has issued TIPS with maturities of 5, 10, and 30 years. In spite of the growth of the volume of TIPS outstanding, the market for inflation-linked remains less liquid than for conventional Treasury bonds. Trading activity for TIPS tends to spike in conjunction with auction results and the release of data on the consumer price index.

INDEXATION

The bonds are indexed to the non–seasonally adjusted consumer price index (NSA CPI). The non–seasonally adjusted index is used because it is not subject to revision. The seasonally adjusted CPI is revised periodically as seasonal adjustment factors get recalculated. The use of the NSA CPI for indexing purposes introduces a seasonal pattern to how fast the principal for TIPS increases. Increases for the NSA CPI tend to be quite rapid in March through May and slow or even negative during the months in the second half of the year. A significant part of the seasonality in the NSA CPI is due to patterns seen in retail gasoline prices, which tend to rise sharply in the spring.

---

[1]BNY Mellon, *Special Report: Inflation*, June 2014, https://www.bnymellon.com/_global-assets/pdf/our-thinking/special-report-inflation.pdf.

When the NSA CPI declines for a given month, the principal of TIPS issues also declines. At maturity, if the inflation-adjusted principal is less than the security's original principal, the investor will be paid the original principal. This provides some limited protection in the event of deflation. It should be noted, however, that the track record of the CPI suggests that deflation over a multiyear period is fairly unlikely. Over the 25-year period ending in 2015, the average annual increase for the CPI was 2.4%.[2]

The change in principal is calculated daily. The rate of increase over a given month is based upon how much the NSA CPI increased two months earlier. For example, the increase in the value of the principal over the course of July is determined by how much the CPI increased in May. This two-month lag structure is needed because the May CPI is the last CPI report available before July 1. CPI reports for a given month are typically released in the third week of the next month. So the May CPI will typically be released in the third week of June and will determine accretion (the growth rate) of the principal on each TIPS issue from July 1 to July 31. Using the data for the NSA CPI the Treasury Department publishes an index ratio for each TIPS issue. The index ratio is calculated for each day and reflects how much the principal has grown since issuance.

Mathematically, the index ratio for a particular TIPS issue can be expressed as follows:

$$IRt = RCPI(t)/RCPI(0)$$

where IR(t) is the index ratio on day t, RCPI (t) is the reference CPI on day t, and RCPI (0) is the reference CPI for the issue in question on its issue date. As we noted, there is a lag structure between the NSA CPI and the reference CPI. For example, the reference CPI on July 1 is the April NSA CPI and the reference CPI on August 1 is the May NSA CPI. For the 31 days between July 1 and August 1 the reference CPI changes by 1/31 of the difference between the April and May NSA CPI. The value of the principal on any given day is its value when issued times the index ratio for that issue on that day.

TIPS issues pay interest twice a year. The interest rate is announced by the Treasury Department prior to the auction of each issue and reflects market conditions in the period ahead of the auction. It is applied to the value of the principal. For example, if July 15 is the date for one of the two annual interest rate payments, the interest rate is applied to the value of the principal for that date.

REAL YIELDS AND INFLATION BREAKEVENS

Investors and traders who are active in the TIPS market pay close attention to the inflation breakeven for each issue. The inflation breakeven is the difference in interest rate of nominal Treasury bond (nominal yield) and the interest rate of a TIPS issue of similar maturity. For example, a five-year Treasury might have a yield of 3% while five-year TIPS are yielding 1%. The breakeven inflation rate is 2%, meaning that inflation has to

---

[2]Bureau of Labor Statistics, "Consumer Price Index Summary," June 2015.

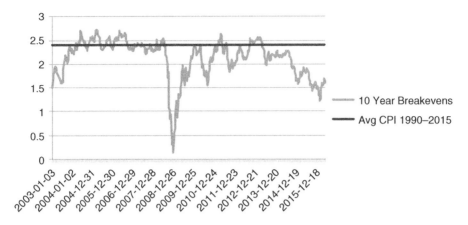

FIGURE 12.1   Ten-year inflation breakeven: Federal Reserve constant maturity series

rise by at least 2% per year over the remaining life of the issue for the return on TIPS to exceed that on the nominal Treasury. It should be noted that the inflation breakeven is not a pure measure of inflation expectations since it also incorporates other factors such as liquidity premia.

A trader or investor might form a judgment that the breakeven on inflation-linked bond is cheap, meaning that he or she expects inflation to exceed the inflation breakevens implied by current rates. If, for example, the investor expects inflation to average 2.5% while inflation breakevens stood at 2%, he or she would have an interest in owning TIPS rather than nominal Treasuries.

The Federal Reserve maintains constant maturity series for breakeven inflation for 5-year and 10-year TIPS. Figure 12.1 shows the 10-year series. It shows the average annual increase in the CPI over a 25-year period (1990–2015).

As the graph shows, there are periods when inflation breakevens in the 10-year sector fluctuate within a fairly narrow band around its long-term average. There are other periods when significant deviations occur. Some of these deviations reflect changing market perceptions about future inflation. For example, periods of significant decline in oil prices also tend to be periods when inflation expectations fall.

However, breakevens can drop for reasons that have little to do with inflationary expectations. Periods of financial stress often provoke strong demand for the safe and liquid assets. Nominal Treasuries are the asset class that investors seek out during such periods. This works to compress the spread between the yields between nominal Treasuries and TIPS. Sometimes, as during the height of the financial crisis in 2008, the compression in spreads will produce declines in breakevens that are not credible when compared with the inflationary history of the United States.

For TIPS investors the distortions to breakevens during periods of financial stress can be looked upon as opportunities. Historical experience suggests that a long-term dip in inflation (as measured by the CPI) below 1% is quite unlikely, but this is what breakevens were priced for in late 2008. Moreover, TIPS investors need to consider that the Federal

Reserve adopted an official inflation target of 2% in 2012.[3] This target is defined in terms of the *personal consumption expenditure* (PCE) deflator, an alternative measure of consumer price inflation. In recent years, the CPI has run about 0.4% faster than the PCE deflator.[4] Should the Federal Reserve achieve its inflation target of 2% for the PCE deflator, the CPI would likely rise slightly faster than that.

With the CPI having increased by an average of 2.4% per year in the past 25 years and the Federal Reserve having an inflation target that implies the continuation of a similar rate of increase, the fair value for 10-year breakevens is probably within a range between 2.0% and 3.0%.[5] Moves outside that range need to be analyzed carefully and often represent good trading opportunities.

In recent years, real yields have generally been very low and for some maturities negative. The Federal Reserve's real yields data for its 5-year constant maturity series show negative real yields throughout the period from March 2011 to August 2014. This reflected very easy monetary policy as embodied by a near-zero fed funds rate and forward guidance from the Federal Open Market Committee (FOMC) that the fed funds rate would be kept at that level for an extended period of time. The commitment to keep official rates near zero had the effect of pushing down both real and nominal yields for longer maturities. The FOMC's goal was to stimulate the economy by boosting those sectors such as housing that are sensitive to medium- and long-term interest rates.

SEASONALITY OF CONSUMER PRICES

For TIPS issues close to maturity, investors need to carefully consider seasonal patterns. Table 12.1 shows the average change in the CPI by month over the 10-year period ending in 2015.

As the data show, increases in the NSA CPI are much stronger in the first half of the year than the second. The NSA CPI often falls during the fourth quarter. This pattern is due in large part to seasonal movements in gasoline prices, which in turn reflect the maintenance patterns of refineries, which must comply with environmental regulations that call for cleaner-burning and more expensive gasoline blends during the summer months. The seasonal pattern in the NSA CPI is often useful to investors trying to predict how much the principal of an issue will grow as it approaches maturity.

DIVERSIFICATION PROPERTIES

The risk-return properties of inflation-linked bonds and the correlation of those returns with the returns of other asset classes are important factors for investors to consider. A number of studies indicate that the returns on inflation-linked bonds are weakly or

[3]Jeremie Banet, "Did a Bond Market Indicator of Inflation Collapse?" *Barron's* (July 11, 2016), http://www.barrons.com/articles/will-the-fed-undershoot-its-inflation-target-1467998545.
[4]Ibid.
[5]Ibid.

TABLE 12.1 Average Month Change
in the NSA CPI (2006–2015)

Month	CPI Change
January	0.72
February	0.91
March	1.35
April	0.84
May	0.79
June	0.59
July	0.11
August	0.14
September	0.09
October	−0.43
November	−0.66
December	−0.53

negatively correlated with returns on other asset classes such as nominal bonds, equities, real estate, and commodities. A weak correlation with other asset classes implies that TIPS are a good source of diversification for a portfolio composed of those types of assets.

TAX TREATMENT

Interest payments on TIPS and increases in the value of the principal from inflation indexation are subject to federal tax but exempt from state and local taxes. The taxation of "phantom income" on accrued but not realized increases in the value of the principal on TIPS has been a negative feature from the perspective of investors. The Internal Revenue Service has a form that TIPS investors must fill out to calculate the amount of this income.

RISKS

While TIPS possess good diversification properties and help to protect investors against inflation, they are not without risk. As with any bond, their price fluctuates with interest rates. Moreover, in recent years the real yields implied by TIPS prices have at times been negative. While a drop in real yields implies a gain for an existing investor, very low or negative real yields are a potential source of discouragement for new investors.

There are also some event risks with respect to inflation that participants in the inflation-linked bond market need to consider. These event risks are largely tied to government policy changes with respect to the structure of the tax system. The CPI measures consumer prices after sales taxes. If the United Stated shifts from the current largely income-based system of taxation to one based upon consumption, this would result in a significant upward impact on consumer prices as the shift is implemented. Another potential policy change that would cause a potentially large rise in the CPI would be the adoption of a carbon tax, whether at the federal level or state and local level.

Technical changes to the consumer price index are also a source of risk that investors should consider. Over the past 20 years, the Bureau of Labor Statistics (the federal agency in charge of producing the CPI) has implemented a series of technical changes in order to improve the accuracy of the CPI as a measure of consumer price inflation. These changes have had the effect of slowing the growth rate of the CPI by slightly over 0.5% per year.[6] Additional tweaks to the CPI remain under consideration.

ISSUANCE SCHEDULE

The Treasury Department issues TIPS through a series of auctions over the course of the year. In recent years, it has auctioned a new five-year issue in April, with a reopening in August and December. Ten-year TIPS have been auctioned in January and July, and auctioned as a reopening in March, May, September, and November. The 30-year TIPS are auctioned in February and reopened in June and October. The auctions are conducted through primary dealers in a manner similar to auctions for nominal Treasuries.

I BONDS

The Treasury Department also sells *I bonds*, which are linked in a similar way to the CPI. Unlike TIPS, they cannot be sought and bought on a secondary market. The purchase limit for I bonds is $10,000 per Social Security number per year. Unlike TIPS, which use every month of CPI data to determine the growth rate of principal, I bonds only make use of the May and November CPI reports to determine accretion.

OTHER COUNTRIES

In 1981, the United Kingdom was the first major industrialized country to issue inflation-linked bonds. Australia followed suit in 1985, and was joined by Canada in 1991, Sweden in 1994, France in 1998, Italy in 2003, Japan in 2004, and Germany in 2006. Several emerging-market countries have also issued inflation-linked bonds, including South Africa, Turkey, Brazil, and Mexico.

REASONS FOR ISSUING INFLATION-LINKED BONDS

There are several reasons why countries choose to issue inflation-linked bonds. Issuing inflation-linked bonds provides diversification in debt instruments. There are potential

---

[6]Bureau of Labor Statistics, "Consumer Price Index Summary," June 2016.

savings if inflation is lower than anticipated. There are also indications that inflation-linked bonds draw in certain investors that are less aggressive participants in the auctions for nominal Treasuries. Inflation-linked bonds are an especially attractive asset class for defined-benefit pension plans. Such plans can use TIPS to defease their liabilities.

The issuance of inflation-linked bonds also provides central banks with a daily gauge of their credibility with the markets when it comes to controlling inflation. To the extent to which this helps central banks in conducting monetary policy, there may be macroeconomic benefits from having the information regarding inflationary expectations that is embedded in TIPS breakevens.

BOND MATHEMATICS

Concepts such as duration and convexity can be applied to inflation-linked bonds. For inflation-linked bonds, duration is a measure of sensitivity of price to changes in real yields. Compared to nominal bonds, coupon payments tend to be relatively small and principal repayment relatively large for inflation-linked bonds. This implies that duration is higher for inflation-linked bonds.

SUMMARY

Inflation-linked bonds are an asset class with properties that are quite distinctive compared to other asset classes such as nominal bonds and equities. They tend to perform well relative to those other categories when inflation is rising. They appeal to investors seeking to control their risk exposure to inflation. Moreover, the returns on TIPS have a low correlation with other asset classes, including equities and conventional bonds. This implies that TIPS can improve the risk/return properties of portfolios that include those other types of assets.

The U.S. market has grown steadily since its inception in 1997, with the amount of TIPS held by the public now in excess of $1 trillion.[7] In 2015, gross issuance of TIPS was $155 billion.[8] In light of projections of substantial future federal deficits, it is likely that TIPS issuance will continue to be substantial.

In recent years, inflation has been low in most countries issuing inflation-linked bonds. Breakevens have declined, partly because of a perception that inflationary risks have declined. This has provided investors with an opportunity to take out relatively cheap insurance against future inflation.

---

[7]U.S. Department of the Treasury, "Foreign Portfolio Holdings of U.S. Securities," June 30, 2015, https://www.treasury.gov/press-center/press-releases/Documents/05.31.16%20TIC%20Final %20Report%20on%20Foreign%20Portfolio%20Holdings%20of%20U.S.%20Securities.pdf.
[8]Ibid.

CHAPTER 13

Mortgage-Backed Securities

Patrick Byrne

The U.S. agency mortgage-backed securities market is one of the largest and arguably the most difficult sector of the investment-grade universe to analyze and understand. Since the issuers in the agency MBS market carry either an implicit or full guarantee of the U.S. Treasury, credit risk on these bonds is minimal. However, unlike other domestic fixed-income instruments, the primary risk in MBS is the early redemption of the bond triggered by prepayment of the underlying mortgage pools. While the risks associated with investing in MBS can be quantified, seldom do these risk events transpire exactly as expected, since the investor is subject to the capricious behavior of homeowners. Successful investing in the mortgage-backed securities market is thus as much an art as it is a science.

Retail buyers beware: The mortgage-backed marketplace is not a friendly place for those not well versed in its nuances. MBS is primarily an institutional marketplace where sophisticated buyers come to reap the rewards on large blocks of securities via in-depth analysis of these complex products. Traders often speak of "odd lots" as any block of bonds smaller than $5,000,000. Historically, price transparency was virtually nonexistent on many types of esoteric MBSs, and spreads on secondary issues can be exceedingly wide. In recent years, the Financial Industry Regulatory Authority (FINRA) and Interactive Data Corporation (IDC) have created a suite of aggregated data products for asset- and mortgage-backed securities to benefit investors and other market participants. Investors can now access the FINRA website to gauge market activity and review price levels by product types. Nevertheless, valuation of agency MBSs remains uniquely more complex than most other fixed-income products. Not only does an investor need to be concerned with the spread that MBSs trade at, he or she must also consider the security's pricing speed (the prepayment assumption on the underlying mortgages). As new types of mortgage related loans are securitized and new structures developed, the market becomes more complicated and mysterious to the average investor. New technology and methods of analyzing and understanding mortgage products further aid professional investors, further disadvantaging novice participants.

Should the retail investor then avoid this market at all costs? Not necessarily. The investor who takes the time to learn about this market may be compensated with higher yields than would be received on alternative fixed-income securities. Mortgage-backed securities can provide investors with high credit quality and great value relative to Treasury or agency securities. As noted above, the MBS investor is paid to take prepayment risk rather than credit risk.

The mortgage-backed securities market has seen momentous growth over the past three decades. Total volume of outstanding mortgage securities exceeded $4.9 trillion at the end of 2015, according to *Barclays Index Data*.[1]

The importance of MBSs to the domestic investment-grade fixed-income universe (i.e., U.S. Treasury, government agency, investment-grade corporate, asset-backed, commercial mortgage–backed, and residential mortgage–backed securities) cannot be overstated. The MBS market is second only in size to the U.S. Treasury market and currently represents the second largest sector of the Barclay Aggregate Index at roughly 29%. Adding in asset-backed securities and commercial mortgage-backed securities, we see that securitized instruments make up nearly 32% of the index. This is quite remarkable when considering that many investors know little, if anything, about this sector.

MORTGAGES: THE BUILDING BLOCKS OF MBSs

Homeowner mortgage loans are the building blocks of the mortgage-backed securities market. Mortgage bonds are backed by the cash flows generated by pools of individual mortgage loans. Sixty-five percent of American households have secured mortgage loans to purchase a home. Before venturing into the complex world of securitization, it is necessary to understand the concept of mortgage lending.

A mortgage is the pledge of property to a creditor as security for the payment of a debt. The borrower (*mortgagor*) is obliged to make a preset series of payments, representing repayment of principal, interest, and fees. If the borrower fails to make these payments, the lender (*mortgagee*) has the right to foreclose on the property. In other words, if you don't pay the loan back along with all the associated fees and interest, the lender can take your house and sell it to recoup his investment. Mortgages are usually paid off over time in incremental payments that steadily reduce the principal of the loan. This is called *amortization*.

If a homeowner borrows $200,000 for 30 years with payments due every month for 360 months (30 years × 12 months per year) at a 3.5% interest rate, the payment schedule would look like this:

> Principal borrowed: $200,000
>
> Total payments: 360
>
> Annual interest rate: 3.50%
>
> Monthly payment amount: $898.09

---

[1]Barclays Index Data.

TABLE 13.1 Amortization Principal and Interest

Payment #	Payment	Principal	Interest	Cum. Principal	Cum. Interest	Principal Balance
1	$8,606.64	$8,106.64	$500.00	$8,106.64	$500.00	$91,893.36
2	$8,606.64	8,147.17	459.47	16,253.81	959.47	83,746.19
3	$8,606.64	8,187.91	418.73	24,441.72	1,378.20	75,558.28
4	$8,606.64	8,228.85	377.79	32,670.57	1,755.99	67,329.43
5	$8,606.64	8,269.99	336.65	40,940.56	2,092.64	59,059.44
6	$8,606.64	8,311.34	295.30	49,251.90	2,387.94	50,748.10
7	$8,606.64	8,352.90	253.74	57,604.80	2,641.68	42,395.20
8	$8,606.64	8,394.66	211.98	65,999.46	2,853.66	34,000.54
9	$8,606.64	8,436.64	170.00	74,436.10	3,023.66	25,563.90
10	$8,606.64	8,478.82	127.82	82,914.92	3,151.48	17,085.08
11	$8,606.64	8,521.21	85.43	91,436.13	3,236.91	8,563.87
12	$8,606.64	8,563.87	42.82	100,000.00	3,279.73	0.00

From Table 13.1 we can make several important observations:

1. The monthly mortgage payment remains constant at $898.09.
2. Each payment is divided in some way between principal and interest.
3. The portion of the monthly mortgage payment applied to interest declines each month, while the portion applied to reducing the principal balance increases. The first payment of $898.09, for example, consisted of $314.76 in paydown of the principal balance, and $583.33 toward the payment of interest. By the 360th and last payment only $2.61 of the $898.09 payment went to pay interest while $898.09 was applied to the remaining principal, bringing the balance down to 0.

WHAT ARE MORTGAGE-BACKED SECURITIES?

Mortgage-backed securities are debt obligations secured by pools of (typically residential) mortgages. Pools are formed by mortgage originators and servicers by combining loans with similar maturities, interest rates, and properties. By grouping a large number of similar mortgages together, the uniqueness of each mortgage is blended into the pool; 500 mortgages of $200,000 apiece create a pool of $100 million. The pool can now be described by its statistical averages such as weighted average maturity (WAM) and weighted average coupon (WAC). The entity creating the pool can make sure no single loan constitutes too large a portion of the pool by limiting the size of the individual mortgages in the pool. (Although conforming loans can be no larger than $417,000, a limited percentage of loans above the $417k amount can be included.) The issuers or servicers then sell the packaged loans to one of the federal housing agencies, such as FNMA or GNMA. A new MBS is created from the pool and pays a rate of interest based on the WAC. Arrangements are made for a servicing agent to collect the mortgage payments from the mortgagors and wire them to the paying agent. The paying agent then uses the collected interest to pay the coupon interest on the MBS to the bondholders. The cash flow of the mortgage payments thus "passes through" to the holders of the mortgage bond, hence the term *pass-through security*.

U.S. housing policy has been the catalyst for the development of the agency pass-through security. Prior to the late 1970s, the vast majority of mortgage loans were held in the portfolios of the originating institutions. By the early 1980s, with rates moving precipitously higher, S&Ls, thrifts, and other financial institutions were well aware of the perils of holding mortgage loans in a rising rate environment. High bankruptcies, insolvencies, and default rates all pose potential threats to the U.S. housing market. The evolution of pass-through MBS enabled mortgage originators to take these risks off the table by selling their loans to be securitized and sold as bonds in the secondary market. This process in turn freed up capital to make new loans, leading to lower mortgage rates and increased availability of credit for homebuyers. With the acceptance of agency MBSs as a high-quality alternative to Treasuries, agencies, and corporate bonds, there has been a massive increase in the size of the mortgage-backed securities market.

THE ISSUING AGENCIES

The Government National Mortgage Association (GNMA) is a wholly owned U.S. government corporation within the U.S. Department of Housing and Urban Development (HUD). The main focus of Ginnie Mae is to ensure liquidity for U.S. government–insured mortgages including those insured by the Federal Housing Administration (FHA), the Veterans Administration (VA), and the Rural Housing Administration (RHA). The Ginnie Mae pass-through program began in 1970. With this program, Ginnie Mae does not buy or sell loans or issue mortgage-backed securities, but instead guarantees investors the timely payment of principal and interest on pools of FHA-insured or VA-guaranteed mortgage loans. So, Ginnie Mae is directly involved in enhancing the availability of credit for FHA and VA qualified homebuyers. The Ginnie Mae guarantee has the full faith and credit of the U.S. government and therefore is perceived to be the safest federal agency. Ginnie Mae markets its pass-throughs under the labels of *Ginnie Mae I* and *Ginnie Mae II*. Ginnie Mae I MBSs are the most popular. When the market refers to Ginnie Mae pass-throughs, unless noted otherwise it is assumed that they are speaking about Ginnie Mae I. With Ginnie Mae I, payment is made on the 15th day of each month. Ginnie Mae II MBSs allow for larger and more geographically dispersed pools, and multiple-issuer pools are permitted. Issuers are permitted to take greater servicing fees, and a wider range of coupons is permitted as well. The minimum pool size is $250,000 for multi-lender pools and $1 million for single-lender pools. With Ginnie Mae II, payment is made on the 20th day of each month.

The majority of mortgages securitized as Ginnie Mae MBSs are those guaranteed by FHA. FHA mortgagors are typically first-time and/or low-income borrowers. While Ginnie Mae was a boon to the available credit for FHA and VA borrowers, it did little for conventional mortgage borrowers. As a result the Federal Home Loan Mortgage Corporation was formed to perform the same magic for conventional loans. Fannie Mae was also given powers to purchase conventional mortgages.

The Federal Home Loan Mortgage Corporation (FHLMC), a government-sponsored enterprise (GSE), was created in 1932 after many bank failures. FNMA and FHLMC do not carry the full faith and credit of the U.S. government, but it is widely believed that the U.S. government would step in to rescue either entity if the situation was warranted. Fannie Mae and Freddie Mac are currently regulated by the Office of Federal Housing Enterprise Oversight (OFHEO), which is part of the U.S. Department of Housing and Urban Development. In 1970, the government authorized Freddie Mac to develop an active secondary market for conventional loans. The principal way Freddie Mac is involved in the pass-through MBS market is through a program known as the Gold PC (Participation Certificate). With the Gold PC, payment is made on the 15th day of each month, 10 days earlier than the MBS of its sister, Fannie Mae.

The Federal National Mortgage Association (FNMA) is a publicly owned government-sponsored enterprise chartered in 1938 to purchase mortgages from lenders and resell them to investors. In 1972, Fannie Mae began purchasing conventional mortgages. FNMA guarantees the timely payment of debt service on all of its MBSs. Fannie Mae pass-throughs are marketed simply as Fannie Mae MBSs and payment is made on the 25th day of the month.

WHY ARE MBSs ATTRACTIVE?

The trading of mortgage-backed securities benefits all market participants as well as the American homeowner. The movement of individual mortgages from originators to investors is facilitated by dealers and brokers. This movement of securities and funds enhances the nationwide housing market by satisfying the demand for mortgage credit throughout the country, increasing the velocity of capital invested in mortgages and helping to keep mortgage rates low. Investors in mortgage-backed securities profit from the attractive yields, liquidity, diversity of structures, and high credit quality.

Higher Risk-Adjusted Yields (Returns)

Even when considering that MBSs are highly complex and possess substantial negative convexity and prepayment risk, these vehicles offer investors superior returns. In today's markets, the drawbacks are more than compensated for by the incremental yield spread of MBSs above comparable-maturity Treasuries.

Credit Quality

MBS pass-throughs are secured in the first instance by the cash flows generated by the mortgage pool. The guarantee provided by the issuing agency insures that bondholders are protected from defaults by mortgagors within the pools. This second line of defense is reinforced in turn by the backing of the federal government. Government National Mortgage Association (GNMA) MBSs carry a full-faith-and-credit guarantee of the United States. Historically, the Federal National Mortgage Association (FNMA) and the Federal Home Loan Mortgage Corporation (FHLMC) were assumed by the investment community to have some implied U.S. government guarantee. On September 6, 2008, the Federal Housing Finance Authority (FHFA) used its authority to place Fannie Mae and Freddie Mac into conservatorship. This was in response to the substantial deterioration in the housing markets that severely damaged Fannie Mae's and Freddie Mac's financial condition and left them unable to fulfill their mission without government intervention.

A key component of the conservatorships is the commitment of the U.S. Department of the Treasury to provide financial support to Fannie Mae and Freddie Mac to enable them to continue to provide liquidity and stability to the mortgage market. Long-term, continued operation in a government-run conservatorship is not sustainable for Fannie Mae and Freddie Mac because each company lacks capital, cannot rebuild its capital base, and is operating on a remaining finite line of capital from taxpayers. Until Congress determines the future of Fannie Mae and Freddie Mac and the housing finance market, the FHFA will continue to carry out its responsibilities as conservator.[2]

Diversity of Structures

The diversity of MBS structures makes it easy to accommodate the needs of all types of investors. MBSs can be structured as long-, short-, or intermediate-term securities. Amortization windows can be short or long and coupons can be fixed or floating.

Liquidity

The immense size and trading volume in the MBS market has provided institutions with an extremely active and liquid secondary market, rivaling that of U.S. Treasuries. It is important to note, however, that this liquidity does not in any way carry over into the retail marketplace. Buyers of odd lots should consider MBSs as a purchase for life, and only sell if an emergency arises. Significant transaction costs will be assessed to the small investor attempting to sell into this largely institutional market. Figure 13.1 provides an illustration.

TERMINOLOGY

The following is a summary of some of the key descriptive metrics of pass-through MBSs.

Coupon versus Weighted Average Coupon (WAC)

The interest rate on an individual MBS is determined primarily by the weighted average of the mortgage rates on the underlying loans in the pool. Assume this average rate, known as the weighted average coupon (WAC), of a given pool is 3.881%. If the costs to the issuing agency of servicing the payments of the mortgages in the pool were to total 38 basis points, the interest rate assigned to the MBS would be 3.50%. Essentially, 38 basis points of interest paid by the mortgagors in the pool is kept by the issuer to cover its expenses and the differential of 3.5% passes through to the bondholders.

---

[2] Federal Housing Finance Agency, FHFA.gov.

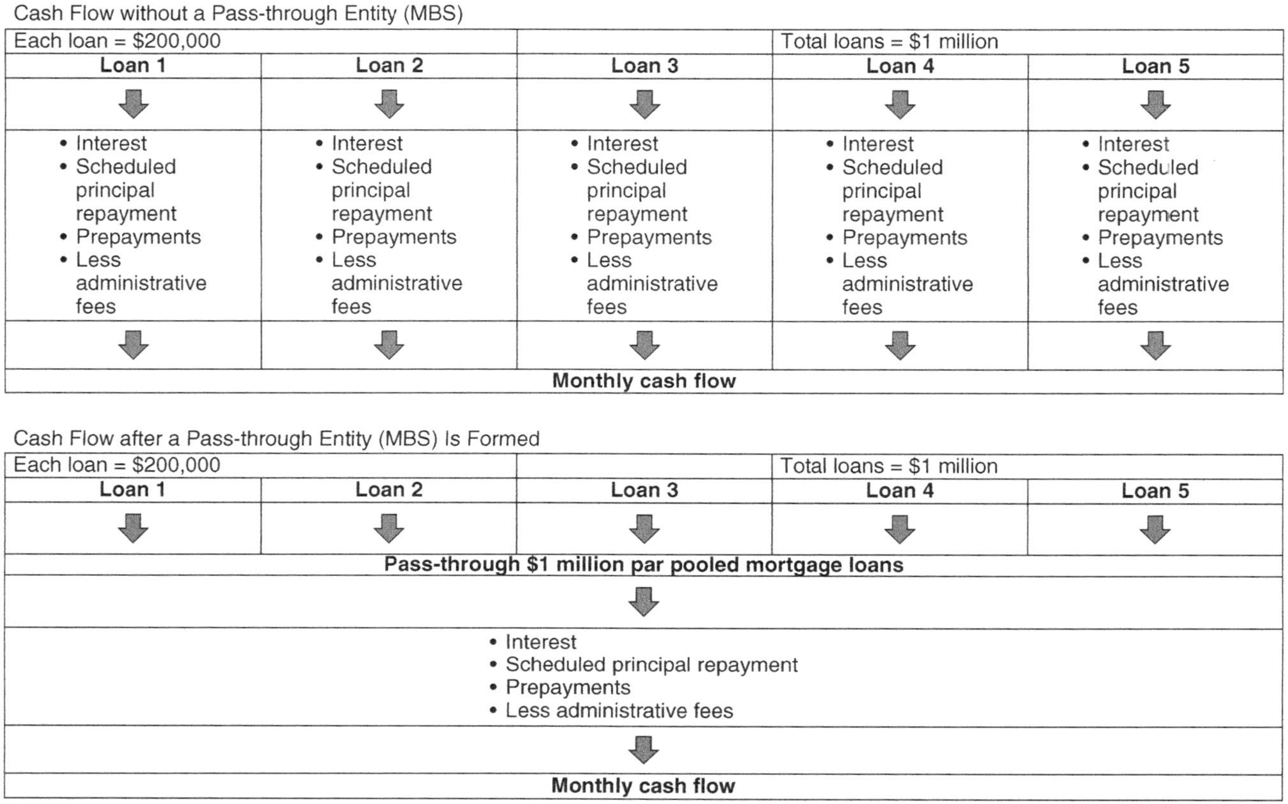

Cash Flow without a Pass-through Entity (MBS)

Each loan = $200,000		Total loans = $1 million		
Loan 1	**Loan 2**	**Loan 3**	**Loan 4**	**Loan 5**
⇨	⇨	⇨	⇨	⇨
• Interest • Scheduled principal repayment • Prepayments • Less administrative fees	• Interest • Scheduled principal repayment • Prepayments • Less administrative fees	• Interest • Scheduled principal repayment • Prepayments • Less administrative fees	• Interest • Scheduled principal repayment • Prepayments • Less administrative fees	• Interest • Scheduled principal repayment • Prepayments • Less administrative fees
⇨	⇨	⇨	⇨	⇨
		Monthly cash flow		

Cash Flow after a Pass-through Entity (MBS) Is Formed

Each loan = $200,000		Total loans = $1 million		
Loan 1	**Loan 2**	**Loan 3**	**Loan 4**	**Loan 5**
⇨	⇨	⇨	⇨	⇨
		Pass-through $1 million par pooled mortgage loans		
		⇨		
		• Interest • Scheduled principal repayment • Prepayments • Less administrative fees		
		⇨		
		Monthly cash flow		

FIGURE 13.1 How a pass-through security is created

Weighted Average Maturity (WAM)

The weighted average maturity (WAM) of a pass-through is the weighted average maturity of the individual loans underlying the bond. The *weighted average life* (WAL), however, measures the average time remaining for the principal balances of a mortgage pool to be paid off. If the WAL is not calculated, an estimation of the WAL called the *calculated loan age* (CAGE) often takes its place. Unlike the actual loans in the pool, the CAGE estimate assumes all the loans in the pool were issued with 30-year terms. In other words, the WAL calculation and the CAGE estimate may differ because a portion of the underlying pool loans may have had an initial maturity of less than 30 years. Furthermore, some of the borrowers may have engaged in curtailments or partial accelerated prepayments of principal.

Delay

A stated delay of 49 days quantifies the time necessary for servicers to process mortgage payments. For example, debt service for June is paid July 19. As compared with July 1, the actual delay can be seen as only 19 days.

Pool Factor

The factor is the outstanding mortgage balance as a percentage of the original balance. The factor continuously declines as the mortgages are amortized and prepaid. By multiplying the original loan amount by the factor, we arrive at the current outstanding balance.

TYPES OF UNDERLYING LOANS

The vast majority of agency pass-throughs are collateralized with single-family loans. Single-family loans can be broken down into the following categories.

Government (FHA and VHA) and Conventional Loans

Ginnie Maes are collateralized by government loans, mortgages made by the FHA and VHA. Fannie Mae and Freddie Mac pools consist almost exclusively of conventional loans. Conventional loans (nongovernment loans) can be further broken down into conforming and nonconforming loans.

Conforming and Nonconforming Loans *Conforming loans* are by definition those loans that are eligible for securitization by both Freddie Mac and Fannie Mae. In addition to meeting certain agency guidelines, such as homebuyer payment–to-income (PTI) ratio levels and loan-to-value (LTV) ratios, conforming mortgages have an inflation-indexed cap. The current maximum loan size for a conforming loan is $417,000. The maximum loan size is adjusted periodically to reflect increases in housing prices throughout the United States. Mortgage loans that meet the credit requirements for conforming loans but are higher than the maximum conforming limit are considered *nonconforming loans*. They are also referred to as jumbo mortgages. Loans of acceptable sizes may also be considered nonconforming due to credit quality or because they do not meet the stringent underwriting or documentation standards of Fannie Mae and/or Freddie Mac.

Nonconforming mortgages carry higher interest rates, typically 25 to 50 basis points higher than conforming loans, and are securitized in the non-agency marketplace.

Payment Schedule and Stated Maturity

Mortgage loans can be further broken down into the following categories, based on their payment schedules and/or maturity structures.

Fixed-Rate Loans Fixed-rate loans represent the most popular collateral structure for pass-through MBSs. The most common term is 30 years, although 15-year loans are often seen as well.

Adjustable-Rate Mortgages (ARMs) An ARM is a mortgage loan whose rate is reset at periodic intervals based on a designated base rate or index. The rate to the borrower is the base rate (index) plus a spread measured in basis points.

Adjustable-rate mortgages arrived on the scene in the early 1980s. ARMs appeal to homebuyers looking to minimize their mortgage payments, at least in the early years of the loan, and to borrowers seeking flexibility in loan structure. In order to entice borrowers, originators often offer ARMs at below-market "teaser" rates. Buyers anticipating lower interest rates may be enticed by adjustable rates as well. Not surprisingly, demand for ARMs has historically been greatest during periods of high real mortgage rates.

Fixed/Adjustable Hybrids (Hybrid ARMs) Today, loans can be tailed to suit the needs of myriad borrowers. A hybrid ARM is a mortgage that combines fixed with adjustable rates. For example, the mortgage rate can be fixed for a period of time, say five years, after which time the mortgage morphs into an adjustable rate that floats with some agreed-upon index, resetting every 12 months. The most common hybrid ARMs issued are *2/28* and *3/27* loans, which are fixed-rate loans for the first two and three years, respectively, followed by adjustments over the balance of the 30-year term of the mortgage.

AGENCY PASS-THROUGH TRADING

To Be Announced (TBA)

Most agency pass-throughs are bought and sold on a TBA basis. A TBA is a contractual obligation to buy or sell mortgage pools of a specific agency and coupon at a specified price and settlement date. The TBA market allows loans to be sold by originators, and borrowers to lock in interest rates, even before the loans are closed. In fact, many of the mortgage loans may not even be signed (and the mortgage pools created) at the time of sale. The TBA market is a forward or delayed-delivery market, where securities settle on a standard forward settlement date. Standard settlement dates are set by the Bond Market Association (BMA).

Although certain general parameters are set, a buyer of TBAs does not know the details of the pool because the actual mortgages constituting the pool are not specified at the time of sale. Rather, the buyer knows only the issuing agency, the coupon, par amount, price, and settlement date. The seller is required to deliver the complete pool information no later than two days prior to settlement. Only single-family mortgage agency pass-through securities are eligible for trading in the TBA market. While the largest volume of trading in the TBA market is for settlement within 30 days, delivery can be delayed up to 180 days. The settlement of a TBA trade usually entails one of the following three situations: a pair-off, a delivery of actual collateral pools, or a net-out in the Mortgage Backed Securities Clearing Corporation (MBSCC) process.

Pass-Through Vintages

When purchasing a pass-through, the buyer can request a particular loan obligation year. Just as a particular vintage of a fine wine may be known for certain desirable traits, in the same way a particular MBS issuance year may be in demand for certain prepayment characteristics sought by a sophisticated investor.

Combined Pools

This involves the combination of outstanding pass-throughs to create a security with a larger pool. These new and improved pools provide investors with greater geographic diversity and lower servicing and administrative costs.

Specified Pools (Collateral)

As the mortgage market continues to mature, the stratification of mortgage pools continues to increase. The specified pool market is a large and active market where, unlike the TBA market, the buyer knows exactly what pool is being purchased along with its characteristics, such as WAC, WAM, age, and prepayment history. In June 2003 Freddie Mac and Fannie Mae began providing additional disclosures on the loans backing their MBS pools to further aid investors in prepayment analysis. This information includes loan credit scores, or FICO scores, the original loan-to-value (LTV), the purpose of the loans, property type, occupancy status, and information pertaining to the servicer. Both Fannie Mae and Freddie Mac have periodically increased the amount of disclosure of pool information available for agency MBS pools, including loan-level data.

The credit score or FICO score gives the investor insight into credit history of the borrowers underlying the pool of mortgages. A FICO score generally ranges from the low 300s to the mid-800s. A score closer to 800 indicates creditworthiness and the ability to refinance, whereas a score below 700 may indicate a diminished ability of the homeowner to refinance. It is important to note that we are not concerned about a low FICO score's effect on the credit quality of the MBS, since most pass-throughs maintain either direct or indirect government backing. Pass-through investors are focused solely on determining the ability of a borrower to prepay a mortgage. It should be noted that higher default rates increase the involuntary prepayment component of the overall prepayment rate.

The loan-to-value (LTV) is used to determine the original mortgage loan as a percent of the equity stake the borrower has in the property. The LTV is negatively correlated with the FICO score; the higher the LTV, the lower the FICO score. This is intuitive, since a lower-quality borrower would tend to need a larger mortgage.

Loan purpose distinguishes between two types of transactions: a purchase or a refinance. Determining the percent of refinancing within a pool of mortgages will be useful in determining how long a borrower has been in a property and will give the investor added clues about future prepayment rates. Refinancings can be further broken down into rate/term refinancings where the borrower is reducing his monthly payments and cash-out refinancings where the borrower is taking some of his equity out of the property.

Property type indicates whether a property is a single-family or multifamily residence, a condominium, co-op, or planned unit development (PUD).

Occupancy status delineates whether the property is owner occupied, a vacation home, or an investor property. There are different prepayment characteristics associated with various types of owners.

Servicer information describes the institution servicing the mortgages within the pool.

The investor examines the characteristics of the pool and using this extra degree of knowledge then makes a relative value decision. Specified pools normally trade with a pay-up to a TBA pool (a premium in price or reduction in return). *Note:* Pools with unfavorable characteristics will not trade below TBA prices in institutional markets since they can be delivered into the TBA marketplace.

Trading TBAs

The current coupon pass-through (generally the coupon that trades the closest to par), whether it be a Ginnie Mae, Fannie Mae, or Freddie Mac security, is generally as liquid as the 10-year U.S. Treasury note. The TBA market is concentrated around the current coupon and extends above and below. The forward market generally extends a few months out. The TBA markets trade in an organized grid as in Table 13.2.

The first column denotes the type of pass-through and the available coupons, known as the "coupon stack." The second column gives the investor the corresponding prices for the various coupons for current delivery. The following columns give the prices for extended settlement. For example, the 3.7% coupon for June settlement is priced at 103-10. The same pass-through settling in July is priced at 103-03 while August settlement is priced at 102-39. The declining prices represent funding issues, since the purchasers of the September and October pass-throughs are forgoing positive interest carry.

TABLE 13.2 TBA Markets

GNMA	August	September	October
4	91–16	91–06	90–29
4.5	95–10	95–00	94–22
5	98–11	98–00	97–20
5.5	100–29	100–17	100–05
6	103–00	102–21	102–09
6.5	104–21	104–13	104–03
7	106–06	106–01	105–27

PREPAYMENT RISK AND ANALYSIS

In the corporate, municipal, and emerging markets, bond investors seek higher returns by analyzing the creditworthiness of issuers, searching for undervalued diamonds in the rough. In contrast, agency pass-throughs are gilt-edged, given their direct or implied government guarantee. Given this superior quality, the astute MBS investor can realize enhanced returns only by analyzing and predicting prepayments.

Mortgages are prepaid when homes are sold or when the loans are refinanced. Home sales occur for numerous reasons and occur at various times throughout the term of a mortgage. Refinancings, however, typically occur when rates move lower. This will cause funds to flow back to the MBS investor at the worst of all possible times, when interest rates have fallen. These funds must now be reinvested at the now-lower prevailing rates.

Home Sales Turnover

Prepayments are tied to a large degree to the sale or turnover of homes. The analysis of the turnover of homes and its effect on prepayments is quite arduous, considering many variables, such as the overall state of the economy, interest rate levels, demographics, and seasonality. Specific MBS pools must be looked at closely to determine the seasoning of the underlying loans.

Refinancing

Mortgage refinancings are closely tied to the level of interest rates, more specifically mortgage rates, and the relationship of those rates with the coupons on the underlying loans collateralizing the MBS. With refinancings, we are concerned exclusively with premium coupons, that is, those mortgage-backed securities with rates greater than those of current mortgage pools. All things being equal, accommodative Federal Reserve policy and the ensuing falling interest rates will create a surge in the rate of prepayments on these premium coupons. As mortgage rates drop substantially below the weighted average coupon (WAC), the prepayment rate may accelerate even further. However, at some point burnout sets in and prepayments decelerate substantially. If mortgage rates continue their descent, a publicity effect sets in as more people discover the economic benefit of refi and the pace of prepayments will pick up again.

It is worth noting that there are other reasons for prepayments, such as defaults of underlying mortgages, and curtailments—partial prepayments by borrowers with extra cash on hand who want to build up equity at a more rapid pace. These account for a small portion of prepayments but are nonetheless worth noting.

How Do We Measure Prepayments?

A partial prepayment amount is the difference between the scheduled principal payment amount and the actual principal received. A full prepayment, such as occurs when a loan is refinanced or a home sold, is simply the outstanding principal balance of the loan. At one time the market utilized an approach called "12-year prepaid life" to analyze prepayments. This approach assumed no prepayments for the first 12 years in the life of the pass-through and a full prepayment at the end of year 12. This simplistic and outdated method ignored the most relevant factors affecting prepayments, such as interest rates and underlying loan rates. FHA experience at one time was a widely utilized prepayment analysis tool as well. This method used historical data on prepayments and defaults of FHA-insured 30-year mortgages to project future prepayment speeds. While FHA experience is no longer utilized as the method of choice for MBS professionals, some of its properties are used in the PSA model discussed shortly.

Modern prepayment analysis has evolved and improved over time through the use of increasingly sophisticated models. Some of the modern-day tools used to estimate prepayments follow.

Single Monthly Mortality   Single monthly mortality (SMM) is the simplest method of measuring prepayments. SMM refers to the percentage of the outstanding principal balance that is prepaid and is the building block for prepayment calculation. For example, assume an initial mortgage balance of $1,000, a scheduled principal payment of $10, and an actual principal payment of $20. The prepaid principal of $10 (principal received of $20 minus the $10 scheduled payment) divided by the new principal balance of $990 or $20 − 10/ ($1,000 − $10) gives us the SMM of 1.01%.

Conditional (Effective) Prepayment Rate   The conditional prepayment rate (CPR) annualizes the SMM (SMM multiplied by 12). Using the preceding example, if a particular mortgage pool prepays at a constant rate of roughly 1% per month, the CPR is calculated to be 12%.

Public Securities Association Convention   In the mid-1980s the Public Securities Association (PSA) model was introduced to the market to explain the aging patterns generally observed with MBSs. Logically, one would assume that prepayments are rare in the early years of a mortgage, but become more frequent as the loan becomes more seasoned. The base PSA curve (denoted as 100% PSA) assumes prepayments begin at 0% at the inception of the loan and increase by .2% per month thereafter, until leveling off 30 months after origination at a constant speed of 6% CPR. This model, referred to as 100% PSA, then becomes our baseline for comparison of projected prepayment rates. For example, a rate of 25% PSA means that the CPR in a particular month is a quarter of that implied by the 100% PSA model. A rate of 200% PSA means that the CPR is twice that implied by 100% PSA, or 0.4% in month 1, 0.8% in month 2, and so on, until it levels off at 12% in the 30th month. Both CPR and PSA convention can be used as prepayment measurement units. The main difference between the two approaches is that PSA adjusts as the loan ages while CPR does not. The decision to use one method over the other is a function of the type or age of an individual loan.

OAS ANALYSIS AND MBS

One of the major challenges facing all fixed-income investors is assigning a value to a bond's embedded options. As we discussed in earlier sections, a bond containing an embedded call option must provide additional yield to compensate the investor for the uncertainty around the redemption date created by the call. *Option-adjusted spread analysis* (OAS) is a tool used by investors to value the option component of a callable bond. Basically, OAS approximates and then removes that portion of a bond's yield spread attributed to the embedded option.

For example, assume a callable bond is trading at a spread to Treasuries of +120 bps. If the OAS analysis determines that 50 bps of the yield spread can be attributed to the bond's call option. then the remaining 70 bps of the spread above Treasuries can be attributed to the bond's other risk factors, such as liquidity and credit. This bond would therefore carry an OAS of +70. Using this information, investors can more easily compare the security to other bonds (both callable and noncallable) to better assess relative value. A higher OAS suggests a greater amount of compensation (excess yield) after removing the impact of the embedded option(s).

The same analysis is utilized when considering mortgage-backed securities. With MBS, the borrower's right to prepay the loan at any time is essentially a continuous call option, sometimes referred to as an American style call. As in the prior example, OAS is used to approximate that portion of the yield spread not attributable to the borrower's prepayment option. This is an easier task with traditional callable bonds where issuers generally call securities to realize savings generated by changes in market interest rates. As we have learned, trying to predict the prepayment behavior of a large diverse pool of mortgage borrowers is eminently more difficult since prepayment speeds are driven by a number of factors, including market interest rates, general economic conditions, trends in the housing market, and changes in personal issues like borrower age or marital status. Each institutional dealer who creates an OAS model must include certain assumptions in order to arrive at their prepayment projections. These prepay model programs are proprietary and unique to each dealer. As a result, an MBS could be offered by multiple dealers at the same price but different OAS levels!

How Is the OAS Figure Determined?

OAS analysis evaluates the cash flows for an MBS based on multiple interest rate scenarios. Starting with the modeler's prepayment assumptions, each different interest rate path is converted into a prepayment scenario. That is, for a pool with a given coupon structure, what percentage of borrowers will refinance in any given month if market rates drop 100 bps? These assumptions are then translated into a series of cash flows. A value for the security is derived by discounting the theoretical cash flows to the present and averaging them. This value is then quoted as an average spread to the Treasury spot curve. While OAS can be a useful tool to assess the relative value of an MBS, investors need to consider that many prepayment assumptions are required in the OAS model and this analysis should be supplemented with other models to obtain a more accurate estimate of the MBS's inherent value.

THE FUTURE OF FANNIE MAE AND FREDDIE MAC SECURITIZATION

The Federal Housing Finance Agency's (FHFA) 2014 Strategic Plan for the Conservatorships of Fannie Mae and Freddie Mac includes the strategic goal of developing a new securitization infrastructure for Fannie Mae and Freddie Mac for mortgage loans backed by 1- to 4-unit (single-family) properties. To achieve that strategic goal, Fannie Mae and Freddie Mac, under FHFA's direction and guidance, are developing a *common securitization platform* (CSP) that will support their single-family mortgage securitization activities, including the issuance by both enterprises of a single mortgage-backed security (single security). The CSP will be a common information technology platform that will use industry-standard software, systems, and data requirements and will be adaptable for use by other market participants in the future. Investing in a single platform to support single-family securitization and the single security will benefit both enterprises and taxpayers in the long run. The goal is one to-be-announced (TBA) market, uniting the liquidity of Fannie Mae TBA securities with Freddie Mac TBA securities. The single security is expected to have the features of Fannie Mae MBSs and the disclosure elements of Freddie Mac Gold PCs. Investors are expected to be able to exchange their legacy Freddie Mac 45-day TBA Gold PCs for a new Freddie Mac TBA-eligible single security. How long it takes for the single security to develop remains to be seen as of this writing.[3]

---

[3]Federal Housing Finance Agency, "The 2014 Strategic Plan for the Conservatorships of Fannie Mae and Freddie Mac," May 13, 2014, http://www.fhfa.gov/AboutUs/Reports/Pages/2014-Conservatorships-Strategic-Plan.aspx.

CHAPTER 14

Corporate Bonds

Marvin Loh

The corporate bond market is one of the largest bond markets in the world with approximately $8 trillion[1] in outstanding securities. The size of the corporate bond market has almost doubled over the past 10 years, making it the second fastest growing bond market in the United States, behind only the U.S. Treasury market, which is also the world's largest.[2] With average trading volumes of $20 billion per day, the corporate bond market has become an important investment option for bond buyers looking for better income opportunities than those offered in the Treasury market under the zero-interest-rate policy pursued by the Federal Reserve.[3] Despite its size and economic performance, retail investors play a limited direct role in the corporate market, which remains dominated by institutional investors such as pension funds, insurance companies, mutual funds, and ETFs. While households own only an estimated 10% of outstanding corporate bonds directly,[4] the biggest growth in ownership of corporate bonds over the past several years has come from the mutual fund and ETF communities, which is in effect a proxy for household interest in the asset class.

While the corporate bond market is considered the second largest bond market, it often trades like a much smaller market. By this we mean that there are a large number of outstanding individual bonds, which makes the average size per bond much smaller than the government bond market, which theoretically is not much larger. For instance, while the Treasury market is the world's largest bond market, with $13 trillion in outstanding securities, there are only approximately 300 outstanding issues. In contrast, the $8 trillion in corporate bonds are divided among approximately 30,000 individual securities, making the average-sized bond much smaller and therefore much less liquid. Figure 14.1 provides and illustration.

---

[1] SIFMA, including high-yield market.
[2] SIFMA.
[3] Bank of International Settlements.
[4] SIFMA.

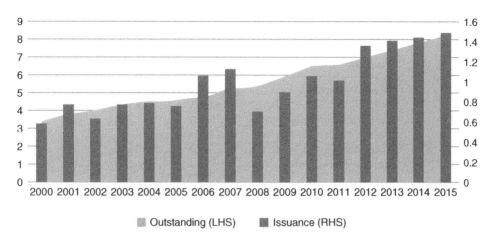

FIGURE 14.1 Four years of record issuance propels corporate bond market (in trillions)

Another way to look at it is by comparing the corporate bond market to the stock market, which often shares similar issuers. For instance, many of the companies that make up the S&P 500 often have debt outstanding in addition to their equity issuance. The stock market capitalization of these 500 large and recognizable companies presently tops $18 trillion by last count, over 2× larger the corporate bond market, despite there being over 60× more corporate bonds outstanding. While each company only has one type of common stock outstanding, that same company can have dozens, hundreds, or even over 1,000 outstanding individual bonds. In addition, each one of those bonds will likely have nuanced differences that will impact the income and returns derived by the investor. The rapid growth of the corporate bond market over the past decade has also created a potpourri of bond types, providing investors with an almost limitless number of combinations of issuers and structures in creating a corporate bond portfolio. However, to effectively navigate the plethora of options, investors must not only comprehend the interest rate risk that all bond buyers assume, they must also understand (1) the numerous corporate bond structures that exist, (2) the credit risk that they are assuming, and (3) that there is greater economic and liquidity risk than in the Treasury market.

WHAT IS A CORPORATE BOND?

In its simplest form, a corporate bond is an IOU from a company given to the investors that have agreed to lend the company money. These obligations are by no means standard, with variations on the security structure, the financing terms (coupon, maturity, and face value), restrictions on other forms of indebtedness, and additional compensation in the event of credit downgrades, to name just a few. While many corporate bonds

TABLE 14.1 Largest Non-financial Corporate Borrowers (in $millions)

Borrower	Outstanding	# Issues
General Electric	176,576	697
AT&T	142,607	135
Verizon Communications	98,835	76
Apple	71,536	46
Ford Motor	65,856	265
Anheuser-Busch InBev	57,202	20
Comcast	50,798	58
Microsoft	41,059	33
Walmart	40,864	39
Oracle	40,276	30

Source: Bloomberg

are registered with the SEC, many corporations take advantage of private issuance and sell certain bond issues directly to large, financially sophisticated organizations such as life insurance companies and pension funds. These transactions are registered with the Securities and Exchange Commission (SEC) differently from the way public bonds are issued and sold and are regulated under Rule 144A of the SEC.

There are a number of reasons that companies issue debt to raise money. They could use the funds as a normal course of business such as for working capital purposes or to finance a business expansion. A larger company may find itself issuing new debt often if they have a large debt portfolio and have a regular need to refinance maturing bonds. Recently, the market has seen the rise of mega-bond deals, multi-tranche transactions structured to raise proceeds in excess of $20 billion at one time, whose proceeds are often used to fund M&A activity. In fact, the two largest bond deals ever were sold by Verizon and Anheuser Busch Inbev over the past few years, both to fund merger-and-acquisition activity. Another trend has been the use of debt financing to fund shareholder-friendly actions, such as to pay dividends and buy back stock. While these activities may leverage a company's balance sheet in favor of shareholders, its debt-paying abilities may remain strong if operations supports this additional debt. Regardless of the use of proceeds, a bond's terms and structure will dictate the company's obligations to its debtholders.

While a stockholder's equity interest in a company allows them to potentially receive growing compensation based on a firm's profitability, a corporate bondholder receives no additional earnings-driven upside. Instead, a fixed-rate bondholder can expect to only receive scheduled interest payments (the coupon) and the principal due on the loan (par amount) at maturity. Under the terms of the loan agreement, the company is obligated to make these payments over the life of the bond. While there is no additional upside to this stream of expected income, bondholders have a priority claim to a firm's assets and are paid prior to stockholder distributions. Legally, the corporation must pay its bondholders the promised coupon interest on all of its outstanding bonds before any funds are declared as dividends, which makes preferred bondholders and equity holders subordinate to corporate bondholders.

TYPES OF BOND STRUCTURES

There are many types of bond structures that investors must become familiar with, several of them relatively new to the market. In addition to coupon and term structures, corporate bonds have varying forms of security, different types of collateral that may back the bonds as well as imbedded options that may enhance bondholder returns but can also be detrimental in certain circumstances. Within the lexicon of bond terms, investors will find secured bonds, senior secured notes, mortgage bonds, collateral trust bonds, equipment trust certificates, sales/leaseback bonds, subordinated indentures, junior subordinated notes, contingent convertible notes, and many additional esoteric structures. Broadly speaking, most bonds generally fall into either the secured or unsecured bond camps.

Secured Bonds

A secured bond refers to a security that holds a legal claim against certain assets should the company default on its obligation. Since the corporation has pledged certain collateral for the benefit of the bondholders, these bonds are generally considered more secure than bonds that hold no collateral. The waterfall of payments that a corporation adheres to is as follows:

- Secured (collateralized) bondholders
- Unsecured bondholders
- Subordinated debtholders
- Preferred stockholders
- Common shareholders

This additional security will cost the bondholders somewhat in a lower yield, as the security is considered to have a lower risk of default and/or higher recovery value in the event of default.

There are numerous types of secured bonds within the market, each distinguished by the different type of collateral securing the issue. Corporate first mortgage bonds (not to be confused with mortgage-backed bonds) are securities that have some form of real estate provided as collateral. Proceeds may be used to construct or rehabilitate these facilities, which can vary from power plants to warehouses to factories. Utilities are some of the most common issuers of mortgage-secured corporate bonds. Another form of secured debt is called an enhanced equipment trust certificate (EETC). The security for an EETC is large industrial equipment, with airplanes and railroad cars some of the most common types of collateral. EETCs are used by the companies to pay for the lease and eventual purchase of equipment.

An important part of the process of creating an equipment trust bond is the role of the trustee. The trustee serves as an intermediary between the corporation that builds the equipment and the corporation that uses the equipment. For example, an aircraft manufacturer may build aircraft for an airline. The airline does not need to purchase the jets outright, instead choosing to lease the planes. This can happen if the manufacturer provides lease financing or if the buyer finds a financial firm to provide lease financing. In the case of an EETC, the trustee has control of the planes, purchasing them from the manufacturer and leasing them to the airline. In order to facilitate the purchase of the aircraft, the trustee would sell EETCs, paying the interest and principal due on the securities with the lease payments made by the airline. The trust certificates are sold by the airline, even though they do not own the airplanes that are being used as collateral, with the aircraft remaining under the control of the trustee.

Another form of a secured bond is the collateral trust bond. These are similar to EETCs, except that instead of physical equipment, the bonds are secured by financial assets, such as other bonds or stocks. These securities arise when a company holds stocks or bonds of other companies on their balance sheet. If the company were to issue a collateral trust security, it would need to segregate the pledged financial assets with a trustee, who would control them for the benefit of the trust certificate holders. As the value of these assets will vary, there will likely be a requirement to provide additional security if the portfolio value drops below a certain level.

Unsecured Bonds

While secured bonds provide a lower default profile, the vast majority of corporate debt falls within the unsecured category. A *debenture* is a general term for an unsecured bond that is backed by the basic earning power of the corporation. That earning power is reflected in the issuer's credit rating and the bond's specific credit rating (if the issuer has paid a rating agency to rate the bond's creditworthiness). If revenues and earnings from operations are sufficient to cover the debt service (regular payment of the coupon interest), holders of the debentures will continue to receive their coupons and the principal when due. Should the corporation experience a business downturn that lowers its earnings to the point where there are insufficient funds to cover the next coupon payment, it may be in danger of defaulting on that payment. Without any backing other than the corporation's cash flow, the debentures carry the greatest risk of a downgrade in their credit rating. Since unsecured bonds carry more risk, they usually pay a higher interest rate than secured bonds. There are a number of reasons that a borrower would choose to issue unsecured debentures. A smaller borrower may find that it does not have enough assets to issue collateral debt, or larger borrowers may be well known enough to not need to encumber their assets in issuing debt. Just because a borrower issues unsecured debt, it does not mean they are not creditworthy. For instance, U.S. Treasury securities are essentially unsecured bonds, backed only by the pledge of the U.S. government to make required payments.

Unsecured debentures may be further divided into smaller subsections, with senior unsecured the highest in the unsecured credit stack and subordinated debentures at the lower end of the spectrum. Subordinated debentures may even be further divided into senior subordinated and junior subordinated debentures. Subordinated debentures (junior subordinated and senior subordinated) are forms of debenture that differ only in the hierarchy of their being redeemed should the corporation find itself in bankruptcy. As the names imply, the subordinated debenture is ranked next (lower) in line for claims over the corporation's assets. Of all of the corporation's creditors, those holding subordinated debentures come last in line and may receive very little once any banks, secured, and more senior unsecured bondholders have received their share of the remaining assets. The reason that a company may issue such delineated securities varies, but a large, lower credit borrower may find that the indenture of its more senior bonds does not allow the issuance of additional bonds. The issuance of junior bonds may allow the company to raise funds without violating these existing indentures. Financial firms often have many classes of bonds, but their need for subordinated bonds may be regulatory in nature. Capital levels are critical for a bank and the equity-like features of certain subordinated debt may help satisfy regulator-defined capital adequacy ratios. Of course, the investor in debentures and subordinated debentures is typically rewarded for the increased risk with a higher coupon and yield.

Variable-Rate Bonds

Not all corporate bonds have a fixed coupon payment. Instead, some bonds have interest rates that change based on the market rate of interest. They are known as *floating-rate notes* (FRNs) and first made their market appearance in the 1970s. The FRN was issued by Mortgage Investors of Washington in 1973, when they sold a $15 million, seven-year floating-rate senior subordinated note. This was followed by a $650 million issuance by Citicorp in 1974. Other financial firms followed, and the market exceeded $1.3 trillion by 1974. After this initial spurt, FRN issuance dried up rapidly and not one bond was offered for the next three years. Citicorp issued another bond in 1978 and, from there, issuance was sporadic. The early years of the 1980s saw double-digit interest rates and increased market volatility, both of which contributed to increased investor demand for variable-rate bonds. From there, the market for these types of bonds took off and today they are an established segment of the fixed-income market. Issuance and demand, however, remains highly dependent on the expectations over the future path of interest rates, and as the chart in Figure 14.2 indicates, FRN issuance has varied from as much as 50% of total issuance in the mid-2000s to as low as mid-single digits in 2015.

Financial firms are the most active issuers within the floating-rate universe as they often utilize asset/liability matching techniques by issuing floating-rate debt in proportion to assets that have a floating-rate component. Most floating-rate debt has a maturity within 10 years and longer maturity FRNs often have call options or mandatory sinking fund provisions. The coupon for a floating-rate bond is tied to some widely published index, such as LIBOR or the fed funds rate. There are also FRNs that are tied to an inflation index, such as the CPI, which gives investors a specific investment vehicle to express their inflation view. The interest rate is therefore determined by the underlying index and usually adds a spread to this index, which represents the credit risk of the

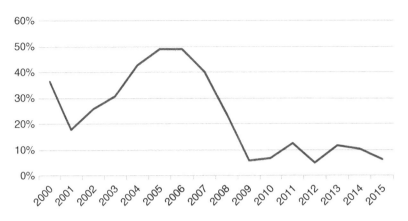

FIGURE 14.2   Percent of FRN to total issuance
Source: SIFMA

borrower. For instance, Goldman Sachs has a 10-year FRN that has quarterly interest payments that are established by adding 170 basis points to the three-month LIBOR rate. If this three-month LIBOR rate was 1% during the next reset period, the interest rate would be 1.00% + 1.70% or 2.7% per annum for the next quarterly interest cycle. Most FRNs reset the interest rate during their interest payment cycles, although they could theoretically be reset daily, weekly, monthly, quarterly, semiannually, or any other formula desired.

Many floaters are also structured with a "cap" or a "floor" or at times both caps and floors. A cap is the maximum rate that the borrower will pay regardless of how high the reference rate goes. This feature protects the issuer in the event that overall interest rates rise precipitously higher than expectations. A floor is the minimum rate that the borrower will pay, again regardless of how low the reference rate falls. This feature protects the lender or bondholder in the event that rates fall significantly. The cap and floor illustrates one of the primary risks for bondholders, in that unlike a fixed-rate security, the income stream from the security will be variable. In addition, while the maturity of the security can be longer term in nature, short-term interest rates, which form the basis of establishing the income stream, will generally be lower and therefore the initial income stream will also be lower. However, since the rate is reset fairly regularly, the volatility on the security will also be lower, and the price should not deviate very far from par unless there is a credit event.

Step-Up Bonds

Step-up bonds are similar to variable-rate securities in that the interest rate of a bond may change during the life of the security. There is, however, a fundamental difference in that the changes in interest rate are not determined by an index, but rather these changes in rate are defined in the indenture. In its simplest form, a step-up bond will have its interest rate rise based on a predetermined schedule. Most step-up bonds also have a call feature, which introduces reinvestment risk to the investor. A step-up bond will generally have a lower coupon at issuance, but provide the potential for a greater weighted average rate over the life of the bond. Of course, those higher coupons may not be realized if the security is called by the issuer. It is worth noting that the probability of a call for a step-up is higher than a simple callable bond. If rates rise rapidly, the issuer may choose not to call the bonds if the stepped-up coupon is below current market rates. For investors that expect the call to be exercised, they may face duration risk by owning a longer-term security than they expected to be called. Certain step-ups may also be triggered by a rating downgrade below a certain level, an event that will again be defined in the indenture. Such credit protection is usually demanded from borrowers rated triple-B camp or lower. Other step-ups are mostly found as a feature tied to a medium-term note (MTN), with financial firms accounting for the bulk of the step-up universe.

Medium-Term Notes

One of the more burdensome aspects of issuing public debt securities, or any public securities for that matter, is the Securities and Exchange Commission registration process. Market conditions must also be cooperative as the timing of the registration process is difficult to predict. In an attempt to address these concerns, the SEC put Rule 415, the Shelf Registration Rule, into effect in 1982. Rule 415 allows that new securities can be sold for up to two years after an existing registration statement is approved, effectively allowing an issuer to sell an issue off the shelf. This allowed many corporations issuing bonds to register the issue with the SEC and then sell securities from the issue at any time during the next two years. Shelf registration substantially reduced the cost of offering new bonds and gave corporations far greater flexibility in selecting when to enter the market to raise additional funds.

One product that arose from the Shelf Registration Rule was the medium-term note (MTN) program. An MTN program can take many forms, but they are usually notes that are sold by well-known borrowers that have need for a regular and continuous flow of capital. Initially, MTN programs filled a void between shorter term funding opportunities, such as commercial paper, which was 1 year or shorter, and traditional longer-term debt issuance. Therefore, much of the MTN universe evolved in the 2- to 5-year maturity segment, which continues to be a sweet spot for MTN issuance. MTNs are not limited to these maturities, however, with 10-year MTNs fairly common and the occasional appearance of the 100-year MTN.

Investors should view MTNs as another form of corporate bond, with many of the same characteristics discussed in this chapter. As such, an investor needs to thoroughly understand the credit, structure, and payment mechanics as they would any other fixed-income security. While most MTNs are fixed-rate, non-callable debentures, they could also be floating-rate securities with either call or put features. One of the more popular features found in MTN programs is the survivor put option, where beneficiaries can sell the bond back to the company in the event of death, providing a useful estate planning tool. The flexibility of an MTN program also allows buyers to dictate certain features that they would like to see in the security. In these instances, a buyer could approach the investment bank that is running the MTN program and request certain attributes through a reverse-inquiry process. If the issuing corporation is amenable to the terms of the structure and the interest and maturity schedule fits their balance sheet, a bond can be created for the specific investor. Many MTN programs are sold on a weekly basis and create the potential for a number of smaller, potentially specialized issues. This may impact the liquidity for the issue in the secondary market, with investors giving up active secondary market liquidity for the conveniences of buying an MTN.

Embedded Options

In its simplest form, a bond would have a fixed interest rate, which is paid in regular intervals until maturity, at which point the investor's original principal amount would be returned. This simplest bond has a fixed interest rate, is not callable, and therefore provides investors with a reliable income stream so long as there is no credit event. While there is no lack of these simple bullet structures (practically all Treasury securities fit into this category), the bullet has been joined by a litany of other structures. In the 1980s corporations began to issue bonds with various embedded options. As the name implies, these options are embedded in the bond and cannot be removed from the structure of the security. They are part of the entire package—fixed-income instrument plus an option—and are not traded separately. Thus, the valuation of bonds with embedded options is an exercise in valuing the fixed-income portion and the option separately and combining their values into the market price of the optionable bond.

Callable Bonds   Callable bonds are the most widely used embedded option associated with corporate bonds, as a simple Bloomberg search indicates over 24,000 USD-denominated callable bonds trading in the market. An embedded call option on a bond gives the issuer the right, but not the obligation, to call the entire issue, or part of it, at the issuer's discretion. In the case of a bond, the issuer can be viewed as the owner of the option while the bondholder is the option writer. Of course, the issuer will only exercise the option when it is economically advantageous for them to do so. The most common reason for the option holder to exercise the call option would be when it is in the money. In the case of bonds, this occurs when the market interest rate falls below the level of the bond's coupon rate. In that event, the corporation would be able to reduce its interest charges by issuing a lower coupon bond and calling the existing higher coupon bond. Of course, options are a zero-sum game, so the investor who wrote the option is now the loser in this scenario. Their loss is that they now face reinvestment risk, both losing the higher income stream and receiving the proceeds from the bond at the very time when interest rates are their lowest.

When an investor purchases a callable bond, he or she is essentially undertaking two simultaneous transactions. At the same time that the investor is purchasing a fixed-income instrument from the issuer, he or she is also selling the issuer a call option on that bond. The investor becomes the writer of the option and must fulfill the obligation to deliver the bond at the predetermined call price if and when the issuer chooses to exercise the option. The call price and the dates upon which the call price changes over time (if any) are clearly spelled out in the bond's indenture.

The use of call options vary with the general tone of interest rates. When interest rates were high, such as in the 1980s and 1990s, bonds were often sold with call options that often also had provided features such as call premiums and call protection. In these instances, if an issuer were to exercise its call option, it would have to pay a premium over par to compensate the bondholder that would lose the bond, presumably at the worst possible moment. Additional protections were demanded by bondholders that would not allow the bonds to be called for a specific period of time. These bonds would be referred to as NC5, NC7, NC10, and so on, referencing that they were non-callable for 5 years, 7 years, 10 years, or any other time period.

More recently, with overall interest rates at historical lows, corporations have not been as aggressive in pushing for scheduled calls. Instead, corporations have sought flexibility in the event of a merger that would require that they redeem existing debt. In order to maintain this flexibility, bonds would essentially need a continuous call feature, which would certainly be punished by investors who would demand a much higher interest rate. The *make-whole call* (MWC) was subsequently developed as a way to give the company additional flexibility without paying a much higher interest rate. Under an MWC, a company can pay off its remaining debt early so long as investors are made whole. The most common structure of an MWC is to discount the remaining cash flows at a predetermined rate. That rate is often a spread to the relevant Treasury bond benchmark at the time of the redemption. So long as the spread is set below the rate at which the bonds are presently trading, the investor will theoretically gain economic value from the call. As an example, the Verizon 3.5% bonds due 11/1/2024 were sold in late 2014 as a callable bond with a make-whole provision. The bonds would be callable at par on 8/1/2024, but could be called earlier if investors were made whole. In the case of these bonds, the make-whole clause requires that the remaining principal and interest be discounted at a Treasury yield +25 basis points. Since the bonds were issued to yield 135 basis points over Treasuries, the make-whole provision should sufficiently compensate investors. While there are examples of MWC provisions negatively impacting bondholders, many indentures have a greater of (a) par or (b) the MWC results to protect bondholders.

The market price of a callable bond must equal the value of the fixed-income portion (the *bullet*, or non-call bond) minus the value of the call option:

Price of Callable Bond = Price of Non-callable Bond–Value of Call Option

Why do we subtract the value of the call option? Think of the purchase of the callable bond this way: When you buy the callable bond, the issuer is paying you for the call option, thereby reducing the price of the bond. Let's say that the price of the bond is 98. If the bond had been a bullet, you would have paid a price of par. The existence of the call option lowers the market price of the callable bond relative to a bullet from a similar issuer with a similar credit rating, coupon, and maturity. Since you are selling a call option back to the issuer, you will receive the premium payment for that option. In our example, the option premium is 2. Thus, you pay 100 for the bullet and receive 2 for the option, making the net position in the transaction 98—the price of the callable bond. This lower price is your compensation for assuming the higher risk of investing in a bond that can be called away from you prematurely. The lower price also translates into a higher yield. The higher yield of the callable bond is the compensation you can and should expect for assuming call risk.

As we have seen in previous chapters, valuing a pure fixed-income instrument is relatively straightforward. Valuing an embedded call option is not as simple. However, over the past 20 years, methods for valuing embedded bond options have been created and those methods are widely used today by traders, analysts, and institutional investors. The most common method makes use of the implied forward rates derived from the U.S. Treasury yield curve and an assumption of interest rate volatility to generate a series of future interest rate paths. These paths represent a set of possible up and down movements in the forward yield curve for U.S. Treasury securities. The method is often referred to as the *binomial lattice* or *lognormal method*. Working backward through time from maturity, when the bond's price is known to be par, the process computes the price one period prior to maturity using the forward rate generated for that point in time, the bond's coupon cash flow, and its next period price—par. When all of the points on the lattice have been populated with theoretical future bond prices, the final price at time zero—today—is the bond's theoretical price based on the model's initial assumptions.

The model's power rests in the fact that it can be used to take into account the existence of the embedded option. This cannot be accomplished using the classic discounted cash flow formula for the price of a bond. At those points in time when the bond is callable at a specific price, we can substitute the call price for the theoretical price based on the forward rate. Using the new call price, we end up computing a slightly different current market price from the model. This price should match the traded price of the callable bond. In this way, we can use the likelihood of the bond's being called because of a decrease in future interest rates as an input into where it should be trading today. If the model produces a theoretical price that differs from the current traded price of the callable bond, we can modify the assumptions that produced our implied forward rates. Assuming we have used the bond's future call prices in our valuation process, the reason for the price discrepancy would be that we have been using Treasury bond rates to discount corporate bond cash flows. Since Treasury yields are normally lower than corporate yields, we have been overvaluing this corporate bond. At this point, we must go back and compensate for the lower Treasury rates we have been using by increasing the forward rate each period by a certain number of basis points. This amount will be added to the forward rates until the average price of all the cash flows equals the bond's current market price. The basis point spread we have added to our forward Treasury rates is known as the *option-adjusted spread* (OAS). OAS can be viewed as representing the bond's nominal yield spread over the entire Treasury curve after statistically removing the value of the embedded call option. Since the spread is positive and produces a yield that is higher than a Treasury yield, the resulting corporate bond price will be lower than that of a similar Treasury. This makes sense and is the reason why OAS is often considered a proxy for credit risk—the difference in price being due to the corporate bond's higher credit risk compared with the Treasury bond.

Putable Bonds The opposite of a callable bond is a putable bond, where the investor is the owner of the option and the issuer is the writer of the option. Unlike callable bonds, which are fairly common, there are far fewer putable bonds in the market. A simple Bloomberg search list only 1,600 putable securities versus over 24,000 callable bonds. The disparity between these two embedded options is fairly straightforward in that putable bonds favor the bondholder, providing the issuers with a disincentive to issue them. While corporations certainly want to increase the likelihood of selling the entire par amount of the bond issue, they do not want to give potential investors any more incentives to purchase the bonds than are absolutely necessary. As further proof of this, many putable bonds are onetime puts, meaning the option to put (sell) the bond back to the issuer takes place on only one date at the predetermined price. If the option is not exercised, it expires and the bond essentially becomes a bullet.

When an investor purchases a putable bond, the two simultaneous transactions are the purchase of a fixed-income instrument from the issuer and the purchase of a put option on that bond. In this case, the corporation becomes the writer of the option and must fulfill the obligation to purchase the bond at the predetermined put price when the bondholder chooses to exercise the option. The put price and the dates on which the put price changes over time are also spelled out in the bond's indenture. Because of the dual transaction, the market price of the putable bond must equal the value of the fixed-income portion (the bullet bond) plus the value of the put option:

Price of Putable Bond = Price of Nonputable Bond + Value of Put Option

Why do we add the value of the put option? When you buy the putable bond, you are paying the issuer for the put option, thereby increasing the price of the bond. When you buy the putable bond, you pay a certain price for it. Let's say that price is 102. If the bond had been a bullet, you would have paid par. The existence of the put option increases the market price of the putable bond relative to a bullet from a similar issuer with a similar credit rating, coupon, and maturity. At the same time, you are purchasing a put option from the issuer. As the buyer of the put option, you pay the option premium to the seller (the issuer). Let's say the option premium is 2. Thus, you pay 100 for the bullet and pay 2 for the option, making the net position in the transaction 102—the price of the putable bond. The higher price is your cost for assuming the lower risk and the concomitant advantage of investing in a bond that can be sold back to the issuer at your discretion. Of course, that discretion can be quite limited, but it does exist and will cost something. The higher price also translates into a lower yield. The lower yield of the putable bond is what you can expect for the issuer's assumption of put risk. The binomial lattice method, which was outlined for callable bonds, can also be used to value an embedded put option. The same set of implied forward Treasury curves is generated but the put option is assumed to be exercised in the future at any time where interest rates have increased and the bond's theoretical price has fallen below the put price. After removing the value of the put option, the theoretical bond price is compared to its current market price and a certain number of basis points are added to each forward rate to make the two prices equal. The additional basis points are the bond's OAS.

Convertible Bonds

A convertible bond (or *convert*) is a security that starts its life with many bond-like characteristics but also has an embedded option that allows the investor to convert the bonds into common stock of the issuer. We will limit our discussion to bonds that convert into equity of the issuer, although there are some instances where conversion could be into another company's stock. As such a convertible is best described as a hybrid security that exhibits different types of behavior depending on the value of the embedded option. The reasons an issuer may issue a convertible bond vary, but the lower interest rate paid on the issue will be one of the main issues. Depending on its credit quality and existing leverage ratio, a convert may help to raise funds when traditional debt issuance is overly restrictive. A convertible may also allow a company to avoid the immediate dilution created by an equity sale while also providing tax benefits from interest expense versus a dividend payment, which is not tax deductible. For an investor, a convertible can be viewed as a safer way to participate in the equity market, with some downside protection in the embedded interest payment and most of the upside from stock appreciation. This possible upside appreciation sets converts aside from traditional bonds in that their value could be much greater than par at maturity, versus other debentures that will only return par at maturity.

Before we begin our convertible discussion, there are a few distinct terms that are unique to the convertible world that that we have not used before.

Conversion Ratio/Conversion Price/Conversion Premium The conversion ratio/price/premium are essentially different ways of looking at the same coin. All three figures are defined in the indenture and refer to the price of the underlying stock that would trigger an economic conversion. Put another way, the conversion ratio establishes the number of shares of common stock to which the bond can be converted. The conversion premium is the percentage premium over the common stock price at issuance that drives the conversion ratio and price.

As an example, if a company were to issue a 1% coupon convertible bond with a 25% conversion premium to its current stock price of $10, the bonds would have conversion ratio of 80:1 and a conversion price of $12.50. This is calculated by dividing $1000 (par value for bonds) by 80 shares (conversion ratio), which yields a $12.50 conversion price. If the underlying share price were greater than $12.50, the investor would have a bond worth more than par, as anything less would provide an arbitrage opportunity. For instance, buying the bond for $980 would be an arbitragable event because the investor could convert it to 80 shares at $12.50, or $1,000, without taking any risk. If the share price were less than $12.50, the investor would simply keep the bond and collect the 1% coupon payment per year.

When a convert is issued, it will have bond-like components such as interest rate and final maturity. As with all bonds that have embedded options that benefit the investor, the interest rate will be lower than a comparable straight bullet bond. A convertible bond can fall into one of three basic categories and may actually transition across all three of these categories during its life. Those three stages are (1) a yield instrument, (2) a hybrid instrument, and (3) an equity alternative instrument. The particular category in which a convert finds itself is tied to where the actual stock price is relative to the conversion price. From this perspective, the embedded equity option may find itself out of the money, at the money, or deep in the money.

If the convertible has a conversion price that is well above the current price of the stock, the option is out of the money. The further out of the money the option becomes, the less value the option provides and the more bond-like the convertible behaves. These converts are often referred to as broken, as there is little chance that the option will be of any value. Therefore, in order for an investor to buy this security, it has to offer a yield similar to other comparable traditional fixed-income securities.

If a convert has an underlying share price that trades close to the conversion price, these securities are considered balanced. The pricing and movement of these converts are hybrid in nature and influenced by both the share price of the underlying stock and bond-specific factors such as interest rates and changes to its credit profile. Most convertibles are issued as balanced securities and can remain in this category for the life of the security.

In the event that a convertible has an underlying security that trades well above the conversion price, these bonds are considered equity alternatives. These bonds with a deep-in-the-money option are most sensitive to changes in equity valuation and have very little sensitivity to general interest rates or changes in the issuer's credit profile. These bonds have a very limited premium to their parity level and will likely be converted into stock at maturity.

Investors should be aware that most convertibles are also callable bonds, with the issuer having the ability to force a conversion if the underlying stock exceeds the conversion price by a predetermined percentage. This would occur because the issuer does not want to pay the interest expense to a bond that is effectively equity from the company's perspective. Convertibles can also be issued with any priority ranking from senior unsecured to junior subordinated. There are additional variations within the asset class, such as mandatory conversions and reverse conversions, which give the issuer flexibility in the timing and securities delivered at conversion.

Contingent Convertible Capital Bonds (CoCo Bonds)

Another type of security that could potentially be converted to equity is the contingent convertible capital bond or CoCo bond. Unlike the convertible bonds discussed earlier, a CoCo conversion is often an undesirable event for the bondholder. What is unique about CoCos is that the conversion may also be an undesirable event for the issuer. This is because CoCos are hybrid securities that were developed to absorb losses of the issuing banks when capital levels fall below certain levels. Since these securities are relatively new, having been conceived after the financial crisis, there are still only a limited number of CoCo bonds and we have not seen how they perform during periods of stress or upon conversion. The main reason for the development of the CoCo market has been to satisfy regularly capital requirements, without immediately raising expensive equity capital. The premise for the CoCo bond is that during periods of duress, a bank can increase its capital levels by triggering a contingent capital event with the CoCo bonds. The CoCo structure has been utilized more actively by European banks, although there are several U.S. dollar–based transactions that may find themselves in the corporate bond arena.

Among the most appealing aspects of the CoCo bond are the high yields that they offer, with most transactions priced with a 7%+ coupon, several 100 basis points above traditional bank debt. The most important features of a CoCo are what triggers a conversion and how the loss absorption mechanism works. As stated, the primary purpose of the CoCo is to be a readily available source of bank capital at a time of crisis. How that time of crisis is determined varies across deals, but generally falls into one of two camps. The more prevalent method is to rely on a formula to set off the trigger. This is usually some form of a capital ratio threshold being broached, such as the book value of common equity Tier-1 capital as a ratio of risk-weighted assets. Triggers that rely on the book value assumptions are only as effective as how often values are determined and vary across banks. As we learned during the financial crisis, many banks that were stressed or even defaulted were solvent from an accounting perspective that based the value of assets on a backward-looking valuation.

Some of the shortcomings of book value triggers can be addressed by using market value triggers, such as the market value of a bank's equity to its total assets. While using market values ameliorates some of the inconsistences of using an accounting-based trigger, it opens up additional complexities such as market manipulation. Concerns over a situation where short-selling the stock causes the trigger to be exercised, thereby further diluting shares to the benefit of the short seller, have been raised by regulators and market participants.

Yet another trigger mechanism that does not rely on either accounting or market thresholds is to simply let bank regulators decide when the point of non-viability is reached. This solution is also not without problems, as home regulatory bias may make the regulators hesitant to activate the trigger. The lack of clarity on when a trigger event will occur may also undermine the market confidence over a bank or banking system at a time of stress when CoCos are intended to add to confidence.

Once a trigger is activated, there are a few possible ways for the loss-absorbing capital to be utilized. Earlier transactions focused on converting CoCo bonds into the issuing bank's equity at a conversation rate. This rate could either be based on the market price of the stock when the trigger is breached or a pre-specified price when the issue was sold. The former would likely be more dilutive to shareholders, which would provide an incentive for existing shareholders to not influence the triggering event. The opposite is true if a predetermined ratio is used, which is less dilutive and would reduce the incentive to avoid triggering a conversion.

Another loss-absorbing method is to have a principal write-down of the CoCo if a triggering event occurs. These write-downs could either be full or partial, although most have full write-down provisions. Some of these write-downs are either temporary or permanent, as defined in the indenture. As can be seen, there are many variations to this relatively new and untested asset class. While the coupon offered to investors is high, a thorough understanding of the conversion process is essential in determining an investor's comfort level. The market for CoCos has remained within the retail and high-net-worth space, with institutional investors taking a cautious approach for the moment.

HOW ARE CORPORATE BONDS PRICED?

One of the more confusing aspects of the corporate bond market is that there are many conventions used in pricing different parts of the market. Depending on the type of bond (investment grade, high yield, floating-rate note, etc.), the bond trader may quote the price of a bond in one of several different, yet related ways. The first thing to remember in bond investing is that all things are relative. Rarely do investors choose a bond for investment without comparing it to alternative bonds to determine which one is best for their individual needs or their portfolios. While whom you trade bonds with in the secondary market continues to evolve, brokers and dealers remain a critical part of the price discovery process. The vast majority of corporate bonds are traded over the counter, meaning that there is not a consolidated quote system to establish the current price as is the case with equity securities. In addition, given the vast number of corporate bonds in existence, there will be times when a specific security has not traded for days, or possibly even weeks. Given these dynamics, the dealer community was usually the primary source for corporate bond trading, as they would inventory bonds until another buyer or seller could be located. Recent developments in technology have allowed for buyers to find sellers through matching networks, which has reduced the role of dealer community, although certainly not eliminated their important function. It is estimated that 75% of institutional investors have used electronic networks, although the market share of these networks is only 20% of total trading.

Given that a specific bond may not have traded for several days, if not weeks, the general level of interest rates may have changed since the last trade of the bonds. Additional market information like supply, economic data, and overall risk appetite may also be impacting the demand for corporate bonds. Traders therefore compare bonds from a relative value perspective. A corporation may have many bonds currently outstanding—some with very similar characteristics. When deciding which bond to purchase, the trader will attempt to determine which bond can be resold at a higher price. If the trader could not do this accurately, she would not be a trader for very long. The ability to determine the right market price for a bond depends greatly on the prices of other bonds. The comparison of these alternative investments is critical in establishing the current price of a security. In the investment-grade corporate bond market, bonds are typically compared to U.S. government Treasuries. Treasuries play a critical role in helping establish prices for many asset classes as it is considered the highest quality most liquid security in the world and is therefore viewed as the risk-free rate for the market. This risk-free rate is used for equity valuation purposes in discounted cash flow models, capital asset pricing models, and discounted dividend models. In the investment-grade corporate market, a spread to Treasuries often captures the premium needed to compensate an investor to buy a corporate bond, which is less liquid and has default risk that Treasury securities do not.

Like the corporate bond market, there are many different types of Treasury securities, which are all priced with individual features. This difference in Treasury bond pricing also means that there are many different interest rates within the Treasury market. In pricing corporate bonds, we are most concerned with the benchmarks, or on-the-run (OTR) bonds within the Treasury bond market. *On-the-run* refers to the fact that these bonds are the most recently issued bonds of their maturity. In its regular debt refinancing schedule, the Treasury issues bonds of various maturities, from one month to 30 years. As the most liquid, highest-rated bonds in the bond market, these newly issued bonds are the benchmarks for comparison of relative risk and return. The on-the-runs are often referred to as the current coupon Treasuries because the coupon rate of interest at which they are issued also reflects the most current rates prevailing in the market for bonds of each maturity. The current OTRs are the 1-month, the 3-month, 6-month, and 12-month Treasury bills and the 2-year, 3-year, 5-year, 7-year, 10-year, and 30-year Treasury notes and bonds. Bond traders always keep an eye on what's happening in the Treasury market as an indicator of where bond yields are headed.

Price

Let's say you are looking for a price on a corporate bond and you contact your broker. She will quote you a price for the bond, say $95\frac{1}{2}$, which should not be confused as a monetary price for the security. In other words, you are not being told the bond will cost you $95.50. In the bond markets, prices are quoted as a percent of par, like the coupon interest payments. The $95\frac{1}{2}$ quoted by the broker translates into "$95\frac{1}{2}$ percent of par." With par being $1,000 on most U.S. corporate bonds, the actual dollar amount you will pay to purchase this bond will be $955, plus accrued interest.

Yield

The yield on a bond is the simple return one could expect to receive if the bond was purchased at a particular price and was held for a specific amount of time. Even though certain assumptions must be made in order for the promised yield to be the actual yield received on the investment, the concept of yield is one of a discount rate that equates the present value of the expected future cash flows to the current market price. Thus, price and yield are two sides of the same coin, and one can be calculated from the other. Indeed, the level of one will directly determine the level of the other. Instead of our hypothetical bond being quoted at a dollar price of $95\frac{1}{2}$, it could just as easily have been quoted at a yield of, say, 5.2% percent. The $95\frac{1}{2}$ dollar price produces a yield of 5.2% percent, so the trader can quote the bond to a buyer or seller either way. Traders often refer to price and yields as levels. Since there is more than one way to quote the market value of a bond, the term *level* is less confusing, especially if a yield is being quoted.

Spread

As we stated earlier, the investment-grade market is often quoted as a spread to a Treasury security. Let's say that instead of a price of $95\frac{1}{2}$ or a yield of 5.2% percent, the trader tells you the bond is trading at "200 over." Since traders view the market in relative terms, neither price nor yield provides any relative value markers to compare. Both of those ways of quoting a bond's market value are measures of the bond's present value and discount rate. The value of Treasury bonds is not explicitly taken into account. However, when the trader says a bond is trading at "200 over," it means that the yield of the corporate bond is 200 basis points higher than the yield of a comparable maturity Treasury bond—the corporate bond's benchmark. By expressing a bond's market value as the difference between its yield and the yield of a similar maturity Treasury, the trader is at once telling you the relative value between two securities and the market value of the corporate bond. That relative value—the difference between the yields of the two bonds—is known as the spread. That spread can quickly be translated into a yield for the corporate bond by adding the spread to the yield on the benchmark Treasury. For example, if the Treasury bond was yielding 3.5% and the spread was 200 basis points over (typically written as +200), the yield on the corporate bond would be 5.5% percent. The trader could then calculate the bond's price from the yield of 5.5% percent, which as expressed above prices the security at 95 ½.

Traders use the concept of spread because at a single time, they can transact in bonds and get a sense of relative value. It's the relative value they're after. If they see spreads widening (corporate bond yields increasing relative to Treasury yields) or tightening (corporate bond yields decreasing relative to Treasury yields), that information gives them insight into the market's perception and expectation of future movements in the economy and interest rates. Some traders hedge their corporate exposure by shorting the comparable Treasury bond, and therefore are only concerned with where the spread of a bond is moving. Ultimately, traders will not really know the exact price at which they are buying and selling. They only know they were done (consummated the transaction) at 200 over. The numerous trading systems in existence translate the settlement price based on the spread that is provided to the system. As long as both sides agree on the final spread and benchmark security, the trade takes place. One final note about spread: We all know that in any financial market the rule is to buy low and sell high. Thus, as in the stock market, we expect the bid price of a bond to be lower than its ask price. This is indeed the case. However, when quoting the bond's value in yield or spread, remember that the yield moves in the opposite direction from the price. The bid yield should therefore be higher than the ask yield. Likewise, the bid spread should be higher than the ask spread. If you are quoted 200/180 (often written +200/+180) on a bond, you are being given the bid–ask yield spread.

Dollar Pricing and Other Pricing Conventions

While most investment-grade bonds are priced as a spread to Treasuries, this is not always true for all corporate bonds. The convention for high-yield bonds has been to provide a straight dollar price for the security. Using our example, the dollar price of 95 ½ would be the quoted level for a high-yield bond. As we have learned, with either the dollar price, yield, or spread (and the comparable benchmark being used for the spread), we could calculate the other components of the equation. Therefore, with a 95 ½ price, we would also be able to determine that the yield was 5.5% and the spread was +200, thereby allowing us to determine relative value of the high-yield security. The main reason that high yield is not quoted in spread is that it typically does not correlate as closely to the Treasury market as higher quality bonds. Therefore, using the Treasury market to determine relative value is not as clear cut as with investment-grade bonds. In fact, high yield is often viewed relative to the equity markets, with a greater correlation to the returns of the S&P 500 than returns of the government bond market. That does not mean that we cannot gather information by comparing high yield to Treasuries; it simply means that we will need to look at other factors in establishing a price for the bonds. This is why when an investment-grade bond becomes distressed for any number of reasons, the price of its bonds will decline and may start to get quoted in dollar price rather than on a spread basis.

A final note on pricing conventions in the corporate bond market: As bonds have become more complex, with added optionality built into securities, traders may utilize different spread conventions. As we discussed earlier, the option-adjusted spread can be used to gauge the implied cost of imbedded options. There are other spread calculations that an investor may come across, including G-spread, Z-spread, and I-Spread. The G-spread uses an interpolated point on the Treasury curve to calculate the spread. This may be useful for a longer-term bond that is not correctly reflected by comparing its spread to either the 10-year or 30-year benchmark. Also, relatively large changes in yield across the Treasury curve may make using the G-spread a more accurate reflection of corporate risk. The Z-spread is a constant spread that will make the price of a security equal to the present value of each cash flow discounted to a curve of zero-coupon bonds at each cash-flow point. The I-spread utilizes the benchmark swap curve rather than the cash curves. In each of these instances, these additional spread metrics are in addition to the Treasury spread information provided.

Additionally, floating-rate securities are often priced to money market securities. There can be any number of money market indices that are used to spread-off-of to determine the current effective rate for a floater. While LIBOR is the most common, there are securities that use a constant maturity Treasury index (CMT), a specific Treasury bill rate (3m, 6m, or 12m), fed funds, prime rate, composite commercial paper rates, or foreign money market rates such as the Eurodollar synthetic forward rates. They key is to understand the spread and the index that will be used to calculate the interest rate that will be used to set the coupon rate.

STAKEHOLDERS IN THE CORPORATE BOND MARKET

There are numerous players in the corporate bond market, each one critical in the sale of new issues and providing liquidity for a functioning secondary market. We will examine the main roles played by the trustee, rating agencies, and various buyers and sellers of corporate bonds.

Trustee

The issuance of a corporate bond includes several parties—the corporation (issuer) itself, an investment bank that assists the corporation in the creation and sale of the bond issue, and the corporate trustee. A trustee is typically a large commercial bank (or, more correctly, the trust department of such a bank) or a trust company that handles the general administrative functions of the bond issue. Included in these functions are payment of the coupons to the bondholders of record, assuring that the amount of the bonds sold by the investment bank does not exceed the total issuance specified by the corporation, notification of early redemption on the part of the issuer, handling the redemption of the bonds from current bondholders, holding the securities pledged as collateral in collateral trust bonds, and, perhaps most importantly, making sure the issuer complies with all the covenants in the bond's indenture. In this last function, the trustee acts as a fiduciary. That is, the trustee is responsible for acting exclusively in the best interest of the bondholders. Should the issuer fail to make the specified coupon or principal payments when due, the trustee may declare the company to be in default. The trustee must also make sure that any promise by the company to maintain adequate levels of debt service coverage is honored. Reporting requirements are also an important role for the trustee, where the inability of the company/issuer to file timely financial reports could be deemed as an event of default. In each of these cases, the trustee must act in such a way as to protect the rights and interests of the bondholders.

Rating Agencies

The two main risks to a corporate bond investor are interest rate risk and credit risk. Interest rate risk is borne by all fixed-income investors, and one's view on the future path of interest rates determines the optimal maturity for an investor. The other risk for a corporate investor is changes in the bond's creditworthiness—in other words, credit risk. The obvious manifestation of this risk is a change in the bond's market value with no commensurate change in the general level of interest rates. What determines a bond's creditworthiness is the issuer's ability to make full and timely payment of interest and principal when due. Bond investors must have confidence that the bond they have purchased will provide the promised cash flows. If not, the market value of the bond will reflect a much higher required return (yield) to compensate for the additional risk of the issuer not making the expected payments.

While there is no substitute for doing individual credit work on bonds that you are considering buying, the large number of issuers and issues means that a helping hand is often useful. A corporation issuing a new bond will often hire a rating agency, such as Standard & Poor's (S&P), Moody's Investors Service, or Fitch, to analyze the credit risk of the bond prior to its issuance and assign a rating. These agencies look at many factors of the issuer's operations when making their determination. Because bonds from the same corporation can have different types of assets pledged as collateral, or varying degrees of seniority, the rating assigned to the bond is that of the bond itself—not the issuing corporation. The ratings agencies also provide a general corporate family rating for larger borrowers, with individual bonds notched upwards or downwards from the corporate rating based on collateral and seniority. Since the majority of the most liquid corporate bonds come with rating, utilizing the ratings agencies allows investors a method to compare the relative creditworthiness of different borrowers.

The general rating scale used by each ratings agency is unique to each ratings agency, although it is generally acknowledged that investment grade is considered for a bond in the triple-B or better category, while a non-investment-grade, or junk bond carries a rating below triple-B. Ratings agencies can disagree on ratings as they perform their credit analysis in isolation, utilizing factors that are unique to their firm. Therefore, it is not unusual for ratings for an individual bond to vary across the different agencies, although those variations generally do not drift more than a few ratings categories. A bond that has an investment grade rating from one agency and a junk rating from another agency is called a *crossover bond*. Some investors may utilize the lower of these ratings in determining its portfolio suitability, which in the case of a crossover bond would not be acceptable to a strictly investment-grade investor. Other investors may blend the various ratings in coming up with a composite rating, which may be considered investment grade if two out of the three agencies rate a borrower IG while one has it as non-investment grade. A few other ratings terms are *fallen angels* and *rising stars*. A fallen angel is an investment-grade bond that has been downgraded into junk status, while a non-investment-grade borrower that gets upgraded into the IG area is called a rising star. Table 14.2 lists the rating categories for the major rating agencies and the definition of each one of these categories.

We will stress again that there is no substitute for doing individual credit work and fully understanding the investment that you are buying. Relying solely on the rating has had mixed results, particularly after some fairly high-profile credit mistakes. Most recently this has included the generally high ratings for banks going into the financial crisis, which ultimately tested their solvency despite their investment-grade ratings. The structured finance market has seen its fair share of incorrect ratings, with model assumptions around the housing market resulting in wholesale downgrades in that asset class. Going back into the middle 2000s, the ratings agencies were ultimately incorrect in their assessments of Enron and WorldCom, both very high-profile borrowers. Having said this, the ratings agencies play an important role in the markets, and their ratings and ratings changes directly impact the prices of corporate bonds. Despite the incorrect ratings assessments listed previously, ratings remain a generally good barometer for credit performance. Moody's transition studies indicate that over a 40-year period, over 90% of bonds with a triple-B rating remain investment grade after one year. That figure declines to 60% after a 5-year period, making the point that surveillance of a portfolio is as important as the original construction. Data from S&P indicates that the vast majority of defaults arise from the weakest single-B and lower categories, again advocating for a regular review of existing bond positons.

In terms of what agencies look for when evaluating a bond's credit risk, we can look toward the five Cs of credit: capacity, capital, collateral, conditions, and character. *Capacity* refers to the ability of the company to generate sufficient cash flow to cover all of its required debt service (interest and principal payments on all bond issues and bank loans).

TABLE 14.2 Rating Categories

	Moody's	Standard & Poors	Fitch	Ratings Definition
Investment Grade	Aaa	AAA	AAA	This rating category is considered the highest of all rating categories. An issuer rated in this category has the lowest credit risk and exhibits the highest capacity to meet its obligations.
	Aa1	AA+	AA+	This ratings category is also considered high quality and exhibits a strong ability to meet its financial obligations. It differs from the highest rating category by just a small margin.
	Aa2	AA	AA	
	Aa3	AA−	AA−	
	A1	A+	A+	The single-A category is also considered a strong rating category. Their risk is considered upper medium grade and they are more suseptible to changes in economic and company circumstances.
	A2	A	A	
	A3	A−	A−	
	Baa1	BBB+	BBB+	This category is considered medium grade and posesses some speculative characteristics and moderate credit risk. These borrowers' ability to meet financial obligations is more easily impacted by changing economic and company circumstances. These ratings are considered the weakest of the investment grade ratings.
	Baa2	BBB	BBB	
	Baa3	BBB−	BBB−	
Non-Investment Grade (or Junk)	Ba1	BB+	BB+	This category is the strongest of the non-investment grade group. As such they are considered speculative and subject to substantial credit risk. These borrowers face major ongoing uncertainties or exposure to adverse business, financial, or economic conditions which could lead to their inability to meet financial commitments.
	Ba2	BB	BB	
	Ba3	BB−	BB−	
	B1	B+	B+	This category is also speculative and subject to high credit risk. While they are presently able to meet obligations, any adverse business, financial, or economic conditions could lead to the obligor's ability to meet its financial commitments.
	B2	B	B	
	B3	B−	B−	

(*continued*)

TABLE 14.2 *(Continued)*

	Moody's	Standard & Poors	Fitch	Ratings Definition
Non-Investment Grade (or Junk) *(continued)*	Caa1	CCC+	CCC+	The triple-C category is considered speculative with a very high degree of credit risk and vulnerable to non-payment. Payment is reliant on favorable eonomic and business conditions and adverse conditions are likely to result in non-payment.
	Caa2	CCC	CCC	
	Caa3	CCC–	CCC–	
	Ca/C/D	CC/C/D	CC/C/D	These lowest-rated obligations are either at default or very near default. They are likely expected to default and the difference in ratings relates to the expected levels of recovery.

Capital refers to the amount of equity invested in the company by its owners. Lenders will require a threshold minimum of equity in the company's capital structure (debt and equity) as an indication of the owners' confidence in the enterprise and their financial risk at stake in the enterprise's success or failure. *Collateral* refers to assets of the company pledged to the lender as a secondary source or repayment. *Conditions* refer to the economic climate in which the enterprise must conduct its business and whether it is currently favorable or unfavorable. *Character* refers to the borrower's willingness to repay and is an assessment of whether the borrower will try to honor or avoid their obligation under difficult circumstances. There are also sector-specific nuances that either support or penalize the companies within the industry. The banking sector is a prime example of understanding industry-specific factors, especially after the litany of new regulatory rules were passed after the financial crisis. The once assumed too-big-to-fail ratings uplift has also been largely removed from a bank's ratings as regulators have distanced themselves from needing to provide emergency support in solvency situations.

While we have provided a detailed explanation of the ratings categories found in the corporate bond space, there are additional ratings applicable for short-term ratings. Moody's utilizes Prime 1 (P-1), Prime 2 (P-2), Prime 3 (P-3), and not Prime as its short-term ratings while S&P utilizes an A-1, A-2, A-3, B, C, and D scale. The short-term market is very quality focused, with A-1/P-1 ratings often required to access the market.

Buyers

There are two broad categories of investors in the fixed-income markets: institutional investors and individual investors. Within the institutional bucket, the composition of the various investors has varied over time, and more recently has shifted away from the traditional pension and insurance company buyers. Mutual funds and ETFs have become more active buyers recently, reflecting an interest from the retail investor that chooses not to own individual bonds. Other institutional investor classes have also seen growth over the past few years, such as investors. One constant for each of these investors in the investment-grade arena is the desire to generate stable, lower-volatility-income, corporate and international that offers a spread pickup to increasingly low government yields.

Insurance companies and pension funds were once the predominant owners of corporate bonds, holding an estimated 70+% of outstanding issues in the 1970s. However, as pensions have become scarcer and alternative investment vehicles like ETF and mutual funds have grown, the share of these market participants has shrunk by over one half during the past several decades. The bond market nonetheless continues to be an important investment asset for these institutional investors. In the case of life insurance companies, bonds account for a major holding in the portfolios that back the company's life insurance policies. The coupon interest and reinvestment of that interest are used to pay death benefits on policies and to generate a level of return that creates the policies' cash value. The uncertainty of stock dividends makes equity investments more challenging to manage, although low yields have forced a greater use of stocks by insurance companies. Another reason insurance companies purchase bonds for their portfolios is to form the collateral for their investment products, such as guaranteed investment contracts (GICs). When an investor purchases a GIC, a guaranteed rate of return is promised by the contract. The upfront premium paid to the insurance company by the investor is used to purchase securities whose returns will allow the company to guarantee the promised return of the GIC. The insurance company must then immunize its liability by locking in a minimum rate of return regardless of subsequent changes in the general level of interest rates. Pensions also need to plan on making regular disbursements to members, and the stability of principal and income is tantamount to accomplishing this task. Pensions therefore must have sufficient cash on hand each period and will match their investment income to cash flow needs. The portfolio creation and management process allows the pension fund to ensure that cash will be available when retirement payments are due.

While pensions and insurance company market share in the corporate bond market have fallen, mutual fund and ETF assets have grown significantly during this period. It is estimated that these two investor groups presently own approximately 15% of outstanding corporates, growing from an almost de minimus level just a few decades ago. Since retail investors make up a large portion of the mutual funds and ETFs world, it is safe to say that retail has become a larger player in the corporate marketplace. Within these investor classes, there has been an increased use of passive investment strategies. Many ETFs track a broad-based fixed-income index, such as those compiled by Barclays Capital and Merrill Lynch/Bank of America. This greater focus on passive management has had an impact on the marketability of all bonds. There are now certain larger more liquid securities that are more frequently traded as part of passive strategies. As a result, these bonds are generally more liquid, carry a liquidity premium, but also may be more volatile given the easier ability to trade them during stressful market environments.

Other corporate borrowers and international buyers have also become larger investors in the corporate bond market. Other corporate borrowers are particularly interesting, in that companies are effectively investing excess cash in other companies, possibly competitors. The inability to generate returns on government yields is a primary reason for corporate treasurers to invest in other companies' debt. Many companies also find themselves cash rich, but many of those funds are locked offshore based on tax code. Therefore, a firm like Apple is a large issuer of corporate bonds despite the fact that it has over $30 billion in cash and investments on its balance sheet. Technology and pharmaceutical firms are some of the most cash-rich sectors investing in the corporate market. Foreign buyers have also become active in the corporate market, as developed market yields plummet under the zero-to negative rate regimes pursued by global central bankers. The desire to hold U.S.-based assets also remains a theme for foreign buyers, particularly as the U.S. dollar has generally strengthened over the past several years.

Individual Investors

The goals of individual investors are similar to those of institutions even though the funds available for investment are generally much smaller. An individual investor in bonds may have a need for regular current income and/or longer-term stability of principal. The minimum denomination of $1,000 for most U.S. corporate bonds puts them in reach of many smaller investors. Along with the relative size of their investments, the major difference between institutional and individual bond investors is the amount of market information, research, and analytical tools available to each. Institutions typically have the wherewithal to invest in systems that allow them to find and analyze various bonds for potential investment. They can also have their holdings valued on a regular basis, in many cases, daily. Individuals normally are not as focused on the daily movement of their bonds since they are typically held to maturity. Of course, this becomes somewhat problematic when the individual has purchased a bond with an embedded option. Without the systems to properly evaluate the potential risk and return characteristics of a given bond, many individuals are rudely awakened when they find their bond has been called. A general rule should be to make sure you receive a prospectus on the bond before you purchase it or you have a system or service that allows you to analyze the risk and return relative to other bonds. Most online brokerage accounts, as well as your broker or wealth manager, should have such systems available. Among individual investors, there are varying levels of both investing experience and relative wealth. For most individuals, bond investing comes in the form of indirect investment via mutual funds and, perhaps, a pension plan, 401(k), ETF, or other retirement vehicle. Mutual funds allow individuals to buy shares of a portfolio of securities. In this way, a small amount of money can be spread across a diversified group of bonds. Pension plans and 401(k) plans are similar in that the investor's retirement funds can be spread across a diversified set of holdings.

Investors with larger amounts to invest are sometimes called high-net-worth individuals. These people often take advantage of the growing business of private wealth management, which is provided by banks and investment firms. The private wealth manager will handle the bond investments of the individual and may suggest certain bonds as appropriate to the investor's risk and return requirements. At the end of the day, the vast majority of bond investing is done for the benefit of individuals, whether it is done personally or through institutions on their behalf.

PRICE TRANSPARENCY

As with most types of fixed-income securities, corporate bonds do not normally trade on a listed exchange. The vast majority of corporate bonds trade over the counter from dealer to dealer. Therefore, historically, the fair value of corporate bonds has been difficult if not impossible to uncover. Both the Securities and Exchange Commission (SEC) and the National Association of Securities Dealers (NASD) were determined to rectify this situation, searching for ways to increase investors' access to bond pricing information. The regulators felt that access to price information would enhance investors' ability to make better investment decisions, and encourage greater numbers of investors to enter the fixed-income arena. On July 1, 2002, the NASD, in an endeavor to increase price transparency in the corporate market, introduced the Trade Reporting and Compliance Engine (TRACE). TRACE, developed by the NASD, facilitates the mandatory reporting of over-the-counter secondary market transactions in eligible corporate securities, including investment-grade and high-yield debt, medium-term notes, and convertible bonds. All broker-dealers who are members of the NASD have a responsibility to report transactions in corporate bonds to TRACE. In April 2004, the NASD announced that under an enhanced proposal, TRACE would disseminate data on more than 23,000 individual securities, bringing investors immediate sale information on 99% of all transactions in TRACE-eligible securities that are publicly traded. "This proposal to increase access to bond pricing information will enhance investors' ability to make better investment decisions," said Douglas H. Shulman, NASD's president in charge of markets, services, and information. "In a very short period of time, TRACE has provided unprecedented transparency to the market, enhancing market fairness and integrity." As more information became available, market aggregate statistics are also now available. Investors can now find an end-of-day recap of corporate bond market activity including the number of securities and total par amount traded as well as advances, declines, and 52-week highs and lows. In addition, the ten most active investment-grade, high-yield, and convertible bonds are also provided. All of this data can be found on the FINRA website (www.finra.org/marketdata.)

HIGH-YIELD ("JUNK") BONDS

The high-yield market is synonymous with non-investment-grade bonds, sometimes referred to as junk bonds. While not the most flattering description, *junk* was an appropriate description during the early phases of the market. Since there was not much demand for non-investment-grade securities in the 1960s and 1970s, most junk bonds were former investment-grade deals that found themselves in a more challenging operating environment. Some of these borrowers were downgraded into the junk category, earning the moniker of fallen angels. The real growth and development of the high-yield market occurred in the 1980s, as merger-and-acquisition activity fueled the subsequent development of an active primary and secondary market. Some of the bankers and companies during that period have evolved into financial legend, with the likes of Drexel Burnham and the RJR Nabisco leveraged buyout sprouting numerous books and even Hollywood movies.

Although the junk market has seen its highs and lows, it is now an integral part of the capital raising process. It is estimated that 20% of the $8 trillion corporate bond market is rated speculative or non-investment grade. While fallen angels continue to help populate the junk ranks, the new issuance market accounted for an average of $300 billion annually over the past several years, or up to 25% of total issuance. From a definitional standpoint, the high-yield market is comprised of borrowers that are rated Ba1/BB+/BB+ or less by the rating agencies. As Table 14.2 references, these bonds are considered speculative, with the expectations of default rising the further one moves down the ratings scale. Use of proceeds mimics all of the reasons found in the high-grade market, from funding business expansions, borrowing for working capital purposes, financing M&A activity, and refinancing existing debt. Industry representation is also widespread, with all economic sectors accounted for, and media, telecom, health-care services, and oil and gas maintaining the largest share of the asset class. See Figure 14.3 High Yield Market (Definitional).

The investor class varies a bit from investment-grade bonds in that there is even less retail representation in the high-yield market. The greater degree of analysis needed to evaluate a speculative-grade borrower has made institutional lenders the primary high-yield buyer. Insurance companies, pension funds, and mutual funds/ETFs are each estimated to account for approximately one quarter of the market. The remainder is a mixture of hedge funds, foreign buyers, and crossover buyers, such as investment-grade funds and even equity funds. Regardless of who owns junk bonds, the attraction is fairly obvious: the higher yield and higher return offered over other fixed-income asset classes. The asset class also offers some interest rate diversification, as high yield has historically had less correlation to the Treasury market and more correlation to equity markets. These correlations vary over time, although they have averaged 35% since the financial

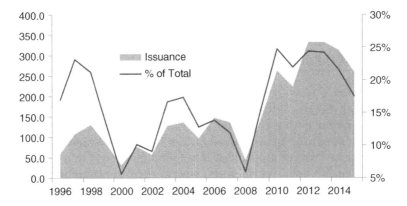

FIGURE 14.3 High-yield market grows in total issuance and importance
Source: SIFMA

crisis, varying as high as 70% and as low as –22%. This is one of the reasons that high yield is quoted in dollar price rather than on a spread basis.

The structure of high-yield bonds is similar to what is found for investment grade bonds, with seniority, collateral, and bond covenants an important part of the investment process. Given the more fragile nature of the borrowers, high-yield investors may find themselves able to extract better credit terms than what may be found in the investment-grade market. This may include more securitized debt, additional bonds tests, coverage tests and limitation on liens, sales leaseback transactions, and business combinations. The ability of investors to demand more restrictive covenants is often determined by the overall demand for the asset class. As high-yield cycles become more overheated, the quality of indentures has a tendency to deteriorate, often leading to a more borrower-friendly environment. The payment in kind (PIK)/PIK toggle structure often makes its way into indentures when restrictions become more lax. This feature allows an issuer to make interest payments in the form of additional bonds rather than cash. This allows the company to preserve cash and leverage its balance sheet without needing to find additional pools of capital. While the additional bonds usually have higher interest rates associated with them, they are often used when a company's cash flows become stressed.

So, are junk bonds truly junk? There is certainly more credit risk associated with speculative borrowers than investment-grade borrowers. One-year default rates for speculative-grade borrowers have averaged 4% since the 1980s according to Moody's, while the default rate for all borrowers is just 1.6% during that period. Where we are in the credit cycle has proven critical in evaluating default trends, with spec default rate rising to 12% during the financial crisis versus 5% for all bonds. Of course investors demand compensation for this additional risk, and the average yield in the high-yield market has been 350 basis points above investment-grade bonds over the past decade. Various points in the cycle have seen that difference shrink to under 200 bps and gap out to over 1,400 bps, as witnessed in 2008/2009. An additional risk that has arisen in the high-yield market has been market liquidity, which is transforming all financial asset classes. We have seen the high-yield asset class become extremely illiquid during periods of market stress, although liquidity tends to return to the market once the volatility passes. Today, the high-yield bond market is an important part of the broader corporate bond market, allowing corporations to raise working capital and providing investors with opportunities to diversify their bond portfolios.

EMERGING BOND MARKETS

Emerging market bonds have held a prominent role in the development of the modern financial markets over the past several decades, although often not with the most complimentary spotlight. Some of the more notable headlines that investors have been faced with included the cycle of defaulting bank loans in the 1980s from Latin American countries that led to the creation of the Brady Bond market, which allowed these economies to restructure while transferring risk from the U.S. banking system to the broader investment community. The Asian financial crisis in the late 1990s resulted in IMF bailouts for three countries, although many more countries in the region were impacted as their currencies and financial markets collapsed. The tightening of the global credit conditions during the Asian financial crisis effectively spread to Russia, which after a tense spring and summer with creditors defaulted on its debt in August 1998. The carnage of these crises was also not limited to these regions, as the resulting global capital flows worked against the hedge fund Long Term Capital Management, which ultimately needed a $3.6 billion bailout from a consortium of the world's largest banks. While these are some of the more notable crises to impact emerging market investors, there is no lack of recent events, such as Argentina's defaulted bonds and decades-long fight with various holdout investors. Most recently, Brazil's state-run oil company, Petrobras, is embroiled in a widespread corruption scandal that is likely to result in an impeachment trial of the country's president while implicating a wide swath of politicians and corporate executives.

Given this seedy history, why would investors even consider venturing into the emerging market debt space at all? First, the previous examples were chosen for their notoriety in the annals of financial markets, but ultimately make up a small portion of the geographic definition of the emerging markets. Second, the emerging markets provide vast income and growth opportunities, with some of the fastest growing debt markets over the past decade. Finally, and likely most important for investors, emerging markets offer additional income opportunities that are becoming more difficult to find in the developed markets, as sovereign yields remain at their lowest levels in modern financial history. See the illustration in Figure 14.4.

We have structured this section to provide a brief introduction to U.S. dollar–denominated bonds issued by corporate borrowers domiciled in an emerging market.

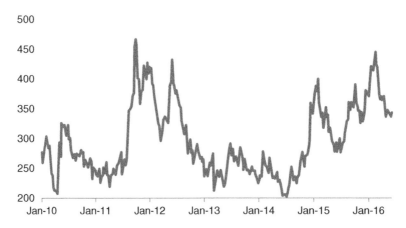

FIGURE 14.4 EM offers spread over comparable Treasuries (Barclays EM aggregated yield versus 10-year Treasury)
Sources: Bloomberg, Barclays Capital

These bonds can refer to Yankee bonds issued by EM borrowers, although our definition may also include the Eurodollar bond market. Both Yankee and Eurodollar bonds may be issued by countries and companies domiciled within both developed and developing economies, although our discussion will be focused on the emerging markets. It is worth noting that the EM bond market has grown exponentially over the past decade and the portion that we will discuss in the upcoming pages is just a small portion of this market, which includes both local currency and non-USD hard currency obligations. Given the globalization of the financial markets, U.S.-based corporate bond investors will encounter USD-based EM obligations, requiring an understanding of the asset class as part of the investment process.

WHAT IS AN EMERGING MARKET?

An emerging market is one that is defined as not having yet emerged, in contrast to a developed market, which we would assume has already developed. Other definitions of EM include countries and markets that fall between developed markets, such as the United States, Western Europe, and Japan, and frontier markets, which are even less developed than emerging markets. Even other definitions include wealthy markets that have legal or regularly frameworks that lag developed counties. We like to think of emerging markets as those countries that have the potential to exhibit higher levels of economic and social advancement than the developed world. The financial markets associated with these countries are also earlier in their lifecycle, which while providing opportunities also exhibit unique risk from less liquidity, potentially greater volatility, and evolving legal and regulatory frameworks. While these definitions may seem confusing, leading to the inclusion of up to 50+ possible economies in an EM basket, debt issuance is dominated by four large economies, which is where investors should focus their efforts. These economies are China, Brazil, Russia, and Mexico, which account for over 40% of outstanding issuance.

Market Sizing

There are many ways to look at the EM debt market, although we will focus on the debt that USD corporate investors are most likely to encounter when constructing their investment portfolio. The EM debt markets have grown exponentially over the past decade, reaching over $6 trillion in 2013 according to the World Bank, a six-fold increase since 2000. Hard currency debt, or bonds issued by these emerging markets borrowers denominated in currencies other than their home market was estimated to be between $1 and $3 trillion, with the U.S. dollar the major funding currency, although the euro and Japanese yen are also represented. Further dissecting this data reveals that USD EM corporate bonds market may be up to $1 trillion in size according to Bloomberg, equal in size to the high-yield market. Various other studies have indicated that cross-section of the bond market has been the fastest growing since the financial crisis, which therefore warrants investor consideration.

TABLE 14.3   Rapid Growth of USD EM Debt Markets (in billions)

	Investment Grade	High Yield	Total
2009	47	549	596
2010	84	665	749
2011	79	732	811
2012	120	925	1045
2013	150	874	1024
2014	167	884	1050
2015	119	825	944

Source: Bloomberg

There are numerous reasons that EM corporate borrowers have been active issuers of hard currency bonds. Since the debt markets in many emerging markets are not overly developed, these borrowers have had to rely on bank debt as a primary source of capital. While bank lending remains the dominant source of funding in many markets, its share of total financing has declined over the past decade, consistent with the overall decrease in bank credit. This fall in bank balance sheets occurred at the same time as interest rates were falling globally as central banks pursued zero-interest-rate policy and other forms of quantitative easing. This created a demand for additional debt, especially higher yielding ones, as investors were suddenly competing against monetary authorities for debt. While central banks initially focused their bond-buying efforts on sovereign bonds, this has been expanded to the corporate bonds in various jurisdictions. The U.S. dollar is the most common hard currency used for funding as the USD occupies a unique role in global finance. Not only are the U.S. capital markets the most developed in the world, the dollar's role as a reserve currency means that it is found in many markets outside of the United States. Therefore, it is estimated that over 80% of hard currency borrowing is in U.S. dollars.

Credit and Market Analysis

In many ways, analyzing an EM corporate credit is similar to analyzing domestic corporate obligations. Industry analysis, fundamental corporate analysis, financial statement review, and market pricing signals are variables that investors in both domestic and EM corporate bonds should consider. This financial analysis should also take into consideration the impact of changing exchange rates, as it may have an outsized impact on a company's ability to service its debt. This is particularly relevant as the U.S. dollar has strengthened over the past few years, which may make it more difficult for a company to service its debt. This occurs when a borrower must repay its liabilities in a foreign currency while collecting revenues in its local currency. In the case of the U.S. dollar, it has strengthened 18% over the past two years, possibly raising the debt service cost of an EM corporate by a similar proportion unless it generates USD-based revenues or has hedged this exposure.

The rating agencies are active in the emerging markets, so using their ratings analysis while adhering to the caveats discussed earlier remains relevant for EM investors. The ratings of EM borrowers vary extensively, as a county's economic prospects have a direct bearing on EM corporate credit. For example, the country ratings for the four largest borrowers range from double-A-rated China to double-B-rated Brazil. How a country manages it finances has a direct bearing on these ratings, with China maintaining $3 trillion in reserves while Brazil maintains external debt at 2× its current account receipts. Since many EM economies are tied to the export of commodities, volatility in those products can also rapidly change the economic prospects for a country. The ratings agencies provide a rating for a country's local currency obligations and its foreign currency debt. This foreign currency rating is usually lower than the local currency rating, reflecting the risk associated with foreign currency translation. These ratings agencies often use these country ratings as a ceiling for all EM debt emanating from that jurisdiction, with the concept that there is risk associated. Country ratings often act as a ceiling for all EM debt obligations, reflecting the risk that possible capital and exchange controls could impact the ability to convert currency to pay external creditors. Since there are more non-investment-grade-rated EM corporates, these sovereign-specific issues must be taken into consideration along with the credit review process. While EM presents greater liquidity and risk issues than investment-grade corporates, the rapid growth of this market and its potentiality to generate greater income and return prospects justifies its portfolio consideration.

CHAPTER 15

Preferred Stock

Sarah Swammy

Preferred stock is a hybrid security with features common to both stocks and bonds. These securities are attractive to investors because they offer periodic income (fixed or variable payments), competitive returns (yields), liquidity (traded on major exchanges) and portfolio diversification. Preferreds are generally issued by companies that have outstanding common stock and normally issued with a par value of $25, which may correlate to the issuer's current market price and dividend. The main difference between common and preferred stocks is the manner in which dividends are paid. Common stock holders receive dividends only at the discretion of the issuer, based on the issuer's earnings and payout ratio. Preferred shareholders are entitled to receive dividends at a predetermined rate (either fixed or variable) by agreement. This agreement is similar to a bond indenture, and sets forth the respective rights and obligations of the preferred buyer and corporate issuer, but unlike most bonds, preferred shares do not have the same form of a guarantee to pay and thus are subordinate to bondholders. The dividends must be paid to preferred shareholders in full before any dividends can be paid to holders of common stock. In other words, payment of the preferred dividends is senior to the payment of dividends to common stockholders. The dividend is paid to preferred stockholders at a set rate as a percentage of par.

In addition, preferred stock investors have seniority over common stockholders in the event of a corporate liquidation (bankruptcy). In that event, preferred stockholders must be paid the full par value of their shares, plus any accumulated but unpaid dividends, before common stockholders receive anything.

Common Stock Features
- Ownership stake in company
- Greater potential for capital appreciation
- Typically has voting rights

Preferred Stock Features

- Ownership stake in company
- Likely to receive regular dividends
- Higher priority in event of bankruptcy
- Issued with a specified dividend rate

Several types of preferred stock will be examined in this chapter.

Although preferred stock is considered part of an issuer's equity base, it tends to trade more like debt. This is because the preferreds value is based primarily on its dividend yield, rather than a change in the underlying value of the business. The yield, expressed as an annual rate, can be compared to the coupon payment on a bond. The annual yield can be ascertained by dividing the annual dividend payment per share by its price per share. For example, let's assume that the current market interest rates for issuers rated "BAA" range from 5.75% to 6.25%; if the preferred stock of XYZ Corp. (which we will assume is rated BAA) has a par value of $25/share and pays an annual dividend of $1.50/share, it will have an annual yield of 6% ($1.50/$25 = 6%). For this reason, preferred stock prices are very sensitive to changes in prevailing interest rates. In a rising interest rate environment, the market yields on preferred issues will also rise. Accordingly, holders of preferred stock that offers a below-market yield will experience a decline in market value. The amount of the decline will be based in large part on the dividend yield and term of the security in addition to any change in the creditworthiness of the issuer.

PERPETUAL PREFERRED STOCK

Traditional perpetual preferred issues, unlike bonds, do not have a maturity date. Unlike a bond, there is no guarantee that the investment will ever be redeemed at par. As a result, perpetual preferred issues can be more volatile and riskier than the longest maturity bond. The perpetual preferred issuance is booked as equity on an issuer's balance sheet. Preferred stocks generally are issued at par values of $25, $50, or $100. However, today most issues are priced at $25. Financial services issues, including banks and REITs, have accounted for the largest percentage of issuance over the past 20 years, followed by utilities and, to a far lesser extent, industrials. Banks have particularly utilized preferreds due to preferential regulatory capital treatment where it may count preferred issues as Tier-1 capital.

There are two types of perpetual preferred stock, fixed and floating rate. Fixed-rate preferred stocks carry a fixed dividend that can be stated in dollar terms or as a percentage of the par value of the security. Floating-rate preferred stocks pay dividends that vary with short-term interest rates.[1]

---

[1]NASDAQ, "Financial Glossary: Interest Rate," http://www.nasdaq.com/investing/glossary/i/interest-rate.

DIVIDEND-RECEIVED DEDUCTION (DRD)

An important characteristic of the perpetual preferred market is that most of these issues qualify for a 70% tax exclusion on their dividends. This is known as the dividend-received deduction (DRD) and is designed to avoid multiple taxation of dividends paid from one corporation to another. To be eligible, you must be a U.S. corporation that receives a dividend from another U.S. corporation, or U.S.-based subsidiary of a foreign corporation that is already subject to U.S. income tax. Eligible corporations are entitled to exclude 70% of preferred stock dividends from gross income. A preferred issue with a 6% yield, for example, would only have 30% of the cash dividend subject to tax. If you assume a corporate tax rate of 35% on the taxable part of the payout, the corporate holder would retain 89.5% of the yield after-tax, instead of 65% (as in the case of a fully taxable investment). The following formula can be used to calculate the equivalent yield that would be necessary on a fully taxable security (to corporate investors assuming a 35% tax rate) to provide the same after-tax return as a preferred with the DRD exclusion for any given dividend rate:

$$\frac{0.70 \text{ (Dividend Rate)} + 0.30 \text{ (Dividend Rate)}(1 - 0.35)}{(1 - 0.35)} = \text{Dividend Rate} \times 1.377$$

Assuming a dividend rate of 6%, the taxable equivalent rate would be 8.26%. An eligible corporate account would need a return that exceeded 8.26% to best a DRD preferred paying 6%, on an after-tax basis. Table 15.1 exemplifies the taxable equivalent yield of various coupon levels containing the DRD exclusion.

The standard formula for calculating the effective taxable yield of a DRD preferred regardless of coupon or tax rate is:

$$\text{Effective Taxable Yield} = \frac{(D \times .70)}{(1 - T)} + (D \times .30)$$

where

D = dividend rate
T = tax rate

TABLE 15.1   Taxable Equivalent Yields with Dividend-Received Deduction

Preferred Coupon	After-Tax Return	Taxable Equivalent Yield
5.00%	4.48%	6.89%
6.00%	5.37%	8.26%
7.00%	6.27%	9.64%

Here's a shortcut formula for converting DRD yields to taxable and tax-exempt adjusted yields:

To convert to Taxable Equivalent → multiply DRD rate × 1.377

To convert to Tax-Exempt Equivalent → multiply DRD rate × .895

Another factor to note is that the security must be held for at least 46 days in order to receive the tax exclusion. As a result of the tax ramifications to the corporate investor, DRD issues generally carry lower dividend rates than other types of preferreds. It should be noted that subchapter S corporations are ineligible to take the DRD exclusion.

The 70% exclusion can be taken only on qualified perpetual preferreds issued after October 1, 1942. These issues are referred to as "new-money" preferreds. A number of utility preferreds issued prior to that date are known as "old-money" preferreds and do carry a DRD exclusion but only approximately 42%. The Internal Revenue Code provides a formula that takes the current tax rate level into account in calculating old-money DRD. At that time, the issuing utilities had already deducted a portion of the dividend on their own returns as an expense. Old-money issues that are refunded, or refinanced, remain at the reduced exclusion rate.

FIXED TO FLOAT

Another group of preferred issues are called adjustable- or floating-rate preferreds. These issues carry dividend rates that can reset quarterly at a spread to one or more benchmark government markets or to the London Interbank Offered Rate (LIBOR). In addition, many of these issues have maximum and minimum coupon limits that they can pay. There is no guarantee that these floaters will remain at par (issue price) as the coupon changes to reflect the interest rate environment at any point in time. For example, a floater with a maximum cap of 8% would probably fall in price if general market rates exceeded 8%.

NONCUMULATIVE PREFERRED STOCK

Many issues of preferred stock are noncumulative with respect to dividends. If the dividend is noncumulative, the issuer is under no obligation to pay any arrearages in the future. Not all preferred stock is noncumulative.

CUMULATIVE PREFERRED STOCK

A cumulative preferred stock is a type of preferred stock with a provision that stipulates that if a preferred dividend is not paid when due, it accumulates and must be paid in full before the company distributes dividends to common stockholders.

For risk-averse investors, purchases in noncumulative preferreds should be limited to higher-rated issues.

CONVERTIBLE PREFERRED STOCK

Convertible preferred shares are corporate fixed-income securities in which an investor has an option to convert its shares into a prescribed number of shares of the issuer's common stock after a predetermined date or on a specific date at a prescribed price per share. The conversion option allows the holder to participate in the upward movement of the underlying common stock. Many convertibles have a specific period in which they can be converted. The following example will help clarify some of the terms relating to convertibles:

XYZ 6.00% convertible preferred priced at an initial public offering of $50 per share

Convertible any time into 4.8605 shares of XYZ common

Conversion price of $10.287

Current price of common: $13.40

Current price of preferred: $72.74

The conversion ratio is the number of common shares that the convertible holder would receive.

$$\text{Conversion Ratio} = \frac{\text{Convertible Preferred Par Value}}{\text{Conversion Price}} = \frac{50}{10.287} = 4.8605$$

Parity exists when the price of the convertible preferred is equivalent (when exchanged) to the current price of the common stock as depicted here:

$$\frac{\text{Par Value of Convertible}}{\text{Conversion Price}} = \frac{\text{Current Price of Convertible}}{\text{Current Price of Common}}$$

In this example, with the convertible issue currently priced at $72.34, the common stock price would have to be $14.96 to achieve parity.

$$\frac{50}{10.287} = \frac{72.34}{14.96}$$

If the market conversion price ($14.96) is greater than the actual common stock price ($13.40), the convertible is selling at a conversion premium. The conversion premium ratio is the percentage increase needed to reach parity. In this case it would be:

$$\frac{14.96}{13.40} = 11.64\%$$

If the convertible preferred is selling above parity, it is valued at a premium. Convertible preferreds usually trade at a premium over parity as buyers are willing to bid up the higher-yielding instrument with the expectation of realizing some of the potential upside performance in the price of the common stock.

Another factor that should be noted is that the issuer may be able to force the conversion at some point in time, depending on where the price of the common is trading. In addition, the conversion price may be subject to adjustments upon certain events. It is important to examine the final prospectus in order to avoid any surprises.

There are also mandatory convertible securities that differ from those discussed above in that they require the purchase of a variable number of shares of the common stock of the issuer by the preferred holder on or before a specified date. This is done regardless of where the common stock is trading and, as a result, investors bear the risk of losing part of their original investment.

FEATURES OF PREFERRED STOCK

Call Features

Although traditional preferred stocks generally do not have a specified maturity date, most issues include a provision that gives the issuer an option to redeem shares periodically. These provisions are usually exercised in a declining rate environment when it is cost-effective for an issuer to call in higher dividend paying stock. While in theory perpetual preferred stock has unlimited term, most are redeemable after a set period of time, for example, 5 years, 10 years, and so forth. Most issues have call protection for five years, meaning that the issuer may not call the issue for five years. Preferred stock is usually called at par value, and some call provisions may include a premium over par. Investors who purchase preferred stock at a premium to par or the stated value should be fully aware of call features that could sharply reduce the effective return or could even generate a negative return.

The prorated yearly loss is then subtracted from the annual dividend or payout in order to properly calculate the true return on investment of the security. The following formula can be used to calculate the yield to call:

Given a $25 par preferred issue with a 6.125% coupon, or $1.53 dividend rate with a call at par 4 years and trading at $26.625, the yield to call would be 4.52%, not the 6.125% dividend rate.

Voting Rights

Generally, preferred shareholders do not have voting rights unless preferred dividends have been in arrears for a specified period of time, generally six quarterly payments. At that point, nonvoting preferred shareholders may elect some number of directors (at least two) to the company's board of directors. Voting rights are continuous until the cumulative dividends have been paid in full. Once any arrearage has been paid, the preferred shareholders are no longer eligible to vote. In the case of noncumulative dividends, voting rights would end after the regular quarterly dividend has been paid for a year.

Sinking Funds

A preferred issue may include provisions for a sinking fund. This provision requires the issuer to retire a certain percentage of the total issue over a specified period of time. Eventually, the entire issue will be retired during the time period prescribed. It should be noted that issues with sinking funds can also carry other call options for the issuer. Issuers can meet the sinking-fund requirement by calling the required number of shares on the sinking fund payment date or by purchasing shares in the open market. The primary difference between call features and sinking funds is that with a standard call feature, the issuer may call its issues on a voluntary basis while a sinking fund is mandatory and must conform to a set schedule as described in the prospectus.

Foreign Issuers

In 2003, new federal legislation reduced taxes on dividend income and capital gains on certain preferred securities held more than 60 days. The new tax rates consist of a 5% tax on lower income brackets and a 15% tax on the higher brackets. This favored tax treatment applies only to the types of domestic issues discussed earlier (perpetual, sinking fund, and convertible preferreds). There are also some foreign ADR issues that would qualify. An American Depositary Receipt (ADR) is a receipt issued by a U.S. depositary bank that represents shares of a foreign corporation held by the depositary bank. ADR issues trade in dollars and in a manner similar to domestic issues. To qualify for this favored tax treatment, a foreign issuer would have to be incorporated in a possession of the United States or be party to a comprehensive income tax treaty with the United States. The preferred stock must be perpetual, trade in the U.S. markets, and have all its dividends paid out of earnings. Qualified dividends do not include those paid by foreign entities that are either a foreign investment company, a passive foreign investment company, or a foreign personal holding company.

In addition, the tax-advantaged rates do not apply to dividends received in tax-deferred retirement accounts. Non-U.S. preferred securities now account for a significant part of the market and are usually issued by highly rated financial institutions. They are generally initially priced at $25 and listed on U.S. equity exchanges. Since the securities are priced in dollars, they do not possess currency risk. Historically, foreign issues have offered higher yields than equivalently rated domestic issues. Examples of some of the foreign issuers who regularly offer these securities include: ING, Royal Bank of Scotland, Abbey National, and ABN AMRO. There are several types of non-U.S. securities to choose from under the preferred umbrella, including perpetual $25 par stock, baby bonds, perpetual trust preferred securities, and exchangeable capital securities.

ANTICIPATING THE RISKS

Call Risk

As discussed earlier, most preferred stocks contain call provisions. This option benefits issuers, since they have the right to exercise the call option at a time of their choosing. Generally, this will be during a period of declining interest rates, when you (the investor) will be hard-pressed to find a replacement investment of similar quality offering as high a dividend. Since many preferreds contain only a five-year non-call period, the price appreciation of these securities will be limited when compared to traditional long-term non-callable bonds. While preferreds can appreciate, the potential upside is potentially limited by the issuer's call option. Since the securities can be called away by the issuer at the expiration of the non-call period, the security will not appreciate far above the call price as that date approaches, regardless of the price appreciation occurring in the general market.

Credit Risk

As with all corporate instruments, there is always a risk that the issuer will default on its obligations. While preferred stockholders have seniority with respect to dividends and assets over common stockholders, their rights are subordinate to bondholders and other general creditors of the corporation. As a result, it is imperative that an investor assess the creditworthiness and financial standing of the corporate issuer. Many investors undertake careful review of individual companies to determine their ability to make timely dividend payments. Most, however, rely largely on the publish ratings from the three major national credit rating organizations (Moody's, Standard & Poor's, and Fitch). Historically, these agencies' independent credit ratings have been utilized by most investors as an important factor when evaluating the credit quality of the securities they are considering. In the aftermath of the financial crisis of 2008–2009, investors have taken a more critical eye on the evaluations from these large ratings organizations. Their views remain an important data point for investors, but there is additional competition from other ratings firms, as well as heightened individual analysis on specific issuers. Investors should perform their own credit and structure analysis before making any investment decision.

Liquidity Risk

Liquidity risk deals with the following question: How quickly can an issue be sold for a price that closely approximates its fair market value? The easiest way to evaluate the liquidity of an issue is to look at the spread between the quoted bid and offer prices. Market makers play an important role in the liquidity of any particular preferred stock. The hybrid nature of a preferred contributes to its liquidity profile. A preferred security trades like an equity on exchange; however, the transparency of liquidity is similar to that of a traditional bond. The bond market is primarily a dealer-to-dealer market where dealers contact each other to find the best price available for a security. Market makers in preferred securities can operate in this same manner to find liquidity within the spread of any particular security. In many cases market makers are willing to buy and sell preferred securities within the quoted spread of a certain issue without advertising or "showing" those positions. Liquidity is based on a number of factors, including the size of the issue, whether it is listed on an exchange, and the particular features of the security, to name a few. Of course, during periods of adverse news (a credit downgrade, for instance) liquidity may temporarily dry up and the security will not trade until a new market level is established. But for buy-and-hold investors, liquidity is not as significant an issue.

Interest Rate Risk

Since preferred stock is essentially a fixed-income security, frequently with a long duration, its price will normally fall with any increase in market interest rates. Furthermore, as mentioned earlier, the conventional five-year call limits the potential for upward price appreciation in a period of falling interest rates. This negative convexity poses potential concern for the preferred investor; the issue may significantly underperform other types of fixed-income securities in a changing interest rate environment. For example, in a period of rising interest rates, the preferred's long duration will cause it to fall in price more quickly than other shorter-duration instruments. This risk may be mitigated to some degree by the relatively high dividend payment.

PREFERRED STOCK ISSUANCE AND TRADING

The secondary market is where owners of outstanding securities may either buy or sell their preferred stock. The primary market is where broker-dealers initially sell securities to investors on behalf of the issuing corporation. Once sold in the primary market, these securities are now traded by investors in the secondary market. The secondary market includes securities that trade on exchanges, such as the New York Stock Exchange (NYSE). In addition, many issues trade over-the-counter (OTC) through a network of dealers who buy and sell the securities that are not exchange-listed. Most OTC securities are traded through the NASDAQ system.

Preferreds can generally be identified in stock tables by a series that is differentiated by letters in the alphabet—for example, series A, B, C, and so forth. When you're checking the stock listings, a preferred stock might have the company ticker symbol followed by an underscore and the letter P (or Pr), denoting that the stock is preferred rather than common. This is followed by the appropriate letter series signifying the specific issue.

CONCLUSION

Preferred stocks are similar to bonds in that there is a fixed or variable payment to the holder backed by the earning power and cash flow of the issuing corporation. There are a number of factors that can affect the price of a preferred, including the direction of interest rates, the creditworthiness of the issuer, the structural features and tax implications of an individual issue, and the liquidity of a given issue. Corporations are large buyers of perpetual domestic issues due to the favorable tax treatment of the dividends. They can realize after-tax yields significantly higher than fully taxable investments.

While preferred stocks have historically been purchased primarily by institutions, the emergence of the $25 par security changed the landscape dramatically. The $25 per-share price comes in a variety of forms and requires less of an investment commitment for the individual investor. Combine this retail-friendly issuance denomination with the price transparency for exchanged-traded issues (most larger, well-capitalized issuers have their preferred stock listed), relatively low transaction costs, favorable tax treatment on many forms of issuance, and high dividend yields, and we have a fixed-income product well-suited to the retail fixed-income investor.

CHAPTER 16

Distressed Debt Securities

Michael McMaster

OVERVIEW OF DISTRESSED DEBT SECURITIES

Investing in distressed debt securities involves a more comprehensive analytical skill set than more traditional securities investing—like Treasuries, municipals, and investment-grade corporate bonds. While traditional investments require an investor to understand market risk and credit risk, distressed debt investors require additional skills depending upon the distressed debt scenario. The distressed debt investor may need to be a little bit research analyst, bankruptcy lawyer, accountant, cash flow modeler, forecaster, asset evaluator, and gambler. In addition, patience and confidence in their valuation methodology are essential qualities for distressed securities investors.

While there is no established definition of distressed debt securities, these securities are generally debt securities issued by corporations, governments, or municipalities that are undergoing severe financial stress and either are currently in bankruptcy proceedings or are in need of financial support, restructuring of debt, a reorganization of the company, and/or relief, which may include a plan of reorganization under Chapter 11 or a plan of liquidation under Chapter 7 of the U.S. Bankruptcy Code.[1,2] Factors that may place the issuers under such financial stress may include, but are not limited to, the following:

- The issuer has experienced operational difficulties due to competition, loss of customers, declining profit margins, customers being forced to cut back in orders, new government regulation, recession, and so on.
- Global market liquidity problems (e.g., financial crisis of 2008).
- Issuer is highly leveraged with a large amount of outstanding debt, which drains cash flow.

---

[1]Martin J. Whitman and Fernando Diz, *Distress Investing: Principles and Techniques* (Hoboken, NJ: John Wiley & Sons, 2009).
[2]Evan Goldschneider, "Distressed Debt Securities," *Investing in Fixed Income Securities: Understanding the Bond Market,* Gary Strumeyer, ed. (Hoboken, NJ: John Wiley & Sons, 2005).

- The company is experiencing cash flow difficulties due to the timing on receipt of cash payments.
- Issuer is unable to make interest payments on debt or is expected in the near future to be unable to meet interest payment obligations.
- Issuer is unable to make principal payments on debt or is expected in the near future to be unable to meet principal payment obligations.
- Issuer's financial condition has made them unable to access the short-term commercial paper markets for funding.
- Issuer's financial condition has made them unable to access longer-term capital markets for funding.
- Issuer's financial condition has made them unable to access bank loan market for funding.
- Company has significant exposure to lawsuits and judgments (e.g., companies with asbestos liabilities).
- Accounting irregularities or restatements.
- Sovereign or municipal issuer cannot stimulate economic growth and increase private investment, employment, and/or tax revenue.
- Sovereign or municipal issuer generates consistent budget deficits and funds the deficits by issuing more debt.

Distressed debt securities are rated below investment grade by the two major ratings agencies, Moody's and Standard & Poor's. A below-investment-grade rating is below Baa3 for Moody's and BBB– for Standard & Poor's. The vast majority of these securities, if they maintain a rating, will be well below the investment-grade breakpoint and are more likely to be rated C or D or be unrated due to default. Some of the securities may have been investment-grade rated when they were first issued, but experienced financial difficulties and a significant downgrade after issuance to result in a below-investment-grade rating. Others may have been issued as "junk" bonds or below-investment-grade rated and experienced further financial difficulties to become distressed securities. They can be publicly traded securities that are held by all types of investors or privately issued securities that were issued under the private placement exemptions of the Securities Act of 1933 and are held by institutional investors. Bank loans, while not securities, can also constitute a portion of the distressed debt market.[3]

WHAT CONSTITUTES "DISTRESS"

For the vast majority of below-investment-grade companies, access to capital is a critical, everyday function. Once a company is classified as distressed, the willingness of investors or banks to either invest or lend is greatly diminished. While it is somewhat subjective as to whether a company is a distressed security while it is still paying its debt

---

[3]Daniel McNulty, "Why Hedge Funds Love Distressed Debt," Investopedia.

obligations, once a company misses an interest payment, principal payment, or declares a debt moratorium (i.e., a delay in the payment of its debt obligations), the debt clearly enters the realm of distressed debt.[4,5,6] For example, consider Company A with poor financial ratios (e.g., poor interest coverage, which is a ratio used to determine how easily a company's earnings can sustain its debt, and weak EBITDA—earnings before interest, taxes, depreciation, and amortization) results. Company A is a diversified chemical manufacturer with several noncore assets up for sale. The chemical industry is very cyclical and the company is at a downturn in the business cycle. Company A has enough free cash flow to remain current on interest payments but it is unlikely it will be able to make the principal payments it has coming due in six months. The company has several options:

1. Miss the principal payment and be in default.
2. Initiate an exchange offer to existing debt securities holders to extend the maturity (while presumably increasing the coupon) of the bond offering coming due in six months.
3. Sell noncore assets and use the money generated to remain current on the company's debt obligations.

Obtaining a bank or syndicated bank loan is not a viable option because the company's ability to pay its obligations will be severely discounted, resulting in either no banks being willing to provide loans or, in the unique case where a bank or bank syndicate (or hedge fund) will loan funds to this company, the interest rate and terms of loan being so egregious as to prevent the company from accepting such terms. In options 1 and 2, Company A would no doubt be considered a distressed issuer. In option 3, though, the sale of assets may help the company raise cash and the amount of such funds may enable the company to make such a principal payment. If it makes such a principal payment, Company A's prospects will look better to investors, presumably justifying a tighter trading spread compared to U.S. Treasuries or an equivalent benchmark.

TRADING MARKET FOR DISTRESSED DEBT

The distressed debt investor is willing to assume a greater amount of risk than most traditional investors. They are looking for a much greater yield that a traditional investment-grade investor and in some cases a "homerun" investment, so they are willing to assume greater risk in search of the greater reward with large upside on their investment.

Distressed debt securities have very poor market liquidity. The financial problems of the issuer have scared away traditional investors. In addition, most mutual funds, pension

[4]Whitman and Diz, *Distress Investing*.
[5]Goldschneider, "Distressed Debt Securities."
[6]McNulty, "Why Hedge Funds Love Distressed Debt."

funds, and retirement plans cannot own distressed debt securities. Hence, the illiquidity leads to the main investor base being hedge funds and "vulture investors"—those looking to capitalize on another's problems. The bid–offer spread on distressed securities—which is indicative of the liquidity and risk involved in investing in such securities—can be very wide and range anywhere from 2 to 5 points for the more liquid names up to a 10-point bid–offer spread for the extremely distressed or illiquid. In addition, these securities generally trade on a dollar price rather than a yield to maturity. This is reflective of the intrinsic value that the investor sees in the securities and/or assets of the company in a recovery scenario and the fact that the investor does not believe that the securities will continue to pay interest and/or principal until maturity. Distressed securities trade at a significant discount to par and may trade as low as cents on the dollar (e.g., $5, $10, $30, $40 to a $100 par price depending upon the specific credit, liquidity, and risk involved), although exceptions may exist. These securities generally trade on a spread over Treasuries, or their equivalent benchmark, of more than 1,000 basis points.

The distressed debt investor is looking for a high return scenario and sees opportunity where others view dire straits. While these scenarios are highly speculative and differ from situation to situation, generally, the distressed investor has the necessary resources to do the research and investigative work needed to arrive at a potential value of the issuer's securities and/or its assets. The investor can then calculate a probability analysis of each scenario occurring and the likely value within each scenario. Again, this is highly speculative investment and the investor base needs the "stomach" to withstand the rollercoaster ride that can occur with investments in distressed debt securities.

If the distressed debt investor believes that the distressed issuer may be able to withstand the current financial stress and become profitable, then purchasing equity securities may be the better investment. However, if the investor believes that there is a likelihood that an issuer may have to restructure and/or file bankruptcy, then debt securities are the preferred investment exposure to the issuer as debt securities will have priority of payment over equity securities when an issuer files bankruptcy. The equity securities holders will be wiped out in a Chapter 7 or 11 bankruptcy filing. This does not guarantee that the distressed debt investor will receive full payment under the debt instrument or even return of their original investment. It is possible that the issuer may have claims (such as tax liability) that have a priority over the debt securities in the payment of claims under the U.S. Bankruptcy Code and could use up all of the cash that is generated from a liquidation of assets. It is up to the distressed debt securities investor to understand the company's financial situation, total assets and liabilities, amount of claims and tax liability, the amount of debt outstanding, the priority of the debt securities over other claims and tax liability, and the estimated value of the assets and liabilities after payment of prioritized claims in determining what value would remain to pay the debt securities.[7,8,9]

---

[7]Whitman and Diz, *Distress Investing*.
[8]Goldschneider. "Distressed Debt Securities."
[9]McNulty, "Why Hedge Funds Love Distressed Debt."

TRADING STRATEGY ON THE DISTRESSED DEBT

The distressed debt investor may be seeking different objectives depending upon the issuer's scenario. For example, Issuer A may be a company that the distressed debt investor believes to be able to withstand short-term financial difficulties and the investor believes has securities that are undervalued. In this case, the investor may be waiting for the company to have a few quarters of positive results under the belief that the market will digest this news and the securities will rise in value and the investor can then sell the securities at a profit. In another scenario, the distressed debt investor may see a company that is highly leveraged. The company may have a good, viable business with growth and valuable assets and growing revenue, but it is saddled with high interest debt. The distressed debt investor may look to buy all of the outstanding debt and control the company's debt securities. In this case, the investor may believe it could negotiate with the company to exchange its debt for equity—and now you have a company with revenue and growth that is no longer saddled with payment obligations on high-interest debt securities. In the alternative, maybe the investor believes they can negotiate with the issuer to reduce the interest rate or swap a certain amount of outstanding principal on the debt securities for equity whereby the company now has reduced debt and the investor now still controls the debt but also owns equity in the issuer. It's also possible the distressed debt securities investor has in mind to change management or gain some control on the board of directors to influence company management and will use their control of the debt securities to pressure the company to implement corporate change. These are simplistic scenarios as outlined, and in most real-life scenarios the issues are much more complicated, but the scenarios outline what an investor may be seeking under various distressed debt situations.[10,11,12]

PUERTO RICO: A DISTRESSED SITUATION

Puerto Rico is a commonwealth territory of the United States and its debt securities trade in the municipal securities market. Puerto Rico debt securities were attractive investments due to their triple-tax-exempt status—they are exempt from federal, state, and local income taxes—in all 50 states. Puerto Rico General Obligation bonds were investment-grade rated by both Moody's and Standard & Poor's as recently as early February 2014. Since then, both rating agencies have downgraded Puerto Rico's debt multiple times to Caa3 by Moody's and CC by Standard & Poor's. Puerto Rico has defaulted on certain debt securities and has indicated that it will not be able to make the interest or principal payments required under its bond issuances and will default on

---

[10]Whitman and Diz, *Distress Investing*.
[11]Goldschneider, "Distressed Debt Securities."
[12]McNulty, "Why Hedge Funds Love Distressed Debt."

more issuances in the future (with July 1, 2016, looming as another possible default date as of the time of this writing). Currently, Puerto Rico securities trade as low as the price of 50 (with a par of 100). Investors who purchased their bonds at par are left with the prospect of having the value of their investment portfolio reduced to a fraction of their original investment. In addition, with Puerto Rico now in default, they are left with the possibly of having to accept reduced interest payments over a longer period of time or possibly a reduced principal amount under a plan of debt restructure. However, distressed debt investors view Puerto Rico as an opportunity and the vast majority of bonds trading today are between hedge funds and large, institutional customers.

How did Puerto Rico get in a situation where its debt securities trade as distressed? It began when tax breaks to U.S. companies with operations in Puerto Rico ended and these companies began to move back to the United States or other tax-beneficial locations, resulting in a loss of tax revenue and jobs. Unemployment in Puerto Rico has reached approximately 12% as compared to the overall U.S. unemployment rate at just under 5%. High unemployment and a stagnant economy has forced many of its citizens to take advantage of their U.S. citizenship and move to the mainland United States for employment. With declining corporate and personal income tax revenue, Puerto Rico resorted to issuing debt to balance its budget. The addition of this method of deficit financing to Puerto Rico's already heavy debt burden has pushed the total amount of the debt outstanding to over $70 billion. Given the dwindling tax base, declining per-capita income, and the continuing population exodus, it is clear that Puerto Rico will be unable to meet its obligations to its bondholders as well as its pension liabilities and other creditors. The only possible resolution is for a massive restructuring of all of Puerto Rico's debt and the imposition of austerity measures in the budgeting process.[13],[14]

THE SOVEREIGN DEBT CRISIS

Another well publicized distressed debt scenario that made headlines over the past few years has been the Greek debt crisis. During the global financial crisis in 2008 and 2009, certain European countries experienced a sovereign debt crisis. The most widely known countries were Portugal, Italy, Ireland, Greece, and Spain—also referred to as the PIGS. These euro member states were unable to repay or refinance their debt. In addition, they were unable to bail out the troubled banks within their home country. They required the assistance of the European Central Bank (ECB), The International Monetary Fund (IMF), and other European countries. Each country had its own problems that led to its sovereign debt crisis. Whether it was a real estate bubble that left banks with huge

---

[13]Nathan Bomey, "Puerto Rico Crisis Serves as Warning to Investors," *USA Today*, July 6, 2015.
[14]Alvin Baez, "Everything You Need to Know about the Puerto Rico Debt Crisis," *The Fiscal Times*, March 29, 2016.

amounts of defaulted loans, ballooning government debt and deficits, poor management of fiscal policy and economic growth programs, the financial crisis and recession of
2007–2012, failure of the Eurozone countries to react and implement stimulus packages,
or a combination of these factors, these countries faced significant financial difficulties and fear spread that a contagion of defaults in sovereign debt could occur without
bailouts of these countries' debt and the debt securities of the PIGS began trading as
distressed debt.[15]

GREECE

In this section, we will focus on the issues surrounding Greece's sovereign debt crisis,
the bailouts, and the fears of default on its sovereign debt, all of which causes Greece's
sovereign debt to trade as distressed debt. Greece is part of the European Union (EU)
and has implemented the euro as its currency. This means that the EU—via the European Central Bank (ECB)—sets monetary policy (i.e., interest rates), but each member
country sets fiscal policy (i.e., amount of debt outstanding). The issue this created is that
the smaller European member countries that may have previously issued debt at higher
interest rates now effectively had the ability to issue debt at lower rates. Whether it was
the perception that Greek credit was stronger as part of EU or the market simply chas-
ing higher yields in sovereign debt, Greece was issuing debt at lower interest rates than
it could when it was not an EU member. Greece—which has high pension liabilities, a
stagnant economy, and low tax receipts—ran up deficits year after year. These factors,
along with the effects of the financial crisis of 2007–2008, the severe recession, and low
foreign investment and wages, all lead to a lack of economic growth, large deficits, and a
huge amount of debt. As interest rates made it cheap to borrow money, Greece continued
to borrow money by issuing debt via the sovereign debt market to finance these budget
deficits. The combination of these factors along with a crisis of confidence in the Greek
government, both with their inability to reverse the trends of a failing economy as well
as the lack of accuracy of Greek economic statistics being released by the government,
led to downgrades in Greek debt to "junk" status in 2010. The capital markets began
to digest all this news and the market for Greek debt froze under fears of a sovereign
default of Greece under the mountain of Greek debt. Subsequently, multiple bailouts
have been necessary by the ECB, the IMF, and certain European countries. The terms
of these bailouts required strict austerity measures that required the Greek government
to implement cutbacks in spending. All of this has led to worsened economic conditions and the need for further bailouts. At this time, it appears that the distressed debt
investors will eventually have to deal with restructured terms that will include reduced

[15]*New York Times,* "Greece's Debt Crisis Explained," May 25, 2016. Reporting contributed by Liz
Alderman, James Kanter, Jim Yardley, Jack Ewing, Niki Kitsantonis, Suzanne Daley, Karl Russell,
Andrew Higgins, and Peter Eavis.

interest, extended maturities, lower principal amount returned, and/or a combination of all of these.[16,17,18,19]

FINAL THOUGHTS ON DISTRESSED DEBT SECURITIES

As we have seen throughout this chapter, distressed debt investors have a number of issues to consider when deciding to invest in a certain security. They must understand the credit, be able to value the security and the underlying assets, have the ability to understand the implications of the U.S. Bankruptcy Code, and have the ability to compute a value that the debt securities have, both from the market that the securities trade in and in a restructuring or liquidation scenario, and have an exit strategy for any such investment. They must also be able to withstand the lack of liquidity such securities may have in the market as well as the great deal of uncertainty that comes with trafficking in distressed debt securities. Even with the great research and valuation tools that an investor may have with respect to a specific issuer, its assets, and the market for the issuer's securities, there can be a tremendous amount of risk and uncertainty transacting in the distressed debt market and there are plenty of highly sophisticated investors in the distressed market who have been wrong on a distressed credit and wish they had the opportunity to reverse the decision to invest or the price at which they invested.

---

[16]Ibid.

[17]Kerin Hope, "Greece to Miss Deadline For Reporting Historic Deficit Stats," *Financial Times*, September 29, 2014.

[18]Louis Story, Landon Thomas Jr., and Nelson D. Schwartz. "Wall St. Helped to Mask Debt Fueling Europe's Crisis," *New York Times*, February 14, 2010.

[19]Sudhanva Shetty, "The Greece Debt Crisis Explained," TheLogicalIndian.com, July 5, 2015.

CHAPTER 17

Securitization

Daniel I. Castro, Jr.

SECURITIZATIONS IN GENERAL

The term *securitization* generally refers to two separate, though related, activities. First, a financial institution is said to have securitized a pool of financial assets when it creates securities backed by the cash flows from those assets and sells some or all of these securities to investors. The financial institution may or may not retain responsibility for *servicing*—providing on an ongoing basis some or all of the services necessary to collect payments from borrowers, monitor performance of the loans, and distribute the cash flows generated to investors. Second, securitization may also refer, more narrowly, to the process of creating multiple securities with different payment priorities from a pool of underlying loans. For example, a pool of loans may be transformed into a senior tranche that is first in line to receive cash flows and a junior tranche that is last in line to receive cash flows.

Securitization provides economic benefits that may lower the cost of credit to households and businesses. Financial assets are securitized for a number of reasons: Assets can be removed from the originator's balance sheet; issuers can obtain a lower cost of funds, which can be passed on to consumers and businesses; originators can get regulatory capital relief; issuers can enlarge and diversify their investor base; and sometimes securitization is the only viable financing option available. One of the key characteristics of securitization is that the investor is not investing in the company originating the assets, but rather, they are investing in a pool of financial assets that when properly structured can achieve higher ratings than the company originating those assets. A higher rating can be achieved because the assets are removed from the bankruptcy estate of the seller, a "true sale" of the assets has occurred, and a first priority security interest in the assets has been perfected.

One reason that securitizations can achieve high ratings is through the use of credit enhancement. Credit enhancement can take many forms: overcollateralization, subordination, reserve funds, corporate guarantees, bond insurance, and so on. The amount of credit enhancement required by the rating agencies will depend on the credit quality of the underlying asset pool, its historical credit performance, and volatility. In addition to credit enhancement, there is typically additional support called *excess spread* embedded in the deals: the difference between the weighted average interest rate on the assets and the weighted average coupon on the bonds, that difference less servicing fees. The combination of legal structure and credit enhancement allows the securities to be tailored to investors' risk and maturity appetites, and allows rating agencies to rate the securities as high as AAA/Aaa.

SECURITIZATION BASICS: STRUCTURES, COLLATERAL TYPES, AND RISKS

The securitization process starts when a financial institution, such as a bank or finance company (commonly referred to as a sponsor or seller/servicer), sells or transfers a pool of assets (collateral) such as auto loans, credit card receivables, or mortgage loans to a bankruptcy-remote, special-purpose vehicle (SPV). It is critical that the SPV cannot be drawn into any bankruptcy proceedings, and it is designed to insulate the assets from the bankruptcy or insolvency of the sponsor. The most effective way to insulate the assets is to sell the assets to an issuing trust.[1] Law firms are asked to opine on whether a true sale of assets has occurred—"true sale opinion"—and whether the SPV could be consolidated with the sponsor—"non-consolidation opinion"—in the event the sponsor becomes insolvent or bankrupt. Investors in the securitization are now insulated from the credit risk of the sponsor. At this point the trust sells the asset-backed security (ABS), via an underwriter, to investors.

The securitization process is also a method for improving liquidity by raising cash through the sale or pledge of assets. The SPV or trust is created with the sole purpose of purchasing assets and paying for them by issuing securities, ABSs, and selling them to investors. The assets in the issuing trust generate enough cash flow to pay principal and interest to bondholders and to pay a servicing fee to the seller/servicer, which is usually the sponsoring company. The payment stream to the bondholder is funded by the payment of principal and interest on an underlying pool of consumer loans. ABSs backed by mortgage loans (one type of consumer loan) are generally referred to as residential-mortgage-backed securities (RMBSs). ABSs generally fall into two categories: mortgage-related ABS (i.e., RMBS) and non-mortgage-related ABS (i.e., consumer ABS or just ABS).

To create an ABS, consumer loans of varying dollar amounts, loan types, and geographic locations are pooled together and sold to a bankruptcy-remote SPV, typically a trust. The trust pays for the loans by issuing certificates backed by the assets held in the trust. These certificates are issued in different *tranches* or classes, with each tranche

---

[1]In this chapter when I use the term *ABS*, I mean asset-backed securities issued by a trust, unless I indicate otherwise. ABSs issued by a trust may have different features than ABSs issued by other types of entities.

TABLE 17.1 Representative Auto ABS Structure

Note Class	Rating (M/S/F)	Principal	% of Deal	Enhancement[a]
A-1	Aaa/AAA	$200,000,000	20.0%	5.0%
A-2a	Aaa/AAA	275,000,000	27.5%	5.0%
A-2b[b]	Aaa/AAA	125,000,000	12.5%	5.0%
A-3	Aaa/AAA	250,000,000	25.0%	5.0%
A-4	Aaa/AAA	100,000,000	10.0%	5.0%
B	Aa1/AA+	30,000,000	3.0%	2.0%
C	Aa/AA	20,000,000	2.0%	0.0%
Total		$1,000,000,000	100.0%	

[a]Credit enhancement also provided by 0.50% Reserve Fund and excess spread.
[b]Floating-rate class.

differing in yield (the amount of return on the certificates), maturity (the length of time before the certificate is expected to pay off), and payment priority (the order in which investors are paid principal and interest). Generally, principal will be paid from the top tranche down in sequential order, and any losses will be allocated to the securities at the bottom of the capital structure and working up the structure. Table 17.1 is illustrative of a typical Auto ABS deal structure.

As explained earlier, issuing ABS with a higher credit rating than the company that originated the collateral requires the legal separation of the assets from the company that originally owned them. In order to achieve a high credit rating, credit enhancements and liquidity are provided through either internal or external sources. Credit enhancements and structural protection are the foundations for protecting investors from credit risk, legal risks, market and interest rate risks, currency risks, and anything else that may be a threat to investors receiving timely payments of interest and return of principal as promised.

ABSs/RMBSs typically have multiple sources of credit enhancement. Subordination of tranche cash flows, to protect more senior classes in a structure, as in Figure 17.1, is the most used form of credit enhancement. ABS securitizations also build credit enhancement through an *overcollateralization* structure. When the face value of the deal's assets (underlying consumer loans) is greater than the deal's liabilities (bonds issued by the deal), then the deal is overcollateralized. At a deal's inception, if the total bonds issued are less than the initial collateral asset balance, initial overcollateralization has been created. For example, a securitization with $500 million of issued securities could be backed by loans with an outstanding principal balance of $525 million (Figure 17.1).

Overcollateralization also can be built by using excess interest to pay down the bonds faster than the collateral. Most ABS trusts are backed by loans with coupons greater than the coupons of the securities issued by the ABS trust. The difference between the interest income the deal's collateral generates (after paying any monthly expenses and fees to parties administering the trust) and the interest expense the deal pays to bondholders is the deal's excess spread. When the excess spread is diverted to accelerate

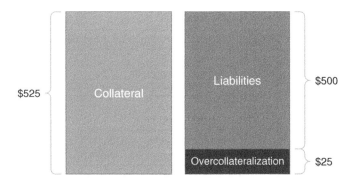

FIGURE 17.1 Securitization with $500 million of issued securities

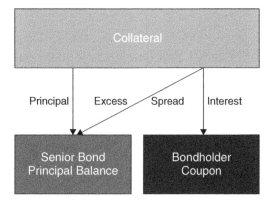

FIGURE 17.2 Overcollateralization

pay-down of senior bond principal, the deal is "turboing" to build overcollateralization (Figure 17.2).

Table 17.2 lists some of the basic characteristics shared by most ABSs. The borrowers, known as *obligors*, usually are either consumers who have taken out loans (autos, credit cards, home equity loans, student loans, etc.) or businesses (auto dealers, farmers, doctors, etc.) who have taken out commercial loans. The primary collateral used in ABS are loans and leases, which may be secured or unsecured and may already be existing or may be originated in the future. The preferred method of transferring collateral to the issuing entity is a *true sale* of the assets, but sometimes the collateral is pledged to the trust and the trust has what is called a *first perfected security interest* in the collateral. Simply put, a first perfected security interest means that the trust has the legal right to the proceeds of the assets and is first in line to receive them. Collateral pools may be closed, meaning that they are fixed as to their composition on the day the ABS is issued (e.g., auto loan ABS), or they may be revolving (e.g., credit card ABS), meaning that as the

TABLE 17.2   Basic Characteristics of ABS

Obligors	▪ Consumers and/or commercial borrowers
Collateral	▪ Loans or leases ▪ Existing or to be created ▪ Secured or unsecured
Transfer of Collateral	▪ Sale or pledge ▪ Closed or revolving pool
Issuing Entity	▪ Trust—grantor, owner, master, business, REMIC ▪ Other special-purpose vehicle or special-purpose entity
Security Issued	▪ Notes ▪ Certificates ▪ Un-certificated interests ▪ Residual interests ▪ Equity

assets pay down, the cash received is used to purchase additional assets for a specified period of time, rather than pay down ABS investors' principal balance.

The issuing entity for most ABSs is a trust, which comes in many forms: grantor trust, owner trust, master trust, business trust, and REMIC to name a few. If the issuing entity is not a trust, then it is usually an SPV or SPE (special-purpose entity), whose sole purpose is to buy collateral and issue ABSs. ABSs may be issued in many formats, including certificates, notes, un-certificated interests, residual interests, and equity.

ABS investors pay to buy a structured security with a specific cash flow structure. ABS cash flows can be tailored to meet almost any variety of investor demand. Principal repayment may take on the classic bullet payment structure used by most corporate bonds, where all the principal is paid back on a single payment date at maturity, or it may pay back principal in amortizing fashion, based on the cash flows of the underlying collateral pool. Furthermore, ABS cash flows may be paid back on a sequential basis, from most senior to most junior tranches, or on a pro-rata basis, where each tranche receives its pro-rata (proportional) share of principal at each principal payment date. In addition, ABSs are subject to both voluntary prepayments and defaults (involuntary prepayments), which have the effect of accelerating principal payments and shortening the weighted average life (WAL) of the security.

Interest payments for ABS are either fixed-rate or floating-rate. In the early days of the ABS market, almost all ABSs were issued with fixed-rate coupons. Floating-rate ABSs were introduced later, and over the past dozen years or so, most ABSs have been issued in floating-rate format. Most floating-rate ABSs are indexed to 1-month, 3-month, and 6-month LIBOR, but other floating-rate indexes also occasionally are used, such as T-bills, the prime rate, the Cost of Funds Index (COFI), and commercial paper indexes. On occasion, ABSs have been issued in a zero-coupon format.

ABS payment frequency is usually monthly or quarterly, but semiannual and annual payments are also used.

TABLE 17.3 Structural Characteristics of ABS

Cash Flows	■ Principal payment
	  ■ Amortizing or bullets
	  ■ Sequential or pro-rata
	  ■ Prepayments and defaults
	
	■ Interest payments
	  ■ Fixed-rate, floating-rate, zero coupon
	  ■ Choice of indexes

Credit Enhancement	■ Internally generated—overcollateralization, subordinated classes, excess spread ■ Externally generated—reserve fund, letter of credit, surety bond, corporate guarantee
Other Structural Elements	■ Interest rate swap ■ Currency swap

Table 17.3 summarizes some of the structural characteristics of ABS.

The primary source of cash flow supporting the ABS is the underlying collateral pool. The assets constituting the collateral pool may be loans, receivables, bonds, or other financial assets. If a collateral pool was simply purchased or transferred to a trust in its raw form, it would look like a portfolio of assets on a typical bank or finance company balance sheet. This portfolio would generate principal and interest payments, and suffer delinquencies and defaults. As discussed previously, the first step in creating a security with a higher rating than the company originating the collateral and sponsoring the ABS is to create a bankruptcy-remote entity that insulates investors from the sponsoring company's fortunes. The next step is to run the collateral pool's projected cash flows through the ABS structure and provide credit enhancement to protect investors from potential losses. This is where the credit arbitrage is created. By adding one or more forms of credit enhancement, the ABS credit quality and rating will be higher than the sponsoring company. There are very few AAA-rated companies in the United States, but almost all ABSs have one or more tranches that achieve a AAA rating. As a result, securitization provides sponsoring companies with a lower-cost funding alternative to issuing unsecured corporate bonds, and provides investors with high credit-quality securities.

Publicly issued ABSs generally are rated by one or more of the three major ratings agencies: Standard & Poor's, Moody's Investors Service, and Fitch Ratings. A critical difference between ABS and corporate bonds is the fact that structured finance securities such as ABS are designed to achieve a specific rating from the rating agencies based on its collateral, structure, legal protection, and credit enhancements, among other things. Credit enhancement generated from the asset pool or structure is generally referred to as internal credit enhancement while credit enhancement provided by third parties outside the structure is referred to as external credit enhancement. Finally, structural enhancements also provide investors with additional protection against the risk of loss.

TRACE REPORTING

The Financial Industry Regulatory Authority (FINRA) implemented the Trade Reporting and Compliance Engine (TRACE) for securitized products in May 2011. The Trade Reporting and Compliance Engine is the FINRA-developed vehicle that facilitates the mandatory reporting of over-the-counter secondary market transactions in eligible fixed-income securities. All broker-dealers who are FINRA member firms have an obligation to report transactions in corporate bonds to TRACE under an SEC-approved set of rules.[2] FINRA and Interactive Data Corporation created a suite of aggregated data products for asset- and mortgage-backed securities to benefit investors and other market participants. Investors can now gauge the activity levels in the marketplace as well as price levels by various sub-product types.[3] On November 12, 2012, FINRA began disseminating transaction information for agency pass-through mortgage-backed securities traded *to-be-announced* (TBA). FINRA began disseminating information for so-called specified pool transactions in agency pass-through mortgage-backed securities and SBA-backed securities in July 2013.[4] On June 1, 2015, TRACE began providing investors with post-trade price information for asset-backed securities, including those backed by auto loans, credit card receivables, and student loans.[5]

This new end-of-day service represents the full asset- and mortgage-backed securities markets and is derived using only actual transacted prices from TRACE, the U.S. over-the-counter bond market mandated regulatory reporting and dissemination facility.[6] The Structured Trading Activity Report displays an aggregate summary of market activity in the U.S. structured products markets by product type, including volume traded (as measured by remaining principal balance), number of trades, and number of unique securities traded.[7]

Although the intention of TRACE is to provide greater information on trading activity and greater transparency to the market, the press has reported that the inclusion of ABS beginning in June 2015 has had the effect of hurting liquidity in the ABS market. According to *Asset-Backed Alert*, broker-dealers have reduced inventory levels and pulled back from secondary market trading activity because "it appears the incentive for those institutions to make markets has diminished…"[8] According to the article, one researcher estimated that banks reduced their overall presence by about 10% in 4Q 2015 and structured product trading revenues fell by 5–10%. One trader was quoted as saying, "TRACE

---

[2]See more at: http://www.finra.org/industry/trace#sthash.dIhYLIDj.dpuf.
[3]FINRA website: http://www.finra.org/industry/trace/structured-product-activity-reports-and-tables.
[4]FINRA News Release, June 1, 2015.
[5]Ibid.
[6]FINRA website: http://www.finra.org/industry/trace/structured-product-activity-reports-and-tables.
[7]See more at: http://www.finra.org/industry/trace/structured-product-activity-reports-and-tables#sthash.Q7hKCjwv.dpuf.
[8]"TRACE Reporting Sends Dealers to Sidelines," *Asset-Backed Alert*, December 18, 2015 p. 1.

has drastically cut our desire and ability to make markets in asset-backed bonds. The couple of ticks of profit we're getting many times isn't worth the effort."[9]

At the margin, there may be some truth to the notion that TRACE has further eroded liquidity in the structured finance markets, but the larger issue of liquidity in the fixed-income markets began in 2007. The liquidity crisis that started in the summer of 2007 and led to the larger Financial Crisis in 2008–2009 resulted in intermediaries (banks and broker-dealers) having significantly less appetite for risk assets on their balance sheets. The lower appetite for risk assets led directly to reduced inventories of not just structured finance securities (ABSs, RMBSs, CMBSs, and CDOs), but also corporate bonds and other fixed-income securities. Reduced inventory levels across the board starting in 2007 has had the effect of weakening liquidity across fixed-income markets since the financial crisis. TRACE may have further exacerbated the weak liquidity, but the lion's share of inventory reductions that lead to reduced liquidity is a function of lower risk appetite combined with higher (some would say punitive) capital-reserve requirements imposed by regulators following the financial crisis.[10]

FINRA is currently considering expanding TRACE to include additional securitized products, including collateralized mortgage obligations (CMOs), non-Agency MBSs, commercial mortgage–backed securities (CMBSs), and collateralized debt obligations (CDOs).

---

[9]"TRACE Reporting Sends Dealers to Sidelines," *Asset-Backed Alert*, December 18, 2015 p. 14.
[10]On April 8, 2014, the FDIC board of directors approved a Final Rule on the Basel III capital standards. This rule is substantially the same as the Interim Final Rule approved by the FDIC on July 9, 2013. The FDIC Board wanted to consider the Basel III rule in relation to the strengthening of the supplementary leverage ratio standards (for the largest, most interconnected banking organizations). See more at: https://www.fdic.gov/regulations/capital/capital/index.html.

CHAPTER 18

Asset-Backed Securities

Daniel I. Castro, Jr.

Starting in about 1985, non-mortgage asset-backed securities (ABSs) were created and offered to the public. One of the very first deals was a securitization that was backed by auto loans and equipment leases. Since that time, we have seen ABS collateralized by myriad financial assets, including auto loans, credit card receivables, home equity loans, and student loans. We have also seen the creation of ABS backed by off-the-run assets such as burglar alarm and cell tower receivables, mutual fund fees, tax liens, property and casualty insurance policies (catastrophe bonds), and loans for timeshare condos. The famed Bowie Bonds, collateralized by David Bowie's music royalties, received much outsized attention from the press. While the issuance of ABS collateralized by intellectual property (i.e., music and film royalties) comprises an insignificant part of the ABS market, it is worth mentioning as it hammers home the point that all sorts of financial assets can be securitized.[1]

Since 1985, the ABS market showed consistent growth during its first decade, followed by explosive growth in the mid-1990s through the mid-2000s. Issuance peaked from 2005 through 2008 and then dropped dramatically following the financial crisis. ABS issuance first topped $100 billion in 1996, $200 billion in 2001, and topped out at almost $300 billion in 2007. The Fed's **Term Asset-Backed Securities Loan Facility** (TALF) program helped restart the market in 2009, but still bottomed in 2010 before rebounding in 2012.[2] (See Figure 18.1.)

According to SIFMA, as of December 31, 2015, $4.3 trillion of non-mortgage ABS has been issued. SIFMA data also shows that ABS bonds outstanding peaked at almost $2 trillion in 2007 and have fallen to just under $1.4 trillion ABS outstanding at year-end 2014. Clearly ABS is a major source of funding for issuers, a significant part of the fixed-income market, and a major holding for many institutional investors. (See Figure 18.2.)

---

[1]Chapter on asset-backed securities, by Daniel Castro, in Gary Strumeyer's *Investing in Fixed Income Securities: Understanding the Bond Market* (Hoboken, NJ: John Wiley & Sons, 2005), 406.

[2]Securities Industry and Financial Markets Association website: https://www.sifma.org/uploadedfiles/research/statistics/statisticsfiles/sf-us-abs-sifma.xls.

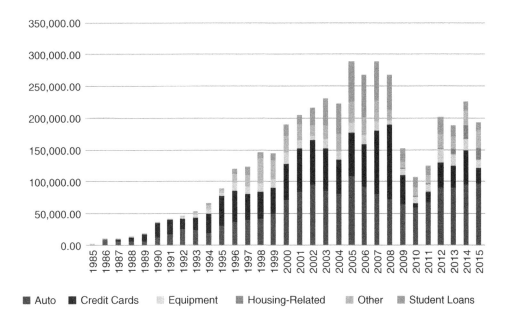

FIGURE 18.1 U.S. ABS issuance

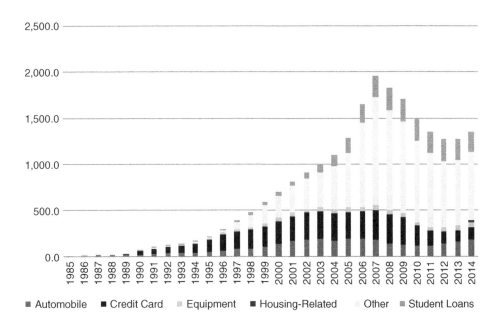

FIGURE 18.2 U.S. ABS outstanding

What follows is a description of how the two largest ABS sectors, Auto ABS and Credit Card ABS, originate, structure, and issue their securitizations.

AUTOMOBILE SECURITIZATION

ABSs backed by automobile loans were the first major sector of the non-mortgage ABS market, beginning in 1985. Today, auto ABS is the largest new-issue market among non-mortgage ABSs. Figure 18.3 shows issuance from 1985 through 2015.[3]

Auto ABS issuance peaked at over $108 billion in 2005 and dropped to $59 billion in 2010 after the financial crisis. Figure 18.4 shows auto ABS outstanding at year-end from 1985 to 2014.[4] Auto ABS outstanding peaked at over $195 billion in 2005–2006 and bottomed out at roughly $116 in 2010–2011 and has been rising since 2012.

Collateral

Automobile ownership is a hallmark of American society. Census estimates suggest that there were about 1.8 vehicles per household in the United States in 2013.[5] Outside of a few large urban areas, autos are necessary for transportation throughout the United

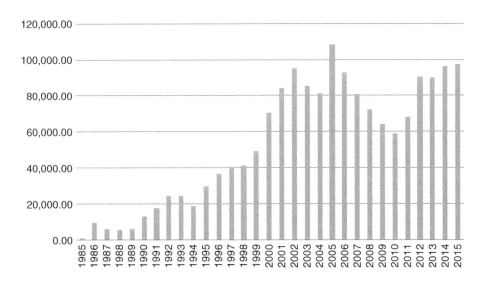

FIGURE 18.3 Auto ABS issuance (in millions)

---

[3]SIFMA.
[4]Ibid.
[5]Governing.com.

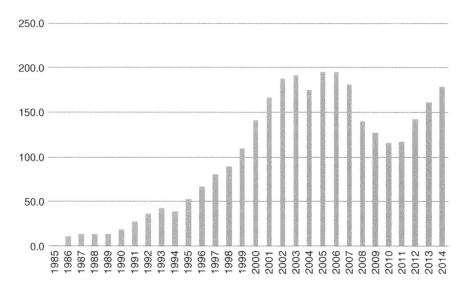

FIGURE 18.4 Automobile ABS outstanding (in $ billions)

States. Autos are often associated with particular lifestyles and sometimes social status. Defaults on auto loans are substantially lower than on unsecured loans, such as credit cards, and default and repossession of a vehicle is a hardship for almost anyone.

Auto loans are originated by banks, credit unions, and finance companies, including captive financing subsidiaries of all of the major automobile manufacturers and specialty finance companies focusing on retail auto loans. Auto loans are one of the most basic of consumer loans. Auto loans typically have 2- to 7-year (24- to 84-month) terms, are fully amortizing, are fixed-rate, and are collateralized by the physical vehicles being purchased. Auto loans provide financing for both new and used vehicles. Down payments for new vehicles come from both cash and trade-ins and typically represent anywhere from 10% to 20% of the auto's value. Stronger quality buyers sometimes put down 5% or less, and some borrowers may choose to put down 30% to 40% or more. Voluntary prepayments typically are the result of a trade-in or outright sale of the vehicle; involuntary prepayments are the result of defaults.

Collateral Credit Quality Segments Auto ABS market participants break the auto loan market down into three credit quality segments:

1. *Prime:* Expected cumulative losses of 3% or below. Primary lenders are banks and captive finance companies financing mostly new cars. FICO scores are typically above 680.
2. *Mid-prime:* Expected cumulative losses between 3% and 7%. Main lenders are banks and captive and specialty finance companies financing more new than used cars. FICO scores typically range from 640 to 680.

3. *Subprime:* Expected cumulative losses over 7% (and typically up to 15%). Lenders are primarily specialty finance companies (and some banks) financing mostly used cars. FICO scores are generally below 640.

Prepayments The market standard for auto loan prepayments is "ABS," which, depending on whom you are talking to, stands for either *absolute prepayment speed* or *asset-backed speed*. If an auto securitization had an ABS of 1.3, it would mean that 1.3% of the securitization's loans were prepaying monthly. This prepayment metric is unique to auto loans and distinctively different from the conditional prepayment rate (CPR) metric used in the MBS market—CPR measures prepayments on an annualized basis as a percentage of the security's pool balance.

Historically, auto loan prepayment speeds are relatively stable and generally insensitive to interest rate changes. In contrast to mortgages, auto loans have short terms and small balances, so a reduction of interest rates would have a small impact on the payment size. Besides, auto loans are not generally refinanced anyway because used car loan rates are higher than new car rates primarily due to the rapid depreciation of automobile values. An additional factor keeping prepayment speeds down is the proliferation of below-market interest rate incentive financing programs over the past dozen years or so, which has reduced consumers' incentive to prepay their loans.

Prime auto loans historically have prepaid between 1% and 1.5% ABS; mid-prime auto loans prepay slightly faster, up to 1.8% ABS; and subprime auto loans prepay the fastest, up to 2% ABS. FitchRatings says their historical experience for subvented, below-market-rate auto loans is 0.50% ABS, 1.80% for market rate collateral, compared with an overall prepayment speed of 1.20% ABS.[6]

Structures

Auto ABS securitizations are structured similarly to other ABS transactions: The sponsor creates a *special-purpose vehicle* (SPV) to isolate the auto loans from its bankruptcy or insolvency. Auto loans earmarked for securitization typically have a first-perfected security interest in the loan receivables as well as the underlying vehicles. The assets also are isolated from the seller-servicer to achieve bankruptcy-remote status. Several legal opinions are provided addressing bankruptcy and insolvency, that cash flow from the loans will not be impaired or diminished, the tax status of the SPV, and that a first-perfected security interest in the underlying assets has been established for the benefit of investors.

The two most widely used structures for auto ABS are the *grantor trust* and the *owner trust*. Depending on the trust structure, multiple classes of securities (e.g., Class A, Class B, Class C), fixed- or floating-rate bonds, varying amortization schedules, maturities, and ratings can be tailored to meet investor appetite.

---

[6]FitchRatings, *Rating Criteria for U.S. Auto Loan ABS*, October 15, 2015, p. 16.

Grantor Trusts The original format used in the auto ABS sector was the grantor trust. As the more basic of the two trust formats, a grantor trust only requires one trustee and allows non-bank (i.e., unregulated) issuers the flexibility to retain or sell subordinated classes/tranches of securities. The grantor trust structure only allows pro-rata principal distributions to each investor based on their percentage ownership of the entire transaction. As a result, all classes in the structure, whether senior or subordinate, receive principal payments at the same rate. The pro-rata feature means that each class maintains a constant percentage of subordination unless subordinated classes are partially written down due to high defaults (very rare).

Owner Trusts For more than a dozen years, owner trusts have been the most popular format for auto ABS. Owner trusts are more complex, providing the ability for cash flows to be carved up and be reallocated among senior and subordinated investors. The owner trust structure allows for tranches of varying average lives, credit ratings, and cash flow characteristics that can be tailored to meet investor needs, thereby broadening the investor base. The creation of money market tranches eligible for purchase under Rule 2a7 has been popular with money market investors. Investors prefer tight principal repayment windows and the owner trust structure can accommodate that desire by creating sequential classes where all principal payments are allocated to the most senior class outstanding before allocating principal payments to the next class once the most senior class is paid down. Using a sequential pay structure in an owner trust, classes with one-year, two-year, and three-year average lives follow the money market tranche at the top of the structure.

Closing Date Cash Flows The sponsor sells and assigns the pool of auto loans/contracts to the securitization SPV. Legal opinions supporting a *true sale* of assets and a *non-consolidation opinion* that trust assets will not be consolidated in the event of insolvency are rendered. The Seller (SPV) transfers the auto loans and pledges a security interest to the Issuer (typically an owner trust). The Issuer funds its purchase of the auto loans by issuing *notes*. Most auto ABSs issue Class A, Class B, and Class C notes, which are characterized as senior, mezzanine or subordinate, and subordinate, respectively.

On a monthly basis, the typical cash flow waterfall (priority of payments) for auto ABS looks like this:[7]

1. Return of servicer advances
2. Servicing fee
3. Trustee and other fees
4. Net swap payments (if applicable)
5. Class A, B, and C interest paid sequentially
6. Class A-1, A-2, A-3, etc. paid sequentially

---

[7]The cash flow waterfall shown here is not exhaustive; it is illustrative of the major cash flows.

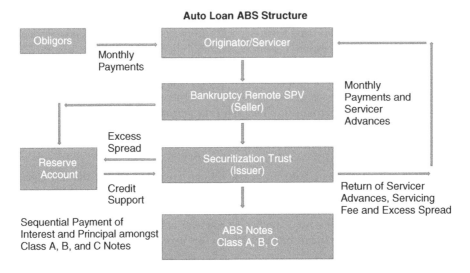

FIGURE 18.5   Auto loan ABS structure

7. After Class A notes paid down to zero, Class B principal
8. After Class B notes paid down to zero, Class C principal
9. Required deposits to reserve account to maintain required amount
10. Remaining funds released to seller

Credit Enhancement

Similar to other securitization markets, investors are primarily protected by internal credit enhancement. The first line of defense, as in other securitization markets, is excess spread. Every month, the excess cash flow after investors and fees are paid is used to cover losses. Credit enhancement is provided by subordination of all tranches below any given tranche as well as a *reserve account* (in most deals), typically established by an *initial deposit* from a portion of the proceeds from the sale of the notes. Occasionally, some trusts do not fund the reserve fund initially or only partially fund them. When that happens, excess spread is used to fund the reserve account, which may take months to be fully funded. Most auto ABSs utilize a reserve account for both credit support and liquidity. Reserve Accounts can be set at a fixed amount or decline with a floor. Minimum cash reserve account balances typically range from 0.25% to 2% of the collateral balance.[8] If a reserve fund is used, it is usually replenished with excess spread. When an auto ABS is backed in part or in whole by subvented loans at below-market rates, auto ABS will include a Yield Supplement

---

[8]For example, Ally Auto Receivables Trust 2015-1 and CarMax Auto Owner Trust 2015-3 have reserve accounts sized at 0.25% while AmeriCredit Automobile Receivables Trust 2015-1 has a reserve account sized at 2.0%.

Account to fund the difference between market interest rates and below-market rates. Yield Supplement Accounts are not credit enhancement, but rather they effectively bring the subvented loans up to market rates.

Mid-prime and subprime deals sometimes incorporate triggers and/or a third-party guarantee or bond insurance—prime collateral generally does not use triggers or bond insurance. Triggers are used to enhance the credit support if the collateral fails to meet specified performance levels. When poor collateral performance hits a trigger level, auto ABS typically requires an increased in reserve fund levels, which are funded by excess spread.

When auto ABSs issue money market tranches, the notes usually pay a floating-rate coupon. Since the underlying auto loans are fixed-rate, an interest rate swap is usually incorporated to mitigate interest rate risk. Securitization documents generally require that if the swap terminates for any reason, the coupon to investors will become a fixed-rate payment payable by the Trust.

Auto ABSs, similar to other ABS securities, have a *cleanup call* provision that provides a call option to the issuer when the collateral balance falls to 10% (typically). Factors such as the higher cost of servicing a small collateral pool and capital tied up in reserve funds make the cleanup call an attractive option for most issuers. Exercising the cleanup call is also attractive because it can free up seasoned loans to be included in a new issue ABS, which can be useful for improving both pricing and credit enhancement levels. Most issuers do exercise the cleanup call, but some don't. Not exercising the cleanup call can potentially extend a transaction by a year or more, depending on the amortization and prepayment speed of the collateral.

Credit Analysis

In order to determine the adequacy of the credit enhancement described earlier, credit analysis is critical. The first step is to assess the legal and structural protections. If the legal structure and opinions are not adequate, nothing else really matters. Next, a thorough understanding of structural enhancements (e.g., triggers) and credit enhancements (excess spread, subordination, overcollateralization, reserve funds, etc.) and fees (servicing, trustee) explained earlier is necessary. Once that is done, an analysis of collateral quality is required. The following characteristics, among others, must be evaluated to determine potential credit losses:

- Pool diversification by geography
- Loan quality
- Loan type
- Loan size
- APR
- Down payment
- Advance on vehicle value (LTV)
- Loan seasoning/original term/remaining term
- Stratification of loan yields

- FICO score distribution
- New vehicle percentage
- Vehicle types
- Prepayment history
- Delinquency history
- Gross loss history
- Recovery history/loss severity
- Servicer financial strength (servicer risk)
- Underwriting standards

CREDIT CARD SECURITIZATION

Credit card ABSs were introduced to the market in 1987. Today, credit card ABS is the second largest sector of the non-mortgage ABS market (after auto ABS) with issuance volume of over $51 billion in 2014.[9] The dollar volume of credit card ABS issued correlates closely to consumer lending and varies considerably over time. According to SIFMA, Table 18.1 shows the issuance of credit card ABS from 2006 to 2014.

Most of the major credit card lenders are the largest credit card ABS sponsors, including JPMorgan Chase, Bank of America, Citigroup, American Express, and Capital One, among others. Since none of these banks have AAA ratings, credit card ABS sponsors generally incur lower funding costs in the ABS market than they would in the unsecured corporate bond market. Additional benefits include diversifying their funding sources and improving liquidity.

Unlike other underlying asset types in the ABS market, credit card loans/receivables do not have a fixed amortization period or payment amount. Auto loans, student loans, mortgages, and other types of consumer or business loans typically have a fixed maturity

TABLE 18.1 Issuance of Credit Card ABS (in $ millions)

Year	Issuance
2006	67,049
2007	99,527
2008	118,119
2009	46,089
2010	7,372
2011	16,152
2012	39,699
2013	34,885
2014	52,911

---

[9]*Securitization Weekly*, Bank of America Merrill Lynch, August 14, 2015, p. 59.

or term (3 years, 5 years, 10 years, 30 years) over which monthly loan payments are spread. Credit card loans, on the other hand, can be added to or paid down subject to certain constraints, such as their credit limit and minimum monthly payments (typically 2% of the outstanding balance).

Most credit card ABSs are supported by either (1) general-purpose credit cards such as VISA and MasterCard, (2) travel and entertainment cards such as American Express, or (3) retail credit cards such as Gap, Dillard's, Nordstrom, or Staples. Although the vast majority of credit cards are unsecured, secured credit cards are offered (with low credit limits and high interest rates) to subprime borrowers with poor or no credit history. According to the Federal Reserve, charge-off rates (annualized percentage of credit card account balances written off as uncollectible) for bank credit cards were over 10% as recently as 2010, and have fallen to roughly 3% in 2015.[10] Thirty-day delinquencies on bank credit cards, according to the Federal Reserve, were over 6% as recently as 2009, and have fallen to roughly 2% in 2015.[11]

In addition to charge-offs and delinquencies, credit card ABS investors should also pay close attention to the portfolio yield, excess servicing spread, and payment rates of credit card portfolios. The portfolio yield is the annualized income generated primarily from finance charges and fees as a percentage of receivables outstanding. *Excess servicing spread* is a strong indicator of credit card portfolio profitability and is measured as the difference between portfolio yield and expenses (coupon to investors, servicing fees, and charge-offs). The payment rate is the percentage of credit card debt paid back each month by cardholders. The payment rate is the best indicator of a credit card portfolio's credit quality. Generally speaking, the higher the payment rate, the higher the credit profile of the portfolio. Stronger borrowers will pay their debt back faster, and weaker borrowers tend to make smaller payments or the minimum payment due each month. Despite that, most credit card issuers prefer customers who carry large balances with lower payment rates because they generate higher income from finance charges.

In order to be earmarked for a securitization, credit card accounts and their related receivables must meet eligibility requirements. Most bank-issued credit card ABSs define *eligible accounts* as having the following characteristics:[12]

- Is in existence and maintained by the bank or an affiliate;
- Is payable in United States dollars;
- Has not identified as an account the credit cards or checks, if any, that have been lost or stolen;
- The accountholder of which has provided, as his or her most recent billing address, an address located in the United States (or its territories or possessions or a military address);

---

[10] "Charge-Off and Delinquency Rates on Loans and Leases at Commercial Banks," http://www .federalreserve.gov/releases/chargeoff/chgallnsa.htm.

[11] Ibid. See http://www.federalreserve.gov/releases/chargeoff/delallnsa.htm.

[12] Eligible account characteristics sourced from *eligible account* definition found in Citibank Credit Card Issuance Trust, Chase Issuance Trust, and Capital One Multi-Asset Execution Trust.

- Has not been, and does not have, any receivables that have been sold, pledged, assigned, or otherwise conveyed to any person (except pursuant to the receivables purchase agreements or the pooling agreement);
- Which is a VISA or MasterCard revolving credit card account;
- Does not have any receivables that have been charged off as uncollectible;
- Does not have any receivables that have been identified as having been incurred as a result of the fraudulent use of any related credit card or check;
- Relates to an accountholder who is not identified by the bank or an affiliate or the transferor in its computer files as being the subject of a voluntary or involuntary bankruptcy proceeding; and
- Is not an account for which the accountholder has requested discontinuance of responsibility.

Most bank-issued credit card ABSs define *eligible receivables* as having the following characteristics:[13]

- Which has arisen in an eligible account;
- Which was created in compliance in all material respects with the bank's or an affiliate's lending guidelines and all applicable requirements of law, the failure to comply with which would have a material adverse effect on investor certificate holders, and pursuant to a lending agreement which complies with all requirements of law applicable to the bank or an affiliate, the failure to comply with which would have a material adverse effect on investor certificate holders;
- With respect to which all material consents, licenses, approvals, or authorizations of, or registrations or declarations with, any governmental authority required to be obtained or given by the bank or an affiliate in connection with the creation of such receivable or the execution, delivery, and performance by the bank or an affiliate of the related lending agreement have been duly obtained or given and are in full force and effect as of the date of the creation of such receivable;
- As to which, at the time of its transfer to the master trust trustee, the transferor or the master trust will have good and marketable title, free and clear of all liens and security interests (including a prior lien or security interest of the bank or an affiliate, but other than any lien for municipal or other local taxes if such taxes are not then due and payable or if the transferor is then contesting the validity thereof in good faith by appropriate proceedings and has set aside on its books adequate reserves with respect thereto);
- Which has been the subject of either:
  - A valid transfer and assignment from the transferor to the master trust trustee of all its right, title, and interest therein (including any proceeds thereof), or
  - The grant of a first priority perfected security interest therein (and in the proceeds thereof), effective until the termination of the master trust;

---

[13]Eligible receivables characteristics sourced from *eligible receivables* definition found in Citibank Credit Card Issuance Trust, Chase Issuance Trust, and Capital One Multi-Asset Execution Trust.

- Which at and after the time of transfer to the master trust trustee is the legal, valid, and binding payment obligation of the accountholder thereof, legally enforceable against such accountholder in accordance with its terms (with certain bankruptcy and equity-related exceptions);
- Which, at the time of its transfer to the master trust trustee, has not been waived or modified;
- Which, at the time of its transfer to the master trust trustee, is not subject to any right of rescission, setoff, counterclaim, or other defense of the accountholder (including the defense of usury), other than certain bankruptcy and equity-related defenses;
- Which constitutes an "account" under and as defined in Article 9 of the UCC;
- As to which, at the time of its transfer to the master trust trustee, the transferor has satisfied all obligations on its part to be fulfilled; and
- As to which, at the time of its transfer to the master trust trustee, the transferor has not taken any action which, or failed to take any action the omission of which, would, at the time of its transfer to the master trust trustee, impair in any material respect the rights of the master trust or investor certificate holders therein.

Credit Card ABS Structures

Credit card securitization requires the transfer of receivables from credit card accounts into a bankruptcy-remote trust, which in turn issues credit card ABSs. The credit card ABS trust funds the purchase of a revolving pool of credit card receivables assigned to the trust. In order to replenish receivables from inactive and closed accounts, the receivables from new accounts are assigned to the trust on an ongoing basis. Every month, the trust receives cardholder payments related to the assigned accounts. After covering interest, principal, servicing fees, and other expenses each month, the trust uses cardholder payments and other proceeds to purchase new receivables arising under assigned accounts and existing receivables assigned to the trust. It is important to note that, although the receivables in the designated credit card accounts are transferred to the credit card ABS trust, the accounts are not, and they continue to be maintained and managed by the originator. As the account owner, the originator continues to maintain its relationship with the cardholders and, because the accounts are revolving accounts, the originator continues to maintain its relationship with the cardholders and continues to make credit granting and underwriting decisions in connection with ongoing extensions of credit in accordance with the credit card account terms.

The trust itself is required to maintain a minimum receivables balance. In credit card ABS, the seller of the receivables must retain an interest in the trust consisting of required receivables and excess receivables. Daily fluctuations in receivables balances are absorbed by the seller's interest in the trust, and it also receives an allocation of cardholders' payments and defaults. Generally, credit card securitizations require a minimum seller's interest of 4% to 7% of the trust note balance.[14] The seller's interest is

---

[14] "DBRS: Methodology—U.S. Credit Card Asset-Backed Securities," February 2014, p. 19.

typically higher for private-label (retail) credit card ABS because merchandise returns are generally higher in retail portfolios. The seller's interest is recorded on the seller's balance sheet.[15] Generally, if the seller's interest falls below the level required to satisfy the minimum seller's interest test, the sponsor must add receivables in an amount that restores the seller's interest to the minimum level. This is one reason why credit card issuers cannot securitize all of their credit card receivables; they must keep a sufficient quantity back to enable them to transfer additional receivables into credit card trusts if necessary. For example, the Capital One Credit Card Portfolio, at year-end, is shown in Table 18.2.[16] Capital One during this period before the financial crisis securitized between roughly 60% and 65% of its credit card portfolio. This was typical of bankcard issuers at the time—it was rare to see more than 70% of a credit card portfolio securitized. After the financial crisis, they only securitized between 30% and 50% of their portfolio, far more conservative than before the financial crisis.

Given the revolving nature of credit cards, credit card ABSs typically have a revolving period followed by an amortization period. During the revolving period, principal collections are used to buy additional receivables or add to the seller's interest—investors only receive interest payments during the revolving period. Because principal and interest payments vary considerably from month to month on credit card portfolios, the seller's

TABLE 18.2 Capital One Credit Card Portfolio

Year	Total Credit Card Portfolio	Securitized Credit Card Portfolio	Percent Securitized
2014	$28.8 billion	$14.1 billion	49.0%
2013	$30.8 billion	$9.8 billion	31.8%
2012	$34.2 billion	$10.3 billion	30.1%
2005	$49.5 billion	$32.3 billion	65.3%
2004	$48.6 billion	$31.0 billion	63.8%
2003	$46.3 billion	$27.8 billion	60.0%

Source: Capital One Multi-Asset Execution Trust Prospectus Supplement, October 16, 2006, Annex I, page A-I-1, and Capital One Multi-Asset Execution Trust Prospectus Supplement, August 19, 2015, Annex I, pp. A-I-1–A-I-3.

---

[15]Since 2010, securitized credit card receivables remain on bank and finance company balance sheets. Generally Accepted Accounting Principles (GAAP) were updated by Statements of Financial Accounting Standards 166 and 167, requiring on-balance-sheet treatment of assets over which a firm maintains control to affect their performance and for which a firm also maintains either (or both) upside and downside exposure. (Adam J. Levitin, *Skin-in-the Game: Risk Retention Lessons from Credit Card Securitization*, Georgetown University Law Center, April 2013).
[16]Capital One Multi-Asset Execution Trust Prospectus Supplement, October 16, 2006, Annex I, p. A-I-1, and Capital One Multi-Asset Execution Trust Prospectus Supplement, August 19, 2015, Annex I, pp. A-I-1–A-I-3.

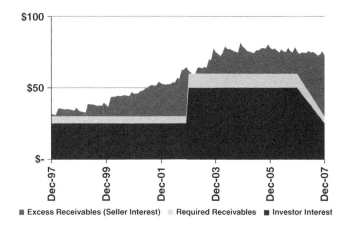

FIGURE 18.6 Receivables Allocation

interest grows or shrinks to accommodate varying receivables balances (see Figure 18.6). Following the revolving period, the amortization period commences, where principal collections on the receivables are used to repay credit card ABS investors. Many credit card ABSs utilize a controlled amortization period, where equal principal payments to investors are made over a specified time, often a year. Other credit card ABSs are structured so that principal payments are like corporate bond payments and principal is paid at maturity. This method is achieved using a controlled accumulation period where principal collections are paid into a trust account and held until maturity, when it is paid to investors.

Figure 18.6 shows how receivables might be allocated in a typical (hypothetical) credit card trust.[17]

Credit enhancement for credit card ABS is similar to other securitizations, and generally it is provided through internal credit enhancements (rarely, external credit enhancement has been used in the form of a third-party guarantee). The primary difference is that the revolving structure and reinvestment period can be ended by what are known as *early payout* or *amortization events*. Internal credit enhancement for credit card ABS can include any of the following:

- Discounted receivables—credit card receivables can be transferred into the trust at a discount, which in turn creates overcollateralization and/or incremental yield on the collateral.

---

[17]Bank of America Merrill Lynch Research, *Credit Card ABS—Market Overview and Update*, January 2, 2009, p. 29.

- Excess spread—the difference between portfolio yield and trust expenses

Hypothetical Excess Spread Calculation:

Portfolio yield		17%
Investor coupon		−5%
Servicing fee		−2%
Charge-offs		−4%
Excess spread	=	6%

- Subordination.
- Reserve accounts (usually supports Class C only)—a reserve account is a specific amount of cash set aside to provide liquidity and cover losses from the collateral pool. Reserve accounts may be filled by an up-front cash deposit or from excess cash flow from the trust's assets.

The primary protection provided to credit card ABS investors is early amortization. If there are problems with the seller/servicer, legal issues, or the collateral performance (portfolio yield, charge-offs, payment rates) deteriorates, early amortization triggers are created to end the revolving period prematurely, and immediately divert principal payments to repay investors before their credit enhancements are exhausted. Typical payout or amortization triggers include:

- Collateral events:
  - Excess spread below specified minimum
  - Seller interest or receivables balance falls below specified levels
- Seller/Servicer events:
  - Failure to make deposits or transfer receivables
  - Breaches of representations and warranties and/or covenants
  - Occurrence of receivership/bankruptcy
- Legal events: Trust becomes an investment company.

When credit card ABSs were first issued, the standalone trust was the primary structure used. In a standalone trust structure, a single pool of receivables supports each transaction. Subsequent transactions from the same issuer would require a new trust and a new pool of receivables. In 1991, the master trust structure was introduced to the credit card ABS market. A master trust structure allows an issuer to issue multiple sets of securities from the same trust. The master trust and all of the securities it issues are all supported by a large group of receivables. For an issuer, a master trust is much more cost effective than creating a new trust for every new issue, and a larger pool/portfolio should be much more representative of an issuer's overall credit card business than several smaller standalone portfolios. A master trust would simultaneously issue Class A, B, and C certificates.

In 1998, the owner trust structure was introduced within the framework of the master trust. Initially, the owner trust structure was created to improve the salability of the subordinated Class C debt. This was accomplished by selling the Class C to an owner trust, which in turn issued notes that could be purchased by a broader group of investors. In 1999, the owner trust structure was enlarged to encompass the entire structure of the deal. A "collateral certificate" would be issued from the master trust to an owner trust so that the underlying cash flows could be further tranched up. Master trusts were the predecessor of *de-linked* trusts, which is the most frequently used structure today. The master trust issues a collateral certificate to the de-linked trust. The collateral certificate represents an undivided interest in the master trust, receives pro-rata principal and interest payments, and pays its pro-rata share of losses and servicing fees.

Over the past few years, the credit card ABS market has evolved to a de-linked structure utilizing an *issuance trust* (see Figure 18.7).[18] Some market participants refer to this structure as the *master owner trust* (MOT) structure.

Utilizing the issuance trust structure allows an issuer to both issue traditional credit card ABS, where the Class A, B, and C notes all have matching maturities, and issue de-linked notes, where senior, mezzanine, and subordinate notes have differing, unmatched maturities. This more flexible structuring technology allows issuers to be more opportunistic in tapping investor demand and provides more flexibility on when to issue various bonds with disparate sizes, maturities, and ratings.

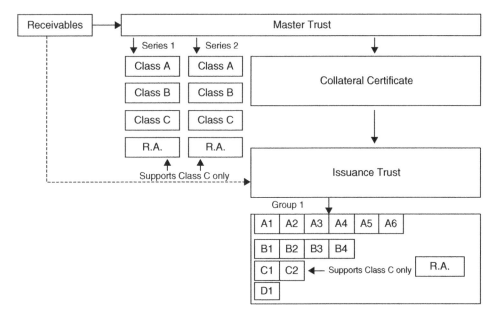

FIGURE 18.7   Basic credit card de-linked structure

---

[18]*Source:* B of A Merrill Lynch Global Research, *Basic features of Consumer ABS*, March 13, 2012, p. 17.

The master trust/owner trust/de-linked structure provides numerous benefits versus older structures. Some of those benefits include:

- Ability to participate in relatively large subordinated classes.
- Ability to purchase public, ERISA-eligible classes in all rating categories.
- Ability to issue specific rating categories and/or specific maturities when market conditions and/or investor demand favors such rating categories and/or maturities and not others.
- Issuance of Class A (triple-A rated), Class B (single-A rated), Class C (triple-B rated), and Class D (below investment grade or unrated) can occur on separate dates (Class A, Class B, and Class C can only be issued if a sufficient amount of subordinated classes are outstanding).
- Collateral includes a certificate representing an interest in receivables of a related master trust and for certain de-linked trusts receivables.
- Entities with de-linked and master trusts use the de-linked trusts to issue notes.

Table 18.3 summarizes the major structural differences between older and newer credit card structures.

In 2016, credit card ABS remains a core sector of the ABS market. The performance of securitized credit card accounts is robust with charge-offs near record lows in 1Q, 2016 at just above 2.5% and delinquencies near 1%, according to a credit card index managed by Fitch.[19] Although new issuance has dropped from prior years, according to life-to-date TRACE transaction data, credit card ABS constitutes 33% of ABS secondary trading volume by current face amount.[20]

TABLE 18.3 Credit Card ABS Structural Innovations: Credit Card Owner Trust Structural Features

Attribute	New Structure	Old Structure
Assets	Participation interest in credit card receivables	Credit card receivables
Legal form for liabilities	Notes	Certificates
Registration	Public for all classes	Public for Class A and Class B only
Enhancement structure	Both series specific and shared enhancement structure allowed	Series specific enhancement only
Cash flow sharing among liabilities	Yes	Principal only
Size, timing, and maturity flexibility	At the tranche level	At the series level

---

[19] *Asset-Backed Alert*, April 29, 2016, p. 5.
[20] "Merrill Lynch Securitized Product Strategy," May 13, 2016, p. 64.

CHAPTER 19

Non-Agency Residential Mortgage-Backed Securities (RMBSs)

Daniel I. Castro, Jr.

RMBS OVERVIEW

Residential mortgage-backed securities (RMBSs) are bonds where the payment stream to the investor is funded by the payment of principal and interest on an underlying pool of residential mortgage loans. RMBSs generally fall into two categories: agency MBSs issued by *government-sponsored enterprises* (GSEs) such as Federal National Mortgage Association (Fannie Mae) and Federal Home Loan Mortgage Corporation (Freddie Mac), or by the government agency known as Government National Mortgage Association (Ginnie Mae); and non-agency or private-label MBSs sponsored by private entities without government support. Ginnie Mae is backed by the full faith and credit of the U.S. government while Fannie Mae and Freddie Mac also provide certain guarantees and have special authority to borrow from the U.S. Treasury. The GSEs' and Ginnie Mae's government support mitigates their credit risk and provides exceptionally strong liquidity. This chapter focuses on non-agency RMBSs.

THE CREATION OF RMBSs

The RMBS securitization process starts with the origination of mortgage loans. Similar mortgage loans—the collateral—are then aggregated into mortgage pools. The trust raises funds to pay for the loans by issuing certificates backed by the assets held in the trust. A typical RMBS transaction involves the creation and deposit of the pooled mortgage loans into an investment vehicle with an independent trustee and the sale of RMBS certificates to certificate holders.[1] To create RMBSs, residential mortgage loans of varying dollar amounts, property types, and geographic locations are pooled together and sold

---

[1]Typically, a grantor trust elects *real estate mortgage investment conduits* (REMICs) treatment for tax purposes.

to a bankruptcy-remote *special-purpose vehicle* (SPV), typically a trust. Once mortgage loans are transferred to a trust, they are combined with other elements of credit enhancement (described ahead) to form the collective trust assets held for the benefit of certificate holders. These RMBS certificates give certificate holders rights to the cash flows arising from the securitized mortgage loan collateral held in the trust. In other words, RMBS certificate holders buy undivided interests in the cash flows generated by the mortgage pool, not discrete interests in a subset of specific whole-mortgage loans.[2]

Structure of RMBSs and Allocation of Risks

These certificates are issued in different *tranches* or classes, with each tranche differing in yield (the amount of return on the certificates), maturity (the length of time before the certificate is expected to be paid off), and payment priority (the order in which investors are paid principal and interest). Generally, principal will be paid from the top tranche down the cash-flow waterfall in sequential order, and any losses will be allocated to the securities at the bottom of the capital structure first, and then working up the structure. Figure 19.1 is illustrative of a typical non-agency RMBS deal structure.

RMBSs can be structured in different ways (e.g., different subordination structures, different pool structures),[3] and can be backed by various types of mortgage products

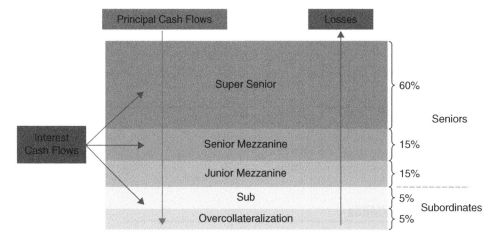

FIGURE 19.1   Non-Agency RMBS Deal Structure

---

[2]RMBSs often comprise multiple pools and in some cases there is cross-collateralization across the various pools. Cross-collateralization occurs when cash flows generated from the mortgage loans in one pool are used to pay certificate holders of another pool within the same RMBS deal.

[3]Subordination structure refers to how the cash flows and potential losses are distributed among the securities issued as a result of the securitization. Pool structure refers to the fact that the trust may divide the underlying mortgage loans into one or more pools to support different subordination structures. See, e.g., "Understanding Residential ABS: A Comprehensive Guide to Collateral, Structure and Related Credit Derivative Markets," *Wachovia Capital Markets, LLC*, February 14, 2007, pp. 24–26.

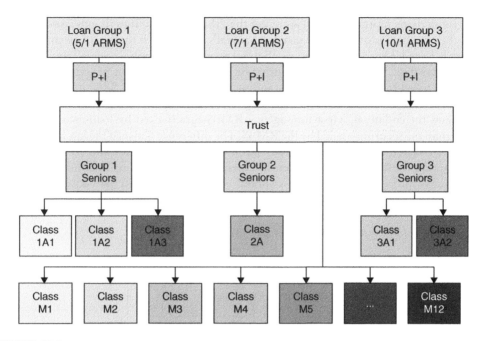

FIGURE 19.2 Typical hybrid ARM RMBS structure

(e.g., prime, Alt-A, subprime, first-lien, second-lien, and home equity line of credit).[4] However, certificate holders and insurers in all types of RMBSs are exposed to certain risks, such as credit risk, interest rate risk, prepayment risk, regulatory risk, market risk, and fraud risk.[5]

Figure 19.2 illustrates a typical multiple-loan group structure for hybrid ARMs. Using Figure 19.2 as an example, Class 1A2 is backed by Loan Group 1. Loan Group 1 is 5/1 ARMs, so the relevant performance structures and collateral characteristics used would be those for 5/1 ARMs.

Credit Enhancement

RMBSs typically have multiple sources of credit enhancement. Subordination of tranche cash flows to protect more senior classes in a structure, as in Figures 19.1 and 19.2, was the most-used form of credit enhancement. Mortgage securitizations also built credit enhancement through an *overcollateralization* structure. When the face value of the deal's

---

[4]Prime and Alt-A loans generally were made to borrowers deemed to be the most creditworthy, while subprime loans were made to borrowers with credit blemishes. First-lien, second-lien, and home equity line of credit mortgages represented the status of the loans in terms of seniority of the mortgage holder, where first-liens are paid first, followed by second-liens followed by home equity lines of credit.

[5]Borrower fraud is another risk to non-agency RMBS investors. Fraud risk is often not covered by the originator/conduit/sellers' representations and warranties.

assets (underlying mortgage loans) is greater than the deal's liabilities (bonds issued by the deal), then the deal is overcollateralized. At a deal's inception, if the total face amount of the bonds issued is less than the initial collateral asset balance, initial overcollateralization has been created. For example, a securitization with $800 million of issued securities could be backed by loans with an outstanding principal balance of $880 million.

Overcollateralization can also be built by using excess interest to pay down the bonds faster than the collateral. Most non-agency RMBSs are backed by loans with coupons greater than the securities issued by the RMBS. The difference between the interest income the deal's collateral generates (after paying any monthly expenses and fees to parties administering the trust) and the interest expense the deal pays to bondholders is the deal's excess spread. When the excess spread is used to accelerate pay-down of senior bond principal, the deal is "turboing" to build overcollateralization. See Figures 19.3 and 19.4.

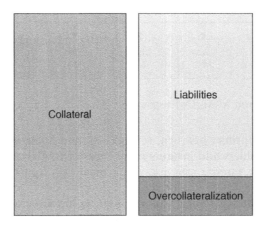

FIGURE 19.3   Overcollateralization

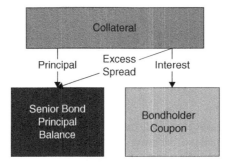

FIGURE 19.4   Collateral

MORTGAGE QUALITY TYPES

The mortgage loans backing RMBSs may fall into several quality classifications, including the following:

Prime mortgages typically conform to GSE standards and have prime quality borrowers who make a minimum 20% down payment (giving them *loan-to-value* (LTV)[6] ratios of 80% or lower, strong credit scores (720 FICO or higher), and full documentation (full appraisals, verification of income and assets). Prime borrowers generally exhibit the strongest credit credentials, having substantial credit histories and a demonstrated capacity to make mortgage payments, giving them the lowest risk of default.

Jumbo mortgages may or may not be prime, but the size of the loan is larger than the size limits imposed on the GSEs by the FHFA, their regulator.

Alt-A mortgages generally have borrowers with relatively high credit scores, but typically have nonconforming aspects such as lower documentation or non-owner-occupied status, and nonconforming underwriting ratios that do not meet GSE standards. *Option-ARM* borrowers are the riskiest segment of Alt-A because they sought the lowest initial payments available, and, due to negative amortization, may have allowed their principal balances to grow over time. Option-ARM borrowers do not necessarily have to demonstrate their current ability to make a payment based upon full amortization.

Subprime mortgages generally have riskier borrowers with lower credit scores (typically under 660 FICO) and little or no documentation. Subprime mortgages generally have higher LTV ratios (over 80%) and high *debt-to-income* (DTI) ratios (over 35%). The subprime mortgage market has historically been the financing source of last resort for prospective borrowers with impaired credit or lack of credit history or an overleveraged balance sheet.

Scratch-and-dent mortgages take many disparate formats, including delinquent loans, re-performing loans, repurchases, and loans with documentation or other deficiencies, among others. These loans typically have defects, and their borrowers are generally the weakest in the mortgage market.

Residential mortgages typically are either fixed-rate or adjustable-rate. Fixed-rate mortgages vary in length, with 30-year and 15-year loans the most prevalent. For example, a 30-year fixed-rate mortgage will have equal monthly payments, based on a fixed interest rate, that amortize its principal balance over its 30-year term. Adjustable-rate mortgages (ARMs) have interest rates that reset periodically—generally monthly, quarterly, semiannually, or annually—based on the level of an index such as LIBOR

---

[6]The ratio of the loan amount over the value of the property. The difference between the value of the property and the loan amount represents the borrower's equity in the property.

and a margin or spread. Interest rate resets on hybrid ARMs commence after an initial fixed-rate period ranging from 2 to 10 years. RMBSs backed by fixed-rate loans may have a fixed-rate coupon or a floating-rate coupon, while RMBSs backed by ARMs typically pay floating-rate or variable-rate coupons.

PARTICIPANTS IN THE CREATION OF AN RMBS

RMBSs are bonds where the payment stream to the holder is funded by the payment of principal and interest on an underlying pool of residential mortgage loans. The creation of an RMBS involves the efforts of multiple distinct entities.

Mortgage Originator

A mortgage originator is the entity that provides the mortgage loan to the borrower. A mortgage originator is usually a commercial bank, mortgage bank, thrift, credit union, or finance company. The originator is responsible for all aspects of creating a mortgage loan, including processing loan applications, documentation, underwriting, and compliance with state and federal laws. Underwriting decisions (i.e., whether to make a particular mortgage loan) are made with reference to the originator's "underwriting guidelines." Originators offer various types of mortgage loans and may have specific underwriting guidelines for each type of mortgage offered. If underwriting guidelines are met and a loan is approved, the originator's last responsibility to the borrower is to disburse the funds for the mortgage loan. After mortgage loans have been funded, the originator may keep them on its balance sheet, sell the loans into the secondary market, or sell them directly into a securitization.

Mortgage Servicer

After the funds for a mortgage loan have been disbursed, the servicer is responsible for sending statements and bills to borrowers and collecting mortgage principal, interest, and escrow payments from the borrower. The mortgage servicer may be the same institution or an affiliate of the originator, or the mortgage servicing rights may be sold to third parties. The servicer uses the payment collections to remit funds to various parties. Escrowed funds are distributed to pay taxes and insurance. In the case of mortgage loans that have been securitized, principal and interest payments are distributed to the securitization vehicle (typically a mortgage trust) that issued the RMBS so that investors in the RMBS can be paid. The servicer often has reporting responsibilities to the trustee, which are stipulated in a *pooling and servicing agreement* (PSA).

The Sponsor

The sponsor is an entity that sells or transfers assets (mortgage loans) to the bankruptcy-remote issuing entity. A sponsor could be an affiliate of the originator (or the originator itself) or the sponsor could be a third party that purchases loans in the secondary market and earmarks them for securitization. If and when the sponsor subsequently sells its loans into a securitization, it transfers the ownership of the loans to the depositor.

The Depositor

The depositor is the entity that deposits the mortgage loans into the issuing trust that issues the securities. On the closing date, the depositor transfers all of its rights, title, and interest in and to each mortgage loan to the issuing trust. The depositor is usually required by the PSA to deliver, or cause to be delivered, to the trustee the mortgage notes endorsed to the trustee on behalf of the certificate holders.

The Issuer

The issuer is typically a bankruptcy-remote trust that is created for the sole purpose of issuing RMBSs. The governing document for the issuing trust is typically the PSA.

CREDIT RATINGS

RMBS bonds are typically rated by some or all of the three major *nationally recognized statistical ratings organizations* (NRSROs)—Moody's, Standard & Poor's (S&P), and Fitch. The credit rating assigned to each tranche is designed to reflect the likelihood that the bond will experience losses in the future. A bond's credit rating depends substantially, but not exclusively, on a combination of (1) the credit quality of the underlying mortgages, (2) the aggregate level of credit enhancement available to each tranche, and (3) the structural and legal protections provided by the bond's cash flow and legal structure. Table 19.1 reflects the range of credit ratings assigned by each of the three leading NRSROs (AAA = safest, D = riskiest).[7]

For non-agency RMBSs, typically two or three of the NRSROs assign credit ratings to most tranches in a given transaction. Each tranche carries a different risk profile based on its position in the cash-flow waterfall and the degree of credit enhancement to protect against cash flow delays, shortfalls, and losses. RMBS tranches can range in credit quality from AAA (the highest rating) all the way down to unrated. AAA-rated tranches found in RMBS transactions can be: (1) "super senior" AAA tranches; (2) "senior" AAA tranches; (3) "mezzanine" AAA tranches; or (4) "junior" AAA tranches. In the lower

---

[7]Each NRSRO has a unique definition of what each rating means. Ratings are determined by a combination of both qualitative and quantitative factors, which vary by ratings agency. Some ratings agencies focus more on probability of default and others focus more on expected losses. A detailed explanation of the rating process and definitions of all ratings are provided by each ratings agency on their respective websites.

TABLE 19.1 Comparison of Ratings Grades by NRSRO

Grade	Moody's	S&P	Fitch
Investment Grade	Aaa	AAA	AAA
	Aa1	AA+	AA+
	Aa2	AA	AA
	Aa3	AA-	AA-
	A1	A+	A+
	A2	A	A
	A3	A-	A-
	Baa1	BBB+	BBB+
	Baa2	BBB	BBB
	Baa3	BBB-	BBB-
Below Investment Grade	Ba1	BB+	BB+
	Ba2	BB	BB
	Ba3	BB-	BB-
	B1	B+	B+
	B2	B	B
	B3	B-	B-
	Caa1	CCC+	CCC
	Caa2	CCC	CCC
	Caa3	CCC-	CCC
	Ca	CC	CC
	C	D	D

part of the credit structure of RMBSs are tranches rated AA, A, BBB, and below. The most junior class, the residual tranche, is typically unrated, and is commonly referred to as the "first loss piece," because the initial losses of the underlying mortgage loan pool are allocated to this tranche first. As described earlier, subordinate tranches are next in line to absorb losses because they sit next in priority between the senior tranches and the residual tranche.

RISK FACTORS AFFECTING RMBSs

When an investor purchases a debt security, cash flow can be generated from three potential sources in exchange for an initial principal investment: (1) principal cash flow, (2) interest cash flow, and (3) resale cash flow. The value or loss of value from the three potential sources of cash flow can be broken down into four components of risk. Investors seek to be paid (earn a return on their investment) for undertaking a combination of these risks. The four risk components are explained here.

Credit Risk

RMBSs' credit risk is determined by the mortgage borrowers' ability and willingness to repay principal and how well protected those underlying collateral losses are by the security's credit enhancement. RMBSs' intrinsic value is based upon projecting the bond's cash flows with an expectation of future credit risks driven by the underlying collateral's projected *conditional default rate* (CDR) and expected loss severity. The credit risks associated with mortgage borrowers can be mitigated, sometimes even largely removed, through the securitization structure. Within the capital structure of an RMBS, the most-senior bonds are exposed to less risk because the subordinate bonds, which are more highly exposed to credit risks, act to protect the senior bonds from incurring losses. In the simplified example in Figure 19.5, two vastly different effects of a defaulted loan within a capital structure are displayed. Defaults may produce involuntary principal prepayments (i.e., prepayments that are made with the proceeds from the liquidation of a defaulted mortgage). This prepayment will reduce the weighted average life (WAL) of senior tranches, which receive principal from the defaulted loans' recoveries. Simultaneously, the subordinate bonds absorb the majority of losses and their prices are reduced accordingly.

Interest Rate Risk

Bond prices rise when interest rates fall and vice-versa. However, given the presence of convexity/prepayment/extension risk (see ahead), prices sometimes will rise less than a typical corporate bond when interest rates decline and may drop more when interest rates rise. Interest rate risk is created when market interest rates, such as LIBOR, rise to the point where the security coupon no longer provides an attractive return. This risk can be mitigated with floating-rate coupons tied to a market index.

Convexity/Prepayment/Extension Risk

These risks are a result of prepayment behavior. Homeowners typically have scheduled monthly mortgage payments that pay down principal, as well as the right to voluntarily

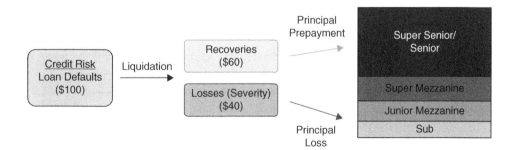

FIGURE 19.5 Effects on a Defaulted Loan

prepay a portion or all of their mortgage at any time. Most prepayment activity was projected to be voluntary, as homeowners refinanced or sold their homes. When interest rates fall, homeowners often refinance their mortgages. However, if home prices also fall, refinancing or sale may not be an economically viable option for many homeowners. When higher-than-projected prepayments occur, principal outstanding declines faster than originally projected and shortens the WAL of the bond. Since this happens when rates are low, reinvestment opportunities for investors are diminished. When interest rates are rising, homeowners may decide to make fewer prepayments than originally expected, lengthening the WAL of the security. When prepayment speeds slow to a fraction of initial projections, for example, from 25 VPR[8] (voluntary prepayment rate) or higher to low single digits, investors who intended to purchase a three-year asset instead end up with a bond two or three times as long and experience the phenomenon known as extension. When a bond extends, the risk of credit deterioration also increases due to the longer exposure time to credit risk. In the examples in Tables 19.2 through 19.4, we see that when securities extend, the prices will be reduced if the discount rate is greater than the coupon rate. Extension compounds the detrimental price effects of RMBS mark-to-market valuations because investors demand a significant market liquidity risk premium (spread) driving the discount rate far above the coupon rate, which now discounts the cash flows over an even longer, extended period of time.

TABLE 19.2   Extension Is Favorable When Coupon > Discount Rate

Coupon Rate			Discount Rate		
5.0%			2%		
Principal	Total Interest	Total Cashflows	Year to Maturity	Discount factor	Price
100	5	105	1	1.020	102.94
100	10	110	2	1.040	105.73
100	15	115	3	1.061	108.37

TABLE 19.3   Extension Can Still Be Favorable with Principal Losses When Coupon > Discount Rate

Coupon Rate			Discount Rate		
5.0%			2%		
Principal	Total Interest	Total Cashflows	Year to Maturity	Discount factor	Price
100	5	105	1	1.020	102.94
98	9.8	107.8	2	1.040	103.61
96	14.4	110.4	3	1.061	104.03

---

[8]25 VPR (voluntary prepayment rate) means that 25% of the deal's then-outstanding principal balance voluntarily prepays each year.

TABLE 19.4 Extension Is Not Favorable When Coupon < Discount Rate

Coupon Rate			Discount Rate		
2.0%			5%		
Principal	Total Interest	Total Cashflows	Year to Maturity	Discount factor	Price
100	2	102	1	1.050	97.14
100	4	104	2	1.103	94.33
100	6	106	3	1.158	91.57

Credit/Liquidity Risk

All of the previous risks will impact the liquidity (usually measured by bid–ask spread in the secondary market) of RMBSs. Credit/liquidity risk is the risk that the market demand for a security will result in a transactional price/yield that is not equivalent to the security's fundamental value. Market prices incorporate a *liquidity premium* in order to compensate investors based on the ease of converting the security into cash. The liquidity premium is a direct function of supply and demand.

OPERATION OF THE RMBS MARKET

The primary market for private-label RMBSs works in similar fashion to the primary market for other fixed-income securities, such as corporate bonds. Broker-dealers either solely or in a syndicate sell RMBSs via prospectuses and prospectus supplements for public deals and via offering memoranda for private deals. New-issue pricing is typically at or very near par, except for low-investment-grade or below-investment-grade tranches, which are often sold at discounts to par in order to produce the yields required by investors for the higher level of implied risk. Spreads and their associated coupons and yields are typically determined by broker-dealer trading desks based on their traders' assessment of where similar securities are trading and market demand for the securities offered. Once the initial sale and distribution of securities has taken place, subsequent buying and selling of RMBSs takes place in the secondary market. Each tranche of an RMBS has a unique identifier known as a CUSIP (Committee on Uniform Securities Identification Procedures) number. The CUSIP number consists of nine characters (numbers and letters) that uniquely identify the security. When RMBSs are traded, both buyer and seller typically refer to the CUSIP number to identify the security being transacted.

Secondary trading for private-label RMBSs is conducted almost entirely over-the-counter (OTC), meaning all sale transactions are conducted bilaterally between two parties without the assistance of a centralized *market maker* or exchange. In the RMBS market, buyers and sellers negotiate the purchase and sale of securities directly with one another via established trading relationships. RMBSs are typically bought and sold by broker-dealers who quote prices at which they are willing to buy and sell securities. Investors trade RMBSs through broker-dealers and not directly with each other.

Large broker-dealers may carry substantial inventories of RMBSs to facilitate market liquidity while smaller broker-dealers may not carry any RMBSs on their balance sheets and may instead engage in riskless trading by *crossing bonds* between investors and getting paid the bid–ask spread for their efforts. Depending on market conditions and their own preferences, broker-dealers could increase their secondary trading or withdraw from the market at any time, ultimately impacting the market's liquidity. As a result of the bilateral nature of non-agency RMBSs trading and the lack of centralized reporting until 2014, value determinations for RMBSs tend to be less transparent relative to exchange-traded securities.[9]

Given the nature and complexity of RMBSs, substantial product and market expertise is required in order to transact in these securities. Different investors have different appetites for the myriad risks described earlier in this report. Despite what any particular investor's opinion may be about prices, almost all investors *mark-to-market* their portfolios at the end of each month, and those marks come from a generally recognized price source. Market practice is that generally recognized price sources are either a broker-dealer that regularly transacts in the specific securities at issue and is performing the function of determining the price of securities or a third-party pricing service. Various types of investors and other market participants are not generally recognized price sources.

RMBS CONTRACTS

Several contractual agreements enable the pooling of mortgage loans, the creation of the trust, and the transfer of mortgage loan collateral to the trust. Among other elements, the relevant contracts generally include some defined set of representations and warranties made by the seller with respect to the mortgage loans. There may be multiple transfers of mortgage loans and multiple contractual agreements that govern these loan transfers before the mortgage loans are ultimately deposited into the trust. An RMBS *sponsor* acquires mortgage loans, subject to review, from multiple third-party mortgage originators pursuant to *mortgage loan purchase agreements* (MLPAs) with those originators that contained particular loan-specific representations and warranties provided by the originators (the *originator MLPAs*). After purchasing mortgage loans from third-party originators, the sponsor pools them together and ultimately transfers them to one or more special-purpose vehicles, which served as the *depositor*—the entity that sells the mortgage loans to the trust—pursuant to separate MLPAs (the *securitization MLPAs*). Sponsors typically make separate representations and warranties about the mortgage loans in the securitization MLPAs. The representations and warranties in the originator MLPAs are often similar but not identical to the representations and warranties in the securitization MLPAs.

---

[9]The Trade Reporting and Compliance Engine (TRACE) was implemented for securitized products in May 2011. However, the data captured was primarily agency MBSs until recently.

Next, a *pooling and servicing agreement* (PSA) or *selling and servicing agreement* (SSA), depending on the transaction, establishes and governs the trust and transfers to the trust the rights and benefits of the mortgage collateral, including the representations and warranties in the securitization MLPA.

In the United States, the mortgage finance market developed a nonrecourse, true-sale model whereby the right and title to the mortgage loans, along with the risks and benefits of ownership of the loans, are sold and transferred to the trust.[10] This model of mortgage finance is known as a *true sale*, because the mortgage loans are removed from the originator's balance sheet, and as *nonrecourse*, because mortgage loan sellers retain only limited risks relating to the mortgage loans through the provision of loan-level representations and warranties.[11] The trust owns the mortgage loans,[12] and the RMBS certificate holders own beneficial interests in the trust that entitle them to a share of the income generated by the securitized mortgage loans.

Under this nonrecourse, true-sale model, there are several ways to manage the credit risk associated with the ownership of the mortgage loans in the trust. First, most transactions include a senior-subordinate structure, or *tranching* of credit risk, where lower tranches absorb losses first. Second, some transactions have internal credit enhancement features, such as overcollateralization and excess interest coverage, which are designed to absorb some amount of collateral losses before those losses impact RMBS certificate holders. Third, many transactions include external credit enhancement features, such as private mortgage insurance for individual mortgage loans, letters of credit and/or swaps, and financial guaranty insurance on entire tranches or classes of securities. Financial guaranty insurance is specifically designed to cover losses associated with the nonperformance of the collateral due to adverse macroeconomic developments, adverse personal circumstances, or other causes unrelated to origination errors or defects. Finally, through representations and warranties and associated repurchase obligations, risks relating to specific origination defects, to varying extents, based on the scope of the representations and the agreed-upon conditions for repurchase, remain with the mortgage loan seller.

In agency securities, mortgage sellers have greater repurchase risk compared to non-agency RMBSs.[13] This is for two reasons. First, there is typically a difference in the scope of representation and warranty coverage, with agency securities benefiting from

---

[10]"U.S. Residential Subprime Mortgage Criteria: Legal Criteria for Subprime Mortgage Transactions," *Standard & Poor's Financial Services*, September 1, 2004, available at http://www.stan dardandpoors.com/prot/ratings/articles/en/us?articleType=HTML&assetID=1245350612130, accessed December 17, 2014, at the section titled "First Tier: True Sale." Moreover, rating agencies generally required a "true sale opinion" from counsel confirming that the assets were truly transferred to the trust. Ibid.

[11]Ibid.

[12]The trustee holds title to the collateral (mortgage loans) for the benefit of certificate holders.

[13]For example, Fannie Mae stated in its selling guide that "no fraud or material misrepresentation has been committed (by any lender employee, any agent of the lender, or any third party including, without limitation, the borrower), by act or omission, in connection with the origination of the mortgage or servicing prior to the sale, regardless of the level or type of documentation, verification,

broader representations and warranties than non-agency RMBSs. Second, as further explained ahead, agency securities lack a "material and adverse" effect requirement, meaning that mortgage loans may be put back to sellers without showing an actual adverse effect. This requirement increases the repurchase risk retained by the seller of the mortgage loans.

REPRESENTATIONS AND WARRANTIES

Representations and warranties are intended as a limited-recourse obligation of the mortgage seller. For nonrecourse, true-sale transactions, certificate holders and/or insurers assume the credit and prepayment risks associated with the mortgage loans, except for the limited-recourse available to them through the provision of loan-level representations and warranties. Thus, the allocation of risk rests heavily on the type and scope of representations made, and not made, in non-agency RMBSs, and the conditions requiring repurchase of breaching mortgage loans.

Because RMBSs are nonrecourse, true-sale transactions, each specific risk not kept by the mortgage loan seller through the repurchase obligation is transferred to certificate holders and, where applicable, insurers. Consequently, the representations and warranties provided by the mortgage loan seller do not operate as a guarantee of future performance of the mortgage loans, but rather focus on specific characteristics of the loans at the time of securitization. If investors want greater protection against potential future losses, they have available to them various credit enhancements and alternative securitization/mortgage financing models such as covered bonds and agency MBSs.

Types of Representations and Warranties

Some representations and warranties cover the seller of the mortgage loans. These will include statements regarding the organization and good standing of the seller, the seller's power and authority to enter into agreements, that there are no lawsuits or actions pending that would hinder the seller's ability to perform its duties, and other statements related to the seller. Most representations and warranties are made in respect to individual mortgage loans. Representations regarding mortgage loans typically include the following:

- Loans are not delinquent in payments.
- The seller is the sole owner and has the right to transfer the mortgages.
- The mortgages are in compliance with all applicable laws.
- The mortgages have valid and enforceable liens.
- The mortgage notes and mortgage loans are enforceable.
- All mortgages have been recorded in appropriate jurisdictions.

---

or corroboration of information that may be required by this Guide or any contract with that particular lender." See Fannie Mae 2007 Selling Guide, § I.202.01.

- The mortgages have not been canceled, satisfied, or rescinded.
- There is no pending litigation.
- The borrower is not deceased.
- The mortgage loan is covered by title insurance.
- The property has hazard insurance.
- The property is in good condition and free from material damage.
- Disclosure of underwriting standards used to originate mortgage loans.
- The originator verified the borrower's income, employment, and/or assets in accordance with its underwriting guidelines.

The representations and warranties also include a *mortgage loan schedule* (MLS), which is a listing of all the mortgage loans included in the securitization. The MLS will include, among other things:

- Location of the property
- Loan type
- Identity of the originator
- Loan amount
- Interest rate
- Interest rate caps and floors on adjustable-rate mortgages
- Lien position
- Term of the mortgage loan
- The appraised price of the property
- Occupancy status
- Borrower FICO scores (since financial crisis, the representation often also says that the FICO scores are no more than four months old)
- Prepayment penalties if any
- Other key terms listed in mortgage note

The MLS Representation: Understood and Intended as a Data Verification Representation

The data representations above are generally covered by a representation that says "The information on the mortgage loan schedule relating to the terms of the mortgage loan and mortgage note is true and correct in all material respects." Since the beginning of the non-agency RMBS market, the MLS was included to identify the mortgage loans being sold via securitization. The MLS is a listing of the mortgage loans in a securitization that contains certain loan-level characteristics collected from the mortgage loan files, such as rate, term, and maturity date.[14] From the inception of the non-agency RMBS

---

[14]For example, the MLS requirements specified in the WMC Mortgage Corp. and JPMAC Trust MLSA as of July1, 2005, provides for 44 loan-level characteristics, and an additional 11 characteristics with respect to adjustable-rate mortgage loans. Examples of these characteristics include several mortgage loan identification numbers, the gross coupon, the servicing fee rate, the maturity date, the original principal balance, and the property type.

market, the common understanding, at least until the financial crisis, among RMBS market participants was that the MLS representation warranted that the information on the MLS was an accurate reflection of the information contained in the relevant mortgage loan files.[15] The understanding and practice of the MLS and the representation that it is true and correct was not controversial. After the financial crisis, with the onset of massive litigation regarding losses on RMBSs, some certificate holders and insurers acting as plaintiffs have suggested a contrary interpretation. Under this novel interpretation, the MLS does not necessarily have to reflect what is in the originator's records or what is in the loan files; the MLS has to reflect the objective truth even if the borrower committed fraud in their loan application.

The basic purpose of the MLS is to identify the mortgage loans that are part of a trust at the time of securitization. They contain only a subset of the information available to certificate holders in separate "data tapes," which often serve as a condensed guide to the characteristics of the underlying mortgage loans. In some respects, the MLS is an artifact of a different era. Whereas previously not all certificate holders had the capability to analyze all of the information contained in the (separate) data tape, today—due primarily to advancements in computing power—they can. But its purpose remains: It is meant to be a transcription of certain contents of the mortgage loan files. Post–financial crisis, some market participants have argued that even if the MLS perfectly reflects the information in the mortgage loan files, if that underlying information is false for any reason, including due to borrower fraud, then the MLS representation is breached. This interpretation of the MLS representation is inconsistent with industry practice and understanding.

Fraud Risk

The risk of fraud is present in any form of consumer lending, and mortgage origination is no exception. Prudent RMBS investors consider fraud risk when analyzing RMBSs. There is no industry-standard method of allocating fraud risk in RMBS transactions. In some cases, certificate holders might demand some structural credit support to cover the potential for fraud.[16] Some securitizations had fraud support built in via carved-out subordination. Historically, the most common way to deal with fraud is to have

---

[15] For example, a 2008 Moody's publication stated the following: "The information on the mortgage loan schedule relating to the terms of the mortgage loan and the mortgage note is true and correct in all material respects. The information on the mortgage loan schedule and the information that was provided to Moody's are consistent with the contents of the originator's records and the underlying loan files." See "Moody's Criteria for Evaluating Representations and Warranties in U.S. Residential Mortgage Backed Securitizations (RMBS)," *Moody's Investors Service*, November 24, 2008, p. 4.

[16] Some securitizations had fraud support built in via carved-out subordination. See F. Fabozzi and J. Dunlevy, "Real Estate-Backed Securities" (Frank J. Fabozzi Associates, 2001), p. 70.

representations and warranties regarding fraud, especially in relation to higher risk collateral such as subprime mortgages and second-lien mortgages. Certificate holders might demand that the seller provide explicit coverage for fraud through an express "no fraud" representation.

Even among transactions in which the mortgage loan seller provided explicit protection against fraud, there are material differences in the scope of the representation. Certain representations warrant only against fraud committed by "the Mortgage Loan Seller or Related Originator," not borrowers. Others extend the fraud protection to include "any other party ... involved in the origination of the Mortgage Loan ... including without limitation the Mortgagor, any appraiser, any builder or developer."[17] In either case, the mortgage seller retains certain specifically delineated risks of fraud in the origination of the mortgage loans underlying the trust. Absent one form or another of the no-fraud warranty, the risk of undetected fraud generally passed to certificate holders and insurers, who factored the risk of fraud into their own credit analysis. It is important to note that no-fraud representations are not standard or boilerplate like most representations and warranties, they are not included in most securitizations, and they are negotiated for when certain parties want to acquire additional protection.

The "Material and Adverse" Clause

The "material and adverse" clause is a component of the process through which certain parties may be required to repurchase a mortgage loan from the trust. The market practice for determining whether a repurchase obligation has been triggered requires two steps: (1) confirming that a breach of a stated representation or warranty occurred; and (2) determining that the breach *materially and adversely* affected the value of the interests of the trustee, certificate holders, and/or insurers, as the case may be, in the related mortgage loan. If a specific representation and warranty was breached, then it also has to meet the material and adverse standard. The typical language laying out this process from a typical trust is as follows:

> *PSA § 2.03—Upon discovery by any of the parties hereto of a breach of a representation or warranty set forth in the Mortgage Loan Purchase Agreement with respect to the Mortgage Loans* that materially and adversely affects the interests of the Certificateholders in any Mortgage Loan, *the party discovering such breach shall give prompt written notice thereof to the other parties.*[18]

The "material and adverse" clause is therefore a precondition to repurchase embedded in non-agency MBS contracts that strictly confines the mortgage seller's obligation

---

[17]WMC Mortgage Corp. and JP Morgan Acquisition Trust MLSA, July 1, 2005, § 7.01.hh.
[18]Emphasis added.

to cure, repurchase, or substitute a mortgage loan to circumstances when a breach of a representation or warranty causes an actual adverse effect—that is, the monetary non-performance of the mortgage loan. In other words, a mere breach, without causing actual injury, does not give rise to a repurchase obligation.

Without this limiting "material and adverse" qualifier, mortgage sellers could potentially be subject to repurchase demands for technical violations of the representations and warranties that do not have any impact whatsoever on the interests of the trustees, certificate holders, and/or insurers. A mortgage loan can default for various reasons unrelated to alleged origination errors or defects, including a change in employment status, a drop in income, divorce, poor health, and negative equity, among other causes. These defaults can, and often do, occur in the absence of any alleged material origination errors or defects. In fact, as mortgage loans age, it becomes much less likely that any alleged origination error or defect had any bearing on, or was a factor in, a default. By including a "material and adverse" requirement in the relevant agreements, the contracting parties made clear, consistent with industry practice, that there must be some causal connection between the breach and default. Otherwise, the agreements would run afoul of the allocation of risk effectuated by a nonrecourse, true-sale securitization.

A comparison of the governing documents for agency securities is further illustrative. The relevant provision for agency securities required "the immediate purchase of a mortgage" for a "lender's breach of any selling warranty."[19] As a result, the risk transference was different in agency securities than in non-agency MBSs: Mortgage sellers retained greater risks associated with the collateral in agency securities than in non-agency MBSs.

Recent behavior of the mortgage securitization market further illustrates this point: As the mortgage securitization market has reawakened from its eight-year slumber, market participants have engaged in a vigorous debate concerning what representations ought to be made to non-agency MBS certificate holders. In July 2008, the American Securitization Forum[20] (ASF) announced the public launch of its Project Restart. The ASF described Project Restart as a "broad-based industry-developed initiative to help rebuild investor confidence in mortgage- and asset-backed securities."[21] Around the launch of Project Restart, many certificate holders agitated for the inclusion of a no-fraud representation covering any and all fraud occurring in the origination process, whereas issuers believed that certificate holders should accept fraud risks alongside other risks associated with the mortgage loans. That this debate occurred notwithstanding that virtually all non-agency MBSs had included both an MLS and a no-default representation demonstrates that no market participant seriously considered, at least before it became convenient to do so in the context of post–financial crisis litigation, that those representations guaranteed against fraud.

---

[19]Fannie Mae 2006 Selling Guide, § I.208.01.
[20]The ASF is a broad-based professional forum through which participants in the U.S. securitization market advocate their common interests on important legal, regulatory, and market practice issues.
[21]"ASF Project Restart: ASF Model RMBS Representations and Warranties, Request for Comment," *American Securitization Forum*, July 15, 2009, p. 2.

OPACITY AND COMPLEXITY OF SECURITIES

Structured finance securities in general, and RMBSs in particular, are complex securities by the nature of their bond structure. Further complicating their understanding, RMBSs are backed by various types of complex loans, whose performance, while available, appears rather opaque to an untrained observer. Understanding the structural nuances of RMBSs and the elements of risk can take years of market participation. Layering an understanding of the underlying mortgage loans and the varying impact of credit, prepayments, and loan terms on top of the structural complexity requires a high level of expertise. A person who is not a professional in fixed-income RMBSs, even one who otherwise is a sophisticated investor, looking at limited descriptive information, would have a difficult time at best knowing a conservative investment in RMBSs from a risky one.

CHAPTER 20

Commercial Mortgage-Backed Securities (CMBSs)

Daniel I. Castro, Jr.

OVERVIEW OF COMMERCIAL MORTGAGE-BACKED SECURITIES

Commercial mortgage-backed securities (CMBSs) are bonds where the payment stream to the holder is funded by the payment of principal and interest on an underlying pool of commercial mortgage loans. Typically, the loans serving as collateral for CMBS include loans for office buildings, apartment buildings, hotels, shopping centers, warehouses, health-care facilities, industrial properties, and other commercial real property. The loans are generally 10-year fixed-rate term loans (5-year and 7-year maturities are less common) with a 30-year amortization schedule that have a balloon payment due at maturity.

To create CMBSs, commercial mortgage loans of varying dollar amounts, property types, and geographic locations are pooled together and sold to a trust. The trust pays for the loans by issuing certificates backed by the assets held in the trust. These certificates are issued in different *tranches* or classes, with each tranche differing in yield (the amount of return on the certificates), maturity (the length of time before the certificate is expected to be paid off), and payment priority (the order in which investors are paid a return on their investment). Generally, principal will be paid from the top tranche down in sequential order, and any losses will be allocated to the securities at the bottom of the capital structure and working up the structure.

Typically, two or three credit ratings agencies such as Moody's, Fitch, and/or DBRS[1] assign credit ratings to most tranches in a given transaction. CMBS tranches can range in credit quality from AAA (the highest rating) all the way down to unrated. Three basic classes of AAA-rated tranches are typically found in a CMBS transaction: (1) the

---

[1] Dominion Bond Rating Service (DBRS).

"super-senior" AAA tranches;[2] (2) the "mezzanine" AAA tranche (often referred to as the "AM" tranche); and (3) the "junior" AAA tranche (often referred to as the "AJ" tranche). The mezzanine AAA tranche typically offers 20% credit enhancement, meaning that 20% of the securitization is subordinated to this tranche. The junior AAA tranche typically has a 12–15% credit enhancement.

In the lower part of the credit structure of CMBSs are tranches rated AA, A, BBB, and below. In the typical CMBS transaction, there will also be what is known as a *B-piece* at the bottom of the capital structure rated BB/Ba or lower, which are non-investment-grade ratings. B-pieces, also known as junior bonds, have more exposure to the risk that the underlying loans will not perform than the more-senior classes. The most-junior class is commonly referred to as the "first loss piece," because the initial losses of the underlying commercial real estate loan pool are allocated to this tranche first.

Many investors find CMBSs attractive because tranches can be tailored to meet their needs. Lower rated tranches can have higher returns than most fixed-income alternatives, providing desirable relative value. CMBSs are more liquid than direct commercial real estate investments, thereby enabling exposure to commercial real estate in tradable securities. The CMBS market came into being following the closure of the Resolution Trust Corporation (RTC) in 1995. From its inception until the financial crisis, the CMBS market had steady issuance growth. CMBSs issued through 2008 are generally referred to as CMBS 1.0, and CMBSs issued after the financial crisis are generally referred to as CMBS 2.0. U.S. CMBS issuance from 1995 through 2014 is shown in Figure 20.1.[3] Due to the credit concerns and volatility created by the financial crisis, CMBS issuance stopped from a period in mid-2008 until late 2009.[4] When the CMBS market restarted slowly in 2009–2010, collateral was underwritten much more conservatively, marking the start of CMBS 2.0. In addition to tighter underwriting standards, credit enhancement levels below super-senior tranches were generally pushed up by 50% or more by the ratings agencies. Investors demanded lower leverage on collateral and greater credit support on bonds.

CMBS MARKET PARTICIPANTS

Seller

The seller is the originator of the commercial mortgage loans that are sold into a securitization. Sellers are typically banks, insurance companies, finance companies, and

---

[2] In most CMBSs, the super-senior tranches typically have approximately 30% credit support, and are subdivided into four tranches usually named "A1" through "A4." The A1 through A4 tranches are "time" tranches whose sizes are determined by the maturity schedule of the underlying loan collateral. Generally speaking, investors in the A-1 tranche are fully paid their principal before an investor in tranche A-2 is paid any principal, and so on.

[3] SIFMA.

[4] "The Developers Diversified Deal Was Not Only the First Deal Fostered via TALF, It Was Also the First CMBS Deal of Any Kind in the U.S. since Mid-2008," *Commercial Mortgage Alert*, November 20, 2009.

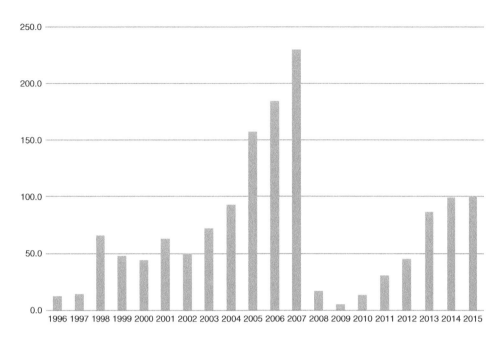

FIGURE 20.1 U.S. CMBS issuance

mortgage bankers. The seller generally enters into a mortgage loan purchase agreement (MLPA) to sell the loans to the securitization depositor (same process as in the RMBS market).

Depositor

This is an SPV set up by the underwriter sponsoring the securitization that purchases the mortgage loans and immediately sells the commercial mortgage loans to the *issuance trust*.

Servicer/Master Servicer

Pursuant to the PSA, the servicer is responsible for servicing the performing mortgage loans and acts for the benefit of the certificate holders. The servicer collects loan payments, escrow, and reserve payments from borrowers, advances funds on delinquent loans, and sends reports to the *trustee*, among other duties. The servicer passes collections on to the trustee, advances late payments to the trustee, provides performance reports to certificate holders, and sends nonperforming loans to the *special servicer*. In the event of servicer default, the trustee is generally obligated to find a replacement servicer or fulfill all responsibilities of the servicer itself, including advancing principal and interest.

The investor reporting process for CMBS has been in place for over two decades and is well known to most investors. A *master servicer* is appointed on each CMBS transaction per the terms of the related *pooling and servicing agreement* (PSA). One of the functions performed by the master servicer is to collect information regarding the loans in any given transaction so that it can be made available to CMBS investors. In some cases, the master servicers report the information directly to investors, and in all cases the master servicers deliver it to the trustee for dissemination to investors.

Special Servicer

Special servicers are appointed in the PSA for the purpose of servicing any loan that became "specially serviced." The special servicer is responsible for servicing defaulted mortgage loans. The special servicer negotiates workouts and restructurings and works through the foreclosure process on defaulted loans. Special servicers are usually appointed because of their distressed asset expertise. The special servicer tries to maximize recoveries and has latitude to accept a discounted payoff of the loan, waive a particular breach, or agree to a consensual sale of the property with the borrower, among other things. They prepare reports on the specially serviced loans, which are then made available to investors via the trustee. The December 18, 2015, issue of *Commercial Mortgage Alert* (*CMA*) published a list of approved U.S. primary, master, and special servicers on pages 16–18. Among other information, the primary contact and phone number for each servicer is provided on the list.

Issuer

A CMBS issuer is typically a *real estate mortgage investment conduit* (REMIC); specifically, it is a trust that owns the pool of mortgage loans and elects to be treated as a REMIC for tax purposes. The REMIC trust is formed pursuant to the PSA and it holds the commercial mortgage loans on behalf of certificate holders. The trust issues multiple classes of notes and certificates with differing maturities and ratings. REMICs are not subject to federal income tax if they are in compliance with IRS rules. To qualify as a REMIC, substantially all of the assets of the trust must consist of qualified mortgages and permitted investments.[5] REMIC provisions are built into the PSA so that the trust activities will not violate REMIC requirements.

Trustee

The trustee holds legal title to the collateral for the benefit of certificate holders. The trustee also ensures that the master servicer and special servicer act in accordance with the pooling and servicing agreement (PSA). The trustee is responsible for administering the loan pool on behalf of the REMIC trust. The trustee is responsible for replacing the servicer, if necessary, and the trustee has backup advancing obligations for principal and interest. Trustees' duties include preparing and delivering reports to

---

[5]U.S. Code § 860D—REMIC defined.

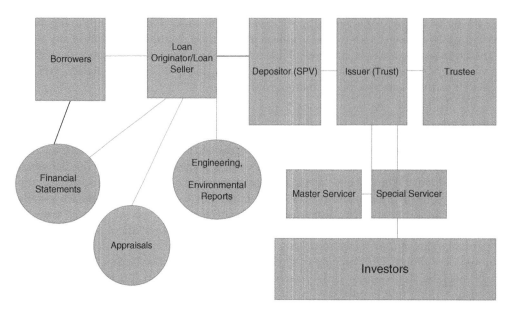

FIGURE 20.2 CMBS market participants

investors, including acting as a portal through which the reports prepared by the master servicer and special servicer are provided to investors. Trustees provide the various reports and information via websites, as well as by response to email and telephonic inquiries. The top trustee, as of mid-2015, was Wilmington Trust, which was trustee of over half the issuance at the time. Wells Fargo was the top certificate administrator for U.S. CMBSs during the same time-period with 71.9% market share by dollar volume.[6]

Figure 20.2 is a diagram of key CMBS participants.

Underwriter

The underwriter has overall responsibility for structuring the CMBS, selling the notes/certificates to investors and maintaining secondary market liquidity for CMBS notes and certificates.

Ratings Agencies

Ratings agencies explicitly say that their ratings are merely informed opinions and that they should not be relied upon to make investment decisions. On top of that, the ratings agencies make a huge effort to explain the rating process for both corporate

---

[6]*CMA*, July 24, 2015, p. 9.

bonds and all types of asset-backed securities (ABS), including CMBSs. Corporate bonds and CMBSs are different types of debt securities, with different risks and different ratings methodologies that by definition cannot be the same or equate to identical levels of risk.

The Credit Rating Agency Reform Act of 2006 requires that the SEC provide an annual report on Nationally Recognized Statistical Rating Organizations (NRSROs) to the Committee on Banking, Housing, and Urban Affairs of the Senate and the Committee on Financial Services of the House of Representatives. The Rating Agency Act added Section 15E(a)(3) of the Exchange Act, which requires the Commission to issue rules requiring an NRSRO to make certain information publicly available on its website or through another comparable, readily accessible means. Exchange Act Rule 17g-1(i) specifies that the information consists of the NRSRO's current Form NRSRO and Exhibits 1 through 9 to Form NRSRO. These exhibits contain information about each NRSRO's performance statistics; procedures and methodologies for determining credit ratings; procedures to prevent the misuse of material, nonpublic information; organizational structure; code of ethics (or explanation of why it does not have a code of ethics); conflicts of interest; procedures to manage conflicts of interest; credit analysts; and designated compliance officers. The Annual Report also lists Internet website links where detailed information is publicly available on ratings methodologies and models, and ratings transitions or ratings migrations for various ratings categories, including corporates and ABSs. It is a legal requirement that the ratings agencies' policies, procedures, methodologies, and performance be posted and available for all to see.

For most investors, ratings are simply a gatekeeper to what they may potentially invest in. Generally speaking, investors typically have investment guidelines that specify what types of securities they can purchase and what ratings those securities must have. Prudent investors, however, do not rely on credit ratings in lieu of fundamental credit analysis. A rating is really a checklist item that investors check off to make sure a security is eligible for purchase before they conduct their analysis to determine if they are comfortable with the securities' credit risk. In addition, virtually every prospectus, prospectus supplement, and/or offering circular for CMBS contains a section with a description of significant mortgage loans and the related mortgaged properties. Typically, this is a detailed write-up of each of the 10 largest commercial mortgage loans and the properties associated with them, which includes pictures of the properties and all relevant information. I can't think of a better reality check than a detailed description and related cash-flow and risk metrics for the largest loans/properties in a CMBS deal.

UNDERLYING COLLATERAL

CMBS valuation is based on the analysis of security cash flows. Analyzing security cash flows involves analyzing the underlying commercial real estate loan cash flows, which in turn relies on an analysis of the underlying commercial property and the borrower. In other words, before the CMBS can be analyzed, the commercial mortgage loans must be analyzed, and before the loans can be analyzed, the underlying properties must be evaluated.

Properties

Before evaluating commercial properties, the commercial property market each property is located in must be considered. Within each commercial property market segment (office, retail, hotel, multifamily, etc.) the location, supply and demand, economic conditions and trends, and demographic trends will impact the viability of the property. In addition, analysis of planned new construction and construction underway should be considered.

The performance of the property within its market segment is critical. The cash flow, location, access, physical amenities, parking facilities, physical condition, occupancy (if applicable), and third-party reports (engineering, environmental, appraisal) are some of the important information needed to assess the quality and viability of the property. If the property is a hotel, the number of rooms, restaurants, size of the gym, mix of business/leisure customers, and presence of conference facilities should also be considered. For office buildings and shopping centers, tenant creditworthiness, lease terms, expected rollover, and competitiveness of lease rates should be factored in. The net cash flow of the property is of paramount importance. In particular, the potential for cash flow volatility or deterioration must be assessed. Net operating income (NOI) is the cash flow generated through a property's normal operations, which is intended to reflect the property's typical cash flow performance.

Commercial property appraisals are governed by the Uniform Standards of Professional Appraisal Practice (USPAP). Valuation methodology under USPAP includes the sales comparison approach, the cost approach, and the income approach.[7] The sales comparison approach incorporates the sales prices of comparable properties similar to residential mortgage appraisals. The cost approach evaluates the dollar amount it would cost to replace the property. The income approach is based on the property's cash flow. Appraisers using the income approach typically calculate the capitalization rate (*cap rate*)—the ratio of NOI to the property's value, in a given market. Dividing the NOI of the subject property by prevailing market cap rates is a common method of valuation. In developing the appraisal, "an appraiser must collect, verify, and analyze all information necessary for credible assignment results."[8] Commercial appraisers tend to favor the income approach, which requires the following information:[9]

- Analyze such comparable rental data as are available and/or the potential earnings capacity of the property to estimate the gross income potential of the property.
- Analyze such comparable operating expense data as are available to estimate the operating expenses of the property.

---

[7] *USPAP 2014–2015 Edition*, Standards Rule 1-4, p. U-19.
[8] Ibid.
[9] Ibid.

- Analyze such comparable data as are available to estimate rates of capitalization and/or rates of discount.
- Base projections of future rent and/or income potential and expenses on reasonably clear and appropriate evidence.[10]

Loans

Commercial mortgage loans are typically made by banks, insurance companies, conduits (bank and finance company conduits originating loans for securitization), GSEs, and REITs, among others. Underwriting commercial mortgage loans starts with an evaluation of the property market and the property itself, as described earlier. In addition to evaluating the property securing the loan, the quality, credit, and experience of the borrower must be evaluated. Due diligence on a prospective borrower (generally a company) includes understanding the company's business, financial structure, earnings, history, and competition, among other things. Ultimately, the stability of cash flow generated by the property and/or business is the most important factor.

The strength of the property and borrower must then be analyzed in the context of the loan structure. Although the classic commercial mortgage loan is a 10-year fixed-rate term loan with a 30-year amortization schedule and a balloon payment due at maturity, most recent CMBSs have had a preponderance of 5-year and 10-year loan terms with either a 30-year amortization or interest only (IO) payments and a balloon payment at maturity. However, any of several loan attributes are subject to negotiation, such as the loan amount, loan term, interest rate, amortization rate, recourse versus nonrecourse debt, up-front fees and/or points, prepayment options and penalties, and so on. In addition, cash management safeguards, such as reserves (for taxes and insurance, capital expenditures, and tenant improvements), lockboxes, and triggers for trapping cash, are structural elements that can mitigate loan risks.

The primary measures used to evaluate commercial mortgage loans are debt yield (DY), debt service coverage ratio (DSCR), loan-to-value (LTV) ratio, cap rates (discussed earlier), reserves, credit support, and loan covenants. The DY is simply the cash-on-cash ratio of net cash flow (most conservative) or NOI divided by the mortgage loan amount. Essentially, the DY shows how much the property is earning relative to the size of the loan on the property. A high DY is less risky than a low DY.

DSCR is the net operating income (NOI) of the commercial property divided by interest and principal payments (debt service). DSCR measures how much cash flow is generated to service the debt on a given property. For example, a DSCR of 1.15 means that the cash flow can service the debt and has 15% excess cash flow; a 1.40 DSCR means that after a debt is serviced, cash flow equal to 40% of the debt is leftover. The trend of the DSCR on a given loan is highly correlated with the probability of default—as DSCR rises the probability of default decreases and as DSCR falls the probability of default increases.

---

[10]Statement on Appraisal Standards No. 2, *Discounted Cash Flow Analysis*.

LTV is simply the loan principal balance divided by the property value. A high LTV demonstrates higher risk to the lender—if the property value declines, the collateral value may be insufficient to pay off the loan balance. For example, a $5.4 million loan collateralized by a $6 million commercial property has a 90% LTV, which is relatively high. If the property value were to drop to $5 million, there would not be enough collateral to pay off the loan, if necessary. If the loan had been $4.2 million instead of $5.4 million, the LTV would have been 70%. With a 70% LTV, if the property declined in value from $6 million to $5 million, the LTV would rise to 84% and there would be sufficient collateral to pay down the loan. LTV is a strong indicator of whether the collateral value is sufficient to pay off the loan at maturity, which is particularly critical with balloon loans used for commercial properties.

As explained earlier in this chapter, cap rates can be used to calculate the implied value of a property. Calculating a property's cap rate based on actual performance and comparing it with prevailing market cap rates can be a good indicator of the loan risk within the property's market segment.

Credit support includes any additional collateral supporting the loan and any borrower guaranties. Reserve funds can help mitigate credit risk and are often in place to cover capital improvements (e.g., a new roof, paving parking lots, etc.) or unanticipated expenses. Sometimes two loans are issued to finance a given property. The senior "A-note" is typically securitized, while the junior "B-note" is targeted for investors seeking higher yields and willing to take on greater risk. Loan covenants are ongoing loan conditions such as minimum cash flow levels or maximum levels of leverage allowed. Any professional involved in the commercial property market is familiar with these risk considerations, and they also know that they are critical to understanding the value of the property that is supporting the loans. The underlying collateral is the building block for all CMBSs and any evaluation of CMBSs starts and ends with the underlying collateral.

CMBS 2.0

When the CMBS market restarted after the financial crisis, loan underwriting improved significantly. Commercial loans were originated with lower leverage and enhanced representations and warranties. In addition, greater disclosure resulted in increased transparency. CMBS 2.0 loans had lower LTVs, higher DSCRs, and larger loan sizes while the transactions became smaller and had far fewer IO loans. Ratings agency requirements for credit enhancement increased. When CMBS 2.0 was gaining traction in 2010 and 2011, Moody's reported that DSCRs had risen from roughly 1.25 in 2007 to 1.46 in Q1 2011.[11] Moody's also reported that in Q1 2007, 20% of commercial mortgage loans had LTVs over 120% and more than 30% of loans had LTVs between 110% and 120% compared to CMBS 2.0 loans in Q1 2011 that had only 5% of loans with LTVs above

---

[11] *CMBS 1.0 vs 2.0*, FT Alphaville, Cardiff Garcia, May 4, 2011.

110% and none above 120%.[12] Moody's also pointed out that in 2007 the average DY based on Moody's cash flow was 8.3% compared to a Q1 2011 DY average of 10.5%.[13] So debt yields increased over 26% from 2007 to 2011.

In 2012, CMBS 2.0 issuance was increasing and commercial mortgage loan originators started relaxing underwriting standards, raising LTVs, reintroducing mezzanine debt to CMBS, and increasing interest-only loans.[14] On April 21, 2014, Moody's announced "U.S. CMBS conduit loan leverage reaches CMBS 2.0 record high." Moody's reported that conduit CMBS transactions had an average LTV ratio of 107.3% in the first quarter of 2014.[15] According to Kroll Bond Rating Agency:

> *Regarding new issuance, origination standards in 2015 continued to ease, as competition among loan originators remained steadfast throughout the year. Consequently, CMBS metrics weakened as leverage and interest-only exposure climbed to new post crisis highs. Absent a market dislocation, we expect credit standards to continue to slip at a pace that isn't too dissimilar from 2015, as borrowers shop origination firms (approximately 40) for the most favorable credit terms.[16]*

In 2010 and 2011, CMBS 2.0 helped restore investor confidence and issuance restarted. In 2012, issuance gained momentum, competition increased, and underwriting standards began to weaken. Issuance grew through 2014 and competition grew stronger while underwriting standards continued to erode. In 2015, issuance leveled off and origination standards eased at a slower rate. Commercial mortgage underwriting in 2016 is better than it was back in 2007, but the trends are moving back in that direction.

CMBS STRUCTURES

It should be abundantly clear from the previous discussion that properties and commercial loans are hugely disparate compared to residential mortgage loans. As a result, the structuring process is far more complex. There are various structures employed in the CMBS market related to varying collateral types such as large loans and agency multifamily loans, but the most common structure is the conduit structure used for fixed-rate balloon loans. CMBSs use a senior-subordinate structure similar to other securitizations with triple-A-rated tranches at the top of the structure and single-B and unrated tranches

---

[12]Ibid.

[13]Ibid.

[14]Edward L. Shugrue III, "CMBS—Party Like It's 2007," *CRE Finance World*, 15(1), (Winter 2013).

[15]U.S. CMBS Q1 Review: "As Conduit Lending Competition Heats Up, CMBS Market Faces Risk of 'Boiling Frog Syndrome,'" Moody's Investment Service, April 21, 2014.

[16]*KBRA 2016 CMBS Outlook*, December 11, 2015 p. 1.

at the bottom of the structure. As in other securitization types, subordination levels are determined by the rating agencies (CMBS ratings are dominated by Moody's, Fitch, and DBRS). The CMBS market has been very dynamic in terms of credit enhancement levels required by the ratings agencies. In the mid-1990s when the market began, triple-A enhancement was above 30% and had gotten down to 12% just prior to the financial crisis. When CMBS 2.0 debuted after the financial crisis, triple-A credit enhancement was typically 20% and early 2016 deals are showing triple-A credit support of 30%. The variability of credit enhancement from double-A down to single-B ratings was not as great as at the triple-A level, but as collateral quality and investor expectations have evolved, ratings agency subordination levels have adjusted across the capital structure. At any point in time over the past 30 years, credit enhancement levels and the structures of CMBS transactions have been quite variable.

Super-Senior Aaa/AAA Classes

Prior to the financial crisis when triple-A credit enhancement levels fell to less than 15%, many investors became less comfortable that they were adequately protected. To make investors more comfortable, issuers created two new classes with higher credit enhancement levels of 30% and 20%, respectively. The tranche with 30% credit enhancement was dubbed the "super-senior" and the tranche with 20% credit enhancement was named the "mezzanine" triple-A Class or AM Class. The tranche below the super-senior and mezzanine classes was renamed the junior triple-A or AJ class. As a result, prior to the financial crisis, you could see a CMBS transaction having super-senior Aaa/AAA tranches with 30% credit support, an AM Aaa/AAA tranche with 20% credit enhancement, and an AJ Aaa/AAA tranche with 12% credit enhancement. Under this new paradigm, losses were allocated sequentially among triple-A classes.

Every tranche below (junior to) the super-senior provides credit enhancement to the super-senior by absorbing credit losses prior to such losses being experienced by the super-senior, thereby reducing the super-senior's credit risk. The super-senior has more credit enhancement than required by the ratings agencies to achieve a triple-A rating (the enhancement available to the Class A-S tranche in Table 20.1 example ahead), hence the super-senior designation. The super-senior's relatively reduced credit risk, as compared to the junior tranches, means that investors receive a lower interest rate and yield on that tranche than investors in the junior tranches. The size of a super-senior tranche is determined substantially by the quality and diversification of the underlying collateral assets—the higher the underlying collateral asset quality, the greater in size the super-senior tranche can be.

Table 20.1 is a representative structure from conduit deals in early 2016.

In the diagram in Table 20.1, the A-1 through A-6 classes are super-senior classes with 30% credit enhancement, and the A-S class is a senior tranche with 24% credit enhancement. In this structure, the super-senior classes are time-tranched to appeal to different investors (super-senior tranches often have tranches with 3-, 5-, 7-, and 10-year average lives) and some classes are larger than others, which may provide greater liquidity.

TABLE 20.1 Representative CMBS Conduit Structure

Note Class	Rating(M/F)	Principal	% of Deal	Enhancement
A-1	Aaa/AAA	$30,000,000	3.0%	30.0%
A-2	Aaa/AAA	50,000,000	5.0%	30.0%
A-3	Aaa/AAA	60,000,000	6.0%	30.0%
A-4	Aaa/AAA	200,000,000	20.0%	30.0%
A-5	Aaa/AAA	300,000,000	30.0%	30.0%
A-6	Aaa/AAA	60,000,000	6.0%	30.0%
A-S	Aaa/AAA	60,000,000	6.0%	24.0%
B	Aa2/AA	55,000,000	5.5%	18.5%
C	A2/A	60,000,000	6.0%	12.5%
D	Baa2/BBB	50,000,000	5.0%	7.5%
E	Ba2/BB	25,000,000	2.5%	5.0%
F	B/B	10,000,000	1.0%	4.0%
G	N/R	40,000,000	4.0%	0.0%
Total		$1,000,000,000	100.0%	

Mezzanine Classes

Mezzanine classes constitute all classes rated below Aaa/AAA that are investment grade (rated no lower than Baa3/BBB–). In the representative conduit structure given earlier, the mezzanine classes are Classes B, C, and D. The mezzanine classes are subordinate to the Aaa/AAA rated classes and senior to the subordinated classes described ahead. These investment-grade classes provide greater yield and risk than the highest rated tranches, but they are not considered high yield, which separates them from the subordinated classes described in what follows.

Subordinated Classes or B-Pieces

Subordinate classes include all tranches rated below investment grade or unrated. In the representative conduit structure given earlier, the subordinate classes are Classes E, F, and G. Subordinate classes are the last bonds in the cash flow waterfall and the first bonds to absorb losses. Since B-piece investors are in a first-loss position, CMBS structures generally make them the "controlling class" under the governing documents. B-pieces are not public securities so B-piece investors are given access to more information than public investors in higher-rated classes, and they have more control over distressed properties/loans managed by the special servicer.

CMBS IOs

Interest-only (IO) classes can be created in CMBS in the same way as in other structured finance markets such as RMBS. A portion of the excess servicing spread from an individual class or the entire collateral pool is allocated to an IO class. Payments to IO investors are based on a notional balance of the class or collateral pool and the coupon on the IO.

INDUSTRY PRACTICES FOR THE MARKETING AND SALES OF CMBSs

Prevailing financial industry practices for the buying, selling, trading, and repo financing of CMBSs in the primary and secondary markets are, for the most part, the same as they are for other structured finance sectors. The major (large) broker-dealers are typically staffed with investment bankers who structure and put together new issues that are either sold to investors directly or *syndicated* to other broker-dealers for sale to their investor clients. A trading desk known as the syndicate desk handles the initial sale of CMBSs. This desk is also known as the primary trading desk.

Most new issues of CMBSs are, and were, large transactions, often consisting of billions of dollars of bonds and typically syndicated among several broker-dealers. At initial issuance, for each CMBS transaction a disclosure document is prepared containing information regarding the characteristics of the CMBS as well as the risks involved in investing in the certificates. The disclosure documents for public transactions that are registered with the Securities and Exchange Commission (SEC) are commonly known as a prospectus and prospectus supplement. For unregistered or private transactions that are offered only to certain types of investors at initial issuance, the disclosure document is known as a private placement or offering memorandum.

CMBSs that are not new issues trade in the secondary market. Every broker-dealer that trades CMBSs in the secondary market has a secondary trading desk that buys and sells CMBSs with investors and other market participants. It is common industry practice for secondary trading desks to issue daily offering sheets listing the bonds they are offering for purchase. Secondary trading desks generally determine CMBS offering prices based on recent trading levels, credit performance of specific bonds, liquidity, and other market factors that impact investor demand for CMBSs. Traders will also take into consideration market benchmarks, such as the Markit CMBX Indices, but ultimately market prices are determined by the balance of available CMBS (supply) and investor appetite (demand), which can be influenced by myriad factors, including competing investments, interest rates, and macroeconomic data.

CHAPTER 21

Collateralized Debt Obligations (CDOs)

Daniel I. Castro, Jr.

INTRODUCTION TO CDOs

This chapter, in general, describes how typical collateralized debt obligations (CDOs) are structured and how they operate. It should be kept in mind, however, that every CDO is unique and there can be significant variation in the specifics of each deal.

A CDO is an entity—and typically a bankruptcy-remote special-purpose vehicle (SPV), also referred to as a *special-purpose entity* (SPE)—that purchases a pool of assets (*collateral assets*) financed by the issuance of debt and equity securities (*CDO securities*). The collateral assets can be any of a variety of debt instruments that generate cash flow from which the CDO can make payments to the holders of its CDO securities. Collateral assets can include RMBSs, CMBSs, leveraged business loans, trust preferred securities, and other cash-generating debt obligations. CDO securities in turn are issued in tranches, with each tranche assigned a different priority to the payment of principal and interest by the terms of the CDO's governing documents.

CDOs are structured finance products designed to securitize diversified pools of debt securities. ABS CDOs are typically backed primarily by RMBSs, with small amounts of other ABS. The purpose of a securitization is to repackage and redistribute risk, and the act of securitization is the process of converting assets into securities backed by those assets. CDOs finance the purchase of their asset portfolios by issuing debt and equity. The debt is issued in ranked classes with higher-ranking classes having payment priority over lower-ranking classes, and all of the debt having payment priority over the equity. Consequently, each CDO debt class has a higher credit rating than the average credit rating of the portfolio of loans,[1] so the CDO can borrow at a lower rate than it earns on its portfolio.[2] The difference, or spread, between the relatively high-yielding assets and the lower-yielding (lower-cost) liabilities is paid to the CDO's equity investors. The CDOs discussed in this summary are cash-flow CDOs backed by RMBSs and other ABSs.

---

[1]This creates a ratings arbitrage.
[2]This creates a cash-flow arbitrage.

Depending on the size of a deal, a CDO may be supported by the cash flows of dozens or even hundreds of RMBSs. RMBSs are purchased by CDO managers in the primary or secondary market at prices negotiated between buyer and seller. Most RMBSs included in CDOs are backed by first-lien mortgages; however, RMBSs may be backed by second-lien loans as well. The credit quality of the RMBS generally ranges from prime to Alt-A to subprime.

RMBSs pay coupons to their debt securities either at fixed rates of interest or at a floating rate equal to LIBOR plus an established premium in excess of the LIBOR rate (typically expressed in basis points) as stated in the RMBS's offering documents. By paying a floating interest rate and using floating-rate mortgages as collateral, floating-rate RMBSs are able to avoid a fixed-asset, floating liability mismatch. When fixed-rate RMBSs are used, an interest rate swap is utilized to mitigate the fixed-asset, floating liability mismatch.

The governing documents for CDOs typically have criteria specifying the eligibility of certain assets that can be collateral assets (*eligibility criteria*) and limitations on the proportion of the total portfolio that can be concentrated in any particular asset class (*concentration limitations*). Eligibility criteria may address, among other things, asset ratings, the weighted average rating factor (WARF) for the asset pool, default status, issuer jurisdiction, and cash-security or synthetic-security issuance form. Concentration limitations may address, among other things, loan types, geographic concentrations, issuer concentrations, and ratings.

CDOs are typically structured to offer investors multiple tranches with varying levels of risk and return. The securities issued by a CDO typically are tranched into several classes of senior notes (rated AAA to A), mezzanine and subordinated notes (rated BBB to B), plus equity that is unrated. CDO classes above the equity piece are given ratings by the ratings agencies. When ratings are assigned, the agencies look to the strength of the collateral, as well as the legal and structural protections for those classes embedded in the deal structure, when conducting their analysis. The rating of each class is a function of the relative seniority of the class's claim on the CDO's assets, the relative quality and quantity of the CDO's assets, and the level of subordination of more-junior classes in the CDO (also known as credit enhancement). Generally, most CDOs allocate the interest and principal proceeds generated by their securities portfolio on periodic distribution dates according to a payment waterfall. Payments of principal and interest to the various note classes issued by the CDO are made sequentially in the order of their subordination subject to specific rules by which the payments may be reordered in the event of overcollateralization or coverage test triggers. The equity receives the difference between the interest earned on the portfolio and the interest paid on the CDO notes (as discussed in the following section), provided that certain collateral quality tests are met. If these collateral quality tests are not met, the residual interest proceeds could be diverted from the equity to purchase additional collateral, prepay principal on the notes, or fund a collateral reserve account. In general, losses realized in the portfolio are borne by the classes in reverse order of seniority, with the equity bearing the first loss.

TABLE 21.1 Representative CDO Structure

Note Class	Rating(M/S)	Principal	% of Deal	Enhancement
A-1	Aaa/AAA	$325,000,000	65.0%	35.0%
A-2	Aaa/AAA	75,000,000	15.0%	20.0%
B	Aa2/AA	25,000,000	5.0%	15.0%
C	A2/A	15,000,000	3.0%	12.0%
D	Baa2/BBB	10,000,000	2.0%	10.0%
E	Ba2/BB	10,000,000	2.0%	8.0%
Equity	N/A	40,000,000	8.0%	0.0%
Total		$500,000,000	100.0%	

CDO securities are typically issued in tranches with each tranche assigned a different priority to the payment of principal and interest by the terms of the CDO's governing documents. A typical CDO structure is shown in Table 21.1.

The Super-Senior

The Class A-1 tranche is referred to as the *super-senior*. Every tranche below (junior to) the super-senior provides credit enhancement to the super-senior by absorbing credit losses prior to such losses being experienced by the super-senior, thereby reducing the super-senior's credit risk. The super-senior has more credit enhancement than required by the rating agencies to achieve a triple-A rating (the enhancement available to the Class A-2 tranche in the previous example), hence the super-senior designation. The super-senior's relatively reduced credit risk, as compared to the junior tranches, means that investors receive a lower interest rate and yield on that tranche than investors in the junior tranches. The size of a super-senior tranche is determined substantially by the quality and diversification of the underlying collateral assets—the higher the underlying collateral asset quality, the greater in size the super-senior tranche can be.

The Mezzanine and Subordinate Notes

Between the super-senior and the preference shares or equity (see ahead) there are several tranches of CDO securities: Class A-2 Notes, Class B Notes, Class C Notes, Class D Notes, and Class E Notes. The Class A-2 Notes are subordinate to the Class A-1 notes and senior to the other note classes and the equity. The Class B notes are subordinated to the Class A-2 notes and senior to the notes below it in the structure and the equity, and the rest of the mezzanine tranches work in similar fashion.

The Preference Shares

The preference shares (which are generally called the CDO's equity) are the first-loss position for credit losses experienced by the collateral debt securities. However, in terms of cash flow timing, the equity receives all of the transaction's residual cash flow in each payment period (i.e., excess cash flow after paying various fees and expenses plus any principal and interest due on the super-senior, mezzanine, and subordinate notes during that period). Equity holders typically receive most of their cash flow early in the deal—and continue to receive cash flow so long as the cash flow on the underlying assets is greater than the cash flow out to the transaction's liabilities (super-senior, senior, and mezzanine classes), including counterparty fees. The preference shares' rights to the residual cash flow are nonetheless subject to certain conditions (often called *triggers* or *tests*) that operate to terminate the preference shares' rights to receive residual cash flow and redirect it to accelerate principal repayments on more-senior classes of CDO securities if certain conditions are not met.

PRIORITY OF PAYMENTS

In addition to the credit enhancement provided by the subordination of junior classes, certain classes are also protected by various tests or triggers built into the structure of the transaction. CDOs typically have asset coverage tests. If these tests are violated in relation to a payment date, the effect is typically to redirect collateral proceeds away from payment to lower-rated tranches in order to pay down the principal balance of the senior-most CDO security outstanding until such time that such coverage tests are met. A CDO may have a coverage test for each rated class of securities (e.g., a Class A test, a Class B test), or it may have tests that cover multiple classes (e.g., a Class A/B test, a Class C/D test). Coverage tests are designed to protect senior noteholders by accelerating the pay-down of principal by diverting cash flow away from the subordinated class and thereby increasing subordination (i.e., credit enhancement). The higher the coverage ratios, the better off senior noteholders are, since higher ratios represent greater credit enhancement in the form of overcollateralization.

Each of the asset coverage tests described earlier is satisfied if it meets a specified *overcollateralization* (O/C) ratio. The O/C ratio is calculated as the principal amount of collateral assets outstanding divided by the principal amount of the CDO securities outstanding, starting from the senior-most position in the capital structure (i.e., the super-senior) down to the classes named in the particular test. If, on any given determination date in respect of a payment date, one or more of those tests is not satisfied, then collateral proceeds are diverted from the lower-ranking CDO securities (including the preference shares) and redirected to pay down principal of one or more senior tranches or to fund a collateral reserve account structured to build back the required coverage. In CDOs requiring diversion of collateral proceeds to more-senior tranches, collateral proceeds are paid first to the super-senior, and if the super-senior is already paid down, then to the lower classes sequentially due principal payments. The O/C ratios for the various class coverage tests in most CDOs range from 100.5%, for lower-rated classes to 104% or more for Class A tests. The O/C tests are dynamic in nature because the O/C ratio changes as the aggregate value of assets fluctuates and tranches pay down. The O/C tests are designed to be self-correcting. As cash flow is diverted to accelerate the pay-down of the senior class, the overcollateralization ratios improve and in most cases, after some period of time, the O/C tests are subsequently satisfied and cash-flow redirection ends.

CDO MARKET PARTICIPANTS

The Issuer

The issuer is a special-purpose vehicle (SPV) established to facilitate the transaction. The SPV is set up as a bankruptcy-remote entity, which limits investors' ownership to the cash flows generated by assets in the SPV. The SPV typically issues securities that are sold to investors and, sometimes, affiliated parties, then uses the proceeds to buy the collateral, and then puts it into a structure. The super-senior—the top portion of the structure—is often held by the underwriter. The bottom piece—equity or preference shares—may be purchased by investors, such as a hedge fund, the CM, or an affiliated party.

The Collateral Manager

The performance of a CDO and the value of its CDO securities depends significantly on its collateral manager's decisions regarding, most importantly, the selection of the CDO's collateral assets. As the ratings agency Fitch has explained, "[H]istory has shown that performance across similar portfolios can vary markedly under different managers" and "the manager's performance is vital to the performance of all rated tranches of the CDO, particularly the most subordinate."[3] As such, "[a]n important pillar of Fitch's ratings process for a CDO is an assessment of the capabilities of the originator, servicer or [collateral] manager...to service or manage the CDO."[4] The other major ratings agencies—Standard & Poor's and Moody's—also considered the quality of the CDO collateral manager to be an important factor in rating CDO securities.[5]

As a general matter, investors and counterparties in the CDO market are keenly interested in the reputation and prominence of the collateral manager for a given CDO. For example, a highly regarded and active collateral manager is more likely to participate in the market regularly and thereby have better access to pricing and other information not widely available in these over-the-counter markets. Active engagement in the market by a collateral manager also provides the manager with a wider network of potential counterparties from which to source collateral for a transaction and obtain ancillary agreements (such as swaps, hedges, and puts) to facilitate a transaction, reduce its risk, and ultimately improve the price of a transaction.

---

[3]Kenneth Gill et al., *Global Rating Criteria for Collateralized Debt Obligations: September 2004*, Fitch Ratings Credit Products Criteria Report 2, 19 (Sept. 13, 2004).
[4]Ibid. at 19.
[5]See Falcone and Gluck, Moody's Investor Service, *Moody's Approach to Rating Market-Value CDOs* (Apr. 3, 1998); Bell and Rose, Standard & Poor's, *The Fundamentals of Structured Finance Ratings* (Aug. 23, 2007).

Generally speaking, a *collateral manager* (CM) is solely responsible for independently making all investment, credit, purchase, and trading decisions for a CDO, subject to parameters specified in the transaction's governing documents. In typical CDOs, the CM ensures that the collateral in the deal meets all criteria set forth in the deal documents in terms of composition, credit quality, coupon, that all deal tests are met, and that collateral maturity fits within the life of the deal, among other tasks. The first thing a CM does is to select and purchase the initial collateral pool. In most CDOs, the underwriter/placement agent enters into an engagement letter with the prospective CM to specify the role of the CM in connection with the formation and offering of the CDO, including the selection of the initial collateral pool.

CDOs, typically, are not fully ramped at closing—often they are 60–90% ramped at closing. As the CM buys assets, he or she is selecting for the optimal combination of assets at best credit quality and best market price that meet all deal criteria and tests. Sometimes the CM is selecting assets from the broader market, other times from a more limited portion of the market—potentially from funds the CM managed itself, from a third-party fund, or from the structuring agent/placement agent. After closing, typically the CM continues to select assets in the same manner, and manages the overall collateral pool so it complies with all deal parameters as assets pay down, pay off, or default and are replaced. In so-called *static deals*, the CDO can be fully ramped up at closing, so the CM never purchased additional collateral. On a daily basis, the CM is managing the portfolio of assets, managing the transaction itself, checking against all the deal tests and limits, ensuring that underperforming collateral is replaced, and that the deal performs as it should, subject to market conditions.

Actively managed CDOs (non-static CDOs) have a reinvestment period, which typically is 2 to 5 years long, subject to termination if certain specified events occur (events of default, ratings downgrades, removal of CM, etc.). During the reinvestment period, principal collected on collateral assets can be reinvested in new eligible collateral debt securities, subject to specified conditions. The CM in a *managed CDO* also is permitted to direct the trustee to sell certain collateral assets in discretionary sales during the reinvestment period. Most CDOs are managed CDOs as opposed to static CDOs. The CM is relied upon to make sales and purchases of collateral assets during the life of the CDO. In actively managed CDOs, the CM is of paramount importance—the manager goes well beyond just monitoring collateral performance; he is expected to actively trade bonds in the pool to protect the credit profile or simply to improve the collateral pool's profile. Depending on the deal, there may be limits as to how much collateral turnover can happen in a year or specific circumstances that the manager believes can be met (like the ability to reinvest proceeds of a sale within a specific time frame).

In a static CDO, the transaction works similar to traditional ABS where the collateral pool is selected (usually 100% ramped at closing), held constant, and pays down over the life of the transaction. The CM is afforded little or no discretion to purchase collateral assets after the deal closing—the manager is primarily limited to replacing underperforming or downgraded collateral. Some investors like the static design because the bonds are usually of shorter maturity and the collateral pool is transparent because it usually does not change. In a static deal, the manager is not as important as in a managed deal.

Generally, the CM also may direct the issuer to sell or otherwise dispose of any collateral asset that defaults.

On the closing date, the issuer typically enters into a *collateral management agreement* (CMA) with the CM. The CMA governs the CM's rights and responsibilities, such as those described in the prior four paragraphs. In consideration of the performance of the obligations of the CM, he may be entitled to all or a portion of the *senior management fee* and/or all or a portion of the *subordinate management fee*.

The Structuring Agent

The structuring agent sets up the SPV, puts together the deal documents, structures the deal, engages parties to the transaction, and shepherds the deal to completion. The structuring agent is usually the underwriter.

The Placement Agent

The placement agent is in charge of the sales function—placing the securities (particularly the mezzanine tranches) with investors. (Sometimes the equity is really placed as part of the banking/structuring function, and the super-senior bonds are part of underwriting the transaction.) Typically, the CM does not even learn who takes down the mezzanine bonds—that is the placement agent's proprietary sales/client information. The CM is often a fiduciary for unknown investors. The placement agent is usually the underwriter or an affiliate of the underwriter.

The Underwriter

The underwriter takes down (buys) the super-senior class. The underwriter is responsible for taking on the risk of placing all classes of securities to investors and purchasing whatever securities in the deal that are not sold.

The Warehouse Provider

Prior to closing, a CDO's assets typically are accumulated during the warehouse period. An account generally referred to as the *warehouse* is usually set up on the balance sheet of the investment bank that is serving as the underwriter/placement agent for the CDO. In most CDOs, the party that has been engaged to become the CM at closing purchases collateral using funds from the warehouse. The collateral may be acquired from third-party sellers, often via the underwriter/placement agent, from the balance sheet of the underwriter/placement agent, from an investment vehicle(s) managed by the future CM, or from other sources. Although the CM generally is responsible for selecting the initial collateral, the warehouse provider/underwriter/placement agent typically is heavily involved in the collateral acquisition process because of their knowledge of the structuring process and investor considerations. Furthermore, since the warehouse provider is taking the collateral risk prior to closing, they typically must sign off on the selection and pricing of the initial collateral.

In most transactions, a collateral manager employs another institution—often the underwriter or its affiliate—to finance the CDO's initial collateral assets (i.e., warehouse them) for some period of time prior to the collateral manager, causing the issuer to purchase them on the CDO's closing date. Based on market practice, the warehouse provider typically—and perhaps always—has the ability to refuse to allow an asset to be added to its warehouse. In most cases, the collateral manager seeks the warehouse provider's approval of positions selected for the warehouse by the collateral manager at prices designated or obtained by the manager. Generally speaking, most positions selected by a collateral manager are approved for CDO warehouses, but it is not uncommon for warehouse providers to reject selected positions.

During the accumulation phase prior to a CDO's closing, it is commonplace for an underwriter to suggest assets from its own inventory (including new-issue assets in its deal pipeline) for inclusion among the CDO's collateral assets. Unless otherwise agreed to by the parties, it is always the collateral manager's sole decision, acting on the issuer's behalf, whether or not to cause the issuer to purchase assets recommended by the underwriter.

CDO market participants—including collateral managers—understand underwriters providing a warehouse to be pursuing their own interests when they review assets selected for a CDO warehouse, and not fulfilling any kind of responsibility to the issuer. An underwriter/warehouse provider typically conducts such credit analysis of a selected asset as is sufficient to determine whether there is a substantial risk that the asset would default during the expected term of the warehouse, and reviews the price set or negotiated by the collateral manager to determine whether it is priced reasonably given the market for such similar securities (or, in rarer circumstances, consistently with contemporaneous, market-clearing prices for the same security to which the warehouse provider has access). Because of the short duration of the typical warehouse provider's risk to assets earmarked for transfer to a CDO (relative to the CDO's risk to those assets during the expected life of a transaction), the underwriter/warehouse provider's analysis of the assets selected by the collateral manager is understood by market participants to be more limited than the analysis conducted by the collateral manger on behalf of the issuer (which would be expected to hold the assets for many years).

Consistent with the concept that the warehouse provider's collateral-asset review primarily protects its pre-closing risk while it is funding the warehouse, neither underwriters nor warehouse providers typically have any rights of review or approval with respect to assets selected for the CDO by the collateral manager *after* closing. As a result, in most circumstances where a warehouse provider objects to a bond being financed in the warehouse *prior* to closing, the collateral manager would still have the authority to purchase that previously rejected bond for the deal, *post*-closing.

The allocation of risk and revenues (including credit risk, prepayment risk, and the risk of the deal not closing) between the warehouse provider, CM, and other parties, such as the lead equity investor, typically are specified in a warehouse agreement or risk-sharing agreement (*warehouse agreements*). The warehouse agreements are negotiated between the parties and executed prior to the warehouse provider purchasing the collateral. When the CDO closes, the issuer sells the notes and equity and uses the proceeds to purchase the collateral from the warehouse as well as pay fees and expenses related to the formation and structuring of the CDO.

The Trustee

The trustee holds title to the assets in the SPV for the benefit of investors (owners of the assets). If a replacement CM were needed, the trustee would be responsible to find a replacement. The trustee steps in when things go bad; if there is a dispute, they deal with it. If there is a vote, they administer it. The trustee is also responsible for producing the monthly trustee report, which gives a snapshot of the collateral, its performance, and deal cash flows. Because the trustee must produce the trustee reports, they typically also serve as the issuing and paying agent or collateral administrator (the equivalent of the servicer in an ABS or MBS transaction). In consideration of the performance obligations of the trustee, he or she is entitled to receive the *trustee fee* from the issuer.

The Surveillance Agent

The surveillance agent (SA) prepares monthly reports for the *initial holder on the pledged collateral debt securities* and distributions made with respect to the Class A notes, Class B notes, and the subordinate securities, as reasonably requested by the initial holder. In consideration of the performance of the obligations of the surveillance agent, he may be entitled to a portion of the senior management fee and/or a portion of the subordinate management fee.

The Ratings Agencies

The ratings agencies are officially known as *nationally recognized statistical rating organizations* (NRSROs)—they conduct due diligence on the CM and trustee, and sign off on the legal and credit structure as part of the rating process. In the CDO market, typically two or three credit rating agencies such as Moody's, Standard & Poor's, and/or Fitch assign credit ratings to most tranches in a given transaction. As explained in more detail previously, each tranche carries a different risk profile based on a combination of (1) the credit quality of the underlying collateral, (2) the structural and legal protections provided by its position in the cash-flow waterfall and legal structure, and (3) the degree of credit enhancement to protect against cash flow delays, shortfalls, and losses. CDOs can range in credit quality from AAA (the highest rating) all the way down to unrated. Since the issuance of ABS CDOs effectively shut down after 2007, a comparison of ratings scales used in 2007 is shown in Table 21.2.

Some market participants claim that the ratings agencies are the standard industry source of information about the creditworthiness of securities and their issuers. Some observers have said that investors in U.S. structured finance securities (non-agency RMBSs, ABSs and CDOs) relied heavily on the ratings of the nationally recognized statistical rating organizations (NRSROs) when making investment decisions. Some market participants also claim that the confidence in the ratings of U.S. RMBSs and CDOs

TABLE 21.2 Comparison of 2007 Ratings Grades by NRSRO

Grade	Moody's	S&P	Fitch
Investment Grade	Aaa	AAA	AAA
	Aa1	AA+	AA+
	Aa2	AA	AA
	Aa3	AA−	AA−
	A1	A+	A+
	A2	A	A
	A3	A−	A−
	Baa1	BBB+	BBB+
	Baa2	BBB	BBB
	Baa3	BBB−	BBB−
Below Investment Grade	Ba1	BB+	BB+
	Ba2	BB	BB
	Ba3	BB−	BB−
	B1	B+	B+
	B2	B	B
	B3	B−	B−
	Caa1	CCC+	
	Caa2	CCC	CCC
	Caa3	CCC−	
	Ca	CC	
		C	
	C		DDD
	/	D	DD
	/		D

collapsed after the three leading ratings agencies, beginning in the summer of 2007, reviewed and downgraded, often in concert, thousands of classes of U.S. RMBSs and related ABS CDOs, and repeatedly made material changes to their credit enhancement requirements for these securities. The implication is that investors (1) relied heavily on the rating agencies, (2) lost confidence in the ratings when the agencies correctly downgraded securities and updated their rating standards, and (3) partially blame the ratings agencies for their losses.

I respectfully disagree with the implication that investors can and should utilize credit ratings as the basis for investment decisions. A credit rating is simply the opinion of a ratings agency about the creditworthiness of a specific bond, not a substitute for an investor making his or her own evaluation of the bond's suitability for investment. Credit ratings are most appropriately viewed as a checklist item. For certain investors, particularly in regulated industries, if the security has a rating in a certain range, it is eligible for purchase (it meets the checklist). Just because a security has a rating making it eligible for investment, does not mean it is an appropriate security for purchase for a given investor. A credit rating does not address market risk, liquidity risk, reinvestment risk, or event risk (e.g., terrorist attacks). Prudent investors or their advisors should evaluate a security based on their own metrics, techniques, and analyses to decide if the credit risk, along with the other risks, is suitable for them.

Being aware of the problems in the RMBS and CDO markets, investors also knew that the potential for additional downgrades was very real. It was not so much that investors lost confidence in the ratings agencies; it was really a case of the market being uncertain about the magnitude of future downgrades now that the ratings agencies were reevaluating deal performance and rating criteria. Unfortunately, the market did not know what the changing criteria were going to be. In July 2008, the SEC published "Summary Report of Issues Identified in the Commission Staff's Examinations of Select Credit Rating Agencies" (SEC report). In this report, the SEC criticized various policies, procedures, and practices for rating RMBSs and CDOs, and effectively forced the agencies to take further actions and update their criteria, policies, and procedures.

Among the findings of the SEC report were the following:[6]

- There was a substantial increase in the number and in the complexity of RMBS and CDO deals since 2002, and some of the ratings agencies appear to have struggled with the growth.
- Significant aspects of the ratings process were not always disclosed.
- Policies and procedures for rating RMBSs and CDOs can be better documented.
- The ratings agencies are implementing new practices with respect to the information provided to them.
- The ratings agencies did not always document significant steps in the ratings process—including the rationale for deviations from their models and for rating committee actions and decisions—and they did not always document significant participants in the ratings process.
- The surveillance processes used by the ratings agencies appear to have been less robust than the processes used for initial ratings.

A number of the SEC's findings were not generally known to the market. For example, "Internal documents at two of the rating agencies appear to reflect struggles to adapt to the increase in the volume and complexity of deals."[7] All of the ratings agencies examined by the SEC in 2007 had implemented or announced that they would implement measures designed to improve the integrity and accuracy of the loan data they receive on underlying RMBS pools.[8] Although this was a positive development, it increased market uncertainty because the new measures were not yet known.

---

[6]SEC report, pp. 1–2.
[7]Ibid. at p. 12.
[8]Ibid. at p. 18.

COLLATERAL PRICING

As discussed earlier, the vast majority of CDOs utilize a warehouse provided by the under-writer/placement agent to accumulate collateral. Most warehouses, prior to the financial crisis, needed three to six months to accumulate enough collateral to price and close a CDO, but some warehouses lasted up to a year. Typically, the price paid for collateral when purchased by the warehouse was the same price used to transfer the collateral to the issuer at closing. Over the course of the warehouse period, market values could rise or fall, but generally the transfer price was the same price paid when the collateral was purchased by the warehouse.

In fact, on many occasions, a CDO's OC may state that the

> *Collateral Debt Securities consist primarily of RMBSs, many of which the Issuer has purchased at a significant discount to par, due to a variety of factors, including, but not limited to, such securities being part of an out-of-favor or stressed asset class or being distressed, undervalued or orphaned. The OC language often goes on to say that the transfer price paid by the Issuer (in cash and/or Offered Securities) for such Collateral Debt Securities may not reflect the current market value of such Collateral Debt Securities.*

This was typical market practice and disclosure in 2007.[9] In fact, there are even examples where the OC expressly stated that the market value of the assets on the closing date would be (or was expected to be) materially lower than the price at which they would be acquired by the CDO on the closing date.[10] Even in cases where the underwriter, placement agent, warehouse provider, CM, and/or other parties to a CDO conclude, prior to closing, that the market value of the initial collateral had declined or would decline as a result of post-pricing date developments, industry participants would not have expected that the price of the initial collateral would have been adjusted. Initial collateral simply does not get repriced to the market value as of the closing date.

Investors considering the purchase of rated tranches of cash-flow CDOs typically make investment decisions based on many factors, including the credit quality of the collateral, the rating, the structural protections, and the coupon payable on the bonds, but not on the market price of the underlying collateral. Consistent with the fact that investors did not focus on the market value of the collateral, it was not market practice

---

[9] "The price paid by the Issuer for the initial portfolio of Collateral Debt Securities purchased from CALYON on the Closing Date will not be based on the fair market value of such securities on the Closing Date" (VOLANS Funding 2007-1, Ltd. OC), p. 45.

[10] "Current Market Value of Collateral Assets to be acquired on Closing Date is Materially Lower than Price Issuer Paid on Closing Date .... Although a material decline in the market value of such Collateral Assets has occurred since the date of purchase or binding commitment by the Warehouse Provider, the Issuer will still be obligated and/or enter into such Collateral Assets at the agreed-upon purchase prices ..." (Pinnacle Point Funding II Ltd. OC dated June 7, 2007), pp. 46–47, at ¶25.

to disclose in the O/C the market value of the collateral as of the closing date. In addition, market practice is that the monthly trustee reports for cash-flow CDOs do not generally disclose the market value of the collateral.

The ratings agencies made adjustments for market value by determining how much *par credit* to allow for securities being purchased into a CDO. If collateral is purchased at a price below certain thresholds, it is defined as a *discount security* and for the purpose of calculating the *net outstanding portfolio collateral balance of a discount security* the ratings agencies only give credit for par multiplied by the dollar price percentage paid. In addition, if collateral is downgraded below investment grade, a discount percentage will also be applied to the par credit for purposes of calculating the O/C test as specified in the O/C.[11] Subject to certain conditions specified in the O/C, for purposes of the O/C tests, the discount percentage (percentage of par credit allowed for a given rating) was as shown in Table 21.3.

In addition to making par credit adjustments for both discount securities and downgraded securities, the ratings agencies had an additional tool—adjusting credit enhancement levels—that has the ability to largely equalize for adverse market conditions or other factors that might adversely affect ratings and investor returns. If the ratings agencies were not comfortable that par credit adjustments and structural protections did not adequately protect investors, they could always increase credit enhancement levels by requiring more overcollateralization and/or a larger equity piece.

Factors Affecting CDO Prices

In addition to the cost of the liabilities and the yield on assets, the key variables affecting the return to CDO equity and bond investors are default rates, timing of defaults, recovery rates on the portfolio collateral, prepayment rates, and interest rate risk.

The degree to which the timing and rate of defaults deviates from the expected timing or rate (such as, for example, higher-than-expected defaults or lower-than-expected recoveries) will determine the degree to which the return to the equity investor is affected. The coupon spread of each class of CDO debt is determined at the time the debt is issued.

TABLE 21.3 Par Credit Allowed by Rating

Moody's Rating	Discount Percentage	Floor Percentage	Standard & Poor's Rating	Discount Percentage	Floor Percentage
Ba1, Ba2, or Ba3	90.0%	0.0%	BB+, BB, or BB−	90.0%	5.0%
B1, B2, or B3	80.0%	0.0%	B+, B, or B−	80.0%	0.0%
Below B3	50.0%	0.0%	Below B−	70.0%	0.0%

[11] The discount percentage is only applied to securities in each ratings category that exceed the floor percentage.

However, the yield spread over the respective indices on the portfolio of securities varies over time as securities pay down and new bonds are purchased.

Broader market factors such as interest rates, volatility, and supply and demand will also influence CDO pricing. For example, prepayments on RMBSs are sensitive to interest rate changes. Higher interest rates typically slow prepayment speeds and, consequently, may extend the expected maturity of CDO debt. Conversely, lower interest rates typically increase prepayments and may shorten the expected maturity of the underlying assets, and consequently the CDO debt. Traders at broker-dealers tend to base their pricing views primarily on where similar CDO bonds or equity has recently traded (technical factors). Many investors take a more fundamental approach by modeling how the underlying collateral will perform, given their assumptions regarding defaults, recoveries, and prepayments within the CDO's cash flow structure. Both fundamental and technical factors will have an impact on CDO pricing. In times when CDOs are being actively traded, technical factors will dominate pricing discussions, while in times when CDOs are less frequently traded, fundamental factors will provide a better guidepost to CDO valuation.

CDO TRADING

The primary market for CDOs works in a similar fashion to the primary market for other fixed-income securities, such as corporate bonds. Broker-dealers, either solely or in a syndicate, sell CDOs via *offering memoranda* (OM) and/or *offering circulars* (OC) for private 144a deals (CDOs are not generally publicly offered, so there are no prospectuses). New-issue pricing is typically at or very near par, except for below-investment-grade tranches. By comparison, below-investment-grade tranches often are sold at discounts to par in order to produce the yields required by investors to compensate for the higher level of implied risk. Equity tranches are typically priced to produce a higher yield than the lowest-rated tranche. Spreads and their associated coupons and yield are typically determined by broker-dealer trading desks based on traders' assessments of where similar securities are trading and the market demand for the securities offered. Once the initial sale and distribution of securities has taken place, subsequent buying and selling of CDOs takes place in the secondary market. Each tranche of a CDO has a unique nine-character alphanumeric identifier known as a Committee on Uniform Securities Identification Procedures (CUSIP) number. When CDOs are traded, both buyer and seller typically refer to the CUSIP number to identify the security being traded.

Secondary trading for CDOs is conducted almost entirely over the counter (OTC), meaning that all transactions are conducted bilaterally between two parties without the assistance of a centralized *market maker* or exchange. CDOs are typically bought and sold by broker-dealers, who quote prices at which they are willing to buy and sell securities. Investors trade CDOs through broker-dealers and not directly with each other. Large broker-dealers may carry CDO inventories to facilitate market liquidity while smaller broker-dealers may not carry any CDOs on their balance sheets, but may instead engage in riskless trading by *crossing bonds* (arranging for sale to one investor prior to committing to purchase from another) between investors and getting paid the bid–ask spread for their efforts. Depending on market conditions and their own preferences, broker-dealers could increase their secondary trading or withdraw from the market at any time, ultimately affecting the market's liquidity. Because of the bilateral nature of CDO trading and the lack of centralized reporting, value determinations for CDOs tend to be less transparent relative to exchange-traded securities.

In contrast, exchange-traded securities are subject to the rules and regulations of the exchange on which they are traded, which typically includes some form of a centralized recordkeeping and price quotation system. As a result, exchange-traded securities are typically characterized by greater price transparency. Moreover, the exchange itself is acting as the intermediary in all transactions, helping alleviate counterparty risk by standing on both sides of every transaction.

Given the nature and complexity of CDOs, substantial product and market expertise is required in order to transact in these securities. Despite what any particular investor's opinion may be about prices, almost all investors *mark-to-market* their portfolios at the end of each month, and those marks come from a generally recognized price source. Market practice is that a generally recognized price source is either a broker-dealer that regularly transacts in the specific securities at issue and is performing the function of determining the price of securities, or a third-party pricing service. Investors who have financed their holdings via repo or other financing typically mark-to-market their collateral on a daily basis, due to the potential for margin calls.

Deal Analysis and Intex

When investors are evaluating CDOs in the secondary market, they often review the deal documents (indenture, OM) and trustee reports, and typically use analytic tools to value the tranches of a given deal. For over two decades the most commonly used analytic tool used by market participants has been Intex. Intex is a cash-flow modeling system widely used in structured finance markets to analyze deal cash flows under various assumptions and scenarios for CDOs, ABSs, RMBSs, and other types of securities. Intex would show deal parameters such as principal balances, coupons, cash-flow triggers, collateral tests, and information reported on trustee reports. Intex also embedded a deal's cash-flow waterfall so that traders and investors could generate cash flows under different assumptions and use those cash flows to determine securities valuations under various scenarios. Market participants also used Intex to check the performance status of the underlying collateral and the status of O/C tests and other performance measures such as defaults, loss severities, prepayments, principal write-downs, interest shortfalls, and credit support levels.

For many years prior to the financial crisis, Intex was a trusted tool for market participants to analyze and evaluate CDOs, and it is still a trusted tool today. Cash flows were updated in a timely fashion and the cash-flow modeling accurately captured how principal and interest would flow to various tranches under whatever scenarios investors wanted to evaluate.

Intex warehouses an enormous amount of current and historical deal and collateral information for each of its securities, including data and program code for cash flow structures necessary to conduct a full valuation of each security. Intex provides information on the CDO deal or tranche-level static variables, including CUSIPs, original ratings, issuers, deal and tranche balances, coupons, gross margin spreads, underwriters, collateral managers, collateral type, trigger information, and other variables. All data are housed in monthly files, with updated performance information provided by trustees.[12]

Intex CDO data is captured on its CMO descriptor indicator (CDI) and CMO descriptor update (CDU) files. "CDI is a static file used for both the initial descriptive and cash flow information of the transaction, while CDU files contain, depending on the reporting period, the quarterly or semi-annual bond and collateral information such as payments, balances, and triggers. Historical CDU files provide snapshot information at the specified month."[13] It is critical to note that "(s)ince SF ABS CDOs are 144A deals, collateral asset information from Intex is not as consistent and uniform as for purely public deals."[14]

MOTIVATION FOR ISSUING CDOs

Collateral managers have several motivations for issuing CDOs such as increasing assets under management, the cash-flow arbitrage, the ratings arbitrage, stable term funding, and reducing exposure to market volatility—these reasons are in fact the primary motivations for structuring, issuing, and managing a CDO for most participants. Almost all CDOs lock in the price of the collateral to be sold into the CDO well before the closing date. Once that price is locked in, it is not adjusted and the market value could move higher or lower, between when the transfer prices were established and the CDO's closing date.

Some asset managers want to develop a more stable financing structure. Many RMBS portfolios were financed via repo positions, leaving asset managers subject to margin calls. A CDO provides term-financing without having to mark-to-market for funding purposes. Repo financing typically has a term of 30 days or less and then needs to be rolled over into a new repo that may have a different interest rate and/or a different haircut. Repo financing also is subject to margin call and has the risk of not being rolled over at all.

As discussed earlier in "The Ratings Agencies," downgrades and announced changes to policies, procedures, and criteria at the ratings agencies can create significant uncertainty regarding additional downgrades. By taking legacy RMBSs, which were exposed to downgrade risk, and repackaging them into a new, freshly rated CDO, the market should have more confidence in those ratings. The ratings agencies should have taken

---

[12] Larry Cordell, Yilin Huang, and Meredith Williams, "Collateral Damage: Sizing and Assessing the Subprime CDO Crisis," Federal Reserve Bank of Philadelphia, Working Paper No. 11-30/R, May 2012, p. 10.

[13] Ibid.

[14] Ibid.

into consideration the new paradigm and applied updated/evolving rating policies, procedures, and criteria to a newly created CDO, making it less subject to downgrades than existing RMBSs rated under less robust criteria.

In a cash-flow arbitrage ABS CDO, the issuer and CM can achieve nonrecourse term financing of the CDO's underlying assets. "If the CDO's assets perform poorly, debt tranche holders have no recourse, other than to the CDO assets, and cannot make a further claim against the equity tranche. This is in contrast to the repo market where financing is short term and the creditor has recourse to the borrower if the collateral is insufficient to extinguish the debt."[15]

In addition to having a more stable source of funding and more liquidity than its underlying collateral, CDOs offer an arbitrage opportunity. Assets purchased into a CDO typically have higher yields than the interest payments due to investors in CDO tranches. The arbitrage is created from the positive spread between the primarily non-investment-grade assets and the investment grade liabilities. The CM also can use a CDO to increase its assets under management—"CDOs are another means, along with mutual funds and hedge funds, for an asset management firm to provide its services to investors. The difference is that instead of all the investors sharing the fund's return in proportion to their investment, investor returns are also determined by the seniority of the CDO tranches they purchase."[16] One reason many investors prefer CDO investments over mutual fund or hedge fund investments is that a CDO's division and distribution of the risk of its assets can be sold to parties with different risk appetites. From the CM's perspective, management fees on a CDO are more stable than they are for a mutual fund or a hedge fund. On static CDOs, where management fees are significantly smaller than on managed CDOs, this is not a significant consideration. A CDO's "non-call provisions have the added benefit of locking in asset management fees, most of which are generally payable only after interest payments have been made on rated notes. Furthermore, since the fees accrue on the par amount rather than on the market value (or NAV) of the collateral, the volatility of these fees is further reduced."[17]

In addition to the cash-flow arbitrage is the concept of ratings arbitrage, where you can repackage unrated assets, put them into a CDO with structural protections, legal protections, and credit enhancement, and thereby create securities with ratings as high as triple-A, much better liquidity, and lower funding costs. To a good degree, cash-flow CDOs also insulate both asset managers and investors from market value volatility. "The cash flow CDO structure allows asset managers to focus primarily on managing the credit quality of the underlying portfolio rather than the volatility of its market value, or net asset value (NAV)."[18]

---

[15] JP Morgan *CDO Handbook*, p. 11 (May 29, 2001).
[16] Douglas J. Lucas, Laurie S. Goodman, and Frank J. Fabozzi, "Collateralized Debt Obligations and Credit Risk Transfer," 2007, p. 5.
[17] The Barclays Capital Guide to Cash Flow Collateralized Debt Obligations (March 2002), p. 5.
[18] Ibid., p. 4.

Events of Default Under the Indenture

All CDOs contain language defining events of default. The idea underlying an event of default is the concept that certain catastrophic events or conditions (generally ones that cannot be corrected) should allow noteholders or the trustee on their behalf to accelerate the maturity date of the CDO securities and direct the near-term liquidation of collateral assets, among other remedies. This simply means that the collateral will be sold off, typically by way of auction, and the proceeds will pay down the CDO securities in accelerated fashion in accordance with the waterfall in the indenture.

The *indenture* defines the conditions that constitute an event of default for CDO transactions. Depending on the CDO, there could be 6 to 10 possible events of default. The following are examples of three of them that are often included in most deals:

1. An event of default based upon a default in the payment of any principal, when due and payable of any secured note (or, in the case of a default in payment resulting solely from an administrative error or omission by the trustee, the administrator, any note-paying agent, or the note registrar, such default continues for a period of five business days).
2. An event of default based upon the failure on any payment date to disburse amounts available in accordance with the payment waterfall and a continuation of such failure for five business days (or, in the case of a default in payment resulting solely from an administrative error or omission by the trustee, the administrator, any note-paying agent or the note registrar, such default continues for a period of five business days).
3. An event of default based upon a default in the performance, or breach, of any other covenant (it being understood that noncompliance with any of the coverage tests, the collateral concentration limitations, or the collateral quality tests will not constitute a default or breach) or of any representation or warranty of the issuer under the indenture or if any certificate or writing delivered pursuant hereto proves to be incorrect when made, which default or breach has a material adverse effect on the secured noteholders and continues for a period of 30 days (or, in the case of a default, breach or failure of a representation or warranty regarding the collateral, 15 days) of the earlier of knowledge by the issuer or the collateral manager or notice to the issuer and the collateral manager by the trustee or to the issuer and the collateral manager by the holders of at least 25%, of the then-aggregate-outstanding amount of the secured notes of any class, specifying such default, breach, or failure and requiring it to be remedied and stating that such notice is a "Notice of Default" under this indenture.

Remedies Available Under the Indenture

CDOs are purposely designed to protect investors in multiple ways: through structure, through credit enhancement, through collateral tests, through interest coverage tests, through overcollateralization tests, and through clawback mechanisms. When breaches become more serious, they may give rise to a cause for removal of the collateral manager. Only in extreme circumstances can the remedies that become available upon the occurrence of an event of default be invoked. When errors in calculating amounts owed to noteholders are made in payment reports and payments are then made in error, the appropriate remedies involve correcting any misclassifications, recreating the cash flows as they should have been had no mistakes been made, clawing back any misallocated funds pursuant to the indenture, and redistributing funds according to the corrected allocations. Acceleration and collateral liquidation based on an event of default—which effectively is the "nuclear option," since it essentially involves blowing up the entire CDO with no ability to return to the status quo prior—are not available as remedies for such types of breaches and would be unacceptable to most participants in the CDO market except in the most extreme situations, as it would essentially grant senior noteholders the right to exercise the nuclear option at potentially great losses to the junior noteholders any time there was an error, no matter how immaterial. Most indentures used in the CDO market lay out a series of remedies that are consistent with respect to ordinary course errors. Accordingly, most indentures require a correction of errors, a clawback of any funds distributed incorrectly, and payment of the monies it should have received; indentures typically try to avoid direct acceleration and liquidation of the collateral debt securities.

Removal of Collateral Manager

The *collateral management agreement* for most CDOs says that the agreement may be terminated and the collateral manager may be removed at the direction of the controlling class under any of the following events or circumstances:

> *The Collateral Manager breaches in any material respect any provision (including, without limitation, any breach of any material representation or warranty) of this Agreement or any terms of the Indenture applicable to it, which breach has a material adverse effect on the Issuer or the Holders of any Class of Notes and is not cured within 30 days after the earlier of (a) the date on which any professional employee of the Collateral Manager directly involved in the performance by the Collateral Manager of its duties hereunder has actual knowledge of it and (b) the Collateral Manager's receipt from the Issuer or the Trustee of notice of such breach; or in the case of a breach that is not capable of being cured within 30 days, the breach is not cured within the period in which a reasonably diligent person could cure such violation or breach (but in no event more than 120 days).*

The language here is similar to the language in most CDO indentures, except for the fact that it permits removal if the breach is material with respect to the "holders of *any* class of notes" as opposed to all secured noteholders. If I were an investor in the controlling class and I believed that the collateral manager made material errors that significantly harmed me, then I would certainly seek to replace the collateral manager before even considering the "nuclear option." Moreover, if I were an investor anywhere else in the structure, I would want the controlling class and the trustee to remove and replace the collateral manager.

CDOs are among the most complex securities in the fixed-income market. This chapter should have demystified the critical aspects of CDOs, including the structure, collateral, market participants, pricing, and trading of CDOs. This chapter also explained why parties are motivated to issue CDOs, what potential events of default are, and how the CDO indenture provides remedies to protect investors.

CHAPTER 22

Structured Investment Vehicles (SIVs)

Daniel I. Castro, Jr.

INTRODUCTION TO SIVS

This chapter, in general, describes how typical SIVs are structured and how they operate. It should be kept in mind, however, that every SIV is unique and there can be significant variation in the specifics of each investment vehicle. The first SIV, Alpha Finance, was established in 1988 by Citibank. At their peak in mid-2007, Moody's said there was almost $400 billion outstanding and they were rating 36 SIVs.[1] According to a Bank of America presentation, the $400 billion of assets was funded via CP ($130 billion), MTNs ($235 million), and capital ($35 billion).[2]

The liquidity crisis that began in the summer of 2007 impacted subprime residential mortgage-backed securities (RMBSs) initially and then spread to collateralized debt obligations (CDOs), asset-backed commercial paper (ABCP), and SIVs, followed by several other market segments. In late 2007, SIV asset portfolios deteriorated to the point where the major ratings agencies downgraded the commercial paper and medium-term notes of several SIVs. The first four SIVs to fail all had material concentrations of subprime MBS and/or mortgage-related CDOs. These failed SIVs were Cheyne Finance, Rhinebridge, Golden Key, and Mainsail II—each of these SIVs was forced to liquidate or restructure in 2007.[3] Falling asset values and a loss of liquidity caused the collapse of the SIV market in 2008. Sigma Finance, a $27 billion SIV managed by London-based Gordian Knot, was the last SIV to shut down in October 2008.[4]

An SIV is a *bankruptcy-remote special-purpose vehicle* (SPV) that issues to investors debt securities that are secured by the assets purchased by the SIV. SIVs have been typically

---

[1]Henry Tabe, "SIVs: An Oasis of Calm in the Sub-prime Maelstrom: Structured Investment Vehicles, International Structured Finance: Special Report," Moody's Investors Service, July 20, 2007, p. 1.

[2]Bank of America, "SIVs—Past, Present and Future," June 2008, p. 4.

[3]The Financial Crisis Inquiry Commission, "Financial Crisis Inquiry Report," January 2011, p. 253.

[4]"Sigma Collapse Marks End of SIV Era," *Financial Times*, October 1, 2008.

established under either U.S. or U.K. law, and domiciled in tax havens such as Jersey or the Cayman Islands. SIVs that issued debt securities in the United States typically set up subsidiaries in Delaware. An SIV is a type of ABCP conduit. An SIV issues short-term commercial paper and medium-term notes (MTNs) to fund the purchase of longer-term assets held in the SPV. SIVs are designed to be perpetual, open-ended, self-contained investment vehicles. An SIV is a levered financing vehicle designed to earn the spread between its long-term assets and its short-term liabilities.

SIVs try to operate in a market-neutral environment by hedging interest rate and currency risk. Essentially, SIVs are relatively complex finance/operating companies, and they require substantial investments in technology, operational logistics, and staffing. SIVs need strong analytical, hedging, and modeling capabilities. In addition to initial operating expenses, issuers face substantial legal costs. As a result, it is generally recommended that an SIV grow to at least $2 billion in order to cover typical startup costs of $5–$10 million.[5] It should be noted that based on the numbers cited in the first paragraph of this chapter, SIVs' average asset balances at the market's peak in mid-2007 were over $11 billion.

Sponsor/Investment Manager

The investment manager of the SIV is also referred to as the *sponsor*. The sponsor of an SIV is typically a bank or an investment company. The primary responsibilities of the investment manager include managing the assets (investment and reinvestment), the liabilities, credit and liquidity risk, and hedging interest rate risk and currency exposure. The investment manager gets paid a fee for its services. In addition to being the investment manager, the sponsor usually performs the roles of risk manager, treasurer, operations manager, counterparty, and legal counsel. Sometimes the sponsor also plays the role of capital raiser and liquidity provider.

Given the startup costs of an SIV, the sponsor has strong incentives to perform well so that it recovers its initial investment. In addition, the high fixed costs of running an SIV mean that poor performance could jeopardize the sponsor covering its operating costs and potentially reduce its fee income. Since most sponsors have multiple ABCP programs, poor performance on an SIV may impact the sponsor's reputational risk and how their other programs are perceived.

SIV STRUCTURE

Most SIVs issue short-term commercial paper and medium-term notes to fund the purchase of longer-term assets held in the SPV. SIVs' general business model is to capture the spread between its underlying assets (average life of roughly 3 to 5 years) and its liabilities (average life ranging roughly from 6 months to 1 year).

---

[5]Daniel Castro, Theresa O'Neill, and Joshua Anderson, "Structured Investment Vehicles (SIV)," Merrill Lynch ABS Product Analysis, March 6, 2002, p. 4.

Traditional multi-seller ABCP programs operate from a bankruptcy-remote conduit that purchases assets (loans and receivables) from multiple companies. Financial institutions, such as banks, are typically the sponsor of these programs and also provide the conduit with a committed liquidity line. Some sponsors also provide credit enhancement through a letter of credit that absorbs credit losses. A primary difference between ABCP programs and SIVs is that SIVs do not have committed lines from their sponsor banks backstopping liquidity of all their short-term liabilities. Most SIVs had committed liquidity lines, but those lines only provided partial coverage (often in the range of 10%) of their maturing commercial paper. Instead, SIVs rely on a dynamic liquidity management process that utilizes liquidation of assets to pay investors if necessary.

In addition to being bankruptcy remote, SIVs are also insolvency remote. This means that investors in SIVs only have limited recourse to the SIV upon the borrower's (the SIV) insolvency—the creditor (investor) only has recourse to the net proceeds of the assets supporting the SIV.

As mentioned earlier, ABCP programs typically have liquidity and credit enhancement provided by their sponsors, which in turn ties their ratings to their sponsors. SIVs, on the other hand, are backed primarily by highly rated securities, and credit enhancement is provided by subordination in the form of *capital notes*. The amount of credit enhancement required is determined by the ratings and composition of the underlying collateral (assets). Since the asset portfolio is dynamic, meaning that its composition can change over time, the required credit enhancement is also dynamic. A portion of the capital notes may or may not be held by the sponsor. The balance, sometimes all, of the capital notes are sold to third-party investors.

SIV Assets

SIVs invest in high-quality, highly rated assets (primarily Aaa/AAA) that have good liquidity, such as bank and insurance company debt and senior classes of structured finance securities, including credit card ABSs, auto loan ABSs, student loan ABSs, home equity loan ABSs, RMBSs, and CDOs. Standard & Poor's data shows that historically over 80% of SIV assets were rated AAA or AA.[6] Credit default swaps (CDSs) of MBSs and ABSs (synthetic MBSs and ABSs) are also among SIV assets. Although sponsors can buy and sell assets within their operating guidelines, most assets are typically held to maturity. Moody's data shows that SIV assets peaked at roughly $400 billion in July 2007 and that just four months later, SIV assets had fallen by $100 billion to just $300 billion outstanding.[7]

In similar fashion to CDOs' eligibility criteria, SIVs have operating guidelines that, among other things, govern investment activity and concentration limits to asset types, issuer jurisdictions (United States, Europe), cash securities, synthetic securities, rating

---

[6] "SIV Outlook 2007: Another Bumper Year Ahead for SIVs After Assets Approach $300 billion in 2006," Standard and Poor's, February 26, 2007.
[7] "Moody's Update on Structured Investment Vehicles, International Structured Finance: Europe, Middle East, Africa: Special Report," Moody's Investors Service, January 16, 2008.

categories, issuers, and individual investments. Most SIVs provide weekly reports to the ratings agencies to show that the vehicles maintain adequate capitalization. Most SIV managers mark-to-market their asset portfolio value daily in similar fashion to repo collateral in the repurchase financing market.

SIV Liabilities

SIV liabilities typically are a combination of ABCP and medium-term notes (MTNs) issued in both the United States and Europe. Multi-seller ABCP conduits are able to concentrate their ABCP's maturities to three months or less due to their committed liquidity lines. SIVs do not have that luxury, so generally they spread the ABCP maturities across the money market spectrum in order to reduce liquidity risk. MTNs typically have maturities out to three years and their coupons can be either fixed rate or floating rate. In general, SIV liabilities have weighted average maturities ranging anywhere from 6 months to just over a year.

Capital Notes

Equity capital is provided in the form of junior notes called *capital notes* that range in maturity from one to five years and typically average between three and four years. Capital notes, in combination with "residual spread,"[8] provide credit enhancement to the SIV since they are in the first loss position after the "excess servicing" or residual spread. The combination of ABCP, MTNs, and subordinated capital helps broaden the SIV investor base by providing a wide menu of investment options attractive to disparate pockets of investors.

The ratings agencies determine the size of the capital notes based on the composition and quality of the assets, and the maturities of both assets and liabilities versus the potential for credit losses and mark-to-market losses. Since neither the assets nor the liabilities of an SIV are static, the determination of the amount of capital required is dynamic. Historically, two primary methods have been used to determine capital requirements. The first method is a matrix approach, based upon the assets' ratings. Higher-rated assets require less capital and lower-rated assets require more capital. The second method is a model-based approach based on various assumptions and inputs, which include, among others, rating transitions, default probabilities, asset correlation, and asset composition. Regardless of the method used to determine the amount of capital required, the result was that SIVs were highly leveraged. According to Moody's, the ratio of the book value of assets to equity ranged from 2.5 to 28.3 times for all SIVs; the average was 13.6 times.[9]

---

[8]Residual spread, often called "excess servicing," is the difference between the interest generated by the assets less interest paid on liabilities and fees.

[9]"Moody's Special Report: Moody's Update on Structured Investment Vehicles," January 16, 2008, p. 13.

Many capital notes have an annual option allowing the final maturity to be extended. In addition, most capital notes with longer maturities have a "put feature" that can be exercised after five years. The put feature is subject to the condition that it can only be exercised if it does not adversely impact the senior debt ratings of the SIV. When the SIV market was first established, capital notes were unrated private placements; as the market evolved many SIVs sought private ratings for their capital notes to improve marketability and liquidity.

Liquidity

Liquidity is absolutely critical to SIVs' viability as an investment vehicle and must be maintained at all times. Maturing debt must be refinanced and rolled over, meaning that when commercial paper and MTNs mature, new CP and notes must be issued to pay off the maturing securities. If the amount of debt that can be refinanced is exceeded by the amount of maturing liabilities, an SIV must be able to borrow against its liquidity facilities.

In addition to committed bank lines, SIVs maintain additional liquidity by holding certain amounts of assets that are generally referred to as *liquidity-eligible assets*. These liquidity-eligible assets are highly rated securities that meet specific issuer, diversification, and maturity requirements. These securities are considered to be easily salable (liquid), and for market-value purposes, they are given a small haircut (about 2%) to estimate conservatively the value they would provide if sold quickly (fire-sale pricing).

In order to operate in a market-neutral environment, SIVs hedge interest rate risk and currency/foreign exchange risk via swaps with highly rated counterparties. SIV operating guidelines have provisions for rating requirements of counterparties and remedies for ratings downgrades. Both liquidity providers and swap counterparties are generally required to have the highest ratings of A-1+/P-1/F-1+ from S&P, Moody's, and Fitch, respectively. Operating guidelines also usually specify exposure limits for various counterparty risks.

Figure 22.1 shows a generic SIV structure. The SIV manager is responsible for managing the assets, liabilities, capital, investment risks, and liquidity among other things. In order to hedge interest rate and foreign exchange risks, the SIV manager will engage in interest rate and currency swaps with various counterparties. The SIV manager also maintains relationships with multiple highly rated liquidity providers. If an SIV has problems and an enforcement event occurs, a *security trustee* is appointed to oversee the operations of the SIV (further discussion follows).

All SIVs issue CP, MTNs, and capital notes. Within each of those security classifications, an SIV can choose many variations. CP is typically issued with maturities anywhere from three to nine months. CP usually ranges from 30% to 35% of the total structure, but could be higher or lower. MTNs are usually rated Aaa/AAA, but mezzanine and junior MTNs may also be issued with ratings anywhere from Aa/AA to Baa/BBB. MTNs are typically 55% to 60% of the structure, but could be higher or lower. Capital notes are usually 7–10% of the structure, but could be higher or lower.

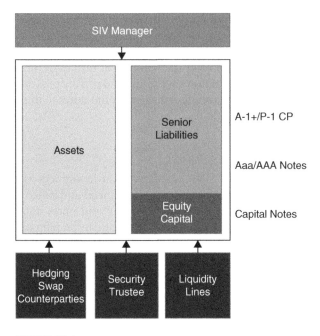

FIGURE 22.1 SIV structure

STRUCTURAL PROTECTIONS

Another similarity SIVs have with CDOs is the presence of various tests and triggers. These structural mechanisms are designed to reduce or mitigate various risks. SIVs must pass various operating tests in order to maintain normal operations. Different SIVs have different tests; there may be tests for ratings downgrades, net asset values, liquidity, capital losses, interest rates, and foreign exchange rates, among other things. The failure to pass one or more tests may trigger various restrictions on the SIV's operations and it may cause the cash-flow waterfall to be redirected. Depending on the test that is failed and the magnitude of the failure, the limitations on the SIV's operations may be modest or more significant. Typically, in situations where there is a breach of asset ratings or quality composition, capital requirements are increased.

SIVs generally operate in four specific operating modes:

1. *Normal operating mode.* The SIV may increase funding and purchase additional assets. The SIV manager has discretion, within its operating guidelines, over what investments it makes and debt it issues. Most SIVs have asset valuation and liquidity tests designed to limit its risk exposure. If these tests are not satisfied, the test failure may result in a change of operating mode for the SIV.

2. *Restricted investment operating mode.* This might occur in a weakening market where asset valuations are decreasing and capital is reduced. Some SIVs have triggers that can initiate de-levering before a more serious defeasance trigger is violated. The SIV may not add any additional funding, although it can refinance. Some SIVs successfully refinanced their liabilities in the repo markets while in restricted operating mode by selling assets to third parties via a repurchase agreement.[10] The SIV can use the repo proceeds to repay maturing debt and effectively shift the leverage from ABCP and MTN investors to the repo counterparties. The SIV may not invest in any new assets. SIVs may also be restricted from increasing the overall risk profile of the asset portfolio.

3. *Restricted funding or defeasance mode.* A *defeasance event* might be triggered by a rating downgrade or a drop in net asset value. A defeasance is a process through which an SIV becomes less levered. A defeasance event causes the suspension of cash flow or dividends to the capital note holder. At the same time, assets may be sold in a partial unwind and/or new liabilities may not be issued. These actions will decrease leverage, with the goal of ensuring the required amount of capital is available and the liabilities, if downgraded, regain their original ratings. Defeasance is specifically designed to reduce the SIV's risks and allow it to keep operating. If defeasance is not successful, more serious tests, such as a *capital loss limit test,* may be violated and result in an enforcement event.

4. *Enforcement or liquidation mode.* When an SIV goes into enforcement mode, the investment manager is relieved of its duties and a security trustee is appointed to run the SIV and liquidate its collateral. The SIV has to draw on liquidity in order to redeem liabilities. An enforcement event is far more severe than a defeasance— it requires an irreversible unwinding of the entire asset portfolio. Enforcement events are designed to protect ABCP and MTN investors. An SIV enforcement event is analogous to an *amortization event* in credit card ABS, where, when triggered, investors are paid back as rapidly as possible. In the case of an SIV, an enforcement event causes a sale of the portfolio. Some SIVs have provisions that allow investors to vote on whether to liquidate the assets and/or the manner of the liquidation. While enforcement events on SIVs have varied over the years, some of the more common events are listed here. Some tests have a cure period, but most are automatic when triggered.

   a. Automatic events:

      i. Default in payment of principal or interest on ABCP or MTNs (excluding administrative error).
      ii. Bankruptcy or insolvency of the issuer.
      iii. SIV ratings fall below specified threshold.
      iv. Default of the SIV under one of its liquidity facilities that causes the commitment of the liquidity facility to be terminated.

---

[10]In a repurchase agreement (a repo), the selling party agrees to repurchase the asset at a later date, at a specified price.

   b. Events with a cure period (typically five days);
      i. *Interest rate limit test.* Test ensures the net worth of the SIV is minimally impacted by interest rate changes.
      ii. *FX risk limit test.* Test ensures net worth of the SIV is minimally impacted by foreign exchange rates.
      iii. *Liquidity requirement test.* Test ensures adequate liquidity.

Insolvency Event

An insolvency event is a different circumstance than an enforcement event. In an enforcement event, ABCP and MTN investors are expected to continue receiving interest and principal payments until the assets are liquidated. When an insolvency event occurs, ABCP and MTN investors may not receive interest or principal payments. Under an insolvency event, liquidation is typically conducted as rapidly as possible, in contrast to an enforcement event where liquidation is generally done in a more orderly manner.

This chapter provided a general overview of how typical SIVs are structured and how they operate. The market began in 1988, peaked 9 years later, and then collapsed after 20 years in 2008. The liquidity crisis coupled with falling asset values was too much for the SIV market to bear. The failure of the SIV market provided lessons about liquidity, structures, and investor protections that have been incorporated into other structured finance sectors. In the post–financial crisis world, investors in other structured finance sectors are better protected from the various risks that fixed-income securities are exposed to.

CHAPTER 23

Collateralized Loan Obligations (CLOs)

Demystifying a Versatile Asset Class

Mendel Starkman

WHAT IS A COLLATERALIZED LOAN OBLIGATION (CLO)?

CLOs are a type of investment fund. Similar to a mutual fund, a CLO is a professionally managed fund that invests in a pool of financial assets, specifically corporate loans. Unlike a mutual fund, however, a CLO is a structured fund. Instead of each investor owning a share with the same risk and return as all other investors, the CLO offers various investment tiers, each with a different risk-and-return profile. This chapter discusses the characteristics of a CLO, including its structure, underlying loan pool, and collateral manager.

At its core, the fundamental purpose of a CLO is to provide an efficient source of financing to below-investment-grade corporate borrowers. Corporations require funding for various purposes, including general business and growth opportunities, capital planning, or to finance acquisition activity. CLOs provide a meaningful source of funds from which these companies can borrow.

On the other side of the equation are institutional investors, who find that CLO tranches provide an attractive return for their level of risk. Investors may not be willing or able to lend directly to speculative-grade companies. Instead, a CLO provides investors with a professionally managed, well-diversified pool of such loans, with the added protection of loss shock absorbers that are inherent to the CLO structure.

The CLO market connects the equation. Investors who have available funds are able to provide them to the CLO, which in turn lends them to companies that want to borrow. The innovation of CLO technology enables such an interaction, opening a sizeable source of funds to borrowers while crafting a risk-and-return profile that is attractive to investors.

CLOs have a relatively long and impressive track record. The CLO market began to emerge in the late 1990s and early 2000s. Issuance picked up significantly from 2005 through 2007, paused for several years during and after the financial crisis, and then roared back to life in 2012. Moody's Investors Service calculated that only 0.8% of the CLO tranches that they have rated since 1996 have incurred (or were expected to

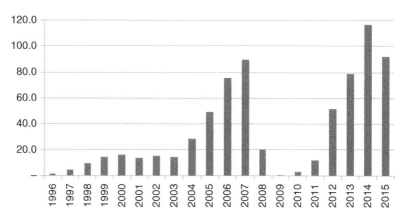

FIGURE 23.1   Annual issuance of U.S. broadly syndicated loan CLOs, 1996–2015
Source: Wells Fargo

incur) principal losses.[1] While certain improvements have been made to CLOs due to lessons learned during the crisis, their resilient performance through market cycles provides meaningful perspective for potential future performance (Figure 23.1).

It should be noted that CLOs come in several different flavors. This chapter focuses on U.S. *cash flow* CLOs that are backed by broadly syndicated leveraged loans (these transactions are also referred to as *arbitrage CLOs*). However, the concepts described still broadly apply to other types of CLOs, which include:

- *Balance sheet CLOs*—CLOs constructed as a means for a financial institution to transfer an existing loan portfolio into a new off-balance-sheet entity.
- *European CLOs*—CLOs managed by European collateral managers and primarily backed by loans to European companies.
- *Middle-market CLOs*—CLOs backed by loans to smaller companies (the European equivalent of a middle-market CLO is referred to as a *small- and medium-enterprise (SME) CLO*).

STRUCTURES AND STRUDELS: AN INTRODUCTION TO STRUCTURED FINANCE

CLOs are card-carrying members of the structured finance family. But before examining the specific characteristics of CLOs, it is worth beginning with a brief introduction to structured finance in general (which we will slant toward an application to CLOs). To explain the basic concept of structured credit, one can pay a visit to their local bakery shop.

---

[1] "CLO Interest: Losses to Remain Infrequent on U.S. Cash Flow CLO Tranches," Moody's Investors Service, September 24, 2014.

A typical investment fund, such as a mutual fund, can be thought of as a pie. Each investor owns a slice of the pie proportional to his investment. For example, let's say a fund had a total value of $100, and five investors each invested $20 into the fund. Each of the five investors in this example owns a proportionate 20% slice of the fund. Should the fund experience losses, the entire pie would shrink, and all investors would sustain a loss proportional to their investment. In our example, if the fund value declined by $20, and now had a remaining value of only $80, any one of the investors would still own a 20% slice of the fund. But since the value of the entire fund has decreased, an original investment of $20 would now be worth only $16. Each investor sustained an equivalent proportional loss in their investment.

Continuing with the analogy, structured finance can be thought of as a layer cake, in which each investor owns a different horizontal layer of the cake. For example, imagine that a cake had five layers, in which each layer represented 20% of the height of the cake. If someone were to take a knife and slice off the entire bottom-most layer of the cake, 80% of the cake would remain perfectly intact. However, now it would be a four-layer cake instead of a five-layer cake.

This analogy illustrates the broad concept behind structured finance. Similar to the layers in the cake, imagine an investment fund that is worth $100, but in which five investors each invested $20 into different, equally sized layers of the fund. If the fund were to sustain $20 of losses, it would be comparable to the bottom-most layer being sliced off the cake. The investor in the bottom-most layer of the fund would absorb the full $20 of loss, thereby wiping out his entire investment. In contrast, the four other investors would not sustain any losses at all. (See Figure 23.2.)

The key difference is that the pie-like nature of typical investment funds attributes losses *proportionately*, while the layer-cake-like nature of structured finance attributes losses *sequentially*. Specifically, losses in structured finance are allocated from the bottom up, otherwise referred to as being in *reverse-sequential order*.

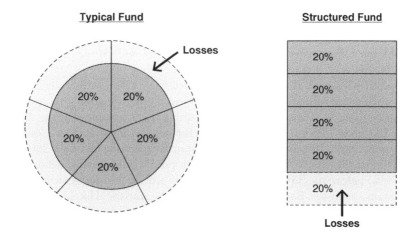

FIGURE 23.2 Illustration of investment fund ownership and loss allocation

Why, then, would anyone want to invest in the bottom-most layer of a structured fund? Wouldn't everyone want to invest in a higher layer and have the protective buffer that the lower layers provide against losses?

The answer relates to the classic balance of risk and reward. Clearly, the lowest layer of a structured fund is the most risky, because it is the first to absorb any losses. But correspondingly, it is also designed to yield the most. On the opposite extreme, the highest layer of the fund is the least risky, because it does not absorb any losses until the value of all of the other layers has been exhausted. It is therefore correspondingly designed to yield the least. The layers in between, with varying degrees of risk, are issued with yields that are appropriate for their respective levels of risk.

In an actual structured finance transaction, each investment layer is referred to as a *tranche* (based on an Old French word meaning "slice"). The existence of junior tranches provides a greater buffer to protect the senior tranches from loss. Another way of saying this is that the more senior the tranche, the greater the *subordination* that exists beneath it to protect against losses. The junior-most tranche has no subordination (i.e., no tranches exist beneath it to buffer from losses) while each more-senior tranche is protected by progressively greater amounts of subordination.

BON APPETIT: REENGINEERING FOR RISK APPETITE

One aspect of structured finance that is often misunderstood is how a structure can include tranches that are rated investment grade (including a large proportion with the highest possible rating of AAA), when in the case of a CLO all of the assets that act as collateral are speculative-grade loans. Don't the ratings of the tranches need to more closely reflect the risk of the asset pool that supports them?

The answer relates to a fundamental difference between the risk of the loans and the tranches. The ratings of the loans in the pool consider the risk, as measured by probability of loss of each individual corporate loan. Because the loans are speculative-grade credits, the probability of loss for any given loan is relatively high. Recall, however, that the tranches have an added buffer to protect against losses, due to the subordination of more junior tranches. Consequently, a tranche's risk is not whether there will be *any* losses in the loan pool, but rather, whether losses on the loan pool will exceed the tranche's *entire* loss buffer. In this way, a tranche's risk largely becomes a matter of statistics. What is the likelihood that losses in the pool, net of any recovery value, will erode all of a given tranche's available subordination and result in a loss to the tranche?

This can be illustrated with a simplified example. Let's assume that the senior-most tranche of a CLO has 35% subordination. Let's further assume that after a loan defaults, it recovers, on average, 50 cents on the dollar. In order to erode all of the subordination to the senior-most tranche, 70% of the entire loan pool would need to default (and then recover at 50%) before the 35% of subordination is eroded and the senior-most tranche begins to sustain any losses. Based on historical data, the statistical likelihood that 70% of a diversified corporate loan pool will default is very remote, indicating that an investment in this senior tranche is expected to be much less risky than a direct investment in the underlying loan pool.

Due to the alchemy of financial engineering, the structure is able to issue tranches whose risk is significantly lower than the risk of the collateral pool itself. In essence, it is possible to issue tranches that have AAA-grade risk, even though they are backed by a pool of single-B-rated loans, because there is a very low probability that the losses on those loans will exceed all of the tranche's available subordination. For this reason, the tranches are able to achieve credit ratings that can be meaningfully higher than the credit ratings of the underlying loans.

CHASING WATERFALLS

Until now, our focus has been on the inherent seniority order of a structured credit product, and the protection afforded to each tranche through the subordination of more-junior tranches. Underlying the structure, however, is a portfolio of assets that serve as collateral. Structured products are each collateralized by a single type of asset class, but that asset class differs based on the type of securitization. Structured finance collateral pools can range from residential or commercial mortgages, to credit card receivables, auto loans, or student loans, to other more esoteric forms of loans (for example, aircraft leases or railcar receivables). For CLOs, the pool generally consists of loans to relatively large companies, with a single CLO typically investing in loans issued by 100 to 300 different obligors. Some examples of household names that have had loans represented in CLO pools include: American Airlines, Chrysler, Dell Computers, Hilton Hotels, MGM Resorts, PetSmart, and Sea World.

With any fixed-income product, the lender (or investor) receives payments of interest on a regular basis, and payments of principal that are based either on a preset payment schedule or on the instrument's maturity date (similar to a mortgage or a student loan). CLOs are no different. They invest in a pool of loans, and thereby play the role of lender to a range of corporate borrowers. In turn, these corporate obligors make periodic payments of interest and principal back to the CLO.

A CLO's payment structure follows a sequential tranche system, but as opposed to loss allocation (which is implemented from the bottom up), payments follow a top-down sequential order. The senior-most tranche receives payments first, followed by the second-priority tranche, and so on. If on any payment date, available funds are insufficient to pay all of the tranches, it is the junior-most tranche that is left holding the bag. This sequential prioritization of the tranche payments is referred to as the payment *waterfall*.

The CLO maintains a ledger that separately tracks interest and principal receipts. Interest payments received from the loan pool are used for the CLO's *interest waterfall* to sequentially pay the periodic interest due to each of the tranches. Principal payments received are used for the CLO's *principal waterfall* to sequentially repay the principal balance of each of the tranches (Figure 23.3). In normal operation, principal and interest waterfalls are almost always kept separate. (However, there can be circumstances, particularly in times of distress, when interest proceeds would be used to cover shortfalls in principal payments, or vice versa.)

Priority	Payable to:	Amount
	Available Interest Proceeds:	5,783,840.36
(A)	to the payment of accrued and unpaid taxes and governmental fees:	—
(B)	to the payment of accrued and unpaid Administrative Expenses:	—
(B)(i)(a)	to the Bank under each of the transaction documents:	21,097.93
(B)(i)(b)	to the payment of any Petition Expenses	—
(B)(i)(c)	to Moody's and S&P for fees and expenses in connection with any rating of Rated Notes pro rata:	—
(B)(i)(d)	to the payment of all other Administrative Expenses as directed by the Collateral Manager on their respective amounts:	50,893.00
(B)(ii)	upon discretion of Collateral Manager, deposit to the Expense Reserve Account lesser of: OERS or OEEA:	—
(C)	to the payment of any accrued and unpaid, current and prior, Senior Collateral Management Fee:	191,799.34
(D)	to the payment of any Interest Rate Hedges, including any termination payments to a Hedge Counterparty:	—
(E)(i)	to the payment of accrued and unpaid interest on the Class A-1a Senior Notes inc. Defaulted interest, pro rata:	1,578,740.80
(E)(ii)	to the payment of accrued and unpaid Interest on the Class A-1b Senior Notes inc. Defaulted interest, pro rata:	195,000.00
(F)	to the payment of accrued and unpaid interest on the Class A-2 Senior Notes, inc. Defaulted Interest:	465,451.35
(G)	if either Senior Coverage Test is not satisfied	—
(G)(i)	to the payment of principal of the Class A-1a Notes (pro rata):	—
(G)(ii)	to the payment of principal of the Class A-1b Notes (pro rata):	—
(G)(iii)	to the payment of principal of the Class A-2b Notes:	—
(H)(i)	to the payment of acrrued interest on the Class B Mezzanine Notes . . . :	370,771.66
(H)(ii)	and inc. Defaulted Interest . . . :	—
(H)(iii)	and Interest on Deferred Interest:	—
(I)	in the event that any Class B Coverage Test is not satisfied:	—
(I)(i)	to the payment of principal of the Class A-1a Notes (pro rata):	—
(I)(ii)	to the payment of principal of the Class A-1b Notes (pro rata):	—
(I)(iii)	to the payment of principal of the Class A-2b Notes:	—
(I)(iv)	to the payment of principal of the Class B Mezzanine Notes:	—
(J)	to the payment of any Class B Mezzanine Deferred Interest:	—
(K)(i)	to the payment of acrrued interest on the Class C Mezzanine Notes . . . :	284,506.95

FIGURE 23.3 Interest waterfall excerpt from sample CLO payment date report
Source: U.S. Bank

THE CAPITAL STRUCTURE: THE INTERSECTION OF STRUCTURED AND CORPORATE FINANCE

Earlier, we illustrated the concept of subordination thorough the example of a layer cake with equally sized horizontal slices. In fact, the tranches of a structured fund are not equally sized. The senior-most tranche is by far the thickest. In a modern CLO, it can comprise 60–65% of the total structure (meaning that 35–40% of subordination is provided the combined value of all the more junior tranches). Each of a CLO's other tranches typically represent 5–10% of the structure. Altogether, CLO structure will often have a total of 6 or 7 tranches.[2]

The tranches of a CLO are typically structured so that each one is designated with a different rating category by the major credit rating agencies. The rating for the senior-most tranche is AAA, followed by the second-priority tranche at AA, and so on. At the lower-end of the capital structure, the rated tranches typically dip into below-investment-grade territory, with ratings as low as double-B, or even single-B. The junior-most tranche, however, is known as the *equity tranche* and is left unrated.

CLO tranches are generally issued as floating-rate notes, with the stated coupon rate being represented as a spread over three-month LIBOR. The first-priority tranche, being the least risky, earns the lowest spread over LIBOR. (Because the senior-most tranche is the thickest tranche, it also has the greatest influence on the CLO's overall interest costs.) Each lower-ranking tranche is progressively more risky and therefore earns a somewhat higher stated spread over LIBOR.

The only exception is the junior-most tranche, which does not have a stated payment rate. Rather, the junior-most tranche represents the equity of the CLO's capital structure and it earns the *residual* interest and principal proceeds that remain after all other tranches have received their payments. (Another term used to describe the residual cash flow is *excess spread*, which refers to the excess proceeds available within the CLO after all payments due to the more senior tranches.)

In a way, a CLO structure resembles a corporate balance sheet, in which assets equal liabilities plus shareholder's equity (Table 23.1). The corporate loans held by a CLO are its assets while the interest-bearing tranches represent the debt and the junior-most tranche represents the equity. A company uses its revenues to service the periodic interest payments on its outstanding debt, and the remaining proceeds belong to the shareholders (either through retained earnings or dividends). In the same way, the proceeds received from the CLO's loan pool are its revenues, from which payments are made to the

---

[2]The subordination to a tranche is technically not provided by the value of the tranches that exist beneath it, but rather by the extent to which the CLO's *loan pool* exceeds the value of the tranche in question. While the loan pool's excess is roughly approximated by the value of the more subordinate tranches, the tranches themselves do not actually provide the buffer from losses. Therefore, for loss buffer considerations, it generally does not matter how many subordinate tranches, or the balance of those tranches, exist beneath a particular senior tranche.

For example, let's assume that a CLO's loan pool has a value of $500 million, and that the senior tranche of the CLO—the Class A notes—has a value of $325 million. The excess value that exists to support the Class A notes would be $175 million, which is the value of the loan pool that is in excess of the amount required to directly support the Class A notes ($500 million loan pool *minus* $325 million Class A balance *equals* $175 million of excess value). Put differently, the loan pool could lose $175 million of its value and still remain with an ending value (of $325 million) sufficient to fully repay the $325 million Class A notes. The subordination to the Class A notes would therefore be calculated as the excess loan value (i.e., the total pool value *minus* the tranche value), divided by the total pool value. In this example, this would result in Class A subordination of $175 million / $500 million, or 35%.

TABLE 23.1   Sample CLO Capital Structure

Galaxy XX CLO

Manager:	PineBridge Investments, LLC
Underwriter:	Goldman, Sachs & Co.
Trustee:	U.S. Bank National Association

Security	Principal Amount ($)	Original Subordination	Coupon	Initial Ratings	
				Moody's	Fitch
Class A Notes	352,000,000	36.0%	3mL + 1.45%	Aaa	AAA
Class B Notes	63,250,000	24.5%	3mL + 1.95%	Aa2	NR*
Class C Notes	33,000,000	18.5%	3mL + 2.60%	A2	NR*
Class D Notes	31,350,000	12.8%	3mL + 3.50%	Baa3	NR*
Class E Notes	26,950,000	7.9%	3mL + 5.50%	Ba3	NR*
Subordinated Notes (Equity)	48,950,000	N/A	Residual	NR*	NR*
Total Initial Pool Balance:	550,000,000				

Pricing Date:	5/19/15
Closing Date:	6/25/15
End of Non-Call Period:	7/20/17
End of Reinvestment Period:	7/20/19
Stated Maturity Date:	7/20/27

*NR indicates *not rated*.
Sources: Bloomberg, Intex

debt tranches, with any remaining residual cash flow generally distributed to the CLO's equity tranche.

BEING FRIENDLY: DEBT VERSUS EQUITY

Since the debt tranches of a CLO are only entitled to receive their stated interest rate (i.e., the tranche's spread over three-month LIBOR) and the ultimate return of their principal, there is no potential for upside in payments. If the CLO performs well, then the debtholder will earn the quarterly coupon payments to which they are entitled and ultimately receive back their principal balance. If a CLO underperforms, the debt investor would have downside risk in the form of lost interest or principal payments.

A CLO's equity tranche, on the other hand, is not paid a stated coupon, but rather earns all of the cash flow that remains after the debt tranches are paid. Therefore, while the equity tranche has the greatest risk of payment variability and downside, it also has the potential for meaningful upside.

This dichotomy of risk profiles between debt and equity creates an implicit divergence of interests within the CLO's investor base. For example, a skew toward loans that are more risky and higher yielding would be of greater benefit to the equity investors, while not directly benefitting the debtholders.

When analyzing a CLO's structure and the investment style of the CLO manager, certain aspects may be considered more "debt-friendly," as they would maximize the protection of the debt tranches at the possible expense of extra yield for the equity tranche. Other aspects may be considered more "equity-friendly," as they would involve some additional degree of risk in an effort to achieve a somewhat higher return. The role of a CLO manager includes a perspective of both elements, ensuring that the interests of all investors are appropriately balanced throughout the life of the transaction. An investor needs to access the potential sources of risk and opportunity in each CLO and ensure that the transaction meets the intended risk profile of their investment.

CLO COVERAGE TESTS: TAKE YOUR PIK

Another noteworthy aspect of a CLO structure relates to the ongoing measurement of *coverage tests*. These are ratios for each debt tranche that measure the extent to which it is supported by the loan collateral. There are two types of coverage tests:

The objective of an *overcollateralization test* (also referred to as an OC or *par coverage* test) is to ensure that sufficient collateral exists to repay the principal balance of the CLO tranches. (See Figure 23.4.) The test measures the par balance of the loan pool relative to the par balance of each debt tranche. A ratio result of less than 100% for a given tranche level means that the par balance of the loans does not fully support the par balance of that tranche.

The objective of an *interest coverage test* (also referred to as an IC test) is to ensure that sufficient interest cash flow exists to support the ongoing interest payments due to the CLO tranches. The test measures the interest expected to be received from the loan pool relative to the interest payments due to be paid on each debt tranche. A ratio result of less than 100% for a given tranche means that the interest payments to be received from the loans are insufficient to fully service the upcoming payments due to that tranche.

In order to ensure that the CLO's debt tranches are sufficiently supported by the loan pool, the OC and IC ratios are required to be maintained at or above certain predetermined levels. Failure to maintain these levels for a given tranche causes the temporary diversion of cash flows away from more junior tranches to prepay the senior-most debt tranche. This cash flow diversion continues until the failed test is brought back into compliance with the required predetermined level.

Mathematically, failing ratios can be brought back into compliance either by reducing the denominator or by increasing the numerator. In the case of a failing OC test, for example, the test can be cured either by paying down a portion of the debt tranches, which reduces the denominator, or by adding additional amounts of collateral, which increases the numerator.

In the event of a failed OC or IC test, the tranches that are junior to the tranche level with the failing test would not receive any current payments (as their interest payment

Step I: Initial Class E OC Test Result

The Class E OC Test (including all tranches through the Class E Notes), has cushion of 4.88% in the initial result

Ratio Calculation			Result	Required Ratio	Test Status	Test Cushion
$550.0 Loan Balance/ $352.00 Class A Notes +$63.25 Class B Notes +$33.00 Class C Notes +$31.35 Class D Notes +$26.95 Class E Notes	=	**$550.0 Loan Balance/** $506.55 Debt Tranches	108.58%	103.70%	**PASS**	4.88%

Step II: Assume the loan pool losses of $27.5 of par value

The ratio's numerator is reduced by $27.5 due to realized par losses (or as a result of OC Test "Haircuts")

Ratio Calculation			Result	Required Ratio	Test Status	Test Cushion
$522.5 Loan Balance/ $352.00 Class A Notes +$63.25 Class B Notes +$33.00 Class C Notes +$31.35 Class D Notes +$26.95 Class E Notes	=	**$522.5 Loan Balance/** $506.55 Debt Tranches	103.15%	103.70%	**FAIL**	−0.55%

Step III: Divert subordinate cash flow (as available) to bring the test back into compliance

$2.68 of subordinate cash flow prepays the Class A Notes, curing the OC Test by reducing the ratio's denominator

Ratio Calculation			Result	Required Ratio	Test Status	Test Cushion
$522.5 Loan Balance/ **$349.32 Class A Notes** +$63.25 Class B Notes +$33.00 Class C Notes +$31.35 Class D Notes +$26.95 Class E Notes	=	$522.5 Loan Balance/ **$503.87 Debt Tranches**	103.70%	103.70%	**PASS**	0.00%

FIGURE 23.4 Illustration of hypothetical OC test curing calculation

would instead be diverted to prepay the senior tranche). Rather, those tranches would *pay-in-kind* (PIK), which essentially provides them with an IOU. The outstanding balance of the non-paid tranche would be increased by the amount of the missed payment, and that amount would be due (to the extent available) on a later payment date.

The CLO's debt investors receive meaningful protection from the OC and IC tests, and the possible diversion of more-junior cash flows. It also acts as a somewhat self-curing mechanism in the event of a failed OC test, because it introduces funds from the CLO's interest waterfall to be used instead to support the transaction's principal waterfall.

It should be noted that many CLOs also have an additional overcollateralization test, often referred to as the *interest diversion test*. This test is typically calculated only at the junior-most debt tranche level, and acts as an early warning before any of the actual OC tests are breached. The failure of this test has two key differences within the CLO structure from a failed OC or IC test. First, instead of diverting all of the more-junior cash flows, this test typically only diverts half of them. Second, the diverted funds are used by the CLO to invest in extra loans, rather than to prepay the debt tranches.

THE LIFE AND TIMES OF A CLO

Chronologically, there are several important milestones in the lifecycle of a CLO (Figure 23.5).

First is the *marketing period*. In the weeks prior to the issuance of a new CLO, the manager and the CLO underwriter meet with prospective investors and discuss the transaction's intended structure, tranche spreads, documentation, and collateral composition. Investors provide their feedback, upon which the manager and the underwriter may choose to adjust the intended transaction to satisfy the investor requests and secure orders for the marketed tranches. Often, a loan *warehouse* is opened prior to the

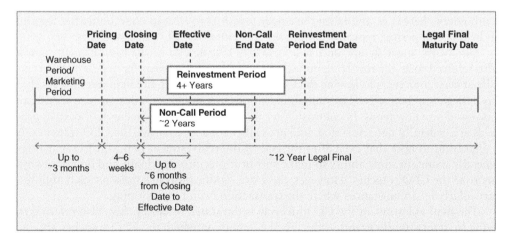

FIGURE 23.5 CLO lifecycle illustration

marketing period, and the CLO manager is provided with a budget to begin purchasing loans that will ultimately be included in the CLO's loan pool. The existence of a warehouse provides investors with a degree of certainty as to which specific corporate obligors will be included in the CLO, and at what price the manager is able to source the loans.

Next is the *pricing date*. On this day, coupon rates are set for each of the CLO tranches, and allocations are made to investors who placed orders for investment in the transaction. Depending upon the demand for particular tranches, investors may be filled on their entire order, or the CLO may be oversubscribed, causing investors to be allocated less than they had ordered.

Following the pricing date is the *closing date*, also referred to as the *issue date*. This is the day on which the CLO legally begins to exist and the CLO tranches are issued as securities. The CLO tranche trades that were allocated to investors on the pricing date all settle on the closing date. Investors provide funds and formally invest in the CLO tranches. In turn, the CLO uses the funds to purchase any loans that had been warehoused for the CLO prior to that point and continue investing in other loans.

The next key milestone for a CLO is its *effective date*, often up to six months or longer after the closing date. This period represents the time it takes for the CLO manager to fully select and acquire its complete initial loan pool. The entire period during which the manager purchases the pool is known as the *ramp-up period*, which begins when loans begin to be purchased into a warehouse (often during the marketing period), and continues until the effective date, when the loan pool is fully invested. Prior to becoming effective, the quality and characteristics of the CLO's loan pool must meet or exceed certain predetermined metrics and the expected ratings of each debt tranche must be confirmed by the relevant credit rating agencies.

Another important date in the lifecycle of a CLO is the end of the *non-call period*, the period during which the tranches are not subject to optional redemption, refinancing, or repricing. At times, the equity investors may benefit from redeeming the CLO or from amending the stated coupon of the CLO's debt tranches. To protect the interests of debtholders, there is no ability for the equity investors to elect to do so until after the end of the non-call period, typically about two-years after the CLO's closing date.

One of the most significant dates for a CLO is the end of the *reinvestment period* (also referred to as the revolving period). During the reinvestment period, which is typically at least four years following the CLO's closing date, the CLO manager ensures that any cash proceeds (received from loan maturities, prepayments, sales, or recoveries) are reinvested into new loans. In contrast, after the end of the reinvestment period, cash proceeds are generally not reinvested, and are rather used to amortize the CLO tranches. It is important to note that even after the end of the reinvestment period, CLO managers generally maintain some ability to make substitutions into new loans and do not always amortize the CLO tranches. However, there are significant restrictions on such abilities, particularly in circumstances where the transaction is underperforming.

The final milestone in the CLO lifecycle is the *stated maturity date*, also referred to as the *legal final maturity date,* which is the date upon which the CLO tranches are due to be repaid in full. This date typically occurs at least 12 years after the *closing date*. Due to the structure of a CLO, which begins to pay down the tranches after the end of the reinvestment period, most tranches of a CLO are no longer outstanding at the time of the stated maturity date. However, any remaining loans in the CLO pool would be sold at such time and the sale proceeds would be used to pay down any remaining outstanding debt tranches (with any residual value belonging to the equity). In order to prevent the CLO from being required to sell loans, and thereby subject to risk from the market value of the loans at such time, CLOs are generally restricted from investing in any loans that mature after the stated maturity date.

THE LOAN MARKET

With a background in the creation and structure of a CLO, we now turn our attention to the underlying collateral pool. While the CLO's structure regulates the risk, return, and payment timing of the tranches, it is ultimately the performance of the underlying loan collateral that drives the CLO.

The collateral pool of a CLO is comprised of loans to speculative-grade corporate borrowers. CLOs predominately invest in single-B rated loans (which are between four and six notches below investment grade), although CLO pools also often include some proportion of double-B and triple-C-rated loans. The loans are frequently referred to as *leveraged loans*, due to the fact that the issuing companies operate with a relatively large proportion of debt in their corporate capital structures. Companies often issue loans at the same time as they issue high-yield debt, and may use the entire new financing package to fund a leveraged buyout (LBO) or for other purposes.

Loans are issued by a diverse range of obligors, incorporating virtually every industry sector and domestic geographic location. Most loans are floating-rate instruments, which accrue on a quarterly basis and pay a stated rate (also referred to as a *spread* or *margin*) over three-month LIBOR.

With limited exception, CLOs generally make investments in a company's *senior-secured, first-lien loans*. This means that in the event of a default, the lenders (in this case, the CLO, which acts as a lender) have a senior claim to the assets of the company and should therefore expect a higher recovery value as compared to the recovery prospects of the company's more subordinate, second-lien loans or unsecured debt. Recovery prospects may be based on the liquidation value of the company's hard assets or on its enterprise value as it continues operations.

The size of the loan market has grown significantly over time as loans have gradually grown in acceptance as a mainstream asset class. (See Figure 23.6.) Demand for loans is due in part to the fact that they are secured instruments with floating-rate coupons. This stands in contrast to other corporate debt instruments that are often unsecured or issued with fixed-rate coupons. Loan issuance picked up after the financial crisis, as the economic recovery spurred companies to issue additional loans to fund M&A activity or to optimize their corporate liability structures. In addition, there has been meaningful demand for loans from open-ended mutual and exchange-traded funds (ETFs) in addition to CLOs and privately managed accounts.

The loan market is sizeable and an active secondary market exists. Loan trading, however, is more operationally intensive, and trade settlement times tend to be longer than for corporate bonds or other non-loan securities.

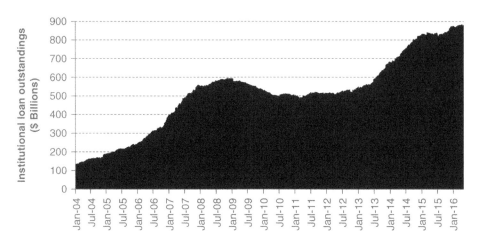

FIGURE 23.6 Institutional loan outstanding amount, 2004–2015 ($ billions)
Source: Thomson Reuters, S&P/LSTA Leveraged Loan Index

Historically, loan agreements have included positive or negative covenants to which the borrower is required to adhere, with breaches of such covenants generally constituting a default. There are two broad types of covenants. *Incurrence covenants* restrict the borrower from taking certain actions that could dilute the value, control, or protection of the existing debtholders. These may include limitation on the borrower assuming additional debt, paying dividends, or repurchasing shares. *Maintenance covenants* require the borrower to continually uphold a specified degree of healthy performance, such as maintaining earnings by at least a certain proportion above their debt expenses.

Over the past few years, fewer covenants have been included within loan agreements, resulting in the advent of loans that are so-called *covenant-lite* (or *cov-lite*). A primary risk of covenant-lite loans is the prospect for lower recovery values, as lenders would need to wait for the borrowing company to deteriorate to the point of missed debt payments rather than being able to react to the earlier occurrence of a breached maintenance covenant. The jury is still out on the fundamental prospects for covenant-lite loans. Empirical evidence suggests that covenant-lite loans have not historically experienced lower post-default recovery values.[3] However, historical data may not be predictive of future recovery prospects for cov-lite loans (Figure 23.7). There were relatively few historical observations of covenant-lite loan defaults, resulting in a limited dataset. In addition, the unique government policy intervention that existed during the previous recovery cycle may have influenced the historical observed recoveries while future recovery cycles may perform differently.

The growth of the loan market, and the rise of covenant-lite loans in particular, has attracted the attention of banking regulators. In 2013, U.S. banking regulators issued

---

[3]"Covenant-Lite Is Back, Along With Its Risks," Moody's Special Comment, January 17. 2012; "Covenant-Lite Issuance Casts a Cloud Over Future Default Levels," Standard & Poor's, July 14, 2014.

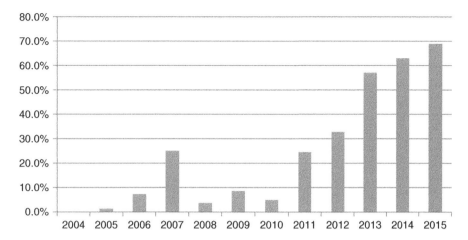

FIGURE 23.7 Percentage of annual primary first-lien loan issuance by covenant-lite loans, 2004–2015
Source: Wells Fargo, S&P LCD

guidance on leveraged lending practices, which defined certain expected characteristics for bank-originated leveraged loans. Essentially, underwriting banks are expected to issue prudent loans that are able to repay over time. While the specific balance of characteristics is generally left to the discretion of the underwriting bank, certain broad examples were provided. These included a maximum total leverage multiple (including total debt to EBITDA), and an expectation of the borrower's ability to repay the debt within a specified time horizon. The extent to which this guidance changes underwriting standards for future loan issuance has yet to be fully realized.

CLO REPORT CARDS: PERFORMANCE METRICS

How can an investor tell how a CLO is performing? Fortunately, CLO reporting is very transparent. Investors receive monthly trustee reports as well as quarterly payment date reports. These reports show the CLO's current tranche balances, the identity of all loans held in the pool, and various metrics that represent the quality of the loans. The reports also show the metrics relative to each of the required portfolio guidelines (which are technically referred to as the *concentration limitations*), as well as certain high-level averages that represent the quality of the underlying loan pool (which are technically referred to as the *collateral quality tests*). If one were to look at the summary page of a monthly trustee report, one would typically see the following data and metrics:

- Current tranche balances
- Current coverage test results (i.e., overcollateralization, interest diversion, and interest coverage tests)
- Collateral characteristics and limits (e.g., the percentage of loans that are second lien or covenant-lite, presently in default, or rated CCC+ or below)

In addition, the report contains several other key metrics, which fluctuate some-what each month based on the then-current composition, performance, and active-management of the underlying loan pool.

Several of the primary metrics that are reported in a CLO's trustee report are described in the following:

The *weighted average rating factor (WARF)* is a standard Moody's measure of the CLO pool's average credit quality. Each rating subcategory, from AAA to D, is given a numeric value (on a scale of 1 to 10,000).[4] The scale is applied to each individual loan in the pool, from which a weighted-average pool rating is calculated (Table 23.2). Typically,

TABLE 23.2 WARF: Moody's Default Probability Ratings versus Moody's Rating Factors

Moody's Default Probability Rating	Moody's Rating Factor
Aaa	1
Aa1	10
Aa2	20
Aa3	40
A1	70
A2	120
A3	180
Baa1	260
Baa2	360
Baa3	610
Ba1	940
Ba2	1350
Ba3	1766
B1	2220
B2	2720
B3	3490
Caa1	4770
Caa2	6500
Caa3	8070
Ca, C	10000

Source: Moody's Investors Service

[4]The weighted average rating factor (WARF) value is based upon the long-term cumulative default rate expected for positions within each rating category. For example, a WARF value of 2,720, which is the WARF value for single-B credit quality, represents a 27.2% cumulative default rate over a 10-year period, based upon Moody's idealized default probability rates ("Moody's Global Approach to Rating Collateralized Loan Obligations," Moody's Investors Service, December 14, 2015).

CLO WARF measures have tended to be in a range from 2500 to 3000, representing a weighted-average loan pool credit quality between single-B and single-B-minus.

The *weighted average life (WAL)* is a measure of the CLO pool's tenor. It is calculated by measuring the average time until maturity for each loan, weighted by the balance of the loan.

The *weighted average spread (WAS)* is a measure of the CLO pool's rate of return, calculating the weighted-average floating spread over LIBOR for each loan in the pool. (For example, if a loan pays three-month LIBOR + 3.50%, then the 3.50% spread would be included in the WAS calculation.)

The *diversity score*, as implied, it is a measure of the CLO pool's diversification. The value of the metric is based on a Moody's model that generates a numeric value for the pool, based upon inputs such as each loan's issuer, industry, and geographic location (Figure 23.8).

The probability of defaults occurring in a CLO's loan pool is in part a function of time. The longer a loan is outstanding, the greater the probability that the obligor may become distressed. Due to this, one can consider how the metrics described earlier may balance against one another. For example, while a lower-credit-quality portfolio has a greater probability of default, there may be offsetting factors, such as a shorter remaining life or greater diversification, which could each act to offset the loan pool's overall probability of default.

THE CLO MANAGER

A CLO's underlying loan pool is actively managed by a professional collateral manager. Several different types of investment firms act as managers to CLO funds. These include traditional asset or fund managers, such as BlackRock or Neuberger Berman, as well as insurance companies, like Prudential and New York Life. Some CLOs are managed by the credit investment arms of private equity firms, such as Apollo, Carlyle, or GSO/Blackstone, while others are managed by credit teams within hedge funds, such as Och-Ziff. CLOs may also be managed by standalone investment companies whose primary business is to manage credit and/or loan funds, either in the form of CLO portfolios or as privately managed accounts.

The CLO manager plays an integral role in the performance of the transaction. Essentially, their mandate is to prudently invest the CLO's available cash balances into loans in accordance with all of the CLO's investment guidelines and within the limits required by the CLO's various metrics (such as constraints on OC ratios, triple-C percentages, or WARF values). In order to do this, the manager employs a credit team of portfolio managers, analysts, and traders, who evaluate, transact, and conduct ongoing surveillance on corporate credits that are appropriate for investment by the CLO.

Typically, the CLO manager's analyst team is divided according to individual sector expertise. For example, one credit analyst may cover health-care companies while another specializes in energy credits and a third focuses on names in technology, media, and telecom. The CLO management company may rely on their analyst team to support

Coverage and Collateral Quality Tests

Coverage

Test Name	Current Threshold	Current	Result	Prior
Senior Interest Coverage Test	120.00%	244.77%	Pass	282.89%
Class C Interest Coverage Test	112.50%	220.94%	Pass	254.33%
Class D Interest Coverage Test	107.50%	197.57%	Pass	226.00%
Class E Interest Coverage Test	102.50%	174.06%	Pass	197.25%
Senior Overcollateralization Test	121.40%	132.47%	Pass	132.38%
Class C Overcollateralization Test	114.10%	122.72%	Pass	122.63%
Class D Overcollateralization Test	108.10%	114.70%	Pass	114.62%
Class E Overcollateralization Test	103.70%	108.59%	Pass	108.52%
Class E Reinvestment Test	105.10%	108.59%	Pass	108.52%
5.1(c) Test	102.50%	156.27%	Pass	156.17%

Quality

Test Name	Current Threshold	Current	Result	Prior
Moody's Weighted Average Recovery Rate Test	47.5%	50.0%	Pass	50.0%
Weighted Average Life Test	7.50	5.07	Pass	5.11
Diversity Test	65	74	Pass	73
Maximum Moody's Rating Factor Test	2,963	2,729	Pass	2,664
Minimum Weighted Average Spread Test	3.75%	4.01%	Pass	4.27%

FIGURE 23.8 Summary metrics from a sample CLO trustee report
Source: U.S. Bank

their CLO effort in addition to their other funds that invest in speculative-grade corporate credit.

CLOs represent an opportunity for managers to add fee-generating assets under management (AUM). With each new CLO, the manager adds several hundred million dollars of AUM, and is often able to tap into an investor base that does not otherwise invest in the manager's non-CLO funds. CLO managers typically earn a total management fee of 0.50% per annum on the outstanding balance of the CLO's assets. (The total fee is split between a "senior" fee that is paid prior to any of the CLO tranches, and a "subordinate" fee that is paid just before the distribution to equity investors.) Later in the life of the CLO, there is also the potential for the manager to receive an incentive fee to the extent that the realized equity return exceeds a pre-specified hurdle.

QUALITATIVE ANALYSIS OF A CLO

When analyzing a CLO, there are two main qualitative aspects that warrant consideration: due diligence of the CLO's collateral manager and thorough review of the transaction documentation.

Meet and Greet: Collateral Manager Due Diligence

An investment in a CLO is often intended to be held for the medium or long term, so the investor is effectively entering into a long-term relationship with the CLO manager. The manager's expertise, strategy, and actions can have a significant impact on both the performance and tradability of the CLO's tranches throughout the life of the investment. On the positive side, a manager can select strong credits, maintain consistent equity returns, manage steady transaction amortization, and maintain open communication with the CLO's investor base. On the negative side, a manager can be slow to act on deteriorating problem credits or try to enhance equity returns by dipping into more yieldy loans that represent weaker credits. They may also take actions that do not fully balance the interests of all investors in the structure.

Prior to making an investment, due diligence should be conducted to assess the extent to which the manager has the requisite expertise, staffing, systems, and processes to properly manage the CLO. In addition, the investor should consider the manager's investment style and track record, and their views regarding the loan market. The qualities of different CLO managers can vary widely in these areas, which are briefly touched upon in what follows.

Expertise and Staffing An investor should assess the experience of the manager's credit analysts, traders, and portfolio managers, and any recent turnover within the research team. It is also worth considering the size of the team relative to the number of credits that are followed, the depth of analysis that is conducted, as well as whether the analysts' time is shared with the manager's other funds or asset classes.

Investment Style and Track Record Getting a sense of the manager's investment style and track record involves discussion, analysis, and ongoing review. Some styles are more readily apparent. For example, some managers select loan portfolios with fewer credits while others construct granular portfolios with many credits. Other investment styles may be more difficult to detect, such as an affinity or aversion to loans from particular industry sectors, or the regular use of allowed risk buckets (such as those for triple-C-rated or second-lien loans).

The manager's historical track record can be difficult to ascertain from data alone. It is possible that key performers may have shifted positions since the track record was established and past equity returns or loss experience may not tell the whole story. For example, strong historic equity returns may have resulted in part from investments in more risky loans, heavy trading activity, or structural features within individual CLOs. The investor should carefully evaluate historic performance data to determine whether it represents how the manager would be expected to perform in the future.

Systems and Processes CLO management is a data-intensive business. Each manager actively follows hundreds of corporate loan investments, public and/or private corporate financial data, loan prices, and CLO transaction metrics. An investor should assess the manager's approach to data management and how seamlessly the data is incorporated within their investment and surveillance processes.

The investor should also evaluate the manager's normal business processes. An understanding of the manager's credit selection process is of foremost importance. Other processes worthy of discussion include the manager's approach to credit surveillance, particularly how they address troubled credits, and how purchases or sales are allocated across funds.

The CLO investor should meet with the manager and request sufficient information from which they can assess the entirety of the manager's platform. Investors who are interested in stable, consistent future performance, and a more readily-understood risk profile, would need to consider these qualitative factors, and not simply take the information in the CLO's marketing materials at face value.

The Devil in the Details: CLO Documentation Review

The other key aspect of qualitative CLO analysis relates to a review of the transaction's documentation. While the general structure of a CLO's tranches, payment waterfall, and loan investment guidelines have all become more consistent across post-crisis CLOs, a thorough review of the documentation will still reveal meaningful differences between transactions. The degree of flexibility that the documents provide to the manager can affect the composition and risks of the loan portfolio, the pace at which debt tranches are ultimately repaid, and the benefit to investors from the CLO's inherent structural protections. Overly restrictive documents, on the other hand, could prevent the CLO manager from taking investment actions that would be beneficial to the CLO's performance. Differences in documentation would likely have the most pronounced effect on performance in circumstances where the underlying loan pool became distressed.

Two main documents delineate the terms of a CLO: the *offering circular* and the *indenture*. The offering circular is a marketing document that describes key provisions of the CLO in relatively easy-to-read summary sections and also includes the disclosures necessary for the sale of securities. The indenture is the formal governing document, which includes all of the legal terms and definitions that are relevant to the transaction.

The following is a brief guided tour through some of the key considerations that pertain to CLO documentation.

Investment Guidelines The documents prescribe investment guidelines that define the parameters of the instruments into which the CLO pool is allowed to invest. Certain investments are never permitted. For example, the pool may be required to consist entirely of loans, and not contain corporate bonds, structured finance securities, or other debt instruments. Other investments may be permitted, but only within certain constraints. Typical limits might include a requirement that at least 90% of the loan pool consist of senior secured loans, that no more than 60% of the pool can consist of covenant-lite loans, or that no more than 2% of the pool be exposed to any individual borrower. These sections of the document place parameters around the expected constitution and quality of the collateral pool.

Trading Activity The documents also describe the circumstances under which the CLO manager is allowed to invest (or reinvest) available cash balances, and when they would be required to stop investment activities and allow the loan pool to naturally pay down. Broadly speaking, the manager is allowed to invest during the reinvestment period, and not invest after the end of the reinvestment period. However, there may be restrictions on investment activities even during the reinvestment period, particularly if the transaction is underperforming. Likewise, limited investment activities may still be permitted even after the end of the reinvestment period. The document may also set parameters for how the manager may address the workout of distressed loans, and under what circumstances a loan's maturity date can be amended and extended. These sections of the document can have a meaningful influence on the total lifespan of the CLO's collateral pool, and by extension, on the duration of the CLO's tranches.

Priority of Payments An important aspect of the CLO documentation defines the step-by-step order of payments that are made to each of the tranches. This section prescribes how available interest and principal proceeds are disbursed to pay the CLO's management and administrative fees to each of the debt tranches and to the equity investors. It also identifies the points within the payment waterfall when the overcollateralization (OC) and interest coverage (IC) tests are applied, and how the failure of such tests would redirect cash flows away from subsequent steps in the payment order. This section also describes whether the payment sequence would change after the occurrence of extreme events, such as an *event of default*.

OC Test Calculations Several areas of the document describe adjustments made when calculating the CLO's OC tests. Recall that the OC tests measure the par value of the loans relative to the par value of the CLO tranches. However, there can be circumstances in which certain loans are included in the calculation at less than their stated par value. These typically include loans that have already defaulted, loans that were originally purchased at deep discounts from par, or loans that contribute to an excessive amount of triple-C-rated collateral within the CLO. In circumstances like these, the loans are given a *haircut*, meaning that they are considered to have a value that is less than their full par value when being considered within the OC test calculations. These haircuts lead to a reduction in the resulting ratio. The application of OC haircuts is important to understand, because they influence how quickly the tests may fail, which in turn can cause the diversion of junior tranche cash flows for the purpose of supporting the senior tranches.

Deal Document Amendments   Another section of the document defines the required process that must be followed in order to make future changes to the CLO documentation. Unforeseen market events or other circumstances, such as changes in government regulation, may create the need to make amendments to the original terms of the CLO documents. In such cases, the documents describe the notices that must be provided to investors, credit rating agencies, or other parties to the transaction, and who must provide consent prior to the execution of a proposed amendment. It is important for an investor to understand these aspects of the document, because it is possible for certain terms of the CLO to be materially altered even if it were against the will of some investors in the transaction.

Extreme Events   Some sections of the document specify what will occur in the event that certain extreme circumstances impact the CLO. For example, the document describes what would constitute an event of default for the CLO, as well as how the transaction would operate and who would retain primary control after such an event occurred. Other sections relate to what would occur if the CLO manager were to resign (or in some cases, if specific key personnel left the collateral manager's firm).

QUANTITATIVE ANALYSIS OF A CLO

Quantitative analysis of a CLO tranche involves projecting future expected cash flows and measuring risk or return under a variety of possible scenarios. The assumptions used to project future cash flows are the heart and soul of the analysis. The exact scenarios that should be projected depend on both the tranche level and the risks that are being assessed. For example, an investor in a senior tranche may be less concerned about default risk and more concerned about tranche extension risk while an equity investor may have the opposite perspective. Assumptions can be further refined, based upon the quality of the underlying loan pool and the analyst's perspective of what investment actions may be taken by the CLO manager.

As a practical matter, it is feasible to model CLO cash flows in a spreadsheet. However, most market participants utilize third-party software, due to the complexity of CLO modeling and the data requirements necessary to maintain current collateral information for an actively managed underlying loan pool.

The key assumptions that are input into a CLO cash flow model relate to default rates, recovery rates for defaulted loans, prepayment rates, and the characteristics of loans into which the CLO is expected to invest in the future. Each of these assumptions is briefly touched upon in the following.

Default Rates

One of the most significant cash flow assumptions—but arguably the most difficult to estimate—is the portfolio default rate. The relatively long-term nature of CLOs requires a multiyear perspective of the future default experience of speculative-grade corporate credit. Three approaches to modeling future defaults are described ahead: conditional default rates (CDRs), cumulative default rates, and Monte Carlo simulation. All three approaches intentionally focus on the loan pool as a whole, as opposed to an in-depth understanding of each specific underlying credit in the pool. A CLO typically has very limited exposure to any individual loan issuer, so there is generally greater utility in understanding *how many* loans are expected to default over time and the impact they will have on the CLO's payment structure, rather than *which ones* they are likely to be.

Conditional Default Rates (CDRs) The easiest and most common default rate approach is to assume a constant percentage of annual portfolio defaults, commonly referred to as a *CDR*. Market participants have traditionally assumed a constant rate of 2–3%, which is loosely based upon historical experience. In practice, this means that 2–3% of each year's projected outstanding loan pool is assumed to default.

Benefits of this flat CDR approach relate to it being both simple and uniform. Differences in future expected performance can be addressed separately through the discount rate that is applied to the resulting cash flow projections. One drawback is the fact that it does not directly account for the current position in the corporate credit cycle. Corporate defaults tend to fluctuate between periods of higher and lower defaults. Modeling a constant, average rate is therefore less realistic—and could have a different effect on the CLO structure—than more specific default timing assumptions.

A variation of the *flat* CDR approach is to use a *vector* of different CDR values. The CLO's total outstanding life can be divided into several time horizons, each with a different assumed CDR. While this approach may be somewhat more realistic than the previous flat CDR approach, it is still not customized to the characteristics of the specific loan pool.

As an additional variation to both the flat and vector CDR approaches, it may be useful to identify specific risky portfolio characteristics, such as particularly concentrated loan exposures, loans that pose an imminent default risk, or allocations to weaker industry groups. (These loans may possibly be identified on the basis of their current market price, as low marks on the loans may at times be used as a proxy for weaker credit quality.) In such cases, asset-specific default assumptions may be applied to particular loans within these identified risk buckets. The general CDR assumption for the remainder of the loan pool would then be overlaid in addition to the asset-specific assumptions.

Cumulative Default Rates A second approach is to assume that a certain cumulative proportion of the CLO's loan pool will default over the next several years, and then account for the credit cycle by staggering the proportion of that cumulative rate over the course of the projection period. For example, if the analyst wanted to apply a five-year cumulative default rate of 15%, and assume that the greatest stress occurs in the middle of that period, they might apply a cumulative annual vector such as the following: 1% / 2% / 6% / 4% / 2%, which together sums to the intended rate of 15%.

One approach to determine a cumulative lifetime default rate assumption is to rely on historical precedent—by looking at the performance of similar loans over average or specific past time periods. Historical default data, both long term as well as for specific cohort years, is often available from credit rating agencies or other data providers.

The challenge is to determine which historical data is appropriate to apply to a given CLO. Current credit ratings on the CLO's underlying loans may be a good starting point to inform a cumulative default rate assumption, but adjustments may be necessary to account for disproportionate exposures to particular loan types, sectors, or other risks.

The main drawback of historical data is that it may not reliably predict future performance. This is especially true when considering the severe performance of loans during the financial crisis, as well as the unprecedented global monetary stimulus that contributed to the loans recovering so rapidly thereafter. Neither of these factors will necessarily be repeated in the future. In addition, loan underwriting standards may have changed due to a combination of market forces and regulatory pressures. For these reasons, there may have been a regime shift between the available historical data sets and the expected future default (and recovery) experience for loans. Effectively using historical data may therefore be limited in its ability to project future performance.

An alternative to using specific historical data is to project future default rates based upon one's own macroeconomic outlook. An investor may have a view on the future default rate for speculative-grade corporate debt, and they can overlay that perspective onto the expected performance of the specific CLO portfolio. Credit rating agencies and sell-side Wall Street research teams also periodically publish default rate projections, which can be useful for this type of analysis.

There are also challenges to practically applying a broad macroeconomic perspective to a specific CLO portfolio. It is important to consider how the macroeconomic-based default rate was determined, and if there are differences that would limit its application to the CLO. Some macroeconomic rates are inferred from prior recession cycles while others are calculated by regressing variables against historical default rates and then extrapolating those rates into the future. Still others are based on the idea that current loan market prices imply an expected default rate (given an assumed recovery rate). Properly calibrating a macroeconomic default rate with the CLO's collateral pool requires an evaluation of the source and methodology of the default rate projection.

Monte Carlo Simulation A third approach, although clearly the most computationally advanced, is to simulate future default rates by modeling the performance of each loan in the CLO's portfolio to its maturity or default. A rating transition matrix can be used to simulate the probability of each future period's change in credit quality and possible jump to default. This calculation is performed for every individual asset within the CLO and then aggregated to generate different paths of lifetime portfolio defaults. This process is repeated thousands of times and modeled in conjunction with the structural rules of the CLO's payment waterfall to simulate all possible future outcomes for the CLO. A simulation approach can also apply dynamic recovery or prepayment rates that vary as a function of each path's simulated default rate.

To a certain extent, simulations provide for more realistic modeling of CLO cash flows. By predicting defaults on an asset-level basis, the simulation can capture the disproportional shock to the CLO structure from the loss of specific, large, high-yielding, or low-recovery assets. This stands in contrast to the other default rate approaches, which implicitly assume that defaulted assets have average characteristics. (In fact, relative to lower-yielding loans, the higher-yielding assets may actually have a greater probability of default, and their loss may have a more adverse impact on the CLO structure.) Further, simulation results can be used for risk management purposes to quantify more extreme scenarios or specific confidence intervals or to evaluate a tranche's sensitivity to particular cash-flow assumptions.

While simulations provide for superior structural analysis, they are somewhat limited by the data sets that are used as model inputs. Historical rating transition matrices are necessary to conduct the simulation, as are corporate industry and asset correlation rates. These historical relationships tend to change over time, however, and may not be fully relevant for future periods. In addition, from a practical perspective, subscription-based third-party CLO models with Monte Carlo capability can be difficult to come by.

In summary, there are three general approaches to modeling CLO default rates: conditional default rates (CDRs), cumulative default rates, and Monte Carlo simulations. All three approaches can be applied in practice, each with its own benefits and drawbacks. At times, an analyst may find it beneficial to apply more than one approach to the same transaction. Investors should first assess the qualities of the particular CLO structure and loan pool to determine what risks or qualities are most important to evaluate. Then, they can select an analytical approach that best addresses their modeling and valuation requirements.

Recovery Rates

The seniority of leveraged loans within the capital structure of the issuing corporation has historically resulted in high post-default recovery rates. It should be noted that the opposite of a recovery rate is a *loss severity rate*. (The recovery rate measures the percentage of par that is repaid on a defaulted loan while, conversely, the severity rate measures the percentage of par that is not repaid. Severity is also referred to as *loss-given-default*, or LGD.) Market participants have generally assumed flat, average recovery rates of 70% or higher.

Assumed recovery rates should be adjusted to account for loans that are not senior-secured, such as second-lien or unsecured loans. These loans have historically realized lower recovery rates, although they do comprise only a small minority of a CLO's loan pool.

Recovery rates are influenced by various factors such as the company's enterprise value at the time of default, or the value of its assets in the event of liquidation. The recovery value is also affected by the company's capital structure, including any other obligations of the defaulted company that would be paid prior to, or together with, the loan in question. Timing can also play a role in recovery value. With certain loans, it may take longer before a company formally triggers a default (which may be the case in the future with covenant-lite loans). Likewise, the workout process for a defaulted obligor may take a long time to process through the legal system, particularly in periods when many other companies have also defaulted. The longer the delay in realizing the recovery, the greater the chance that the company or its assets decline in value, which in turn could lead to lower recovery rates.

Similar to default rates, there are also several ways to implement recovery rate assumptions. One is to apply flat, average recovery rates. Another is to use a multiyear vector, with lower recovery rates in certain years, but higher rates in other years, to account for changes in the business cycle. Finally, recovery rates can also be modeled within a Monte Carlo simulation as a function of each path's projected default rate.

To account for the longer expected timing of the workout process in times of higher corporate stress, the cash-flow analysis can incorporate *recovery lag* assumptions. These assumptions can have a notable impact on the CLO, as investors may face extension risk from delays in realizing recovery values.

When reviewing historical recovery rate data, it is important to note the method used to measure the recovery rate (Figure 23.9). Often, the loan's recovery value is considered to be the trading price of the loan 30 days after the date of default. However, some data services capture the trading price of the loan on the day of the default itself while others measure the ultimate cash recovery received on the loan regardless of how long it took. Each of these approaches has different implications for the way one may view future recovery prospects. In addition, it is important to note that actual recoveries are sometimes realized in the form of equity or warrants (or other securities) in a reorganized company, rather than as a lump-sum cash payment to the CLO. In contrast, CLO models typically assume that recoveries are received as cash that is then deployed to reinvest or to amortize the CLO's senior notes. Non-cash recoveries have a different impact on the CLO structure and may require adjustments to the cash flow assumptions in order to achieve the intended effect.

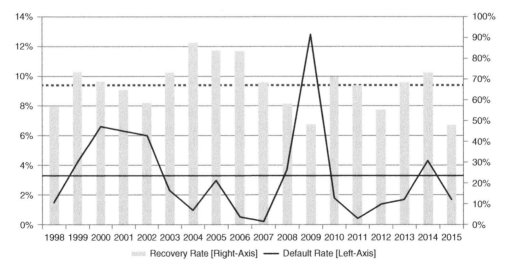

FIGURE 23.9   Historical leveraged loan default and recovery rates, 1998–2015
Note: Annual default rates are par-weighted. Annual recovery rates are issuer-weighted, first-lien recovery rates and based on the loan price 30 days after the default date.
Sources: J.P. Morgan, Moody's Investors Service, S&P LCD, Markit

Prepayment Rates

Loan prepayments occur when the corporate borrower repays a loan prior to its stated maturity date. Loans typically have minimal call protection, which provides the borrower with the option to elect for an early redemption. The company's decision to do so is largely based upon corporate finance considerations. If current market interest rates are lower than the rate being paid on the loan, a new loan would result in a lower interest expense. The borrower may therefore elect to refinance their loan, using the proceeds of the new loan to prepay the original lenders. Alternatively, the borrower may wish to extend the maturity of outstanding obligations in order to secure greater certainty of future funding or to show only long-term debt on their financial statements. At times, a loan prepayment is caused by merger activity. In a prepayment, the CLO receives cash earlier than previously expected, rather than continuing to hold an ongoing exposure to the loan.

Depending on the phase in the CLO's lifecycle, there can be different implications of a prepayment. During the reinvestment period, prepayments can generally always be reinvested, provided that the CLO's metrics are satisfied or at least not made worse as a result of such reinvestment. After the reinvestment period, prepayments can typically be substituted into new loans with similar credit and duration characteristics as the prepaid loan. In circumstances where prepayments are not allowed to be reinvested, the proceeds are used to sequentially amortize the CLO tranches. In general, faster prepayments benefit investors in the CLO's debt tranches, because they receive their money back faster and therefore have less exposure to potential future credit issues. In contrast, slower prepayments generally benefit the equity investors, because the inherent leverage of the CLO structure remains outstanding for longer.

Market participants often assume *conditional prepayment rates (CPRs)* of 15%–20% per annum, which is broadly consistent with average historical experience (Figure 23.10). However, CPRs can fluctuate, often inversely to the state of the market. When market conditions have been favorable, actual annualized CPRs have been in excess of 50%, largely due to heavy refinancing activity. During weaker periods, when capital markets were not readily open to speculative-grade borrowers, annualized prepayment rates have dipped below 10%. CLO pools can also suffer from adverse selection, in which the stronger credits are redeemed from the pool while the weaker credits remain outstanding.

Reinvestment Rates

One other important CLO cash-flow assumption is often given less focus, and it relates to the reinvestment of available cash. Recall that CLOs receive cash through both maturities and prepayments within the loan pool, and as actively managed vehicles, the CLO manager is often able to reinvest those funds into new loans. The characteristics of those new loans (such as the assumed maturity, spread, and purchase price) will have a material impact on both the duration of the debt tranches and the rate of return to the equity investors. For example, an assumption that the manager will reinvest into longer-duration assets would keep the debt tranches outstanding for longer and enhance the equity returns. Assumed reinvestment into higher-yielding loans or into loans at discounted purchase prices can likewise increase the modeled equity returns. When setting

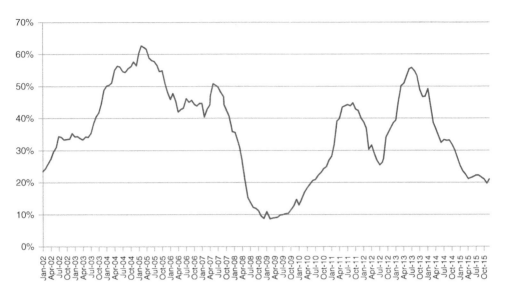

FIGURE 23.10 Historical loan repayment rate, 2002–2015 (trailing 12-month annualized rate)
Source: Morgan Stanley

reinvestment assumptions, an investor should consider the manager's track record and style, as well as the constraints within which the manager is operating. Typically, one would expect the manager to optimize the use of available constraints in order to realize the best results for all investors.

CLO Valuation

Once CLO cash flows have been projected, those projections can be used to value an investment. This is typically accomplished through a standard discounting process. However, since the debt tranches are floating rate, they would normally be discounted at a floating spread over LIBOR, also referred to as a *discount margin* (DM), rather than a fixed internal rate of return (IRR). A fixed-rate tranche, or the equity tranche, would commonly be discounted at a fixed rate.

When discounting the cash flows, it is important to consider the relative stress that was incorporated into the cash flow projections themselves. If the cash flows are already risk adjusted and thereby already represent a conservative or stressful projection, then the discount rate should be lower. On the other hand, if the projections are not risk adjusted, then the risk would need to be captured by the use of a higher discount rate. In addition, for equity tranches, whose cash flows may be very sensitive to specific assumptions, a range of scenarios and sensitivity analysis is appropriate rather than just applying a discount rate to a single projected scenario.

Another approach that is sometimes used to estimate a tranche's value is by calculating its *net asset value* (NAV) coverage. This approach considers the market value coverage of a CLO tranche by assuming that the underlying loan portfolio is liquidated at its current market value and sale proceeds are used to repay the CLO's liabilities. NAV coverage is a useful data point, particularly for more distressed transactions in which some tranches are not fully collateralized on a market value basis. However, it is an incomplete proxy of actual tranche value. The NAV does not account for the CLO's structural features or the fact that the transaction most likely cannot be redeemed or liquidated for many years to come.

A WHOLE NEW WORLD: CLOs IN THE POST-CRISIS REGULATORY ENVIRONMENT

Lessons learned through the financial crisis and the different financial and regulatory atmosphere in the era following the crisis have each contributed to changes in the structure of the markets for loans and CLOs. Two regulations in particular that were part of the Dodd-Frank Wall Street Reform and Consumer Protection Act have had a particularly direct impact on the CLO market.

The Volcker Rule

One of the sections of the Dodd-Frank Wall Street Reform and Consumer Protection Act is commonly referred to as the Volcker Rule. It is named after Paul Volcker, the former Federal Reserve Bank chairman whose ideas inspired that section of the Act. One of the goals of the Volcker Rule was to prohibit banks from investing in hedge funds or private equity funds, which were deemed to be overly risky for the safe-and-sound investment practices that are typically expected of banks.

At first blush, it would seem that this rule is unrelated to CLOs. After all, CLOs are not hedge funds or private equity funds. However, the issue arises from the fact that it is difficult to clearly define what constitutes a "hedge fund" or a "private equity fund."

The definition that the legislators opted to use to define prohibited funds also ended up including most CLOs. However, the regulators did provide an allowance for CLOs, provided that they qualify as so-called *loan securitizations*. This requires, among other things, that the collateral of the CLO be comprised exclusively of loans with no exposure to bonds or other securities.

Historically, banks have tended to be significant investors in CLO tranches. Since the Volcker Rule effectively requires that any CLO in which a bank invests qualifies as a loan securitization, the entire CLO market has generally shifted to be 100% loan-only. (Previously, there had been certain benefits, such as diversification, to the allowance of small proportions of bonds or other non-loans within the underlying CLO portfolio. However, due to the Volcker Rule, CLOs with such allowances are generally no longer issued in practice.)

Skin-in-the-Game: Risk Retention Requirements

Another section within the Dodd-Frank Act set new requirements for securitization sponsors to retain risk in the funds that they issue and essentially requires a CLO manager to retain 5% of the balance of any new CLO issuance. The concept is that if the manager is exposed to investment risk with some of their own skin-in-the-game, they are more likely to select loans that are well-underwritten and expected to perform.

The risk retention requirement makes it much more onerous for managers to issue new CLOs. In the past, managers had sometimes co-invested in their own transactions, but there was no regulatory requirement for them to do so. Issuing more CLOs simply added to the manager's assets under management (AUM) and enhanced the manager's fee revenue. The manager's interests were aligned with investors through both their general reputation as well as the CLO's fee structure of senior, subordinate, and incentive management fees. In contrast, with the new requirements, a typical CLO of $500 million will require the manager to make a $25 million cash investment in the transaction. Consequently, CLO issuance will therefore be transformed into a very capital-intensive business, changing the manager's economic benefit of new issuance and potentially placing CLO management out-of-reach for some managers.

The outcome of the risk retention requirements may be that the universe of active CLO managers will shrink. Existing CLO managers will need to have an adequate source of capital to be able to fund new issuance, and they may need to reevaluate the economic benefits of continuing to issue additional transactions. New CLO managers will find that these requirements further raise the barriers to enter the CLO market. In addition to the staffing, analytical, operational, and marketing issues that new managers have always needed to address, they must now also find a significant source of capital to enable them to bring their CLOs to market. The CLO manager and issuance landscape is therefore likely to evolve as a result of this regulation.

CONCLUSION

CLOs present investors with the ability to gain exposure to leveraged loans in a way that buffers the risk for senior investors and enhances the return for junior investors. CLOs boast a relatively long and impressive track record, which demonstrates their resilience as an asset class. However, past performance should not lead one to underestimate the potential risks. The performance of a CLO ultimately depends upon the performance of speculative-grade loans and the active management of the collateral manager. Investors should do their homework prior to making an investment, including manager due diligence, document review, and quantitative cash-flow analysis, in addition to conducting ongoing surveillance throughout the life of the transaction. With a deeper understanding of a CLO's construction, features, considerations, and risks, an investor can make informed decisions about this attractive and resilient asset class.

CHAPTER 24

Municipal Bonds

Fred Yosca

INTRODUCTION

Municipal bonds are debt instruments issued by states and their political subdivisions such as counties, cities, towns, school districts, and governmental agencies. When you purchase new-issue municipal bonds, you are in effect lending money to finance various public projects such as the construction of hospitals, highways, and schools or the purchase of subway cars and garbage trucks. As the infrastructure of our country continues to age and the population increases, the amount of capital needed to rebuild, rehabilitate, and construct new roads, bridges, mass transit systems, and water and sewer systems will grow. The municipal bond market is the preferred venue in which those financings take place.

What distinguishes municipal bonds from other fixed-income investments is their tax treatment. The interest paid by municipalities on bonds issued to finance public-purpose projects such as the ones cited earlier are exempt from federal income taxes. In most cases, states do not tax the interest income generated by the bonds they issue or the bonds issued by their political subdivisions. For example, a New York resident who purchases a bond issued by New York State or any of its political subdivisions would not have to pay federal or state income tax on the income produced by this bond. For a New York City resident purchasing an instate bond the interest is exempt from New York City income tax as well. Conversely, bonds that are issued for a nonmunicipal purpose, such as the funding of employee pensions, are fully taxable at the federal level.

The last category of tax treatment for municipal bonds concerns bonds that are subject to the federal *alternative minimum tax* (AMT). Bonds whose proceeds are used for private-purpose activities such as financings for corporations or other nongovernmental purposes will be subject to AMT. In these cases, a bondholder will need to include the interest earned on the bond in the AMT calculation when preparing their annual tax return. Should the calculation determine that the taxpayer is subject to the AMT, the interest on the bond is no longer tax exempt for that holder, but is instead taxable at the bondholder's AMT rate.

With a population of over 300 million people living in thousands of towns and cities, there are multitudes of potential issuers of municipal debt. This diversity notwithstanding, most municipal debt falls into one of three general categories: general obligation bonds, revenue bonds, and pre-refunded/escrowed-to-maturity bonds.

1. *General obligation bonds (GOs).* These bonds are backed by the full faith and credit of the issuer. The bond's security is thus derived from the municipality's unconditional pledge to levy taxes sufficient to pay the principal and interest. Voter approval is needed to issue GO bonds. Traditionally, GOs have been perceived as the most secure of municipal credits because of the unconditional nature of the issuer's pledge to "levy taxes without limit as to rate or amount." As we will discuss later, the sanctity of this pledge has been called into question by a variety of market observers, given recent events in cities such as Detroit, MI; Vallejo, CA; and Harrisburg, PA.

2. *Revenue bonds.* These bonds are secured solely by the pledge of a revenue stream derived from a specific source, such as user fees and rents. Revenue bonds are issued to finance projects such as electric power systems, water and sewer projects, airport facilities, highway toll roads, and hospitals. Issuers also securitize assets such as single-family mortgages and student loans into "pass-through" securities payable from the revenues derived from the repayment of these loans. Normally, voter approval is not needed to issue revenue bonds.

3. *Pre-refunded/escrowed bonds.* This class of municipal debt derives its security from a pool of money held in trust by a third party. During periods of low interest rates municipal issuers may have an opportunity to reduce their borrowing costs by retiring older, higher coupon bonds with the proceeds of new bonds issued at materially lower interest rates. This process is similar to that of a homeowner who refinances his mortgage to lower his monthly payment. When the refunding is completed, the proceeds of the new issue are generally invested in U.S. Treasury securities and held in escrow by a trustee. The old bonds are then defeased, which means that they are removed from the issuer's debt statement and are no longer payable from the revenue stream identified in the original indenture. Instead the older bonds are now payable solely from the pool of escrowed Treasury securities. If it suits the issuer's purpose, it may exercise its call option on the refunded bonds and retire them before their stated maturity (see discussion of callable bond structures ahead). If there is no call option, the escrowed bonds will remain in circulation until the maturity date. This latter category of bonds is known as *escrowed-to-maturity* bonds (ETMs). Since the security for pre-refunded bonds and ETMs consists of the pool of government securities, they are considered tantamount to tax-exempt Treasuries and generally carry AAA ratings. One caveat with this class of bonds is that some escrow pools are not collateralized with U.S. Treasury securities, but are escrowed instead with federal agency paper such as FNMA, GNMA, or Federal Home Loan Bank, or in some cases with nongovernment securities.

MUNICIPAL BOND CREDIT ANALYSIS

Ratings Agencies

The vast majority of municipal bonds are considered to be of investment-grade quality by virtue of the ratings given to them by the three main credit rating agencies, Moody's, Standard & Poor's, and Fitch. To achieve an investment-grade rating, a bond must not have any speculative elements that might endanger the timely payment of principal and interest. All three ratings agencies define investment grade using this general criteria. Bonds that do not clear this hurdle are given ratings that are sub-investment grade or speculative. Credit ratings for all three agencies follow the same general alphabetic scale from the highest quality or AAA down to defaulted bonds (C in Moody's parlance, D by S&P and Fitch). The cutoff between investment grade and high yield is Baa3 for Moody's and BBB– for S&P and Fitch.

Although bond ratings are useful in assessing overall credit quality and the historical default rate of investment-grade municipals is statistically insignificant, serious investors may want to make a determination of a bond's creditworthiness on their own. The principal tools for doing so are the Official Statement published at the time of the bond's issuance and the issuer's continuing financial disclosures, which are typically published annually. Both types of documents are publicly available on the Municipal Securities Rulemaking Board's website (emma.msrb.org). (The MSRB is the industry's primary regulatory body.)

The Rise and Fall of Bond Insurance

During the last two decades of the previous century, credit enhancement of municipal bonds in the form of bond insurance was a true growth industry. The basic business model was very sound; an insurance company assumes the default risk over the life of an investment-grade municipal bond in exchange for an upfront payment of premium. Since the default rate on investment-grade munis historically is a fraction of 1%, the insurer's risk was kept to a minimum. When weighing this risk against the substantial reserves held by the insurers, the ratings agencies correctly assigned AAA ratings to insured bonds. Investors loved the double-barreled (belt-and-suspenders) concept of a natural A- or AA-rated credit attaining an AAA rating to such an extent that by 2005 over half the municipal bonds in circulation carried some form of insurance. In fact, demand for AAA-insured bonds became so great that natural AAA credits often went begging for buyers because they lacked that extra level of protection provided by insurance. Unfortunately, the story of insured municipal bonds did not end happily.

During the housing boom of the first years of this century, many of the insurers had diversified into insuring private-label structured housing bonds without really understanding the risks lurking in the underlying mortgage baskets. When the mortgage bubble finally burst in 2008, resulting in wholesale defaults of structured mortgage debt, the insurers had to make the bondholders whole. The huge losses incurred by the insurance companies weakened their capital reserves to such an extent that they lost their AAA ratings. Suddenly, lower-rated munis that were sold to investors as AAA-insured credits reverted back to their original ratings with a commensurate loss in market value. The hard-earned lesson for investors in the municipal space is clear: Credit is king and bond buyers who fail to scrutinize the underlying strength of an issuer do so at their own peril.

Basic Analysis of General Obligations

As we have stated, GOs are payable from the full faith and credit of the issuer and a pledge to levy taxes at a level sufficient to pay in full the principal and interest over the life of the bond. The issuer's ability to honor this pledge is a function of its economic health, the diversity of its revenue sources, the quality of its fiscal management, and the overall level of debt. Of increasing importance to an issuer's credit quality these days is its ability to control the costs of employee retirement benefits, principally pensions and retiree medical insurance. Economic health can be measured by trends in population, valuations of real property, employment rates, and where applicable, income tax collections. Diversity of revenue sources is often a function of the size and organizational structure of the issuer. For instance, a large city such as New York derives the majority of its funding from property taxes, personal income taxes, sales tax, and licensing fees, whereas a small school district depends primarily on property taxes and state aid, the latter being a revenue stream it has no control over. The importance of the quality of fiscal management cannot be underestimated, as even the wealthiest communities will garner lower credit ratings than one would expect if their management teams are not up to the task of balancing the books.

On the other side of the ledger, the size and composition of a municipality's expenditures, including its debt, need to be scrutinized. Obviously, a given issuer must have the revenue base to pay its employees, vendors, and creditors. Frequent issuance of short-term debt to cover deficits in the general fund is an indicator of structural instability, or an imbalance between recurring revenues and recurring expenditures. As stated in the opening paragraph of our discussion, long-term debt is issued to finance capital projects, not to fund current operations. To do otherwise is comparable to a homeowner obtaining a 30-year mortgage to buy groceries. Analysts use several metrics to measure an issuer's ability to support its debt. Debt per capita (total long- and short-term debt divided by population) and total debt as a percentage of full valuation of real property are two of the most frequently used. In addition, most states require issuers to calculate a debt limit for general obligation debt, which is usually a percentage of the full valuation of real property. Typically, overlapping debt, that is, debt issued by other governmental entities that share the same tax base, is included for the purposes of calculating debt limits. It should be noted that in this era of retirement benefit crises, ratings agencies are modifying their concept of total debt to include unfunded pension and retiree medical care liabilities as well as bonded debt.

Basic Analysis of Revenue Bonds

As we have stated, revenue bonds are payable from a single revenue source generated by a municipal enterprise. While this revenue pledge may sound on the surface like a less secure structure than general obligation financing, that is not necessarily the case. Revenue bonds that are issued for so-called essential purposes, such as a water or electric utility, are often considered blue-chip credits for a number of reasons. First, consider the meaning of *essential purpose*; a reasonable person would probably judge the revenue generated by rate payers who need to keep the lights on and the water running from their taps as highly reliable. Second, revenue bond credit structures typically ensure that the flow of funds to bondholders is more than adequate. Most revenue bonds are payable from the net revenue (NR) of the enterprise, or gross revenue–operating expenses. The primary measure of the bond's quality is the *coverage ratio*, which is equal to NR divided by *maximum annual debt service* (MADS). MADS is in turn defined as the greatest amount of principal and interest combined due in any given year during the life of the bond. Obviously this ratio must always equal or exceed 1:1 and the greater the coverage ratio, the better a bondholder will sleep at night. Another protection analysts look for in revenue bonds is the additional bonds test, which caps future issuance of bonds with the same revenue pledge at an amount that will not bring the coverage ratio for all the issuer's debt below a certain level. Finally, it should be mentioned that there is often a hierarchy to an issuer's debt profile. Senior-lien debt has first claim to the NR of the enterprise while junior or sub-lien debt is payable from the residual NR left after the senior bondholders have been paid.

Basic Analysis of Pre-refunded/Escrowed Bonds

As long as the collateral held in escrow is in the form of U.S. Treasuries, pre-refunded and ETM bonds generally earn Aaa ratings from Moody's, AA+ from S&P, and AAA from Fitch. Regardless of whether the issuer has applied to the agencies for a new rating, there is little to concern bondholders regarding credit quality beyond insuring that the escrow agreement is ironclad. Bonds escrowed in other types of securities may carry lower ratings, reflecting the lesser quality of the collateral.

THE EROSION OF THE GENERAL OBLIGATION PLEDGE

An issuer's pledge to levy taxes without limit to support its general obligation debt has always been considered sacrosanct. In theory, this is eminently logical; no municipality would jeopardize its access to the capital markets by defaulting on its debt if it had the option to raise the funds needed by simply increasing the tax burden on its residents. In practice, however, several events in recent decades have shaken investors' faith in the inviolability of GO debt. First, in 1994, Orange County, CA, a large, wealthy, AA-rated issuer, accrued losses of over $1.5 billion from interest rate–derivative products in its investment portfolio. The County declared Chapter 9 bankruptcy in December of that year, an event that shook the municipal market to its core.[1] In the spring of 1995, the County's taxpayers voted down a half-cent increase in the sales tax that would have provided the needed cash to return the County to solvency. Soon thereafter, Orange County defaulted on roughly $800 million in short-term debt. Although troubled credits had defaulted on debt in the past, such as the Washington Public Power Supply System in the 1980s and New York City in the 1970s, never had a municipality as wealthy as Orange County reneged on its obligations.[2]

Although the noteholders were eventually made whole and the County's credit regained its luster, a dangerous precedent was set; the likelihood of an issuer paying its obligations in a timely fashion may depend as much on its *willingness to pay* as it does on its ability to pay.

The second disaster to shake investors' confidence in the GO pledge is the bankruptcy of the City of Detroit. Once one of the nation's largest cities and the manufacturing center of the U.S. automobile industry, Detroit's fortunes declined as the Big 3 automakers lost market share to foreign competitors during the latter part of the previous century. The City's downward economic spiral continued even after the General Motors bankruptcy in 2009 to such an extent that it could barely provide even the most basic of municipal services to its ever-shrinking number of residents. With its tax base and population continuing to decline, Detroit filed for Chapter 9 bankruptcy in July 2013. Historically, conventional wisdom has dictated that the holders of general obligation debt maintain the most-senior role in the hierarchy of a municipality's creditors. However, in the Detroit Chapter 9 case, the judge ruled that the City's pension recipients had the highest standing among the City's creditors. As a result, payments to pension holders were reduced by 4.5% in the bankruptcy settlement while GO bondholders suffered losses ranging from 26% to 66%.[3]

These two cases, along with similar crises in cities such as Stockton, CA, and San Bernardino, CA, have served to alter the trading relationship between general obligations and essential-purpose revenue bonds. In the past, GOs always traded at lower yields than comparably rated revenue bonds of the same duration. In fact, today there are institutional buyers who shun the entire GO asset class with the exception of only the highest rated and most liquid names.

A WORD ABOUT PUERTO RICO

At the time of this writing, the credit crisis on the island of Puerto Rico continues to unfold. The bond ratings of every issuer on the island are all well below investment

---

[1] Sallie Hofmeister, "A Default by Orange County," *New York Times*, December 9, 1994, http://www.nytimes.com/1994/12/09/business/a-default-by-orange-county.html.
[2] "When Government Fails: The Orange County Bankruptcy—A Policy Summary," Public Policy Institute of California (University of California Press, March 18, 1998).
[3] Michael Aneiro, "Bondholders and Pension Risk," *Barron's*, November 8, 2014, http://www.barrons.com/articles/bondholders-and-pension-risk-1415436717.

grade and two of its agencies have already defaulted. The conventional wisdom assumes that most if not all of the issuers in the Commonwealth will be in default by July 1, 2016. (Indeed, the governor of Puerto Rico has stated so repeatedly.) Due to its status as a territory of the United States, Chapter 11 bankruptcy is not available to Puerto Rico. Negotiations in Congress to address the crisis have so far proved fruitless, but the market expects that a debt restructuring agreement among all parties will eventually be reached. Any such restructuring deal will most likely result in serious haircuts to bondholders and the imposition of a financial control board placed over the Commonwealth's operations.

Puerto Rico's woes are best described as a perfect storm: profligate capital borrowing, low income levels, a contracting economy, population flight, and a lack of due diligence on the part of lenders, the financial advisors, and bond counsel. The end result is a crushing debt burden that far exceeds that of any of the 50 states, borne by a commonwealth with per-capita income levels far lower than Mississippi, the most impoverished of the states. In short, it is very difficult to imagine any kind of favorable outcome for the people of Puerto Rico or their creditors.

Significantly, Puerto Rico's woes have caused little damage to date to the broader municipal market. The fact that Puerto Rico is not a state, enjoys universal tax exemption, and has always been perceived as a marginal credit have relegated its debt to a special category that is not readily comparable to more traditional municipal credits. In other words, Puerto Rico's problems are perceived as unique to Puerto Rico. For these reasons, the market is minimizing the chances of contagion to the investment-grade tax-exempt sector.

TYPES OF MUNICIPAL BOND STRUCTURES

For municipal debt to be considered tax exempt, bond issuers are required to match the tenor of their borrowings to the useful life of the projects they finance. Issuers typically also endeavor to provide themselves with a material amount of flexibility in managing that debt. To do so they will take advantage of a variety of bond structures. Some of the most common are described in the following.

Non-callable Bonds

The simplest bond structure has a fixed rate or coupon paid semiannually and a single maturity date. Commonly referred to as a *bullet maturity*, none of the principal of the issue is amortized before the maturity date. The classic municipal bond issue, however, is a serial loan. In this format, a 20-year issue will actually consist of 20 individual bonds, each bearing a specific rate of interest and maturing yearly beginning in year 1 until the entire issue is retired in 20 years. Since the issuer is returning principal as well as interest to bondholders yearly, the issue is being amortized on an annual basis. When preparing the bond issue to come to market, the issuer will tailor the individual amortization amounts to best suit its future anticipated revenue flows. In other words, the yearly debt service cash outflows (principal and interest) must not exceed the issuer's ability to pay them.

Callable Bonds

Most municipal bonds of 10 or more years in tenor usually contain embedded call features. These are options held by the issuer that give it the right to buy the bonds back from investors at a given price, usually 100% of face value or par. The call option is exercisable most commonly beginning 10 years after issuance. For example, a New York City general obligation issued with a date of 1/1/2016 bearing interest at 5% and maturing 1/1/2036 will be callable at 100 beginning 1/1/2026. In this case, the bondholder has what is known as call protection, meaning that the City cannot force him to sell the bond back until 10 years after issuance.

The advantage to the municipality of selling callable bonds is greater flexibility in managing its debt. In the case of the NYC bond described previously, if by 2026 the City can borrow at a rate materially below 5%, say 3.50%, it might elect to take advantage of this lower interest rate environment and sell refunding bonds bearing interest at 3.5%. The proceeds of this new issue will be used to refund the 5% bonds due in 2036 by exercising the call option and the City will have saved 1.5 percentage points in borrowing cost over the 10-year period between 2026 and 2036. When a refunding takes place before the call date, the old 5% bonds will be pre-refunded in the manner discussed earlier in this chapter.

Since callable bonds are so commonplace in the municipal market, their issuance does not result in a premium in borrowing cost to the municipality. The exception to this general rule occurs when bonds are issued with call options materially shorter than 10 years.

Variable-Rate Bonds

Larger municipalities often manage their overall debt portfolio by issuing variable-rate debt. During a period of elevated borrowing costs, a city or state may be reluctant to lock in a high fixed coupon for a long-term financing. Rather than postpone debt issuance until rates come down to a more palatable level, it will instead issue a variable-rate bond. This vehicle may be a long-term security but it pays interest as though it were a short-term bond. This can be achieved in several ways. Variable-rate bonds may pay interest at a spread to an index such as the SIFMA swap rate or a widely quoted market rate such as LIBOR.

THE PRIMARY MARKET

The term *primary market* refers to the process by which new-issue municipal securities enter the marketplace. There are two basic mechanisms by which municipalities sell their debt to the market: competitive and negotiated sales. Both are done as public offerings (as opposed to private placements) and are transacted by the municipal bond dealer firms. The vast majority of general obligation debt is sold to the public through a *competitive sale*. Most municipalities are required to solicit bids for the purchase of the goods and services they require to serve their residents, whether it be a new firetruck or textbooks for a school district. So, too, with their issuance of debt to finance capital projects: Public notice is given by an issuer that it will be auctioning the sale of a bond issue on a given date. Interested parties who wish to purchase the new issue in its entirety must submit bids to the issuer by a given time on that date. The bidder who complies with the terms of the sale and submits the lowest rate of interest is awarded the bonds. The process is analogous to that of a homebuyer who seeks to obtain a mortgage at the lowest possible rate. The interests of the taxpayers are well served because the auction process generally results in the bonds being sold at the lowest possible borrowing cost. In the case of larger competitive sales, teams of municipal dealers will band together to bid the issue. The market risk on the deal assumed by the successful bidding syndicate is shared by its members. Typically the firm leading the syndicate, known as the *bookrunner*, along with several other senior co-managers will have the largest share of the risk as well as the largest share of the profit and or loss resulting from the sales of the bonds to investors.

The second method of accessing the capital markets is known as a *negotiated sale*. Negotiated sales are more commonly utilized by state-level agencies selling revenue bonds or municipalities refunding general obligation debt. The common denominator among negotiated sales is that they tend to be larger and more complex than competitive sales. In a negotiated sale, a team of underwriters is appointed by the issuer prior to the sale. This team is comprised of municipal bond dealers who have submitted proposals to the issuer for underwriting services. It is not uncommon for large new issues, often exceeding $1 billion in size, to have an underwriting syndicate of 20 or more dealers.

The principal difference between the two types of underwritings is that competitive deals must be bought and priced by the winning syndicate before they can be sold to investors. The advantage negotiated underwriters have is that they are able to price the issue and solicit orders from customers and syndicate members in amounts sufficient to account for all the bonds before purchasing them from the issuer. Only when the entire issue is subscribed for do the underwriters propose to buy it from the issuer. Although there are periodic exceptions to the rule, it is unusual for the bonds in a negotiated sale to not be entirely placed with customers at the time the award is received from the issuer.

The primary advantage of buying bonds from a new issue is that all buyers of a given maturity receive the same yield during the underwriting, regardless of the size of the transaction. These offering terms are a matter of public record and this level of price transparency is uncommon in the municipal secondary market. In addition, the compensation received by the underwriters for selling new-issue securities is paid to them by the issuer. This is in contrast to the secondary market where dealers mark up the price of bonds before selling them to investors.

THE SECONDARY MARKET

The secondary market is the forum in which older or seasoned bonds change hands between investors and dealers. Although most individuals are buy-and-hold investors, institutional customers such as mutual funds, money managers, and insurance companies are more active buyers and sellers. The dealer community performs two functions in this process. First, dealers distribute municipal bonds to customers from their inventory as well as from underwritings as previously discussed. Second, they provide liquidity to customers who are sellers. The bonds bought from customers are either sold in turn to other customers or placed in dealer inventories in anticipation of interest from investors. In the latter case, the dealer assumes the market risk on the bonds they now own.

Dealers in municipal securities also do business with each other. Traditionally, much of this inter-dealer trading was done through intermediaries known as brokers' brokers. These firms do not carry inventory; rather their role is to bring buyers and sellers of a particular bond together. Once a broker negotiates an agreement on price between a buyer and a seller, a three-way transaction takes place. Dealer #1 sells to the broker, who marks up the price of the bond by a nominal amount and sells it to Dealer #2. The markup in price on this trade is the broker's remuneration. The dealers involved in a trade through a broker are guaranteed anonymity since the broker is each dealer's counterparty and neither is aware of who is on the other side.

In recent years, the municipal market, like most other fixed-income markets, has become increasingly automated by the rise of electronic communication networks (ECNs). These web-based trading platforms provide access to a broad range of live dealer municipal bond offerings and serve as a forum for sellers to liquidate positions by requesting bids. When shopping for bonds to fill customer inquiries, sales reps can utilize ECN capability to pinpoint offerings that meet their customer's specific investment parameters. With multiple platforms firmly established in the market, the municipal business is sometimes described by pundits as more of a wholesale distribution system than a traditional securities market.

Price transparency has always been a problem for municipal bond investors. Due to the vast number of issuers and the range of credit quality and structures, the vast majority of municipal bonds trade infrequently if at all after issuance. Consequently, there are seldom active bid or offer quotes for a given security. This becomes especially problematic when bondholders need to sell their securities. It can be very difficult for a nonprofessional to judge whether the price he or she receives from a dealer is the best that the market will bear. To address this need, the regulatory authorities have required dealers to report all their municipal trades to the MSRB within 15 minutes of execution. Investors who want to verify the quality of a quote they receive for a given bond can view current trade price information on the MSRB's electronic municipal market access website (emma.msrb.org). By entering the bond's nine-digit identifier or CUSIP number in EMMA's search function, investors can see all of its recent transactions as well as the issue's Official Statement and most recent audited financial statements.

INVESTING IN MUNICIPAL BONDS

Municipal bond investors fall into one of two broad categories; retail or institutional. Retail buyers are generally defined as individuals or their proxies, that is, entities who act on an investor's behalf. Included in this group are registered investment advisors, separately managed accounts at investment firms, bank trust departments, and family offices.

On the other hand, institutional buyers are investing large sums and typically transact in blocks of $5 million or more. Among them are mutual fund companies, insurance companies, hedge funds, and bank portfolios. These buyers focus largely on the primary market where they can purchase bonds in blocks from intact new-issue maturities. Their investment strategies vary, but they typically seek to maximize total rate of return (TRR) on their investments. That is, they will be active sellers as well as buyers in an effort to realize capital gains to supplement the tax-exempt income they earn on their portfolios. For the purposes of our discussion, we will focus on the retail investor.

As noted, most individuals buy municipal bonds to generate tax-exempt income rather than capital appreciation. The stereotypical bond buyer is a wealthy, middle-aged or older person who plans to hold their bonds until maturity. Although this is a gross generalization with many exceptions to the rule, we will see from the discussion ahead that there are legitimate reasons for this profile of a retail municipal buyer to exist.

Municipal Bonds and the Asset Allocation Model

Individuals who are fortunate enough to build an investment portfolio will have changing goals over the course of their lives. After starting a successful business, buying a home, or funding children's educations, a person's focus may change toward saving for retirement. A portfolio heavily weighted toward equities (as opposed to fixed income and cash) is generally favored to generate a higher rate of growth; the more aggressive the strategy, the higher the potential risks and rewards. Hopefully, over time, an individual's net worth grows to a level that will sustain his or her lifestyle long after retirement. At that point, investing strategy becomes more about keeping one's wealth as opposed to building it. To do so, a more conservative approach is in order. A portfolio weighted more toward fixed-income products and away from equities then becomes appropriate. For many investors, the fixed-income product of choice will be medium- and high-grade municipal bonds. One of the two most compelling reasons a conservative investor would buy municipal bonds is their safety. Detroit, Orange County, and Puerto Rico aside, the default rate of investment-grade munis since the Great Depression is a fraction of 1%. Investors sleep well at night knowing that the bonds they have purchased will pay them regular interest and return 100 cents on the dollar at maturity. The other reason for buying municipals bonds is their tax treatment.

Tax-Exempt Bonds versus Taxables

What type of bond is most appropriate for the investor looking to preserve the value of their hard-earned nest-egg? The answer to that question is a function of marginal personal income tax rates. A cursory review of yields on various fixed-income products reveals that municipal bond yields are generally lower than taxable alternatives such as U.S. Treasuries or bonds issued by corporations, yet there is always demand for these lower-yielding bonds. A person choosing between a 10-year AAA-rated tax-exempt and a 10-year AAA-rated taxable corporate bond must put them on equal terms to make an informed purchase decision. To do so, the investor must convert the tax-free yield

(TFY) on the muni into a taxable equivalent yield (TEY). The TEY is based on his or her marginal tax rate (MTR) and this formula:

$$TEY = TFY/1 - MTR$$

For example, the TEY on a NYC Water Rev. 3.10% due 8/1/36 yielding 3.10% (or a dollar price of 100) for a person in the current maximum marginal tax rate (currently 39.6%) is:

$$TEY = 3.10/1 - .396$$
$$TEY = 3.10/.604$$
$$TEY = 5.13\%$$

In other words, this investor would be indifferent between the NYC Water bonds of '36 yielding 3.10% and a comparable quality taxable bond of the same duration yielding 5.13%. If, on the other hand, the quoted yield on the taxable bond is higher than 5.13%, our investor with the 39.6% marginal tax rate would choose the taxable bond because after paying federal income tax on the bond's interest, he or she would still be left with a yield greater than 3.10%.

The analysis shifts in favor of the taxable bond alternative for investors in lower tax brackets. Assume the person considering the NYC Water 3.10% maturing in 2036 yielding 3.10% is in an MTR of 25%. Our formula gives us a TEY of 4.13%. For a person in a 15% MTR, this indifference point drops to a TEY of 3.65%. Clearly, then, the value of the tax exemption on municipal bond interest is the greatest for investors in the highest tax brackets.

MUNICIPAL BOND RISK FACTORS

Although we have described municipal bonds as the sleep-well-at-night portion of an investment portfolio, the asset class is not without risks. Specifically there are three types of risk when buying bonds. In each case, the concept that risk increases with time is essential to understanding the psychology of the bond buyer and the positive slope of the yield curve.

Credit Risk

Put simply, credit risk measures the likelihood of the bondholder receiving the semiannual interest payments and return of principal in a timely fashion. Any failure or delay in receiving these payments on the expected date qualifies as an event of default. The perceived credit risk on an individual bond should be positively correlated to the yield. Credit risk is a function of the creditworthiness of the issuer and is weighted by the tenor of the bond. For example, one would expect an AAA bond due in one year to yield less than the same credit due in 30 years. Similarly, for any two bonds maturing on the same part of the yield curve, one would expect a sub-investment-grade bond to yield far more than a highly rated bond.

For buyers of investment-grade, higher-quality bonds, history would imply that the risk of default is very low. However, deterioration of an issuer's creditworthiness can erode the market value of its bonds, especially if the credit impairment results in a ratings downgrade. For the buy-and-hold investor, a loss of market value stemming from a credit event is not catastrophic as long as principal is paid upon maturity, but for a *total return* buyer who may need to sell during the life of the bond it can prove to be very damaging.

Market or Interest Rate Risk

Since bond prices move inversely to interest rates, the market value of fixed-rate instruments will vary with changes in the U.S. Treasury yields, the benchmark around which the world's credit markets revolve. Generally (and in recent years there have been many exceptions to this rule), yields in the municipal market are positively correlated with the Treasury market, so we may define market risk as the change in a bond's value caused solely by fundamental changes in interest rates.

Market risk can be quantified by calculating the change in the market value of a bond resulting from a one-basis-point or .01% change in its yield. This incremental change, known as the dollar value of a basis point or DV01, increases with the tenor of the security. For example, the DV01 of a one-year security is roughly $.50 per thousand dollars of notional value versus $1.50 per thousand for a 30-year non-callable bond. For callable bonds valued above par, the DV01 is driven by the call feature. Regulatory convention dictates that in quoting a yield for a callable bond, a dealer must calculate which of the potential redemption dates, beginning with the first call date and ending with the maturity date, generates the lowest dollar price. This will ensure that the buyer's true yield, regardless of whether the bond is called, will never be lower than the stated yield. Another term for a bond's DV01 is its duration. The greater a bond's duration, the greater its market risk and in turn the greater the yield required to take that risk.

Event or Extraneous Risk

This is the most intangible of risks taken by investors in any asset class. In recent decades, the integrity of municipal bond holdings has often been shaken by factors totally unconnected to the financial markets. In 2001, the September 11 terrorist attacks changed forever the way Americans viewed the security of their homeland. New York City, where the loss of life and damage to the economy were the greatest, was faced with the task of rebuilding its entire downtown financial district. In the aftermath of the attack, the Port Authority of New York and New Jersey, the owner of the World Trade Center and a major bond issuer, saw the value of its outstanding debt plummet and its access to the primary market evaporate. Fifteen years and billions of dollars later, New York and the Port Authority have regained their financial footing. Similarly, communities ravaged by hurricanes such as New Orleans and the Gulf Coast in 2005 and the greater New York/New Jersey region in 2012 faced major challenges in rebuilding their infrastructure and economies in the storms' aftermaths. In all of these cases, the damage to the credit quality of bond issuers in the affected areas was impossible to anticipate. Unfortunately, the threats posed by stateless terrorist groups and extreme weather remain both unmeasurable and unpredictable and are widely assumed to be realities of life in the twenty-first century.

CASE STUDY

You are the investment officer of a small bank in the City of Springfield. In keeping with the company's philosophy of investing in the local community, the bank's investment portfolio consists primarily of municipal bonds issued by nearby localities. The bank's two largest holdings are

1. City of Springfield Various Purpose General Obligation 5% due 1/1/2036, callable 1/1/2024 at par, purchased at issuance in 2014 at 121.066 to yield 3.00 to the 2024 call.
2. Springfield Water & Sewer Authority Revenue Bonds 3% due 6/1/2026, non-callable, purchased at issuance in 2014 at par. (The service area of the Authority consists of the City of Springfield and two nearby counties.)

Both bonds are rated Aa2 by Moody's, AA by Standard & Poor's, and AA by Fitch.

In late 2016, the local corporate power company announced its plan to close its now-obsolete nuclear power plant, which is located in Springfield. Since its opening 40 years ago, the plant has been Springfield's largest taxpayer and employer. In fact, the property tax revenue generated by the plant has helped make Springfield's public school system one of the strongest in the state. In addition, the large number of steady, well-paying jobs at the plant has been the principal driver of the city's robust local economy and has made it a very desirable place to live. In short, the City's fortunes and the high-grade ratings carried by its debt are closely tied to the power company's presence.

The company estimates it will take two to three years to decommission and dismantle the nuclear facility. By that time, virtually all of the employees at the plant will have been let go or relocated to other facilities around the state. The company also plans to challenge in court any attempt by the City to maintain the plant's property assessment at the current levels.

In regard to the two securities above:

1. Without actually performing the calculations, which bond do you think has the greater duration and why?
2. In what ways will the closing of the power plant impact the credit of both the City GO and the Water & Sewer Authority?

3. Assuming major economic fallout from the plant closing, which of the two bonds faces the greater risk of a ratings downgrade, or in a worst-case scenario, default? Explain your reasoning.

4. Historically, Springfield GOs and Springfield W&S Revs with similar structures and maturities have traded in the secondary market with a 5-basis-point spread in favor of the GO. (That is, the GO trades at a 5-bp-lower yield and commensurate higher price than the revenue bond.) In light of the scenario we have described, would you expect this spread relationship to change? If so, how?

5. *Bonus Question:* What college did the owner of the Springfield nuclear plant attend?

Answers

1. Duration measures the change in the price of a bond for an incremental change in its yield (i.e., 1 basis point). This is sometimes referred to as the dollar value of a .01 or DV.01. The interest rate on the bond, its current dollar price, its call features, and its maturity date all affect its duration. The 3% Water & Sewer bonds are non-callable and mature in 2026. The GO 5% of 2036 are callable in 2024 and were purchased at a yield of 3% and a price of over 121. Unless yields have risen by two full percentage points since the GOs were purchased, this bond is being priced to its 2024 call date. We know that the value of a basis point increases with the tenor of a bond; therefore the 3%/year revenue bonds due in 2026 will have a greater duration than the 5% GOs, which are priced to the 2024 call option.

2. Credit impairment poses a real threat to bondholders of both securities. We assume that the closing of the plant will exact a serious toll on the Springfield economy. As jobs are lost, residents will spend less, which will in turn impact local businesses. The loss of well-paying jobs might force families to sell their homes and relocate. Mortgage defaults will rise as well, reducing home values and property tax collections. If the city is forced to reduce the assessed value of the power plant, its largest taxpayer, general-fund revenues from real estate taxes will be cut sharply. City managers will need to make difficult decisions over expenditure levels and how to deploy their shrinking general-fund revenue base. It is probably safe to assume that Springfield's AA GO rating will be in serious jeopardy and the prospect of a default greatly enhanced.

   The Water & Sewer Authority will be impacted by this scenario as well; its revenues will drop if some rate payers stop paying their bills. As an AA-rated issuer, the cover ratio (maximum annual debt service/net revenue) might provide ample room for the authority to absorb this blow and continue to meet its obligations. Also, the essential-purpose nature of the Authority may limit the extent to which rate payers fail to pay their bills. Finally, we know that the net revenues of the system are dedicated to the payment of debt service before being used for any other purpose. However, a rating downgrade cannot be ruled out.

3. The risk to GO holders is greater because of the City's reliance on property and to a lesser degree, other taxes to pay debt service. The ability to raise taxes will be meaningless if the local economy and the city's real property values contract dramatically. With its historical overreliance on one taxpayer, Springfield lacks the financial diversity to adapt to the utility's decision and faces the prospect of multiple rating downgrades or even a default.

4. The impact of the plant closing will fall more heavily on the GO credit, making it a more risky investment. Investors will therefore demand a higher return to compensate for this perceived increase in credit risk. This will be especially true if the GO rating is downgraded to a level below that of the Water & Sewer Authority. As a result the trading relationship between the two credits will invert and the revenue bonds will out-trade the GOs.

5. Yale University.

CHAPTER 25

Equities

David Weisberger

WHAT IS AN EQUITY?

Equity securities, also known as *stock* or *shares*, along with bonds are one of the two primary means for corporations to raise additional capital. Unlike bonds, however, stocks do not represent a debt that needs to be repaid. Rather, equity securities represent a defined ownership interest, or a specific claim against earnings of either a corporation or a fund that holds financial assets. There are several types of equity securities, all of which represent a defined interest in the issuing company and are perpetual: There is no predefined date where they *mature* or cease to exist.

TYPES OF EQUITIES

Equity security types are defined by the nature of the issuing company and the particular rights that are assigned to the individual securities. The following sections describe the primary types of equities: common stock, preferred shares, depository receipts, and investment companies (mutual funds).

Common Stock

The most basic form of equity is called *common stock* or *ordinary shares*. Common stock usually has specifically defined voting rights attached to ownership that allow stockholders to cast votes for the company's board of directors as well as for or against changes to the corporate charter.

Some companies issue multiple *classes* of common stock with different voting rights. For example, Alphabet Inc., the parent company Google, has three share classes:

1. Class A, ticker GOOG, which has one vote per share
2. Class B, no ticker, as these shares are privately held by the founders and other insiders, which have 10 votes per share
3. Class C, ticker GOOGL, which have no voting rights

The rationale in this case for establishing multiple classes of common stock is that the original ownership group, Class B, wanted to retain voting control over the direction of the company.

Preferred Shares

Preferred shares are a form of equities that represent a priority claim on a company's assets over common stockholders, and are typically issued with a fixed dividend but without voting rights. A company must pay all dividends associated with preferred shares before paying any dividends to common stockholders.

Depository Receipts

Depository receipts are securities issued by international banks denominated in a country's local currency, but based on the ordinary shares of a foreign company. For example, *American depository receipts* (ADRs) are denominated in U.S. dollars. Similarly, *global depository receipts* (GDRs) are issued and trade in various countries and allow investors in those countries to trade foreign company stocks in their local currencies.

Investment Companies (Mutual Funds)

A mutual fund is an investment vehicle that is made up of a pool of funds collected from many investors for the purpose of investing in securities such as stocks and bonds. When purchasing a mutual fund, investors are in essence buying a share of a cross-section of a diversified pool of financial assets. Investors thus gain access to a professionally managed portfolio, which would be impossible to create with a small amount of investment capital. Each shareholder or unit holder participates proportionally in the income gain or loss of the fund. Mutual fund units, or shares, are issued and can typically be purchased or redeemed as needed at the fund's current net asset value (NAV) per share (calculated by dividing the total value of all the securities in its portfolio by the number of fund shares outstanding).

There are generally two types of mutual funds, open ended and closed ended.

Open-ended funds issue new shares and repurchase old shares to meet investor demand. These funds thus buy and sell units on a continuous basis, allowing investors to enter and exit at their convenience. The units are bought and sold at the net asset value declared by the fund as of the close of business that day.

Closed-ended funds issue a fixed number of shares. Thus, unlike open-ended funds, investors cannot buy and sell shares based on the fund's NAV; instead the investor must purchase shares in the secondary market at current market prices, which may be greater than or less than NAV based on supply and demand.

WHY DO COMPANIES ISSUE EQUITIES?

Corporations issue stock in order to raise capital for ongoing operations, for research and development, or to fund acquisitions. A company has several alternatives when looking

TABLE 25.1 Advantages/Disadvantages of Capital-Raising Alternatives

Impact On:	Common Stock	Preferred Stock	Bond/Loan
Balance Sheet	No impact.	Perpetual liability for dividend payment if fixed.	Liability for principal and interest.
Ownership Control	Dilution of ownership if voting rights attached to common stock.	No dilution unless security is convertible to common stock.	No dilution unless security is convertible to common stock.
Future Profit Exposure	Dilution of owners' claim on future retained earnings.	No dilution unless security is convertible to common stock.	No dilution unless security is convertible to common stock.
Financial Flexibility	Ability to use stock to purchase other companies plus lack of debt means future ability to issue debt is unimpaired.	No specific financial flexibility, but there is no liability associated with the initial sale of the securities, only the future dividends.	Debt securities need to be repaid.
Tax	Some mergers can be accomplished using stock without tax consequences.		Interest payments are often deductible.

to additional raise capital. These include commercial loans, the issuance of corporate bonds, or the sale of equity. Both commercial loans and bonds represent a liability as they both must be repaid. When selling equity the company does not incur a liability, but instead dilutes the ownership interests of the company by increasing the ownership claims to corporate earnings and assets.

Corporations must continually choose between these capital-raising methodologies when evaluating how to raise capital. There are advantages and disadvantages to the capital-raising alternatives for the corporation depending on the type of method chosen, including balance sheet impact, ownership structure, financial flexibility, and tax liability. (See Table 25.1.)

In order to maximize both short- and long-term earnings for their investors, corporations are constantly evaluating these tradeoffs when they are in need of financing.

EQUITY MARKET PARTICIPANTS

There are several types of participants in the equity market, including various types of investors, speculators, and market makers. Investors in the equity markets include individuals investing for retirement or other future needs, pension funds investing to provide income to retirees, insurance companies interested in growing their assets, and investment companies that provide professional investment management services to their clients. Generally, investors buy equities in order to profit from the combination of long-term price appreciation and dividends paid by the companies whose stocks are purchased. There are two additional categories of investors that are somewhat different, however. Strategic investors purchase stock to obtain control over a company, often with the goal of merging the existing operations of their own company with those of the company whose stock they purchase. Activist investors are people who believe that the company's stock is undervalued, but that changes in corporate strategy are necessary to unlock that value. In all cases, however, investors purchase equities with the idea of owning the stock for a relatively long period of time.

Speculators, on the other hand, include participants that look to profit on short-term movements in equity prices, either up or down. Examples of speculators include arbitrageurs, day traders, automated quantitative traders, and dedicated short sellers. There are many forms of arbitrage trading that, in its simplest form, buy or sell stocks when simultaneously selling or buying correlated securities. Day traders are professional traders who buy and sell stocks based on a variety of technical indicators, news stories, or other techniques. Automated, quantitative traders include a wide array of trading strategies that range from very high-frequency strategies to computer models that predict multiday price moves in stocks. Short sellers are professional traders who bet against companies by selling their stock short with the expectation that the price will decline.

One of the more important types of participant in the equity market is the market maker. Those trading firms that almost continuously maintain orders to buy and sell the stocks in which they make markets help to keep the spreads between bids and offers tight, which keeps trading costs lower for all participants.

Unlike long-term investors, market makers and speculators such as hedge funds and day traders engage in a variety of trading strategies. Day traders buy and sell securities on a short time horizon during the day; market makers use sophisticated computer systems to profit from the bid–offer spread; proprietary trading firms and hedge funds either employ traders or build trading models designed to profit from short-term price discrepancies between highly correlated individual stocks or baskets of stocks. These short-term investors are mostly interested in price appreciation or, in the case of short sellers (selling stock that is not owned), betting that the stock prices will fall.

Equities as an asset class are attractive because historically they have outperformed the rate of inflation. As illustrated in the chart in Figure 25.1, equities have provided a higher real rate of return than bonds, bills, gold, or the U.S. dollar over the past 200 years:[1]

---

[1]Jeremy Siegel, "Real Returns Favor Holding Stocks," *AAII Journal*, August 2014, http://www .aaii.com/journal/article/real-returns-favor-holding-stocks.touch.

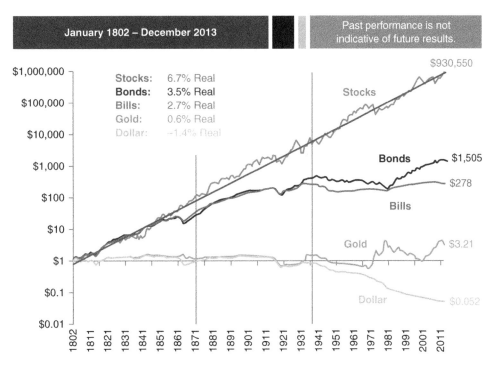

FIGURE 25.1 Total real return indexers
Source: Jeremy Siegel, "Real Returns Favor Holding Stocks," *AAII Journal*, August 2014, http://www.aaii.com/journal/article/real-returns-favor-holding-stocks.touch.

EQUITY MARKETS

The equity market consists of the primary market and secondary market. The primary market involves the initial public offering (IPO) where the stock is first offered to the public and listed on a stock exchange. Firms may wish to issue additional equity at a later date; this is commonly known as a *secondary offering*, not to be confused with secondary market trading. The secondary market, which normally starts immediately after the IPO, is characterized by the continuous buying and selling of equities during the trading day.

The IPO Process

The IPO process is highly regulated and normally conducted by one or more underwriters and a selling group comprised of broker-dealers. Underwriters, as the name implies, guarantee some or all of the risk of the IPO and are responsible for leading the IPO process.

The underwriter is compensated through the underwriter's spread, which is the difference between what the public pays for the security and the proceeds that the issuing company receives. The underwriting spread is made up of the following components: the management fee for handling the IPO; the *selling concession*, which is carved out for payment to broker-dealers that actually sell stock to its customers (whether in the selling group or as an underwriter); and the underwriter's direct compensation for taking on the deal risk.

The underwriter is responsible for the creation of all legal documents that are provided to potential investors. The most important document is the prospectus, which includes audited financial information, descriptions of the company's business and corporate structure, as well as potential risks to the company's business prospects. The Securities and Exchange Commission (SEC) requires that underwriters must disclose all known risks to the company's business model. As a result underwriters conduct extensive due diligence on the company, including documented discussions with company management, auditors, and customers.

Following due diligence, the company's management along with the underwriters and selling group members may conduct a *roadshow*. Roadshows are presentations that are made by an issuer's senior management, often accompanied by representatives of the lead underwriters, to market the upcoming security to prospective investors. The roadshow is intended to generate interest in the IPO, and gives potential investors an opportunity to ask detailed questions regarding the issue.

Listing Standards

The next step in the process is selecting a listing exchange. The IPO is then conducted pursuant to the guidelines of that particular exchange. While most equity securities post IPO trades on multiple stock exchanges, each company is *listed* on only one exchange in each country. In the United States, the New York Stock Exchange and the NASDAQ stock exchange are the largest primary markets for corporate stock while the ARCA exchange (Archipelago exchange) and the BATS exchange (Bats Global Markets, Inc.) are the largest primary listing markets for exchange-traded funds (see Chapter 27 for more). In the United States, the exchanges have regulatory responsibilities, including the supervision of listing standards, which include minimum financial requirements set by each listing exchange and are monitored by the exchanges themselves. The listing standards include:

> *Pre-tax earnings*—income, net of expenses, from continuing operations before income taxes
>
> *Cash flows*—cash received from continuing operations net of cash expenses
>
> *Market capitalization*—over a minimum threshold, calculated by multiplying the shares outstanding on the company's balance sheet by the market or IPO price
>
> *Revenue*—All earned income from continuing operations before expenses
>
> *Total assets*—All investments, cash, production equipment, real estate, intellectual property, or other items of value owned by the company
>
> *Stockholders equity*—The total value of all stock in the company, calculated by subtracting all liabilities from the other assets of the corporations

Total number of shareholders

Market value of publicly held shares, calculated by multiplying the number of total outstanding shares by the market price of the shares

Once the IPO has been completed the equity shares trade in what is termed the *secondary market*. The secondary market for equities can include both private and public trading. Privately traded stock, usually referred to as *private equity*, is restricted to qualified investors and trades far less frequently with limited disclosures and information. The term *qualified investor* refers to the SEC definitions of an investor's experience and liquid net worth.

Publicly traded equity securities comprise the vast majority of equity trades and come in two varieties: order driven and quote based. Order-driven markets are by far the most popular. In these markets, client orders are accepted by the stock exchanges and are either posted, matched, or rejected. This is done by aggregating all priced orders into an *order book*, which is then displayed to the public as a *best bid and offer* (BBO). These quotes, along with matched trades, are collectively referred to as *market data*, which is the information behind the ticker commonly seen scrolling across the screens of financial websites and news programs. Today's order-driven markets are fully automated: Every individual order is required to be entered into an order management system at a broker-dealer, which in turn sends the order to an exchange.

MECHANICS OF ORDER-DRIVEN MARKETS

Consider the following sequence of orders sent to a stock exchange in stock "XYZ":

1. Client A—buy order at 100.50 for 200 shares
2. Client B—sell order at 100.52 for 500 shares
3. Client C—buy order at 100.49 for 800 shares
4. Client D—sell order at 100.53 for 500 shares

At this point, the exchange will be displaying a BBO of 100.50 bid and 100.52 offered and the order book will have additional liquidity available at the lower bid of 100.49 and higher offer of 100.53. Typically, this is represented in trading screens with the BBO expressed as: XYZ 100.50 100.52 200 × 500 (verify how volume is displayed. i.e., should it state 20x50) (Common convention for equity tickers is to list the bid price followed by the offer price and then the bid size "x" offer size in smaller print.)

The full order book, often called a *montage*, would look like this:

Shares	Bid	Offer	Shares
		100.53	500
		100.52	500
200	100.50		
800	100.49		

If, at this point, a buyer willing to pay 100.52 enters an order of 500 shares or less, the exchange will match that order with the par 100.52 best offer and a trade will occur. To illustrate, consider the following sequence of orders:

5. Client initiates buy order for 200 shares at 100.52.

The exchange would report a trade of 200 shares at 100.52 and the BBO would change to: XYZ 100.50 100.52 200 × 300. The order book would also change to look like this:

Shares	Bid	Offer	Shares
		100.53	500
		100.52	300
200	100.50		
800	100.49		

6. Client initiates buy order for 500 shares at 100.51.

No trade would occur, but the BBO would change to: XYZ 100.51 100.52 500 × 200.

Shares	Bid	Offer	Shares
		100.53	500
		100.52	200
500	100.51		
200	100.50		
800	100.49		

7. Client initiates sell order for 1000 shares at 100.50.

The market would report two individual trades: 500 shares at 100.51 and 200 shares at 100.50 and the BBO would change to: XYZ 100.49 100.52 800×300.

Shares	Bid	Offer	Shares
		100.53	500
		100.52	200
		100.51	300
800	100.49		

Quote-driven markets are also often referred to as dealer markets, since they are characterized by competing quotes displayed by market makers. Market makers post quotations based on both the orders that they have received as well as their own trading interest. Unlike the order-based markets described earlier, market makers generally display quotes for a standard amount of shares rather than for individual order amounts. In the largest U.S. market of this type (OTC markets[2]), this is referred to as a *tier size* and represents the minimum size required for market makers to trade in any particular stock. In most dealer markets, market makers are required to register with the market in order to post quotes. Broker-dealers accept an affirmative obligation to both bid and offer for stocks in which they make markets. This is in direct contrast to order-driven markets where any broker-dealer that connects to the market can place an order. This exclusivity is provided to market makers in exchange for meeting this two-sided markets obligation as described previously.

Most of the exchanges worldwide, including those in the United States, operate on an order-driven basis. It is important to know that the primary exchange for equity securities also conducts both opening and closing auctions. In the opening and closing auctions, either the exchange system or a designated market maker aggregates all buy and sell orders to set the price. The price is set in order to maximize the number of shares that can trade while fulfilling the most orders possible.

The closing auction on the primary exchange is a very important price point, as it is used for pricing the closing value of all stock indexes and derivative products such as stock options. When investors look at historical price data for equities, it is typically the closing auction price.

HISTORY OF EQUITY TRADING

There have been a number of milestone events that have greatly influenced the equity markets. This section discusses some of the organizational, historical, technological, and regulatory changes that had a major impact.

Timeline of Milestone Events:

1602—Amsterdam Stock Exchange established (Dutch East India Company)

1711–1720—South Sea bubble

1792—Buttonwood Agreement forms the New York Stock Exchange and fixes commissions

1801—Rules created the subscription room of the London Stock Exchange

1867—Tickertape invented

1929—Crash of '29

---

[2]OTC Markets Inc., a registered alternative trading system, handles the majority of OTC transactions in unlisted foreign and domestic equities. For more information see http://www.otcmarkets.com/home.

1933/4—The Securities Exchange Acts passed to create the National Market System in the United States

1971—NASDAQ debuts with electronic display of stock quotes

1975—"Mayday" deregulation of equity commissions

1977—CATS OS debuts in Toronto

1982—CME introduces S&P 500 futures

1987—Crash of '87

1996–98—NASDAQ scandal leads to order handling rules and Reg ATS

2001—Decimalization

2007—Reg NMS

The Buttonwood Agreement Leads to the Formation of the NYSE

During the industrial revolution, stock markets became an important means for emerging corporations to raise capital. In 1792, in lower Manhattan, the leading stock brokers in New York City formed a members-only association by what is known as the "Buttonwood Agreement." That agreement, under which all the signatories agreed to trade directly with each other and to fix a floor on commission rates, established the precursor to the New York Stock Exchange, which was formalized years later. While the NYSE was not the first stock exchange in the United States (Philadelphia has that distinction), it soon became the most important. After the invention of the telegraph enabled faster communication between investors and New York City, stock trading grew rapidly and the NYSE became the dominant exchange.

The Tickertape

The invention of the tickertape in 1867 further sped the development and expansion of stock trading. By the 1880s, there were over a thousand tickertape machines installed in offices in New York City alone. The development of this technology facilitated the establishment of brokerage offices throughout the country.

Margin

When a buyer of stock purchases equity on margin, they are borrowing the money to complete their purchase from the brokerage firm they are using. The buyer is only required to deposit funds in their account sufficient to cover the margin requirement. Today, due to a rule called Regulation T, which was adopted by the U.S. Federal Reserve in 1974, the margin requirement for most equities is 50%. Thus, if a person was to purchase 100 shares of stock XYZ at $50, they would only need to deposit $2,500, and would therefore be borrowing $2,500 to enable the purchase of $5,000 of this stock. If the price of the stock were to decline substantially, the margin requirement would force the investor to either deposit more money to maintain the position or sell enough of the position to make up for the decline in value.

During the late 1800s and early 1900s, there were no regulations governing the use of margin. Speculators in those days could purchase stocks on extremely low margins, in some cases as low as 2%. While not the primary cause of volatility in markets, excessive margin debt did contribute to magnifying financial shocks and severe dislocations, experienced often in those days. Prior to the Great Depression, there were so-called financial "panics" in 1873, 1884, 1890, 1893, 1896, 1901, 1907, and, after the end of World War I, the depression of 1920–21. Financial panics were all marked by dramatic declines in the value of the stock market and other speculative assets that led directly to significant losses to investors and corporations as well as to spikes in unemployment.

The Crash of 1929 Leads to Change

Despite these financial panics, there were very few changes in the equity markets in this era. After the depression ended in 1922, the decade of the "Roaring Twenties" ensued with a strong economy and significant gains in the stock market that accelerated as the decade progressed. It was estimated that, in the year before the onset of the Great Depression, the average stock purchase was made with as little as 10% margin. This meant that as the market was approaching its highs in 1929, 90% of stock purchases were made by borrowed money. As a result, once the stock market crash began, widespread forced selling ensued, causing many investors to suffer a complete loss of their investment.

Founding Legislation of Equity Markets

Starting in the depths of the Great Depression, new legislation began shaping the modern equity markets. The 1933 Securities Act established the first federal regulations on the issuance and trading of equity securities, and in 1934, the Exchange Act established the Securities and Exchange Commission, creating the regulatory framework for stock exchanges and brokers. This legislation was followed by amendments in 1938 that created the National Association of Securities Dealers (the precursor organization to FINRA), the *self-regulatory organization* (SRO) that is primarily responsible for the oversight of client-facing broker-dealers. In 1940, the Investment Company Act established the regulatory environment for mutual funds. The establishment of this regulatory framework produced a lengthy period of growth in the equity markets. By the end of the 1960s, trading volumes had grown too large to be accommodated by the back-office processes of that day, which handled the settlement of trades. In order to settle an equity trade, the buyer must deliver the agreed-upon funds to the seller's account and the seller must transfer the securities purchased to the account of the buyer. At that time, the process was manual, where equity securities were represented by physical stock certificates and were tracked by related documents such as "floor reports," "contract sheets," and "transfer statements." The paperwork associated with physically renaming the owner of stock certificates was cumbersome and labor intensive.

The entire system became so unwieldy that there were an ever-increasing number of failed trades, substantial theft, and, ultimately, over 200 brokerage houses were driven out of business.

Subsequently, a new phase of rulemaking began, which culminated in the 1975 amendments that established the National Market System we have today. Among other things, these amendments authorized the creation of the Securities Information Processor (SIP), which was created to be the central, consolidated live stream and aggregator of every exchange's best quotes (bids and offers) as well as reported trades. The data comes from all the exchanges and is processed and fed back out as one stream of data. This is often referred to as the *consolidated tape*, and it is considered the official vehicle for disseminating price information in the U.S. equity market.

Market Data under the National Market System

At the time that the National Market System (NMS) was established, there were three primary listing markets: the New York Stock Exchange, the American Stock Exchange, and the NASDAQ market. The rules creating the NMS mandated that all stock quotes and trades be aggregated. They established the Consolidated Tape Association Plan/ Consolidated Quotation Plan (CTA/CQ Plans) for the two exchanges and the OTC UTP plan for the NASDAQ market (NASDAQ did not become a registered exchange until 2006). These plans governed the collection, processing, and distribution of quotation and transaction information for all NMS securities and were broken out into three tapes (tapes A, B, and C representing the NYSE, AMEX, and NASDAQ, respectively). The data is collected from all market centers where NMS securities are traded, including securities exchanges, ATSs, and other broker-dealers. All of this data must be provided to a centralized Securities Information Processor (SIP) for each tape data consolidation and dissemination. The current SIPs are run by the New York Stock Exchange for tapes A and B and NASDAQ for tape C, and that data is made available to all market data vendors, broker-dealers, and technology platforms that want such access.

Commissions and "May Day"

In addition to the creation of the National Market System, 1975 was also the year that the SEC mandated the deregulation of fixed commissions. This occurred on May 1 of that year and was dubbed "May Day" by the financial industry. Starting on that date, the original agreements that bound members of the New York Stock Exchange to fix commissions were declared void, and the law mandated that all commission agreements be negotiated. Initially, the law was seen to have limited impact, since brokerage firms operated as a somewhat closed community. While the established brokerage firms made minor modifications to commission rates, offering some small discounts to large clients and even raising fees to small clients, newer firms were more innovative. Over the next decades, "discount" brokerage firms changed the industry by driving down commission costs to the levels seen today.

NASDAQ

Another major innovation in the equity markets was the debut of NASDAQ in 1971, the first all-electronic market. NASDAQ was a *dealer market* and, as such, did not have a trading floor. Thus only market makers were allowed to post quotes via the NASDAQ display system for public dissemination. Although NASDAQ market makers displayed their quotes electronically, up until the late 1990s most actual trades were still consummated via telephone. As a result, bulge bracket firms with extensive client lists and large trading desks dominated the trading of NASDAQ stocks for the first 25+ years of its history.

The decade of the 1970s saw a lingering recession that depressed investor interest in the evolving equity markets. In 1982, the bear market reached a generational bottom and the market proceeded to start an extended bull run. It was in this year that the stock index futures contract on the Standard and Poor's (S&P) 500 stock index was introduced.

Stock Index Futures and the Crash of 1987

Creation of the S&P 500 stock futures was an extremely important development in the history of the modern stock market. The index itself was (and still is) created by S&P to represent the most liquid and largest public companies in the United States. The futures contract is traded on the Chicago Mercantile Exchange (CME) and is *cash settled*, whereby, upon the expiration of a contract, the buyers and sellers exchange the cash difference between the purchase (or sale) price and the actual price of the index.[3] The ability to trade one single futures contract to gain upside or downside exposure to equity price movements was revolutionary. The S&P futures quickly became one of the more liquid vehicles for trading equity market risk and was heavily used by a wide array of investors and speculators. Its popularity led to the creation of several new trading businesses, including index arbitrage and a variety of derivative products.

One of the most innovative derivative products using the S&P 500 futures during the 1980s was called *portfolio insurance*. This product was sold to a variety of large institutional investors and asset managers to protect their clients against substantial losses in the case of a large downturn in the market. Financial models were designed to signal to portfolio insurers when they should sell futures contracts to hedge their risk. It was generally considered that the S&P 500 futures contracts were so liquid that firms selling insurance would always be able to sell sufficient futures contracts in order to hedge. This assumption was proved incorrect in the fall of 1987. The stock market had been on a virtually uninterrupted 5-year bull run, but stresses were beginning to show and in the third week of October the market dropped by roughly 9%. This left portfolio insurers with a substantial amount of futures to sell the following Monday. On Monday, October 19, the market crashed.

---

[3]The actual price of the S&P 500 Index at futures expiration is calculated by multiplying the official opening price on the Friday that the contract expires of each of the constituent stocks in the index by the official weight in the index of each stock.

Following the crash of 1987, there were several new regulations implemented, including market-wide *circuit breakers* that were designed to pause trading during times of severe price moves, as well as special reporting to document the amount of program trading. Program trading was defined as any computer trading program that traded more than 15 stocks simultaneously with a market value exceeding $1 million, and included all index arbitrage and computerized trading for the accounts of brokerage firms. Specific rules were put in place to prohibit most program trading during times of severe market stress.

In addition to these measures, there was a major effort to reduce the settlement period for equity trades to three days from the previous five days, meaning the brokerage firm must now receive payment no later than three business days after the trade was executed. Conversely, when securities are sold, they must be delivered to the brokerage firm no later than three business days after the sale. The crash of 1987 helped to galvanize this effort since the SEC was concerned about the risks of unsettled trades during periods of extreme market movements. In the SEC's words:

> *Unsettled trades pose risks to our financial markets, especially when market prices plunge and trading volumes soar. The longer the period from trade execution to settlement, the greater the risk that securities firms and investors hit by sizable losses would be unable to pay for their transactions.*[4]

The NASDAQ Scandal and the Order Handling Rules Lead to Modern Markets

As the 1990s unfolded, technological changes were accelerating in many businesses, and the stock market was no exception. Retail stock trading was revolutionized by the introduction and rapid growth of online brokers. Regional stock exchanges started to experiment with new technologies such as an all-electronic market (Cincinnati stock exchange) to compete with the NYSE. The NYSE, while continuing to require its specialists to be directly involved in all trades, facilitated the development and use of handheld computers by floor brokers, which allowed firms an electronic method of communicating with the floor. NASDAQ market makers transitioned away from exclusive reliance on the telephone for trading, using new software systems such as Tools of the Trade to update their quotes as well as to trade with other market makers. Those market makers began using a newly developed *inter-dealer* electronic market terminal developed by Instinet. Technological advances further accelerated after a NASDAQ market trading scandal in 1996.

In that year, there were multiple allegations made against the largest NASDAQ market makers. They were accused of colluding to keep bid–offer spreads artificially wide, of using the Instinet terminal to trade without passing on the benefit to their clients,

---

[4]SEC Investor Publications, "About Settling Trades in Three Days: T+3," https://www.sec.gov/investor/pubs/tplus3.htm.

and of putting their firm's profits ahead of their "best execution" duties. This resulted in a settlement with the SEC and a series of new regulations referred to as the *order handling rules*. These rules included regulations that forced brokers to display most limit orders they received from clients, gave client orders priority over the brokers' proprietary orders, and forced market makers to make public their best quotes. These new rules led directly to the NASDAQ market implementing a new system called SuperMontage, and resulted in the transition of the NASDAQ market from a dealer quote–based market to an order-driven market. With the SuperMontage system in place, for the first time both orders and quotes were fully executable electronically by a central matching engine. During this same time period, in order to promote innovation, the SEC also passed Regulation ATS, which facilitated the development of new electronic markets.

The cumulative impact of these regulations was both to promote more electronic order-based systems at the large brokerage firms and to spur the proliferation of alternative trading systems (ATSs) and electronic communication networks (ECNs). (ECNs are a particular type of ATS that display their bids and offers to their subscribers.) In the 1990s, the market became extremely fragmented as many ECNs emerged to compete with the New York Stock Exchange and the NASDAQ market. They included Instinet, the Island ECN, Brut and Strike (multiple broker–owned), REDI, Archipelago, and the Attain ECN.

Over the following years, however, these ECNs combined with each other and ultimately were either purchased by exchanges or became exchanges themselves. Brut and Strike combined, Instinet and Island merged, and both of these new entities were purchased by NASDAQ. REDI and Archipelago combined and, after becoming a publicly traded company, was purchased by the NYSE to form the largest exchange operator at the time. The Attain ECN was purchased by a consortium of brokers and became Direct Edge, and the BATS ECN, which was formed in the following decade, eventually became the BATS Exchange. Those two entities merged, forming the BATS Exchange Group, which is the exchange group with the largest equity volume traded at the current time.

This fragmentation of the market into competing electronic order books also spurred the development of the *smart order router* (SOR). The SOR is a trading technology that scans every market to see which has both the best available price and sufficient quantity to satisfy the order, and then sends orders to those markets. SORs are used by traders seeking liquidity as a more expedient alternative to sending one order at a time to each market seen onscreen. SORs helped traders achieve a best execution standard at a time when conventional trading systems failed to show available liquidity from all ATSs and markets.

Decimalization

The next major change to the equity market in the United States was that of decimalization, where equity prices are quoted using a decimal format rather than fractions. The decision radically impacted the market, making it easier for investors to interpret and react to changing price quotes. This led to significantly tighter spreads. For example, prior to decimalization the minimum quoted spread was 1/16 of a dollar, called a *teeny*, representing .0625 cents per share. After, the minimum quoted spread was .01 cent. The average quoted spread for stocks fell by almost the same amount, thus dramatically lowering the cost of trading. The lower trading costs resulted in a significant increase in trade volume, particularly in NASDAQ securities. By 2001, NASDAQ securities traded only on fully electronic order-driven markets. The rise of SOR technology facilitated this volume increase by helping to link the electronic markets together.

Smart Order Routing

Smart order routers were built mainly to handle marketable orders, defined as buy orders at or above the best offer and sell orders at or below the best bid. To illustrate the benefit of SOR technology, the following table contains a modified version of the earlier BBO example that was in the order-driven market example. Consider the situation where stock XYZ is traded in four different markets. In this example, the stock's order book can be shown by what traders refer to as a *montage* that depicts the orders on the order book displayed as follows:

Market	Shares	Bid	Offer	Shares	Market
			100.55	500	NASDAQ
			100.54	1000	NASDAQ
			100.53	500	ARCA
			100.53	500	NASDAQ
			100.52	500	Instinet
			100.52	500	Island
Island	200	100.50			
Instinet	800	100.49			
NASDAQ	500	100.49			
ARCA	2500	100.48			
NASDAQ	500	100.48			

In this scenario, the actual NBBO is XYZ 100.50 100.52 200 × 500 but, depending on the technology used by the trader, they might not have had this full visibility into the market. For example, if a trader was using the NASDAQ proprietary workstation of the time, they would have only seen a best bid of 500 shares at 100.49 and a best offer of 500 shares of 100.53. If that trader had received an order to buy 2000 shares up to 100.55, then the most likely event would have been the trader buying 500 shares at 100.53, 1000 shares at 100.54, and 500 shares at 100.55, all on the NASDAQ system, for an average price of 100.54. If, however, the trader used an SOR that was connected to the Island ECN, the Instinet ECN, the ARCA ECN, as well as to NASDAQ's SuperMontage system, the results would have been much better. Since the SOR was capable of accessing all of the orders on all of the markets, instead of being limited to NASDAQ alone, the SOR would have bought 500 shares from Island at 100.52, 500 shares from Instinet at 100.52, 500 shares from ARCA at 100.53, and 500 shares from NASDAQ at 100.53, for an average price of 100.525. In this example, the SOR would have saved 1.5 cents per share on the 2000-share order.

In addition to SORs, brokers have developed algorithmic trading programs designed to trade large orders. Those algorithms were designed to trade larger orders by splitting them up into smaller pieces and then trading them either by using SORs or through direct connections to systems such as the New York Stock Exchange's DOT system. Most early algorithms either used schedules based on patterns such as historical volume, or were programmed to participate at a particular percentage of the actual volume traded. These algorithms also spurred the growth of internal crossing systems, which allow brokers to match client trades.

Prior to the development of algorithms, one of the primary functions of large broker-dealers was to match large institutional buy and sell orders. Sales traders, handling institutional orders throughout the trading day, either worked to find a natural match to the order from another client, or worked in conjunction with NYSE or NASDAQ traders to execute the order. As the use of algorithms became more widespread and broker crossing systems were developed to facilitate matching institutional orders it became harder for sales traders to compete with computers in matching buyers and sellers. Many of these systems evolved into *alternative trading systems* (ATSs) and expanded beyond crossing orders and actually attracted other sources of order flow. In addition to the broker-operated systems, several other ATSs were developed, including several designed to match large orders. Due to the fact that these trading venues did not display any orders, they became known as *dark pools*. Dark pools have become an important tool for institutional investors by facilitating the matching of natural buyers and sellers while displaying less information to the market.

Even after decimalization the New York Stock Exchange (NYSE) still operated on a floor-based trading model. They required all trades, even those that could match electronically, to be approved by the specialists on the floor. Despite publishing bids and offers electronically, it was not always possible to execute trades against those quotes. This model helped the NYSE maintain over 80% market share, by traded volume, in the securities where they were the primary listing exchange. Competitors such as regional stock exchanges, NASDAQ, and the ECNs in operation at that time complained that the NYSE's membership rules and large market share enabled them to ignore other quotes and discourage real competition. By the middle of last decade, these complaints helped lead to a sweeping set of regulatory changes to the U.S. equity markets: Regulation NMS.

Regulation NMS

Regulation NMS introduced several important changes; the most important from a structural point was the Order Protection Rule, which essentially forced all exchanges to honor the fully executable quotes on other exchanges. It did so by introducing the concept of a *protected* quote, which meant that no exchange could execute a trade at a price inferior to that being displayed at an exchange whose quote was electronically executable.

The rule also introduced a prohibition on knowingly locking a market, which prohibited exchanges from accepting and displaying bids or offers at a price that could be satisfied by routing to a different exchange. The impact of these rules was that the NYSE was now forced to make their quotes electronically executable, which in turn led to significantly increased trading volumes overall, but decreased market share for the NYSE.

In addition to increased trading volumes, the transformation of the NYSE to a fully electronic model and the impact of Reg NMS accelerated the trend toward algorithmic trading. The ability to access all markets electronically made it possible to computerize all types of trading strategies with speed and precision. By the time Reg NMS was fully implemented and all quotes were accessible electronically, all large broker-dealers had fully developed suites of algorithmic trading tools. Virtually every institutional investor's trading desks had linkages to those systems and the percentage of trading handled by computers rapidly increased.

MODERN MARKET STRUCTURE—ORDER TYPES

One of the unique features of the equity market is the ability of traders to enter a variety of order types when attempting to buy or sell stock. At the most basic level, orders are characterized by features such as price considerations, the discretion the broker-dealer or market center maintains when holding the order, when the order is eligible to be traded, as well as special trading restrictions that vary by market.

The most basic types of orders are market and limit orders. Market orders are orders to buy or sell stock without regard to price. These orders tend to always get executed since they are the most aggressive. Limit orders, however, are orders with a specific price limit beyond which the order cannot be executed. For a buy limit order, the price specified is the highest price that the order will pay, and for a sell limit order, the price specified is the lowest price that the seller is willing to accept. When evaluating limit orders, participants categorize them as marketable or nonmarketable, depending on how the price relates to the *national best bid and offer* (NBBO).

The concept of discretion is relevant to both brokers and to individual market centers. From the perspective of a broker-dealer, it is important to know whether the order is considered *held* or *not held*. Held orders essentially means that the broker-dealer has no discretion over how to work the order, meaning that such orders must either be executed immediately or posted onto an exchange for public display. Not held orders, however, can be handled by the broker on a best-efforts basis, but brokers in either case are always responsible for proving that they are meeting the obligation of best execution for their clients.

In the U.S. equity market, stocks can trade in the pre-market, during market hours, or after the markets have closed during extended hours. All stocks in the National Market System have an official opening price determined by an opening auction and an official closing price determined by a closing auction. Orders, therefore, can be placed with a restriction to be executed exclusively in the official opening auction called *on open*, in the official closing auction called *on close*, during market hours, called *day*, or during the pre-market and during extended hours. Orders can also be sent to a market for immediate execution or cancellation, called *immediate or cancel* (IOC).

MODERN MARKET STRUCTURE—COMPLEXITY

Today's U.S. equity market is quite complex. There are 12 exchanges and over 40 alternative trading systems in operation. Most of these exchanges and alternative trading systems are located in one of three data centers in northern New Jersey. The ICE group runs the NYSE, NYSE market, and Archipelago in Mahwah, New Jersey, while the NASDAQ OMX group runs the NASDAQ, Boston, and Philadelphia stock exchanges in Carteret, New Jersey. The BATS Group runs the BATS and Direct Edge exchanges in Secaucus, New Jersey, which also houses the National Stock Exchange. Trading firms, meanwhile, have built their own infrastructure in all three data centers in order to be closer to the exchange matching engines. This practice, called co-location, is the modern equivalent of the booths located on the floor of the old New York Stock Exchange. Historically the large brokerage firms strategically placed their trading booths in close proximity to the specialist posts on the floor to quickly garner information being disseminated. Modern co-location is no different; the co-location of market making, algorithm, and smart order routing technology provides faster access to both the exchange matching engines and the market data that exchanges provide via their direct feeds.

MODERN MARKET STRUCTURE—MARKET DATA

Each exchange provides their own market data via direct feeds to facilitate trading in their market. They also provide market data to the consolidated tape delivered via the SIP as part of their regulatory requirements established by the CQA/CTA/UTP plans described earlier. The direct feeds differ from the data provided by the consolidated tape in two important ways. First, the exchanges provide data on all the levels in their order books via the direct feeds, but only provide the top-of-book data to the SIP. The Regulation NMS order protection rule only applies to the highest bid and lowest offer per individual exchange, which are often referred to as the top-of-book quotes. Second, there is only one instance of each of the three SIPs, which means in many cases, even if the SIP software was infinitely fast, that there would be a major speed advantage to the direct feeds. To understand this, consider the configuration of the major exchanges (shown in Figure 25.2) and how a co-located server in the Secaucus data center would receive data from the BATS and Direct Edge exchanges directly versus from the SIP for Tape A located in Mahwah. A co-located server in Secaucus trading in IBM, for example, would receive data from BATS and Direct Edge in a few microseconds due to their location. If the same server was receiving data from the Tape A SIP, the data would need to traverse the distance from Secaucus to Mahwah and back. The distance involved, due to the speed of light, would take roughly 400 microseconds. While such a delay does not sound too extensive, in today's market, it is sufficient to provide a competitive disadvantage to algorithms and SORs that do not subscribe to direct market data feeds.

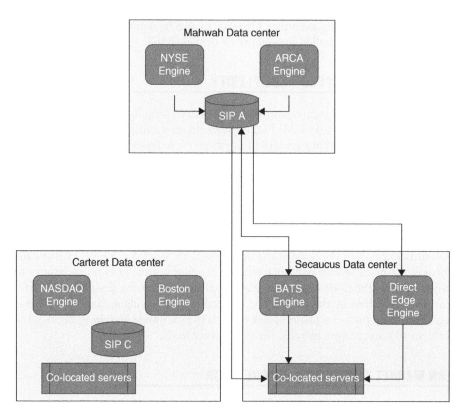

FIGURE 25.2   Example of data being transmitted across servers

HIGH-FREQUENCY TRADING

The development of automated order-driven exchanges and the proliferation of electronic algorithmic trading led directly to the emergence of disruptive competitors to the incumbent banks and institutional brokers. These new trading firms, called *high-frequency traders* (HFTs), developed sophisticated technology that utilized high-speed networking, quantitative models, and modern server technology to make trading decisions orders of magnitude faster than the human traders that used to dominate the markets. Twenty-five years ago, the leading equity trading firms by volume were all well-known, established firms that employed hundreds of traders. Today, most of the largest market makers, by volume, on the NASDAQ and BATS exchanges are HFT firms as well as all of the designated market makers on the New York Stock Exchange. Most observers believe that roughly 50% of the equity market volume in the United States is traded by HFT firms. These firms employ servers that are located inside of the data centers where the stock exchange systems are housed. They utilize direct data feeds provided by the stock exchanges in combination with technology designed to minimize the latency between receipt of market data messages and the sending and modification of orders sent to the exchanges.

The emergence of high-frequency technology has been transformational for the equity market. Virtually all firms have embraced aspects of the technology, including co-located servers and the use of direct data feeds. This has led directly to lower trading costs for investors, due to tighter bid–offer spreads and significantly more volume traded.

Strategies of HFT Firms

Market Making HFT firms dominate the business of providing liquidity to aggressive buyers and sellers as market makers. These firms place buy and sell orders on multiple exchanges in a wide range of securities at the same time. In order to manage their risk and to avoid mispricing orders, these firms need to employ state-of-the-art technology to react to changes in the market.

Proprietary Trading Since the invention of the tickertape in 1867, there have been proprietary traders that scanned the tape for clues on the future direction of stock prices. This type of proprietary trading was chronicled in the classic book, *Reminiscences of a Stock Operator*, a fictionalized account of Jesse Livermore, a famous investor whose insights are still widely quoted. For example, in Jack Schwager's *Market Wizards*,[5] *Reminiscences* was quoted as a major source of stock trading learning material for experienced and new traders by many of the traders whom Schwager interviewed. One of the more fascinating things about that book was how similar the concepts the author expressed are to today's quantitative proprietary trading. In the book the author described trading in the following way[6]:

> *Observation, experience, memory and mathematics, these are what the successful trader must depend on. He must not only observe accurately but remember at all times what he has observed. He cannot bet on the unreasonable or on the unexpected, however strong his personal convictions may be about man's unreasonableness or however certain he may feel that the unexpected happens very frequently. He must bet always on probabilities, that is, try to anticipate them. Years of practice at the game, of constant study, of always remembering, enable the trader to act on the instant when the unexpected happens as well as when the expected comes to pass.*
>
> *A man can have great mathematical ability and an unusual power of accurate observation and yet fail in speculation unless he also possesses the experience and the memory. And then, like the physician who keeps up with the advances of science, the wise trader never ceases to study general conditions, to keep track*

---

[5]Jack D Schwager, *Market Wizard*, (Hoboken, NJ: John Wiley & Sons, 2012).
[6]Ibid.

of developments everywhere that are likely to affect or influence the course of the various markets. After years at the game it becomes a habit to keep posted. He acts almost automatically. He acquires the invaluable professional attitude and that enables him to beat the game at times! This difference between the professional and the amateur or occasional trader cannot be overemphasized. I find, for instance, that memory and mathematics help me very much. Wall Street makes its money on a mathematical basis. I mean, it makes its money by dealing with facts and figures.

Similarly, modern proprietary HFT firms utilize computer models to buy and sell stocks based on quantitative signals. There is a wide range of such strategies, including trading based on technical price signals that are the modern equivalent to the mathematics described earlier. Obviously, modern computers can calculate these indicators in fractions of a second in sharp contrast to manual calculations of the past, which took days.

Another type of proprietary trading strategy is called *statistical arbitrage*. This strategy attempts to determine when securities get mispriced by the market. This is accomplished by comparing a stock price with the prices of other stocks or groups of stocks, and buying the underperforming and selling the outperforming stocks. Such strategies have been augmented by algorithms that scan digital news and social media to assure that the price divergence is truly an aberration and not created by a fundamental change. In addition, these strategies attempt to uncover whether the price divergences are created by detectable large orders. In this case, the strategy may be to trade aggressively in the same direction as those orders in order to profit from the likely continued movement. Such order-detection algorithms are usually very short term and have become less profitable as the sophistication of institutional algorithms has increased.

Index and ETF Arbitrage   As explained earlier, algorithms that can scan multiple markets across baskets of securities are used to implement arbitrage strategies. These strategies attempt to profit by either buying or selling stock index futures or buying or selling either the correlated ETFs or the underlying baskets of stocks that make up the index. Arbitrage strategies typically involve large trading volumes and minuscule margins, minimizing the mispricing of both indexed futures and ETFs. This assures that those instruments are rarely mispriced and provides a distinct benefit to consumers of these products.

The evolution of equity trading technology has continued to improve the quality of the market over time. Whether it was the introduction of the telegraph, the tickertape, screen-based trading, automated order-driven markets, or even high-frequency trading, all these innovations have helped increase trading volumes and the efficiency of the equity markets. While it is true that some of these technologies caused disruption and, in some cases, forced long-tenured participants out of the business, for the most part, firms have adapted. Today, the vast majority of brokers have adopted co-located servers processing direct data feeds in their suite of electronic trading products. In essence, most firms have adopted some aspects of HFT in their infrastructure, in the same way as all surviving firms adopted the telegraph, the ticker tape, market data terminals, and so on.

There are two key roles that the equity market plays in the economy. First, it provides a means for companies to raise capital in order to grow their business without the liability of taking on debt. Second, the equity market provides a method for various types of investors to earn a rate of return commensurate with the growth of the companies they invest in. Over the past 200-plus years, the U.S. stock market has undergone dramatic changes, but for the most part has done a good job of performing both of those roles, and yet the market has evolved. Advances in regulation have formalized the process of offering and trading stocks as well as establishing rules that govern the types of investment vehicles that can be provided to the public. The establishment of the SEC and the creation of the National Market System created a more stable environment for the equity market to develop and subsequent rules culminating with Regulation NMS have established a dynamic and competitive marketplace. Technological innovations starting with the telegraph, the tickertape, electronic market data, and now including exchange systems capable of microsecond-level timestamps have led to the lowest bid–offer spreads and trading costs in history. At the same time, financial innovations such as stock futures and ETFs have improved the ability for investors to manage risk and for traders to execute their strategies. All of this progress has been good news to most investors in the market as well as to the companies that rely upon equity issuance for capital.

CHAPTER 26

Cash Equities in the Secondary Market

Eric Blackman and Robert Grohskopf

INTRODUCTION

This chapter discusses the secondary cash business within an institutional equities division of a full-service broker-dealer such as Morgan Stanley or Deutsche Bank. The discussion will focus on how the secondary cash business is often structured, including roles and responsibilities, and how products and services are delivered to the institutional clients of the broker-dealer. The secondary cash equity business deals with products and services related to stocks previously issued and currently trading in the marketplace. Although the secondary cash business is presented here as a standalone entity, it has connectivity with and contributes to the success of other business units within the broker-dealer, such as investment banking, prime brokerage services, and equity derivatives.

The discussion begins with an explanation of the organizational structure of an institutional investment manager (known as the *buy-side*, e.g., mutual fund, pension fund, or insurance company). The functional roles, responsibilities, and interactions among the participants, which include research analysts, portfolio managers, and buy-side traders, will also be discussed. The next section will focus on the secondary cash business of the broker-dealer (referred to as the *sell-side*). Also discussed are the functional roles, responsibilities, and interaction of these players, which include research, research sales, sales traders, and position traders. It is essential to have a comprehensive view of both the buy-side and sell-side in order to fully appreciate the workings of the cash equity market business.

THE INSTITUTIONAL CLIENT

The organizational structure of most large buy-side clients, such as mutual funds, pension funds, and insurance companies, contains the following three functional roles: *portfolio manager, research analyst*, and *trader*. The responsibilities of each of these functions, as well as the interactions among them, are discussed ahead. The reader is encouraged to refer to the Institutional Client portion of Table 26.1, and Figure 26.1, as visual references during the discussion of the institutional client.

TABLE 26.1 Institutional Client and Full-Service Broker-Dealer Roles

	Institutional Client		
Function	Underlying Focus	Time Horizon	Generalist/Industry Specialist
Research Analyst	Fundamental Analysis	Long Term (12+ Months)	Industry Specialist
Portfolio Manager	Fundamental Analysis	Long Term (12+ Months)	Generalist
Trader	Technical Analysis	Short Term (Transactional)	Industry Specialist
	Full Service Broker-Dealer		
Research Analyst	Fundamental Analysis	Long Term (12+ Months)	Industry Specialist
Research Sales	Fundamental Analysis	Long Term (12+ Months)	Generalist
Sales Trader	Technical Analysis	Short Term (Transactional)	Generalist
Trader	Technical Analysis	Short Term (Transactional)	Industry Specialist

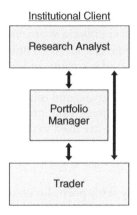

FIGURE 26.1 Internal interactions at a large institutional investor

THE PORTFOLIO MANAGER

The portfolio manager is responsible for constructing and managing the investment portfolio or fund. They determine the industry sectors in which to invest, the investment weightings of each sector, and the individual stocks to buy or sell. The fund's mandate provides overall investment guidelines that must be followed when constructing and adjusting the composition of the investment portfolio (e.g., investing in small-cap, mid-cap, or large-cap issuers, or sector concentrations such as Cyclicals, Energy, or Tech). The performance of the portfolio manager is normally evaluated by comparing the fund's investment returns to the returns provided by a relevant market index, such as the S&P

500 Index or the Wilshire 5000 Index or sector benchmark such as the UTY Index for Utilities. Performance is one of the key determinants that may ultimately attract new investor capital.

The management of an investment portfolio is driven by the portfolio manager's ongoing view of the long-term fundamental value of equities within the investment universe as a whole and its views of the relevant market sector fundamentals. The portfolio manager is often a generalist who leverages the in-depth, fundamental valuation analysis performed by sector research analysts. Large institutional clients have teams of research analysts to support the portfolio investment process.

THE RESEARCH ANALYST

Research departments within buy-side firms are organized according to industry sectors. Research analysts cover specific industries, such as autos, banks, or airlines, and cover individual companies within the industry (e.g., Ford, Wells Fargo, or Delta Airlines). The individual companies followed by the research analyst are referred to as the *coverage universe*. The research analyst develops an investment opinion of the company's stock with an expected or target stock price over either a short-term horizon (one year or less) or a longer-term investment horizon (typically 12 to 18 months). This investment opinion is developed through in-depth analysis of company and industry-related factors and trends against the backdrop of overall economic fundamentals. The analyst will examine company earnings reports, financial statements, and other company fundamentals to build a detailed financial forecasting and company valuation model. Meetings with senior management of companies under coverage are used to assess the quality of the management team and company strategy. Industry- and company-specific news events are monitored closely and evaluated. Industry and company expertise from outside sources is frequently drawn upon as well.

Research analysts work closely with portfolio managers and in-house traders communicating relevant information/analyses to further refine their models to try to enhance overall portfolio returns.

THE BUY-SIDE TRADER

Equity trading desks at large institutional buy-side firms are also usually organized by industry sectors. Similar to research analysts, traders become experts in the stocks within their assigned industries. However, their primary focus is transactional and short-term in nature, in stark contrast with portfolio managers and research analysts, who have a significantly longer-term view focusing on company and industry fundamentals and valuations. Traders are tasked with understanding the trading characteristics of their assigned companies, and, through constant interaction with the marketplace, determine how to best execute a buy and sell order. Characteristics to consider include the stock's average daily trading volume, historic price volatility, observed intraday trading patterns, current supply-and-demand profile, as well as trading patterns and relative price movements. When a portfolio manager decides to buy or sell a stock, a trade order is sent to the appropriate sector trader. The order identifies the stock and quantity of shares to be bought or sold and contains price instructions. It is the trader's responsibility to determine the appropriate order execution strategy, taking into account the size of the order (number of shares to be executed), the trading characteristics of the stock, and conditions within the marketplace. The trade order is then routed to a broker-dealer for execution in the marketplace.

THE BROKER-DEALER (SELL-SIDE)

The secondary cash equity business of a large full-service broker-dealer is designed to provide value-added equity products and services to buy-side client. As shown in Figure 26.2, broker-dealers are organized into functional areas responsible for delivering three main products and services: research, research sales, and trading/execution. The functional roles are *research analyst, research salesperson, sales trader,* and *position trader.* The product and service categories are research, execution, and corporate access.

The secondary cash equity business is client service driven. The goal is to provide value-added products and services, providing solutions to the institutional client while at the same time generating commission/trading revenue. Institutional clients commonly budget commission dollars for broker-dealers based upon their determination of the value-added to their investment objectives by a given broker-dealer. The buy-side research

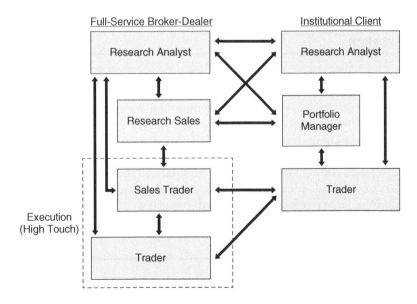

FIGURE 26.2 Interactions between full-service broker-dealer and large institutional client

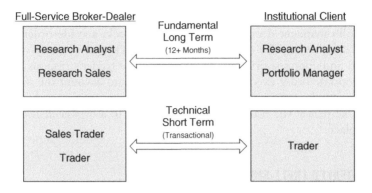

FIGURE 26.3 Interactions between full-service broker-dealer and large institutional client

analysts, portfolio managers, and traders collectively determine the annual commission payout proportioning to a particular broker-dealer. It is important for the broker-dealer to coordinate sales coverage and product delivery efficiently to maximize commission revenue while ensuring quality service to the client overall. This section will discuss the following topics related to the secondary cash equity business at the broker-dealer: functional areas and related roles and responsibilities, products and services delivered to the institutional client, the interactions of these roles with their counterparts at the institutional client, and the internal interactions among the broker-dealer's functional areas. Please refer to Table 26.1 and Figure 26.3 as visual references during the discussion of the secondary cash equity business at a full-service broker-dealer.

EQUITY RESEARCH

Equity research provides the buy-side clients with insightful investment ideas and recommendations, supported by a detailed analysis related to the economy, financial markets, industry sectors, and individual companies within these sectors. Equity research departments at large full-service broker-dealers typically employ economists, equity strategists, and company research analysts to this end. These departments produce reports and studies on the U.S. and global economies, financial markets, portfolio strategies, topical thematic investment considerations, industry sectors, and individual companies.

Analysts covering individual companies produce the majority of research reports and thus account for a large portion of the research budgets at full-service broker-dealers.

THE RESEARCH ANALYST

Sell-side research analysts utilize fundamental analysis to evaluate companies in their coverage universe, estimating the potential value of the company and determining an expected per-share stock price (the *target price*). They examine the company's financial statements, the overall market for the firm's products or services, its competition, industry- and company-specific risks, as well as macroeconomic and regulatory considerations. These data points serve as inputs into a detailed financial model to assist in the valuation of companies covered by the analyst.

Research analysts develop and maintain professional relationships with senior management at the companies in their coverage universe to augment the analyses described earlier. When valuing a company, it is imperative for the research analyst to clearly understand senior management's strategy and assess the probability of successful implementation and the potential impact of that strategy. Development of these strong relationships goes a long way to that end and serves as a key ingredient to a successful corporate action program as discussed later in this chapter.

Research analysts publish industry- and company-specific research reports for distribution both internally and externally to the firm's institutional clients. These reports typically address a specific topic, such as the impact of an important announcement by or about the company or an analysis of the company's quarterly earnings release. The research report will normally include the analyst's 12-month price target for the stock, the analyst's investment opinion (buy, sell, or hold), data on important stock valuation metrics, and the analyst's detailed financial and valuation models and ratings rationale.

Internally, the research analyst interfaces with both the research sales and trading teams. While they work more closely with research salespeople, who are responsible for selling the firm's research product, a meaningful dialogue and exchange of ideas and information also takes place with the firm's trading desk in accordance with compliance requirements.

RESEARCH SALES

The traditional role of a research salesperson is to sell the firm's research product to its institutional client base. Research sales is organized by client accounts with each salesperson responsible for between 15 and 25 institutional clients (known as their "account package"). A research salesperson acts as the channel connecting the firm's research to the appropriate consumer at the institutional client and thus must have a general understanding of all the firm's product offerings across all sectors.

The research salesperson must also have an understanding of the investment processes used by each portfolio manager as well as their investment needs, with the ultimate goal of providing a high-value research offering that ultimately the client will pay for in the form of trading commissions.

Another important product offered by the research sales team is *corporate access*. Through corporate access, portfolio managers and buy-side research analysts may be introduced to members of senior management of companies in which they invest or may potentially invest. It is important that the research sales team works hand-in-hand with its internal research analysts to coordinate the delivery of the analysts' industry and company expertise to the institutional client. The research sales team also works closely with the sales traders responsible for executing trades on behalf of their clients.

EXECUTION

Execution is the completion of a buy or sell order for an equity security. (Broker-dealers provide institutional clients with their trading expertise related to specific markets, industries, and individual stocks as well as access to sources of market liquidity in order to optimize trade execution. Broker-dealers seek to uncover sources of liquidity, provide best execution, and not cause significant adverse price movements. In the United States, there are 11 stock exchanges and over 40 alternative trading systems (ATSs). An ATS is an SEC regulatory term for a non-exchange-trading venue. In addition, liquidity to facilitate the execution of client orders can be provided internally at broker-dealers by matching client orders (known as *natural order flow*) or by committing firm capital and playing the role of *principal intermediary*.

Trading in the United States has continued to become increasingly automated, fast-paced, and further fragmented among the numerous trading venues. In order to access these pools of liquidity with the necessary speed and efficiency, electronic trading platforms and electronic trading tools are utilized. Broker-dealers typically spend considerable time and resources developing and upgrading these platforms and tools in order to provide the most efficient trading services it can offer.

Electronic trading tools generally use three components: execution algorithms (algos), smart order routers (SOR), and direct market access (DMA). Algos are complex mathematical formulas that determine and execute trading strategies to fit a particular market order, such as a volume-weighted average price (VWAP) model, which would be written to automatically buy or sell a given stock over the trading day to achieve VWAP for that day. Algos determine the manner and timing of a trading strategy, the *how-and-when-to-trade* decisions. SORs determine where the best sources of liquidity to access are in order to direct automated trading systems to that venue; for example, a given stock may find more liquidity in the FINRA ADF versus the NYSE. DMA provides the electronic connectivity directly to sources of liquidity, such as exchanges and ATSs.

Many full-service broker-dealers provide their institutional clients with three execution channels: high touch, program trading, and electronic. Clients can choose to use the channel that is best suited for a given buy/sell order or group of orders. High-touch execution will be the example used to highlight the execution product. High-touch trading best illustrates the interaction between buy-side traders and their broker-dealer counterparts and generally accounts for the largest portion of secondary cash commissions paid by institutional clients.

High-touch execution has two functions: sales trading and position trading.

Sales Trading

Sales traders are the primary execution point of contact for the institutional client. Sales trading is organized by client account groupings, with each sales trader usually responsible for between 15 and 25 clients (the account coverage package). Developing, maintaining, and managing close client relationships based on competency and mutual trust is an important responsibility of the sales trader. High-touch execution is a relationship-driven business. This is especially true when a buy-side trader is deciding which broker-dealer to use for execution of a difficult or complex trade order or when the broker-dealer will be asked to use firm capital to facilitate trade execution. Sales traders are generalists, providing value-added content and order execution services across all industries to their clients' trading desks. Although sales traders provide high-level research product summaries to buy-side traders, the content delivered daily to their clients focuses more on technical aspects of the market, industry sectors, and the trading characteristics or behavior of individual stocks. Sales traders are in frequent contact with their clients' traders throughout the day, either electronically or by telephone. Contact during the trading day usually centers on important developments in the market or in individual stocks, updates on live trade orders, or developments in sources of liquidity that might be of interest (e.g., a new sell order from another client the buy-side trader might wish to purchase).

Order execution is the important responsibility of the sales trader. This activity is transactional in nature, as sales traders execute their client orders in the marketplace. Sales traders can also act as the intermediary between the position traders and the buy-side trader. This can occur, for example, when the position trader is committing capital to facilitate (or enable) a trade. Here, based on the client's objectives, the sales trader may help negotiate the terms of the order.

Position Trading

Position traders specialize in industry sectors such as autos, banks, and airlines, and are responsible for the following activities: commitment of firm capital, position risk management, and execution. Position traders have an expertise in understanding the trading characteristics and price patterns of specific stocks in their industry sectors. Their activities are generally short-term and transactional in nature, focusing on timely and accurate trade execution.

Position traders should have well-developed relationships with their buy-side trading counterparts and strive to be a trusted source of expertise in the stocks they trade. Position traders communicate frequently and directly with buy-side traders (either electronically or by phone), providing industry- and company-specific content such as important news or events, expected stock price impact, observed trends, and the trading supply-and-demand profile for their covered stocks.

Order execution is the important activity performed by the position trader. In some cases, the position trader may take over execution of an order the sales trader may be having difficulty with. In another case, where the trader has other clients wishing to buy or sell the same stock, he or she will attempt to bring all the parties together, thus organizing and executing a large crossing trade at a mutually acceptable price. The position trader can thus interface and negotiate directly with the buyers and sellers or work through the sales traders. The role of the position trader is vital to providing additional liquidity available for its clients. They frequently act as an intermediary to match actual or prospective buyers and sellers in the stocks they trade.

The commitment of firm capital in trade execution and risk management of open stock positions are two activities that are performed exclusively by position traders.

Position traders commit firm capital for their institutional clients as the buyer or seller of last resort in order to enable (or facilitate) the execution of a trade. This is one particular activity that is highly valued by institutional clients and may occur, for example, when a client needs to buy a stock that is not readily available for sale in the marketplace or through other clients of the broker-dealer. The position trader can step in as the seller, providing liquidity otherwise unavailable in the market by selling the stock short. Price and trade quantity are negotiated with the buy-side trader and are based on many factors, such as trading volumes, current short interest, current market conditions, anticipated price movement of the stock, and other client-related considerations. The trade is then negotiated with the buy-side trader and can occur directly with the position trader or through the sales trader assigned to the account. For the position trader, this transaction results in a short position in the stock. If the client had been a seller of the stock in this example, the capital commitment would have been a long position for the position trader.

The position trader is also responsible for managing any potential position risk that may result in a loss due to adverse price movements associated with positions created through capital commitment activities. Capital commitment involves *negative selection* on the part of the position trader, meaning the client selects the stock, quantity, and timing of the trade, and the position trader responds by providing liquidity when other buyers or sellers are not available. The position trader will manage the risk associated with the position with an offsetting trade of the stock in the marketplace or directly with clients. They also may hedge the risk by buying and selling other instruments such as futures, options, or swaps.

ADDITIONAL PRODUCTS AND SERVICES

The following products have been referenced within the previous sections: corporate access and execution channels for program trading and electronic trading. Each of these is discussed in the following.

Corporate Access

Corporate access makes senior management of a client company available to the broker's institutional client base (usually portfolio managers, research analysts, and senior management). Institutional investors want to meet with senior management to better understand the company's strategic vision, and to evaluate the quality of the senior management team as well as to discuss specific company- and industry-related issues. On the other side of the coin, senior executives of the client company may want to meet with current and prospective investors in order to strengthen and broaden the investor base of the company. Corporate access represents a significant portion of the commission wallet for institutional clients and is an important product offering of a large broker-dealer's secondary cash business.

Various functional roles within the broker-dealer may work together to execute this match-making service such as research analysts as well as investment bankers to leverage their relationships at the companies they cover to obtain senior management participation in these events. Research salespeople utilize their institutional client relationships to identify and arrange participation from the appropriate portfolio managers and buy-side research analysts. A marketing coordinator will usually work with the groups to coordinate the *corporate access event*.

There are four types of corporate access events: non-deal roadshows (NDRs), investor conferences, investor field trips, and the bespoke event. In an NDR, company management typically travels to various geographic regions and meets one-on-one with institutional clients at the client's offices. Each one-on-one meeting typically lasts 60 minutes, and numerous client meetings are held over the course of the NDR. The one-on-one meetings tend to be highly valued by portfolio managers and research analysts as it gives them singular access to corporate management. Likewise, corporate management teams can get valuable feedback from their institutional investor base.

Conferences are arranged at a single location for the senior management teams of companies within an industry to interact with many institutional clients. Conferences will usually have industry panel discussions, individual company presentations, and one-on-one meetings usually lasting 35 minutes. The sell-side research analyst covering the industry is actively involved in these conferences, interfacing between company management and institutional clients. Sell-side research analysts will typically write up and publish notes on the conference for distribution both internally and to the institutional client base.

Investor field trips provide a venue for a group of institutional clients to meet with senior management at the company's facilities. Investor field trips are usually industry specific.

Bespoke events are arranged at the request of a single institutional client. It provides portfolio managers and buy-side research analysts with access to senior management of a specific company. The client usually travels to the company's headquarters for the meeting and gives the client an opportunity to kick the tires.

Execution Channels: Program Trading and Electronic Trading

Full-service broker-dealers provide two additional trade execution channels: program trading and electronic trading. In program trading, individual orders are grouped into a portfolio of orders for execution by the broker-dealer. An example of this is when a client has a meaningful adjustment to or rebalancing of the composition of an investment portfolio that will potentially result in a basket of buy and sell orders across many individual stocks. The basket of orders, referred to as a program, may be executed in the marketplace by the broker-dealer on behalf of the institutional client and is known as an *agency program*. Alternatively the buy-side trader may request that the broker-dealer commit firm capital and become the counterparty to each of the individual transactions. This is known as a *principal program*. With a principal program, the trader must manage the risk associated with the resulting long or short stock positions as mentioned earlier.

The electronic trading channel enables buy-side traders to execute their orders directly in the marketplace utilizing electronic platforms and tools provided by the broker-dealer. Orders executed through the electronic trading channel completely bypass both the sales and position traders, and firm capital is not committed. Commission rates for orders executed in the electronic trading channel are typically in the range of $0.002 to $0.004 per share as compared to a range of $0.02 to $0.04 per share for orders executed in the high-touch channel. However, the aggregate potential quantity of shares executed through the electronic trading channel is many multiples of the quantity executed through the high-touch channel.

CONCLUSION

It is important to note that the structure, roles, responsibilities, and products of a secondary cash equities business as detailed in this chapter can vary across different financial institutions. It is also worth noting that recent regulatory scrutiny on the cash equities business (e.g., electronic trading, dark pools, and high-frequency trading) will have both short- and long-term impacts on the functioning of these businesses. For example, in 2015 the SEC enacted the Systems Compliance and Integrity Rule (Reg. SCI). This rule requires some broker-dealers who use electronic trading platforms (alternative trading systems (ATSs) or dark pools) to adhere to a much stricter set of requirements with the goal of reducing systemic risk. As a result, some electronic trading groups have implemented new controls that actually stop execution through these platforms just prior to the established rule trigger to avoid the stricter requirements. In an industry that has historically focused on maximizing order flow to increase revenues, rejecting order flow for regulatory risk management purposes demonstrated the need for firms to monitor and perhaps revise their operating models to respond to the changing regulatory landscape. The ever-changing regulatory environment, combined with disruptive financial technologies such as Blockchain and cryptocurrency (FinTech), will play a significant role in the evolution of the equity markets in the future and their place in the capital markets ecosystem.

CHAPTER 27

Exchange-Traded Funds (ETFs)

An Overview

Reginald M. Browne

An exchange-traded fund is a financial instrument, similar to a mutual fund, that is comprised of a basket of securities designed to track the performance of an index such as the S&P 500. However, unlike mutual funds that price daily at the market close based upon the fund's closing *net asset value* (NAV), these open-ended trusts trade continuously on public exchanges, with their prices fluctuating throughout the day based on supply and demand like common stock.

ETFs may be indexed to track any of the major market indices across asset classes, geographic regions, and market sectors. ETF sponsors employ several strategies designed to produce market returns based on an investor's risk objectives such as leveraged ETFs, which use credit to amplify market movements. A recent ETF strategy is the *smart-beta* ETF, which applies a rules-based strategy structured to reduce risk and enhance index returns by adjusting the weighting of the components in the fund. There are also actively managed ETFs, which seek to replicate returns on actively managed portfolios but do not track an index per se.

CONSTRUCTING AN ETF: MARKET PARTICIPANTS AND THEIR FUNCTIONS

Regardless of strategy type or investment focus, structuring an ETF requires the interaction of a number of different players including: the issuer or asset manager, the authorized participant, the custodian, and the market maker.

Issuers (Asset Managers)

The ETF issuer, or asset manager, selects the investment strategy that an ETF will follow. For example, if the ETF is based on an index, the issuer will select an index that the ETF will attempt to mimic. The best-known ETFs track established, widely followed benchmarks such as the S&P 500 or the MSCI EAFE (captures large- and mid-cap equity representation across developed-markets countries around the world, excluding the

United States and Canada). There are also many ETFs that track customized benchmarks to match the performance of narrower, more specialized areas of the market. Since 2008, the SEC has permitted the creation of ETFs that track actively managed or rules-based portfolios. In such ETFs, the issuer is required to define the investment style and its targeted portfolio composition.

The issuer, with the assistance of legal counsel, determines the ETF's structure. Structures (regulated by the Investment Company Act of 1940) include: open-end funds, which comprise the majority of ETFs issued; unit investment trusts (UITs), which, while less widely used, is the structure used by SPDR 500 (SPY), one of the largest ETFs listed in the United States; and finally, the least common structure, the limited partnership or grantor trust, mostly used for commodity-based ETFs. Each of these structures has its own set of legal, regulatory, tax, and accounting implications. The issuer will consider each fund's investment focus, holdings, and investor base to determine an optimal structure.

The issuer is also responsible for registering the ETF with the SEC to qualify it for the public market. The issuer begins this process by recording the fund's investment objective and submitting it for approval to the SEC. This filing will contain detailed information about the fund's fees, objectives, risks, management oversight, as well as the ETF's symbol. Once approved by the SEC, this filing becomes the basis for the fund's Prospectus and Statement of Additional Information.

The issuer is also responsible for the ETF being in continual compliance with its prospectus filing (i.e., following its stated investment objectives and rebalancing when a change in the underlying index occurs). The issuer will also determine the team of ETF professionals that will be engaged to administer the ETF, including authorized participants, custodians, and market makers.

Authorized Participant

An authorized participant is a firm that has entered into a legal agreement with the issuer to create and redeem units of the ETF. Most authorized participants are large financial institutions, market makers, or specialists.

The authorized participant is a key player in the creation/redemption process through which ETF shares are originated and redeemed. In this process, the authorized participant acquires the securities that the ETF will own and delivers shares to the issuer via its custodian in the proportions that will enable the ETF to track its benchmark. The custodian then delivers to the authorized participant a block of ETF shares, called a *creation unit*. Creation units are very large (typically between 20,000 to 50,000 ETF shares), and can be held by the authorized participant, sold to other authorized participants, or broken into shares for sale to investors.

Authorized participants play an ongoing role in the creation and management of ETF shares. For instance, if there is demand in the market for additional ETF shares, the authorized participant creates them by purchasing shares of the underlying portfolio and exchanging them for more creation units. Conversely, if there are too many ETF shares, the authorized participant can reduce the supply by disassembling them into their components. The authorized participant can also act as a market maker for the ETF, arbitraging slight differences between the ETF's market value and the value of its underlying component securities, or NAV—that is, creating shares when the ETF is overvalued and eliminating them when the ETF is undervalued. This increases liquidity in the ETF shares and keeps their market value closely aligned with the value of the underlying assets.

Custodians

Most ETFs have an independent, third-party custodian bank that acts as a trustee for the benefit of the exchange-traded fund. As the trustee, the custodian bank holds and reconciles the actual portfolio positions. It directs the authorized participants to trade the underlying portfolio assets to take into account changes in the index. The ETF portfolio will be rebalanced as new securities are added and removed from the underlying index, as well as to reflect dividends, stock splits, and corporate events like mergers and acquisitions. The custodian bank ensures that the ETF holdings adhere to the investment mandate defined by the corresponding index definitions.

Market Makers

ETF market makers provide market liquidity via public exchanges. Each market maker calculates independent fair value for the underlying assets of each ETF. Using these independent calculations, the market maker generates continual and executable quotes via public exchanges. Often, in new or thinly traded ETFs, the market displayed in an ETF is by a sole market maker, unlike in corporate stocks where the market is composed of the best bid and best offer by retail and professional dealer orders. ETF market makers play an essential role in the displayed quote and liquidity of the ETFs on the various exchanges.

ETF REGULATIONS

Most ETFs are regulated as *investment companies* under the Investment Company Act of 1940. ETFs registered under the 1940 Act are open-end investment companies—that is, they can issue additional shares at any time. The 1940 Act has many requirements, including strict antifraud provisions, disclosure of portfolio holdings, a minimum level of diversification, limits on leverage, and a prohibition on short-selling. ETFs are registered with the Securities and Exchange Commission and must comply with the various provisions of the Investment Company Act of 1940 and be granted an exemptive relief order to be listed on an exchange. These provisions include specifying the minimum creation and redemption unit size, the in-kind exchange of the underlying representative basket of securities, the mandate for an independent board of directors, and the use of leverage.

There are two basic types of ETFs regulated under the Investment Act of 1940: unit investment trusts (UITs) and regulated investment companies (RICs).

UITs are non-managed funds, that is, the managers have no discretion over which components of an index go into the portfolio; if a security is in the index, it must be in the fund. In addition, UITs have strict diversification requirements; securities that comprise 5% or more of the ETF's index weighting cannot comprise more than 25% of the fund, the ETF can own no more than 10% of a company's voting stock, and sector weightings cannot exceed 50% of the fund. For example, broad-based ETFs can be structured as UITs, but sector ETFs generally cannot. UITs are also prohibited from reinvesting cash from dividends into the fund. Instead, dividends must be transferred to a non-interest-bearing account until they are distributed to shareholders on a quarterly basis, potentially creating a slight drag on returns.

1933 Act ETFs

The Securities Act of 1933 regulates certain types of ETFs, including highly leveraged funds and ETFs that invest in undiversified portfolios and/or communities. There are three basic kinds of 1933 Act ETFs: investment trusts, exchange-traded grantor trusts (ETGTs), and exchange-traded notes (ETN).

Investment trusts permit investments in stocks, bonds, hard assets, and derivatives. There are commodities-based ETFs (e.g., investing in precious metals and commodities and futures). Investment trusts function like other ETFs, with authorized participants creating and redeeming shares to ensure that the NAV continues to reflect the value of its underlying portfolio.

Exchange-traded grantor trusts (ETGTs) are non-managed investment pools that buy and hold a diversified portfolio of securities. Shareholders in this structure have voting rights as they can elect a board of directors and influence management of the trust via proxy votes. Dividends are paid out immediately to investors, rather than held until the end of the quarter as in the case of RICs (Regulated Investment Companies). The unique element of exchange-traded grantor trusts, however, is that shareholders can redeem shares in the trust for the proportional shares of stock held in the underlying portfolio. For example, a shareholder could redeem shares in a technology ETGT, and receive in return shares in components like Yahoo!, Google, or Facebook.

Exchange-traded notes (ETNs) differ from other exchange-traded vehicles. Fundamentally, they are nothing more than a bank's promise to pay the return generated by a specified security index or benchmark, minus any fees. The bank is not obligated to directly invest in the securities represented in the index. Rather, it can meet its obligations to shareholders in any way it prefers (i.e., total return swaps). In addition to the performance of the underlying instruments, ETN values are influenced by the creditworthiness of the issuing bank. For example, if the issuer's credit rating is downgraded, the value of the ETN may fall even if there is no change in the index it tracks. ETNs are extremely tax-efficient vehicles since no interest, dividends, or capital gains are paid until the investor redeems his or her shares.

Shares Outstanding for Open-End ETFs (Limited by Prospectus)

To be listed, an ETF is required to have an initial minimum of 100,000 shares and maintain a minimum of 50,000 shares outstanding during the fund's lifespan. The ETF shares outstanding will increase or decrease as units are created or redeemed by authorized participants as dictated by trading activity.

Cash

As a result of the creation/redemption process, the majority of an ETF's underlying portfolio is comprised of the securities that make up its benchmark. However, as in any investment strategy, an ETF will maintain a cash position (cash component).

Cash may flow into the portfolio as a result of regular dividends, special cash dividends, or any other corporate action that would have resulted in a cash payment. The cash component of an ETF is measured on a daily basis by calculating the amount of cash that has been delivered or received during the prior day's creation/redemption process. Thus the representative deliverable portfolio plus the total cash would equal the value of the prior day's creation unit (NAV × shares per unit).

ETF issuers also calculate estimated cash—that is, the cash that they expect to be delivered during the current day's creation/redemption process. Differences arise between the actual and estimated cash positions as a result of portfolio executions, rebalances, or unanticipated corporate actions.

DETERMINING NET ASSET VALUE OF ETFs

The net asset value of an ETF is determined by totaling the value of the assets it holds, subtracting any liabilities and dividing by the number of shares outstanding. To generate the official valuation, the custodian bank uses a predefined pricing basis for each underlying constituent.

Pricing mechanisms for the main asset classes included in ETF portfolios are as follows:

- *Domestic U.S. equity:* Primary exchange official close price.
- *International equity:* Primary exchange official close price or official last price when the specific country exchange does not have a closing price.
- *Currency:* The rate is determined by the issuer and would fall under: *World Market/Reuters* (WM/R) London fixing (11 a.m. EST), 3 p.m. EST (either WM/R or custodian level), or 4 p.m. EST (either WM/R or custodian level)
- *Fixed income:* U.S. government bonds are valued at the 3 p.m. EST Barclays closing auction price. Other instruments use price provider levels (i.e., IDC) or local market closes.
- *Commodity/futures:* Official closing/settlement price or official last price when no settlement price.

The custodian bank will typically set an ETF's NAV daily after the markets have closed. However, since ETFs trade continuously on the secondary market, their market price per share fluctuates throughout the day to reflect investors' expectations of the value of the underlying portfolio.

As a result, all ETFs report an iNav, or intraday net asset value during trading hours. This is the calculated price given the current last price for the underlying constituents. The iNav calculation is:

(Sum of (Underlying Constituent × Last Price × Currency Rate)

+ Cash Component)/Creation Unit

ETF market makers continually recalculate the ETF's fair market value, purchasing shares when the ETF's share prices falls below fair value and selling them when it exceeds fair value. In this way, the NAV of an ETF stays closely linked to the value of the security it holds.

PORTFOLIO DISCLOSURE

To meet SEC disclosure requirements, ETF issuers in coordination with their custodians provide portfolio-level information for authorized participants, exchanges, and market makers. On a daily basis, after markets have closed, the issuer creates a *portfolio composition file* (PCF), which lists all the securities in the portfolio by name, the number of shares of each per creation unit, as well as any cash in the portfolio. This information is delivered to a central processing group—the National Security Clearing Corporation (NSCC). The NSCC generates a generic file that itemizes deliverable ETF holdings. This generic file reflects the portfolio holdings on a creation unit basis.

UNDERSTANDING DIFFERENT ETF STRATEGIES

The ETF industry has grown rapidly since inception in 1993. In the early days of ETFs, only one fund was listed on the American Stock Exchange in the United States. Now there are more than 4500 listed globally with $3 trillion of assets under management at the time of this writing.[1]

Underlying Indices

When ETFs first appeared in the financial markets in the 1990s, nearly all were designed to passively track major market benchmarks—first, the S&P 500 Index, and later, other broad-based indices like the MSCI EAFE and the Russell 2000. But as the market for ETFs has grown, vehicles tracking hundreds of other indices have sprung up, broadening

---

[1]"$3 Trillion ETF Market Received $347 Billion in New Money in 2015," Market Realist, January 7, 2016, http://marketrealist.com/2016/01/3-trillion-etf-market-received-347-billion-new-money-2015/.

the ETF universe until it provides exposure to nearly every type of asset, geographic market, and sector.

Index methodologies have also evolved over time. Today there are three basic types of indices:

1. *Capitalization weighted:* This is the oldest and most common approach to index construction. Securities within the index are weighted by their market capitalization size, that is, the product of share price times number of shares outstanding. Under this methodology shares in the largest companies comprise a disproportionate share of the portfolio. Some market observers call cap-weighted indexing a closet form of momentum investing, since it systematically overweights appreciated securities.
2. *Price weighted:* Under this methodology, index components are weighted according to their price per share. Higher-priced securities are more heavily represented than lower-priced ones.
3. *Equal weighted:* In this scenario, all index components are weighted equally. An equally weighted S&P 500 index would allocate 0.2% of its assets to each stock in the index, the same amount for mega-caps like Apple as for the smallest-cap stock in the index. Equal-weighted indices typically have a higher turnover due to rebalancing to calibrate larger-capitalization stocks to lower-market-cap stocks with lower-liquidity stocks. Equal-weighted indices generally outperform cap-weighted indices.

PORTFOLIO CONSTRUCTION METHODOLOGY

Exchange-traded funds' investment objectives fall under three general categories: passive index investment, factor-based (smart beta) investment discipline, and active investment.

Passive investment ETFs are created by issuers to provide a standardized portfolio that mirrors the market exposure of a predefined benchmark index. The passive investment has predefined rules for composition, constituent entry/exit, and index rebalancing times. Widely known domestic equity passive index investment strategies include the S&P 500 Index, NASDAQ 100 Index, and Russell 2000 Index. There are also a number of well-known international equity passive indices such as MSCI EAFE, MSCI Emerging Markets Index, MSCI Europe Index, and CSI 300 Index. Passive fixed-income indices include Barclays Capital Aggregate Bond Index (formerly the Lehman Aggregate Bond Index).

Factor-based/smart-beta ETFs are also rule-based investment strategies where the decision process is built around investment factors. Some of the factors that may be incorporated include revenues, dividends, quality, momentum, earnings, value, volatility, and size. Each factor-based/smart-beta index has predefined rules for composition, constituent entry/exit, and index rebalance times. Smart-beta ETFs are designed to provide index-like performance with a performance enhancement derived from exploiting structural market inefficiencies such as the long-term outperformance of small-caps versus large, or of value stocks versus growth.

To construct them, ETF issuers can use existing rule-based strategies from commercial providers. For instance, MSCI Barra's factor-based model overweights securities that meet its criteria for value, quality, low volatility, momentum, dividend yield, and size. NYSE's Intellidex emphasizes price momentum, earnings momentum, quality, management accountability, and value. RAFI Research Affiliates tilts its Fundamental Index toward value and small-cap stocks. ETF issuers can also design their own factor models or customize existing models to emphasize particular factors.

Active investment ETFs have an opened-ended strategy that allows the issuer to manage the underlying portfolio as defined by the investment objective, allowable security type, and approved underlying weightings.

Alternative ETFs emphasize nontraditional investments and may employ strategies typically used by hedge fund managers, including long/short, leveraged, inverse, managed futures, arbitrage, and hedge fund investing. Like the alternative assets they track, these ETFs can provide performance that is not correlated to traditional assets like stocks and bonds, as well as the potential for higher returns; however, again like the assets they track, they may also significantly underperform the public markets and can lose money.

Investment Focus

ETFs can also be categorized based on the investment mandate and underlying asset allocation. The most common types of ETFs include the following:

Domestic Equity   Domestic ETFs all invest to track indices of stocks listed and headquartered in the United States. Within this group are several subgroup strategies, including broad-based, sector-based, and thematic-based strategies, which are designed to match an investor's desired investment objectives.

- *Broad-based:* Broad-based ETFs are structured to track the whole of the U.S. stock market. These ETFs are generally market-cap weighted and may include hundreds or even thousands of individual securities. Some are all-cap funds, that is, they invest in small, medium, and large-sized companies. Others track a specific benchmark like the S&P 500 Index (large companies) or the Russell 2000 (small companies).
- *Sector-based:* Sector ETFs invest in stocks in a specific industry, such as technology, cyclicals, financials, real estate, pharma, or energy. They are designed to let investors take investment positions in areas of the economy they believe will outperform and to diversify by investing in industries not represented in other parts of their portfolios.
- *Thematic-based:* Thematic ETFs invest in stocks of companies that may be affected by a specific issue or trend, even if they are not all in the same industry. For instance, a thematic ETF might invest in companies that appeal to a specific demographic group like women or Millennials.

Global/International Equity   Global and international equity ETFs give investors an opportunity to diversify their portfolios so that they are less vulnerable to risk in their home market and take advantage of growth opportunities in other countries.

Developed-Country Broad-Based ETFs   These ETFs track the stocks of large, established economies in countries with stable governments, reliable banking and legal systems, and well-developed financial markets. The most widely used developed-country broad-based index is MSCI EAFE, but there are others including the FTSE All-World Ex-U.S. and Citigroup Primary Market Index. There are also indices that track developed economy stocks by region (Europe, Pacific Rim, for instance), capitalization size, and country. These ETFs are also available with sector- and thematic-based strategies like their domestic counterparts.

Emerging Broad-Based ETFs   These ETFs track the stocks of roughly 150 countries that are currently less economically developed than the major economies of Europe, Japan, and North America, but which are seeking to become more developed. Two important benchmarks for this category are the S&P Emerging Markets Indexes and the MSCI Emerging Markets Index. More specialized emerging markets ETFs can track regions (Latin America, Emerging Europe), capitalization size, or country. Emerging markets ETFs may also use a sector or thematic investment strategy.

Fixed Income   Fixed-income ETFs are growing in use and popularity given the unique structure ETFs offer in transparency and price determination of fixed-income assets. Due to the bond market's trading structure; there is no consolidated best bid/best offer by dealers in individual bonds as bonds do not trade on an exchange. The bond market has a higher bid–offer spread than equities and quotes in fractions, not in cents. Bond ETFs, however, offer better price transparency by trading on stock exchanges. Innovations in fixed-income indexing, such as the new liquid fixed-income indices (which include only liquid securities), as well as increased demand for fixed-income products, have driven strong growth of ETF adoption. Fixed-income ETF assets now account for close to one-fifth of all ETF assets yet only account for 3% of the total corporate bond market.[2]

Issuers have created many different types of fixed-income ETFs, from broad-based bond ETFs that encompass all sectors of the fixed-income market (such as the Barclays Aggregate Bond ETF and Total Bond ETF) to ETFs that focus on specific sectors, credit quality ratings, and maturities. These include:

- *U.S. government bond ETFs:* These ETFs track the U.S. Treasury market, the largest and most liquid fixed-income market in the world. ETFs may be broad-based or may track specific maturity range indices such as the Barclays 1-3 Year U.S. Treasury Index or the Barclays 20 Year U.S. Treasury Index. Separate indices—and ETFs—are benchmarked to *Treasury inflation-protected securities* (TIPS), which provide both income and inflation protection.
- *Mortgage-backed securities ETFs:* These ETFs track portfolios of home loans guaranteed by the Government National Mortgage Association (GNMA) and the Federal

---

[2]Todd Schriber, "Boring Bonds Boost ETF Asset Growth," Benzinga, March 16, 2016, http://www .benzinga.com/trading-ideas/long-ideas/16/03/7652553/boring-bonds-boost-etf-asset-growth.

National Mortgage Association (FNMA). Mortgage-backed securities typically pay higher interest rates than government securities because of prepayment risk—that is, the risk that homeowners will refinance their loans if interest rates fall.

- *Investment-grade corporate bond ETFs:* These ETFs invest in portfolios of the bonds of extremely liquid, high-quality, established companies. Interest rates are higher than government securities but there is also more risk, since even the highest quality companies may default on interest or principal payments.
- *High-yield corporate bond ETFs:* Even higher interest rates can be obtained by investing in high-yield bond ETFs, which invest in companies rated BBB or lower by S&P or Baa or lower by Moody's. However, there is even more risk than in an investment-grade corporate bond ETF, since these companies are generally in weaker financial condition and more likely to default on interest or principal payments.
- *Aggregate bond ETFs:* These are the broadest based, most diversified bond ETFs, covering securities across sectors, maturities, and credit ratings.
- *Unconstrained bond ETFs:* These ETFs can invest opportunistically across multiple sectors of the bond market.
- *Floating-rate ETFs:* The interest rates paid by floating-rate securities adjust when interest rates rise or fall, giving investors who choose this type of ETF protection against rising rates.
- *Bank loan ETFs:* Bank loans are short-term, floating-rate financing usually issued by below-investment-grade companies. ETFs that track this sector of the fixed-income market offer yields that are above short-term government yields, with the risk protection of shorter-terms and rates that rise with inflation.

Interest Rate Strategy ETFs   As interest rates are perceived to have bottomed out, a number of fixed-income ETF strategies have emerged to manage rising interest rate risk, including:

- *Interest rate hedged ETFs:* These vehicles seek to mitigate interest rate risk by overlaying a portfolio of bonds with short positions in interest rate swaps. When rates rise, the value of the bond portfolio declines, but the value of the short positions increases, offsetting the negative impact.
- *Neutral duration–based ETFs:* ETFs with a neutral duration strategy seek to maximize total return, which is comprised of income and capital appreciation, while hedging interest rate exposure.
- *Negative duration–based ETFs:* These ETFs combine a long exposure to a broad-based bond index with short positions in U.S. Treasuries to provide enhanced returns during a rising rate environment.

International Fixed-Income ETFs   International fixed-income ETFs are available in many of the same categories as domestic ones, from broad-based all-market ETFs to more specialized ones focused on bond market sectors such as government, corporate, and mortgage-backed bonds; short-, medium-, or long-term maturities; and credit ratings. ETFs may track developed-country markets or emerging ones, and may further specialize by region or individual country. Some international fixed-income ETFs are currency-hedged back into dollar terms; others report returns in local currency. Most tracked fixed-income securities are issued in their home markets, but one specialized type of ETF is linked to the performance of Yankee bonds, or foreign company bonds issued in the United States.

Commodity ETFs   Commodity ETFs provide a liquid, convenient way to invest in hard asset classes that provide other diversification benefits, but have historically been hard for individual investors to access. These vehicles make it possible to invest in assets that are vital to the global economy—such as oil, industrial chemicals, precious metals, and agricultural goods—without having to buy and store the bulky materials themselves. Because they're so liquid, they allow investors to trade in and out of specific commodities to take advantage of pricing inefficiencies, protect against inflation, or capture perceived supply/demand trends.

It's important to note that most commodity ETFs track futures contracts linked to commodities rather than the commodities themselves, so their NAV may not always move in sync with the spot, or current, market prices. The main exceptions are precious metals–related exchange-traded products that are backed by physical gold, silver, platinum, and palladium bars stored in bank vaults.

Commodity ETFs come in a variety of forms, with some tracking a broad basket of commodities and others focusing on a narrower group (precious metals, industrial materials) or single commodity (oil, gold).

Because commodity ETFs create exposure through futures contracts, rather than buying physical commodities, some ETFs add value through curve-based strategies. Commodity ETFs hold baskets of commodities futures, which expire at some point in the future and then must be rolled over into another contract. Commodity contracts are priced differently, based on days until expiration and other factors. So a contract for the next month may be higher or lower than that for the current month. A contract for two months out may be higher or lower than that. A curve-based strategy seeks to enhance returns by buying the optimally priced contract at each expiration date.

Leveraged and Inverse ETFs   Leveraged ETFs use derivatives to seek returns that are some multiple of the return of a benchmark's daily return. That is, for a 2× leveraged ETF tracking the S&P 500 Index, if the S&P 500 rose by 1% during a day, the ETF would appreciate by 2%; conversely, an index loss of 1% would trigger the ETF's decline by 2%. By varying the amount of leverage they employ, these ETFs can target different multiples of the return. There are leveraged ETFs that target 1.25, 2, and 3 times the benchmark's daily return.

Inverse leveraged ETFs also employ derivatives, but to achieve a return that is the inverse of the index tracked. That is, if the S&P 500 rises by 1%, a leveraged inverse ETF should fall by 1%. Inverse ETFs can also be levered up or down to achieve different inverse multiples of the benchmark's return, from 1.25 to 3 times. These types of ETFs are useful for hedging long stock positions against risk or for making short-term opportunistic bets against the market.

Both leveraged and inverse leveraged ETFs add significant risk to a portfolio, since they amplify the impact of volatility. It is also important to notice that the multiplier effect applies to each day's return, not the cumulative return over longer periods. A 2× leveraged ETF will return twice its benchmark on any given day, but may return more or less than twice its index for the year.

Alternative ETFs Alternative ETFs emphasize nontraditional investments and may employ strategies typically used by hedge fund managers, including long/short, leveraged, inverse, managed futures, and arbitrage and hedge fund replication strategies.

CONCLUSION

This short summary on exchange-traded funds offers readers an overview of one of the most innovative financial products ever created in the North American markets. Like all investment vehicles, common stocks, corporate bonds, or insurance products, careful review of an ETF's offering documents is necessary to understand the intended outcome of underlying fund's mechanics.

The ETF ecosystem of index providers, ETF sponsors, custody banks, exchanges, market makers, authorized participants, and, yes, ETF investors each play an important role in the continuing evolution of financial opportunities for the individual investor as well as the largest institutional investor. ETF diligence by all investors, in order to understand what is under the hood and understand the best practices for the asset class an ETF is representing, is essential. The reader should have an understanding of the characteristics of the underlying basket of securities of the ETF, its investment objectives, and its investment track record before making an investment in order to understand the expected behavior of the ETF in light of the investor's objectives.

CHAPTER 28

Equity Capital Markets

Underwriting and At-the-Market Equity Financing

Daniel C. de Menocal, Jr.

In the 1980s, the use of continuously offered *medium-term notes* (MTNs) grew in popularity for U.S. corporate borrowers as they could *take down*, or issue notes as needed, from a shelf registration as investor demand allowed. Growing from an $800MM market in 1981[1] to $131B in 2011,[2] MTNs became a way for the issuer to diversify its investor base and access incremental fixed-rate debt periodically. Issued under SEC Rule 415, MTNs are sold from a shelf registration with the filing of a *prospectus supplement* that identified a maximum amount of securities that could be sold *at-the-market* and identifying the named underwriter(s).

In the mid-1980s, this concept of continuous, at-the-market (ATM) issuance off of a shelf registration was adapted to the equity securities market, initially for smaller market capitalized companies. While the MTN model thrived, the equity model failed to gain significant traction among corporate finance managers. It may have been due to a number of factors, including the relative lack of sufficient trading volume, visibility of the issuer's selling activity on the exchanges, or the Street's institutional bias toward marketed equity offerings. The equity ATM issuance strategy didn't really go mainstream until the financial crisis in 2008–2009 when the corporate need for capital in a constrained market led CFOs to explore all liquidity options, including the ATM model, for equity capital. As the ATM strategy gained wider acceptance beginning in 2010, it has since grown to become an important and innovative tool to manage efficient and discreet equity capital formation. A total of ~260 ATM programs were filed in 2015 representing an issuable amount totaling ~$41.7 billion.[3] While seemingly not a significant total versus primary or secondary equity offerings, which numbered over 900 with a total equity issuance of

---

[1] CIBC World Markets, "Medium-Term Notes (MTN)" (1999).
[2] FTSE Global Markets, "In or Out of MTNs" (October 22, 2012).
[3] BNY Mellon Capital Markets, LLC; Bloomberg, LP; Dealogic.

nearly $330 billion, the ATM model still represents an important equity-raising option for U.S. corporations.

Conventional equity offerings are conducted in the public markets through several issuance forms; overnight "bought" deal, marketed deal, and initial public offering (IPO) are common examples. In each case, the underwriter is usually agreeing to purchase the shares from the issuer and in turn reselling the shares to investors. This is the case in a *firm-commitment* underwriting where the underwriters assume the risk once the shares are committed to. Smaller issuers may use a *best-efforts* or a *mini-maxi* structure that mitigates some of the underwriting risks compared to the firm-commitment underwriting. In a best-efforts underwriting, the underwriter will use its best efforts to sell all of the offered shares and, to the extent the total order book falls short of the full offering amount, the issuer may choose to accept the amount sold. In the case of a *best-efforts, all-or-none* offering, as the name suggests, the full deal must be sold. In a mini-maxi offering, similar to the best-efforts, the issuer establishes the minimum amount of equity that must be sold in order to effect the issuance.

Overnight bought deals are typically arranged between the issuer and a small group of underwriters (as few as one and as many as three or four). The underwriter(s) agree to purchase from the issuer at a negotiated price the full amount of the offering immediately following the market close. This can be at a small or large discount to the stock's closing price. These issuances will not have a group of underwriters beyond the book-running manager(s) and the book-running manager is responsible for distributing the shares. In marketed deals, an underwriting syndicate is formed to maximize the distribution of the offering. In each case, firm-commitment underwritings provide the issuer with certainty, as the underwriter is committed for the whole issuance amount on the issuance date.

In contrast, at-the-market equity financing is, in simplest terms, a periodic or continuous offering of equity securities that are sold, on a *commercially reasonable* basis, by a *selling agent* (a broker-dealer engaged to manage the sales) on a securities exchange rather than directly to investors. The power of the issuance strategy is largely dependent upon the liquidity of the stock (average daily trading volume) and share price: The greater the trading volume, the more shares can be sold into the market without disrupting the market price; and the higher the share price, the more issuance proceeds are available to the issuer. Generally speaking, the selling agent will target sales at 10% to 15% of the stock's average daily trading volume, although there may be times of greater or less than that range, depending upon market conditions. The selling agent receives a commission based upon the amount of shares sold.

SECURITIES OFFERING REFORM OF 2005

Prior to the Securities Offering Reform, effective in December 2005, the SEC rules for securities registration limited a shelf filing's effectiveness to two years and imposed other requirements for larger corporations that were no longer practical. One of the more important concepts introduced by the new rules was defining a new category of issuer, the *well-known, seasoned issuer*[4] (WKSI), that could have its shelf registration filed on Form S-3 or F-3 become automatically effective without further SEC review. This gave the issuer the ability to issue securities immediately following the registration if it so chose. It also eased certain communications rules providing a safe harbor for issuers to provide increased communication of factual information over the course of an offering. Further, the rule extended the effectiveness of the shelf registration from two to three years. Most importantly, the reform permitted WKSIs to file an *automatic shelf registration* without being required to identify the amount of securities to be sold, giving the issuer the ability to pay the requisite SEC filing fees on a pay-as-you-go basis as the issuer takes down securities from the shelf. This change, among others, provided issuers with greater financing flexibility and gave the equity ATM financing model an opportunity to evolve into a viable financing tool, especially for larger corporate issuers.

SEC Rule 415, originally adopted by the SEC in November 1983, addresses continuously offered securities, and was, most importantly, modified by the Securities Offering Reform to eliminate certain existing limitations for shelf registrations allowing for primary at-the-market offerings of equity securities. In addition, prior to the 2005 reforms and subsequent revisions in 2008, issuers were limited to filing up to 10% of their unaffiliated market cap. The new rule eliminated this cap, which was a significant inhibiting factor for the ATM equity model especially for small and mid-cap companies. Rule 415 permits the sale of securities registered on Form S-3 or Form F-3 to be sold on an immediate, delayed, or continuous basis and specifies that "the term 'at the market offering' means an offering of equity securities into an existing trading market for outstanding shares of the same class at other than a fixed price."[5]

The Reform also addressed Prospectus Delivery protocol with a new rule, Rule 172, implementing a new *access-equals-delivery* regime that creates an exemption to Securities Act Section 5(b)(1) to allow trade confirmations for secondary offerings to be sent without an accompanying prospectus. The SEC made the assertion that given the breadth of electronic access to the initial filing, including the SEC's EDGAR System,[6] the investor was presumed to have had the opportunity to review the prospectus. In addition, for securities sold by a broker-dealer on an exchange under the amended Rule 153, neither the issuer nor the selling agent would be required to deliver a prospectus to investors

---

[4]Pursuant to Section 13(a) or 15(d) of the Exchange Act, a WKSI is defined as satisfying the following requirements: a Form S-3 or F-3 registrant being current with all reporting requirements for the preceding 12 calendar months; as of a date within 60 days either has a non-affiliated market value of at least $700MM or has issued in the last three years at least $1B in principal amount of non-convertible securities; and is not an ineligible issuer.

[5]SEC Rule 415(a)(4).

[6]SEC.gov/edgar: "EDGAR, the Electronic Data Gathering, Analysis, and Retrieval System, Performs Automated Collection, Validation, Indexing, Acceptance, and Forwarding of Submissions by Companies and Others Who Are Required by Law to File Forms with the U.S. Securities and Exchange Commission (SEC)."

beyond the initial filing at the commencement of the program.[7] This change provided another benefit to the ATM model in that the agent would not be required to deliver prospectuses with each sale.

Taken all together, the Securities Reform of 2005 was a game-changer for the equity ATM model as it provided the model with broader applicability for more prospective issuers, and in time those issuers began to adopt the issuance strategy. One catalyst, the financial crisis beginning in 2007, put the ATM model at the forefront of equity capital-raising strategies for a growing number of companies. Another was the growth in electronic trading venues.

THE RISE OF ELECTRONIC TRADING

Introduced in the mid-1990s, *alternative trading systems* (ATSs) provided an electronic medium to bring buyers and sellers of securities together without the need for a broker intermediary. Initially dealing primarily in debt securities and limited partnerships, the ATS model evolved creating Electronic Communications Networks (ECNs) that provided direct access to the NASDAQ trading system for equities. Traders were able to route buy and sell orders electronically, allowing greater share volume at a lower cost than orders handled by floor brokers. Initially, transparency was an issue as price discovery lacked uniformity and the SEC amended its order handling rules in 1997, which in turn led to an expansion of ECN venues. The new rules imposed two conditions on market makers: They must publicly disseminate their own buy/sell offers as well as limit orders placed by their customers and they must include all quotes provided by any other ECN. The intent was to ensure that the particular ECN was not being used to show better quotes than the NASDAQ exchange.

The rise of the ECN was driven by two key objectives of the participants: (1) the ability to handle large equity orders and (2) maintaining buyer/seller anonymity. Large buy/sell orders could be sliced into many smaller orders and fed through the ECN without identifying the ultimate buyer/seller. The ECN became an important tool for institutional investors such as mutual fund managers to manage their larger portfolio trades without tipping their hand as to their buying or selling intentions.

---

[7]SEC Rule 153: Any requirement of a broker or dealer to deliver a prospectus for transactions covered by paragraph (a) of this section will be satisfied if:

(1) Securities of the same class as the securities that are the subject of the transaction are trading on that national securities exchange or facility thereof, trading facility of a national securities association, or alternative trading system;

(2) The registration statement relating to the offering is effective and is not the subject of any pending proceeding or examination under section 8(d) or 8(e) of the Act;

(3) Neither the issuer, nor any underwriter or participating dealer is the subject of a pending proceeding under section 8A of the Act in connection with the offering; and

(4) The issuer has filed or will file with the Commission a prospectus that satisfies the requirements of section 10(a) of the Act.

The ECN also provided an important component to the ATM model giving the selling agent a means to sell large amounts of an issuer's shares discreetly and at a low transactional cost. The ATM model would not have flourished without the ECN as an electronic link to the exchanges.

As ECNs continued to grow in number and trading volume, the use of so-called *dark pools* also expanded since 2007.[8] Dark pools provide an institutional investor or trader the ability to place limit orders for large blocks of stock anonymously away from the exchange without publicly displaying the price or size of the order, which is the case in the "lit" markets on the exchange. The trade is executed when another anonymous order(s) on the other side of the trade is identified by the dark pool at the same limit price. The ATM model is well-suited to using dark pools as one of the venues for trading by enabling the issuer and selling agent to remain anonymous in selling large amounts of shares and avoiding tipping off the market, thus not potentially adversely affecting the share price. As trades are completed, they are printed to the National Consolidated Tape as over-the-counter transactions between ECNs with no identifiers indicating who the ultimate buyer/seller was.

THE GREAT RECESSION

Corporate liquidity was severely challenged following the collapse of Lehman Brothers on September 15, 2008, which set off a chain of financial crises. Financing options became less readily available as corporations looked to realign their balance sheets, pay down debt, and, for some, acquire distressed assets at bargain prices. The Dow Jones Industrial Index fell from 11,416 on September 15, 2008, to a low of 6,595 on March 6, 2009,[9] a loss of 42.25%.

With companies looking to reduce their balance sheet leverage, the choice between asset sales and equity issuance became problematic. Asset prices had little price support given the lack of market liquidity and, with the sharp declines in stock prices, corporations had a dilemma to deal with in raising equity capital. Steep discounts on secondary equity offerings made that option unattractive for many companies. The ATM model, still somewhat novel to the broader market, became an option that several companies, particularly real estate investment trusts (REITs), used to shore up their balance sheets. In 2008, out of an estimated total of 58 ATM programs filed totaling approximately $9.2B, 22 programs were for REITs (including mortgage REITs) totaling $1.8B. Also notably, Ford filed two $500MM ATM programs in 2008 that it used to repurchase its debt in the open market at significant discounts from par. Five electric utilities also filed inaugural programs totaling $650MM to help pay for construction work in progress, repay short-term indebtedness, and for general corporate purposes. Four airline companies filed ATM programs totaling approximately $900MM used to repay short

[8]Lemke and Lins, *Soft Dollars and Other Trading Activities* (Thomson West, 2013–14 ed.).
[9]Bloomberg, LP.

term indebtedness and for other general corporate purposes.[10] The ATM model became battle-tested.

In 2009, over 120 ATM programs were filed totaling over $39B, a fourfold increase over 2008. REITs accounted for over one-third of the number filed with an issuable amount of over $6B.[11] Banks also adopted the strategy filing 22 programs with an issuable amount totaling over $22B. The largest ATM program filed that year was Bank of America in May, which filed a program for up to 1.25 billion shares (~$12B). The prospectus supplement stated the use of proceeds as only for "general corporate purposes." Other banks, including Huntington Bank, used their programs according to their respective prospectus supplements for the "possible repurchase of debt securities" in addition to general corporate purposes.[12] During 2009, the ATM model began to get attention across the greater corporate finance landscape.

As the economy began to stabilize and market liquidity improved, beginning in March 2009 as investor confidence grew, the utility of ATMs gradually shifted from defense to offense. Firms such as REITs scaled back their debt repurchases and looked to begin acquiring assets at relatively attractive prices beginning in 2010 using their access to the equity market with follow-on offerings as well as ATMs. Asset prices had fallen during the recession and this was an opportunity to be taken advantage of. The president and CEO of Host Hotels & Resorts, Inc. stated on the company's fourth-quarter 2009 earnings call, "Given our successful capital raising efforts, we are well positioned to take advantage of opportunities as they begin to arise."[13] In 2015, companies continued to use the ATM model as a tool to reduce leverage as cited by Sabra Health Care REIT, Inc. in their January 12, 2015, guidance update: Commenting on Sabra's deleveraging efforts, Rick Matros, chairman and CEO said, "Strong demand under our ATM program allowed us to lower our leverage more quickly than we had anticipated"[14] as well as funding capital projects.

The incremental nature of asset acquisition and project financing activity may often match the capital-raising capacity of the ATM model for many companies, making the ATM a useful strategy, especially in the REIT and Energy sectors.

GROWTH OF THE ATM MARKET

As seen in Figure 28.1, the dramatic growth of ATM filings began in 2009, with follow-through in 2010, largely attributable to the financial crisis and the ensuing disruptions in the financial markets. As economic stability grew, the demand for equity eased but the use of the ATM strategy continued to expand, growing steadily each year from 2011 through 2015.

---

[10]BNY Mellon Capital Markets, LLC; Dealogic.
[11]Dealogic data.
[12]Bank of America 424(b)(5) filing (May 8, 2009).
[13]Bloomberg, LP transcript, Host Hotels & Resorts, Inc. Q4 2009 earnings call (February 2, 2010).
[14]Sabra Health Care REIT, Inc. press release (January 12, 2015).

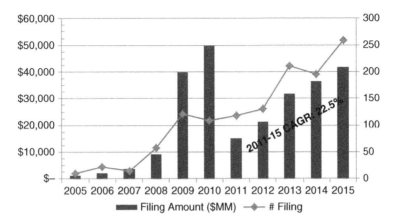

FIGURE 28.1 At-the-market program filings: 2005–2015
Sources: BNYMCM, Bloomberg, Dealogic.

TABLE 28.1 At-the-Market Filings and Value: 2015

Industry	# Filings	ATM Value (MM)
REIT	64	$17,309
Oil & Gas	34	$13,635
Utilities	9	$1,960
Healthcare–Biomed	28	$1,246
Healthcare–Drugs/Pharm	63	$2,477
Healthcare–Other	16	$501
Finance–I/M	10	$541
Other	35	$4,011
Totals	259	$41,681

By year-end 2015, the use of the ATM strategy became an equity tool of choice for three capital-hungry industries, REITs (mortgage and equity), Energy (primarily master limited partnerships, or MLPs), and Utilities, which all together accounted for approximately $33B or ~79% of the total $41.7B ATM program value filed in 2015. Table 28.1 and Figure 28.2 describe the scope of the ATM market FYE 2015.[15]

As mentioned, the Energy/MLP sector is one of the significant users of the ATM strategy due to growing market liquidity coupled with the growing need for capital, and it has fully embraced ATMs since 2012 as seen in Figure 28.3. In fact, this sector's ATM filing amounts have exceeded its follow-on offerings since 2013.[16]

---

[15] BNY Mellon Capital Markets, LLC, Bloomberg, LP, Dealogic.
[16] BNY Mellon Capital Markets, LLC, Dealogic.

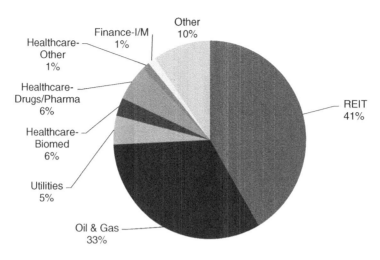

FIGURE 28.2   2015 At-the-market program filings ($MM)
Source: BNY Mellon Capital Markets, LLC, Dealogic.

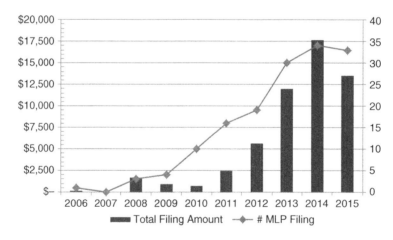

FIGURE 28.3   Energy/MLP ATM filings ($MM)
Source: BNY Mellon Capital Markets, LLC, NAREIT, Bloomberg, LP, Dealogic, Company SEC filings.

To focus on the equity REIT market specifically, one of the most prolific users of the strategy, Figure 28.4 illustrates the growing use of ATMs compared to follow-on offerings from 2006 through yearend 2015 (this dataset excludes mortgage REIT filings). Prior to 2009, ATM programs were a small fraction of the total equity raised by REITs. In 2009, 24% of the total equity offerings filed was with ATMs. For year ended December 31,

EQUITY REIT FILINGS: 2006–2015					
	Total Follow-on Issuance	# Follow-on	Total ATM Filed	# of ATM Programs	ATM as % of Total Equity Filings
2006	$ 13,848,910,000	64	$ 350,700,000	3	2.47%
2007	$ 7,254,420,000	35	$ 321,000,000	3	4.24%
2008	$ 7,947,410,000	45	$ 890,131,500	7	10.07%
2009	$ 18,171,505,000	71	$ 5,739,135,288	41	24.00%
2010	$ 19,372,340,000	77	$ 7,484,930,000	40	27.87%
2011	$ 15,362,680,000	66	$ 7,939,276,150	36	34.07%
2012	$ 24,416,380,000	67	$ 9,216,275,533	45	27.40%
2013	$ 24,800,730,000	91	$ 11,318,926,807	51	31.34%
2014	$ 16,988,245,507	69	$ 12,051,078,490	48	41.50%
2015	$ 17,363,915,289	55	$ 16,156,160,655	58	48.20%
2015	$ 165,526,535,796	640	$ 71,467,614,423	332	30.16%

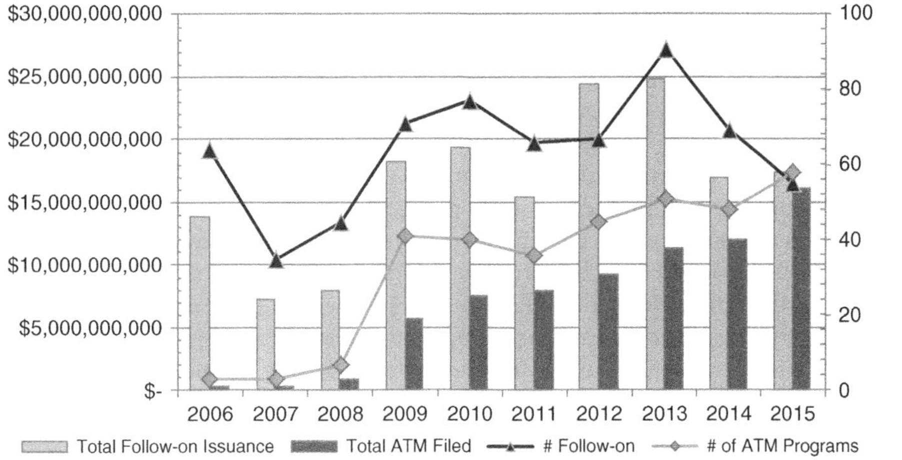

FIGURE 28.4 Equity REIT filings: 2006–2015
Sources: BNYMCM, NAREIT, Bloomberg, LP, Company SEC filings

2015, 48% of total equity filings were for ATMs.[17] One of the principal drivers of the ATM model for equity REITs is the ability to finance property development, short-term debt repayment, and incremental asset acquisitions. Larger M&A activity continues to

---

[17]BNY Mellon Capital Markets, LLC, NAREIT, Bloomberg, LP, Dealogic, Company SEC filings.

be principally financed with follow-on, either marketed or underwritten, offerings given the larger capital-raising capacity.

ATM FINANCING VERSUS FOLLOW-ON OFFERING

ATM financing has distinct advantages and disadvantages to traditional follow-on or marketed offerings. The principal advantage is the potentially lower all-in cost of raising equity. As the term *at-the-market* implies, shares sold under an ATM program are sold at current market prices throughout the trading day. Follow-on offerings typically price at a discount to the prior day's closing price with such discounts ranging from 0% to 5%+ based on our review of recent equity offerings during 2015. The other main cost advantage to the ATM model is the lower underwriting commissions, with ATM program commissions generally ranging from 1% to 2%+ of the amount sold as compared to follow-on equity offering commissions ranging from 3% to 5%+ based on our review of equity offerings filed in 2015. Taken together, the ATM structure may result in a potential total savings of 1% to 10%+ of the amount sold. Discounts and commissions vary widely depending on the issuer, its industry, share liquidity, and general market conditions, so one should consider these factors in context.

Other distinguishing elements of the ATM model include the ability to raise equity capital when, as, and if needed and the ability to be opportunistic as to timing and price. Unlike follow-on offerings where all of the capital is raised at once, ATM programs permit the issuer to raise targeted sums over time to cover known or anticipated expenditures when needed (such as funding development or redevelopment projects) and in effect dollar cost average the share price on equity raised. An issuer may also choose to target a minimum price range in which to issue shares and has the ability to do so with the ATM program as the program may be turned on or off at any time, even intraday. Issuance flexibility is the hallmark of the ATM model. Furthermore, raising capital as needed reduces the effect of *negative carry* as capital is theoretically deployed accretively as it is raised as opposed to a larger follow-on where the funds may be underinvested until they are deployed.

As shares sold using the ATM model are distributed directly into the exchange, the issuer cannot target a particular investor base, be it retail or institutional, unlike a follow-on where the issuer may direct that its shares be marketed to a desired investor base. The ATM selling agent does not know the identity of the ultimate buyer, nor vice versa. The agent's sole objective is to sell shares at the best current market price available, selling into existing market liquidity, and will align its selling strategy to best achieve that objective. As discussed further in what follows, the agent will often slice larger blocks of stock into smaller trades throughout the trading day in order to avoid adversely affecting the price, which could end up favoring smaller retail investor orders. That said, many institutional investors, when targeting a larger block purchase, may also slice their buy order into smaller lots similarly to avoid impacting the market price of the shares.

The main disadvantage with the ATM strategy is price uncertainty vis-à-vis the follow-on offering. The pricing of the follow-on is established on the sales date for the full issuance amount, whereas the total price of an ATM equity raise is the weighted average price of the shares sold over the course of the selling period, which may be as short as a few days or weeks to a month or more. So, if the share price declines over the selling period, the average price will be less than the prices earlier in that period. The converse is true if the share price rises during the period. There is market price risk in the ATM model that should be taken into account when evaluating the two strategies.

Another potential disadvantage with the ATM is the relative market liquidity for the issuer's shares (i.e., How long will it take to raise $X million given the company's average daily trading volume and price?). For some companies, this may be a significant negative factor if their average volume is light (for example, trading less than 100,000 shares/day) and the share price is relatively low. For larger-cap companies, this may not be a significant limiting factor. For example, for a company with an average share price of $45/share and an average daily trading volume (ADTV) of 5,000,000 shares/day, an ATM program could theoretically raise $22.5MM to $33.7MM per day assuming the agent was selling 10% to 15% of ADTV. Similarly, a company with an average share price of $45/share with ADTV of 175,000 could expect a daily capital raise of only $.8MM to $1.2MM. However, a company with a share price of $145/share and ADTV of 175,000 could theoretically raise $2.5MM to $3.8MM per day. In evaluating ATM liquidity, ADTV is the more important metric to consider when reviewing this financing alternative.

DUE DILIGENCE REGIMEN

An important aspect for issuers evaluating the use of the ATM model is the selling agent's continuing due diligence regimen and the extent to which that may engage management over the term of the ATM offering period. An ATM program is designed to be used over a number of months or even years and the need to maintain ongoing due diligence by the selling agent is an important element of the agent's ability to participate in the offering. The agent and its counsel will examine such corporate documents, minutes, resolutions, management letters, financial statements, and such to be able to establish the necessary level of comfort that all questions have been asked and answered. The agent and its counsel must be able to determine that the prospectus at the time of sale is current and accurate in all material respects.

The frequency and scope of the diligence protocol will vary depending on the issuer, its industry, or an agent's institutional requirements. In some cases, an agent may memorialize the diligence protocol in the Sales Agency Agreement; another may require daily *bring-downs* while the issuer is selling shares. Other agents may take a less structured stance on diligence protocol. Market practice requires, however, that if an issuer expects to be in the market, at a minimum, quarterly bring-downs, updated opinions, corporate certifications, and comfort letters will be required by the selling agent.

Under certain circumstances, the diligence process may be temporarily suspended if the company determines that it will not be selling shares in a given quarter. The agent will in any event require a bring-down from the last diligence review when the company chooses to issue shares. While the company is an active seller, it is necessary that the selling agent be attentive to any news relating to the issuer or its industry that may cause concern, and if so, will alert the company and possibly cease selling activity if necessary. The issuer is required under the Sales Agency Agreement to alert the agent if it determines it has material nonpublic information, and if so, the agent will cease selling shares until such information becomes public (and such information typically is "in the market" for 24 hours). The Sales Agency Agreement will typically contain this construct as well.

TRANSACTION PARTICIPANTS AND TYPICAL ATM DOCUMENTATION

At-the-market programs are in effect statutory underwritings and the participants and documentation involved will be substantially similar to any public offering of securities. The main documentary difference between the ATM model and a follow-on offering is the form of the Sales Agency, or Underwriting, Agreement. Given the continuous nature of the sale of securities, the Sales Agency Agreement defines the terms of distributions, conditions precedent to commencing a selling period, and the method of sale (including the option of negotiated block trades) and settlement. The Sales Agency Agreement will define when and how shares will be sold by a selling agent and the issuer will provide for periodic diligence updates as well as legal opinions, comfort letters, and issuer representations and warranties.

The ATM transaction participants and responsibilities include, like follow-on offerings, the following:

- *Issuer:* Diligence participation, secretary's certificate, officer's certificate, NYSE Supplemental Listing Application, press release (if applicable)
- *Issuer's counsel:* Prospectus supplement, Form 8-K, 10b-5 opinion, negative assurance letter
- *Issuer's auditors:* Diligence participation, comfort letter
- *Selling agent(s):* Due diligence, representation letter to the auditors
- *Selling agent's counsel:* Due diligence, Sales Agency Agreement, 10b-5 opinion

ATM deliverables will typically include the following prior to initial filing:

- Prospectus/prospectus supplement (Form S-3 and/or Form 424b-5)
- Sales Agency Agreement and Form 8-K
- Comfort Letter with circle-ups
- Secretary's certificate
- Officer's certificates
- Issuer counsel opinion and negative assurance letter
- Issuer counsel Sales Agency Agreement opinion
- Agent's counsel opinion and negative assurance letter
- Instruction letter to transfer agent

- Issuer opinion to transfer agent
- Certificate of transfer agent
- NYSE Supplemental Listing Application

Other transaction documents may include:

- Diligence materials request
- Management and accounting diligence questionnaires
- Organizational documents
  - Good-standing certificates
  - Board resolutions
  - Incumbency certificates
- Representation letter from selling agent to auditors
- Press release (if applicable)
- "Blood letter" (if applicable)

The timing to put an ATM program in place is largely dependent upon the extent of the due diligence work that needs to be undertaken. The Sales Agency Agreement documentation has been substantially standardized and as such there is not much to be negotiated in the Agreement (Sales Agency Agreements will contain the customary representations and warranties seen in a follow-on Underwriting Agreement and many issuers will tailor the Sales Agency Agreement to the issuer's standard underwriting reps and warranties package). We have seen programs go from start to filing in as little as one week when diligence was current with all documentation agreed upon. Once the filing is made and deliverables confirmed, the company is in a position to commence issuing. Like most public securities offerings, ATM program filings are usually made pre-opening or post-closing of the stock market.

THE SELLING AGENT

The selling agent is the broker-dealer that is responsible for managing the sale of shares when the company commences using the ATM program. Up until 2010, almost all ATM programs filed were managed by one agent, largely due to the relative novelty of the strategy, but also because the bulge bracket Wall Street firms did not want to cannibalize their higher fee follow-on equity business for the lower commissioned ATM business and sought to marginalize the ATM strategy as a low-cap targeted product. As the ATM strategy gained broader acceptance from a growing number of increasingly larger-market-cap companies, these firms ultimately joined the party, tacitly acknowledging the ATM model's place in the CFO's capital-raising toolbox. This was first particularly noticeable in the Equity REIT and Energy markets beginning in 2010.

Figure 28.5 shows the number of agents for each ATM program filed from January 1, 2005, to December 31, 2015, and a trendline for the period.[18] How many agents

---

[18]BNY Mellon Capital Markets, LLC, Bloomberg, LP, Dealogic.

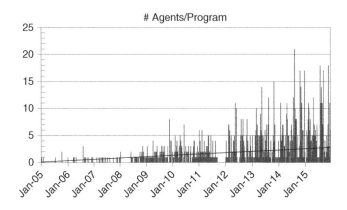

FIGURE 28.5   Number of agents per program: 2005–2015

to appoint on a program is generally determined by the size of the program; the larger the issue, the more agents may be engaged. Determining how many agents to engage, an issuer will consider which of its banks/brokers should be included and what would be fair compensation for each agent. So, for example, the commission for a $100MM program with four agents would be $250k or $500k for each agent, assuming the program is fully drawn equally among the agents and assuming a commission rate of 1% or 2% respectively of the sale amount.

Multi-agented programs are not in and of themselves overly problematic. Each agent enters into a separate but identical Sales Agency Agreement with the issuer and each agent will be listed on the filed prospectus supplement. The company will often appoint one of the agents to act as a lead agent to coordinate the documentation and diligence with counsel on behalf of the other co-agents. The company will generally include all agents on all diligence update calls. Only one agent may be in the market selling on any given trading day.

CORPORATE BOARD AND MANAGEMENT OVERSIGHT

Corporate governance rules vary by corporate jurisdiction and state laws pertaining to board authorization of the sale of equity securities. Some jurisdictions, for example Delaware, require the board to authorize the issuance price prior to confirming the actual sale, which, in the case of an ATM program, would be logistically difficult given the continuous, even daily nature of the ATM model. In such cases where the sales may be made over a period of time, a board may delegate authority to a committee that may include members of the management team to determine the number of shares and the timing of the issuance, or it may authorize a resolution in which the same criteria are defined. The resolution must include maximum number of shares that may be issued, timing, and minimum price.[19]

---

[19]Section 152 Delaware General Corporation Law as amended (June 24, 2015).

Once the company's board of directors authorizes the issuance of equity and means of sale (e.g., follow-on or ATM), the selling agent and its counsel will commence the diligence and documentation process with the assistance of management and its counsel. Management will provide such corporate documents, resolutions, minutes, and financials as may be requested by the selling agent. Upon satisfactory completion of the documentation, all parties will conduct a business and accounting diligence call prior to filing, following which opinions and comfort letters will be released and the SEC filing of the Sales Agency Agreement and the prospectus supplement may be filed. Once the program is filed, management will cooperate with the selling agent for the periodic updating of diligence during the program's term.

Corporate governance protocol defines certain *blackout dates* during which the company's employees or officers are not permitted to trade in the company's shares. Usually, these blackout dates key off of the company's quarterly earnings releases. The company should consult with its outside counsel to similarly define periods when it should be out of the market with its ATM program. Many companies will use its management blackout dates as the defined "no-sale" period for the ATM program. Others have opted to close the selling window between quarter-end and the earnings release. In some cases, an agent may predefine those periods and memorialize it in the Sales Agency Agreement.

Beyond the initial filing of the ATM program documents, the prospectus supplement, and the Sales Agency Agreement, the company has limited responsibilities for filing ongoing program-related documents or notices. Generally speaking, sales made under the program need not be publicly reported other than in its quarterly earnings filings on Form 10-Q or 10-K, unless the amount sold could be deemed material. *Materiality* is not clearly defined by the SEC so the company should consult with its counsel as to what would constitute a material sale of equity in its particular case. Should the sale amount rise to an amount deemed to be material, the company will file a *pricing supplement* pursuant to Rule 424, or a *current report* on Form 8-K, indicating retrospectively the amount that was sold during the quarter. Otherwise, the company will describe the sale of equity in its quarterly filings as it would for any capital-raising activity.

If the issuer is in the market selling shares under the ATM program, and it comes to have knowledge of an event, or an impending event, such as a material acquisition, pending changes in management or the board, material litigation, or any other material nonpublic information that would necessitate the filing of a current report in Form 8-K, the issuer will notify the selling agent immediately to cease all selling activity until such information becomes public (and such information typically is in the market, or *seasoned*, for 24 hours).

The ATM model has no *lockup provision* as is the case for most follow-on offerings. The issuer is, however, proscribed from offering any sale of equity, direct or indirect, while it is in the market, except for certain circumstances such as exercises of stock options or grants or awards, dividend reinvestment or stock purchase programs, or shares issued in consideration related to future acquisitions (being mindful of material nonpublic information that may require the issuer to suspend sales under the program).

While the ATM program selling is active, the company will receive a daily trade blotter from the selling agent at the end of the trading session noting the number of shares sold, the average selling price, trade date, settlement date, and the amount of proceeds net of the agent's commission. The issuer will then notify its stock transfer agent of the sale amount each day and instruct the transfer agent to set up the transfer of the shares, via DTC's DWAC[20] system, versus payment, to the selling agent's account. Upon receipt of the shares, the agent will release the net proceeds to the issuer via fed funds wire.

MARKETPLACE ACCEPTANCE

During the mid-2000s, until late 2010, most institutional investors criticized the ATM model citing a lack of transparency and no ability to vote on the use of proceeds by participating in a follow-on offering. One commentary titled "The Case Against ATMs" submitted to NAREIT's reit.com in April 2010 stated that the "ATMs are an end run around the governance and transparency of the public market."[21] There was much debate at the time about the issuance strategy but companies continued to enjoy the benefits of the ATM model and, as more issuers adopted the strategy, antipathy toward the strategy subsided. Issuers were mostly transparent about their use of proceeds on a retrospective basis after they were in the market, usually on their quarterly earnings calls. Largely due to the prudent use of the ATM, buy-side opposition to ATMs is no longer as contentious an issue as it was just five or six years ago.

We interviewed several sell-side equity analysts in 2009 and 2010 on a no-name basis and each one acknowledged the benefit to the shareholder through lower all-in equity underwriting costs by raising more proceeds from the share sale. The rating agencies also looked favorably on the ATM model as it provided additional flexibility in raising equity, particularly coming out of the turbulent market period of 2008–2009. Moody's February 18, 2011, Credit Opinion for Equity Residential stated: "Credit strengths include: Good near-term liquidity coverage supported by ample bank line capacity and access to multiple forms of capital" and specifically, "EQR's at-the-market share offering program also should continue to add to its capital base over the next three years."[22] The Fitch Ratings review of the outlook for REITs for 2015 cited the following related to ATM financing:

> We believe portfolio focus and tactical diversification, lower risk growth strategies, good liquidity management, minimal share repurchase risk, and enhancements to capital access via at-the-market (ATM) equity programs are key drivers and will continue for the foreseeable future.... We believe issuers will continue to have access to low all-in-cost secured and unsecured debt and opportunistically access the equity markets via ATM programs or follow-on offerings to fund acquisitions and development.[23]

---

[20]Deposit and withdrawal at custodian.
[21]NAREIT, https://www.reit.com/news/articles/commentary-case-against-atms.
[22]Moody's Investors Service.
[23]Fitch Ratings, "U.S. Equity REIT Positive Sector Outlook for 2015" (December 16, 2014).

SIZING AN ATM PROGRAM

There is no established rule for determining the size of an ATM program. We have seen companies file programs for as little as 2% of market capitalization up to as much as 75% of market cap. The general practice has been sizing the program to reflect the issuer's reasonably expected equity needs over the next three to five years. As ATM programs now need not have a definitive term or expiration date, as it can remain active as long as the company's shelf registration is effective, the program can contemplate a longer time horizon for its equity needs to determine an appropriate size. If one looks at the average sizing of 2015's ATM filings in the equity REIT market, for example, it was ~7% of market capitalization with a sample range of approximately 2% to 30%. In our experience, around 10% to as much as 15% of market cap is often the sizing range used by many of our mid-cap clients and around 5% for our larger-cap clients.[24]

The market impact on share price upon filing an ATM program is rarely negative or pronounced. This is largely due to the market's recognition that the ATM is an option to issue equity, not an obligation, and most corporate users of this strategy have been prudent issuers when it comes to utilizing their programs. An important consideration is that any company should be prepared to provide a reasonable case for any potential equity raise as it will get questions about the program from investors and equity analysts.

REGULATION M

Rules 101 and 102 of Regulation M are intended to protect against potential market manipulation by imposing limitations on certain trading activity during an equity offering. These rules prohibit underwriters and their affiliates from directly or indirectly bidding for, or inducing others to bid for, a covered security until the applicable restricted period has ended. Reg M has an exemption for "actively traded" securities (i.e., ADTV of at least $1MM for issuers with a public float of at least $150MM). Thus, ATM programs for actively traded issuers have no Reg M restriction. Selling agents, however, are required to report all ATM trading activity to FINRA for compliance purposes, not for public use.

PROCEDURES AND MECHANICS OF THE ATM PROGRAM

Once filed, the ATM program is effective and the company may issue shares under the program, unless there is cause to suspend issuance due to lack of diligence updates or stale deliverables, company policies, and so forth, by delivering an *issuance notice* to the selling agent indicating the amount (in dollars or number of shares) to sell and the minimum price per share, or *floor price*, below which the agent may not execute trades.

---

[24]BNY Mellon Capital Markets, LLC data.

The issuer will also determine the length of each *selling period*, which may be one day or as many as 10 days. Additionally, the issuer may define any trading parameters (the board may have determined certain price bands or share price performance dictates), usually in consultation with the selling agent and its traders, such as a maximum percentage of the day's volume the agent may execute. The selling agent will acknowledge the issuance notice and its terms to the issuer and will commence selling.

The selling agent's trading desk will often have a pre-market call with the issuer to discuss the tone of the market pre-opening and review any economic or industry-specific news anticipated that day that may have an impact on the market or sector. The trading desk will also want to gauge the issuer's priorities with respect to the issuance. For example, one issuer's priority may be to sell shares with less concern about relative price performance where another issuer may be more focused on relative price performance and will be more patient on the pace of the sales. Yet another issuer may take an opportunistic approach and ramp up or down selling activity at certain price points or certain relative price performance. The trader will offer to provide input on possible selling strategies that may help the issuer clarify its priorities and objectives. The trader wants to fully understand the issuer's objectives in order to best manage the selling of the shares and will want to determine those priorities before trading commences.

The traders execute the sales electronically into the exchange through an ECN or, if appropriate, directly through a floor broker. As the total issuance amount is typically large enough to move the market if executed all at once, the trader will slice a larger sell order into smaller lots, making many smaller trade executions, for example, a few hundred shares up to a thousand or more at a time, often using an algorithm to adjust the pace of selling in line with a specific, targeted percentage of ADTV. The agent may also look to use dark pools of liquidity, discussed earlier, in order to maintain anonymity while selling larger blocks of stock. The trader's job is to find the deepest liquidity for the shares and he or she may end up looking at several venues to find that liquidity. The trader will gauge the tone of the market in order to adjust the pace of the selling activity to ensure minimal adverse price impact, speeding up the selling rate during periods of price strength and easing the selling rate during weaker price performance. It is not unusual for a trader to write over 1000 tickets throughout the trading day (but just one ticket with the issuer), the objective being to minimize the risk that the selling activity has any ill-effects on the share price.

Measuring a trader's selling performance should be gauged using two principal metrics: average daily sale price comparison to the day's VWAP; and relative stock price performance compared to a closely correlated index or peer group. In the former metric, a trader should be expected to meet or beat VWAP on average. Given the volume of shares that the trader is selling, as a proportion of the day's volume, achieving this metric should be attainable, barring some intraday extraordinary trading event or large closing crossing trades at the end of the session. The second metric is an important one to use as it measures relative price performance of the stock vis-à-vis its peers, taking external market movement out of the calculation. If the selling stock moves closely with its peer group, then the trader is generally having little or no adverse effect on the share price. If the share price is underperforming the peer group, the trader will try to determine if its selling activity is affecting the price, such as limiting or even ceasing trading activity for a period of time, or if there is something else having a price impact, such as market noise on the stock. The trader may also use this metric to take advantage of relative market strength in the stock versus the peer group by stepping up the selling pace. If the stock price is underperforming the peer group despite limited or no program selling activity, the trader will usually notify the issuer that something is producing a drag on price and may discuss tailoring the selling strategy with the issuer.

At the end of each trading session, the trader will summarize the day's results on a trade blotter and submit it to the issuer via e-mail. The trader will generally include the following information: trade date, settlement date, number of shares sold, average sale price, total share volume for the day, VWAP, gross proceeds, selling commission, and net settlement price and proceeds to the issuer.

ATM SELLING STRATEGIES

The selling strategies employed by various broker-dealers engaged in the ATM market may vary to a limited or even a large extent. Some traders tend to rely more on algorithmic trading strategies (*algo* trading), employing, for example, a volume-weighted average price (VWAP) algo with a set-it-and-forget-it philosophy. Such algorithms are designed to target VWAP for the day, and, except for extraordinary trading events such as erroneous off-market prints or large block activity at the highs or the lows of the day, will achieve the desired results. Some traders may engage in a smile-and-dial strategy, calling select institutional buyers to cross blocks of stock, usually at or around VWAP for the day. Yet others, arguably most traders, will employ a modified algo approach using a VWAP algo together with a more high-touch managed selling approach using dark pools or other ECNs. Each strategy has its place and one may be more appropriate for certain issuers over others. For example, a smile-and-dial strategy might be more appropriate for less liquid issuers, such as those with a lower ADTV.

The ultimate objective for the trader, and the issuer, is to try to achieve the highest price for the shares sold on behalf of the issuer while avoiding having an adverse impact on the share price vis-à-vis its peer group. Trading anonymity is the important element in achieving this objective.

VARIATIONS OF THE ATM MODEL

Prior to the commoditization of the ATM model today, other forms of continuous offerings of equity were used, although with less broad market appeal. One such model was the *equity line of credit* in which an issuer would enter into a purchase agreement with a purchaser, often an institutional investor or a broker-dealer, that gave the issuer the right, but not obligation, to sell or *put* shares to the purchaser at a predetermined price (often VWAP-based), which price may include a discount.

Equity Line Financing was a similar concept to Equity Line of Credit except it was in effect an underwritten commitment on the part of a broker-dealer to purchase shares at VWAP, less a spread, upon request by the issuer provided the selling price met or exceeded the floor price. The broker then sold the shares electronically, similar to the ATM methodology, putting the broker at risk on the average daily sale price versus VWAP. These programs were largely used by smaller public companies looking for growth capital such as biotech and technology companies as an alternative to structured PIPE transactions (private investment in public equity) and had higher commission rates than the ATM model, reflecting the broker's price risk premium.

Another variation of, or adaptation to, the present-day ATM model was incorporating a *forward purchase agreement* into the ATM program that permits the issuer to sell shares at a current market price and settle the transactions either on a regular way basis (T+3) or at a later date, usually up to one year later. This structure involves a third party, typically an affiliated bank of the agent, to perform the duties of the forward purchaser who borrows the shares to be sold by the agent, creating a short position against an obligation of the issuer to deliver shares. The principal advantage of this structure is to establish a known cost of the equity raised now to fund an obligation in the future rather than taking the market risk in waiting until that future date to execute the equity sale. While not a widely used strategy, it has been used in the Utility, REIT, and Investment Management sectors.[25] Figure 28.6 shows a flowchart illustrating the forward-ATM initial sale.

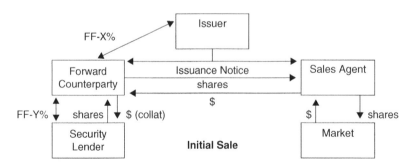

FIGURE 28.6   Forward-ATM initial sale

---

[25]Examples: AvalonBay Communities (December 2015), Piedmont Natural Gas (January 2014), Affiliated Managers Group (August 2013), DDR Corp (June 2013), Westar Energy (March 2013).

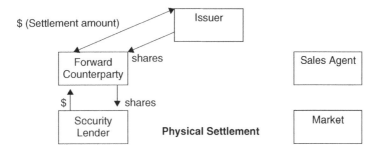

FIGURE 28.7 Forward sale, physical settlement

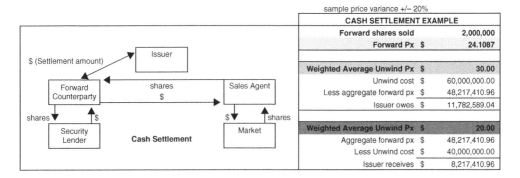

FIGURE 28.8 Forward sale, cash settlement

The forward is usually settled with the exchange of shares issued by the company in exchange for the funds raised by the forward seller as depicted in Figure 28.7.

Alternatively, the issuer may elect to unwind the forward sale and choose to *cash settle* the trades (should the need for the equity diminish) whereby the issuer pays, or receives, the difference between the net forward price and the current market price for the same number of shares as shown in Figure 28.8.

A whitepaper I co-authored with attorneys from Dewey & LeBoeuf in 2010 goes into greater detail on this structure and may be accessed through this URL: http://www .bnymellon.com/foresight/pdf/equityfinancing.pdf.

SUMMARY

At-the-market offerings have evolved over the past 30 years into an effective and efficient source of equity capital that has a useful place in most CFOs' corporate finance toolboxes. With the wide array of electronic trading venues with greater access to liquidity and strategic trading tools the ATM model has become a powerful tool to manage targeted equity raising. Coexisting with traditional underwritten offerings, the ATM will continue to provide capital for project finance, balance sheet management, and incremental acquisitions. It will not replace the follow-on for transformational M&A transactions. The ATM is not designed to do that.

As we continue to see the size and number of ATM filings grow, it demonstrates that corporate adoption of the ATM model and market acceptance of the strategy have affirmed the value of this form of equity issuance.

CHAPTER 29

Interest Rate Swaps

Amir Sadr

The interest rate derivatives market (swaps, options) is the largest segment of the global over-the-counter (OTC) derivatives market consisting of contracts on foreign exchange, interest rates, equity, commodity, and credit default swaps. According to the Bank for International Settlements (BIS), as of June 2015, interest rate contracts comprised $434 trillion (78%) of the notional amounts outstanding, or $11 trillion (71%) of gross market value. Of these contracts 90% were swaps—almost all plain-vanilla swaps—and FRAs, and 10% options. Comparing the gross market value of swaps to the $12.7 trillion of U.S. Treasury outstanding debt should drive home the significance and size of this market.

In the United States, almost every major financial institution and corporation uses interest rate swaps. Commercial banks can use swaps to match the duration of their assets (long-term fixed-rate loans) to their liabilities (short-rate deposits, CDs). Agencies use swaps and swap derivatives to fine-tune and hedge the duration of their mortgage portfolios in response to expected or realized prepayments, and for funding. Corporates usually follow a debt issuance (typically fixed-rate bonds) by swapping these to floating rates at opportune times (steep yield curves). Finally, speculators such as hedge funds and proprietary trading desks use swaps to express views or take advantage of level/slope/curvature of interest rate curves.

Traditionally, swaps and derivatives have been privately negotiated, bilateral, principal-to-principal contracts between two counterparties with maximum flexibility in the details (start date, maturity date, payment frequency, floating index, . . .) of the contract. Despite this flexibility, most swaps have standardized terms, with only the notional, maturity and the fixed rate being negotiated at trade time. Since the 2007–2008 financial crisis and passage of Dodd-Frank Law, the impetus has been to centrally clear standard swaps by having a Central Counterparty (CCP) become the intermediate counterparty to all original counterparties. As of this writing, more than 75% of swaps are centrally cleared, and this allows for netting and mitigation of credit risk inherent in swaps, and avoids the domino effect of one counterparty's default, since the CCP requires initial and daily variation margin from its swap counterparties. Moreover, there is a strong push by SEC and CFTC to execute swaps on a Swap Execution Facility (SEF) which is an electronic trading platform providing bid and offer information to end-users. This has helped to move swaps to a regulated, transparent, and commoditized market.

PLAIN-VANILLA FIXED-FOR-FLOATING SWAPS

A plain-vanilla fixed-for-floating *Interest Rate Swap (IRS)* is an agreement between two counterparties to periodically exchange interest payments on a hypothetical loan, where one counterparty, the fixed-rate payer, pays a periodic fixed coupon, while the other counterparty, the floating rate payer, pays a variable amount that periodically resets based on a benchmark interest rate index, for example, 3-month London Interbank Offered Rate (Libor) for USD, which is considered to be the uncollateralized funding index for banks. As opposed to a bond, each counterparty only pays the *interest payments* on the hypothetical loan, and no principal payment is made either at the beginning or end of the swap, hence the name *interest rate swap*. Figure 29.1 shows the cash-flows of a simple 1-year USD swap with fixed-rate C.

When talking about plain-vanilla fixed-for-floating swaps—*swaps* from now on—the point of reference is the fixed rate: If one is receiving the fixed rate (floating rate payer), one is said to be *receiving in a swap* or simply *receiving*. Similarly if one is the fixed-rate payer, then one is *paying in a swap*, or simply *paying*. Receiving in a swap is akin to being long a bond, since one is receiving a coupon and paying periodic financing (3m-Libor rather than overnight or term repo). Similarly, paying in a swap is akin to being short a bond.

The stream of cash-flows made by each counterparty (fixed/floating payer) is referred to as a *Leg*, and a swap's cash-flows are considered to be made up of a *Fixed Leg* and a *Floating Leg*. For each leg of a swap, the first/last date that interest begins/ends accruing is called the *Effective Date* and *Maturity Date* respectively. Commonly both legs of a

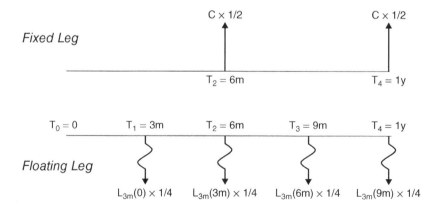

FIGURE 29.1   Simplified cash-flows of a 1y USD swap

swap have the same Effective and Maturity dates, and these are then referred to as the swap's Effective/Maturity dates. Also the interest rates are based on hypothetical loans with same principal, referred to as the *Notional* of the swap.

Each leg of a swap comprises of contiguous *calculation periods*, so a 1y USD swap has 2 semi-annual calculation periods on the fixed leg, and 4 quarterly calculation periods on the floating leg. For USD swaps, the fixed rate is accrued for half a year and paid at the end of each semi-annual calculation period. On the floating leg, at the beginning of each quarterly calculation period (actually 2 London day's prior to that), the 3m-Libor fixing is used as the interest rate and accrued Act/360 for the length of that calculation period, and this accrued interest amount times the notional is paid at the end of the calculation period.

To value an IRS, one needs to compute the net PV of the fixed and floating legs. Given the appropriate discount factor curve, this is straight-forward for the fixed leg as it is a series of known cash-flows. For the floating leg, we first need to compute the forward/fixing value of the unknown index (3m Libor), and then *discount the forward*.

CLASSICAL SINGLE-CURVE WORLD

Prior to the 2007–2008 financial crisis, major banks' credit was not in question, and Libor was universally treated as the true and best measure of risk-free and uncollateralized funding index for banks. With this assumption, pricing a swap boiled down to extraction and usage of the Libor discount curve serving the dual purposes of discounting and extracting forward Libor rates. We shall discuss this historical single-curve method first.

Focusing on the 1y swap shown in Figure 29.1, we can easily price the fixed leg, as the fixed-payer makes two known semi-annual payments $C/2$ with per unit notional with payments in 6 months, and 1 year's time. Armed with a discount function $D(T)$, it is easy to evaluate the fixed leg per unit notional ($T_2 = 6m, T_4 = 1y$):

$$PV(FixedLeg) = C/2 \times (D(T_2) + D(T_4)).$$

The obligation of the float-payer and its valuation are more complex. The 1-year duration of the swap is divided into four quarterly calculation periods, where $0 = T_0 < T_1 = 3m < T_2 = 6m < T_3 = 9m < T_4 = 1y$. At the beginning of each calculation period, $[T_i, T_{i+1}]$, the prevailing 3-month floating index $L_{3m}(T_i)$, is determined (rate-fixing), accrued for 3 months, and paid at the end of that period (T_{i+1}). Specifically, at T_{i+1}, the float-payer pays $L_{3m}(T_i)/4$ which we recognize as the interest component of 3-month forward loan at rate $L_{3m}(T_i)$.

If the floating index reflects the swap counterparties' funding rate, one can replicate this interest only portion by ensuring that one owns unit currency at T_i, and owes unit currency at T_{i+1}. In this case, one can invest the unit currency at T_i at the prevailing 3-month rate, $L_{3m}(T_i)$, and use the proceeds, $1 + L_{3m}(T_i)/4$, as follows: pay $L_{3m}/4$ to settle the floating obligation, and pay the unit principal to whom he owed unit at T_{i+1}.

Therefore, the economic value of the floating payment is $D(T_i) - D(T_{i+1})$, and the value of the floating leg can be computed as:

$$PV(FloatLeg) = \sum_{i=0}^{3}(D(T_i) - D(T_{i+1}))$$

$$= D(T_0) - D(T_4)$$

per unit notional. Note that with this static replication, we do not need to know (or care) what the future interest rates will be. The same formula would hold if we were periodically observing an index (Fed-Funds), and compounding it at successive fixing rates, and pay the compounded interest at the payment date.

Putting it together, the value to the receiver of a 1-year swap in the one-curve world is

$$PV(Swap) = \left[\sum_{i=1}^{2} C/2 \times D(T_{2i})\right] - (D(T_0) - D(T_4))$$

per unit notional, while the value to the payer is the negative of the above.

In general, the value of the fixed leg of N-year swap with annual fixed-rate C paid m times per year, with Effective date T_0, Maturity date T_{Nm} and payment dates $T_1 < \cdots < T_{Nm}$ is:

$$C \times \sum_{i=1}^{Nm} \alpha_i D(T_i)$$

where $\alpha_i = \alpha(T_{i-1}, T_i)$ is the length of each calculation period in years, according to the specified day-count for the fixed leg (for USD swaps, SA, 30/360, $\alpha_i = 1/2$.) The value of the floating leg is $D(T_0) - D(T_{Nm})$, giving the following formula for the value of a receiver swap:

$$\left[C \times \sum_{i=1}^{Nm} \alpha_i D(T_i)\right] - (D(T_0) - D(T_{Nm}))$$

per unit notional.

Swap Leg's Floating Payment

As long as the floating index is the same as swap counterparties' funding index, since the funding index can be locked at the forward rate, we can replace its unknown future value by its locked forward value. Simple algebra shows that

$$PV(\text{Float Payment}) = D(T_i) - D(T_{i+1})$$

$$= (D(T_i)/D(T_{i+1}) - 1) \times D(T_{i+1})$$

$$= \frac{D(T_i)/D(T_{i+1}) - 1}{\Delta T_i} \times (\Delta T_i) \times D(T_{i+1})$$

$$= f([T_i, T_{i+1}]) \times (\Delta T_i) \times D(T_{i+1}).$$

where ΔT_i is the accrual factor for the i-th calculation period. Therefore, in order to value the floating leg's payments, it *mathematically suffices* to assume that its unknown floating rate is equal to the forward rate, accruing it for ΔT_i, and discounting this *assumed* cash flow by $D(T_{i+1})$. This is the usual practice, and is referred to as *discounting the forwards*. For this method to work, one has to ensure that the floating index's tenor and day-count exactly match the floating payment's—true for plain-vanilla swaps. For other swaps, this method fails and only provides a first-order approximation, requiring further *convexity adjustments* to arrive at the correct value.

Par Swap Rates

A *Par Swap* is a swap whose value today is zero, and the *Par Swap Rate* is the fixed rate of this swap. For a swap with Effective date T_0, Maturity date T, since the value of the floating leg is simply $D(T_0) - D(T)$, we form the calculation periods for the fixed leg, $\{T_0, \ldots, T_M = T\}$ to compute the Par-Swap Rate, $S(T_0, T)$, as the fixed rate that makes the value of the swap zero:

$$S(T_0, T) = \frac{D(T_0) - D(T)}{\sum_{i=1}^{M} \alpha_i \times D(T_i)},$$

A graph of $S(0, T)$ versus maturity T is called the *Par-Swap Curve*.

A typical swap is spot-starting: $(T_0 = 0)$. If its effective date is in the future, $T_0 > 0$, then it is a *Forward Swap*, and its Par swap rate is called the *Forward (Par) Swap Rate*.

The reason for calling a swap with zero value as a *Par Swap* is as follows: For a spot starting $(T_0 = 0)$ par swap, note that by rearranging the above equation, we have

$$1 = \sum_{i=1}^{M} S(0, T) \times \alpha_i \times D(T_i) + D(T).$$

The right-hand side is the value of a T-maturity coupon bond with coupon rate $S(0, T)$, where the cash flows are discounted by a series of different spot/zero rates rather than assuming a single constant yield-to-maturity y. So, $S(0, T)$ is the coupon rate of a par-bond, that is par-coupon rate, with *discounting along the curve* rather than flat.

The receiver in a swap is therefore economically long a fixed-coupon bond at par, and an N-year swap is similar to a N-year bond, with similar duration characteristics. When a swaps's fixed rate is the same as market par-swap rates, its value is zero, similar to the bond being worth par if its coupon rate is the same as market yields: *Par swap rates are analogous to bond YTM's.*

Construction of the Swap/Libor Curve

We have seen that as long as the floating index is the same as our funding index (driving our discount function), all we need is the discount curve $D(T)$ to price swaps and calculate swap rates. It would be nice if the market quoted $D(T)$ directly, saving market participants a lot of grief. Sadly, it is not the case. Note that we would like to have the daily discount factors for a good number of years, say 30 years, amounting to about 10,000 prices (one for each day). In reality, at each point of time, there are active and liquid markets for at most 40–50 instruments that provide information about our funding index.

The traditional solution has been to use the bootstrap method to extract the discount factors, albeit with more sophisticated interpolation methods. The interpolation method (Linear in Discount Factors), while simple, is one of the worst interpolation methods. The metric used to make this assessment is to look at the graph of implied 1-day or 3-month forwards. This graph is discontinuous, and highly jagged, forcing one to forecast excessively high implied rates, followed by excessively low implied rates (see Figure 29.2).

There are other simple methods that somewhat alleviate this problem. One such method is linear interpolation in $\ln D(T)$, sometimes referred to as *Log-Linear* or *piece-wise constant forwards* or *Constant-Daily-Forwards (CDF)* method.

For any given $T_1 < T < T_2$, we linearly interpolate in the $\ln D(T)$ space to get:

$$(T_1 < T < T_2)\ D(T) = D(T_1)\left(\frac{D(T_2)}{D(T_1)}\right)^{\frac{T-T_1}{T_2-T_1}}.$$

Over each segment, the instantaneous forward rate, $f(T)$ is constant, and a graph of it versus T looks like a staircase (with discontinuity at segment points). Forward rates of longer tenor are averages of instantaneous forward rates, and also exhibit this staircase behavior, albeit slightly smoother. Other methods include cubic spline interpolation in Zero Rates, which results in short-term forwards that are smooth (3rd-order polynomials).

While bootstrap method combined with an interpolation scheme is the usual method to construct a discount factor curve, there are other (global) methods that would fit

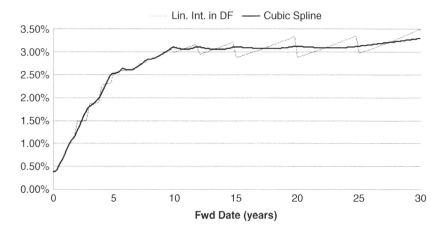

FIGURE 29.2 Forward-3m rates due to different curve interpolation methods

a curve satisfying all the input constraints, and fall into the category of constrained optimization methods. Among these are minimum length methods which minimize the total variation of the instantaneous forward curve and lead to a smooth curve. Another approach is to posit a parametric shape for the forward, zero, or par-swap curve, and optimize the free parameters according to some metric while satisfying the input constraints either exactly, or within user-specified tolerances for each constraint.

Flow or Prop: Descriptive or Normative

The question usually arises as to which one is the "best" curve build method. While a staircase curve makes sense for Fed-funds rates as they are generally constant between FOMC dates, for a 3m-Libor curve, it might seem that we should insist on a continuous and smooth forward curve when building a curve and discard any discontinuous method. However, it turns out that smooth methods result in non-intuitive hedges (see discussion of partial PV01's at end of this chapter). Therefore, *when selecting a curve build method, one has to decide on the right tradeoff between smoothness and the sensibility of the prescribed hedges*. As each trader might have a different opinion on where the right tradeoff is, there has yet not emerged a universally accepted curve build method.

Another consideration in the choice of curve building is its target application. For a market-maker or a flow-trading desk at a broker/dealer, the source of profit is usually the bid–offer of traded instruments. For this group, the market is always right, and the constructed curve has to completely fit all traded instruments, even if one thinks that certain instruments trade rich or cheap. This is also the requirement imposed by control groups within a broker/dealer, so that each book is marked-to-market, so that the proper liquidation value of a book can be ascertained (at least in theory). With this constraint, the constructed curve has to be *descriptive* and perfectly fit the market, whether rational or irrational.

An alternative motivation when building a curve can be to determine the relative fair value of traded instruments. In this paradigm, not all instruments need to fit exactly, and one requires an exact fit for a subset, while using the difference between the modeled value versus the market value as a rich/cheap trading signal. This *normative* view of curve construction is used by proprietary traders as it aides in determining where an instrument *should* trade in contrast to where it *does* trade relative to some benchmark instruments.

THE NEW WORLD: DECOUPLED DISCOUNT AND FORWARD CURVES

In the aftermath of the 2007–2008 financial crisis, the main assumptions of the single curve methodology have come under serious question. Libor has proven to be a manipulable and compromised rate, it is *not* the risk-free rate, and does not reflect the true funding cost of banks's derivatives contracts. More important, in order to mitigate credit risk, many derivative contracts now require the periodic posting of collateral as the value of the contract changes, with the collateral earning overnight risk-free index (Fed-Funds in case of USD) rate, hence the funding cost of a collateralized derivative contract is no longer Libor, but Fed-Funds rate, and future cash-flows need to be discounted using the *Fed Fund* curve.

The OIS curve—used to calculate the policy rate's discount *and* forward rates—has taken on a central role in pricing and risk-management of swaps and derivatives, and has become the de facto discount curve for derivatives. Most of the curve build methodologies (bootstrap, optimization, . . .) have been redirected to extracting the single OIS discount/forward curve. Once the OIS curve is extracted, it is then used as the discounting curve, and the forward curve of other instruments, 3m-Libor, 6m-Libor, and other indices are extracted from market quotes, with discounting off of the OIS curve. Once these forward curves are constructed, the pricing then reduces to OIS discounting of the forward index or fixed rate.

OIS MARKET

The *Overnight Indexed Swap (OIS)* market is based on the policy rate of central banks for each currency, and are based on actual traded deposits. For example in USD, the benchmark is daily Fed-Fund Effective Rate, which is a volume-weighted average of rates on Fed-Fund trades arranged by major brokers, and calculated and published next day by the Federal Reserve in its H.15 report.

OIS Market Instruments

An OIS swap is a fixed-for-floating swap where the floating leg is based on the overnight policy rate. Typical maturities in USD are 1 week, 2 week, 3 week, 1m, 2m, 3m, . . . , 6m, 9m, 12m, 15m, 18m, 2y with longer maturities having low liquidity. The floating payment for each calculation period the daily compounded interest at each overnight rate (weekends/holidays use previous business day's fixing) over the calculation period,

$$[1 + \alpha_1 \times r_1] \times [1 + \alpha_2 \times r_2] \times \cdots \times [1 + \alpha_N \times r_N] - 1$$

where α_i is the length of each *compounding day* according to some day count basis (for example, $\alpha_i = 1/360$ or $3/360$ for Fridays), while the fixed payment is the fixed rate accrued for the same calculation period, resulting in a single net cash-flow for each calculation period. OIS swaps of maturity less than 1-year have one calculation period, while longer-term swaps are broken into annual calculation periods. Below is a list of OIS swaps and their benchmark index for different currencies:

USD: FFER (Fed Funds Effective Rate) as calculated by the New York Fed, Act/360.

EUR: EONIA (Euro Overnight Index Average), the effective overnight rate computed as a weighted average of all overnight unsecured lending transactions in the interbank market, calculated by European Central Bank (ECB) and published by the European Bank Federation, Act/360.

GBP: SONIA (Sterling Overnight Index Average), the weighted average rate of all unsecured overnight cash transactions brokered in London by Wholesale Markets Brokers' Association (WMBA). SONIA closely follows Bank of England's (BOE) policy rate, Act/365.

JPY: TONAR (Tokyo Overnight Average Rate), based on uncollateralized overnight average call rates for lending among financial institutions, published by Bank of Japan (BOJ). BOJ effects TONAR using open market operations to keep it in line with its policy rate (called *Mutan*), Act/365.

CAD: CORRA (Canadian Overnight Repo Rate Average) released by Bank of Canada, Act/365.

For OIS swaps, the funding index coincides with the fixing index, and we can use the OIS swap quotes to bootstrap the single-curve discount-factor and forward curves. Unfortunately, OIS swaps have only a few years of liquidity and we need additional instruments to extract the OIS discount factor curve for the long end of the curve.

Fed-Fund Futures

Monthly futures contracts based on the arithmetic average of the fed fund effective rate trade up to three years. The liquidity however is only in the first year. Since the payment is based on the arithmetic average rather than the compounded rate, a small convexity adjustment needs to be applied to turn FF futures into comparable OIS swaps. The magnitude of this convexity adjustment however is small, and is usually ignored in practice.

Fed-Fund/Libor Basis Swaps

For maturities 2y and longer, the most liquid USD OIS instruments are fed-fund vs Libor basis swaps. These basis swaps are quoted based on quarterly exchange of the 3m daily weighed arithmetic average of overnight Fed fund rate plus spread versus 3m-Libor flat, both legs paid Quarterly, Act/360.

OIS Curve Construction

A combination of a FF/Libor basis swap together with a plain vanilla swap (fixed vs. 3m Libor) can transform the package to a FF (plus spread) vs. fixed, which alongside with other FF-based instruments (OIS Swaps, Fed Fund futures) can then be used to bootstrap an OIS curve. Having constructed the OIS curve, we can use it as the discount curve for all derivatives.

LIBOR MARKET INSTRUMENTS

For the USD swap market, the benchmark floating index is the 3-month London Inter-Bank Offered Rate (Libor). The default settlement date also known as the *Spot date* is two

London business days after trade date, rolled forward if necessary to be a good New York and London business day.

In order to construct a Libor forward curve (Libor Curve), a collection of the following input instruments are used.

FRAs

An $n \times m$ Forward Rate Agreement (pronounced n-by-m FRA \'$fr\ddot{a}$\) is an agreement based on the economic value of a forward deposit starting n months from today, and maturing m months from today, with the payoff based on the difference between the actual "$m - n$"-month rate versus the agreed upon deposit rate K. So a 2×5 FRA is based on the future 3m rate, starting in 2m. At inception, the rate K is chosen so that the FRA has zero value, that is, K is equated to the forward rate. A seasoned FRA has positive or negative value, depending on how the fixed rate K compares to the current market forward rate. The payoff of $n \times m$ FRA occurs at rate fixing date—n-months from now—and uses the actual rate for fixing *and* discounting (called "FRA discounting"). For example if one owns a 2×5 FRA struck at K, the payment in 2 months is:

$$\frac{\alpha \times (L_{3m}(2m) - K)}{1 + \alpha \times L_{3m}(2m)},$$

per unit of notional, where $\alpha \approx 1/4$ is the length (Act/360) of the [2m,5m] period.

While not as liquid as ED futures, FRAs are quoted and can be used as input instruments to a Libor curve. The quote convention for FRAs is sometimes in reference to the floating index: *buying, selling* an FRA is same as paying/receiving in the single period swap.

Libor-OIS FRA

A package of 3m FRA and a 3m OIS swap with the same start and end dates is quoted for certain salient dates such as FOMC meeting dates, and the first few IMM dates. The package is quoted as a spread of the FRA's fixed rate to the OIS swap rate.

Euro-Dollar Futures

Euro-dollar contracts are exchange-traded derivative contracts traded in the International Money Market (IMM) pit of the Chicago Mercantile Exchange (CME, or "Merc"). Each contract settles on two London business days prior to the third Wednesday of the contract month based on that day's Libor fixing.

3M-Euro-dollar contracts settling on the last month of each quarter (March, June, September, December) are actively traded and fairly liquid for the first 3y of contracts (12 of them). Later contracts (up to 40, 10y out) can be traded, but have diminishing liquidity. There are also 6 monthly 3M-Eurodollar contracts for the first 6 months, and also 12 monthly 1M-Euro-dollar contracts, but these are not as liquid as "Quarterly 3m-Euro-dollar Futures Contracts" (ED futures from now on).

Each ED is based on the interest payment of a hypothetical $1 millon 90-day deposit starting on the third Wednesday of quarter-end. A Euro-dollar "tick" is the change in value of the contract due to a 1bp change in the implied interest rate:

$$1 \text{ tick} = \$25 = \$1,000,000 \times 0.0001 \times \frac{90}{360}.$$

ED futures trade based on price, and have an implied future's rate (100-Price). They are forward contracts and have 0 value at trade time. Other than opening a futures (margin) account and posting initial margin, and paying brokerage (about $1 per contract), no money is exchanged when trading them. So if ED1 is trading at 98.00 (implied futures rate 2%), and you buy 100 contracts, you pay no money (except about $100 for brokerage). However, unlike true forward contracts (FRAs) which require no cash exchange until expiration, ED contracts are cash-settled daily.

At each day's end, the Merc computes that day's final settlement value based on the markets at the close, 2pm Chicago time. Every open position will get cash-settled, akin to closing your ED position at settlement price, and immediately initiating an identical new position. For example, having bought 100 ED1 for 98.00, if that day's settlement value is 98.10 (implied rate of 1.90%), you have made 10 ticks, or $25,000 = 100 × 10 × $25, and this amount will be posted to your margin account. Until you close out the position (sell 100 ED1), each day an amount equal to the daily move (in ticks) times the number of contracts in your account is posted or taken from your futures account. When you close out the position (sell 100 ED1), the difference between the sale price and prior day's settlement value is used and posted/taken from your futures account.

ED futures are also referred to in colors. The first 4 contracts are called whites, the next 4 reds, followed by 4 greens, 4 blues, 4 golds, 4 purples, 4 oranges, 4 pinks, 4 silvers, and 4 coppers. So ED5 is sometimes referred to as first red, ED6 as the second red, ED9 as the first green, and so on.

A common trade is to buy/sell a ED *pack:* 1 contract in each series of a specific color. Buying/selling 1 red pack means buying/selling 1 ED5, 1 ED6, 1 ED7, and 1 ED8. The PV01 of a pack is $100.

Trading an *n*-year ED *bundle* is the trading of the first $4 \times n$ EDs. For example buying/selling 1 2y bundle is buying/selling of 1 ED1, 1 ED2, ..., 1 ED8 contract. The PV01 of an *n*-year bundle has $n \times \$100$.

Packs and bundles are quoted based on change on day. For example, "+3 (up 3) on day" means each contract in the pack is priced at prior day's close plus 3 ticks.

Future/Forward Convexity Adjustment

As stated, ED Futures are not exactly forward rate contracts, as they have daily mark-to-market settlement, while true FRAs do not. For FRAs, the P&L of the contract (the difference between the contracted value and the realized value) is only paid at the final settlement date, and hence its value today is the properly discounted value of this future settlement value. In contrast, the P&L of the future contract, while based on the same forward interest rate, is broken out into a series of daily P&Ls and paid daily without discounting. Since interest rates are highly correlated (overnight rates and forward rates in our case), this daily settlement confers an advantage to a short position in the ED future contract, as he earns money and gets to re-invest it daily at overnight rates when interest rates are high and loses money and hence has to borrow overnight money when interest rates are low. This systematic advantage for a short position does not go untaxed by the market: The short is charged for this free lunch in the form of being required to sell the contract at a cheaper level than would have otherwise been if it was a true FRA. Therefore, the implied rate in the future contract (100 − *Price*) is higher than the true forward rate, and this difference is known as the *future-forward convexity adjustment*. The size of convexity adjustment depends on the expected extra P&L of the short position over the life of the contract, which in turn depends on the volatility of the rates, and requires a model to calculate it. In general, it can be shown that the implied future rate is the expected rate at future's settlement. A commonly used formula based on the Ho-Lee model is as follows:

$$\text{Implied Futures Rate} - \text{Forward Rate} = 1/2\sigma_N^2 t^2,$$

for a future contract that settles in t-years, and has Normalized volatility of σ_N. As can be seen, the effect of the convexity adjustment gets larger (t^2 order) for later settlements, and this is one of the reasons that later contracts (3-years and out) are less liquid, as their value depends on the proper modeling of the convexity adjustment. Armed with a convexity adjustment model, one can construct a Libor curve purely based on a strip of ED futures and calculate par-swap rate from this curve. The resulting par-swap rate is called the *strip rate*, and can be compared to quoted par-swap rates to potentially take advantage of differences.

Par Swap Rates

Par swap rates for various maturities are quoted and are used to construct a Libor curve. In USD, the following maturities are quoted: 2y-10y, 12y, 15y, 20y, 25y, 30y. Longer par swap rates (40y, 50y, 60y) are quoted as spreads to 30y rates. Also, USD par swap rates are typically quoted as (swap) spreads to *current* Treasuries with similarly quoted maturity (CT2, CT3, CT5, CT7, CT10, CT30) or interpolated Treasury yields for other maturities. In most other currencies, the swap rates are directly quoted, and not as spreads to government yields. For 1y maturity, the swap rate is derived and calculated from the money market futures (ED for USD). As the 1y point is the crossover point between money market and capital markets, it is often quoted with a different frequency and/or day-count basis than other rates, so care needs to be taken when trading 1y swaps.

Extracting Forward Rate Lock Curves

Assume that the USD OIS discount/forward curve has been extracted from a combination of OIS market instruments: OIS Swaps, Libor/OIS FRAs, Fed-Fund contracts, Fed-Fund/Libor basis swaps. We can then start building a plausible forward/locking curve for 3m Libor as follows: Start the curve with today's fixing of 3m Libor, and 1×4, 2×5, 3×6 FRAs to extract the forward curve for 0m, 1m, 2m, and 3m points. We then use quarterly ED rates (minus convexity adjustments) up to two years to extract 3m-Libor forward rates on the first eight IMM dates. Next we use par swap rates to extract 3m Libors such that the swaps with the quoted par rates price to zero with discounting off of the OIS curve. For example, having generated the curve up to two years, by trial and error, we can set the 2y9m forward 3m Libor to a level so that when the 3y quoted par swap's fixed cash-flows versus floating cash-flows (quarterly 3m Libors for 3y, use linear interpolation if needed) when discounted off of the OIS curve price to zero. Continuing this way, we extract the full forward 3m-Libor forward/locking curve up to end of the par swap curve.

DUAL CURVE CONSTRUCTION

The market instruments for OIS and Libor are interlinked, especially for the long end where the most liquid instruments are OIS/Libor basis swaps. Also, in the short end, IMM or FOMC-dated Libor/OIS FRAs provide valuable information. If one had the OIS discounting curve, it would be easy to construct the forward Libor curve, and vice-versa, but many market instruments only provide information on just the *spread* of the two indices.

While one could try to extract the OIS curve and then Libor curve, it has become the practice to use all the liquid OIS-based instruments, including OIS-Libor basis swaps, in addition to all the Libor-based products *jointly* in a *dual-bootstrap* process to simultaneously extract the OIS and Libor forward curves.

SWAP TRADING—RATES OR SPREADS

USD par swap rates are quoted as spreads to benchmark Current (On-the-Run) Treasuries, and a typical broker or SEF (Swap Execution Facility) swap screen is shown in Table 29.1.

USD swaps can trade either as *rates* or *spreads*.

Trading in Rates

When one is trading *rates*, one is taking duration risk. For example, receiving in $100 million 2y swap has similar risk of buying $100 million 2y Treasuries. Looking at Table 29.1, we see that we can receive 0.761% in a swap, which is equal to yield of the offered side of 2y Treasury (99-31+, 0.633%) plus the bid side of swap spread market, 12.8bp.

TABLE 29.1 A Typical USD SEF/Broker Screen

	Treasury Cpn/Mat	Treasury Price	Treasury Yield (%)	Swap Spd (bp)	Swap Rate (%)
2y	0.625 09/30/17	99-312/99-31+	0.633/0.637	12.8/13.3	0.761/0.770
3y	0.875 10/15/18	99-26/99-262	0.936/0.938	7.6/8.1	1.012/1.019
4y			1.166/1.168	5.8/6.3	1.224/1.231
5y	1.375 09/30/20	99-28+/99-286	1.396/1.398	5/5.5	1.446/1.453
6y			1.588/1.589	3/3.5	1.618/1.624
7y	1.75 09/30/22	99-255/99-257	1.779/1.780	−1/−0.5	1.769/1.775
8y			1.888/1.889	−1.1/−0.6	1.877/1.883
9y			1.997/1.998	−1.3/−0.8	1.984/1.990
10y	2.0 08/15/25	99-016/99-02	2.106/2.107	−1.6/−1.1	2.090/2.096
12y			2.190/2.190	−4/−3.5	2.150/2.155
15y			2.315/2.316	−3/−2.5	2.285/2.291
20y			2.525/2.526	−6/−5.5	2.465/2.471
25y			2.735/2.735	−9/−8.5	2.645/2.650
30y	2.875 08/15/45	98-196/98-20	2.944/2.945	−32/−31.5	2.624/2.630

The reason for using the offered side of the Treasury is that the the other side of the trade (the payer) would have short duration risk upon execution of the swap. U.S. swap traders are not in the business of taking duration risk (that belongs to the cash/Treasury desk), only spread risk. As soon as the trade is done, the trader will cover her short and buy Treasuries, that is, lift the offer of 99-31+. This will leave her with spread risk, where she is paying the bid side (12.8bp) of the swap-spread market. With enough 2-way flows, she will try to pay the bid side of the swap-spread market, and receive the offered side, and make a living out of the bid-offer spread (of the swap-spread market).

Trading in Spreads

A more common inter-dealer trade is to directly enter into a *spread* trade by entering into a swap and simultaneously providing the Treasury hedge.

Buying a spread is the simultaneous purchase of Treasuries (called cash), and paying in swaps. This is also called *paying in spreads*. *Selling* a spread is the simultaneous sale of Treasuries, and receiving in swaps. This is called *receiving in spreads*. To remember it, always recall that in a *spread* trade, whatever you are doing to the Treasury (buy/sell), you are doing to the spread (buy/sell).

The amount of Treasuries is adjusted so that PV01 of the Treasury position (using the PV01 formula) matches the PV01 of the swaps. For example, let the 2y Treasury trade at 99-312/31+, with PV01 of $196 per $1 million face. Also assume that PV01 of 2y swap is 198 per $1M notional. If the trade is done, one agrees on the price of the Treasury, let's say 100-00, compute the yield (0.632%) and compute the swap rate 0.76%(= 0.632% + 12.8bp). One then calculates the PV01-equivalent amount of Treasuries: $100*mm* × 198/196 = $101.23*mm* face.

Note that since the dealer is being provided with the Treasury hedge, she does not have duration risk, and the exact price of the passed-on Treasuries is not as critical as when trading rates. However, she does have spread risk, expressed as *Spread-PV01:* $100M 2y-spread risk, or $19,800 (2y) Spread PV01.

Swap Curve Trading

Similar to Treasury curve, one can express views or hedge exposure to the slope (longer rate – shorter rate) of the swap curve via *curve* trades. For two given swap maturities, one can put on a steepener by *buying* the curve, that is, receiving in the shorter-maturity swap and paying in the longer-maturity, with the notional of each swap chosen so that each swap has the same PV01. Similarly, one can put on a flattener by selling the curve: paying in the shorter-maturity and receiving in PV01-equivalent amount of the longer swap. For example, one can buy the 2's/10's swap curve by receiving in $100M 2y swap and paying in $21.64mm (= 100mm \times 1.98/9.17$) 10y swaps, where PV01(2y) = 1.98, PV01(10y) = 9.17 cents. In this trade, one is immune to parallel moves in the swap curve, but is carrying $19,800-per-01 2's/10's *curve risk:* For each 1bp steepening/flattening of the 2's/10's curve, one makes/loses $19,800.

One can also trade curves forward. A forward swap curve steepener trade consists of receiving in shorter-maturity *forward* swap while paying in PV01-equivalent longer forward swap. For example a 1y-forward 2's/10's steepener consists of receiving in a 2y swap, 1y forward, while paying in a PV01-equivalent 10y swap, 1y forward.

SWAP SPREADS

In the United States, swap traders are primarily trading swap spreads, and hedge most of their duration risk, either with other swaps or with U.S. Treasuries. As such, they are mostly focused on swap spreads, and manage that risk. To understand swap spreads, one has to remember that they primarily represent the average *credit spread* of the Libor Panel—consisting of the banks polled to determine their estimate of Libor—generally thought to be equivalent to AA–, versus U.S. government credit. While many explanations have been offered as to what drives swap spreads, they all come back to relative supply/demand of bank versus government credit. For example, in the early 1990s, Government Sponsored Entities (GSEs) like Fannie-Mae and Freddie-Mac would hedge the duration mismatch in their mortgage portfolios with U.S. Treasuries, resulting in tightening swap spreads. When later in the decade, they switched to use swaps, swap spreads in general widened. Similarly, in a steep curve environment, corporates will swap their fixed-rate debt (either existing or new issue) by receiving in swaps to take advantage of lower short-term funding costs. This increased demand for receiving in swaps results in tightening swap spreads. Another supply/demand driver occurs when the government is running a deficit and issuing more debt via U.S. Treasuries: this results in the tightening of swap spreads. On the flipside, during periods of economic turmoil and flight-to-safety, there is high demand for U.S. Treasuries, resulting in widening swap spreads. As noted, all of these drivers boil down to relative supply/demand.

Another way to understand swap spreads is the financing spread between U.S. Treasuries versus swaps, that is Libor versus repo. The 2y swap spread is the market's expectation of the average UST repo versus Libor rates for the next 2 years. This is the basic understanding of quoted swap spreads, sometimes called *headline spreads* as they are the difference in the yields of the *current* Treasuries versus par swap rates. As a given current Treasury, say CT10, is issued quarterly, it will remain *current* for three months, while the 10-year par swap rate is for a swap that matures in exactly 10 years from trade date, headline swap spreads suffer from calendar roll-down and abrupt shift on auction dates.

Matched-Maturity Spread

A similar measure of swap spreads is the *Matched-Maturity* (sometimes called *Yield-Yield*) swap spreads which measures the yield of a given Treasury security to the par-swap rate of a swap maturing on the same date as the given Treasury. When one buys/sells a matched-maturity spread, one buys/sell a given Treasury and pays/receives in PV01-equivalent amount of a swap with same maturity date. Therefore it is two trades, done as a package. When dealing with short-term treasuries, say Treasury bills or treasuries less than two years remaining maturity, instead of swaps, one can buy/sell a strip of ED futures versus selling/buying the treasury. This yield spread is referred to as the *Treasury-ED (TED) Spread*, expressed usually as the semi-annual yield of both (Treasury, ED) components.

Asset Swap Spread

Another way of trading swap spreads is via *asset swaps* where the swap fixed leg's payment and dates are required to match exactly those of a given bond, and an *asset swap spread* is added to the Libor leg of the swap, with either the notional of the floating leg matching the principal amount of the bond, *Par-Par* asset swap, or the initial dirty price of the bond, *Market Value* asset swap. In either case, the *asset swap spread* is primarily the difference between the funding level for the Treasury, that is its repo rate, versus Libor until the maturity of swap/bond.

Note that in a Par-Par asset swap, the seller has to initially deliver the bond for par, so he is making a loan (assuming premium bond) to the buyer, while in a Market-Value asset swap, the seller's loan is shifted from up-front to the maturity date of the swap. In either case, the asset swap spread is solved for such that the PV of all these cash-flows—including the up-front or back-end loan—is zero when discounted off the swap discount curve (the OIS curve).

For the duration of the swap, a leveraged investor has to finance the bond at the prevailing overnight or term repo rate (plus variation margin) versus receiving Libor–Spread. Therefore, an asset swap's ongoing payment are Libor–Spread versus repo. Said in another way, a leveraged buyer has locked in Libor–Repo spread at the asset swap level, and benefits if the realized spread payments turn out to be higher during the life of the swap.

Zero-Coupon Swap Spreads

The purest expression of swap spreads is the swap rate for a *Zero-Coupon Swap* versus the yield of a similar-maturity zero-coupon Treasury bond, as each instrument has a single cash-flow, and hence their yield spread is just a measure of credit quality for the maturity point. A Zero-Coupon Swap consists of a fixed and a floating leg, with both legs having a single (net) payment at maturity. The floating leg is usually based on the benchmark swap index, Libor-3m for USD, and the final payment is based on the compounded interest of current and future Libor settings:

$$N_0 \times [(1 + L_{3m}(0)/4) \times (1 + L_{3m}(3m)/4) \times \cdots \times (1 + L_{3m}(T - 3m)/4) - 1]$$

where T is the maturity of the swap, and N_0 is the initial notional of the swap. Similarly, the fixed leg's single payment is the compounded interest based on the quoted Zero-Coupon rate. For example, the fixed payment of an N-year swap with semi-annual zero-coupon rate of Z is

$$N_0 \times [(1 + Z/2)^{2N} - 1].$$

In practice, one has to specify the Initial Notional (N_0) or Final Notional (N_{Final}) of the swap, related by

$$N_0 \times (1 + Z/2)^{2N} = N_{Final}.$$

The fixed leg's single payment is then $N_{Final} - N_0$ and is called the Fixed Payment, paid at swap maturity (T).

Swap Spread Curve

A graphical representation of any of the above spreads (Headline, Matched-Maturity, Asset Swap, Zero-Coupon) versus maturity is referred to as the *Swap Spread Curve*, or simply the Spread Curve. One can express views or hedge exposures to different points of the Spread Curve. When engaging in two simultaneous *spread trades* of different maturities, one is said to be trading *Spread of Spreads* or alternatively since each spread trade consists of two trades, one cash (Treasury), and one swap, it is also referred to as a *Box Trade*. For example, when taking views on the slope of spread curve, say between 2y point and 5y point, buying a "2's-5's Spread of Spreads" means buying the 5y spreads (buying 5y cash, paying in 5y swaps), and selling the 2y spread (selling 2y cash, receiving in 2y swaps), thereby profiting from steepening of spread curve between the 2-year and 5-year maturities. The amount of Treasuries (and hence swaps) on each leg is adjusted so that each will have the same Spread PV01. In this way, the trade is immune to parallel moves in the spread curve.

RISK, PV01, GAMMA LADDER

As opposed to bonds where we are dealing with a single yield-to-maturity, in swap-land we are dealing with a series of interest rates (OIS and Libor) which are aggregated to construct a discount (OIS) and forward (Libor) curves. Therefore the value of a swap depends on all the input instruments used to construct these 2 curves.

In order to compute the sensitivity of a swap-related instrument to changes in interest rates, two procedures are commonly used:

1. Parallel PV01: For each (OIS, Libor) curve, bump up all input rates (cash, futures, par-swaps) by 1bp, and revalue the instrument. The change in the value of the swap is called Parallel PV01 (also called Delta) for that curve. A variation is to compensate for different input quote conventions (Act/360 for simple cash, futures rates; SA 30/360 for swaps), and either convert all quotes to a single convention or reconstruct a new discount factor curve by bumping all the implied zero rates.
2. Partial PV01: For each input instrument of the curve, bump up its rate by 1bp while holding all other inputs constant, and revalue the instrument. This gives rise to a series of sensitivities—one for each input—called Bucket or Partial PV01/Delta. The sum of partial PV01's should be close to Parallel PV01, the difference due to instrument's convexity and higher order effects.

Admittedly, interest rates do not move in either fashion: it is rare that only one rate changes while the others don't. Also, even when they move together, interest rates don't move by the same amount: short-term rates (say 2y) typically move more than longer (say 30y) rates. In order to hedge under a real-life rate movement scenario, we can compute the change in value due to a curve shift scenario. The assumed scenario is usually derived from a statistical analysis of historical curve movements using methods such as Principal Component Analysis (PCA).

Armed with Partial PV01's, and the PV01 of each input instrument, we can then compute the amount of each input instrument needed to hedge. An example is shown in Table 29.2.

As alluded to before, the choice of curve build method greatly affects the prescribed hedge. For example, when hedging a $100M 5.5-year receiver swap relative to the Libor curve, the Log-Linear interpolation method, while discontinuous in forward rates, prescribes paying in $49.7mm 5y swaps, and $50.3mm 6y swaps. This is intuitive, and close to what a trader expects. On the other hand, using cubic splines results in a smooth forward curve, but the prescribed hedge for a 5.5-year receiver swap is to receive in $32.5mm 2y swap, pay in $31.5mm 3y swap, receive in $47.9mm 4y swap, pay in $97.5mm 5y swap, and pay in $31.6mm 6y swap! This tradeoff between smoothness in forward rates versus reasonable (local) hedge behavior affects any curve build method, and needs to be considered when choosing one.

Convexity, Gamma Ladder

Swap and option traders are not only interested in the Parallel/Partial Deltas, but also how their deltas change when the market moves, that is, convexity which in swap-land is also

TABLE 29.2 Partial Libor PV01's for a $100mm 5.5y Swap

	Rate	PV01 $/\$mm-Face	Log-Linear Needed Hedge (\$mm)	Cubic Spline Needed Hedge (\$mm)
3m	0.400	25	0.0	−5.5
ED1	0.395	25	0.0	−20.4
ED2	0.505	25	0.0	−19.9
ED3	0.624	25	0.0	−20.2
ED4	0.762	25	0.0	−23.7
ED5	0.910	25	0.0	−10.8
ED6	1.033	25	0.0	−32.4
2y	0.757	198.4	0.0	32.5
3y	1.009	295.8	0.0	−31.5
4y	1.231	391.5	0.0	47.9
5y	1.446	485	−49.7	−97.5
6y	1.631	576.2	−50.3	−31.6
7y	1.768	665.1	0.0	0.0
8y	1.887	751.5	0.0	0.0
9y	1.992	835.5	0.0	0.0
10y	2.088	917	0.0	0.0

referred to as *gamma*. When the market moves, a completely hedged book can gain/lose duration, and needs to be re-balanced. Often when there is a large market movement (market gap), there is not enough time to re-compute partial deltas for a large book. In order to be prepared for such movements, traders pre-compute parallel and partial deltas for a variety of scenarios (typically a series of parallel shifts) to come up with a *Gamma Ladder*. This allows them to quickly re-balance their books under fast market conditions.

CREDIT CONSIDERATIONS: XVA

In addition to OIS discounting, SEF execution, and Central Clearing, the other important change to swap pricing after the financial crisis has been paying careful attention to counterparty credit risk and default potential. This has given rise to a collection of credit adjustments to the non-default price:

$$P_{New} = P_{ND} - CVA + DVA$$

where Credit Value Adjustment (CVA) is the expected cost of counterparty default, and Debit Value Adjustment (DVA) is the expected benefit of own default. Each of these depends on projection of future values of the contract under consideration, probability of (first) default, and recovery value of the remaining cash-flows after default.

The credit scrutiny has not stopped to the above adjustments and there are other adjustments, mainly Funding Value Adjustment (FVA) which is a debated (even in its definition) adjustment used to adjust for the cost or benefit of unsecured funding rate for derivatives trades versus the OIS rate used when the trades or their hedges are collateralized. Consider a collateralized swap: When its value is positive to a counterparty, that counterparty receives OIS for the positive value and can lend this amount at Libor plus a spread, resulting in a Funding Benefit Adjustment (FBA). Alternatively, when the swap has negative value, the counterparty has to secure funds at Libor plus spread and avail these funds the other counterparty, and receive OIS rate on this collateral, resulting in a Funding Cost Adjustment (FCA). Since the value of a swap can vary as market rates change, FVA = FCA − FBA can be either positive or negative.

CHAPTER 30

Interest Rate Options

Amir Sadr

Given an underlying asset, derivatives or contingent claims are contracts with specified payoffs based on the value of the underlying. The simplest contingent claim—after a forward contract—is a *European Style* exercise option which has a specified payoff at a single exercise time t_e in the future. For example, a *call*, $C(t)$, with strike K on an asset $A(t)$ has the following payoff: $C(t_e) = \max(0, A(t_e) - K)$, while a *put*, $P(t)$, has payoff $P(t_e) = \max(0, K - A(t_e))$. While the value of the contingent claim is known at expiration, the goal of *Contingent-Claim Pricing* is to determine its value prior to expiry.

The Black-Scholes-Metron formula was a pioneering result in calculating the price of European-style options. While their methodology used advanced mathematical techniques to come up with the formula, it was shown later by Cox-Ross-Rubenstein (CRR), that the same formula can be obtained and understood using much simpler techniques. This new methodology goes under the name of Risk-Neutral Valuation and is the modern framework for contingent claim valuation. Its basic result is that *any contingent claim's value is its expected discounted value of its cash-flows in a risk-neutral world*. We explain this by using the most basic model: A 1-step binomial model. It is often said (and is indeed true) that all you need to understand option pricing is to fully understand the 1-step binomial model. We shall spend some time to fully explore this simple yet powerful model.

1-STEP BINOMIAL MODEL

Given today's $t = t_0$ price of an underlying asset $A(t)$, consider a European-style contingent claim $C(t)$ with a single expiration time t_e in the future. Assume that the underlying asset has no cash-flows over the period $[t_0, t_e]$, and let us consider the simplest case where the underlying asset at expiration can only take on two values, A_u, A_d, as shown in Figure 30.1. Let C_u and C_d denote the corresponding then-*known* values of the contingent claim in each state at expiration.

Our goal is to construct a portfolio today (t_0) so that its value at expiration, t_e, replicates the value of the contingent claim. Therefore if we are the seller of the option, we

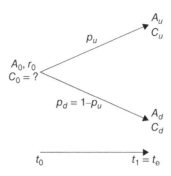

FIGURE 30.1 A 1-step
binomial model

can replicate the option's contingent cash-flows at expiration via this *replicating portfolio*. The fair price of the option today, C_0, would be the cost of setting up the portfolio.

Our portfolio consists of taking a position in the asset, Δ units of it, by financing it via a risk-free loan of size L at the prevalent risk-free rate r until expiration date t_e, so the value of the loan at expiration would be $L \times (1 + r \times (t_e - t_0)) = L/D(t_0, t_e)$ regardless of the state of the world.

At expiry, t_e, if we are in A_u state of the world, we want this portfolio to be worth C_u:

$$\Delta \times A_u + L/D(t_0, t_e) = C_u.$$

Similarly, if we are in A_d state of the world, we want the portfolio to be worth C_d:

$$\Delta \times A_d + L/D(t_0, t_e) = C_d.$$

We have two equations and two unknowns (Δ, L). Solving for these, we get:

$$\Delta = \frac{C_u - C_d}{A_u - A_d},$$
$$L = D(t_0, t_e) \left(C_u - \frac{C_u - C_d}{A_u - A_d} A_u \right).$$

Therefore, today's value of the contingent claim is:

$$C_0 = \Delta \times A_0 + L$$
$$= \frac{C_u - C_d}{A_u - A_d} A_0 + D(t_0, t_e) \left(C_u - \frac{C_u - C_d}{A_u - A_d} A_u \right).$$

The seller of the option can charge C_0 as above, take a loan of size L as above, and use these proceeds to buy Δ units of the asset at spot price A_0. At expiration, in either state of the world, A_u or A_d, the value of his holdings (Δ units of the asset) exactly offsets his liabilities: Repayment of loan plus interest, and cash-settlement value of the option (C_u or C_d).

Note that in the above setup, we did not have to consider the probability of either state happening: as long as A_u, A_d can happen and are the only two possibilities, we are golden!

However, there are restrictions on the assumed future states. A bit of algebra allows us to rewrite the formula for C_0 as an expected value:

$$C_0 = D(t_0, t_e)[p_u C_u + (1 - p_u)C_d],$$

where

$$p_u = \frac{A_0/D(t_0, t_e) - A_d}{A_u - A_d}.$$

No Arbitrage

Lack of arbitrage is equivalent to p_u being a *probability*,

$$0 \le p_u \le 1.$$

which is equivalent to the following restriction on assumed states:

$$A_d \le F_A(t_0, t_e) \le A_u.$$

since for an asset with no interim cash-flows, $F_A(t_0, t_e) = A(0)/D(t_0, t_e)$.

To see this, consider the case $p_u > 1$, which means that the forward is higher than either state in the future: $F_A > A_u > A_d$. In this case, we can sell the asset forward for F_A, and deliver it at t_e by buying it at either A_u or A_d. Regardless, we have made money with no risk!

Similarly, if $p_u < 0$, then $F_A < A_d < A_u$, and we can ensure a risk-less profit by buying the asset forward for F_A, and selling it higher at expiration at A_u or A_d.

Therefore, if there is no arbitrage in the above simple economy, p_u can be considered as a probability, and today's value of the option is simply the expected discounted value of the option payoff under this probability.

Risk-Neutrality

We obtained C_0 by constructing a portfolio that replicates the option payoff, regardless of the probability of each state. We then showed that we can get the same value by taking the expected value under a probability p_u. Other than a mathematical identity—p_u is the probability that gets you the correct option value, as long as you know the option value!—is there another way of interpreting p_u? The answer is in the affirmative: p_u is the probability that a *risk-neutral* investor would apply to the above setting.

Most people are *risk-averse*: between a guaranteed return and a risky investment with identical *expected* returns, they would opt for the former. That is why risky investments (stocks, real-estate,...) need to have a higher than average expected returns. Otherwise, one could simply put one's money in the bank and have the same return with no volatility.

On the other hand, most of us have bought a lottery ticket or played in casinos, *investments* whose expected gain is less than what we paid for. These types of investing are examples of *risk-taking*, where although risky, we are batting for the fences.

In between, there is an investment behavior that considers any investments with the same expected return as equivalent, and does not require a risk premium for risky bets. Consider such an investor given a choice between 2 investments: 1) Invest A_0 at the bank, and get $A_0/D(t_0, t_e)$ at t_e, or 2) Buy an asset at A_0 and either get A_u or A_d at t_e. For a risk-neutral investor, these two investments would be equivalent if

$$p_u A_u + (1 - p_u) A_d = A_0/D(t_0, t_e),$$

or equivalently, when

$$p_u = \frac{A_0/D(t_0, t_e) - A_d}{A_u - A_d}.$$

Therefore, rather than setting up a replicating portfolio and computing its value today, we can simply take the expected discounted value of the option payoff using *risk-neutral probabilities*.

FROM 1 TIME-STEP TO 2 TO ...

The 2-state setup is obviously too simplistic. Assets can take a variety of values at expiration. However, using the above setup as a building block, we can arrive at more complex cases. The trick is to subdivide the time from now till expiration into multiple intervals, and for each state in each interval, generate two new arbitrage-free (bracketing the forward) future states. With enough subdivisions, we can arrive at a richer and more real-life terminal distribution for the asset.

Consider a 2 time-step example shown in Figure 30.2. At node A_u, we have a binomial model and we can solve for the risk-neutral probability p_{uu} and Δ_u and L_u to obtain C_u. Similarly, at node A_d, we have a binomial model and can calculate the option value at that node, C_d. Having obtained C_u, C_d, we can step back to today and again use the binomial model to solve for p_u, L_0, Δ_0, and C_0.

Self-Financing, Dynamic Hedging

As we subdivide the time to expiration into finer partitions, we have to ensure that original portfolio can be dynamically managed to replicate the option value. At each state, we can change the amount of asset we hold by securing requisite funds at the prevailing

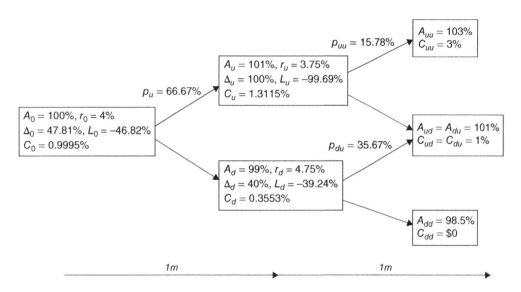

FIGURE 30.2   Example of bond option pricing in a 2-period setting

financing rates. As we do this dynamic rebalancing (changing Δ's), the value of the portfolio entering into each state must equal the value of the portfolio leaving the state, that is, the replicating portfolio should be *self-financing*.

Consider the *up* state (A_u, r_u). As we enter it, we hold a portfolio that consists of Δ_0 units of the asset (now worth A_u at t_1), and a loan of size L_0 plus its interest (worth $L_0/D(t_0, t_1)$ at time t_1). Therefore the value of the portfolio value is:

$$C_u = \Delta_0 A_u + L_0/D(t_0, t_1).$$

On the other hand, $C_u = \Delta_u A_u + L_u$, since (Δ_u, L_u) is the required portfolio to replicate the option payoffs (C_{uu}, C_{ud}) at the next time step, t_2. Therefore, we need to change our holding of the asset from Δ_0 to Δ_u only by changing the size of our loan from $L_0/D(t_0, t_1)$ to L_u, that is, the change in the underlying holding should only be financed by the loan:

$$(\Delta_u - \Delta_0)A_u = L_u - L_0/D(t_0, t_1),$$

ensuring that the portfolio is *self-financing*.

NORMAL DISTRIBUTION

We can continue to subdivide the interval $[t_0, t_e]$ into smaller and smaller sub-intervals. By a judicious choice of state variables at each subdivision, we can ensure that the limiting terminal distribution or its log is Normally distributed. A random variable (r.v.) X is said to have a Normal distribution with mean μ and standard deviation σ, if the probability that it lies in some region $[x, x + dx]$ is approximately

$$\frac{1}{\sqrt{2\pi\sigma^2}}e^{-\frac{(x-\mu)^2}{2\sigma^2}}\,dx.$$

We will use the shorthand $X \sim N(\mu, \sigma^2)$. More precisely, the *Cumulative Distribution Function* (CDF) of an $N(\mu, \sigma^2)$ random variable X is

$$F_X(x) \equiv P[X \leq x] = \int_{-\infty}^{x} \frac{1}{\sqrt{2\pi\sigma^2}}e^{-\frac{(z-\mu)^2}{2\sigma^2}}\,dz,$$

and its *Density Function* (DF) is

$$f_X(x) \equiv \frac{d}{dx}F(x) = \frac{1}{\sqrt{2\pi\sigma^2}}e^{-\frac{(x-\mu)^2}{2\sigma^2}}.$$

A *Standard* Normal r.v. has mean 0 and variance 1: $X \sim N(0, 1)$. The CDF of a Standard Normal $N(0, 1)$ r.v., $N(x) \equiv P[N(0, 1) \leq x]$, is widely available in tabulated form, or from numerical recipes with varying degree of precision.

Log-Normal Distribution

A random variable Y is said to have a Log-Normal distribution, $Y \sim LN(\mu, \sigma^2)$, if its *natural* log is an $N(\mu, \sigma^2)$ r.v., or in other words, $Y \sim e^{N(\mu, \sigma^2)}$. A $LN(\mu, \sigma^2)$ r.v. can only take positive values.

Note that for a Log-Normal $LN(\mu, \sigma^2)$ r.v., the parameters (μ, σ^2) are *not* its mean and variance. A Log-Normal $LN(\ln(\mu^2/\sqrt{\mu^2 + \sigma^2}), \ln(1 + \mu^2\sigma^2))$ r.v. will have mean μ and variance σ^2, and can be compared to a Normal $N(\mu, \sigma^2)$ r.v., as shown in Figure 30.3.

MODELING ASSET CHANGES

Normal distributions are commonly used to model the underlying asset value at option expiration. The focus is on the change in asset value from today until the expiration, with the change expressed either in *percentage/proportional* or *absolute* terms. Specifically, starting with asset value today, $A(t_0)$, a European-style option depends on the unknown/random asset value at expiration, $A(t_e, \omega)$.

Proportional Change

One way to model asset at expiration is to consider its changes over time via:

$$A(t_e, \omega) = A(t_0)e^{r([t_0, t_e], \omega) \times (t_e - t_0)},$$

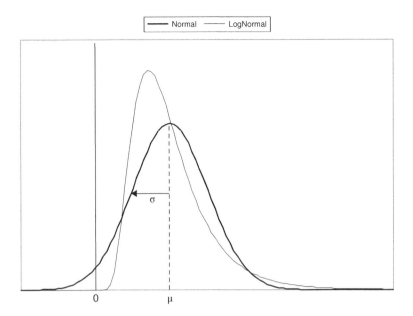

FIGURE 30.3 Comparison of normal versus log-normal distribution functions with same mean, variance (μ, σ^2)

where $r([t_0, t_e], \omega)$ is the continuously compounded random return over investment period $[t_0, t_e]$ for the generic unknown future state of the world ω:

$$r([t_0, t_e], \omega) = \frac{1}{t_e - t_0} \ln \frac{A(t_e, \omega)}{A(t_0)}$$

This measure is also referred to as proportional return, percentage return, or log return. Its standard deviation is referred to as percentage, proportional or log volatility, or just volatility:

$$\sigma = \sqrt{Var \left[\frac{1}{t_e - t_0} \ln \frac{A(t_e, \omega)}{A(t_0)} \right]}$$

Assuming that the percentage return is Normal

$$r([t_0, t_e], \omega) \sim N(\mu \times (t_e - t_0), \sigma^2 \times (t_e - t_0))$$

implies that the asset value at expiration will be Log-Normal:

$$A(t_e)/A(t_0) \sim LN(\mu \times (t_e - t_0), \sigma^2 \times (t_e - t_0)).$$

This Log-Normal distribution is somewhat close to the empirical distributions observed for equities—although the empirical/realized distributions tend to have fatter tails than

Log-Normal—and is commonly used for Equity/FX/Commodity options. The original Black-Scholes-Merton Formula for European call and its variant, Black's Call Formula for futures/forwards, were derived assuming this dynamic for the evolution of asset prices in a risk-neutral world ($\mu = r - 1/2\sigma^2$). Specifically, Black's Call Formula is

$$C(0) = D(t_e)E_{RN}[\max(0, A(t_e) - K]$$
$$= D(t_e) \times [F_A(t_e)N(d_1) - KN(d_2)],$$

where

$$d_{1,2} = \frac{\ln(F_A(t_e)/K)}{\sigma\sqrt{t_e}} \pm \frac{1}{2}\sigma\sqrt{t_e}, \quad F_A(t_e) = A(0)/D(t_e).$$

Absolute Change

Another way to model change is to focus on the absolute change, $A(t_e, \omega) - A(t_0)$, and to model this random change as a Normal r.v.

$$A(t_e) - A(t_0) \sim N(\mu \times (t_e - t_0), \sigma_N^2 \times (t_e - t_0)).$$

Under this model, the underlying can take on negative values at expiration, and while inappropriate for equities/FX/commodities, it turns out to be the lesser of the two evils for interest rates, and has become the dominant base-case model for interest rate derivatives. With this dynamic in a risk-neutral setting ($\mu \times (t_e - t_0) = F_A(t_e) - A(t_0)$), we get the following formula

$$C(0) = D(t_e)E_{RN}[\max(0, A(t_e)) - K]$$
$$= D(0, t_e)\sigma_N\sqrt{t_e}[N'(d) + dN(d)],$$

where

$$d = \frac{F_A(0, t_e) - K}{\sigma_N\sqrt{t_e}}.$$

Note that d is a measure of the *money-ness* of the option as it expresses the distance between the forward versus the strike, $F_A - K$, expressed in units of standard deviation, $\sigma_N\sqrt{t_e}$. A similar interpretation can be given to d_1 for Log-Normal dynamics.

Put-Call Parity

To derive the value of a European put, we would consider two portfolios:

(1) A t_e-expiry call option with strike K, and cash holding equal to the Present Value of K, that is, $KD(t_e)$.

(2) A t_e-expiry put option with strike K, and the underlying asset, $A(0)$.

If the underlying asset has no interim cash-flows until t_e, then the two portfolios will have the same value, $\max(A(t_e), K)$, at expiration t_e. Therefore, they must have the same value today $(t = 0)$, and we must have:

$$P(0) + A(0) = C(0) + KD(t_e).$$

This identity is called put–call parity, and holds for European-style options on underlyings with no interim cash-flows.

In particular, when the strike equals the *At-The-Money-Forward (ATMF)* value of the asset, $K = F_A(0, t_e)$, then the call and put prices coincide: $P(0) = C(0)$.

GREEKS

Recall that Black's Formulae were obtained as special instances of Risk-Neutral Valuation under Normal distributions for proportional or absolute returns. We should not forget that Risk-Neutral Valuation gives the same value as a self-financing replicating portfolio. The question arises as to what happened to the replicating portfolio, and how do we replicate an option's payoff? The answer lies in the *Greeks*.

Recall that in our binomial setting, the replicating portfolio was Δ units of the underlying asset financed via a risk-free loan. The Δ amount had to be (dynamically) changed in response to market movements. In the simple 1-step binomial model, we computed

$$\Delta = \frac{C_u - C_d}{A_u - A_d},$$

which can be interpreted as the sensitivity of the option price with respect to the underlying asset.

In the limit, $\Delta \to \frac{\partial C}{\partial F}$, and the replicating portfolio consists of $\frac{\partial C}{\partial F}$ units of a forward contract on the asset. This is called the *Delta* of the option. The Delta is a number between 0 and 1, and expresses how much of the forward asset is needed to replicate the option payoff. For Log-Normal dynamics, it is measured as $N(d_1)$, while for Normal it is $N(d)$.

As we saw in the 2-step binomial model, the Delta changes. The rate of change of Delta with respect to the underlying is called *Gamma* and is defined as $\frac{\partial^2 C}{\partial F^2}$. Gamma measures the curvature of the option payoff, and is also called the *convexity*.

The intrinsic value of an option is its value at expiration, and the *Time Value* of an option is the difference between the option value and its intrinsic value. Time Value converges to 0 as one gets closer to expiration. *Theta* or time-decay is defined as the rate of change of option value due to time $\frac{\partial C}{\partial t_e}$. An option holder typically loses Time Value as one gets closer to expiry.

Finally, the sensitivity of an option with respect to volatility $\frac{\partial C}{\partial \sigma}$ is called *Vega*.

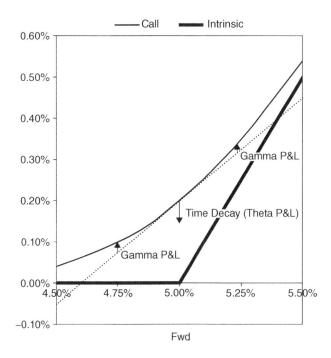

FIGURE 30.4   Gamma P&L versus time decay for a European call option

Gamma versus Theta

As seen in Figure 30.4, Black call formula is a convex function of the underlying, and its delta changes when the underlying moves. The dynamic rebalancing of the replicating portfolio is primarily the result of this convexity, and it confers a systematic edge to the replicating portfolio. Loosely said, a delta-hedged replicating portfolio consisting of a financed position of delta $\left(\frac{\partial C}{\partial F}\right)$ units of the underlying will need to get rebalanced as forwards move. For the option holder, be it a call or a put, it requires reducing/increasing the position as the underlying appreciates/depreciates, that is, the option holder will have to buy-low, sell-high to replicate the option payoff! The amount of this excess P&L of a delta-hedged option is predominantly $1/2 \times$ Gamma $\times (\Delta F)^2$, similar to the convexity P&L of a duration-neutral portfolio of bonds.

A delta-hedged long option position experiences two dominant P&Ls: it loses Time Value every day, and it gains a gamma P&L as the position is rebalanced (delta's changed). Note that the gamma P&L is incurred whether the asset moves up or down. This is shown in Figure 30.4 for a call option. The typical (expected) movement of the forward asset over a short interval time dt is prescribed by volatility as $dF \approx \sigma_N \sqrt{dt}$. Each move in the forwards incurs a gamma P&L, and passage of time leads theta P&L due to loss of Time Value. Black's formula is the correct computation of the expected value of the sum of these two P&Ls over the life of the option.

Digitals

A digital call option $C(t_e)$ has unit payoff if the asset $A(t_e)$ at expiration t_e is above the strike K:

$$DigiCall(t_e, K) = \begin{cases} 1 & \text{if } A(t_e) > K \\ 0 & \text{otherwise} \end{cases}$$

Similarly, a Digital put has a unit payoff if the asset at expiration is below the strike K:

$$DigiPut(t_e, K) = 1 - DigiCall(t_e, K).$$

Cheat Sheet

Tables 30.1 and 30.2 summarize various Black formulae and their Greeks. All of these are for European options *without the discounting from payment date to today*. Recall that

$$d_{1,2} = \frac{\ln(F/K)}{\sigma\sqrt{t}} \pm \frac{1}{2}\sigma\sqrt{t}, \quad d = \frac{F-K}{\sigma_N\sqrt{t}}.$$

$$N(d) = \int_{-\infty}^{d} \frac{1}{\sqrt{2\pi}} e^{-x^2/2} dx, \quad N'(x) = \frac{1}{\sqrt{2\pi}} e^{-x^2/2}.$$

TABLE 30.1 Black Log-Normal Formulae

	Premium	Delta
Call	$FN(d_1) - KN(d_2)$	$N(d_1)$
Put	$KN(-d_2) - FN(-d_1)$	$N(d_1) - 1$
Digi-Call	$N(d_2)$	$\dfrac{1}{F\sigma\sqrt{t}}N'(d_2)$
Digi-Put	$N(-d_2)$	$\dfrac{-1}{F\sigma\sqrt{t}}N'(d_2)$

TABLE 30.2 Black Normal Formulae

	Premium	Delta
Call	$\sigma_N\sqrt{t}[N'(d) + dN(d)]$	$N(d)$
Put	$\sigma_N\sqrt{t}[N'(d) - dN(-d)]$	$N(d) - 1$
Digi-Call	$N(d)$	$\dfrac{1}{\sigma_N\sqrt{t}}N'(d)$
Digi-Put	$N(-d)$	$-\dfrac{1}{\sigma_N\sqrt{t}}N'(d)$

CALL IS ALL YOU NEED

One can continue along the above lines to derive analytical formulae for European-Style options with more complicated payoffs. In practice, however, the call and digi-call formulae are all one really needs to evaluate European-style options. Indeed, any real-world option payoff is economically equal to—or can be approximated arbitrarily closely—via a portfolio of calls and/or digi-calls. Hence calls and digi-calls serve as the salient *building blocks* of European-Style options.

The following is a list of some common European-style (single-exercise) payoffs encountered in practice:

1. Straddle—A put and call with same strike K.
2. Strangle—A K_1-put and K_2-call where $K_1 < K_2$.
3. Collar—Being long a collar is being long a K_2-call, and short a K_1-put with $K_1 < K_2$. The strikes K_1, K_2 are usually chosen around the forward rates, so that the package is worth 0, that is, a costless-collar.
4. Risk-Reversal—Long a call at $ATMF + d$ and short a put at $ATMF - d$ is called a $2d$-total-width (or d on each side) risk-reversal. Under Normal dynamics with no skews, a risk-reversal should be worth zero. Traders track the price of various-width risk-reversals to discover the implied skews in the market.
5. Call/Put Spread—Being long a call-spread is being long a K_1-call, and short a K_2-call, with $K_1 < K_2$.
6. Ratio—Most common is a 1×2 (1 by 2) ratio. Being long a 1×2 call ratio means being long one K_1-call, and short two K_2-calls. Some traders track the implied market skews by setting $K_1 = ATMF$, $K_2 = K_1 + d$, and solving for d that would make the ratio costless, the higher the call-skew, the higher the solved d.
7. Fly—Being long a call-fly is being long one K_1-call, short two K_2-calls, and long one K_3-calls, with $K_1 < K_2 < K_3$, and $K_2 - K_1 = K_3 - K_2$. This is usually used to pin down and express strong views on the setting of Libor at expiration, leading to *Pin Risk* for the option-seller.
8. Digitals—Digi-calls, Digi-puts. Due to their high gamma, these are usually sold as a conservative (from seller's point of view) call or put spreads, with the strikes chosen to be 10–20 basis points apart (called the "width of the ramp").
9. Knock-in Call/Put—A K_1-strike call with K_2-knock-in ($K_1 < K_2$) has the same payoff of a K_1-call, but only if the underlying is above K_2 at expiration. The payoff is zero if the underlying is below K_2 at expiration. This can easily be priced as a K_2-call plus a K_2-Digi-Call with payoff $K_2 - K_1$.

These are shown in Figure 30.5. All of the above products can be priced via Black's Normal/Log-Normal formulae, as the payoffs are simple portfolios of different-strike calls/puts and digi-calls/puts.

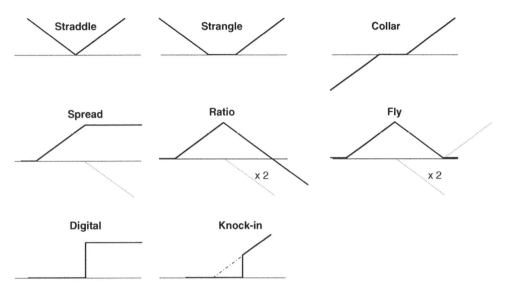

FIGURE 30.5 Common European-style payoffs

INTEREST RATE OPTIONS

The Black-Scholes-Merton Formula, and its Black variant for futures was historically derived for non-interest-rate related underlying assets (Equities, FX, Commodities), and under the assumption that interest rates are non-random. When interest rate options (cap/floors, swaptions) were introduced, traders co-opted these formulas and applied them to interest rates. While everyone recognized that the formulae need to be adjusted since interest rates are not traded assets, and *are* random, nevertheless, in the absence of any other simple alternatives, Black's Formula became and still continues to be the standard option pricing formula for flow products.

For most market practitioners, Black's formula is mostly a quoting mechanism, and also a *guide* on calculating deltas needed to replicate the option payoff under the *assumed* (often too simplistic) dynamics. Just like bonds, ultimately all interest-rate options trade on price. And just like bonds where implied flat yields are calculated, implied vols are calculated to help assess the fairness of the quoted option prices.

For interest rate options, since ATMF straddles have little duration risk, and are predominantly a function of the volatility, ATMF straddles are actively quoted and traded. Option traders are in the business of taking and managing volatility risk, not duration or spread risk, as each option desk will try to maintain a delta-neutral position and takes only volatility risk. By monitoring and trading ATMF straddles, they are then trading volatility itself.

Initially, Black's *Log-Normal* formulae were co-opted for interest rate products. In recent years, however, most traders have switched to the *Normal* dynamics as the base case, and brokers quite often quote Normal vols alongside prices in preference to Log-Normal vols.

MARKET PLAYERS

As with any other derivative, interest rate options can be used for hedging or for speculation.

Hedging, Protection

Mortgage servicing companies often buy swaptions to hedge the negative convexity of their servicing portfolios. Insurance companies typically buy cap/floors to hedge their guaranteed-payoff annuity products.

Speculation, Penny Options, Lottery Tickets

Hedge funds typically utilize interest rate options to express a view on the terminal setting of interest rates at expiration. Rather than entering into a forward agreement, they usually buy cheap out-of-the-money options to cap the downside to the premium paid, while benefitting handsomely if their view is borne out. These buyers do not hedge the interest rate options, except sometimes under a favorable outcome before expiration to lock in profit, or by rolling the strike.

Gamma Trading, Realized versus Implied Vol

The dominant P&L of short-dated (6m and under) options when delta-hedged is due to their gamma. If the actual realized volatility turns out to be higher than the implied volatility paid through the up-front premium, then delta-hedging can be a source of profit for a long position in an option. Similarly, a seller of an option profits when realized volatility is smaller than implied vol.

Vega Trading, Supply/Demand

For longer-dated options (1y and longer expiries), the dominant P&L is due to changes in implied volatility, that is, their vega. These changes in implied vols are primarily due to supply and demand of volatility. For example, a large hedging program by a servicing company can drive up volatilities in one sector, while the hedging needs of exotics desks can pressure a specific sector of the volatility surface. An astute anticipation of these flows allows one to take a position—usually via straddles in order to minimize delta-hedging needs—in vega pieces, and then unwinding the position for profit/loss after a favorable/unfavorable outcome. As these trades can span a few months for the flows to be realized, one needs to consider the volatility carry (loss of time-value) and roll-down (slope of the volatility surface along expiry).

CAPLETS/FLOORLETS: OPTIONS ON FORWARD RATES

A caplet/floorlet is a European option on a rate, typically the benchmark interest rate, say 3m Libor. A typical caplet/floorlet on 3m Libor is based on a single calculation period: $[t_e, t_e + 3m]$. At expiration t_e the market rate is compared to the strike K, and the option payoff is accrued for the duration of the calculation period, and paid at the end of the calculation period $t_e + 3m$. For example, a 6m-expiry 2% caplet on 3m Libor has the following payoff 9m from today:

$$\max(0, L_{3m}(6m) - 2\%) \times \alpha,$$

per unit notional, where $\alpha \approx 1/4$ is the accrual fraction.

Market practice is to use Black's formula to price options on futures. For a given calculation period $[T_1, T_2]$, the risk-neutral formula for a caplet on a rate R is calculated as:

$$C(0) = D(T_2)E[\max(0, R(T_1, \omega) - K)] \times \alpha(T_1, T_2),$$

and it is further assumed that a forward *rate* is a tradeable asset, hence Black's call formula is used to evaluate the $E[.]$ term. Similarly, for floorlets, the payoff $E[\max(0, K - R(T_1, \omega))]$ is evaluated using Black's put formula.

Caps/Floors

A cap/floor is simply a portfolio of caplets/floorlets, all having the same strike. For example, a 2y 2% quarterly cap on 3m Libor is a collection of 8 caplets based on 8 calculation periods: $[0, 3m], [3m, 6m], \dots, [21m, 2y]$, where each caplet's strike is 2%. Each caplet/floorlet is valued using Black's formula using its own (depending on its expiration date) volatility, and the value of the cap/floor is simply the sum of all these values.

An $m \times n$ (pronounced m by n) *forward cap/floor* is a cap/floor starting m years from today, and maturing n years from today. So a 1×2 cap is a 1y cap, starting in 1y; a 3×5 cap is a 2y cap, starting in 3y.

In practice, only prices of a few caps/floors are actively quoted in the form of *cap-floor straddles*. Typical maturities are 1y, 1×2, 2×3, 3×5, 5×7, 7×10 for USD cap/floors. For example, a 1×2 USD "cap-floor straddle" quoted as 25 cents denotes a price of \$250,000 for a package consisting of one \$100mm 1×2 quarterly cap (4 caplets) and one \$100mm 1×2 quarterly floor (4 floorlets). The common strike for all caplets/floorlets is chosen so that all caplet+floorlets pairs (one pair for each expiration) are close to ATMF.

A final note is that for spot-start caps/floors, the first caplet/floorlet is ignored, so a 1y quarterly cap is really a $3m \times 1y$ cap, and has actually 3 caplets: $[3m, 6m], [6m, 9m], [9m, 1y]$. A forward quarterly 1y cap, say 1×2, however has 4 caplets.

Options on Euro-Dollar Futures

Options on Euro-dollar futures trade at Chicago Mercantile Exchange (CME) and are quoted in Euro-dollar ticks (\$25 per contract). Options on Euro-dollar futures are treated as caplets/floorlets, using Black's formula to evaluate them.

Example 30.1 Assume the first ED contract expires in 60 days, and is trading at 98.10. Also assume that $D(60d) = 0.98$. (Euro-dollar options cash-settle on expiration date, not 3m later.) A 98.25 call (called an "82" call) is trading at 5 ticks, so \$125 per contract. Although all ED prices and strikes are quoted in price, we are always thinking of the implied rate/strike, so we compute the forward rate $F = (100 - 98.10)/100 = 1.90\%$, and the strike $K = (100 - 98.25)/100 = 1.75\%$. Also a call on the price is a put/floor on the implied rate, so to analyze a ED Call, we have to use Black's Put formula. The implied Normal vol σ_N must be backed out from the following:

$$\$125 = 0.98 \times \$1mm \times \sigma_N \sqrt{60/365}[N'(d) - dN(-d)] \times (90/360),$$

where
$$d = \frac{1.90\% - 1.75\%}{\sigma_N \sqrt{60/365}} = 0.54325.$$

Trial and error gives us $\sigma_N = 0.681\%$ or 68.1 bp's/annum.

Buying a naked (un-hedged) 60-day ED 98.25 call is a bet that rates will fall through 1.75% in 60 days (no Fed move). If at expiration, 3m Libor sets at 1.50% (so ED settles at 98.50), then we have made 25 ticks, or \$625 per option contract, a 5-to-1 return.

Caplet Curve = ED Options + Cap/Floors

Options on the first few ED contracts are fairly liquid, and can be used to back out the implied volatilities of 3m-Libor rates for the relevant expirations. Since a dealer cap/floor book consists of many expiration dates, with each expiry having its own volatility, a *caplet curve* is needed to mark this book. The caplet curve is a graph of implied-vols of options on the benchmark floating index versus expiration.

For USD, the instruments used to construct this curve are ATMF options (or strikes as close to forwards as possible) on ED1, ED2,..., and a series of cap/floor straddles: 1×2, 2×3, 3×5, 5×7, 7×10. Since each cap/floor straddle consists of multi-expiration caplet+floorlet pairs, with each expiration requiring its own volatility, a bootstrap+interpolation routine is typically used to back out the implied vol for each expiration. A common procedure is to use implied vols from ED futures options for the first few expiries, and use a parametric shape for the rest of the curve.

EUROPEAN-STYLE SWAPTIONS

An m-year into n-year receiver/payer swaption with strike K is an m-year European option to receive/pay the fixed rate K in an n-year swap. Let us focus on a *Right-to-Pay* (RTP) or *payer* swaption. At option expiry, if (and only if) the n-year par swap rate $S(t_e)$ is above the strike K, then it is advantageous to exercise the option and pay K (below market). Otherwise, if $S(t_e) < K$, the option holder will not exercise the option, as it is cheaper to pay $S(t_e)$ in a market swap rather than the higher rate K.

If $S(t_e) > K$, the option will get exercised and the option owner will *pay* K for the next n years. He could also (conceptually) *receive* fixed in a par swap (worth 0), that is, receiving $S(t_e)$ and pay floating for n-years. Netting these two swaps, the floating legs cancel out, and effectively one is paying K and receiving $S(t_e)$ for the next n-years on the payment dates of the underlying swap. Assuming that the underlying swap is semi-annual, let $\{T_1, \ldots, T_{2n}\}$ be the payment dates for the fixed leg of the swap. The economic value of the payer swaption at expiration t_e then is

$$\max(0, S(t_e, \omega) - K)\frac{1}{2}\sum_{i=1}^{2n} D(t_e, T_i, \omega),$$

where $D(t_e, \cdot, \omega)$ is the random discount-factor curve at t_e.

According to risk-neutral valuation, today's price of this option is simply the expected discounted value of the above payoff. This is approximated as follows:

$$P(0) = \frac{1}{2}A(0, \{T_1, \ldots, T_{2n}\})E[\max(0, S(t_e, \omega) - K)],$$

where $A(0, \ldots) = \sum_{i=1}^{2n} D(0, T_i)$ is today's value of an annuity that pays unit payoff on the underlying forward swap's payment dates, and the last term is evaluated using Black's call formula.

Similarly, the formula for a receiver swaption is

$$R(0) = \frac{1}{2}A(0, \{T_1, \ldots, T_{2n}\})E[\max(0, K - S(t_e, \omega))],$$

where the last term is evaluated using Black's put formula using forward swap rates.

Example 30.2 Let the following discount factors be given: $D(1.5y) = 0.98, D(2y) = 0.9775, D(2.5y) = 0.975, D(3y) = 0.9725$, and let the 2y swap rate, 1y forward, $F = 2.0\%$. In order to price a \$100 million 1y into 2y 25-high ($K = F + 0.25\% = 2.25\%$) right-to-pay swaption using 84bp Normal vol, we form:

$$d = \frac{F - K}{\sigma_N \sqrt{t_e}} = \frac{2.0\% - 2.25\%}{0.0084\sqrt{1.0}} = -0.29672,$$

and calculate

$$E[\max(0, S(t_e, \omega) - K)] = \sigma_N \sqrt{t_e}[N'(d) + dN(d)]$$

$$= 0.0084\sqrt{1.0}\left[\frac{1}{\sqrt{2\pi}}e^{-0.29672^2/2} + (-0.29672)N(-0.29672)\right]$$

$$= 0.002248$$

Finally, the price of 25-high payer swaption is obtained as 43.9 cents:

$$P(0) = 1/2(D(1.5y) + D(2y) + D(2.5y) + D(3y))$$
$$\times E[\max(0, S(t_e, \omega) - K)]$$
$$= 1/2(0.98 + 0.9775 + 0.975 + 0.9725) \times (0.002248)$$
$$= \$0.439\%.$$

Swaptions in Practice

Inter-dealer-brokers maintain ATMF straddle prices for various expirations and maturities, and communicate bids/offer prices for specific straddles between dealers. They also maintain a general swaption price grid for all expiries and maturities in electronic format (broker screens), update them periodically during the day, and send a final settlement grid at end of day. Alongside the price, they might also quote the implied Log-Normal or Normal vol, but that is mostly for informational purposes, as at the end of the day, price is king (see Tables 30.3 and 30.4). So a 1m-into-2y swaption straddle is trading at 29 cents ($290,000 per $100 million notional), and this price is equivalent to Black Normal vol of 68.3 bp/annum.

When trading ATMF straddles, a price is agreed on, and the next step is to agree on the forward swap rate. Due to their curve differences, each side might see the ATMF rate at slightly different values. However, since straddles will have little PV01, both sides agree on a rate (perhaps aided by the broker).

If instead of straddles, a receiver or payer swaption is traded, one needs to specify whether the hedge/delta is exchanged or not. The standard hedge, regardless of the option strike, consists of a delta-weighted amount of a forward swap (struck at the forward swap rate, so with 0 value).

TABLE 30.3 A Swaption Straddle Price Grid (Cents)

		\multicolumn{9}{c}{Underlying Swap Term}							
		1y	2y	3y	4y	5y	7y	10y	15y	30y
"Gamma" Expiries	1m	9	29	43	60	78	103	134	175	242
	3m	22	57	87	115	144	188	245	324	446
	6m	34	80	123	162	199	262	339	443	608
"Vega" Expiries	1y	60	119	174	227	276	363	469	608	837
	2y	86	169	246	318	385	502	645	833	1,124
	3y	103	201	291	376	454	594	760	975	1,316
	5y	120	232	337	434	524	680	876	1,118	1,500
	7y	124	238	347	448	542	704	897	1,136	1,497
	10y	120	230	333	428	516	669	855	1,075	1,401

TABLE 30.4 Implied Black Normal Vols (bp)

	1y	2y	3y	4y	5y	7y	10y	15y	30y
1m	43.2	**68.3**	70.4	75.5	80.5	79.9	78.7	77.8	75.8
3m	57.0	77.6	80.4	81.9	83.8	82.5	81.4	81.1	79.0
6m	65.0	77.4	81.6	82.6	83.5	82.8	81.1	79.8	77.4
1y	81.9	83.6	83.9	84.4	84.3	83.5	81.6	79.9	77.7
2y	88.5	89.2	88.6	88.4	88.0	86.4	84.1	82.1	78.3
3y	91.6	91.4	90.7	90.2	89.7	88.4	85.8	83.3	79.3
5y	92.2	91.4	91.3	90.6	89.9	88.0	86.1	83.2	78.6
7y	90.7	89.4	89.2	88.8	88.4	86.8	84.0	80.5	74.6
10y	87.1	86.0	85.5	84.9	84.4	82.6	80.2	76.2	69.7

If the trade is with the delta/hedge, then one first sets the option price, and the forward rate and the size of the hedge are agreed upon later. In this case, similar to trading straddles, since the PV01 of the combined position (option+hedge) are small, minor rate or delta differences as seen by different sides are (usually) amicably settled.

If the trade is done without the delta/hedge, then a sufficient extra (hedging) premium is built into the option price to cover the subsequent hedging bid/offer cost. The natural preference of an option trader is to transact options with delta, thereby just trading volatility.

For swaption expiries and maturities that do not fall on the grid, one typically uses linear interpolation in square root of time-to-expiry on the expiry axis, and linear interpolation on the maturity axis.

Swaption Settlement

At expiration, swaptions can be either physical or cash-settled. For physical settlement, the owner of an in-the-money receiver/payer swaption will enter into a plain-vanilla swap where he will receive/pay the strike as the fixed rate. Physical settlement is the preferred method for swaptions that are sufficiently (say more than 10bp) in the money, even if the originally agreed-upon settlement method is cash.

Cash-settlement involves determining the market par swap rate at expiration time, and then agreeing upon the value of a swap with fixed rate equal to the strike instead of the par-swap rate. As we saw before, the economic value of an in-the-money swaption struck at K when par-swap rate is S is an annuity of $S - K$ bp's for RTP ($K - S$ for RTR) for the length of the swap. Therefore, both parties must agree upon the *size* ($|S - K|$) and the *Present-Value* of this annuity.

Since the strike K is by contract, the swaption counterparties first have to agree on the par-swap rate S at expiration time. This can be mutual agreement, or polling dealers, or some other method as specified in the option confirm. For generic USD swaptions, the standard is to use the 11:00 am fixing of swap rates. Once the size of the annuity ($|S - K|$) is known, the counterparties have to then agree on its PV.

There are two methods to calculate the PV of the annuity. The first method (the standard for USD swaptions) is to use a discount factor curve to PV the annuity. For example for an n-year swap with m coupons per year, with payment dates $\{T_1, \ldots, T_{nm}\}$, each party needs to compute:

$$|S - K| \times \frac{1}{m} \sum_{i=1}^{nm} D(T_i).$$

As each counterparty can have a different discount-curve (even using the same rate S as the n-year par-swap rate), a bit of horse-trading precedes an amicable cash-settlement of the swaption. This method does not have a standard name, and can be referred to as "cash-settlement off the curve" or cash-settlement "USD-style."

The second cash-settlement method is to PV the annuity using the annuity formula from bonds, using the agreed-upon swap rate as the *yield*. This method is the standard for European currencies, and is referred to as "cash-settlement via annuity (or IRR) method." For an n-year swap with m coupons per year, the payoff is

$$|S - K| \times \frac{1}{m} \sum_{i=1}^{nm} \frac{1}{(1 + S/m)^i} = \frac{|S - K|}{S} \left(1 - \frac{1}{(1 + S/m)^{nm}}\right).$$

SKEWS, SMILES

In a perfect Black world, asset prices evolve (Normally, Log-Normally) with a single volatility parameter. The price of options then can be obtained once we know this volatility, or alternatively, given a price, we can back out the implied volatility. In practice, it is observed that option prices with the same expiration date but different strikes give rise to different implied Black volatilities. Typically, for options with strikes lower than ATMF, the implied volatility goes up, and this effect is called *skew*. Also out-of-the-money options in either direction (high or low strikes) generally have higher implied Black volatilities than ATMF options. This effect is called *volatility smile*.

The existence of skews and smiles means that the implied distribution of the assets is more complicated than what is posited by Black (Normal, Log-Normal) model, and has given rise to a cottage industry of searching for the *right* model for skew and smile. Amongst the models proposed are mixture models, Constant Elasticity of Variance (CEV) models, Stochastic volatility models (SABR amongst them), Jump-Diffusion models, and Fractional Brownian Motion models. While each of these models have its merits, they collectively suffer from the fact that they are modeling the wrong thing!

Skews and smiles are predominantly driven by supply and demand. If a majority of clients are worried about higher rates, and are buying high-strike payers to protect themselves, payer swaptions go up in price (and hence in implied vol). Alternatively, if the fear is for low rates, then low-strike receivers go up in premium/vol. On a day-to-day basis, vol traders perceive the skew/smile as a measure of liquidity rather than the implied distribution of rates. Supply/demand patterns change quickly in response to market sentiments/news, and it is implausible to ascribe these changes to market's view on a meaningful distribution of rates for the life of the option.

Maintaining/Populating Volatility Surface, Cubes

For swaptions, it is customary to maintain a Black *volatility cube*, that is, a volatility for each expiration, swap maturity, and strike. Some desks maintain vols for a series of absolute (1%, 1.25%, 1.5%, ..., 9.75%, 10%, ...) strikes, while most desks maintain vols for a series of relative (ATMF, ATMF±25 bp, ATMF±50 bp, ATMF±100 bp, ...) strikes. A similar procedure is used for caplet vol curves.

As one might imagine, the task of maintaining ATMF volatility surfaces (Expiration, Swap Maturity) and cubes (Expiration, Maturity, Strike) is arduous. Depending on the market, there are 10–20 expirations, 10–20 maturities, and 10–20 strike levels (absolute or relative), hence a rates option trader needs to maintain on the order of 1000 live prices! Given that on a typical trading day, only a few (10–20) swaptions and cap/floors trade, most desks keep active watch on certain *anchor* vols, and derive other neighboring vols via linear/ratio interpolation/extrapolation. For example, in USD, 1m2y, 1m5y, 1m10y, 3m10y, 1y1y, and 5y5y can serve as the anchor vols. Once we know these vols, the vol of 1m3y, 1m4y or 2m10y can plausibly (in the absence of actual markets) be backed out via interpolation.

The market for skews is less active than ATMF options. Most desks select a skew model (SABR, CEV, ...) and *calibrate* the few model parameters to any observed skew markets, quoted commonly through *risk-reversals:* The difference between the price of an out-of-the-money payer swaption versus an equally out-of-the-money receiver. For Normal dynamics, in the absence of any skew these prices should be the same, as the Normal distribution is symmetric. Hence, when a difference exists, it is indicative of Non-Normality or skew. Using these skews markets, volatility traders then populate the cube using these few parameters. Hence the role of skew models is primarily to reduce the dimension of the problem from 1000's to 100's (potentially each Expiration/Swap-Term pair can have its own set of parameters).

CMS PRODUCTS

A CMS (Constant Maturity Swap) rate is simply the par-swap rate for a given tenor, and a *CMS Swap* is the periodic exchange of a CMS rate versus either a fixed rate, or more typically versus Libor. For example, a USD 2-year CMS-10y versus Libor consists of a standard quarterly, Act/360 floating leg based on 3m Libor, versus the quarterly fixing and payment (accrued 30/360) of 10-year par swap rate on the CMS leg, with both legs spanning 2 years. Since the tenor of the underlying CMS rate does not coincide with the length of the calculation period, the replication argument for plain vanilla Libor legs does not hold, and one cannot simply discount the forward par-swap rates. Still, there is a strong temptation to do this, and one typically values CMS resets by first calculating the forward swap rate, and then *adjusting* them by a *CMS Convexity Adjustment*. The term convexity adjustment arises in different contexts in interest rate derivatives, and is usually a red flag that a certain level of fudging is going on. Specifically, convexity adjustments are a quick-and-dirty way of getting the right answer by applying the wrong method, for example discounting the forward rates for CMS products. This obviously pre-supposes that we have the right answer, or at least an idea of what the right answer should be!

For CMS-based payoffs, it is first recognized that while the payoff is linear in the underlying CMS rate, a replicating portfolio would consist of forward swap positions. Recalling that receiving in a swap is economically equivalent to paying par for a forward bond, the graph of the forward swap value is a convex function of the underlying swap rate, analogous to the price/yield graph for bonds. For a CMS-based swap, we therefore are hedging a linear payoff (CMS rate) with a non-linear/convex payoff (Forward Swap). The hedge for receiving the CMS-rate is to pay in a PV01-equivalent amount of a forward swap. This hedge, however, confers a systematic advantage to the CMS-receiver, the size of which depends on the curvature/convexity of the forward swap versus the swap rate, and the expected size of the deviation of the realized swap rate at reset-date versus its forward value. As no free lunch goes untaxed in markets, the CMS-payer will charge the receiver for this free lunch by adjusting the forward swap rate upwards by the convexity adjustment. Note that this adjustment is only used to calculate the PV of future payments, the actual payment on payment date is simply the CMS rate observed at the fixing date (with no adjustment).

The fair level of this CMS convexity adjustment will require a model of the distribution of future swap rates at each reset date in a risk-neutral setting. In lieu of this, the following heuristic argument is invoked to obtain a quick and dirty formula. Using bonds as proxies for swaps, we start with the following approximaton:

$$P(y) - P(F) \approx (y - F)P'(y) + 1/2(y - F)^2 P''(y),$$

where F is the forward par-swap rate, and $P(y)$ is the standard Bond Price-Yield Formula. It is recalled that forward prices must equal expected prices in a risk-neutral world, hence $EP(y) = P(F)$, and

$$(E[y] - F)P'(F) = -\frac{1}{2}P''(F)E[(y - F)^2],$$

Finally, we approximate

$$E[(y - F)^2] \approx \sigma_N^2 dt$$

to arrive at the following *CMS Convexity Adjustment* Formula:

$$E[y] - F = -\frac{1}{2}\frac{P''(F)}{P'(F)}\sigma_N^2 dt$$

$$= \left[\frac{1}{F} - \frac{N/m}{(1 + F/m)^{N+1} - (1 + F/m)}\right]\sigma_N^2 t_e,$$

where N, m are the number and frequency of coupon payments for the underlying *forward* $(C = y = F)$ bond/swap, and t_e is the time to its reset. While very heuristic and approximate, the above formula due to its simple structure is widely used and in preference to more elaborate models.

CMS Curve Options

In the past couple of years, options on the slope of swap curve have become popular. These are referred to as *CMS Curve Options*, as they are simple cap/floors on the difference between two CMS rates. For example, a CMS 2y–10y curve caplet with strike K is based on the following payoff

$$\max(0, S_{10y}(t_e) - S_{2y}(t_e) - K).$$

The simplest method of evaluating CMS curve products is to use Black's Normal model—Log-Normal would be inappropriate since spreads can go negative, and zero or negative strikes are not uncommon—for the spread: $S_{1,2}(t_e) = S_2(t_e) - S_1(t_e)$, and extract the Normal vol of the spread from the swaption Normal volatilities via:

$$\sigma_N(S_{1,2}) = \sqrt{\sigma_N^2(S_1) + \sigma_N^2(S_2) - 2\rho\sigma_N(S_1)\sigma_N(S_2)}$$

where $\sigma_N(S_1), \sigma_N(S_2)$ are the swaption normal vols for the CMS rates, and ρ is the correlation between them.

Contingent Curve Trades

While CMS curve options are the most direct way of taking a view on the slope of the swap curve, one may put on a *conditional* curve trade using European swaptions, since curve trades are usually *directional*: The front end of the swap curve is more volatile than the long end as it is more sensitive to central bank policies, and the front end typically *leads* the long end in either increasing or decreasing rate environments. Therefore, in a tightening (rising rate) environment, the short-term swap rates move more than longer-term swap rates, leading to flattening of the swap curve. This is referred to as *bear-flattening*–"bear" since bond prices are dropping in rising rate environments. Similarly, in an easing (falling rate) environment, short-term rates fall more than long-term rates, leading to *bull-steepening*. As such, one would want to be in a flattener in bearish environments, while steepeners are preferred in bullish environments.

To be long a steepener, one can either be long the curve via swaps (long the front end, short the back-end), using either spot or forward swaps. Instead, one can be in a *conditional* steepener by buying a swaption receiver into the shorter maturity, while selling a swaption receiver into the longer maturity. The size of each swaption is chosen so that if they are both in the money at expiration, each swap will have the same PV01, while the strikes of the swaptions are chosen so that the package is zero-cost:

Zero-cost bull-steepener (sometimes called conditional or contingent call-call). Similarly, a zero-cost bear-flattener consists of a pair of payer swaptions with strikes chosen to make the package zero-cost.

BOND OPTIONS

While not strictly a "Rates" product, bond options are sometimes quoted by flow options desks. The typical expiration for these options is relatively short (a few days or weeks), and are usually priced and hedged using Black's Log-Normal formula, driven by *price volatility*. As the market for bond options is relatively thin, this price volatility is backed out from *yield volatility* using the following heuristic argument: Yield log-volatility σ_y measures a one standard deviation percentage change in yields:

$$\sigma_y \approx E\left[\frac{\Delta y}{y}\right],$$

while price log-volatility σ_P measures a one standard deviation percentage change in prices:

$$\sigma_P \approx E\left[\frac{\Delta P}{P}\right].$$

One can relate change in prices due to change in yields:

$$\Delta P \approx \frac{dP}{dy}\Delta y,$$

therefore

$$\sigma_P = \frac{1}{P}\frac{dP}{dy}y\sigma_y.$$

A common approach is to derive the yield volatility from a similar-maturity swaption volatility using simple regression analysis. For example, when asked to quote a 1m option on the current U.S. Treasury 10y bond (CT10), one can perform a regression analysis on the relationship between 10y Treasury yields versus 10y swap rates, and multiply the 1m-into-10y swaption volatility by the slope coefficient to arrive at a plausible yield volatility for CT10. By converting this yield vol into price vol, one can then price bond options using Black's Log-Normal formula using *clean* forward and strike prices. Note that as option prices are based on replication using the underlying, the specific bond's financing (repo) rate rather than a generic risk-free rate should be used in Black's formula.

Conditional Swap-Spread Trades

While a swap spread trade involves a cash bond versus a swap, one can also enter into a *conditional* swap spread trade using swaptions and bond options. It is observed that swap spreads are typically *directional*. In falling rate environments, spreads generally "come in" (decrease), while they "go out" in increasing rate environments. To take advantage of this directionality, one would then like to be in a swap-spread widening trade (long cash, pay in swaps) when interest rates are increasing, that is, a bearish-widener. For a given cash bond, this can be achieved by selling a put option on the bond, while buying a PV01-equivalent amount of a payer swaption with maturity identical to a bond: If both options finish in-the-money, the bond is put to us while we are paying in a matched-maturity swap, that is, we are long the matched-maturity swap spread of the bond when rates are increasing. The strikes of the put and swaption are usually chosen so that the package is cost-less, typically by selecting one strike higher (in yield) than ATMF, and then solving for the other strike.

To take advantage of directionality in decreasing rate environments, one implements a *bullish-tightener* by selling a call option on the bond and buying a PV01-equivalent (if both options finish in-the-money) receiver swaption for a matched-maturity swap, with strikes chosen so that the package is cost-less, resulting in a *zero-cost call/reciever* or bullish-tightener.

A final note that due to relative low liquidity of bond options, most contingent swap-spread trades are implemented using options on treasury futures contracts traded on Chicago Board of Trade (CBOT), with the future contract equated to Cheapest-To-Deliver (CTD) issue divided by its conversion factor.

CHAPTER 31

Commodities

An Introduction and Overview from a Capital Markets Perspective

Bob Swarup

INTRODUCTION

Commodities are an integral facet of the financial markets and the global economy and are the oldest of all spheres of investments, predating bonds, equities, and even money itself.

One could argue without hyperbole that the story of humanity is one of commodities. Long before the small kingdom of Lydia struck the first coins in the 6th century, great nations such as Egypt, China, Phoenicia, and India were already trading wheat, spices, gold, silver, base metals, and other resources. Their interactions created the first economies and the first merchants. Their alliances, wars, and explorations were all driven by a need to have better or greater access to commodities in some form. As the Roman philosopher Cicero noted, it was the Roman merchant who went first to new areas, not the Roman soldier. The legions only came after a reason for conquest had been established.

The reason is simple. Our history and advancement over the millennia have been defined by our access to and control over the natural resources in our environment. Food and drink sustain and thrill us in equal measure while spices add variety. Base materials and metals allow us to craft tools to build our homes, cities, vehicles, and so on. Precious metals add sparkle, greed, envy, and a measure of social stature while energy is vital to propel people, societies, and civilizations forward. Early human history is broken into stages named after commodities: the Stone Age, the Bronze Age, and the Iron Age. Later human history is underpinned by how we harness, craft, and exploit our resources, whether it be the invention of the windmill, the printing press, or the internal-combustion engine. The discovery of flight, the age of electronics, and even the latest advances, such as robots and nanotechnology, would not have occurred without access to the necessary materials. Needless to say, throughout history, competition for the control of natural resources has been the cause of countless wars.

Given these fundamental links to human endeavor and survival, it is only natural that commodities are integral to the evolution of capitalism and financial markets. The first banks sprang into being in ancient times to fund merchants and speculators seeking to lead expeditions to find, exploit, and profit from the commodities needed in their day. Banks extended credit or directly funded these risky ventures (the precursor of equity) in return for gain, whether it be a guaranteed contractual return on monies advanced, a share of the expected profit, or the right to trade these lucrative goods into hungry markets.

The banks' business models soon grew in sophistication to provide participants with ways of managing risk, leveraging their hoped-for profits, or both. In medieval Europe, for example, the desire of Benedictine abbeys to lock in the price of future shearings of the sheep roaming their vast lands led to the development of a large market in wool futures. In 18th-century Japan, a legendary trader known as Munehisa Homma earned the equivalent of over $10 billion in today's terms in a single year by trading the rice markets. The voyages of Christopher Columbus and the Spanish conquistadors to the New World were funded by investors and nations looking for precious commodities and shorter trade routes as were the efforts of European powers to colonize Africa and Asia. Many of today's financial exchanges originated as forums for trading and managing agricultural produce, extracted metals, and energy.

Today, the commodities market is deep and sophisticated, replete with many different types of instruments. Contemporary society is still fundamentally underpinned by trade, making commodities a critical asset class within the global financial ecosystem. Today, commodities are traded to protect against inherent price risk, to speculate from the sidelines on future trends and demand, to use as collateral to fund trade, or to invest in directly to gain exposure.

In this chapter, we outline briefly today's commodities complex, focusing on its fundamentals, the different types of commodities, and the main markets. We examine both physical and derivative investments as well as the different vehicles investors use to access the market. Finally, we examine briefly some of the important macroeconomic trends in the space today, notably the collapse in prices during 2015–2016.

COMMODITY FUNDAMENTALS

Commodities have taken many forms over the centuries, reflecting the demand for natural resources around the world at any given time. In ancient times, for example, tribes and empires traded gold, wheat, pepper, saffron, spices, rice, livestock, shells, and salt. Today, some of these commodities are still in high demand, such as gold and livestock, but, in response to society's changing needs and priorities, others have come into vogue, such as uranium and carbon trading.

Irrespective of the historical period, certain aspects are fundamentally important. Given the importance of commodities to the smooth functioning of an economy and society, product quality, reliability of supply, guaranteed dates of delivery, and the ease of exchange or trade with others (in other words, liquidity) have always been important considerations. Consequently, commodities markets have always been driven by the need to demonstrate reliability and standardization and to safeguard reputation—something that continues to this day in the rules set by financial exchanges. The fact that most commodities are traded without visual inspection makes this even more critical.

This is also important from the view of policymakers—be they kings or regulators—as the trade in commodities has served as the wheels of commerce, driven economic development, and provided valuable revenues for governments. Thus, commodities have also been carefully regulated for much of their history. After all, no one wants to buy a cow only to find that it has three legs.

The commodities markets today are broad and deep, presenting both challenges and opportunities. For the purposes of this chapter, we will hereafter only examine the key commodities traded on financial exchanges along with a handful of other emerging areas of interest, such as renewables.

The key categories of trading commodities today include:

- *Agricultural*—for example, soybeans, wheat, rice, and coffee, also livestock, such as lean hogs and live cattle
- *Energy*—for example, crude oil and natural gas
- *Metals*—for example, gold, nickel, and copper

The prices of these are essentially set by basic economic principles of supply and demand. For example, rapid urbanization and industrialization in China, and the resulting rise of its middle class during the late 1990s and early 2000s, led to an explosion of demand for all sorts of commodities, ranging from base materials for building (e.g., iron ore and copper) to expressions of affluence (e.g., gold) to changes in diet (e.g., a rise in pork consumption). The surge in demand from China led to severe supply shortages and a consequent boom both in physical commodity prices as well as the shares of those companies producing them. Conversely, in 2015, the advent of new technologies in oil drilling, notably fracking, led to a glut of worldwide crude oil and natural gas inventories. The result was a collapse of energy prices and a dramatic fall in the earnings and share prices of producers.

By following these supply-and-demand dynamics, investors can take positions and look to profit from both long-term investing as well as trading. However, commodity trading differs significantly from trading of other markets such as bonds and equities. The sensitivity of commodities to macroeconomic trends and geopolitics has meant that they represent a macro play for many investors on wider dynamics such as political tensions, the pace of technological innovation, and health scares. For example, historically, the price of crude oil has been inextricably linked to the volatile political dynamics of the Middle East. Traders look to leverage the uncertainty created by this volatility by anticipating the price moves generated by events in the region.

This same sensitivity also means that there is a deep pool of producers and users of commodities who seek to manage the volatility of their supply and its economic cost. As we noted earlier, reliability of supply is key. We all drive cars, use electricity, eat food, and so on. Without careful control, price fluctuations can have enormous impacts on key drivers of economic health and consumer sentiment such as inflation and corporate profit margins. For example, in countries such as India, nearly half the inflation bucket is composed of energy in some form as the country imports the vast majority of its fuel. Thus, any volatility in prices has dramatic impacts on both the levels of inflation within India as well as the earnings of many companies. Conversely, producers are also sensitive to these dynamics and would experience wide swings in earnings if they were fully exposed to the prices of the commodities they supply.

To deal with this problem, commodities markets very early on developed sophisticated hedging tools, whereby producers and consumers could control their risk by entering into derivative trades with other market participants, namely speculators, who were looking to profit from rises and falls in the same prices. The size and depth of this market globally means that derivatives such as futures and options are a far more significant part of the financial universe and the investment palette in commodities than other markets. Consequently, access to commodities can be achieved by physically trading them, executing derivative trades, purchasing mutual funds, or utilizing the services of commodity trading advisors (CTAs)

Regardless of the commodity in question, to be regarded as an investable vehicle, certain key criteria apply. These also help to differentiate commodities from other aspects of the financial markets such as derivatives based on interest rates, currencies, and inflation.

- *Deliverability:* The commodity has to be physically deliverable on settlement date. Although contracts are rarely physically fulfilled, the right of the buyer to actually take physical delivery of the commodity *in specie* is inviolate. Thus, crude oil theoretically could be delivered in barrels (or an oil tanker) and gold could be delivered in bars.
- *Liquidity:* This does not mean liquidity in the traditional sense where one might theoretically be able to exit or enter a financial position immediately. Rather, liquidity in commodities means there is a deep pool of buyers and sellers who create a large secondary market for the commodity and its different financial expressions. This liquidity is measured in terms of ease of entry and exit (as with futures contracts, for example).
- *Tradeability:* An investor must be able to buy and sell the instrument in some way, subject to the other criteria mentioned earlier. That may mean a derivatives contract on a major exchange, but it may also mean the physical commodity itself or proxies such as producers, parts of the supply chain, and ETFs. Thus, crude oil can be traded as actual barrels, futures contracts, oil producers, pipeline owners, and so on. In contrast, lithium is harder to trade but may be accessed through mines (i.e., the physical commodity) as well as companies engaged in exploring or producing lithium for consumption.

All the commodities we will now discuss fulfill these criteria. Additionally, these same criteria mean that new commodities are constantly emerging. For example, renewable energy may now be considered a commodity. While no one can control and deliver the wind or the sun, energy from both can be harnessed and supplied to users. There are buyers and sellers of wind energy and electricity, and it can be traded through companies in the marketplace and in related areas such as energy storage.

TYPES OF COMMODITIES

We now examine and outline each of the three types of commodities; agricultural, metals, and energy. While the individual lists of specific products are not exhaustive, they include the majority of the key commodities that matter to investors today.

Agricultural Commodities

Food is fundamental to human existence, so not surprisingly, the agricultural complex is extremely large and diverse. It may broadly be split into two categories:

- Grains, food, and drinks
- Meat and livestock

We summarize the main contracts traded on exchanges in Table 31.1.

Table 31.1 reflects a range of commodities of key interest to economies and investors. Coffee, for example, is the second most widely produced commodity in the world in terms of physical volume after crude oil, as evidenced by the countless Starbucks and other coffee-shops in storefronts across the globe. Cocoa is used to create chocolate—a perennial favorite and bestseller. Grains such as wheat, corn, and rough rice are staples of food around the world. Rapeseed and soybean oil are used extensively to derive cooking oil. Sugar is a staple again of human diets and the different contracts reflect global and U.S. variations. Milk and frozen concentrated orange juice give investors exposure to key drinks around the world. Finally, livestock, namely cattle and hogs, give investors exposure to key meat components of human consumption. All of these contracts also provide producers and consumers ways of hedging their pricing risk and locking in economic certainty around their supply.

It is worth noting that there are many other agricultural commodities that are actively traded outside the major exchanges, such as almonds, pepper, sheep, and avocados. Markets for these products merely reflect the fact that these are all items of significant consumption globally, making them sought after by investors.

Energy Commodities

Providing reliable stores of energy is vital to ensuring stability in every society in today's globalized world (Table 31.2). The demand for energy going forward will only increase with the rise of key emerging-market nations such as China and India.

TABLE 31.1 List of Main Traded Agricultural Commodities, along with Exchanges and Contract Sizes

Commodity	Main Exchange	Contract Size
Cocoa	Intercontinental Exchange (ICE)	10 tons
Coffee C	ICE	37,500 lb
Corn	Chicago Board of Trade (CBOT), EURONEXT	5000 bushels, 50 tons
Cotton No.2	ICE	50,000 lb
Feeder Cattle	Chicago Mercantile Exchange	50,000 lb (25 tons)
Frozen Concentrated Orange Juice	ICE	15,000 lb
Lean Hogs	Chicago Mercantile Exchange	40,000 lb (20 tons)
Live Cattle	Chicago Mercantile Exchange	40,000 lb (20 tons)
Milk	Chicago Mercantile Exchange	200,000 lbs
Oats	CBOT	5000 bushels
Rapeseed	EURONEXT	50 tons
Rough Rice	CBOT	2000 cwt (hundredweight)
Soybean Meal	CBOT	100 short tons
Soybean Oil	CBOT	60,000 lb
Soybeans	CBOT	5000 bushels
Sugar No.11	ICE	112,000 lb
Sugar No.14	ICE	112,000 lb
Wheat	CBOT, EURONEXT	5000 bushels, 50 tons

TABLE 31.2 List of Main Traded Energy Commodities, along with Exchanges and Contract Sizes

Commodity	Main Exchange	Contract Size
Brent Crude	ICE	1000 bbl (42,000 U.S. gal)
Ethanol	CBOT	29,000 U.S. gal
Gulf Coast Gasoline	NY Mercantile Exchange (NYMEX)	1000 bbl (42,000 U.S. gal)
Heating Oil	NYMEX	1000 bbl (42,000 U.S. gal)
Natural Gas	NYMEX	10,000 mmBTU
Propane	NYMEX	1000 bbl (42,000 U.S. gal)
Purified Terephthalic Acid (PTA)	Zengzhou Commodity Exchange (ZCE)	5 tons
RBOB Gasoline (reformulated gasoline blendstock for oxygen blending)	NYMEX	1000 bbl (42,000 U.S. gal)
WTI Crude Oil	NYMEX, ICE	1000 bbl (42,000 U.S. gal)

Crude oil is the dominant commodity in the world and the one that most people are instinctively familiar with from reading the news. It supplies the majority of energy needs globally and some 90 million barrels of crude oil are traded every day. Given its significant strategic importance, crude oil tends to be very sensitive to perceived geopolitical tensions. The many different types of crude oil contracts reflect the different shades extracted globally. Natural gas is another energy source of rising importance along with ethanol, which is increasingly used as a fuel substitute. Other contracts listed in Table 31.2 reflect other key oil products and chemicals that are used as specialist fuels (for example, in furnaces).

There are many other key commodities of interest that are not traded on exchanges. For example, despite its tarnished image, coal is a significant part of global energy consumption and therefore a key commodity. The advent of nuclear power has made uranium another important energy commodity while the need to find alternative environmental solutions has led to significant interest in solar and wind power. Another key commodity to note is electricity, which is in effect the end product of many of these energy sources. The fact that electricity can be transported, stored, and traded (e.g., supplied by a power station to consumers in return for money) means that there is a burgeoning market in electricity derivatives and companies.

Metals

Metals are important for building most of the things we use, from the home we live in to the cars we drive to the technology we use. The industrialization of society means that there is significant demand for many different metals for a range of purposes. Metals can also serve as a tangible asset to provide a store of perceived value that people may prefer in lieu of cash.

In general, metals may be split into two categories:

- *Industrial:* Metals used to produce things
- *Precious:* Metals perceived to act as a store of value

In practice, the lines between the two can sometimes become blurred. Silver, for example, has significant industrial uses beyond just jewelry while platinum is used in catalytic convertors for cars to reduce emissions.

We outline in Table 31.3 the key contracts traded on major exchanges.

Steel, in its various forms, is the most widely used metal in the world, due to its role as a fundamental building material. Aluminum and copper follow after, given their diverse uses. Nickel and zinc became critical metals as they help create more durable, corrosion-resistant materials such as stainless steel. On the precious side, gold has been a storehouse of value for millennia, along with silver. Both were used historically to back currencies and, even today, economic volatility and distress in economies usually result in an increased demand for these precious metals. Therefore, gold and silver are often traded by investors for their macroeconomic sensitivities as well. They are also seen as

TABLE 31.3 List of Primary Traded Metals, along with Exchanges and Units

Commodity	Main Exchange	Unit
Aluminum	London Metal Exchange, New York	Metric ton
Aluminum alloy	London Metal Exchange	Metric ton
Cobalt	London Metal Exchange	Metric ton
Copper	London Metal Exchange, New York	Metric ton
Gold	COMEX	Troy ounce
Lead	London Metal Exchange	Metric ton
Molybdenum	London Metal Exchange	Metric ton
Nickel	London Metal Exchange	Metric ton
Palladium	NYMEX	Troy ounce
Platinum	NYMEX	Troy ounce
Silver	COMEX	Troy ounce
Steel rebar, scrap, billet	London Metal Exchange	Metric ton
Tin	London Metal Exchange	Metric ton
Zinc	London Metal Exchange	Metric ton

stable sources of value, and are thus used by investors as a hedge against inflation or currency volatility.

As with agricultural and energy commodities, there are many other key metals that are not necessarily traded on exchanges. Steel has already been noted, but there is also iron ore, one of the key components of steel, lithium, a staple of modern fuel cells and electric cars, and rare earth metals, which are used in a wide variety of electronics.

COMMODITIES EXCHANGES

Before we delve deeper into the various ways in which commodities exposure is expressed, it is worth touching briefly on commodities exchanges. Simply put, a commodities exchange is a forum where commodities and their associated derivatives are traded. Historically, the importance of trading efficiently in the commodities arena has meant that exchanges have been critical to the development of the sector and continue to be fundamental to the trading of commodities today.

Commodities exchanges help address key issues of reputation, reliability, and standardization. By developing contracts with standardized terms, key quality criteria, and clear deliverables, they allow investors to trade without having to visually inspect the goods. Additionally, standardization makes the commodity market far more liquid and allows people to hedge as well as trade efficiently.

Much of the world's financial ecosystem today sprang from commodities exchanges. The Amsterdam Stock Exchange, for example, originally began as a market for the exchange of commodities before becoming the first-ever stock exchange. Additionally, key financial developments such as the initial derivatives contracts, forward contracts,

TABLE 31.4 Key Commodity Exchanges Around the World

Exchange Name	Examples of Commodities Traded
Chicago Board of Trade (CBOT)	Corn, ethanol, soybeans, wheat, gold, silver
Chicago Mercantile Exchange (CME)	Feeder cattle, lean hogs, live cattle, butter, milk
Dalian Commodity Exchange	Corn, soybean meal, eggs, polypropylene, coke
Intercontinental Exchange (ICE)	Crude oil, electricity, natural gas
Kansas City Board of Trade (KCBT)	Natural gas, wheat
London Metal Exchange	Aluminum, cobalt, copper, lead, tin, zinc
Minneapolis Grain Exchange (MGE)	Corn, soybeans, wheat
Multi Commodity Exchange	Gold, nonferrous metals, cardamom, crude palm oil, cotton
New York Board of Trade (NYBOT)	Cocoa, coffee, cotton, frozen concentrated orange juice, ethanol
New York Mercantile Exchange (NYMEX)	Aluminum, copper, gold, silver, crude oil, electricity, heating oil, natural gas
Tokyo Commodity Exchange	Gold, silver, gasoline, natural rubber, corn, azuki

options, and the ability to short began there also, as people sought ways of managing their risk and expressing investment views on the supply-and-demand dynamics of commodities. In the 19th century, many great financial centers such as Chicago, New York, and London built their reputations on the ability to facilitate trade, ensure quality, manage risk, and set the accepted prices for key commodities.

Today, a number of exchanges around the world allow investors to trade in agricultural products as well as metals, energy, and miscellaneous raw materials such as rubber. Trading is done through a series of standardized contracts that can include spot prices, forwards, futures, and options. Typically, and as demonstrated by the various pools of commodities out there, many exchanges have specialized in particular segments of the market, offering unique contracts. We summarize in Table 31.4 some of the key players today.

In the last decade, there has been significant consolidation among the various exchanges, which has led to an increase in offerings across the board and made it easier than ever for investors and producers to access markets. A large part of this consolidation has been driven by the advent of electronic trading. Today, the two dominant players are the CME group, which acquired the CBOT and NYMEX and is now the world's largest commodities exchange, and ICE, which has in recent years acquired other major players such as the NYBOT, NYSE, Euronext, and Climate Exchange.

COMMODITY CONTRACTS

As noted earlier, the high level of trading activity in commodities is a function of the large pool of participants looking to hedge their pricing exposure for business or purely economic reasons. There are, therefore, many different forms of commodity contracts both on exchanges as well as over the counter (OTC). The latter are bilateral contracts where two parties enter into a bespoke arrangement.

While we cannot go into all the different types of contracts in detail—a book in itself—we can touch on some of the key forms of contracts that are traded. The bulk of these contracts on exchanges in particular are derivatives. In other words, they derive their value from the behavior of the underlying commodity.

Futures and Options

The overwhelming need for hedging in the commodities market means that many derivative contracts are essentially ways of managing the future pricing risk of commodities. A mining company or farmer, for example, may wish to secure a fixed price at which to sell their output for the foreseeable future. Similarly, industrial companies and food manufacturers may wish to avoid volatility in prices and the corresponding fluctuations in their business margins. This is driven by the simple economic rationale that the market and their shareholders will reward them for stable earnings and sustainable growth. As a result, major sectors such as airlines engage in significant hedging operations to ensure that they can buy their fuel at fixed prices, helping them to manage expenses and avoid corporate distress.

The vast majority of hedging operations are carried out on exchanges in the form of futures and options. This improves both liquidity and allows other parties, namely investors, to speculate on future price moves by taking the opposite side to the party hedging its exposure. It is important to note that futures and options are not unique to commodities. They are prevalent in the bond, currency, and equity markets as well, but they are vital in the commodities sphere as they allow singular uses within standardized structures.

An airline may wish to buy a fixed amount of fuel for a fixed period at a fixed price. The futures market allows it do so by entering into a contract with another party that guarantees this. If the price of the commodity falls during the life of the contract, the airline's counterparty will realize a gain since it is receiving cash flows at a higher price.

Similarly, the airline may wish to access additional fuel at a fixed price over a specific future time horizon for business reasons, such as a possible expansion into new routes. Again, it can enter into an option contract with a third party, whereby it has a right to purchase fuel in the future without having to take pricing risk or risk supply disruptions. The airline pays its counterparty a premium for this privilege, and the counterparty accepts the possibility of a gain or loss depending on price movements. In short, both sides are transacting with each other to either make or save money.

The same principle extends across all commodities and participants, including individuals, companies, governments, and financial institutions. In practice, the trades are more complex. Investors may wish to sell contracts to other participants rather than hold them until maturity and may also want to blend different contracts to execute trading strategies. For example, an oil trader might buy and sell contracts simultaneously at two different locations or maturities to take advantage of pricing discrepancies and lock in a guaranteed profit. This is an illustration of the well-known concept of *arbitrage*.

KEY CHARACTERISTICS

As noted, futures and options represent the most popular way of investing in commodities for many people. It is worth delving into some of the key characteristics.

A futures contract, simply put, is an agreement to buy or sell in the future a specific quantity of a commodity at a specific price. As we have noted, the macroeconomic nature of the commodities market suggests a higher level of volatility in the commodities space than in other markets such as bonds and equities. Additionally, the depth of the hedging market means that prices can be inferred and set many years out into the future if needed.

The underlying asset for commodity futures can be any of the agricultural, metal, and energy products, as long as they are traded on an exchange. Futures can also be based on any commodity traded over the counter with another participant who can theoretically make physical delivery. In this case, however, the contract is known as a forward to differentiate it from futures traded on exchanges. For the rest of this chapter, we will consider futures contracts only, partly because of the standardization that makes them the dominant mode of investor expression, and partly because the base mechanics are identical for forwards. As noted earlier, the futures contract may be specific to a particular exchange or traded on multiple exchanges, depending on the commodity in question.

Futures market participants fall into two camps. First, there are commercial or institutional users of commodities that need to hedge their exposure to future price volatility. They take positions in contracts to reduce the risk of financial loss from unexpected changes in prices; profiting directly from the futures contract (or option) is not a primary consideration. Second, there are other participants, typically individuals, financial institutions, and investment firms that act as speculators. They hope to profit from changes in the price of the commodity in the future or to harvest premiums (in the case of options). Their expectations are typically set by analysis, which may be macroeconomic in nature (e.g., geopolitics or supply-and-demand dynamics) or systemic (e.g., seasonality patterns or observed aberrations). Speculators almost never take physical delivery of the commodity under consideration and typically tend to close out their positions before the contract expires or becomes due.

Futures contracts trade in standardized amounts. We have noted in Tables 31.1, 31.2, and 31.3 the typical trading units for specific exchanges. For example, crude oil is traded in increments of 1000 barrels while cocoa is traded in units of 10 tons. This effectively captures how much of the underlying asset the contract represents and is part of the standardization that we discussed earlier. Participants always know in advance how much of a commodity each contract represents. If they wish to buy more, they simply purchase multiple contracts. Buying less is problematic as the contract represents a minimum size. However, the large increase in the number of individual traders in the marketplace has meant that many exchanges have now begun to introduce smaller contracts.

In Table 31.5, we outline an example of a simplified crude oil futures contract at the CME.

Futures contracts also contain large amounts of leverage, which encourages speculation and thereby aids liquidity. Because a futures contract does not need to be funded in full, market participants can multiply their stake in the trade. A buyer or seller of a contract is required to put up a minimum deposit (typically set by exchange rules, the broker, or a regulator). As the value of the contract changes, the amount of money on deposit is continually adjusted (often on a real-time basis) to reflect the current value of the contract. As the value of the contract rises, money is deposited in the participant's account and may be withdrawn as profit. As the value drops, however, money is deducted from the account and credited to the other side. If the contract value falls below the minimum deposit required, then the participant is required to add more money to the account to keep the contract open. This is known as a margin call.

Margins tend to be small, often only a few percent. Therefore, small changes in price can rapidly translate into significant gains or losses on the amount deposited. This is illustrative of the power of leverage. The ability to leverage trades and the inherent price volatility of many commodities, coupled with the significant liquidity provided by trading on an exchange, explains why speculators are drawn to the commodity market.

In the case of options on futures contracts, the loss is limited to the premium paid (if the participant is buying an option) as the participant can choose whether to enter the contract in the future. However, there is still significant leverage as the price of the option will evolve depending on movements in the underlying commodity and contract as well as the time remaining to the expiration of the option.

Contango and Backwardation

Contango and backwardation, typical in nature, are two noted features and an important aspect of commodities futures to touch on.

All futures contracts have an expiration date and therefore need to be rolled on a regular basis. For many contracts, the expiration is at the end of every month. The result is a list of future prices over time for any given commodity. These indicate participants' expectations about the future price trajectory of a given commodity such as crude oil. Similar to how interest rate curves can be plotted, one can map out prices for futures contracts to derive an oil curve.

This is of vital importance to both hedgers and speculators. Analyzing where the future price of a commodity is heading will drive key decisions for both. The futures price may be either higher or lower than the spot price (i.e., the expected price today). When the spot price is higher than the futures price at the expected maturity, the market is said to be in backwardation and one would expect the price to rise as we approach the future delivery date. In other words, the prices converge and investors with a long position would expect to make a profit. Traders in contrast are betting that the commodity will fall in value over time.

In contrast, if the spot price is lower than the futures price, the market is said to be in *contango*. In contango, these prices reflect the fact that there is likely a cost of carry

TABLE 31.5 Standardized Terms for an Example Crude Oil Futures Contract at the CME

Contract Unit	1000 barrels
Price Quotation	U.S. dollars and cents per barrel
Trading Hours	CME Globex: Sunday–Friday 6:00 p.m.–5:00 p.m. (5:00 p.m.–4:00 p.m. Chicago Time/CT) with a 60-minute break each day beginning at 5:00 p.m. (4:00 p.m. CT)
Minimum Price Fluctuation	$0.01per barrel
Product Code	CME Globex: CL
Listed Contracts	Crude oil futures are listed nine years forward using the following listing schedule: consecutive months are listed for the current year and the next five years; in addition, the June and December contract months are listed beyond the sixth year. Additional months will be added on an annual basis after the December contract expires, so that an additional June and December contract would be added nine years forward, and the consecutive months in the sixth calendar year will be filled in.
Settlement Method	Deliverable
Termination of Trading	Trading in the current delivery month shall cease on the third business day prior to the twenty-fifth calendar day of the month preceding the delivery month. If the twenty-fifth calendar day of the month is a non-business day, trading shall cease on the third business day prior to the last business day preceding the twenty-fifth calendar day. In the event that the official Exchange holiday schedule changes subsequent to the listing of Crude Oil futures, the originally listed expiration date shall remain in effect. In the event that the originally listed expiration day is declared a holiday, expiration will move to the business day immediately prior.
Trade at Marker or Trade at Settlement Rules	Trading at settlement is available for spot (except on the last trading day), 2nd, 3rd, and 4th months and subject to the existing TAS rules. Trading in all TAS products will cease daily at 2:30 p.m. Eastern Time. The TAS products will trade off of a "Base Price" of 0 to create a differential (plus or minus 10 ticks) versus settlement in the underlying product on a 1-to-1 basis. A trade done at the Base Price of 0 will correspond to a "traditional" TAS trade that will clear exactly at the final settlement price of the day.
Settlement Procedures	Crude Oil futures settlement procedures
Position Limits	NYMEX position limits
Block Minimum	Block minimum thresholds
Delivery Procedure	Delivery shall be made free-on-board (FOB) at any pipeline or storage facility in Cushing, Oklahoma, with pipeline access to Enterprise, Cushing storage or Enbridge, Cushing storage. Delivery shall be made in accordance with all applicable federal executive orders and all applicable federal, state, and local laws and regulations.

TABLE 31.5 *(Continued)*

Delivery Procedure *(continued)*	At buyer's option, delivery shall be made by any of the following methods: (1) by interfacility transfer (pumpover) into a designated pipeline or storage facility with access to seller's incoming pipeline or storage facility; (2) by inline (or in-system) transfer, or book-out of title to the buyer; or (3) if the seller agrees to such transfer and if the facility used by the seller allows for such transfer, without physical movement of product, by in-tank transfer of title to the buyer.
Delivery Period	(A) Delivery shall take place no earlier than the first calendar day of the delivery month and no later than the last calendar day of the delivery month.
	(B) It is the short's obligation to ensure that its crude oil receipts, including each specific foreign crude oil stream, if applicable, are available to begin flowing ratably in Cushing, Oklahoma, by the first day of the delivery month, in accord with generally accepted pipeline scheduling practices.
	(C) Transfer of title—The seller shall give the buyer pipeline ticket, any other quantitative certificates, and all appropriate documents upon receipt of payment.
	The seller shall provide preliminary confirmation of title transfer at the time of delivery by telex or other appropriate form of documentation.

associated with the commodity. For example, anyone holding gold today would have to pay storage costs, perhaps insurance, and would forgo interest on the money invested if it had been held as cash. Therefore, people are willing to pay more for the commodity in the future. For a trader, however, contango expresses the view that the market expects the price of the futures contract to increase into the future.

Commodity markets can sometimes change in nature between the two, catching investors unaware. A particularly notable example was the $1.3 billion loss incurred by the German industrial conglomerate Metallgesellschaft in 1993. The management had put in place a flawed hedging strategy that profited from backwardation markets. However, a fall in spot prices forced it to close out contracts at a loss. Subsequently, a shift to contango markets meant that the spot price rose over time, forcing the company to incur even larger losses as it covered its commitments.

INVESTMENT VEHICLES

Given the scope for speculation and the potential for significant profits, it is not surprising that there are a range of investment strategies and vehicles out there for investors. Many fortunes have been built on the back of commodities speculation, such as the Rothschilds, Andrew Carnegie, Cargill, and Glencore—all by employing a range of strategies from owning physical commodities to building companies around commodities trading. Their varying fortunes also bear testament to the volatility of these assets.

More recently, over the last couple of decades, commodities have also found a place in many portfolios across both institutional investors (such as pension funds and endowments) as well as individuals for their diversification benefits. Commodities typically have low to zero correlations with other financial markets such as bonds and equities. Indeed, some commodities such as gold actually boom in times of distress, often giving them a negative correlation. Including commodities in a portfolio, therefore, may reduce overall volatility as well as introduce macro hedges within a multi-asset allocation that protect the portfolio in tail events.

Even where people act like speculators, many lack the time, resources, or expertise to directly trade instruments such as futures, acquire mining assets, invest in commodity-linked equities, or the like. Therefore, investment vehicles may provide them with the ability to access specific areas of interest within the commodity complex through leveraging off the expertise of others.

Here we briefly cover some of the chief ways in which investors access exposure to commodities.

Indices

For those looking for broad exposure to commodities to diversify a portfolio, or to gain exposure to some aggregate of global or population growth, indices represent an ideal starting point. They allow investors, for example, to track a basket of commodities over time, focus on specific subsectors (i.e., agricultural commodities), or even focus on individual commodities such as gold.

As with the commodities they track, indices must also be:

- *Tradable:* The commodities must be traded on a designated exchange and have a futures contract.
- *Deliverable:* The underlying commodity for the contracts that go into the index must be able to be delivered if needed.
- *Liquid:* The market for the underlying commodity must be liquid enough to allow investors to move in and out of their positions freely without any liquidity constraints.

There are a number of commodity indices that can be accessed in an investable manner. Notable examples include the S&P Goldman Sachs Commodity Index (S&P GSCI), the Reuters/Jefferies Commodity Research Bureau Index (CRB), and the Dow Jones AIG Commodities Index (DJ/AIGCI). These also have sub-indices that allow investors to track or invest in particular segments such as energy.

The indices all differ in terms of their composition, structure, and methodology. It is important to appreciate the differences between these, especially if investors want to truly understand the commodities exposure they are taking on. For example, the GSCI chooses commodities based on their production value globally while the CRB adopts a tiered methodology, which is part production value weighted and part fixed weights. Still others might choose other metrics such as liquidity. All of these impact the makeup and can tilt the exposure toward energy or other areas. It should also be noted that all indices are representational. In other words, they do not capture all commodities but rather a representative number that should give insights into the future behavior and price movements of the broader commodities universe.

There are also some nuances that bear careful investigation, as they can materially impact investment outcomes. For example, the purpose of any index is merely to track commodity behavior and not take actual delivery. Therefore, the futures contracts tracked need to be rolled over from one month to the next. This rolling process will be impacted by backwardation and contango, and also will provide a rolling yield due to the price differential between one contract and the next. Another example is rebalancing. How often does the index rebalance its components and what's the methodology around this?

The indices sometimes operate as direct futures contracts or may be accessed through other vehicles such as index funds and ETFs.

ETFs and ETNs

Closely related to the above are exchange-traded funds (ETFs) and exchange-traded notes (ETNs). These are liquid instruments that trade like stocks and allow investors to participate in commodity price changes—both on an aggregate basis as well as for individual commodities—on a real-time basis without the necessity of directly investing in the physical commodity or in futures contracts.

Broadly speaking there are two types of commodity ETFs:

1. *Physically backed ETFs:* These hold the commodity directly in physical form, for example, some gold ETFs. They are almost always commodity specific rather than being a basket for ease of execution and storage. They are also biased toward precious metals, as they are typically held by investors who are looking for tangible and secure stores of value and wealth.
2. *Futures ETFs:* These are ETFs comprised of futures contracts. These can be both index-based and individual commodities. Because of their derivative nature, they are very wide-ranging and can represent virtually anything that is traded on an exchange.

ETNs are a new area of growth in this space. They are senior unsecured debt that mimics the price behavior of a particular commodity or commodity index. They are backed by the issuing bank and carry added credit risk. They can also embed leverage, thereby giving less risk-averse investors enhanced exposure to price fluctuations.

Both ETFs and ETNs are popular due to the liquidity, low fees, and low tracking error of the underlying commodity or basket.

Mutual Funds

Mutual funds are another popular way of investing in commodities and offer a diverse range of strategies and exposures. There are several sorts:

- *Index funds:* Some mutual funds invest in the direct commodity or track an index through futures contracts and other derivative investments. They tend to be long-only vehicles, that is, they only allow investors to express bullish views on a commodity or basket of commodities. It should be noted that the tracking is not perfect due to the inability to perfectly replicate the underlying commodity in most cases.
- *Mining and energy funds:* These funds invest in the equities of companies that are linked to commodities, such as miners and oil producers. In some cases they may also invest in other companies in the supply chain such as oil services providers and refiners. The funds typically will have biases in terms of commodities segment (e.g., mining), market capitalization (e.g., large caps, junior miners), and geographies (e.g., North America). It should be noted that these funds benefit typically from a leveraged exposure to the commodity, as equities are very sensitive to commodity prices and sentiment. However, they also introduce additional complexities such as idiosyncratic company risks, stock market fluctuations, and sentiment and business risks (e.g., too much debt)—all of which mean that the investor is not exposed to the pure commodity alone.

Managed Futures

Many commodity vehicles fall into the managed futures space. These are collective investment vehicles, which aggregate money from investors and then invest into commodity linked derivatives. These are predominantly futures, hence the name. The investments may be done through a pooled vehicle (i.e., a fund), or through individual managed accounts so that client monies are kept segregated. Many can also tailor their leverage by running different margin levels or adding additional leverage through their brokers to enhance returns.

Managed futures funds are linked to pure commodities and not to some related equity. They will also typically look to identify technical patterns of behavior that can then be used to predict future price moves or lock in more secure gains. Trading may be discretionary, in that it is directed by the expert judgment of the fund manager, or it may be systematic, in that it is automated, reliant on identifying trends through the analysis of large amounts of data and generally divorced from direct human intervention. The sheer amount of data that needs to be digested and analyzed means that systematic managers tend to dominate.

There are two types of managed futures funds:

1. *Commodity pool operator (CPO):* This is a vehicle, typically a limited partnership, that gathers money in a common pool to invest in commodity-linked futures and

options. These typically are regulated by the Commodity Futures Trading Commission (CFTC) and the National Futures Association (NFA) but may be exempt if they are only open to registered securities professionals and accredited investors (typically high-net-worth individuals or institutions that are perceived to have base-level understanding of risk). A CPO may run its own pool or retain a commodity trading advisor (CTA) to advise on transactions.

2. *Commodity trading advisor (CTA):* This is a regulated firm that is retained by funds and clients to advise on and trade futures contracts, options, and other derivatives related to the commodities space. They are regulated by the CFTC and NFA, and have a higher bar of regulation. The only limited exemption in the United States is if they are advising 15 investors or less, where the requirement is reduced to simply registering with the NFA. CTAs cannot manage funds for multiple investors in one account; hence the typical structure for funds is to have a CPO advised by a CTA.

It should be noted that managed futures funds often overlap with hedge funds—alternative investment vehicles that use sophisticated trading strategies including leverage, trading systems, and structured trades to isolate arbitrages and with the ability to go both long and short investments. Many, however, still choose to view CTAs as a distinct category due to their focus on just commodities. Managers typically trade the whole basket of tradeable commodity contracts or a defined subset, such as agricultural commodities.

The popularity of CTAs has grown in the last two decades as a source of uncorrelated returns for sophisticated investors and institutions. Their ability to go both long and short commodities means that they can capture returns in a down market as well as an up market. The generally larger minimum allocations, typically at least six figures and more often $1 million and above, mean that these strategies are typically available only to wealthier investors. They also embed higher levels of manager risk as the returns are derived ultimately from the manager's understanding of the commodities markets they trade or their ability to design models that can identify sustainable and repeatable patterns of profitable behavior.

Commodity Master Limited Partnerships

Master limited partnerships (MLPs) are a subset of the equity universe and worth a brief mention. They are publicly traded and therefore have some measure of liquidity. At the same time, the underlying is a partnership, conferring tax benefits and a focused niche strategy. Most MLPs are effectively a play on commodity infrastructure, with the underlying assets including oil and gas pipelines and storage facilities.

This has numerous advantages and appeals for investors. MLPs are income producing. This is of great interest to many investors and the underlying infrastructure is perceived as a more stable asset, as typically the cash flows produced are only weakly linked to the commodity's price. Moreover, the MLP is required to distribute 90% of its underlying cash flows to its investors, who then get the tax benefit of no corporation tax, resulting in an enhanced yield for investors, similar to a real estate investment trust (REIT).

Private Equity Funds

Given the huge surge in commodity prices this century and the strong interest in commodities as a way of playing key themes such as globalization and the rise of China, there has been a strong growth in the last decade in private equity funds that focus on the commodities space. These are private vehicles, typically structured as a limited partnership overseen by a general managing partnership that makes all investment decisions. They are intended to be concentrated long-term vehicles with the most common term being of the order of 8–10 years. They are also closed-ended, which means that all the money is raised at a single point in time and investors thereafter cannot redeem till the end of the partnership's life. Furthermore, they are highly concentrated, typically running portfolios of 10–15 positions.

Investors look to these structures when seeking exposure to commodities that are not so easily traded and that are increasing in demand, such as rare earths, which are used in many technological and defense applications; and lithium, which is key to the development of fuel cells for electric cars. They may also seek to enhance their exposure to more mainstream commodities such as oil or agriculture by using these vehicles to invest in companies that are poised for strong growth or that can be restructured to improve the returns to shareholders. The key here is the leveraged return that owning the commodity producer gives the investor, as opposed to owning the commodity directly. Thus, the exposure is never garnered through the physical commodity but rather proxied through producers, refiners, and others in the supply chain. The exposure may be in the form of equity investments into the entities or occasionally private debt issuance to the same.

Given the tight focus, private equity funds tend to follow niche strategies. They will focus on oil and gas, mining, exploration, agricultural produce, and so on. Thus, for example, they may target investments in Africa in a subset of the commodities universe, say precious metals, thereby having both a geographical and commodity focus. The strategy may be further refined to focus just on early stage companies that are exploring new deposits, for example.

Private equity funds in the commodities space will have carefully articulated investment themes and rely heavily on fundamental research as a way of predicting future behavior. The long-term horizon means that they are less sensitive to price fluctuations as they are investing and harvesting over a period of five years and more. Thus, their returns are predicated more on the future path of demand and growth over the long-term, rather than day to day or month to month. Many funds will also have significant operational expertise on board in actual mining or running commodity companies, as returns are generated by working intensively with portfolio companies to achieve growth, find new deposits, develop new clients, and so forth. Risk management is another key area of focus, as many of these funds look to run active hedging programs of their own or mitigate other key risks such as geopolitics through the use of financial instruments or careful analysis and business planning. In today's environment of commodities distress, several are now turning to finding distressed companies that are overleveraged or unable to get financing to effectively buy proxy exposure to commodities at deeply discounted prices.

FUTURE TRENDS

The future of commodities—like any financial market—is not set in stone. First, there is a continual cycle of gain and loss, similar to the business cycle of an economy. In commodities, however, the cycle is much more pronounced due to the high price volatility and speculation on demand and supply. Consequently, as a sector, commodity companies are also much more prone to booms and busts. Financial history is replete with famous financial crises that were driven by commodities. For example, the infamous Tulip-mania in 17th-century Holland was driven by a seemingly insatiable demand for tulips from wealthy investors, which soon found a willing audience of speculators who were willing to trade on his "new commodity" and its demand. The result was a huge boom. Over a three-month period from November 1636 to February 1637, prices rose by a factor of 20 times, with some rare tulip bulbs changing hands for the price of a small house. As the speculative bubble burst, however, prices began to fall and within another three months had returned to their previous levels and lower as demand dried up. Many fortunes were made and many fortunes were also lost.

Second, as demonstrated by tulips and in the last couple of centuries by oil, lithium, and platinum, there are new commodities constantly emerging. As long a good can be produced or sourced, has demand, and obeys the key rules outlined earlier of tradability, liquidity, and delivery, it is a commodity. The latest ones to emerge are renewable energy and electricity futures.

There is a continual cycle of boom, bust, and renewal. And given their macrosensitivity, commodities are uniquely affected by larger trends emerging in the world. We conclude this chapter by noting some of the key trends and dynamics emerging in the space today that bear watching.

BOOM TO BUST AND BACK AGAIN?

The great elephant in the commodities room is China. Over the last two decades, commodities and commodity companies were on a tearaway thanks to the seemingly endless demand from China for all sorts of natural resources. Between 1991 and 2011, China's average annual GDP growth was a whopping 10.5% per annum. The enormous boom fueled an orgy of speculation, investment, and exploration for new resources. This, more than anything else, was responsible for the growth in popularity of commodities and their move into the mainstream as part of the strategic asset allocation for many institutional investors and individuals.

The train began to slow down in 2012 and came to a crashing halt in 2015. China's explosive growth came under growing strain as the vast tracts of debt underpinning all of its development came under pressure. Growth had already started to weaken from 2012 onward, dropping below 8%, but in 2015, it fell below the psychologically important level of 7%.

At the same time, the country has struggled to reorient its economy toward consumption. Chinese consumers are still very much a nation of savers and the lack of a social security framework means that many are unwilling to save less and spend more. The result has been a slowdown in Chinese growth as the government debates how best to reignite the economy as well as manage the debt overhang. In this environment, commodities demand dried up, resulting in steep falls for many.

The stress has been exacerbated by the fact that many commodity companies invested heavily in new mines, projects, capacity, and exploration in anticipation of significant future demand. In the absence of demand and the slowdown in global growth caused by the Great Recession of 2007–09, many have had to write down significant investments, dispose of assets at poor valuations and often with losses on the investment made to date, and deal with an overleveraged balance sheet (thanks to the large amounts of debt taken on to fund these investments). As an example, Glencore—one of the largest commodity conglomerates in the world—has seen its share price fall by over 50% compared to five years ago and by over a third since the beginning of 2015. The company has had to make significant disposals since as it tackles a debt pile estimated at $30 billion.

The fallout has hit many investors hard and led to a number of funds across the board closing down, as they proved unable to cope with losses and the subsequent investor redemptions. For example, crude oil was at $93.96 per barrel at the start of 2014. It rose to over $107 a barrel at the end of June, only to begin a decline that accelerated into 2015. Today, it sits at a mere $41.29 – a decrease of 56% since January 2014. The same pattern is repeated in many other commodities.

The future is uncertain but will depend greatly on the prospects for global growth. Investors will be looking to other countries such as India and the United States, where growth has picked up again, to lead a resurgence. At the same time, supply is excessive for many commodities, leading to a glut that continues to hold down prices. It is a familiar cycle to seasoned investors, and the bravest of them will likely be looking to pick up bargains at today's prices in preparation for the next upswing.

NEW COMMODITIES

Finally, in closure, it is worth touching on some of the new commodities emerging today. Much of our previous discussion—though applicable to all commodities—has focused on established commodities such as metals, crude oil, and so on.

However, the major trend that is reshaping the composition of the commodities universe today and leading to the next generation of hopefuls is climate change. It is now an established fact that temperatures globally have been rising over the course of human history and accelerated in the last century. The Intergovernmental Panel on Climate Change (IPCC)—an international body overseen by the United Nations and tasked with analyzing the socioeconomic impact of climate change—concluded that the likelihood of human influence being the dominant cause of global warming between 1951 and 2010 was somewhere between 95% and 100%. It predicted that in the absence of new policies to mitigate climate change, its projections indicated an increase in global mean temperature of 3.7 to 4.8°C by the year 2100. The impact of such an increase would be widespread environmental devastation and likely impossible to truly imagine.

Consequently, there has been an enormous shift toward developing renewables as well as other avenues such as fuel cells and hydrogen as alternative energy sources. Though these are still some way off in replacing our reliance on crude oil and natural gas, there are increasingly large amounts of funding from both the public and private sectors going into these areas. The most notable example in recent years has been the ubiquitous spread of wind parks across the world and the meteoric rise of Tesla as the future Ford of the electric car world.

But as with much of human history, for these new sources of energy to truly succeed and develop to full potential, a deep financial ecosystem will need to spring up around them that can help manage pricing volatility and enable companies to make the sustainable profits needed to fund continued investment. That points inevitably toward new commodity markets, new futures contracts, and new players.

Some of this has already begun to occur. For example, lithium has become a highly prized commodity in recent years as one of the key ingredients in the longer-lived and more powerful batteries and fuel cells increasingly used in technology and electric cars. Numerous commodity companies have sprung up to explore for new deposits and several commodity-focused private equity funds have begun to explore the space. We have already talked about the growing market in solar power and wind power, both accessible to investors through mutual funds and private equity funds.

In recent years, a burgeoning market has grown in electricity futures, possibly one of the purest expressions of what a commodity can be. In today's markets, power generators sell electricity into the market and retailers buy in aggregate from the market. There is something—electricity—that is physically delivered. The natural volatility of supply and demand plays out in the need for electricity during peak surges (e.g., during key sporting events) and lulls (say in the very early hours of the morning). Therefore, there is something that speculators can trade, deliver, and create a secondary market for—all the characteristics of a commodity. For suppliers and aggregators, the supply-and-demand volatility translates into a pricing volatility that needs to be managed carefully if profit margins and cash flows are not to be impaired. In other words, there is a need to hedge.

Most notably, we are also seeing the advent of new exchanges. The European Climate Exchange (along with others around the world), for example, is pioneering a market based around the trading of futures contracts where the underlying commodity is carbon emissions (calculated in tonnes of carbon dioxide equivalent). In other words, companies can theoretically trade environmental good behavior. A company with higher emissions of carbon dioxide can purchase the right to emit more from another participant that has fewer emissions and therefore, has environmental goodwill to trade. Overall, the goal is to constrain carbon emissions across the economy and the globe as a whole to minimize the impact of climate change. It is a nascent market but its development will be exciting to chart.

Commodities have been around since the dawn of human history and they will be around till the end. The instruments may change and the indices may evolve, but the rationale and the execution remain unchanged. We await the next chapter in this journey.

CHAPTER 32

Currency

Simon Derrick

THE EMERGENCE OF A FOREIGN EXCHANGE MARKET

The reemergence of currency as a medium for facilitating business can be traced back to Frisian and Anglo Saxon traders from around 700 CE. Small, thick silver coins (deniers) were minted on both sides of the North Sea from around this time and have been found scattered along the Frankish trade routes into Frisia.[1] However, even then it was clear that the money produced in different regions would also have different values. In Aquitaine, for example, Frisian coins were much preferred to the debased money coming from what is now France.[2] By the reign of England's Henry VII (1457–1509) the need for traders to exchange one currency for another had grown so strong that a currency exchange was established within Leadenhall market in London. Indeed, Henry VII is recorded as having speculated on the European currency markets himself, using his favored broker, the Bolognese financier Lodovico della Fava, to carry out the trades.[3]

The need to exchange one currency for another is therefore almost as old as the emergence of money as a medium for trade. However, in order to exchange one currency for another there needs to be a price at which the deal can be fixed. This is the *exchange rate*.

THE MECHANISM

Although an exchange rate can in some instances be for a transaction that settles on the same day, within the modern currency markets the normal convention is that the deal will settle in two banking days in order to allow for the smooth processing of the trade. This agreement to exchange the currencies at an agreed price as soon as is practical (on the spot) is known as a *spot transaction* or (in the terminology of the currency markets) *spot*.

---

[1] Michael Pye, *The Edge of the World* (New York: Pegasus Books, 2014), p 57.
[2] Ibid.
[3] Thomas Penn, *Winter King: The Dawn of Tudor England* (New York: Simon & Schuster, 2012), p. 216.

It may be the case that an investor does not wish to buy or sell one currency outright against another but, instead, simply wants to borrow one currency against another over a specific period of time. There are many reasons why this might be the case. One of the most common is that the investor wants to buy a local security (for example, a share in a company) but doesn't want to be exposed to fluctuations in the value of the underlying currency. The mechanism for this is a foreign exchange swap. In a swap the participants agree to exchange currencies on the start date of the transaction at an agreed price (normally the spot price at the time) and then swap them back at the end of the agreed period at a price that has been adjusted to take into account the relative interest rates of the two currencies in question.

It may also be the case that a company does wish to purchase (or sell) a specific currency but does not need the money immediately. It could be, for example, that an exporter knows that it will receive a known payment in a foreign currency in three months but wishes to fix the price now in order to remove any uncertainty. This is achieved by simply combining a spot transaction together with a foreign exchange swap to create what is known as a *forward transaction*.

WHO USES THE FOREIGN EXCHANGE MARKET?

Almost everyone will need to buy or sell a foreign currency at some point in their lives, even if it is just to have some spending money while on a vacation abroad. Any company that exports goods or services will also need to be able to convert their earnings from overseas back into their home currency while those firms that import, for example, commodities from overseas will need to buy foreign currency in order to be able to pay for what they have bought. Governments and supranational organizations may also regularly need to use the foreign exchange markets in order to be able to make aid payments or make contributions to other organizations.

Since the late 1980s investment firms have become increasingly important players in the foreign exchange markets as they have looked to diversify their investment portfolios internationally. These investments can stretch from the largest markets (such as Japan) to some of the newest (in Africa, for example). These have been joined in recent years by the managers of the foreign exchange reserves of a wide number of nations (reflecting the phenomenal growth in currency reserves since 2002).

WHAT ARE THE MAIN CURRENCIES?

Although a few countries (e.g., Panama) simply use another nation's currency instead of having their own, this brings with it some unique problems. In particular, it means that the local authorities have no control over the setting of official interest rates as this will effectively be done by the central bank of the nation issuing the currency. As a result the government could, for example, find itself having to cope with higher interest rates at a time the nation may be facing a recession. Therefore, most nations prefer to have their own currency.

There is one major exception to this. At the beginning of 1999, 11 members of the European Union adopted the euro as their official currency. Since then a further 8 members of the European Union have joined the currency (it is the second most widely traded currency in the world). The European Central Bank (ECB), which is governed by a president and a board of the heads of national central banks, sets the monetary policy of the area. However, significant problems have emerged in the euro area is recent years. In particular it has become apparent that a one-size-fits-all monetary policy can lead to significant economic imbalances in the absence of a region-wide fiscal policy to act as a counterbalance. As a result a number of nations experienced significant booms (often in the housing market) in the early years of this century followed very rapidly by crippling busts.

The most widely traded currency in the world (according the Bank of International Settlements April 2013 triennial central bank survey) is the U.S. dollar. Other widely traded national currencies include the Japanese yen, the UK's pound, the Australian dollar, Swiss franc, Canadian dollar, Mexican peso, Chinese yuan, and New Zealand dollar. Other significantly traded national currencies include the Swedish krona, Russian rouble, Hong Kong dollar, Norwegian krone, Singapore dollar, Turkish lira, South Korean won, South African rand, Brazilian real, and Indian rupee.

EXCHANGE RATE REGIMES

There have been over time (and still remain) different types of regimes under which the exchange rates are managed. Following a meeting in Bretton Woods, New Hampshire, in 1944 a system sometimes described as a "gold exchange standard" was established that became operational in 1945. The chief feature of the system was an obligation for each country to maintain its exchange rate within a defined band (either plus or minus 1%) against the U.S. dollar. Should the currency move outside this band, then members were expected to take appropriate action either by moving official interest rates or by intervening directly in the currency markets to buy or sell. Meanwhile the United States agreed to link the dollar to gold at the rate of $35 an ounce. However, this system began to come under increasing pressure in the second half of the 1960s as high fiscal spending by the U.S. administration took its toll on confidence. With investors buying increasing amounts of gold at the fixed price on offer it was only a matter of time before the system collapsed. This came in August 1971 when President Nixon announced (without having consulted with other members of the international monetary system) that the United States had "closed the gold window." This meant that gold could no longer be bought at a fixed price of $35 per ounce but, instead, at a rate determined on the open market. Despite further attempts to redesign the exchange rate system (in particular the Smithsonian Agreement of December 1971) the writing was on the wall for the Bretton Woods system. After a 10% devaluation of the U.S. dollar in February 1973, Japan along with members of the European Economic Community decided to allow their currencies to *free float*. This meant that their value was set on the open market with prices being driven by shifting supply and demand.

There have been subsequent attempts to manage groups of currencies within defined price ranges (or bands), most notably the European Exchange Rate Mechanism. For such a system to work each nation must essentially keep their official interest rates at the same level. If not, investors will simply move all their money to the nation with the highest interest rates, leaving all the other members of the system having to struggle as their local economy collapses. However, varying economic circumstances over time typically mean that at some point one member or another of the system will need to shift interest rates relative to its neighbors. Once it becomes apparent that this is the case, then money will begin to flow either in or out of the currency (dependent on whether the market believes interest rates are going up or down), forcing the local authorities either to defend their currency or to step aside and allow the currency to break outside of the band. These systems have rarely fared well.

■ ■ ■

Attempts either to keep currencies at a pegged exchange rate against another currency (a fixed exchange rate system) or to heavily manage their value (dirty floats) have also created their fair share of problems over time. One of the key issues for many of the nations impacted by the Asian crisis during 1997 and 1998 was that they found themselves running critically low of FX reserves with which to protect their currencies, forcing them instead to turn to the IMF for help. As a result these nations became keen to keep their currencies competitive in order to rebuild their economies through export growth as well as to build sufficiently large FX reserves to provide a buffer against any future crisis.

By the early part of the next decade the United States had become increasingly critical of Chinese and Japanese currency policies, seeing them as being deliberately designed to keep their currencies artificially weak in order to gain a mercantile advantage. While U.S. officials would probably deny they decided to fight fire with fire, to some outside observers it appeared that at some point in 2001–2002 they adopted a policy of benign neglect toward the U.S. dollar, driven by increasingly low interest rates (relative to inflation). It was the response of the emerging-market nations to this weakening of the U.S. dollar, however, that mattered the most over the long term. In particular, the wave of money coming out of the United States presented the opportunity they were looking for to rapidly build their reserves in order to ensure that they need never find themselves again in the situation they were in during the late 1990s. Moreover, while Asia might have been where the conflict reignited, the post–2001 boom in currency reserves was not limited to the region. Across the emerging and developing world FX reserves grew from $801 billion at the end of 2001[4] to stand at $5.373 trillion by the end of 2009 (i.e., just

---

[4] According to the IMF's "Currency Composition of Official Foreign Exchange Reserves" (COFER) data.

before the start of the Eurozone crisis). By the summer of 2014 this number had expanded further to reach just over $8 trillion.

Three main problems presented themselves to these nations. The first was that the inflows of "hot money" were so substantial and so rapid that the local authorities often struggled to stop their currencies appreciating to what they considered uncompetitive levels (particularly against their regional competitors). As just one example of how overwhelming (and indiscriminate) these flows could be, the Bank of Thailand found itself having to intervene in its local currency markets in late October 2006 in order to slow the appreciation of the Thai baht. What was extraordinary about this was that it came just over a month after a coup d'état had led the bank to temporarily suspend trading in the currency for fear of potential outflows.

The second problem was that the outflows, when they came, could be equally brutal. In the latter stages of 2014 the Central Bank of Russia found itself trying to defend the ruble's managed exchange rate system in the face of significant outflows as the price of oil (one of its major export commodities) collapsed. Having seen its gold and FX reserves fall by $83 billion since the start of that year (around a 16% decline) the central bank announced that the ruble would float freely (adding in a statement that it would intervene in the FX market at any moment with sufficient volumes to cut speculative demand).

The third problem facing these nations was what to do with the foreign exchange reserves they had accumulated. This was a particular problem for China, which by late 2013 had seen the value of its reserves soar to close to $4 trillion. By October of that year it was clear that the weight of opinion in China was moving toward adopting a policy that allowed it to stop accumulating fresh foreign exchange reserves. In an opinion piece for the *Financial Times*, Professor David Li, a former policy advisor to the People's Bank of China (PBoC) and a prominent economist at Tsinghua University, questioned China's levels of exposure to the U.S. Treasury market (around $1.28 trillion at the time) and the argument that this was because of a lack of alternative investments. He argued instead that the State Administration for Foreign Exchange (SAFE) should invest in the shares of multinationals operating in the Chinese market, increase the holdings of all non-U.S. sovereign bonds rated higher than double-A-plus, as well as buying the shares of public utility companies in mature market economies. Professor Li added that the only explanation of why China had yet to reduce its exposure came down to China's relationship with the United States, noting that the Treasury holding represented "both a hostage scenario and a bonding instrument for the two largest economies in the world." He concluded by saying: "We do not know how long long-term political logic can prevail over the economic rationale."[5]

The policy shift itself came in November 2013 at the Third Plenum (the Communist Party's once-a-decade economic planning forum). Summarizing the forum, the *Wall Street Journal* stated on November 13, 2013, that China would relax investment controls

---

[5]David Li, "Beijing Should Cut Back Its Lending to Washington," *Financial Times*, October 15, 2013.

and allow the market to play a "decisive" role in allocating resources. Two days later the Xinhua News Agency stated specifically that the acceleration of Chinese renminbi convertibility and liberalization of interest rates were among the key reform proposals decided on (although it also noted that the party said it planned to achieve these targets by 2020).

If there were any doubts about China's view on continued reserve accumulation, these were dispelled by the comments on November 21, 2013, by Yi Gang, deputy governor of PBoC and head of SAFE. He stated that while ample foreign reserves helped China defend against the impact from external speculation, the marginal costs of accumulating foreign reserve had now exceeded the marginal gains, which was therefore not good for China's development. This point was expanded upon on June 12, 2014, when Huang Guobo (the chief economist of SAFE), said in a webcast: "The excessively large foreign exchange reserves increase domestic money supply and create potential domestic inflation pressures. They also put more pressure on the central bank to raise reserve requirement ratios and sterilize (inflows)." He added that foreign currency reserves accounted for more than 80% of the central bank's assets, leading to a mismatch between its assets and liabilities, fueling foreign exchange risks.

■ ■ ■

Some exchange rate systems have proved durable over time. Hong Kong has run a currency board (the Hong Kong Monetary Authority or HKMA) since October 1983. Under this system the HKMA authorizes note-issuing banks in the Special Administrative region to issue bank notes. These banks in turn are required to hold U.S. dollars to the equivalent value of the notes they have issued (using an internal fixed exchange rate of 7.8 Hong Kong dollars to every 1 U.S. dollar). While this system has come under pressure a number of times since it was established, it has yet to be broken due to the simple fact that the Hong Kong dollar is by definition fully backed by the U.S. dollar. Nevertheless, this system has brought its own set of problems. In particular, Hong Kong interest rates must track those of the United States irrespective of the needs of the local economy.

THE SIZE OF THE FOREIGN EXCHANGE MARKET

While the mechanisms underlying the foreign exchange market are remarkably simple, the fundamental need for individuals, manufacturing companies, and investment firms (along with governments and supranational organizations) to buy and sell (or borrow and lend) currencies ensures that it has become the largest in the world. According to the Bank of International Settlements triennial central bank survey, trading foreign exchange markets averaged $5.3 trillion per day in April 2013. This is up from $4.0 trillion in April 2010 and $3.3 trillion in April 2007. Little wonder then that governments continue to try to manage their exchange rates or that the scale of the forces at play often means they fail in their efforts.

THE FUTURE OF THE FOREIGN EXCHANGE MARKET

The varying economic and political circumstances of different nations and economic regions means that they each have varying monetary and fiscal policy needs. Having a sovereign currency allows these nations to implement these policies with the minimum amount of disruption. As long as this remains the case there will also need to be a price at which one currency can be exchanged for another (the exchange rate). However, it is also clear that there is still little unity as to how these exchange rates should be fixed. Those that have turned their back on floating exchange rates have suffered over time from sharp inflows and outflows of hot money and have often had to contend with interest rates that are simply not suited to their domestic needs. At the opposite extreme those nations that have adopted free-floating exchange rates have increasingly found themselves in political battles with nations they suspected of manipulating their currencies.

Perhaps the most radical experiment has been the decisions of the 17 nations of the euro-area to adopt a common currency. While not the first time that a currency union has been created, this was still a bold rejection of free-floating exchange rates. For the moment the jury remains very much out on whether this experiment can succeed in its current form.

Even if Europe's currency union were to prove successful economically, membership still brings potential problems that would not be faced by those nations with their own currencies. In particular, there remains the question over what would happen should a member nation decide to leave the European Union (the underlying political construct). Some idea of the potential problems that this might pose can be seen by considering the referendum held in the United Kingdom in June 2016 on membership of the European Union. Although the vote by the electorate to leave the EU may well pose significant economic problems for the UK, one issue it will not have to face is what currency it will need to use in the future as it already uses the pound sterling. In contrast, should a user of the euro decide to hold a similar referendum and find that the electorate voted to leave the European Union, then they would face the difficult choice of either reintroducing their own currency or continuing to use the euro but relinquishing any say whatsoever in the policies pursued by the European Central Bank. Either choice would present significant problems for the nation in question.

Europe probably provides the clearest example as to why exchange rates and the way they are set remain such a politically emotive topic. Over 40 years after the failure of the Bretton Woods system, calls still surface on a regular basis for the creation of an updated version of the system. However, the evidence from the past four decades indicates that while it might be flawed, a system of free-floating exchange rates remains the most effective way of determining the price of one currency against another.

CHAPTER 33

Conclusion

Gary Strumeyer and Christian Edelmann

In this final chapter we aim to provide an outlook for the capital markets industry. We live in times of unprecedented change and uncertainty; hence, instead of applying the crystal ball approach, we

- Review the state of the financial system, noting that banks have become safer but that some risks may have shifted into capital markets (section 1).
- Review the impact of potentially unintended consequences of regulation (section 2).
- Conclude with a view that the industry needs to reinvent itself and provide perspectives on how Blockchain could be part of that journey (section 3).

SECTION 1: SAFER BANKS, BUT IS THE FINANCIAL SYSTEM SAFER?

As a result of a wave of regulation after the crisis and significant management action, banks have now become safer. Leverage ratios are down, capitalization levels are up, funding is more stable, and banks hold a higher share of highly liquid assets. Regulators, via stress tests such as CCAR in the United States, also have a much better understanding of the risks banks take and have built a much more strategic regulatory dialogue.

Yet there are some offsetting effects of shifts of risk to the capital markets. Factors like a higher share of electronic trading and more centralized clearing have increased overall operational risks and asset owners have absorbed a much higher share of liquidity and credit risk, as shown in Figure 33.1.

Recent regulatory initiatives have impacted broker-dealers' ability to act as *risk taker*—both from a principal investments and a market-making perspective. Hence we may have started to observe what one day may be called the *demise of the risk taker*. A risk taker is a party that purchases a good with the hope that it will become more valuable at a future date (for example, a ticket broker). In the context of the capital markets, risk-taking involves the practice of engaging in financial transactions in an attempt to profit from fluctuations in the market value of a financial instrument. While risk-taking maintains a negative connotation (i.e., a scalper of sports tickets, or a trader

578

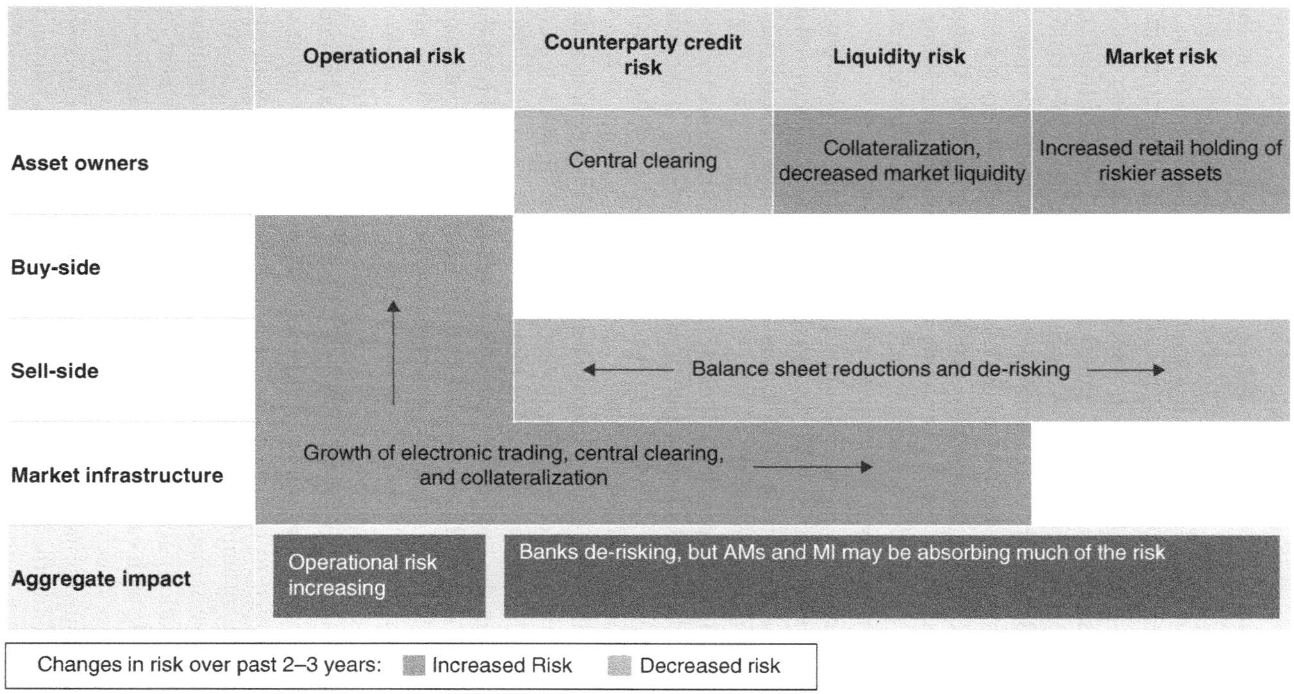

FIGURE 33.1 Shifting risks
Source: Oliver Wyman analysis

irresponsibly assuming excessive risk), risk-taking serves a vital purpose in the markets. Particularly in times of market stress, clients still primarily look to broker-dealers to act on a principal basis (i.e., risk taker) in order to source liquidity.

The *paradox of transparency* has also contributed to a more challenging environment for broker-dealers. What do we mean by the paradox of transparency in the context of the capital markets? Simply put, transparency involves giving market participants access to financial information, including price levels, market depth, and financial reports. Although it's hard to argue against transparency, a prerequisite of free and efficient markets that creates a level playing field, there is a subtle but negative aspect to it where the risk–reward equation is asymmetrical and traders may be discouraged from committing capital (i.e., taking risk) if the profit upside is restricted. The debate is best reflected in the discussion of Finra's TRACE reporting requirement, which undoubtedly makes the market more transparent, but (as many broker-dealers have argued) makes it more difficult for them to recycle risk back into the market within the reporting time windows. There is likely to be an optimal point for market liquidity between the spectrum of complete transparency (and hence limited risk-taking) and a full principal risk-taking model (and hence a world with more information arbitrage opportunities).

These changes have had an impact on liquidity in secondary fixed-income markets. While liquidity levels prior to the global financial crisis may have been inflated, most market participants find the current market a more difficult one to source liquidity in, particularly in a stressed environment.

In light of new (FinTech) providers looking to provide solutions to this liquidity challenge, a spirited debate rages on the role of all-to-all platforms in the future of the fixed-income marketplace. The role of the broker-dealer and hence the principal-based trading model was always driven by the lack of immediate coincidence of wants between potential buyers and sellers of a bond. Various large corporates have thousands of bonds outstanding, which compares to typically one or a few types of stock (equity). Hence equities markets lend themselves toward a trading model of a *centralized limited order book*, whereas this is not the case in fixed income, driven by the diversity of the market.

At the more liquid end we have seen successful marketplace solutions gaining traction. We also observe FinTech solutions looking to tackle the underlying information problem ("Who owns the bonds that I look to buy?"). In combination these solutions are likely to have a positive impact on secondary market liquidity. However, this does not yet mean we will end up in an all-to-all world. The buy-side has traditionally played a price-taker role, and it requires significant change and investments (and in some markets change in regulations) to become a price-maker. A full shift to an all-to-all model would also have significant implications on the middle and back office, as, for example, pension funds and asset managers currently don't have the ISDA (International Swaps and Derivatives Association) agreements and risk/compliance management capabilities in place to directly trade with each other without intermediation by a broker-dealer.

There are also factors such as streamlining of the trading process (typically called robo-bidding or automated principal models), and enhancing liquidity discovery through artificial intelligence. While the use of technology will not solve all trading and liquidity issues, it is clear that such innovation will be pivotal in driving efficiency, reducing risk, and enhancing returns.

However, in the short term, as a result of these changes in liquidity and reflecting the shifting risks in the industry, regulators are now increasingly shifting their focus to the buy-side. The U.S. SEC alone has launched a broad range of initiatives including topics such as liquidity risk management, derivatives, data reporting, and transition planning. Also the FSB recently launched a consultation process in its publication, "Structural Vulnerabilities of Asset Management." These initiatives all look to address the growing regulatory concern with regard to these shifting risks. It will be critical to address these concerns while at the same time ensuring that regulation that was invented for banks deploying their own balance sheets is sufficiently customized to the asset management industry, which typically acts on an agency/fiduciary basis.

SECTION 2: ARE THERE ANY UNINTENDED IMPLICATIONS OF RECENT REGULATION?

Much has been written about the consequences of post-crisis regulation. As argued earlier in this chapter, banks have become safer and their ability to act as risk taker has been reduced. The impact on reduced secondary market liquidity has frequently been cited as an unintended implication of regulation, although we would argue that regulators were very well aware of this likely implication.

Regulations have also largely erased products with inherent opacity and, on the back of that, simple solutions have flourished. What these solutions have in common is their simplicity and responsiveness to customer needs, whether attempting to extract the FX volatility from depository receipts or enabling a retail investor to take efficient physical delivery of gold. There is also an opportunity for new financial instruments to manage certain risks such as one that might solve for the risk of rising medical care. For example, a market for the medical component of the CPI might make sense. Another example would be a market instrument linked to house prices that would allow for insurance against declines in house prices or allow people who are not yet able to afford to buy their own property to get exposure to the market and hence hedge against rising house prices.[1]

Regulation has also forced previously more opaque markets such as the interest rate swap and options markets, which were historically transacting through bilateral agreements, to migrate to *central clearing* solutions such as *swap execution facilities*. Prices are now more transparent, and both credit exposure (counterparty risk) and contagion risk have been mitigated. The accessibility, transparency, and reforms initiated after the LIBOR and ISDA Fix scandals have bolstered confidence in the swaps markets and made them an integral and growing segment of the capital markets.

Yet there may be a few examples where regulation, in many cases in combination with macroeconomic developments, have had unintended consequences. We would highlight two in particular: the challenge of cash management and an emerging financing challenge for the real economy.

---

[1]See Robert J. Shiller, *Finance and the Good Society* (Princeton, NJ: Princeton Press, 2013) for more details.

Managing cash for both investors and corporates used to be among the simplest activities. Banks were typically keen to get clients' deposits and money market funds and offered a capital markets alternative. Today there is a convergence of events occurring in the cash space that may result in hundreds of billions of dollars moving from certain short-term investment products to others.

The *liquidity coverage ratio* (LCR), the *net stable funding ratio* (NSFR), and the *supplementary leverage ratio* (SLR) are impacting how banks manage their balance sheets. The LCR is a stress test that requires large banks to hold a certain amount of high-quality liquid assets (HQLAs) to offset outflows that could occur in a stressed environment over a 30-day period. HQLAs are typically low-yielding. As a result, banks are closely monitoring the amount of HQLAs they need to hold. Overnight deposits (as well as deposits with tenors of 30 days and less) are included as outflows subject to certain factors under the LCR. Consequently, banks will not value overnight and short-term deposits as highly as they historically would have, resulting in comparatively lower rates being paid for these deposits. In addition, the SLR is a new capital ratio that requires compliance in 2018, but has begun to be reported by the large banks in 2015. It will likely result in large banks decreasing or at least closely monitoring their asset base, and consequently their deposit levels. As a result, banks may be pushing certain depositors to invest in off-balance-sheet vehicles such as money market funds.

Yet at the same time, money market reform in the United States is causing many clients to reexamine their investments into prime and tax-exempt funds. Institutional prime and tax-exempt money market funds will become floating-NAV vehicles in October 2016 and will require the ability to impose redemption fees and/or bring down gates preventing any withdrawal activity should the funds' seven-day liquidity levels fall below 30%. Many money market fund investors utilize the vehicles for cash that they may need immediately in an emergency situation. As a result, the possibility of a gate coming down, limiting their ability to access that cash, or a fee being imposed, causing them a loss upon redemption, may make prime and tax-exempt money market funds less attractive to these investors and cause them to reduce or eliminate their positions in these funds. In addition, the concept of a floating NAV, resulting in a potential principal loss in a money market fund, may also give some investors pause, resulting in withdrawal activity from institutional prime/tax-exempt money market funds. Due to these changes, and their expected impact on the attractiveness of these funds to certain investors, there is currently an expectation that a large amount of balances will be withdrawn from them between now and end of 2016. No one knows exactly what that amount will be, or where the balances will go (though much of it is expected to be moved to U.S. Treasury/government money market funds, as floating NAVs will not be a requirement imposed on these funds, and fees/gates are optional), but it is estimated that hundreds of billions of dollars will be in flight as a result of these changes.

All of this is happening at a time when short-term rates are expected to increase in USD, and we expect to see dormant clients reexamining their liquidity options as product yields begin to differentiate more. In summary, this may lead to hundreds of billions of dollars moving quickly across the system, which may have systemic implications that have not yet been fully analyzed and understood.

The second potentially unintended implication of regulation may be a negative impact on the real economy. As secondary market liquidity in fixed-income instruments is increasingly concentrated in a few sectors, large issuers, and on-the-run securities, it may become much more difficult for midmarket corporates to access capital markets, particularly as broker-dealers are also forced to reduce their research capacity given the lower level of client flows they experience and their reduced capacity to take risks, which both negatively impact their revenue outlook. This is likely to be of particular concern in Europe, where the Capital Markets Union (CMU) was intended to accelerate the development of the capital markets and bring it closer to the depth and breadth observed in the U.S. markets.

In that context it is worth noting that while securitized products, in particular U.S. subprime mortgages with poor structures and low-quality assets, were at the heart of the financial crisis, they play a significant role in ultimately providing financing to the real economy as they improve banks' balance sheet turnover and create investment opportunities. These products have advantages such as being generally flexible; they can be tailored to meet investor preferences for ratings, credit risk, prepayment risk, and liquidity, as well as preferences for fixed- or floating-rate bonds, short-, medium-, or long-term maturities, fixed payments or adjustable payments, and amortizing principal payments or bullet principal payments. While the market came to a virtual stop during the financial crisis, in subsequent years, most securitized markets in the United States have recovered with the exception of some formerly prominent markets such as non-agency MBSs and CDOs. The Fundamental Review of the Trading Book (FRTB) will now further negatively impact broker-dealers' economics in structured products, but we believe that revitalizing these markets further, particularly in Europe, will be critical to ensure sustained financing for the real economy.

SECTION 3: A NEED FOR REINVENTION

The pace of change in the capital markets industry will likely remain unprecedented for a while. As we have shown in this chapter, various fundamental forces are in play and they haven't found a new equilibrium yet.

Many of the trends we have outlined put the broader role of broker-dealers into question. They have historically run an integrated model, providing the "3Cs" to their clients: *content*, *connectivity* to markets, and *capital* provision. The relative competitive advantage differs across the various product categories as shown in Figure 33.2.

Many of the traditional sources of competitive advantage are now under threat, creating the potential for disruption of parts of the value chain. Pressure will be particularly high in the more liquid space and the need to differentiate with content in the structured and illiquid space is likely to become ever more important.

Broker-dealers also remain under significant financial pressure as they are starting from already depressed economics. More capacity is likely to be withdrawn (strategic pruning) in the short-to-midterm, which may further negatively impact market liquidity. But that alone is not sufficient. The entire operating model will have to be overhauled, legacy systems decommissioned, and complexity reduced (Figure 33.3).

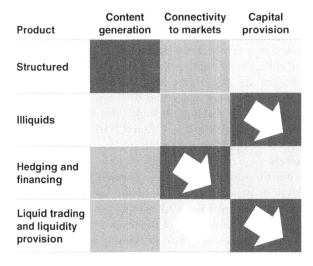

FIGURE 33.2 Sources of competitive advantage
Source: Oliver Wyman proprietary data and analysis

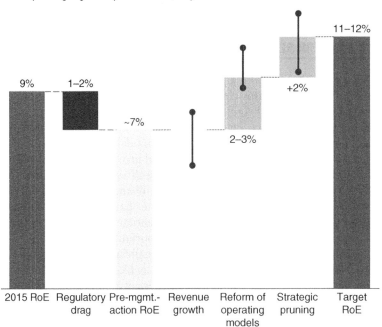

FIGURE 33.3 Sell-side industry ROE outlook
Source: Company filings and annual reports; Oliver Wyman proprietary data and analysis

Blockchain (distributed ledgers) may play a critical role along that journey.[2] The concept of Blockchain has taken the financial services sector by storm, with venture capital and investment pouring into technology startups. Debate over Blockchain's promise, as well as its limitations, is ongoing. For every believer who says Blockchain is the most revolutionary technology platform to emerge since the Internet, there are skeptics who claim it is merely the latest tulip mania.

While in the United States the Depository Trust and Clearing Corp. is fielding proposals for a complete replacement of its credit default swap (CDS) settlement and reporting infrastructure, the Australian Stock Exchange is attempting to address changing regulatory requirements with a Blockchain-based pilot. Regulators such as the Bank of England and the European Securities and Markets Authority (ESMA) have published thoughtful commentary on the feasibility of digital cash and distributed ledger technology. Collectively, the tone of conversations has shifted from "Is this worth exploring?" to "How do we best engage?" Financial commitments to Blockchain are also growing. Investments in Blockchain startups to date have reached $300 million, a figure that is growing swiftly. Investments totaled $125 million in 2015, and this has already been surpassed in the first half of this year.[3] Although predominantly venture capital backed, a handful of companies have attracted significant bank investment. Furthermore, we see growing internal spending by banks, which we estimate totaled $80 million in 2015.[4]

Blockchain applications in wholesale banking and capital markets are seeking to keep the decentralized nature of the network and immutability of the underlying ledger while reinstating accountability and governance models that allow legal recourse and support existing regulatory frameworks. We see the most promise for distributed ledgers existing within a permissioned environment of known participants who can transact privately among one another while selectively granting visibility of their own data to regulators and third parties, such as analytics providers.

The ultimate impact of Blockchain is still debated. Some believe the impact will be limited to the back office and other behind-the-scenes processes. Early efficiency benefits indeed accrue most obviously to the middle- and back-office through data standardization, reduced trade breakage, and simplified infrastructure. However, when real-world assets—represented digitally through tokens or smart contracts—are able to settle between owners at the speed of execution if desired, an innovation tipping point will occur. Settlement flexibility will enable new pricing models and service offerings. However, beyond better data management, the ability to verify assets held on-ledger as truly unique is an innovation not offered by traditional databases. For example, escrow of these digital assets could reduce risk in collateral management; real-time calculation of underlying asset risk could enable more accurate pricing of asset-backed securities.

However, the need for reinvention is not only limited to the sell-side; it equally applies to the buy-side. For them, the main challenge is to adjust to the new liquidity environment

---

[2]The following paragraphs are based on a joint publication by JP Morgan and Oliver Wyman: "Unlocking Economic Advantage with Blockchain" (July 2016).
[3]Coindesk, Oliver Wyman, and JP Morgan analysis.
[4]Oliver Wyman and JP Morgan proprietary data and analysis.

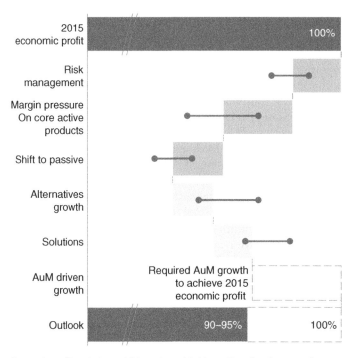

Economic profit excludes variable costs and AuM growth and performance fees

FIGURE 33.4   Asset managers' economic profit evolution (2015 outlook, % of 2015 economic profit)[5]
Source: Oliver Wyman proprietary data and analysis

by upgrading in-house trading and risk management capabilities, reducing dependency on the sell-side, and engaging with new sources of liquidity. In combination with an accelerated shift toward passive products and continued fee pressure in the current low-yield environment, we also expect growing pressure on an industry that enjoyed stellar growth on the back of QE-driven asset inflation post the global financial crisis (Figure 33.4).

Blockchain technology also has the potential to help asset managers tackle some of these challenges.[6] FinTechs and market infrastructure providers are expected to initially offer Blockchain solutions to asset managers but we believe that in time asset managers will also develop their own Blockchain applications. We see four successive waves of deployment for Blockchain technology as shown in Figure 33.5. Initially, we expect the

---

[5] See Oliver Wyman/Morgan Stanley, "Wholesale Banks and Asset Managers: Learning to Live with Less Liquidity" (March 2016).
[6] This paragraph is based on a joint publication by JP Morgan and Oliver Wyman: "Unlocking Economic Advantage with Blockchain" (July 2016).

Wave	Advancements	Examples in development
(1) **Information sharing** 2016–2019	• "Blockchain" used to share and communicate data • Used internally and between trusted external organisations • Distributed ledger solutions tested in parallel with current workflows as proof of concept • Augmentation of existing processes	• CDS trade processing • Payment messaging
(2) **Data solutions** 2017–2025	• "Blockchain" enables an environment to store and manipulate data • Incorporation of distributed ledger technology as part of existing solutions, supporting new efficiencies in operations and workflows • Initial pilots may run in parallel with existing processes, until user confidence is high enough to begin migrating volumes • Users are faced with a choice of infrastructures developed by providers	• Transaction management • Regulatory reporting
(3) **Critical infrastructure** 2020–2030	• "Blockchain" adopted by market participants as main infrastructure for critical functions • Centralized authority still required for administrative functions (e.g., granting access rights, setting industry standards) • Replacement of existing asset, transaction, and payments infrastructure • Participants forced to adopt and integrate new blockchain-based infrastructure	• Custody and settlement • Private markets
(4) **Fully decentralized ?**	• "Blockchain" replaces centrally controlled infrastructure with fully decentralized solutions • Direct engagement in digital asset transactions for organizations and individuals • Legal and regulatory frameworks supportive of asset ownership and transfers via distributed ledgers • Disintermediation of legacy infrastructure owners	• Open, P2P blockchain-powered economy • Digitally issued fiat currency

FIGURE 33.5 Four waves of anticipated Blockchain deployments

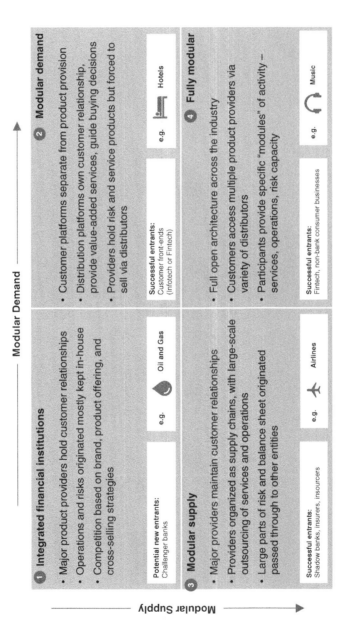

Modular Demand →

Modular Demand →

Modular Supply →

1 Integrated financial institutions

- Major product providers hold customer relationships
- Operations and risks originated mostly kept in-house
- Competition based on brand, product offering, and cross-selling strategies

Potential new entrants:
Challenger banks

e.g. Oil and Gas

2 Modular demand

- Customer platforms separate from product provision
- Distribution platforms own customer relationship, provide value-added services, guide buying decisions
- Providers hold risk and service products but forced to sell via distributors

Successful entrants:
Customer front-ends (Infotech or Fintech)

e.g. Hotels

3 Modular supply

- Major providers maintain customer relationships
- Providers organized as supply chains, with large-scale outsourcing of services and operations
- Large parts of risk and balance sheet originated passed through to other entities

Successful entrants:
Shadow banks, insurers, insourcers

e.g. Airlines

4 Fully modular

- Full open architecture across the industry
- Customers access multiple product providers via variety of distributors
- Participants provide specific "modules" of activity — services, operations, risk capacity

Successful entrants:
Fintech, non-bank consumer businesses

e.g. Music

FIGURE 33.6 Industry structure scenarios

first two waves to be focused on sharing and using data, before expanding to critical infrastructure once confidence in distributed ledger technology grows. The final wave, in which a truly decentralized financial ecosystem arises, is perhaps the most ambitious and the most uncertain.

In summary, both the sell-side and the buy-side are under significant pressure to reinvent themselves, particularly as new competitors look to break up the traditionally integrated value chains. This is a trend we are likely to observe in banking more broadly. We call it *modular* financial services, as shown in Figure 33.6.[7]

Modularization has already impacted various other industries and we are living in a modular world already in parts of the financial services industry. U.S. mortgages, payments, or the Property and Casualty (P&C) insurance industry are the best examples.

Applying the modular concept to the broker-dealer world, one could imagine a world of broker-dealers focusing primarily on content provision with parts of connectivity being provided by alternative trading platforms and parts of the required capital sourced from institutions facing fewer balance sheet constraints than the broker-dealers themselves.

In summary, the industry and the roles the various participants play remain in flux, potentially resulting in significant shifts in economic value in the years to come. But it is incumbent upon regulators and market participants to collectively strike the appropriate balance of risk management, transparency, financial innovation, and creativity to optimize market liquidity and access to funding while mitigating systemic risks. A healthy capital market is ultimately the bedrock of a strong real economy.

---

[7]For further details, see Oliver Wyman, "State of the Financial Services Industry 2016: Modular Financial Services" (January 2016).

A

Absolute change, 530
Absolute prepayment speed, 316
Absolute terms, 528
Access-equals-delivery, implementation, 483
Accounting practices, 112
Accrued coupon interest, 203, 204
Active investment, 475
Active investment ETFs, 476
Additive approach, 187–188
Adjustable-rate mortgages (ARMs), 247, 333–334
Adjustable-rate preferreds, 289
Advanced measurement approach (AMA), 107
African Development Bank (AfDB), 30
Agency benchmark programs, 222, 224–225
Agency bonds, 210–212
Agency debenture FNMA, usage, 187
Agency debt, types, 222–226
Agency market, debt types, 222
Agency mortgage-backed security collateral, 201
Agency pass-throughs, 246–250
Agency program, 467
Aggregate bond ETFs, 478
Agricultural commodities, 550, 552, 553t
Agricultural Credit Act of 1987, 218
Alt-A mortgages, 333
Alternative ETFs, 476, 480
Alternative minimum tax (AMT), 419
Alternative trading systems (ATSs), 124, 128–131, 449, 451, 464, 484

Alternative trading venues, 124, 128–131
American call option, 226
American Depositary Receipt (ADR), 292
American depository receipts (ADRs), 436
American Securitization Forum (ASF), Project Restart, 346
Amortization, 240, 241t, 324–325, 387
Annuity, present value, 541
A-note, 356
Anticipation failure, persistence, 10
Arab Street, rise, 9
Arbitrage, absence, 525
Arbitrage CLOs, 390
Archipelago (ARCA) exchange, 440, 449, 450, 453
Asia Infrastructure Investment Bank (AIIB), 30
Asian Financial Crisis (1997– 1998), 12–13
Asset allocation model, municipal bonds (relationship), 429
Asset-Backed Alert, 310–311
Asset-backed commercial paper (ABCP), 163, 165–167, 166f, 180, 383
Asset-backed securities (ABSs), 305–306, 308t, 309t, 312, 353
Asset-backed speed, 316
Asset-liability management (ALM), 28, 33
Asset-liability risk, 91, 92
Asset managers, 0190, 469–470, 586f
Assets, 30–35, 77, 94–95, 173, 389, 528–531
 true sale, 304, 307–308, 318
Assets under management (AUM), 406, 418

Asset swap spread, 518–519
At-the-market (ATM) deliverables, 492–493
At-the-market (ATM) documentation, 492–493
At-the-market (ATM) equity financing, 481
At-the-market (ATM) financing, follow-on offering (contrast), 489–491
At-the-market (ATM) market, 487–489, 492–493
At-the-market (ATM) model, 496, 499–501
At-the-market (ATM) programs, 485–486, 487f, 487t, 488f, 495, 497–499
At-the-market (ATM) sale, 481
At-the-market (ATM) selling strategies, 499
At-the-market (ATM) strategy, disadvantage, 491
At-the-market (ATM) transaction participants/responsibilities, 492
At-the-money forward (ATMF), 531, 534, 535, 542, 543
At-the-money option, 226
Auction rate securities (ARSs), 157, 180, 181
Auto ABS issuance, 314f
Auto ABS outstanding, 315f
Auto ABS structure, 306t
Auto loans, 315, 318f
Automated trading, 124
Automatic shelf registration, 483
Automobile securitization, 314–320
Average daily trading volume (ADTV), 491, 497–499

B

Backwardation, 559–561
Balance sheet CLOs, 390
Balance sheet constraints, 199–200
Bank Financial Strength Ratings, 173

Bank holding companies (BHCs), CCAR requirements, 97
Banking services, 138
Bank lending, capital market substitute, 24–27
Bank loan ETFs, 478
Bank of International Settlements (BIS), clearing definition, 37
Bankruptcy-remote entity, creation, 309
Bankruptcy-remote SPV, 381–382
Banks, 33, 35–36, 94–95, 168, 173, 174, 578–581
Barclays Aggregate Bond ETF, 477
Barclays Index Data, 240
Basel 1, 95
Basel 2, 96, 106, 107
Basel 2.5, 96
Basel 3 (Basel III), 54–55, 96, 193
Basel Committee (BCBS 239), 117
Basis, 85
BATS, 128, 449, 453
Bear-flattening, 545
Benchmark issues, 198
Bermudan call option, 226
Best bid and offer (BBO), 441
Best-efforts basis, 452
Best-efforts structure, usage, 482
Best execution duties, 449
Bid-ask spread, 340, 374–375
Bid-offer spreads, impact, 448–449
Big data, 119
Bilateral repo, 194–195
Bilateral transactions, implications, 194
Binomial lattice, 264
Black log-normal formulae, 533t, 536
Black normal formulae, 533t
Blackout dates, 495
Black's Call Formula, 530
Black-Scholes-Merton Formula, 530, 535
Blockchain, 585, 586, 587f, 589
B-note, 356
Bond anticipation notes (BANs), 175–176
Bond Market Association (BMA), 248

Bonds, 197–198, 201–204, 257–269, 422–423, 546–547
  computations, 86–88
  creditworthiness, 273
  crossing, 340, 374–375
  forward price (FP), 82–83
  futures basis, 85
  last delivery date, parallel shift (contrast), 87f
  markets, IDB (historic/current role), 132f
  mathematics, 238
  option-adjusted spread, 265
  option pricing, 2-period setting (example), 527f
  weighted average life (WAL), shortening, 338
Book-entry transfer, occurrence, 136
Bookrunner, 427
Book value, triggers (problem), 268
Bootstrap method, 80–82, 81t, 508
Bootstrapped discount factor curve, example, 82t
Bottom-up approach, 107–108
Bowie, David (Bowie Bonds), 312
B-pieces, 359
"Breaking the buck," 181
Bretton Woods, 573
Bring-downs, 491
Broad-based ETFs, 476
Broker-dealers, 36–37, 124, 339, 443, 461–462, 580
Brokered CDs, 173
Bullets, 222, 223, 263, 425
Bullish-tightener, 547
Bull-steepening, 545
Business, 9–11, 55–60, 91–92, 119
Butterfly trade, 75–77, 76f
Buttonwood Agreement, 444
Buyers (corporate bonds), 276–278
Buy order, execution, 464–466
Buy-side, 458
Buy-side institutions, 136
Buy-side trader, 460–461, 465

C
Calculated loan age (CAGE), 246
Calculation layer, 116
Callable bonds, 226, 262–263, 426
Callable CDs, call feature, 174
Callable notes, 225–227
Callables, 222
Call options, 226, 263
Call risk, 293
Canadian Overnight Repo Rate Average (CORRA), 511
Capital, 54, 94, 166, 437t
  notes, 384–385
  reference, 276
  structure, 394–396
Capital adequacy ratio, 25
Capital, assets, management, earnings, and liquidity (CAMEL), 174
Capitalization ratios, standards (improvement), 54
Capitalization weighted indices, 475
Capital markets, 20–42
  development, 47–50
  environment, 21f
  firms, risk buffers, 93–95
  functioning, impacts, 60–63
  growth industry, 4, 5f
  IT architecture, viewpoints, 115
  mission/questions, 6–7
  reinvention, requirement, 583–589
  risk, 89, 114–119
  risk-IT layers, 115–116
  risk management, 90–93, 110–114, 111f
Capital Markets Union (CMU), 583
Capital One Credit Card Portfolio, 324, 324t
Capital project development, 29
Caplets, 537–539
Cap rates, 355
Caps, 537, 538
Carry, 82–83
Cash, 473
Cash and carry, 77–78

Cash bonds, 64
Cash equities, 458, 466–468
Cash-flow CDOs, tranches (purchase), 372–373
Cash flow CLOs, 390
Cash flows, 440
Cash-flow triggers, 375
Cash flow waterfall, 317, 330, 359
Cash injection, 229
Cash settled, 447
Cash settlement, 195
Cash settlement off the curve, 542
Catastrophe bonds, 312
Central Bank of Russia, ruble defense, 575
Central banks, capital market investors, 33–34
Central clearing solutions, 581
Central counterparties (CCPs), 37–38, 39f, 122, 133–134, 141, 503
Centralized limit order, 580
Central securities depositories (CSDs), 38, 122–123, 136–138
Certificate of Deposit Account Registry Service (CDARS), 173
Certificates of deposit (CDs), 172–175
Chapter 7 bankruptcy, 296, 299
Chapter 11 bankruptcy, 296, 299
Character, reference, 276
Charge-offs, 321
Cheapest to deliver (CTD), 85–88
Cheapest-To-Deliver (CTD) issue, 547
Cheat sheet, 533
Chicago Board of Trade (CBOT), 547, 556
Chicago Mercantile Exchange (CME), 38, 143, 447, 556
China, 567–568, 574
Circuit breakers, 448
Clean/Dirty price evolution, example, 68f
Clearing, 37, 133–134, 139
Clearinghouses, 37–38, 122, 132–133
Client porting, 133
Closed-ended funds, 436
Closing date, 400

Closing date cash flows, 317–318
CMBS 2.0, 356–357
Collateral, 185, 187, 248–249, 314–316, 332f
  assets, 361
  availability, 199–200
  certificate, 327
  debt, 369
  events, 326
  first perfected security interest, 307–308
  haircuts, 133
  management/lending, 138
  manager due diligence, 407
  margin holding, 104
  pricing, 372–374
  quality tests, 403
  reference, 276
  squeeze, 199
  types, 305–309
  underlying collateral, 353–356
Collateralization practices, problems, 139
Collateralized debt obligations (CDOs), 228, 311, 361–381, 363t, 370t
Collateralized loan obligations (CLOs), 389–390, 394f, 396t, 397–417, 399f, 406f
Collateralized mortgage obligations (CMOs), 187, 311, 376
Collateral management agreement (CMA), 367, 379
Collateral manager (CM), 365–367, 379–380
Co-location, 453
Commercially reasonable basis, 482
Commercial mortgage-backed securities (CMBSs), 348–360, 352f, 359t
Commercial paper (CP), 163–172, 164–167, 172f, 308
Commissions, 446
Committee on Uniform Securities Identification Procedures (CUSIP), 339, 374

Commodities, 22–23, 473, 548–570, 556t
Commodities Futures Trading Commission (CFTC), 97, 147, 153, 503, 565
Commodity ETFs, 479
Commodity pool operator (CPO), 564–565
Commodity Research Bureau (CRB) Index, 562
Commodity trading advisors (CTAs), 551, 565
Common securitization platform (CSP), 253
Common shareholders, 257
Common stock, 286, 435–436
Companies, equity issuance (reasons), 436–437
Company stockholders, 230
Competitive advantage, sources, 584f
Competitive landscape, change, 56, 58–60
Competitive market, 426–427
Comprehensive Capital Analysis and Review (CCAR), 55, 58, 92, 97, 113, 114f
Comprehensive liquidity analysis and review (CLAR), 106
Concentration limitations, 362, 403
Conditional default rate (CDR), 337, 411
Conditional (effective) prepayment rate, 251
Conditional prepayment rate (CPR), 316, 415
Conditional steepener, 545
Conditional swap-spread trades, 546–547
Conditions, reference, 276
Conduct risk, 91
Conforming loans, 246–247
Consolidated tape, 446
Consolidated Tape Association Plan/Consolidated Quotation Plan (CTA/CQ Plans), 446

Constant-Daily-Forwards (CDF) method, 508
Constant elasticity of variance (CEV) model, 542
Constant Maturity Swap (CMS), CMS-based payoffs, 544–546
Constant (par) net asset value, 182
Consumer price index (CPI), 232, 259, 581
Consumer prices, seasonality, 235
Contango, 559–561
Content, connectivity, and capital (3Cs), 583
Contingent-claim pricing, 523
Contingent convertible capital bonds (CoCo bonds), 267–269
Contingent curve trades, 545–546
Contracts for difference (CFDs), 32
Contract sheets, 445
Contract standardization, 142, 144–145
Conventional loans, 246–247
Conversion premium, 266–267
Conversion price, 266–267
Conversion ratio, 266–267, 290
Convertible bonds, 266–267
Convertible capital instruments (CoCos), 17, 94
Convertible preferred stock, 290–291
Convexity, 71–73, 337–338, 520–521, 544
Core equity capital, 94
Corporate access, 466–467
Corporate board/management oversight, 494–496
Corporate bonds, 254–255, 255f, 270–278
Corporate finance, structured finance (relationship), 394–396
Corporate governance protocol, 495
Corporations, 27–28, 137, 165
Cost of Funds Index (COFI), 308
Counterparties, 185, 192
Counterparty credit risk, 91, 102–105
Counterparty risk, 104, 191–192

Coupon, extension, 338t, 339t
Covenant-lite (cov-lite), 402
Coverage ratio, 423
Cox-Ross-Rubenstein (CRR), 523
Crash of 1929, impact, 445
Crash of 1987, 447–448
Credit, 243–244, 318–319, 500,
    521–522
  risk, 91, 191, 293, 337, 339
Credit analysis, 319–320
Credit card ABS, 320t, 321, 323–326,
    328t
Credit card de-linked structure, 327f
Credit card owner trust structural
    features, 328t
Credit card securitization, 320–328
Credit default swaps (CDSs), 383, 585
Credit Rating Agency Reform Act of
    2006, 353
Credit ratings, 335–336, 336t
Credit-sensitive trading exposures, 101
Credit Support Annex (CSA), 104
Credit support, impact, 356
Credit Valuation Adjustment (CVA),
    103–104
Credit Value Adjustment (CVA), 521
Cross-border settlements, securities
    safekeeping chains, 137f
Crude oil futures contract, standardized
    terms, 560t–561t
Cubes, 543
Cumulative default rates, 411–412
Cumulative Distribution Function
    (CDF), 528
Cumulative preferred stock, 289–290
Currency, 473, 571–576
Current Exposure, 102
Current report, usage, 495
Curvature trades, 75
Curve build method, 509
Curve interpolation methods, 508f
Curve trades, 75
Custodians, 38–40, 122, 136–139, 471
Custody, 38, 138

D
Daily accrued coupon interest, 202
Daily financing interest expense, 202
Dark pools, 45, 125, 128, 130, 452, 485
Data architecture, impact, 117–119
Data capability, support, 117–119
Data governance principles, 117–118
Data management capabilities, 118–119
Data operations, impact, 118
Data processing technologies, usage, 118
Data profiling, 118
Data providers, 40
Data sourcing, 115
Data strategy, impact, 118
Data transmission, example, 454
Data verification representation, 343–344
Day, term (usage), 452–453
DBRS (credit ratings), 348–349
Deal analysis, 375–376
Dealer market, 447
Dealers, functions, 36–37
Debenture, 258
Debit Value Adjustment (DVA), 521–522
Debt capital markets (DCMs), 36, 56
Debt-downsizing adjustment, 16
Debt, equity (relationship), 396–397
Debt-friendly CLO, 397
Debt obligations, 241
Debt securities, repurchase, 486
Debt service coverage ratio (DSCR), 355
Debt valuation adjustment (DVA), 104
Debt yield (DY), 355
Decimalization, 449–450
Decision making, enablers, 109
Decoupled discount curves, 509–510
Deep-in-the-money option, 267
Defaulted loan, effects, 337f
Default events, 378
Default fund, 134
Default management, coordination
    (absence), 139
Default risk charge (DRC), addition, 101
Defeasance mode, 387
Defined benefit, 33

Defined contribution structure, 33
Delay, 246
Delayed-delivery market, 248
De-linked trusts, 327
Delinquencies, 321
De-listing, 230
Deliverability, 551
Deliverable bonds, basket (forward prices), 84
Delivery conventions, 194–197
Delivery *versus* payment (DVP), 194
Delivery-*versus*-payment (DVP), 122, 135
Delta, 520, 531
Delta-normal parametric framework, 98–99
Deposit, 79–80, 138
Depositor, role, 340
Depository receipts, 436
Depository Trust and Clearing Corporation (DTCC), 37–38
Derivatives, 23–24, 102, 139, 142–145, 143f
Derivatives market infrastructure, 138–154, 140f
Descriptive curve, 509
Deutsche Boerse, 125
Developed-country broad-based ETFs, 477
Digi-calls, 534
Digitals, 533
DirectEdge (Direct Edge), 125, 128, 453
Directional spreads, 547
Direct market access (DMA), 464
Direct-pay letter of credit, usage, 177
Disclosed reserves/retained earnings, 94
Discount bond, 68
Discount brokerage firms, 446
Discounted receivables, impact, 325
Discount factors, 65–66, 80–82, 82t, 539–540
Discounting, tools, 64–65
Discount margin (DM), 208, 416
Discount notes (DNs), 222, 223
Distress, components, 297–298

Distressed debt, 298–300
Distressed debt securities, 296–297, 303
Diversification properties, 235–236
Diversity score, 405
Dividend-received deduction (DRD), 288–289
Dividends, 230
Dodd-Frank Wall Street Reform and Consumer Protection Act, 54, 55, 153, 193, 417, 503
Dollar-carry, 83
Dollar pricing/pricing conventions, 271–272
Domestic equity, 476
Domestic U.S. equity, 473
Dow Jones AIG Commodities Index (DJ/AIGCI), 562
Dow Jones Industrial Index, decline, 485
Dual-bootstrap process, 515
Dual curve construction, 515
Due diligence regimen, 491–492
Duration gap, 225
Dynamic hedging, 526–527

E
Early payout, 325
Earnings before interest, taxes, depreciation, and amortization (EBITDA), 298, 403
Economic capital, 52–53
Economies, funding structure, 26f
EDGAR System (SEC), 483
Effective date, 400, 504
Effective expected exposure (EE), metrics/equations, 103t
Effective taxable yield, 288
Election trading, penetration (asset class basis), 46f
Electronic communications networks (ECNs), 124, 130, 428, 449, 451, 484–485, 498
Electronic order book (EOB), 127
Electronic trading, 467–468, 484–485

Eligibility criteria, 362
Eligible accounts, bank-issued credit card ABS definition, 321–322
Eligible receivables, bank-issued credit card ABS definition, 322–323
Embedded options, 262–265
Emerging bond markets, 281–283
Emerging broad-based ETFs, 477
Emerging market (EM), 281–285, 282f
EMIR, 54
Endowments, funds usage, 34–35
Energy commodities, 550, 552–554, 553t, 560t–561t
Energy funds, 564
Energy/MLP ATM filings, 488f
Enhanced equipment trust certificate (EETC), 257–258
Equal weighted indices, 475
Equities, 20–22, 49, 396–397, 435–452
  offerings, 482
  research, 462
  trading technology, evolution, 456
  U.S. equities trading/issuance volumes, 43f
Equity capital markets (ECMs), 36, 481
Equity REIT filings, 490f
Equity REIT market, focus, 488–489
Equity tranche, 395
Escrowed-to-maturity (ETM) bonds, 421
Essential purpose, 423
Euroclear Bank, 38
Eurodollar (ED) contract, expiration (example), 538
Eurodollar (ED) deposits, 174–175
Euro-dollar (ED) futures, 512–513, 537
Eurodollar (ED) options, 538
Euro Overnight Index Average (EONIA), 510
European Bank for Reconstruction and Development (EBRD), 30
European Banking Authority (EBA), 97
European call, 226, 530, 532f
European Central Bank (ECB), 301, 302, 573

European CLOs, 390
European Contagion, 13
European Economic Community, currency free float, 574
European put, value derivation, 530–531
European Securities and Markets Authority (ESMA), 141, 153, 585
European style exercise option, 523
European-style options, 534
European-style payoffs, 534, 535f
European-style swaptions, 538–542
European trade repository open OTC derivative positions, 153f
Europe, multilateral trading facilities (MTFs), 130–131
Evaluation reserves, 94
Excess servicing spread, 321
Excess spread, 305, 326, 395
Exchange Act, 445
Exchange-based trade, example, 41f
Exchange markets, 43–47, 121
Exchanges, 37–38, 128
Exchange-traded contracts, 144
Exchange-traded derivatives (ETDs), 140–142, 144t, 146
Exchange-traded funds (ETFs), 254, 401, 469–480, 563
  arbitrage, 456–457
Exchange-traded grantor trusts (ETGTs), 472
Exchange-traded notes, 472, 563
Exchange-traded securities, 375
Execution, 464–468
Expected exposure (EE), metrics/equations, 103t
Expected loss severity, 337
Expected risk/gain, 10
Expected shortfall (ES), 99–101
Export-Import Bank of the United States (Eximbank), 221
Exposure definitions/measurement, 102–103
Extension risk, 226, 227, 337–338
Extract, transform, load (ETL), 118

F
Factor, 227
Factor-based ETFs, 475
Fail, 195
Fallen angels, 274
Farm Credit Administration (FCA), 218
Farm Credit Debt Securities, 217–218
Farm Credit System, 217
Farm Credit System Associations, 218
"Fed Effective" rate (Fed publication), 159
Federal agencies, 162–163, 210, 211t, 219–222
Federal Agricultural Mortgage Corporation (FAMC) (Farmer Mac), 163, 218
Federal Deposit Insurance Corporation (FDIC), 97, 173–163, 182, 217–218
Federal Farm Credit Bank (FFCB), 163, 217–218, 223f, 225
Federal funds (fed funds), 158–159, 410–411
Federal funds effective rate (FFER), 510
Federal Home Loan Bank (FHLB), 163, 213, 214–215, 216f, 224–225
Federal Home Loan Mortgage Corporation (FHLMC) (Freddie Mac), 163, 210–214, 224, 229–230, 231f, 243, 253
Federal Housing Administration (FHA), 214, 220, 242, 251
Federal Housing Board (FHB), 212
Federal Housing Finance Agency (FHFA), 212, 213
Federal National Mortgage Association (FNMA) (Fannie Mae), 29, 163, 188, 189, 210, 213–214, 477
conservatorship, 229–230
reduction, 230
reference note programs, 224
retained portfolio, reduction, 231f
securitization, future, 253
Federal Open Markets Committee (FOMC), 200–201, 235, 509

Federal Reserve Board, weekly data, 168
Federal Reserve System (Fed), 96, 158, 169f, 170f, 200–201, 510
zero-interest-rate policy, 254
Federal Savings and Loan Insurance Corporation (FSLIC), 220
Financial corporations, 28
Financial crisis (2008), 228–230
Financial crisis (2007/2008), impact, 180–183
Financial crisis, stress events (impact), 55
Financial era definition, accuracy (impact), 9–11
Financial Industry Regulatory Authority (FINRA), 96, 130, 239, 310, 445
Financial institutions, 165
Financial Institutions Reform, Recovery, and Enforcement Act of 1989 (FIRREA), 220–221
Financial intermediaries, 35–40, 190–191
Financial Services Authority (FSA), 125
Financial Stability Board (FSB), 139, 581
Financial system, safety, 578–581
Financing Corporation (FICO), 220, 248–249, 316
FinTech, 580
Firm commitment, 36
Firm-commitment underwriting, 482
First loss piece, 349
First perfected security interest, 307–308
Fitch (rating agency), 348–349
Fixed/adjustable hybrids (hybrid ARMs), 247
Fixed income, 49, 473
Fixed Income Clearing Corporation (FICC), 132, 196
Fixed-income ETFs, 477–478
Fixed-income securities, 22, 279
Fixed-income trading, 193
Fixed leg, 504
Fixed-rate loans, 247
Flat CDR, 411
Flat yield, 66
Flat Yield assumption, 66

Float for fixed, 24
Float for float, 24
Floating net asset value, 182
Floating-rate ETFs, 478
Floating-rate notes (FRNs), 222, 225, 259–260
   total issuance percentage, 260f
   Treasury issuance, 207–208
Floating-rate preferreds, 289
Floorlets, 537–538
Floor price, 497–498
Floor reports, 445
Floors, 537, 538
Foreign exchange (FX), 22–23
Foreign exchange (FX) market, 571–572, 576–577
Forward-3m rates, 508f
Forward-ATM initial sale, 500f
Forward cap/floor, 537
Forward curves, 509–510
Forward price (FP), 77–78, 82–83
Forward purchase agreement, 500
Forward rate agreements (FRAs), 194, 512
Forward rates, 78–80, 515, 537–538
Forwards, 23, 82
Forward sale, cash settlement, 501f
Forward sale, physical settlement, 501f
Forward swap, 507
Forward transaction, 572
Forward yield, 83
Fractional Brownian motion models, 542
Fraud risk, 345–346
Free-floating exchange rates, rejection, 577
Free markets, virtues, 18
Full-service broker-dealer, 459t, 461f, 462f
Fundamental Review of the Trading Book (FRTB), 100, 583
Funding Benefit Adjustment (FBA), 522
Funding Cost Adjustment (FCA), 522
Funding structure, 26f
Funding valuation adjustment (FVA), 104

Funding Value Adjustment (FVA), 522
Fund structures, types, 34–35
Future exposure, 102
Future/forward convexity adjustment, 513–514
Futures, 23, 64, 473, 557–558
Futures ETFs, 563
FX risk limit test, 388

G
G4 10-year interest rates, 8f
G20, impact, 141, 147
Galbraith, John Kenneth, 12
Gamma, 520–521, 532, 532f, 536
Gang, Yi, 576
General collateral (GC), 160–161, 197–198, 208
General collateral finance (GCF), 196
General loan-loss reserves, 94
General obligation bonds (GOs), 420, 422–424
Ginnie Mae I/II, 242
Global capital markets, 3, 7–9, 20, 51f
Global custodians, 39–40, 136–139
Global depository receipts (GDRs), 436
Global equity, 476–477
Global financial asset choice set, 4, 5f
Global financial crisis, 52–53
Global Financial Crisis (2007/2008), 157, 163, 182–183
Global financial system, 12f, 17–19
Gold exchange standard, 573
Gold Participation Certificate (PC) program, 243
Government agency securities, 205
Government final consumption expenditure, 29
Government gross capital formation, 29
Government loans, 246–247
Government National Mortgage Association (GNMA) (Ginnie Mae), 162, 219–220, 477
Governments, 29–30, 33

Government-sponsored enterprises
(GSEs), 29, 210, 211t, 224, 243, 329
debt, issuance, 224
overview, 212–213, 215–219
securities, 162–163
Government wire, 162
Grand Convergence, 12–13
Grantor trust, 316, 317
Great Depression, 10, 219
Great Moderation, impact, 11
Great Recession, 10, 12f, 19, 485–486
Great Society program, 220
Great Transition, 9
Great Transition Age, 11–13, 19
Greece, 302–303
Greeks, 531–533
Gross Basis, 86
Gross settlement, 134
Gross simultaneous settlement, 135
Guaranteed investment contracts
(GICs), 277
Guarantees, 104

H
Haircuts, 104, 134, 187–188
Headline spreads, 518
Hedge funds, 35, 190, 417
High-frequency trading (HFT), 119,
124–125, 454–457
High-quality liquid assets (HQLA),
199, 582
High-yield bonds (junk bonds), 271–272,
279–281
High-yield corporate bond ETFs, 478
High-yield market, issuance growth, 280f
Historical data, drawback, 412
Historical leveraged loan default, 414f
Historical loan repayment rate, 416f
Historical rate spread, 171f
Historical simulation framework, 99
Holding period, selection, 99
Homebuyer PTI ratio levels, 246
Homerun investment, 298

Home sales turnover, 250
Hong Kong Monetary Authority
(HKMA), 33, 576
Household financial assets, investment
company share, 32f
Housing and Economic Recovery Act of
2008, 212
Housing GSEs, 212–213
How-and-when-to-trade decisions, 464
Hybrid ARMs, 247, 331f

I
I bonds, Treasury Department sale, 237
Immediate or cancel (IOC), 453
Impaired mortgages, presence, 180
Implied Black normal Vols, 541t
Implied Repo Rate (IRR), 86
Income collection, 137
Incurrence covenants, 402
Indenture, 378–379, 408
Index arbitrage, 456–457
Indexation, 232–233
Index funds, 564
Index methodologies, 475
Index ratio (IR), 233
Individuals, returns generation, 30, 32
Industry structure scenarios, 588f
Inflation breakevens, 233–235, 234f
Inflation-linked bonds, 232, 237–238
Information providers, support, 40, 42
Information technology (IT) architecture,
114–116, 116f
Information technology (IT)
infrastructure, impact, 117
Infrastructure framework,
strengthening, 50
Infrastructure project development, 29
Infrastructure providers, support, 40, 42
Initial deposit, 318
Initial margin, 104, 133
Initial public offering (IPO), 21, 439–440,
482
Insolvency event, 388

Institutional CDs, 173–174, 181
Institutional client, 458, 459t, 461f, 462f
Institutional investor, internal
    interactions, 459f
Institutional loan outstanding amount,
    402f
Insurers, premiums collection, 32
Interactive Data Corporation (IDC),
    239, 310
Inter-American Development Bank, 222
Intercontinental Exchange (ICE), 38, 152
Inter-dealer brokers (IDBs), 123, 124,
    131–132, 131f, 196–197
Interest cash flow, 336
Interest coverage test, 397
Interest diversion test, 399
Interest-only (IO) classes, 359–360
Interest only (IO) loans, 357
Interest only (IO) payments, 355
Interest payments, 504
Interest rate hedged ETFs, 478
Interest rate options, 523, 535–536
Interest rates, 177, 193–194, 201–202,
    294, 337
  ceilings, 159
  deterministic characteristic, 80
  diversification, 280
  limit test, 388
  tools, 64–65
Interest rate strategy ETFs, 478
Interest rate swaps (IRSs), 24, 503, 504
Interest waterfall, 394f
Intergovernmental Panel on Climate
    Change (IPCC), 569
Intermediaries, role, 41f
Intermediate holding companies (IHCs),
    CCAR requirements, 97
Internal metrics, 107
Internal rate of return (IRR), 65, 416
International Bank for Reconstruction
    and Development (IBRD), 222
International central securities
    depositories (ICSDs), 38, 122,
    136–138

International equity, 473, 476–477
International fixed-income ETFs,
    478–479
International Monetary Fund (IMF), 30,
    282, 301, 574
International Money Market (IMM),
    512
International multilateral organizations
    (MLOs), 29–30
International Swaps and Derivatives
    Association (ISDA), 141, 580, 581
Intex, 375–376
In-the-money option, 226
Inverse ETFs, 479–480
Inverse leveraged ETFs, 479
Investment banks, capital market
    functions, 35–36
Investment companies, 32f, 436, 471
Investment Company Act of 1940,
    177, 470
Investment fund ownership, 391f
Investment-grade bonds, impact, 272
Investment-grade corporate bond ETFs,
    478
Investment grade liabilities, 377
Investment guidelines, 409
Investment leverage, 28
Investment opportunities, breadth/depth,
    48
Investment vehicles, 561–567
Investors, 30–35, 48–50
ISIS/ISIL, rise, 9
Islamic Finance, 17
Issuance notice, 497–498
Issuance trust, usage, 327
Issuance volumes, 43f, 44f
Issue date, 400
Issuers, 27, 49, 127, 138, 469–471
Issuing agencies, 242–243

J

Japan, currency policies, 574
Jumbo mortgages, 333

Jump diffusion models, 542
Junior AAA tranches, 335, 349

K
Kerviel, Jerome, 91, 106
Key risk indicators (KRIs), 111f, 113, 119
Kroll Bond Rating Agency, CMBS
    metrics, 357

L
Last delivery date, parallel shift (contrast),
    87f
Legal events, 326
Legal final maturity date, 400–401
Legs, 504, 506–507
Lehman Brothers, failure, 181
Letter of credit, guarantee, 177
Leveraged buyout (LBO), 401
Leveraged ETFs, 479–480
Leveraged loans, 401
Leverage, ratio, 25, 54–55
Li, David, 575
Limited resources, strategy/management
    (linkage), 107–108
Limit frameworks, 107
Liquidity, 180–181, 244, 381, 388, 551
Liquidity coverage ratio (LCR), 25, 55,
    105–106, 582
Liquidity risk, 94–95, 105–106,
    192–193, 293–294, 339
Listing, 21, 440–441
Loan securitizations, 417
Loan-to-collateral value ratio,
    maintenance, 185
Loan-to-deposit ratio, 25
Loan-to-value (LTV), 246, 249, 333,
    355–356
Local custodians, 136–137
Local settlements, securities safekeeping
    chains, 137f
Lockup provision, 495
Log-linear constant forwards, 508

Log-normal distribution, 528, 529f
Log-normal dynamics, 531
Lognormal method, 264
London Inter-Bank Offer Rate (LIBOR),
    174, 208, 259, 289, 308, 362, 504,
    511–515
  curve, 509
  Fix scandal, 581
  spread, 395
London Stock Exchange (LSE), 125
Long exposure, creation, 145
Long-term capital, 27–28
Long Term Capital Management,
    failure/bailout, 90–91, 282
Loss absorption mechanism, 268
Loss allocation, 391f
Loss exposure, existence, 191
Loss Given Default (LGD), 102, 105
Loss-given-default (LGD), 413
Loss severity rate, 413
Lottery tickets, 536

M
Maintenance guarantee, 212
Maker-taker fee model, 127
Make-whole call (MWC), 263
Managed futures funds, types, 564–565
Margin, 187, 192, 401, 444–445, 559
Marginal tax rate (MTR), 430
Margin valuation adjustment (MVA), 104
Market infrastructure (MI), 35, 61, 120
Marketing period, 399–400
Market maker, 339, 374–375, 471
Market making, 455
Market-neutral environment, SIV
    operation, 385
Market risk, 70, 90–91, 97–102
Market Risk Amendment, 95
Markets, 169f, 188–191, 194, 196, 198
  capitalization, 440
  data/analytics, 127
  discipline, facilitation, 50
  environment scenarios, 101

Markets *(Continued)*
  rates, quoting (example), 81–82
  share, sacrifice (impact), 60f
  transparency, insufficiency, 139
  types, 42–47
  valuations, manipulation, 8
Markets in Financial Instruments
    Directive (MiFID), 37, 54, 55, 131
Market structure, 48, 452–453
Market Wizards (Schwager), 455
Markit CMBX Indices, 360
Mark-to-market (MTM), 192
Master agreements, 141
Master limited partnerships (MLPs),
    565–566
Master owner trust (MOT) structure, 327
Master purchase agreements, 160
Master repurchase agreements (MRAs),
    184–185
Master servicer, 350–351
Master trust/owner trust/de-linked
    structure, 328
Master trusts, 327
Matched-maturity spread, 518
Matched-maturity swap spread, 518
Matching, 132
Material and adverse clause, 345–346
Material and adverse qualifier, 346
Materiality, 495
Matros, Rick, 486
Maturity date, 185, 504
Maturity profile, measures, 95
Maximum annual debt service (MADS),
    423
Maximum PFE/peak PFE,
    metrics/equations, 103t
May Day, 446
Medium-term notes (MTNs), 222, 226,
    261–262, 382, 481
Member fees, 127
Mergers and acquisitions (M&As), 36,
    256, 280
Metals, commodities, 550, 554–555, 555t
Metrics, equations, 103t

Mezzanine AAA tranches, 335, 349
Mezzanine classes, 359
Mezzanine notes, 363
Mezzanine triple-A Class, 358
Middle-market CLOs, 390
Mid-prime credit quality, 315
MiFID II, 37
Mini-maxi structure, usage, 482
Mining funds, 564
Mixture models, 542
Model risk, 91
Modified duration, example, 72f
Modular financial services, 589
Money, 122, 198–199
Money market funds (MMFs), 177–179,
    178f, 179f
Money markets, 157, 180–183
Montage, 450
Monte Carlo simulation, 99, 412–413
Moody's, 163, 167, 348–349
Mortgage Backed Securities Clearing
    Corporation (MBSCC) process, 248
Mortgage-backed securities ETFs,
    477–478
Mortgage-backed security (MBS), 210,
    219, 239, 241–246
  collateral, 201
  OAS analysis, relationship, 252–253
  pools, analysis, 250
Mortgage bonds, 240
Mortgagee, 240
Mortgage loan purchase agreements
    (MLPAs), 340, 350
Mortgage loan schedule (MLS), 343–344
Mortgage quality types, 333–334
Mortgages, 240–241, 247, 331–334
Mortgagor, 240
Multi-agented programs, problems, 494
Multi-dealer platforms (MDPs), 132
Multilateral netting, impact, 134f
Multilateral organizations (MLOs),
    29–30
Multilateral trading facilities (MTFs), 45,
    124, 129, 130–131

Multi-seller ABCP conduits, 384
Multi-seller ABCP programs, 383
Municipal bonds, 419–426, 428–434
Municipal notes, 175–176
Municipal Securities Rulemaking Board (MSRB), 421
Mutual funds, 34–35, 312, 436, 564

N
NAREIT, 496
NASDAQ, 124, 125, 128, 440, 447–449
National Association of Securities Dealers (NASD), 279, 445
National best bid and offer (NBBO), 450, 452
National Futures Association (NFA), 565
National global financial asset returns, 14f
Nationally recognized statistical rating organizations (NRSROs), 168, 335, 353, 369
National Market System (NMS), 446, 452, 457
National Security Clearing Corporation (NSCC), 132, 474
Natural order flow, 464
Negative carry, 490
Negative convexity, 226, 227
Negative duration-based ETFs, 478
Negotiated sale, 427
Net asset value (NAV), 377, 436, 469, 471–474
  floating NAV vehicles, 582
Net obligations, calculation, 132
Net operating income (NOI), 354
Net outstanding portfolio collateral balance, 373
Net revenue (NR), 423
Net settlement, 135
Net simultaneous settlement, 135
Net stable funding ratio (NSFR), 55, 105–106, 193, 582
Netting provisions, right, 104
Neutral duration-based ETFs, 478

"New Conservative Financial Consensus," application, 10, 19
New issue securities, window programs, 162–163
New York Stock Exchange (NYSE), 124, 125, 128, 142, 294, 444, 451
Next-Generation Global Financial System, 16–18
1933 Act ETFs, 472
Nixon, Richard M., 573
Non-agency RMBSs, 329, 331f, 342
Non-bank market makers, proliferation, 59–60
Non-callable bonds, 425
Non-callable T-bills, 161
Non-call period, 400
Non-call provisions, 377
Non-capital expenditure (government final consumption expenditure), 29
Nonconforming loans, 246–247
Non-consolidation opinion, 305, 317
Noncumulative preferred stock, 289
Non-financial corporate borrowers, 256t
Non-financial institutions, 27–28
Non-housing GSEs, overview, 215–219
Non-mortgage asset-backed securities, 312
Non-seasonally adjusted consumer price index (NSA CPI), 232–235. 236t
Normal distribution, 527–528, 529f
Normative curve, 509
Notary services, 138
Notes, issuance, 318
Notification period, 177
Notional, 505
Novation, 134
Nuclear option, 379

O
Obligations, 229–230
Obligors, 307–308
Odd lots, 239
Offering circulars (OCs), 374, 408

Offering memoranda (OMs), 164, 374
Office of Federal Housing Enterprise
Oversight (OFHEO), 212, 243
Office of the Comptroller of the Currency
(OCC), 96
Offset provisions, right, 104
Off-the-run issues, 69, 198
OMX, 453
One-step binomial model, 523–526, 524f
On-the-run (OTR) bonds, 270
Open-ended funds, 436
Open-end ETFs, shares outstanding,
472–473
Opening auction, on open/on close,
452–453
Open interest, 145–146, 145t
Open-market operations, 199
Open Markets Trading Desk (Federal
Reserve Bank of New York),
200–201
Operational data stores, 118
Operational processes, 139
Operational risk, 91, 106–107
Operations, cost (increase), 56, 57–58
Option-adjusted spread (OAS), 252–253,
264
Options, 24, 531
Order book, 441
Order-driven markets, mechanics,
441–443
Order handling rules, impact, 448–449
Order processing system providers, 40
Order types, 452–453
Ordinary shares, 435
Organized trading facilities (OTFs), 141
Originator MLPAs, 340
Out-of-the-money option, 226
Out-right trades, 75
Overcollateralization (O/C), 306, 307f,
332, 332f
  ratio, 364–365, 405
  statement, 372
  test, 397, 398f
Overnight bought deals, 482

Overnight indexed swaps (OISs), 194,
510–512, 515, 518
Overnight repos, 185
Overnight reverse repurchase agreement
(ON RRP) facility, usage, 201
Overseas Private Investment Corporation
(OPIC), 221
Over-the-counter (OTC), 122, 294, 339
  markets, 43–47, 121, 127
Over-the-counter derivatives (OTCD),
139–141, 146–149, 503
Owner trust, 316, 317

P
Panic of 1907, The (Bruner/Carr), 11
Parallel PV01, 520
Par compression risk, 226, 227
Par coverage test, 397
Par credit, 373, 373t
Par-par asset swap, 518
Par swap, 507, 514
Partial call bonds, 227
Partial Libor PV01, 521t
Partial PV01, 520
Passive funds, usage, 35
Passive investment ETFs, 475
Pass-through MBSs, metrics, 244–246
Pass-throughs, combined pools, 248
Pass-through security, 242, 245f, 420
Pass-through vintages, 248
Payer swaption, 538
Paying in a swap, 504
Paying in spreads, 516
Pay-in-kind (PIK), 399
Payment in kind (PIK), 281, 397–399
Payment-to-income (PTI) ratio levels, 246
Penny options, 536
Pension funds, retirement savings
aggregation, 32–33
People's Bank of China (PBoC), 575, 576
Percentage/proportional terms, 528
Percentile threshold, expected shortfall
(contrast), 99–100

Performance metrics, 403–405
Perpetual preferred stock, 287
Personal consumption expenditure (PCE), 235
Phantom income, taxation, 236
Physically backed ETFs, 563
Piece-wise constant forwards, 508
Placement agent, 367
Plain-vanilla fixed-for-floating swaps, 504–505
Pool factor, 246
Pooling and servicing agreement (PSA), 334, 341, 351
Portfolio, 447, 474–480
    manager, 458, 459–460
    strategy (charting), financial era definition accuracy (impact), 9–11
Portfolio composition file (PCF), 474
Portugal, Italy, Ireland, Greece, and Spain (PIGS), 301–302
Position trader, 461
Position trading, 465–466
Positive carry, 83
Post-crisis rules/approaches, 54–55
Post-Great Recession, global capital markets chart, 7–9
Potential future exposure (PFE), 102–103, 103t
Preferred shares, 436
Preferred stock, 286–287, 292–294
Preferred stockholders, 257
Prepayments, 250–252, 316, 337–338, 415
Preprocessing layer, 115
Pre-refunded/escrowed bonds, 420, 423
Presentation layer, 116
Present value (PV), equations, 505–506
Present value of a basis point (PVBP), 70–71, 72f
Pre-settlement risk management, 132
Pre-tax earnings, 440
Price carry, 83
Price differential, 186

Price transparency, 279, 428
Price volatility, 546
Price weighted indices, 475
Price-yield formula, 66–68, 82
Price-yield graph, example, 67f
Pricing date, 400
Pricing supplement, 495
Primary dealers, 36
Primary first-lien loan issuance, percentage, 403f
Primary markets, 42–43, 43f, 426–427
Prime credit quality, 315
Prime mortgages, 333
Principal, 22, 36, 338t, 467
Principal cash flows, 336
Principal intermediary, role, 464
Principal-to-principal contracts, 503
Principal waterfall, 393
Private equity (PE), 417, 441, 566–567
Private Export Funding Corporation (PEFCO), 221
Private foundations, funds usage, 34–35
Private-label RMBS, secondary trading, 339–340
Private placements, 164
Probability, 525
Probability of Default (PD), 105
Process architecture, 111f
Program trading, 467–468
Project Restart (ASF), 346
Property, 249, 354
Proportional change, 528–530
Proprietary trading, 37, 455–456
Prospectus supplement, filing, 481
Prudential Regulation Authority (PRA), 97
Publicly held shares, market value, 441
Public Securities Association (PSA) model/convention, 251–252
Puerto Rico, 300–301, 424–425
Pull-to-par dynamic, 227
Purchase price, 186
Putable bonds, 265
Put-call parity, 530–531

Put feature, 385
PV01, 70–71, 72f, 509, 516, 520–521

Q
Qualified institutional buyers (QIBs), 164
Qualified investor, 441
Quality option, 85
Quasi-sovereign multilateral
    organizations, 29–30
Quote-driven markets, 443

R
Ramp-up period, 400
Rates, trading, 515–516
Rating agencies, 273–276, 275t–276t,
    369–371
Rating Agency Act, 353
Rating-based triggers, 104
Ratings agencies, 42
Real estate investment trusts (REITs), 190,
    287, 355, 485–486, 566
Real estate mortgage investment conduit
    (REMIC), 308, 351–352
Real global financial asset returns, 15f
Realized Vol, Implied Vol (contrast), 536
Real-time gross settlement (RTGS),
    122, 134
Real yields, 233–235
Receivables allocation, 325f
Receiving in a spread, 516
Receiving in a swap, 504
Recovery lag assumptions, 414
Recovery rates, 413–414, 414f
REDI, 449
Refinancing, 250–251
Regional custodians, 138
Regression-weighted butterfly, 77
Regulated investment companies (RICs),
    471–472
Regulation M, 497
Regulation NMS, 451–452
Regulations, 48, 53–55, 581–583

Regulatory framework, strengthening, 50
Regulatory landscape, overview, 95–97
Regulatory reforms, cumulative
    weight, 54
Rehypothecation, 194
Reinvestment rates, 415–416
Reinvestment risk, 226, 227
Remarketing agent, impact, 177
Reminiscences of a Stock Operator, 455
Replicating portfolio, 524
Reporting layer, 116
Representations, 342–346
Repurchase agreements (repo), 34,
    159–161, 181, 184–188, 186f
    additive approach, 187–188, 190t
    bond carry, 201–204
    Federal Reserve, relationship, 200–201
    financing, 376
    rates, 185, 198–199
    subtractive approach, 189, 190t
    transactions, risks, 191–194
    tri-party repos, 161
Repurchase date, 185
Request for quote (RFQ) functionality,
    147
Resale cash flow, 336
Research analyst, 458, 460–463
Research sales, 463
Research salesperson, 461
Reserve Accounts, 318–319
Reserve accounts, 326
Reserve Primary Fund, 181, 330–331
Reserves, 94
Residential mortgage-backed securities
    (RMBSs), 305, 329–342
    fraud risk, 345–346
    market, 339–340, 371
Residual cash flow, 364
Residual interest, 395
Resolution Funding Corporation
    (REFCO), 220–221
Resolution Trust Corporation (RTC),
    220–221
Restricted funding mode, 387

Retail CDs, 172–173
Revenue, 127–128, 440
Revenue anticipation notes (RANs),
    175–176
Revenue bonds, 420, 423
Revenue-earning capacity, reduction,
    56–57
Reverse repo, 160, 201, 203
Reverse repurchase agreement (RRP)
    facility, 201
Reverse-sequential order, 391
Right-to-pay (RTP) swaption, 538
Right-way risk, 105
Rising stars, 274
Risk, 90–108, 90f, 111–114
    allocation, 330–331
    appetite, 107, 392–393
    aversion, 526
    factors, 97–98, 336–339
    information technology (IT)
        architecture, 116f
    measurement, 93–95, 112–114
    risk-adjusted yields (returns), 243
    shift, 480f
    takers, 578, 580
Risk-adjusted framework, shift, 11
Risk aggregation layer, 116
Risk-based capital, 57
Risk capital ratios, 54–55
Risk data, 117–118
Risk-free sovereign, 22
Riskless principal, 36
Risk management, 90–93, 108–110,
    134
Risk-neutrality, 525–526
Risk-neutral probabilities, 526
Risk-neutral valuation, 523, 531, 539
Risk retention requirements, 418
Risk-reversals, 543
Risk-weighted asset (RWA), 54, 57, 94, 97
RNIVs, 101
Roadshow, 440
Roll-down effect, 82–84
Roosevelt, Franklin D., 219

Rule 2a-7, 177, 181–182
Rule 17g-1(i), 353
Rule 144A, 256
Rule 415, 261, 481, 483
Rural Housing Administration
    (RHA), 242

S
SABR, 542
Safekeeping, 38, 137
Sales Agency Agreement, 492
Sales trader, 461
Sales trading, 464–465
Schwager, Jack, 455
Scratch-and-dent mortgages, 333
Secondary markets, 42–43, 43f,
    427–428, 441, 458
Secondary offering, 439
Section 15E(a)(3), 353
Sector-based ETFs, 476
Secured (collateralized) bondholders, 257
Secured bonds, 257
Securities, 122–128, 132–138, 136f
    broker-dealers, 190–191
    financing, 102
    gross settlement, 135
    opacity/complexity, 347
    post-trade process, 123f
    safekeeping, 123, 134–138, 136f
    trustee, 385
Securities Act of 1933, 164, 472
Securities and Exchange Commission
    (SEC), 96, 125, 130, 164, 334, 347,
    360, 483
    Rule 2a-7, 177, 181–182
    Rule 144A, 256
    Rule 415, 261, 481, 483
    underwriter requirements, 440
Securities Industry and Financial Markets
    Association (SIFMA), Master
    Repurchase Agreement, 184, 426
Securities Information Processor (SIP),
    446, 453

Securities market infrastructure, 121–138
  providers, activity overview, 122f
Securities Offering Reform of 2005,
  482–484
Securities trade, 121–132
Securitization, 304–309, 307f, 340
Self-financing, 526–527
Self-regulatory organization (SRO), 445
Seller/servicer events, 326
Selling agent, 482, 493–494, 494f
Selling and servicing agreement (SSA), 341
Selling concession, 440
Selling period, 498
Sell order, execution, 464–466
Sell-side, 458, 467
Sell-side broker-dealer, 461–462
Sell-side industry ROE, outlook, 584f
Semi-annual coupon bond, 67f, 68f, 72f
Senior AAA tranches, 335
Senior Preferred Stock Purchase
  Agreement (SPSPA), 229
Senior-secured first-lien loans, 402
Senior tranches, WAL reduction, 337
Sensitivity measures, 64–65
Servicer, 350–351
Settlement, 134–139, 134f, 185
Settlement banks, impact, 122
Shadow banking sector, 92
Shares, 20, 435
Short exposure, creation, 145
Short History of Financial Euphoria, A
  (Galbraith), 12
Short-term capital, 28
Short-term repo transactions, maturation,
  193
SIFMA data, 312
Single-curve world, 505–509
Single-dealer platforms (SDPs), 132
Single-factor scenarios, 101
Single monthly mortality (SMM),
  measurement method, 251
Sinking funds, 292
SIX SIX, 38
Skews, 542–543

SLM Corporation, 219
Small- and medium enterprise (SME)
  CLO, 390
Small-to-medium enterprises, struggle, 49
Smart-beta ETFs, 469, 475
Smart order router (SOR), 449, 451, 464
Smart order routing, 450–451
Smiles, 542–543
Sovereign Credit Crisis, 10
Sovereign debt crisis, 301–302
Sovereigns, capital market usage, 29–30
Sovereign wealth funds (SWFs), 29, 33
Soybean futures contract, contract terms,
  143t
SPDR 500 (SPY), 470
Special-purpose corporations (SPCs),
  ABCP program creation, 166–167
Special-purpose entity (SPE), 308, 361
Special-purpose vehicle (SPV), 305,
  308, 316
  bankruptcy-remote SPV, 330
Special servicer, 350, 351
Specific wrong-way risk, 105
Specified pools (collateral), 248–249
Sponsor, 382
Spot rate, 80
Spot trade, 22
Spot transaction, 571
Spread, 271, 401, 516–517, 519
Spread of spreads, 519
Spread-PV01, 517
Standalone trust structure, 326
Standard & Poor's 500 (S&P500) stock
  index, 447
Standard & Poor's Goldman Sachs
  Commodity Index (S&P GSCI), 562
Standard & Poor's, short-term rating
  system, 167–168
State Administration for Foreign
  Exchange (SAFE), 33–34, 575, 576
Stated maturity date, 400–401
Static CDO, 366–367
Static deals, 366
Statistical arbitrage, 456

Step-up bonds, 260–261
Sterling Overnight Index Average
  (SONIA), 511
Stochastic volatility models, 542
Stockholders, equity, 440
Stockholders, equity interest, 256–257
Stock index futures, 447–448
Stocks, 435
Storage layer, 115
Stressed Value at Risk (SVar), calculation
  (model methodology development),
  112
Stress events, impact, 55
Stress testing, process (example), 114f
STRIPS, 198, 207
Structured finance, 390–392, 394–396
Structured investment vehicles (SIVs),
  157, 180–181, 381–388, 386f
Structured Trading Activity Report,
  summary displays, 310
Structuring agent, 367
Student Loan Marketing Association
  (Sallie Mae), 219
Sub-custodians, 40
Subordinated classes, 359
Subordinated debt holders, 247
Subordinate notes, 363
Subordination, 326, 393
Subprime credit quality, 316
Subprime mortgages, 333
Subprime RMBSs, liquidity crisis
  (impact), 381
Subtractive approach, 189
Super-senior Aaa/AAA classes, 358
Super senior AAA tranches, 335, 349
Super-senior Class A-1 tranche, 363
Supervision, strength, 48
Supplementary leverage ratio (SLR), 582
Supply/demand, 536, 543
Surveillance agent (SA), 369
Swap data repositories (SSDRs), 153
Swap execution facilities (SEFs), 45, 55,
  141, 146–147, 503–504
Swap/Libor curve, construction, 507–509

Swaps, 24, 504–507, 515–521
Swaptions, 226, 540–542, 540t
Swiss finish, 55
Synthetic call option, 226
Synthetic leverage, 28
Systematically important financials
  institutions (SIFIs), 92
Systems Compliance and Integrity Rule
  (Regulation SCI), 468

T
Tail risk, 88
TAPS programs, 224–225
Targeted multifactor scenarios, 101
Target price, 462–463
Taxable equivalent yield (TEY), 288t, 430
Taxable MMF portfolio composition,
  179f
Tax and revenue anticipation notes
  (TRANs), 175–176
Tax anticipation notes (TANs), 175–176
Tax-exempt bonds, taxables (contrast),
  429–430
Tax-free yield (TFY), 429–430
Tax liens, 312
Tax treatment, 236
Technology capabilities, support,
  114–115
Teeny, 450
Tennessee Valley Authority (TVA), 163,
  219
Term Asset-Backed Securities Loan
  Facility (TALF), 312
Term repos, 185
Thematic-based ETFs, 476
Theta, gamma (contrast), 532
Third Plenum, policy shift, 575–576
Three-lines-of-defense model, 111–112
Tickertape, 444
Tier 1 capital, 94
Tier 1 programs, 168
Tier 2 capital, 94
To be announced (TBA), 247–249, 250t,
  253, 310

Tokyo Overnight Average Rate (TONAR), 511
Top-down approach, 107–108
Total assets, 440
Total Bond ETF, 477
Total rate of return (TRR), maximization, 429
Total real return indexers, 439f
Tradeability, 551
Trade date plus zero (T+0), 135–136
Traded volumes, 129f, 145t
Trade flow (example), CCP (impact), 39f
Trade processing system providers, 40
Trader, 458, 498–499
Trade Reporting and Compliance Engine (TRACE), 62, 279, 310–311, 580
Trade repositories, 40, 42, 154
Trades, 75–77, 122, 187–189
Trading activity, 409
Trading fees, 127
Trading floors, maintenance, 37
Trading venue consolidation, 125
Tranches, 331, 348, 392
Transaction-specific factors, 200
Transfer statements, 445
Transitions, 13–18
Transparency, 62, 580
Treasury auctions, 208–209
Treasury Automated Auction Processing System (TAAPS), usage, 209
Treasury Borrowing Advisory Committee (TBAC), 208
Treasury-ED (TED) spread, 518
Treasury Inflation Protected Securities (TIPS), 198, 206–207, 232–238, 477
Treasury securities. See U.S. Treasury securities
Treasury STRIPS, 207
Tri-party flows, 195f
Tri-party markets, 201
Tri-party repos, 161, 194–197
Triple-A credit enhancement, 358
True sale, 305, 341

Trustee, 273, 350–351, 369, 385
2a-7 funds, 177

U
UCITS regulation (Europe), 34
Uncollateralized obligations, 159
Unconstrained bond ETFs, 478
Underlying collateral, 353–356
Underlying loans, types, 246–247
Underwriter, 367
Underwriting, 481
Uniform Standards of Professional Appraisal Practice (USPAP), 354
Unique product identifiers (UPIs), 154
Unique transaction identifiers (UTIs), 154
United States, 43f, 125f, 129f, 210, 220
    alternative trading systems, 128, 130
    fixed-income trading/issuance volumes, 44f
    Savings and Loan (S&L) crisis, 220
    swap execution facilities (SEFs), 146–147
Unit investment trusts (UITs), 470–472
Unsecured bondholders, 257
Unsecured bonds, 258–259
Urban Development Act (1965), 220
U.S. ABS issuance, 313f
U.S. ABS outstanding, 313f
U.S. Bankruptcy Code, 296, 299
U.S. broadly syndicated loan CLOs, annual issuance, 390f
U.S. CMBS issuance, 350f
U.S. Dollar (USD) EM debt, growth, 284t
U.S. Dollar (USD) SEF/broker screen, 516t
U.S. Dollar (USD) swap, simplified cash-flows, 504f
U.S. Dollar (USD) swaptions, 541–542
U.S. government bond ETFs, 477
U.S. Housing and Urban Development (HUD), 212, 219, 220, 242
U.S. Treasury (UST), 69–70, 69t, 205–208
    bills (T-bills), 161–162, 206, 308

bonds, 82–83, 206, 271
CT2, example, 84
futures, 84–88, 84t
yield curve, 74f

V
Validation, 132
Value at Risk (VaR) (Value-at-Risk),
    98–101, 98f, 112
Variable net asset value, 182
Variable-rate bonds, 259–260, 426
Variable rate demand notes (VRDNs),
    176–177, 180
Variation margin, 104, 133
Vega, 531, 536
Venture capital (VC) funds, 35
Veterans Administration (VA), 220
Volatility cubes, 543
Volatility surface, maintaining/populating,
    543
Volcker Rule, 37, 55, 62, 417
Volume-weighted average price (VWAP),
    464, 498–500
Vulture investors, 299

W
Warehouse agreements, 368–369
Warehouse provider, 367–369
Warranties, 342–346
Waterfalls, 393
Weighted average coupon (WAC),
    241–242, 244
Weighted average life (WAL), 246, 308,
    337, 405
Weighted average maturity (WAM),
    241–242, 246

Weighted average rating factor (WARF),
    362, 404–405, 404t
Weighted average spread (WAS), 405
Well-known, seasoned issuer (WKSI),
    483
When-Issued (WI) note, 69
Window programs, 162
Withdrawal, 138
World Bank, borrowing requirements,
    222
World economic growth (promotion),
    global financial system (impact),
    18–19
World Federal of Exchanges (WFE), stock
    exchanges, 125, 126f
World investment structure, 31f
World Market/Reuters (WM/R), 473
Wrong-way risk, 105

X
XTX Markets, ranking, 60
XVA, 104, 521–522

Y
Yield, 83, 307, 542, 546
Yield carry, 83
Yield curve, 73–76, 74f, 170f
Yield Supplement Account, 318–319
Yield to maturity (YTM), 66, 75
Yield-yield swap spread, 518

Z
Zero-cost call/receiver, 547
Zero-coupon swap spreads, 519
Zero rate, 80

Printed and bound by CPI Group (UK) Ltd, Croydon, CR0 4YY

23/04/2025

14661014-0001